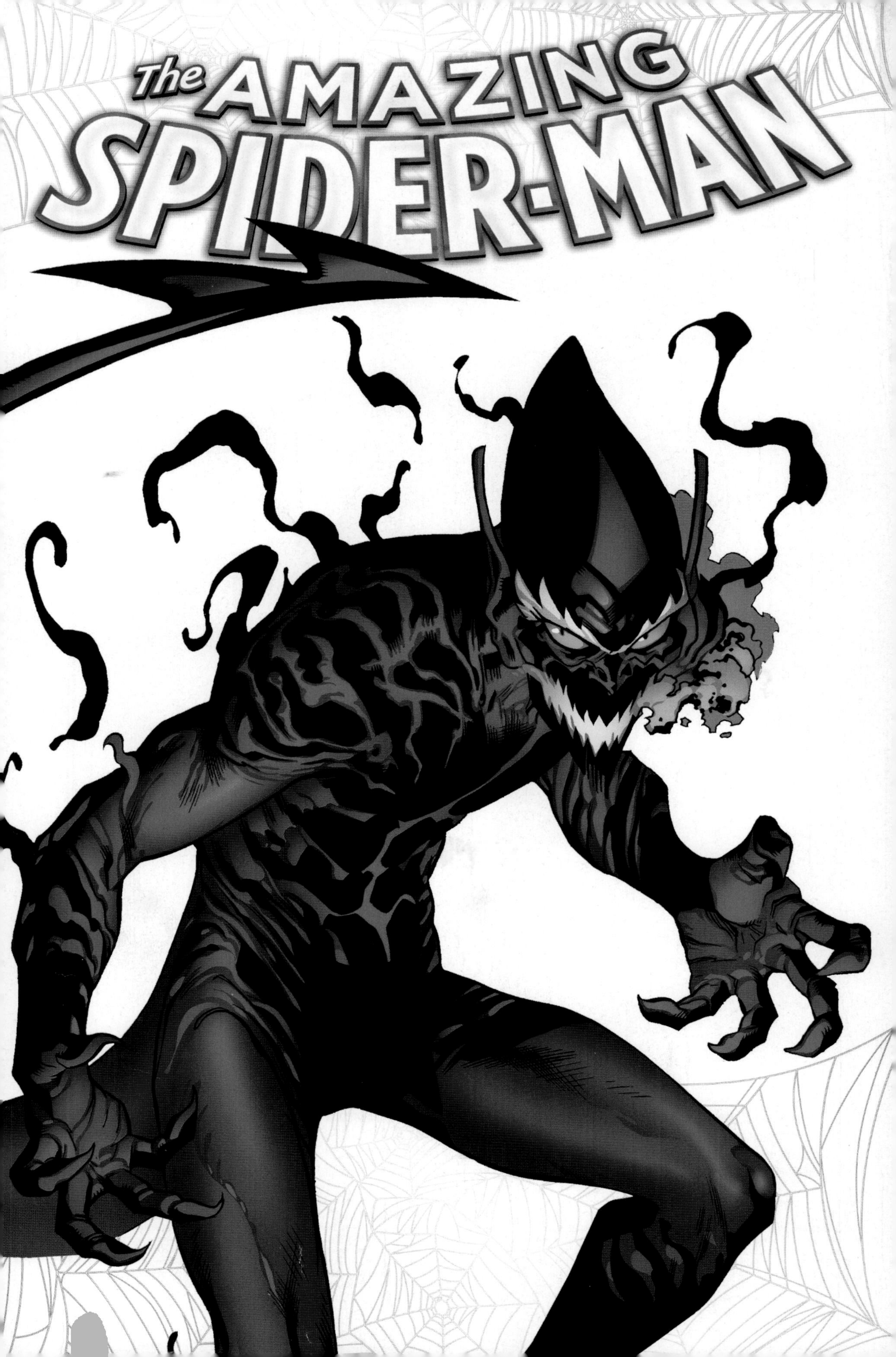

The AMAZING
SPIDER-MAN

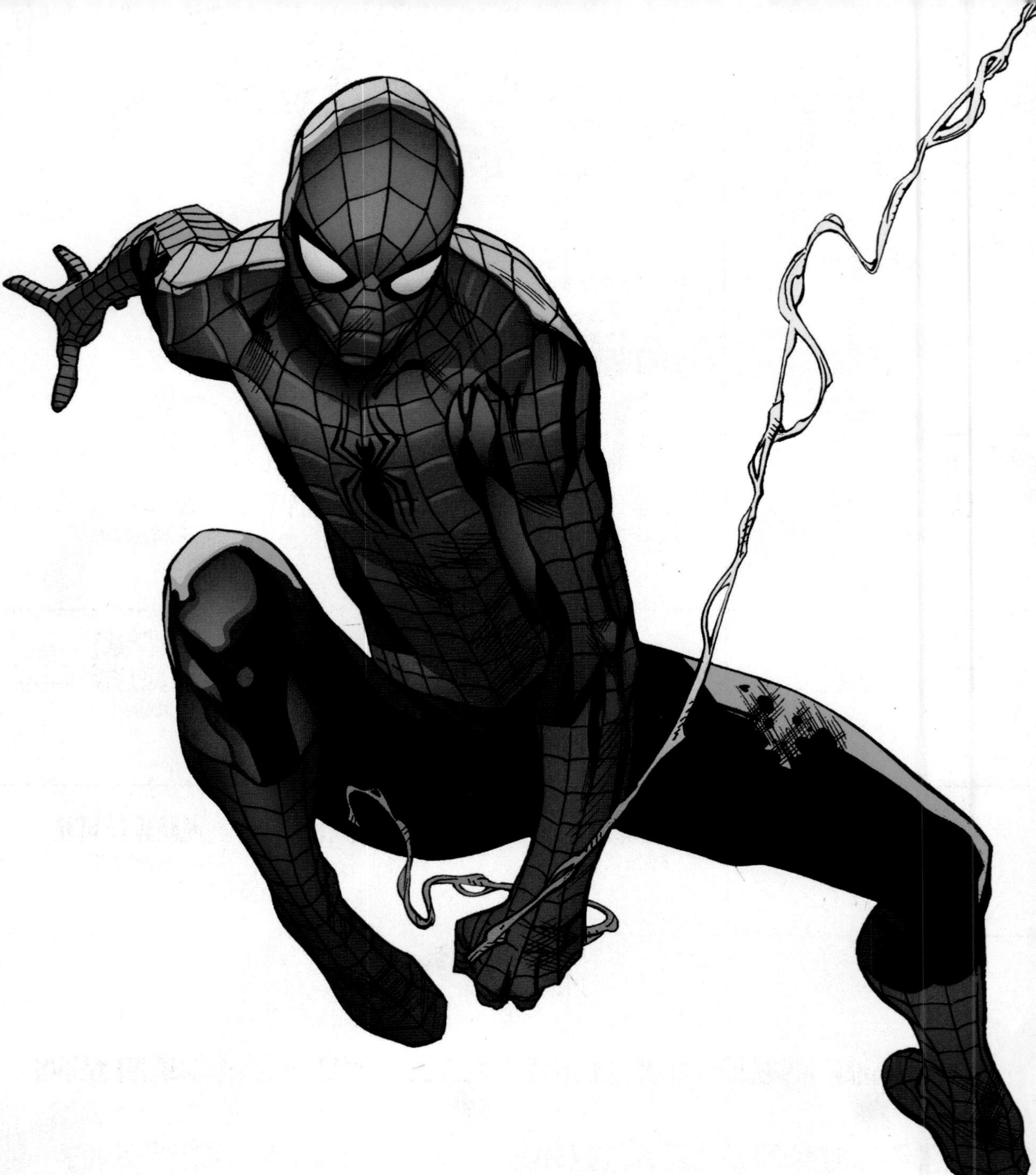

COLLECTION EDITOR **JENNIFER GRÜNWALD**
ASSISTANT EDITOR **CAITLIN O'CONNELL**
ASSOCIATE MANAGING EDITOR **KATERI WOODY**
EDITOR, SPECIAL PROJECTS **MARK D. BEAZLEY**

VP PRODUCTION & SPECIAL PROJECTS **JEFF YOUNGQUIST**
SVP PRINT, SALES & MARKETING **DAVID GABRIEL**
BOOK DESIGNER **ADAM DEL RE**

EDITOR IN CHIEF **C.B. CEBULSKI**
CHIEF CREATIVE OFFICER **JOE QUESADA**
PRESIDENT **DAN BUCKLEY**
EXECUTIVE PRODUCER **ALAN FINE**

AMAZING SPIDER-MAN: RED GOBLIN. Contains material originally published in magazine form as AMAZING SPIDER-MAN #794-801. First printing 2018. ISBN 978-1-302-91354-0. Published by MARVEL WORLDWIDE, INC., a subsidiary of MARVEL ENTERTAINMENT, LLC. OFFICE OF PUBLICATION: 135 West 50th Street, New York, NY 10020. **Printed in the U.S.A.** DAN BUCKLEY, President, Marvel Entertainment; JOHN NEE, Publisher; JOE QUESADA, Chief Creative Officer; TOM BREVOORT, SVP of Publishing; DAVID BOGART, SVP of Business Affairs & Operations, Publishing & Partnership; DAVID GABRIEL, SVP of Sales & Marketing, Publishing; JEFF YOUNGQUIST, VP of Production & Special Projects; DAN CARR, Executive Director of Publishing Technology; ALEX MORALES, Director of Publishing Operations; DAN EDINGTON, Managing Editor; SUSAN CRESPI, Production Manager; STAN LEE, Chairman Emeritus. For information regarding advertising in Marvel Comics or on Marvel.com, please contact Vit DeBellis, Custom Solutions & Integrated Advertising Manager, at vdebellis@marvel.com. For Marvel subscription inquiries, please call 888-511-5480. **Manufactured between 7/27/2018 and 8/28/2018 by LSC COMMUNICATIONS INC., KENDALLVILLE, IN, USA.**

10 9 8 7 6 5 4 3 2 1

RED GOBLIN

ISSUE #794

**DAN SLOTT &
CHRISTOS GAGE**
WRITERS

STUART IMMONEN
PENCILER

WADE VON GRAWBADGER
INKER

MARTE GRACIA
COLOR ARTIST

ISSUES #795-796

**DAN SLOTT &
CHRISTOS GAGE**
WRITERS

MIKE HAWTHORNE
PENCILER

TERRY PALLOT WITH
CAM SMITH (#796)
INKERS

MARTE GRACIA (#795) &
ERICK ARCINIEGA (#796)
COLOR ARTISTS

ISSUES #797-799

DAN SLOTT
WRITER

STUART IMMONEN
PENCILER

WADE VON GRAWBADGER
INKER

MARTE GRACIA
COLOR ARTIST

ISSUE #800

DAN SLOTT
WRITER

NICK BRADSHAW, HUMBERTO RAMOS, GIUSEPPE CAMUNCOLI, STUART IMMONEN & MARCOS MARTIN
PENCILERS

NICK BRADSHAW, VICTOR OLAZABA, CAM SMITH, WADE VON GRAWBADGER & MARCOS MARTIN
INKERS

EDGAR DELGADO, JAVA TARTAGLIA, MARTE GRACIA & MUNTSA VICENTE
COLOR ARTISTS

ISSUE #801

DAN SLOTT
WRITER

MARCOS MARTIN
ARTIST

MUNTSA VICENTE
COLOR ARTIST

VC's JOE CARAMAGNA
LETTERER

ALEX ROSS
COVER ART

ALLISON STOCK, TOM GRONEMAN & KATHLEEN WISNESKI
ASSISTANT EDITORS

NICK LOWE WITH **DEVIN LEWIS**
EDITORS

SPIDER-MAN CREATED BY
STAN LEE & STEVE DITKO

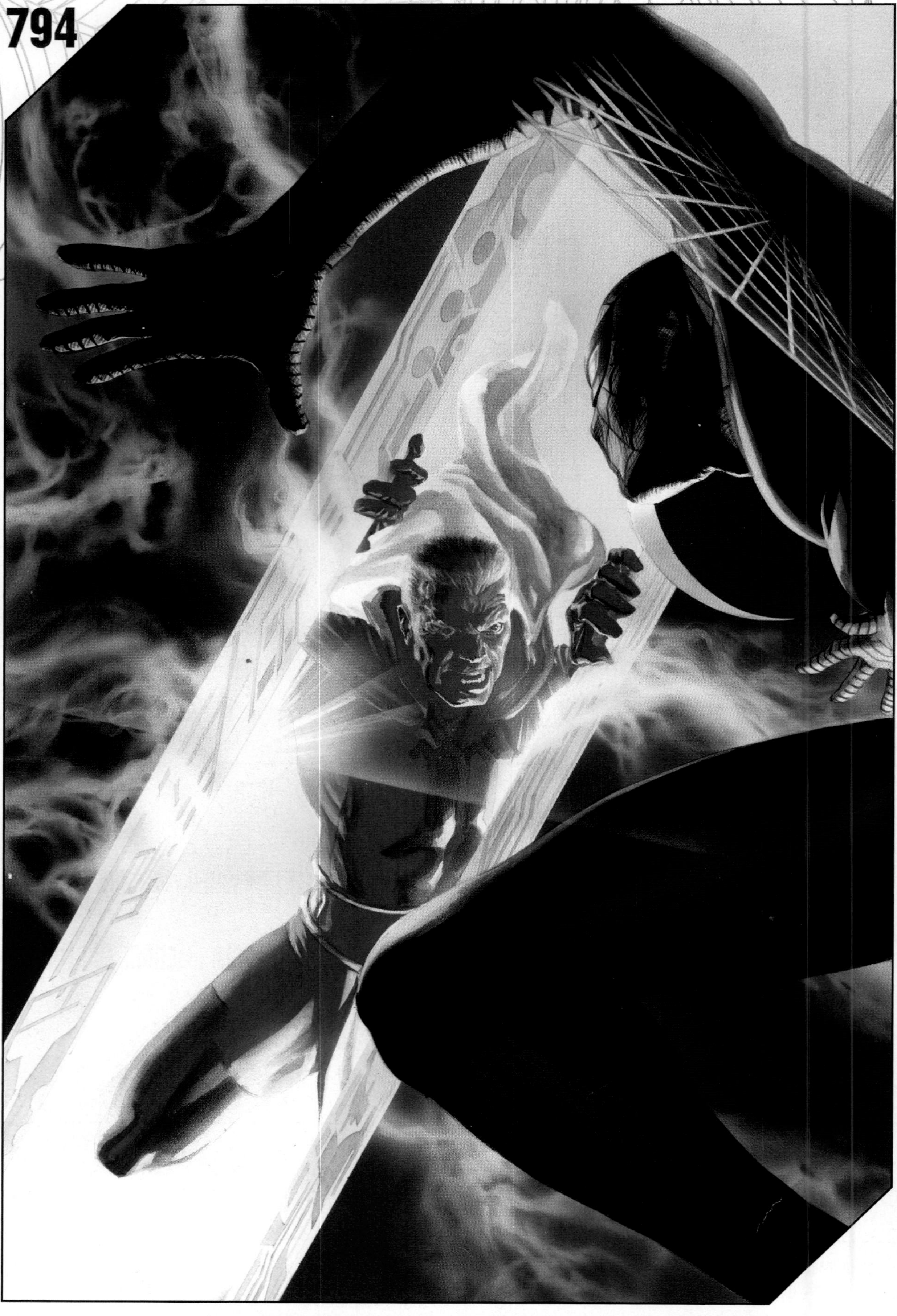

THREAT LEVEL: RED PART ONE "LAST CHANCE"

WHEN PETER PARKER WAS BITTEN BY A RADIOACTIVE SPIDER, HE GAINED THE PROPORTIONAL SPEED, STRENGTH AND AGILITY OF A SPIDER; ADHESIVE FINGERTIPS AND TOES; AND THE UNIQUE PRECOGNITIVE AWARENESS OF DANGER CALLED "SPIDER-SENSE"! AFTER LEARNING THAT WITH GREAT POWER THERE MUST ALSO COME GREAT RESPONSIBILITY, HE BECAME THE CRIME-FIGHTING SUPER HERO CALLED...

the AMAZING SPIDER-MAN

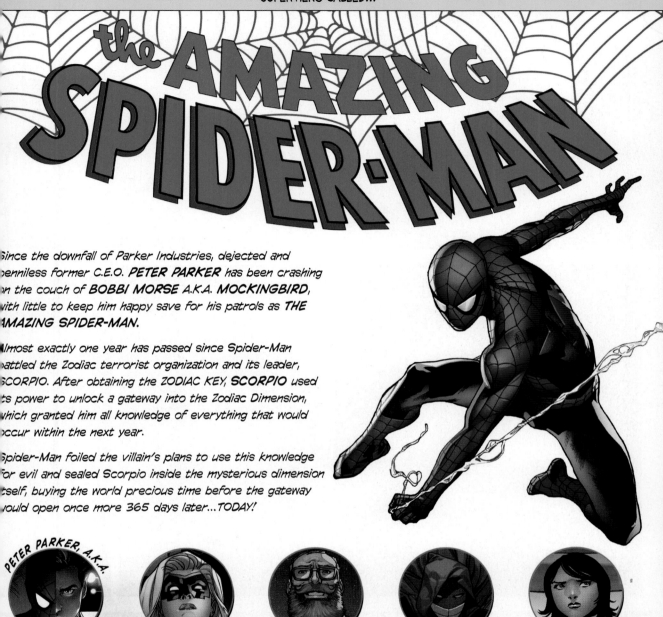

Since the downfall of Parker Industries, dejected and penniless former C.E.O. ***PETER PARKER*** *has been crashing on the couch of* ***BOBBI MORSE*** *A.K.A.* ***MOCKINGBIRD****, with little to keep him happy save for his patrols as* ***THE AMAZING SPIDER-MAN.***

Almost exactly one year has passed since Spider-Man battled the Zodiac terrorist organization and its leader, SCORPIO. After obtaining the ZODIAC KEY, ***SCORPIO*** *used its power to unlock a gateway into the Zodiac Dimension, which granted him all knowledge of everything that would occur within the next year.*

Spider-Man foiled the villain's plans to use this knowledge for evil and sealed Scorpio inside the mysterious dimension itself, buying the world precious time before the gateway would open once more 365 days later...TODAY!

PETER PARKER, A.K.A.
THE AMAZING SPIDER-MAN
MOCKINGBIRD
MAX MODELL
SCORPIO
ANNA MARIA MARCONI

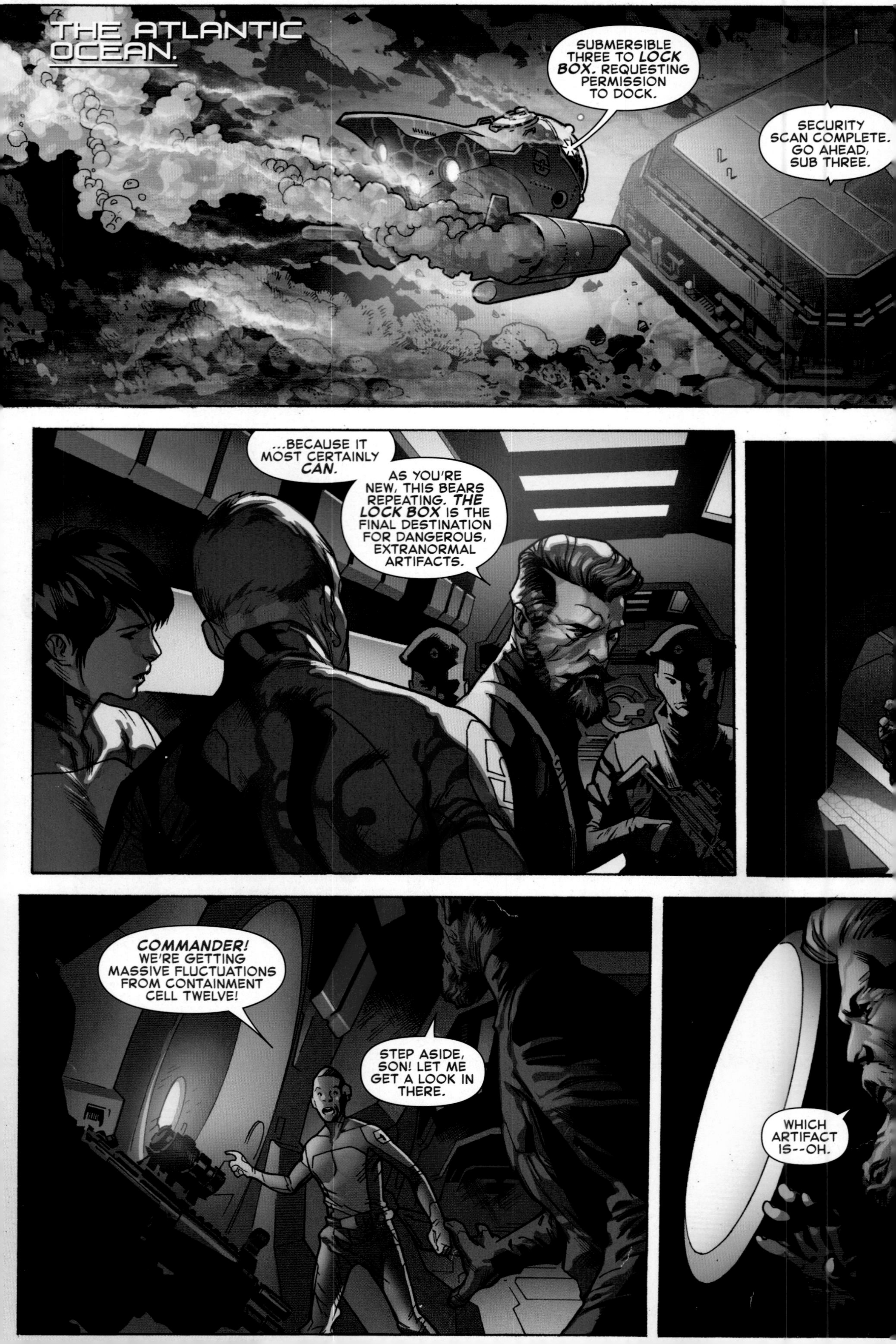
THE ATLANTIC OCEAN.
SUBMERSIBLE THREE TO LOCK BOX. REQUESTING PERMISSION TO DOCK.
SECURITY SCAN COMPLETE. GO AHEAD, SUB THREE.
...BECAUSE IT MOST CERTAINLY CAN.
AS YOU'RE NEW, THIS BEARS REPEATING. THE LOCK BOX IS THE FINAL DESTINATION FOR DANGEROUS, EXTRANORMAL ARTIFACTS.
COMMANDER! WE'RE GETTING MASSIVE FLUCTUATIONS FROM CONTAINMENT CELL TWELVE!
STEP ASIDE, SON! LET ME GET A LOOK IN THERE.
WHICH ARTIFACT IS--OH.

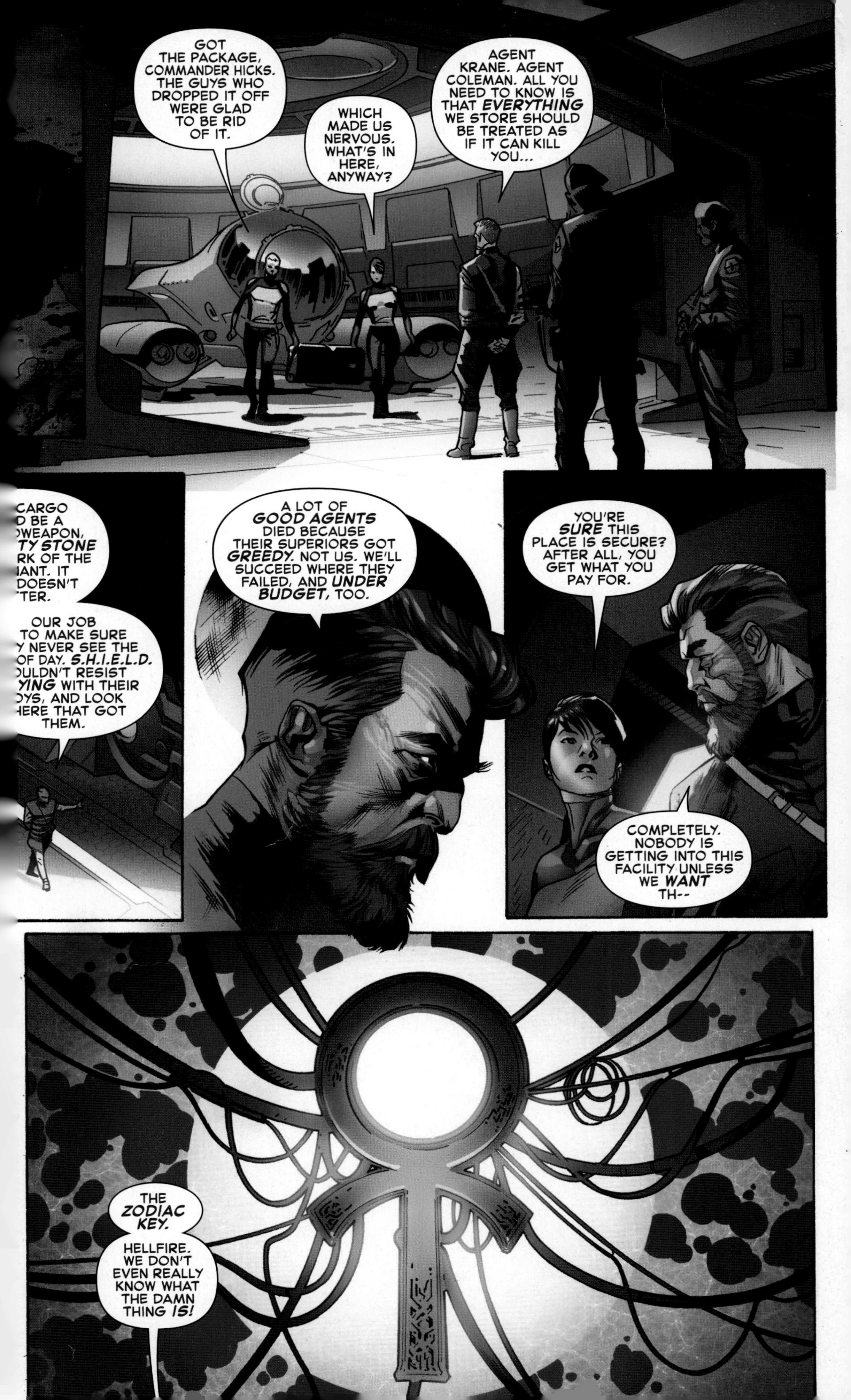

GOT THE PACKAGE, COMMANDER HICKS. THE GUYS WHO DROPPED IT OFF WERE GLAD TO BE RID OF IT.
WHICH MADE US NERVOUS. WHAT'S IN HERE, ANYWAY?
AGENT KRANE. AGENT COLEMAN. ALL YOU NEED TO KNOW IS THAT EVERYTHING WE STORE SHOULD BE TREATED AS IF IT CAN KILL YOU...
CARGO D BE A OWEAPON, TY STONE RK OF THE ANT. IT DOESN'T TTER.
OUR JOB TO MAKE SURE Y NEVER SEE THE OF DAY. S.H.I.E.L.D. OULDN'T RESIST YING WITH THEIR OYS, AND LOOK HERE THAT GOT THEM.
A LOT OF GOOD AGENTS DIED BECAUSE THEIR SUPERIORS GOT GREEDY. NOT US. WE'LL SUCCEED WHERE THEY FAILED, AND UNDER BUDGET, TOO.
YOU'RE SURE THIS PLACE IS SECURE? AFTER ALL, YOU GET WHAT YOU PAY FOR.
COMPLETELY. NOBODY IS GETTING INTO THIS FACILITY UNLESS WE WANT TH--
THE ZODIAC KEY.
HELLFIRE. WE DON'T EVEN REALLY KNOW WHAT THE DAMN THING IS!

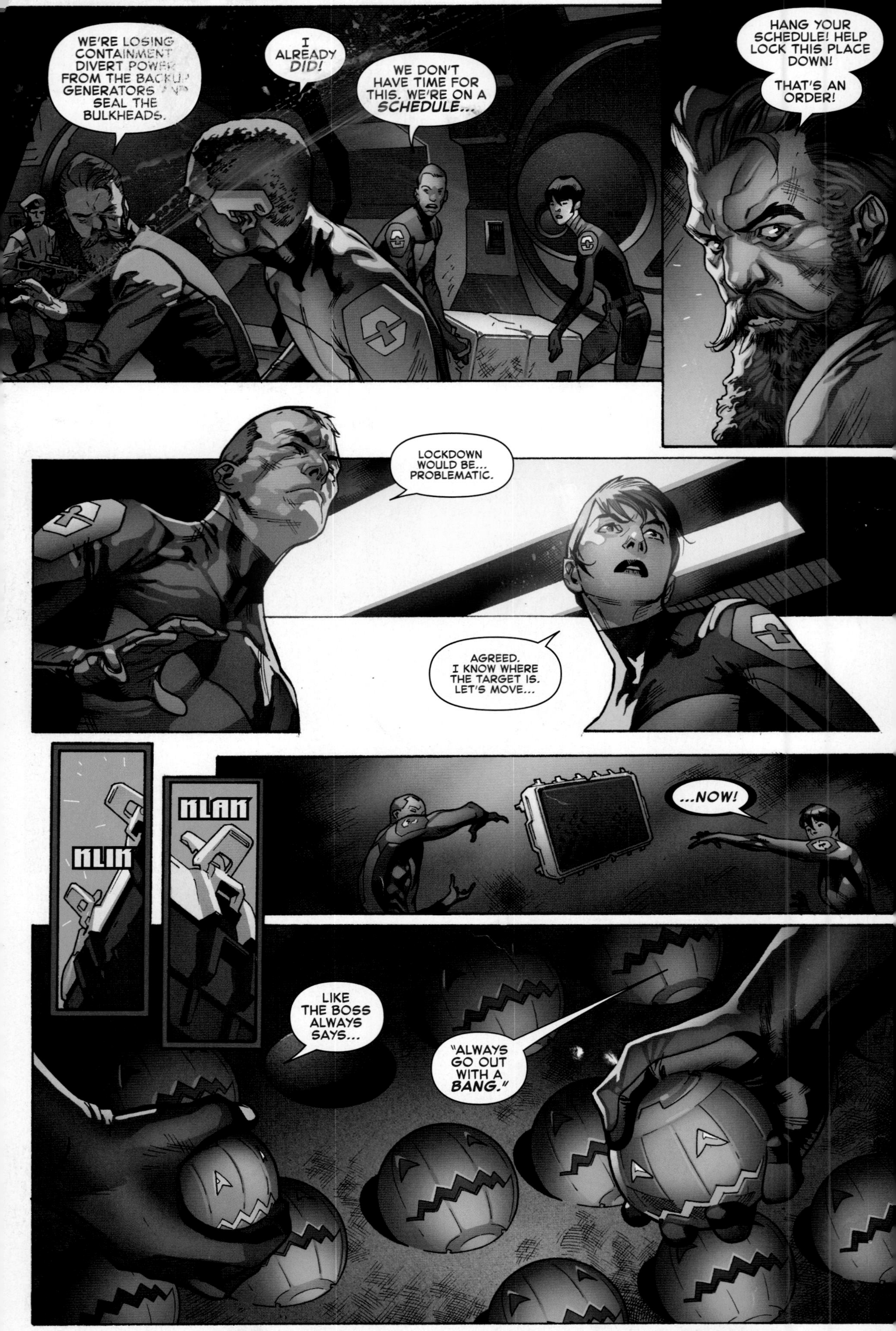
WE'RE LOSING CONTAINMENT! DIVERT POWER FROM THE BACKUP GENERATORS AND SEAL THE BULKHEADS.
I ALREADY *DID!*
WE DON'T HAVE TIME FOR THIS. WE'RE ON A *SCHEDULE...*
HANG YOUR SCHEDULE! HELP LOCK THIS PLACE DOWN!
THAT'S AN ORDER!
LOCKDOWN WOULD BE... PROBLEMATIC.
AGREED. I KNOW WHERE THE TARGET IS. LET'S MOVE...
KLIK
KLAK
...NOW!
LIKE THE BOSS ALWAYS SAYS...
"ALWAYS GO OUT WITH A *BANG.*"

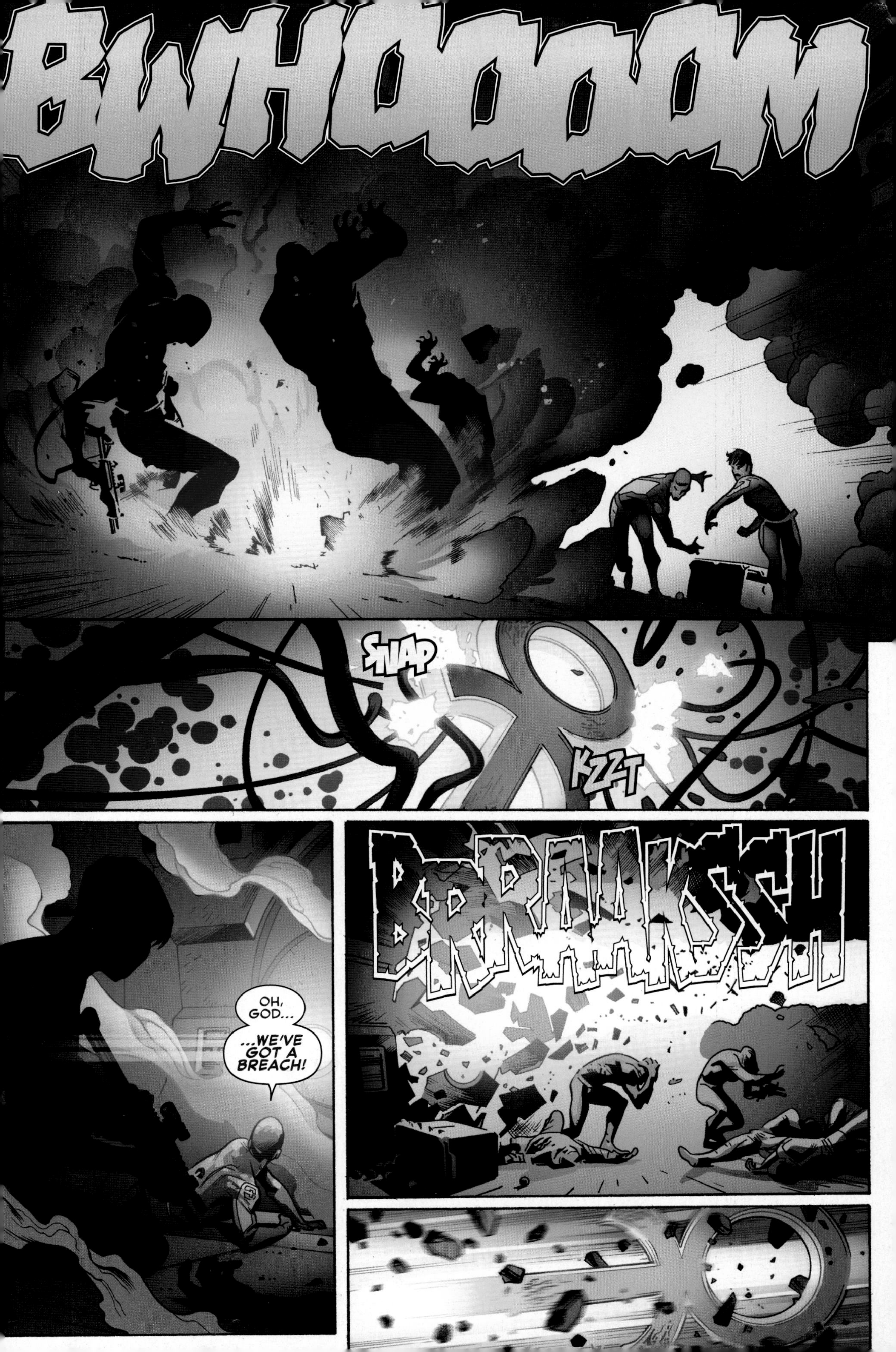
BWHOOOOM
SNAP
KZZT
OH, GOD...
...WE'VE GOT A BREACH!
BRRAKKSSH

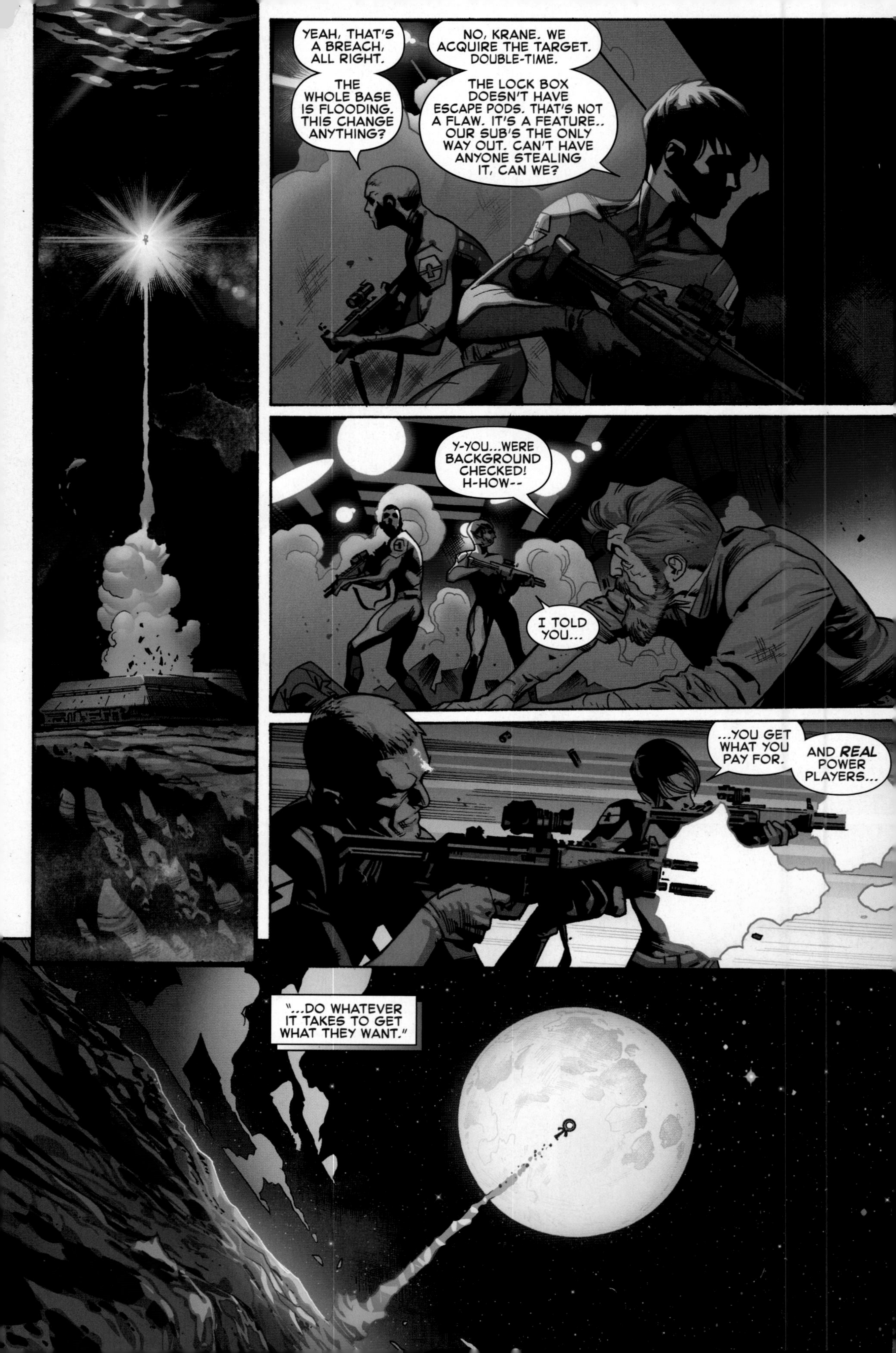
YEAH, THAT'S A BREACH, ALL RIGHT.
THE WHOLE BASE IS FLOODING. THIS CHANGE ANYTHING?
NO, KRANE. WE ACQUIRE THE TARGET. DOUBLE-TIME.
THE LOCK BOX DOESN'T HAVE ESCAPE PODS. THAT'S NOT A FLAW. IT'S A FEATURE.. OUR SUB'S THE ONLY WAY OUT. CAN'T HAVE ANYONE STEALING IT, CAN WE?
Y-YOU...WERE BACKGROUND CHECKED! H-HOW--
I TOLD YOU...
...YOU GET WHAT YOU PAY FOR.
AND REAL POWER PLAYERS...
"...DO WHATEVER IT TAKES TO GET WHAT THEY WANT."

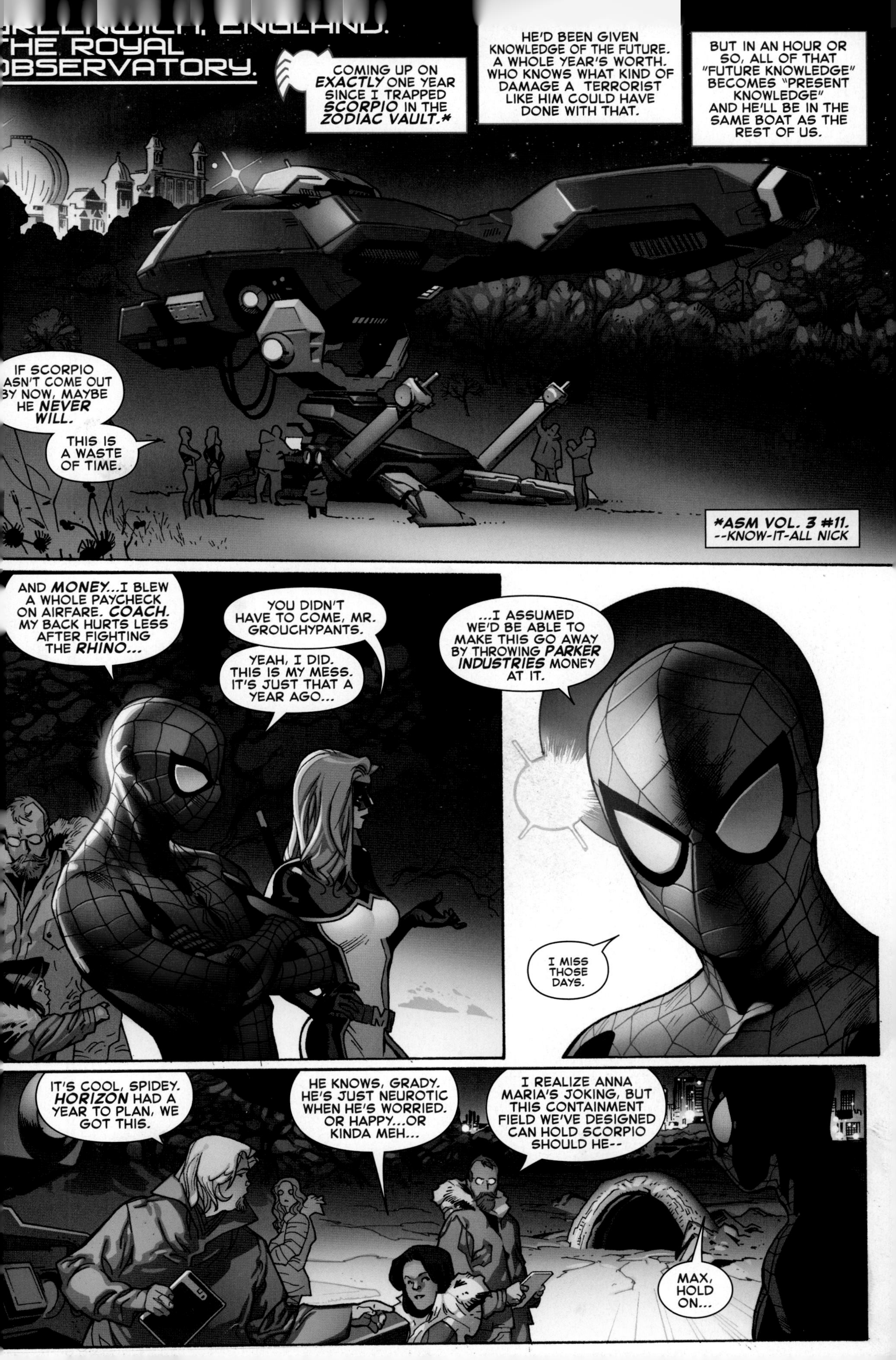
GREENWICH, ENGLAND. THE ROYAL OBSERVATORY.
COMING UP ON EXACTLY ONE YEAR SINCE I TRAPPED SCORPIO IN THE ZODIAC VAULT.*
HE'D BEEN GIVEN KNOWLEDGE OF THE FUTURE. A WHOLE YEAR'S WORTH. WHO KNOWS WHAT KIND OF DAMAGE A TERRORIST LIKE HIM COULD HAVE DONE WITH THAT.
BUT IN AN HOUR OR SO, ALL OF THAT "FUTURE KNOWLEDGE" BECOMES "PRESENT KNOWLEDGE" AND HE'LL BE IN THE SAME BOAT AS THE REST OF US.
IF SCORPIO HASN'T COME OUT BY NOW, MAYBE HE NEVER WILL.
THIS IS A WASTE OF TIME.
*ASM VOL. 3 #11. --KNOW-IT-ALL NICK
AND MONEY...I BLEW A WHOLE PAYCHECK ON AIRFARE. COACH. MY BACK HURTS LESS AFTER FIGHTING THE RHINO...
YOU DIDN'T HAVE TO COME, MR. GROUCHYPANTS.
YEAH, I DID. THIS IS MY MESS. IT'S JUST THAT A YEAR AGO...
...I ASSUMED WE'D BE ABLE TO MAKE THIS GO AWAY BY THROWING PARKER INDUSTRIES MONEY AT IT.
I MISS THOSE DAYS.
IT'S COOL, SPIDEY. HORIZON HAD A YEAR TO PLAN, WE GOT THIS.
HE KNOWS, GRADY. HE'S JUST NEUROTIC WHEN HE'S WORRIED. OR HAPPY...OR KINDA MEH...
I REALIZE ANNA MARIA'S JOKING, BUT THIS CONTAINMENT FIELD WE'VE DESIGNED CAN HOLD SCORPIO SHOULD HE--
MAX, HOLD ON...

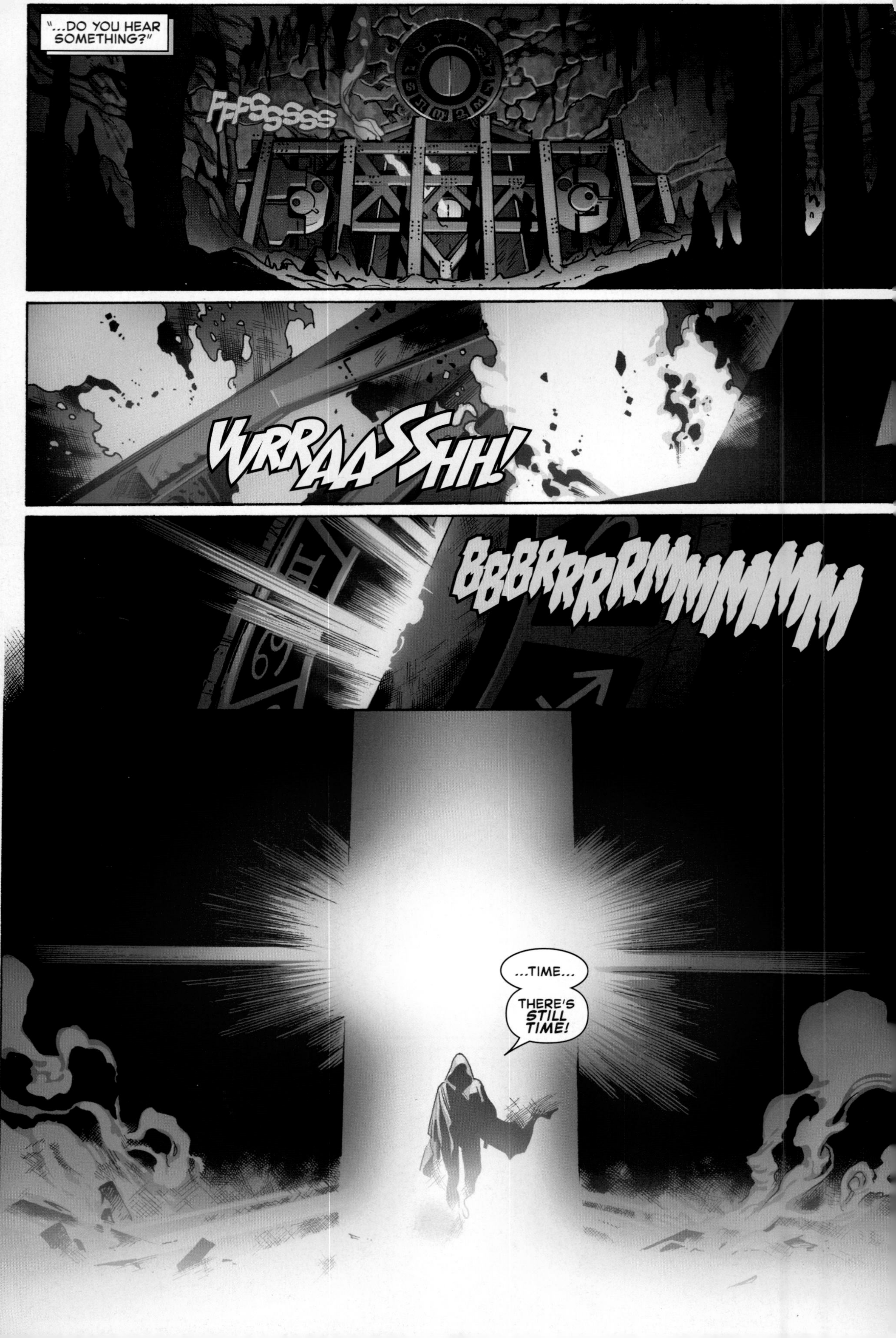
"...DO YOU HEAR SOMETHING?"
FFFSSSSSS
VVRRAASSHH!
BBBRRRRRMMMMMMM
...TIME...
THERE'S STILL TIME!

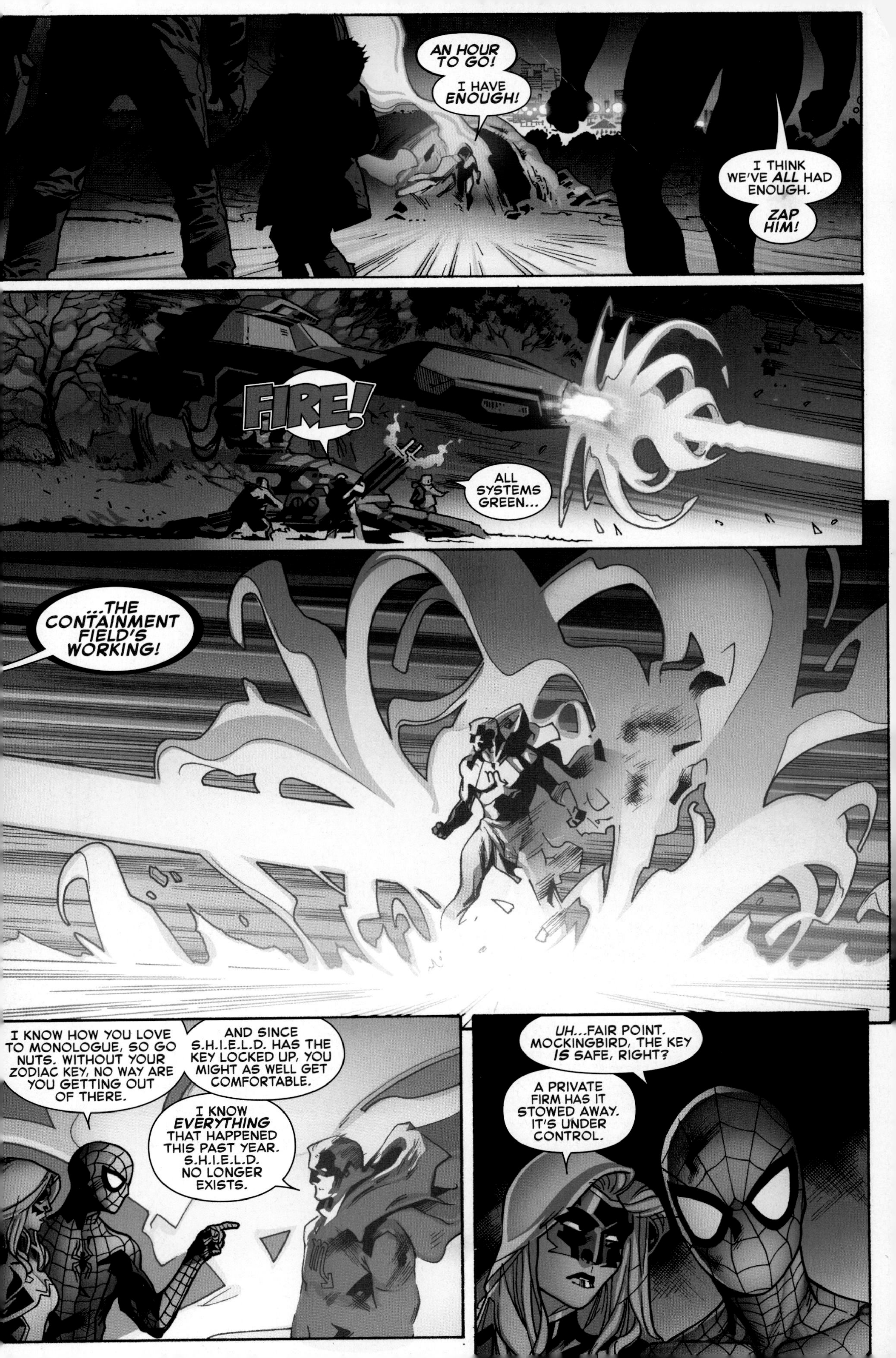
AN HOUR TO GO!
I HAVE ENOUGH!
I THINK WE'VE ALL HAD ENOUGH.
ZAP HIM!
FIRE!
ALL SYSTEMS GREEN...
...THE CONTAINMENT FIELD'S WORKING!
I KNOW HOW YOU LOVE TO MONOLOGUE, SO GO NUTS. WITHOUT YOUR ZODIAC KEY, NO WAY ARE YOU GETTING OUT OF THERE.
AND SINCE S.H.I.E.L.D. HAS THE KEY LOCKED UP, YOU MIGHT AS WELL GET COMFORTABLE.
I KNOW EVERYTHING THAT HAPPENED THIS PAST YEAR. S.H.I.E.L.D. NO LONGER EXISTS.
UH...FAIR POINT. MOCKINGBIRD, THE KEY IS SAFE, RIGHT?
A PRIVATE FIRM HAS IT STOWED AWAY. IT'S UNDER CONTROL.

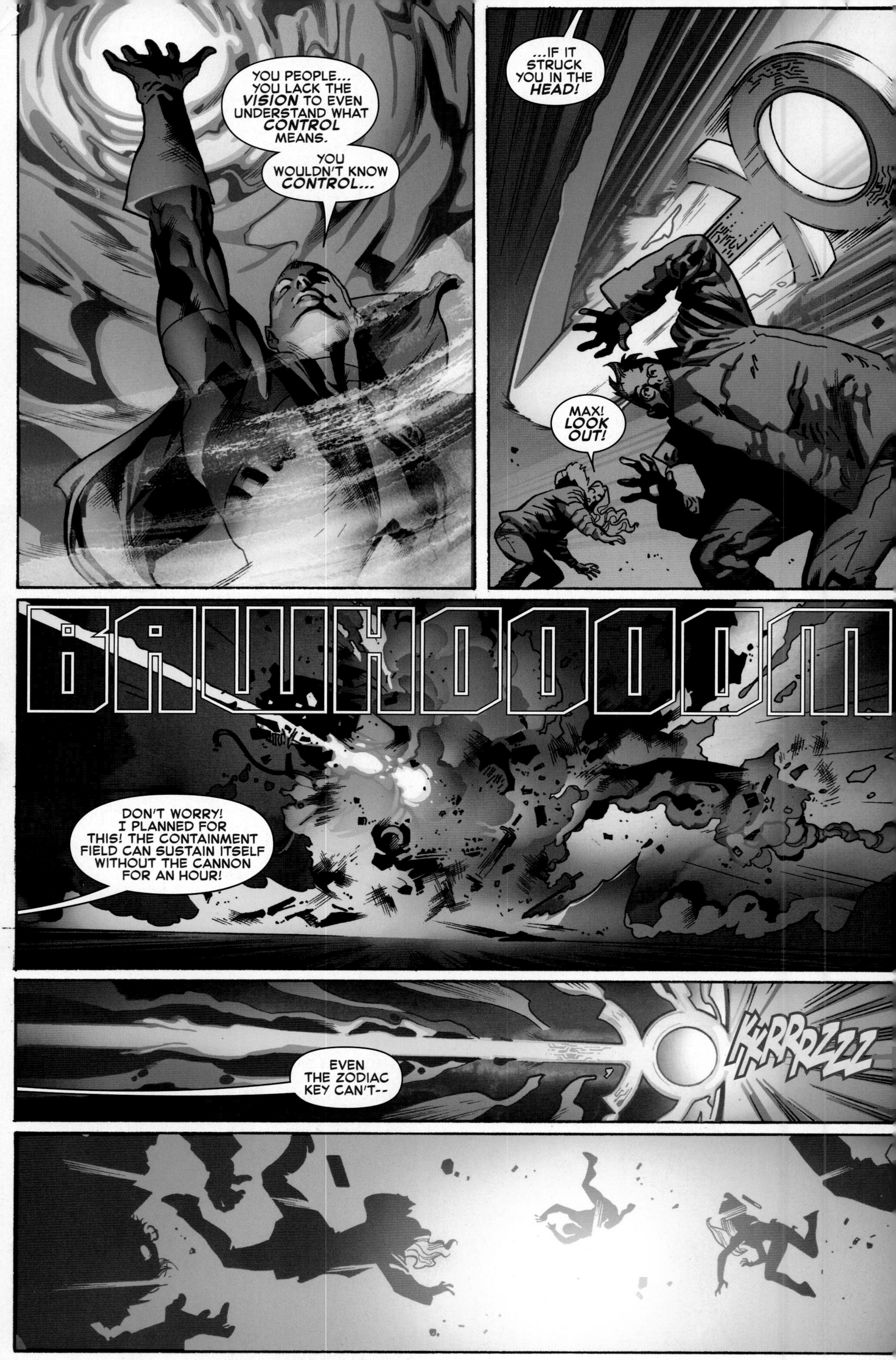
YOU PEOPLE... YOU LACK THE VISION TO EVEN UNDERSTAND WHAT CONTROL MEANS.
YOU WOULDN'T KNOW CONTROL...
...IF IT STRUCK YOU IN THE HEAD!
MAX! LOOK OUT!
BAWHOOOOM
DON'T WORRY! I PLANNED FOR THIS! THE CONTAINMENT FIELD CAN SUSTAIN ITSELF WITHOUT THE CANNON FOR AN HOUR!
KRRRZZZ
EVEN THE ZODIAC KEY CAN'T--

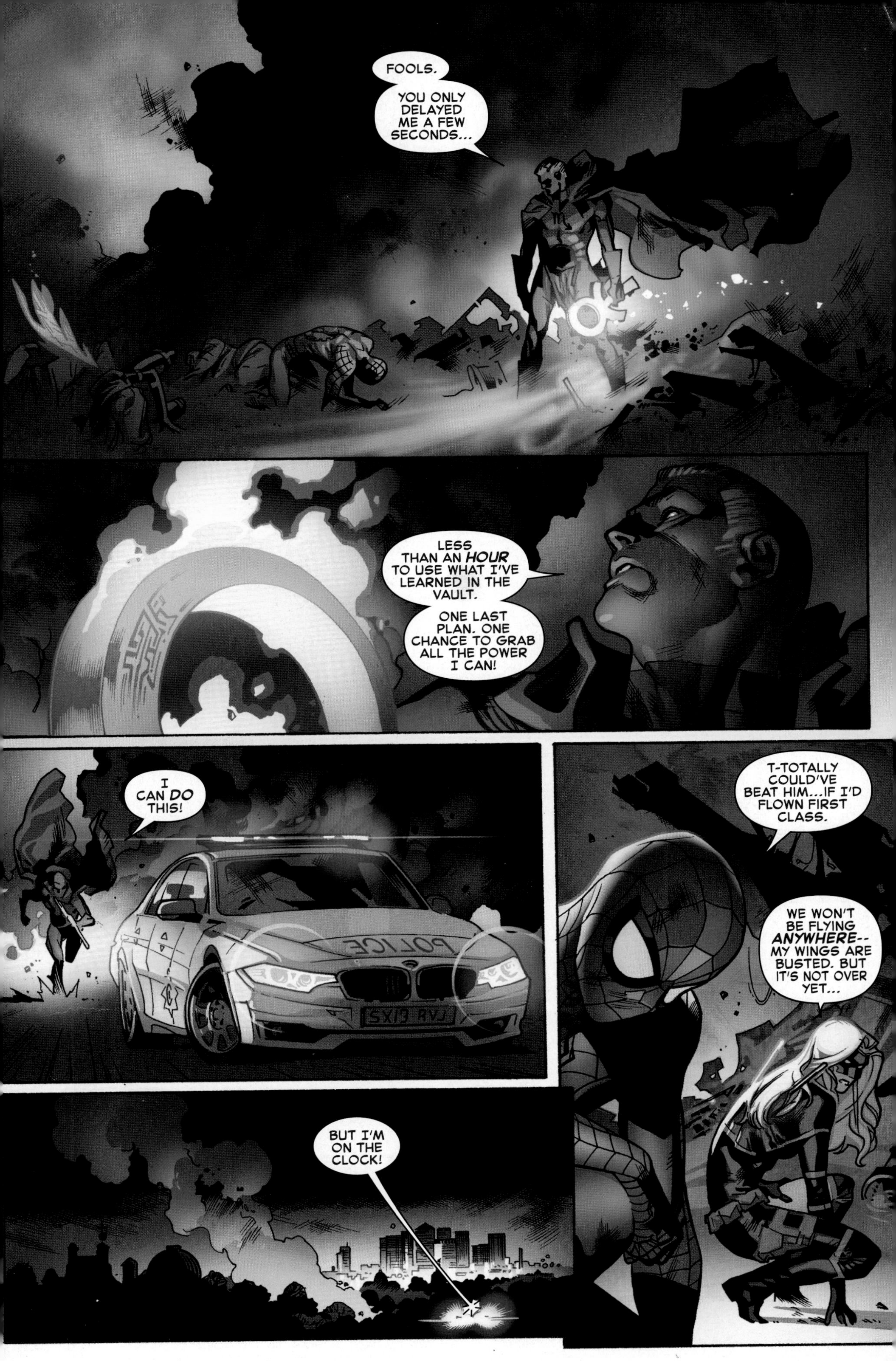
FOOLS.
YOU ONLY DELAYED ME A FEW SECONDS...
LESS THAN AN HOUR TO USE WHAT I'VE LEARNED IN THE VAULT.
ONE LAST PLAN. ONE CHANCE TO GRAB ALL THE POWER I CAN!
I CAN DO THIS!
POLICE
SX13 RVJ
BUT I'M ON THE CLOCK!
T-TOTALLY COULD'VE BEAT HIM...IF I'D FLOWN FIRST CLASS.
WE WON'T BE FLYING ANYWHERE--MY WINGS ARE BUSTED. BUT IT'S NOT OVER YET...

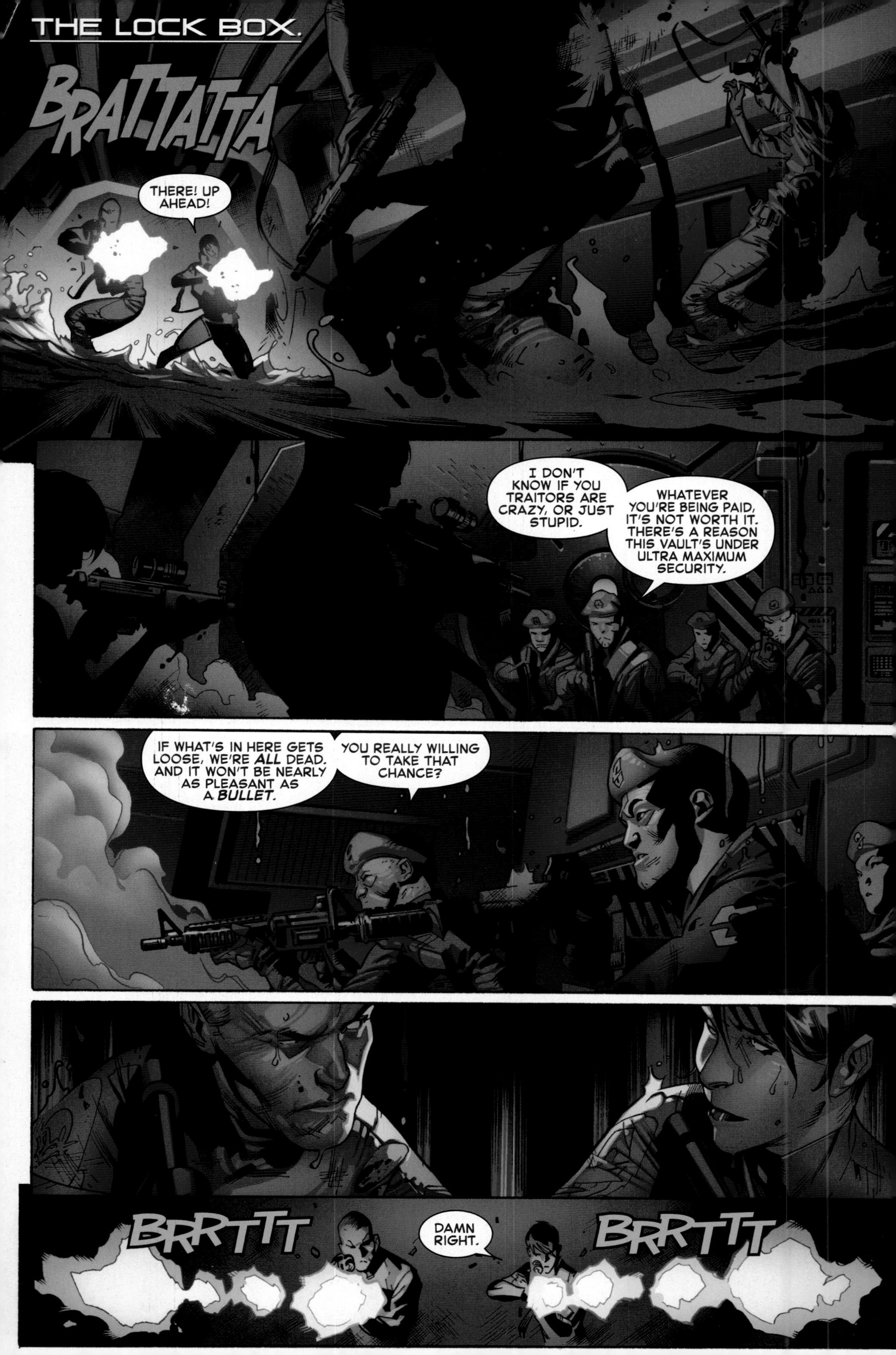
THE LOCK BOX.
BRATTATTA
THERE! UP AHEAD!
I DON'T KNOW IF YOU TRAITORS ARE CRAZY, OR JUST STUPID.
WHATEVER YOU'RE BEING PAID, IT'S NOT WORTH IT. THERE'S A REASON THIS VAULT'S UNDER ULTRA MAXIMUM SECURITY.
IF WHAT'S IN HERE GETS LOOSE, WE'RE ALL DEAD. AND IT WON'T BE NEARLY AS PLEASANT AS A BULLET.
YOU REALLY WILLING TO TAKE THAT CHANCE?
BRRTTT
DAMN RIGHT.
BRRTTT

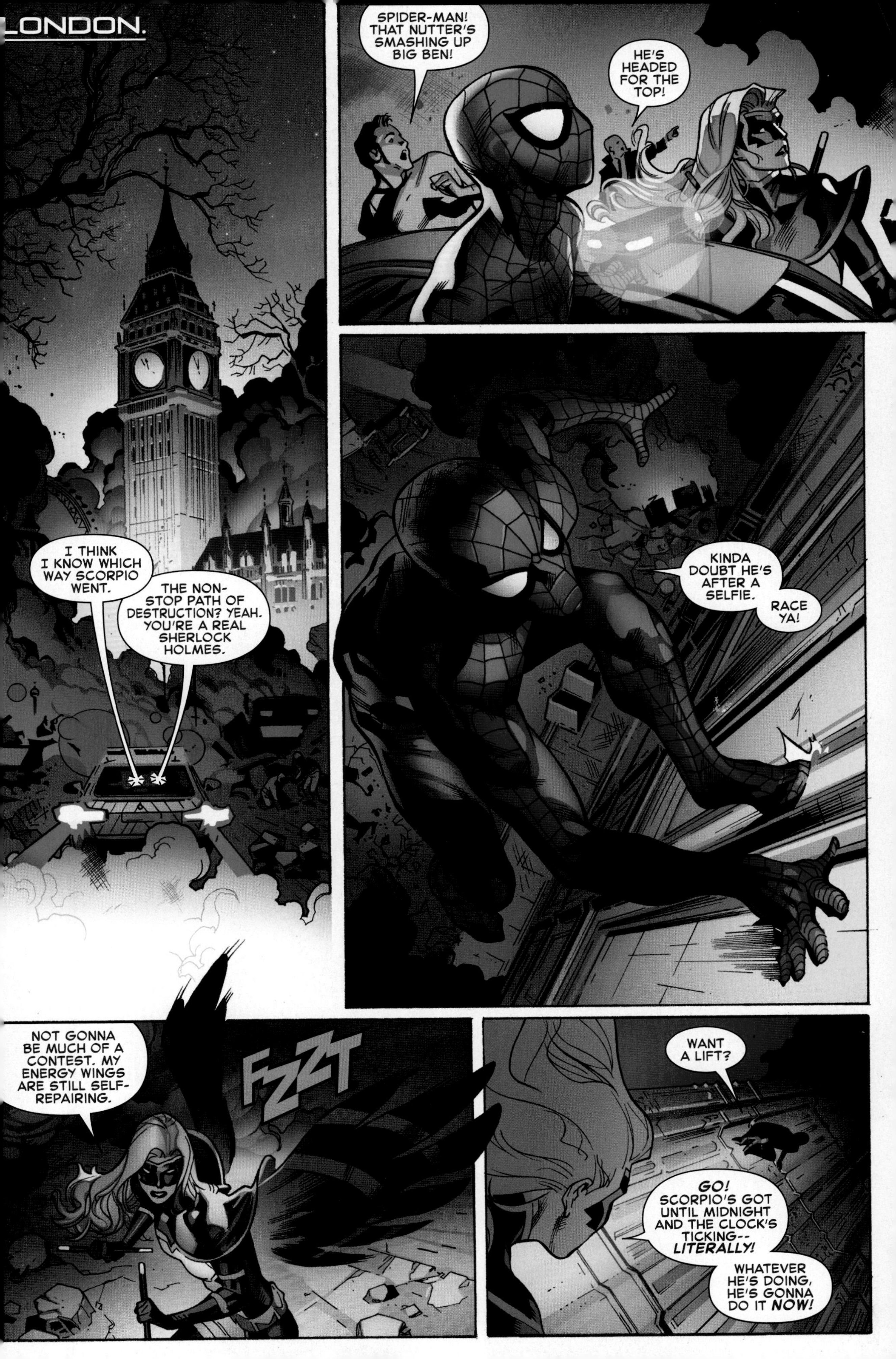
LONDON.
I THINK I KNOW WHICH WAY SCORPIO WENT.
THE NON-STOP PATH OF DESTRUCTION? YEAH. YOU'RE A REAL SHERLOCK HOLMES.
SPIDER-MAN! THAT NUTTER'S SMASHING UP BIG BEN!
HE'S HEADED FOR THE TOP!
KINDA DOUBT HE'S AFTER A SELFIE.
RACE YA!
NOT GONNA BE MUCH OF A CONTEST. MY ENERGY WINGS ARE STILL SELF-REPAIRING.
FZZT
WANT A LIFT?
GO! SCORPIO'S GOT UNTIL MIDNIGHT AND THE CLOCK'S TICKING-- LITERALLY!
WHATEVER HE'S DOING, HE'S GONNA DO IT NOW!

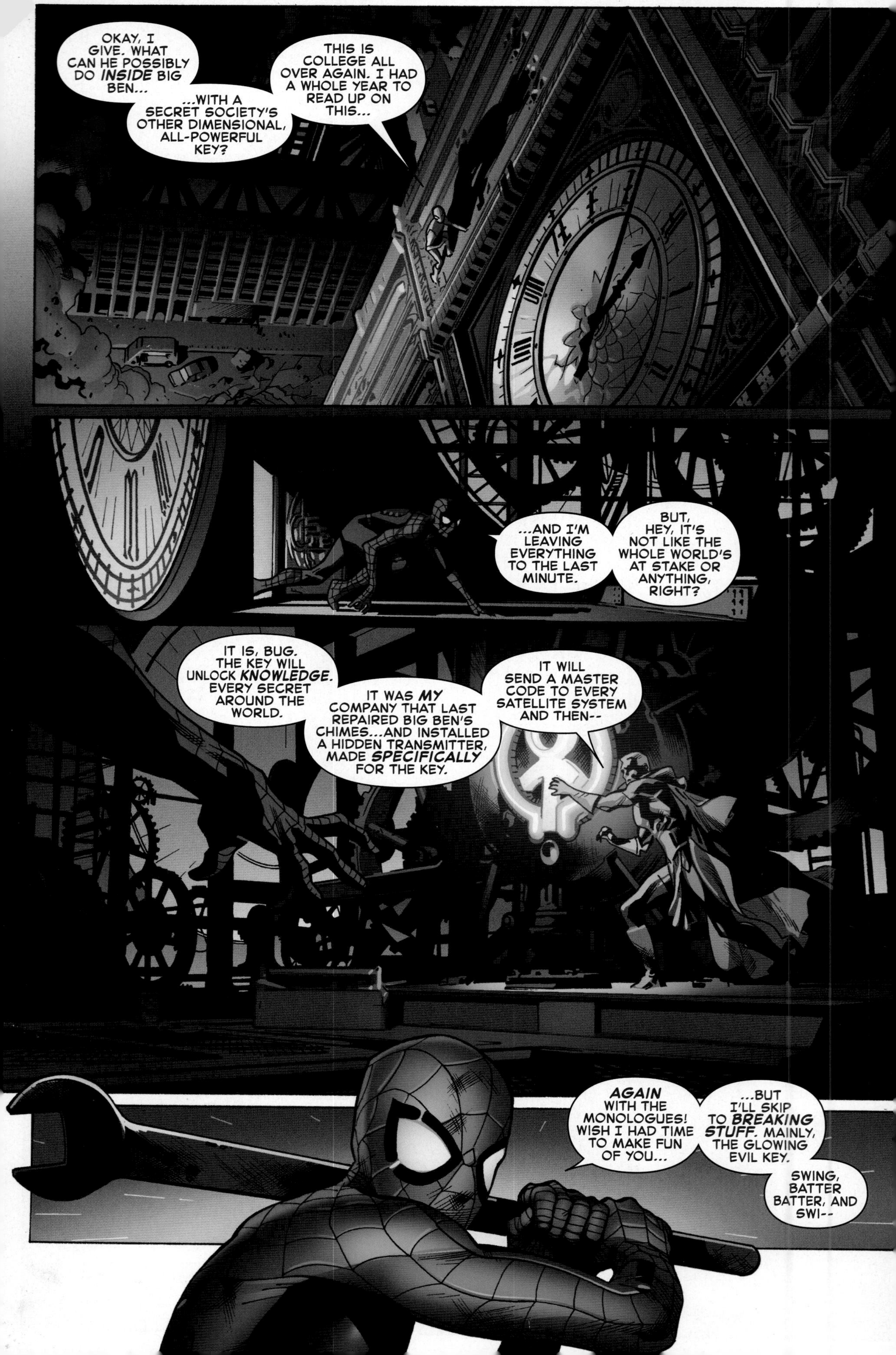
OKAY, I GIVE. WHAT CAN HE POSSIBLY DO INSIDE BIG BEN...
...WITH A SECRET SOCIETY'S OTHER DIMENSIONAL, ALL-POWERFUL KEY?
THIS IS COLLEGE ALL OVER AGAIN. I HAD A WHOLE YEAR TO READ UP ON THIS...
...AND I'M LEAVING EVERYTHING TO THE LAST MINUTE.
BUT, HEY, IT'S NOT LIKE THE WHOLE WORLD'S AT STAKE OR ANYTHING, RIGHT?
IT IS, BUG. THE KEY WILL UNLOCK KNOWLEDGE. EVERY SECRET AROUND THE WORLD.
IT WAS MY COMPANY THAT LAST REPAIRED BIG BEN'S CHIMES...AND INSTALLED A HIDDEN TRANSMITTER, MADE SPECIFICALLY FOR THE KEY.
IT WILL SEND A MASTER CODE TO EVERY SATELLITE SYSTEM AND THEN--
AGAIN WITH THE MONOLOGUES! WISH I HAD TIME TO MAKE FUN OF YOU...
...BUT I'LL SKIP TO BREAKING STUFF. MAINLY, THE GLOWING EVIL KEY.
SWING, BATTER BATTER, AND SWI--

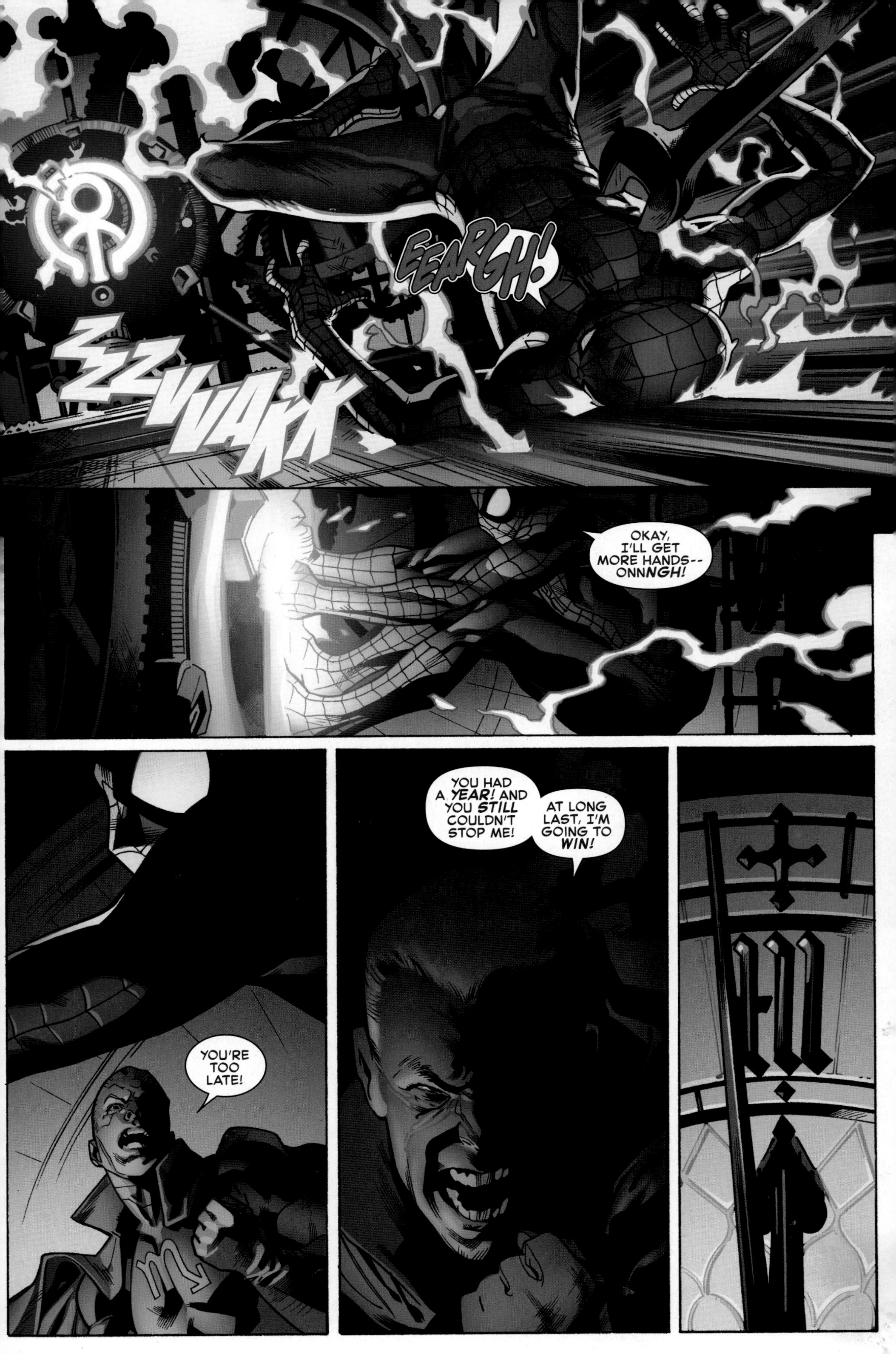
EEARGH!
ZZZVVAKK
OKAY, I'LL GET MORE HANDS--ONNNGH!
YOU'RE TOO LATE!
YOU HAD A YEAR! AND YOU STILL COULDN'T STOP ME!
AT LONG LAST, I'M GOING TO WIN!

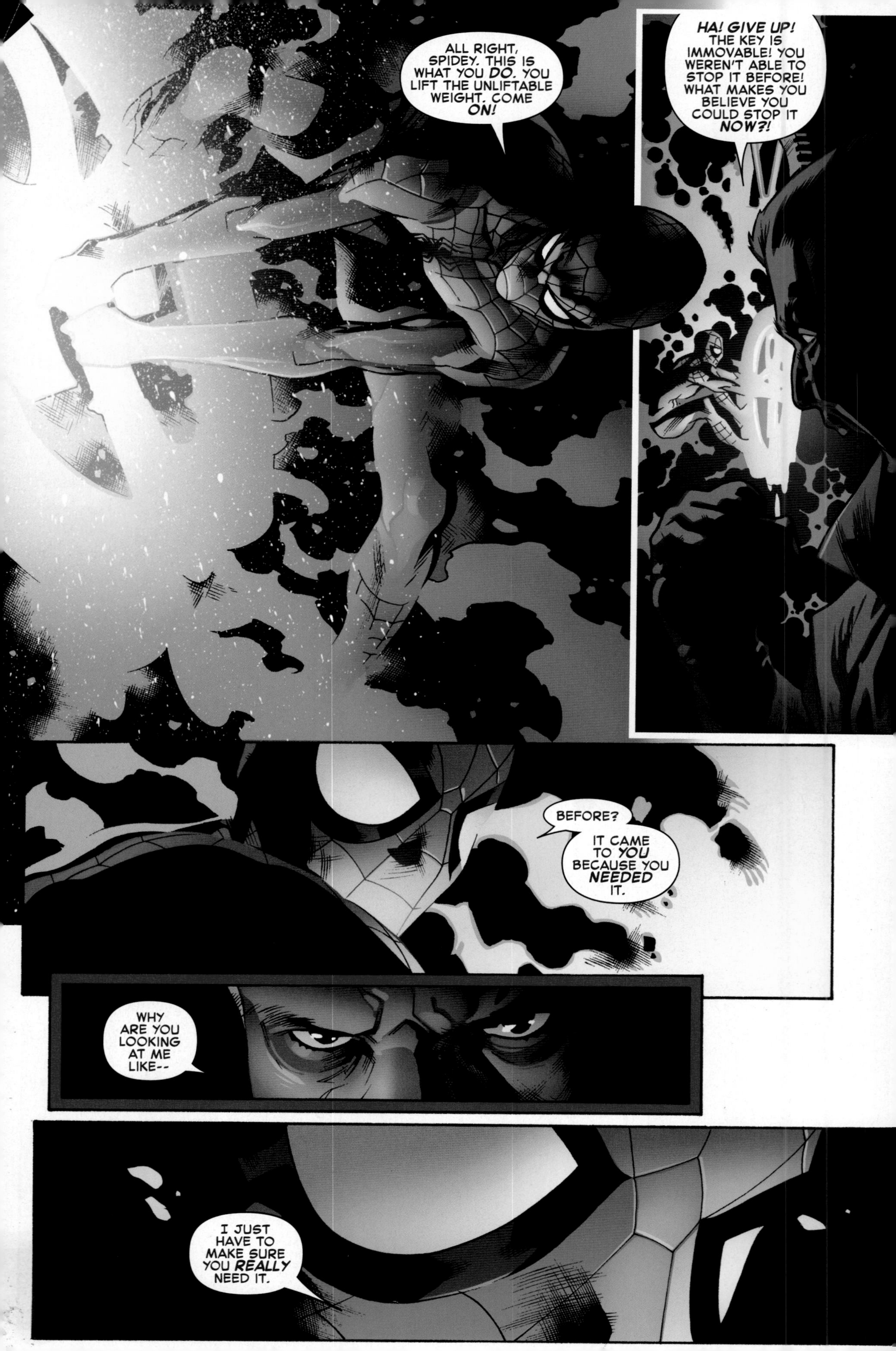
ALL RIGHT, SPIDEY. THIS IS WHAT YOU DO. YOU LIFT THE UNLIFTABLE WEIGHT. COME ON!
HA! GIVE UP! THE KEY IS IMMOVABLE! YOU WEREN'T ABLE TO STOP IT BEFORE! WHAT MAKES YOU BELIEVE YOU COULD STOP IT NOW?!
BEFORE?
IT CAME TO YOU BECAUSE YOU NEEDED IT.
WHY ARE YOU LOOKING AT ME LIKE--
I JUST HAVE TO MAKE SURE YOU REALLY NEED IT.

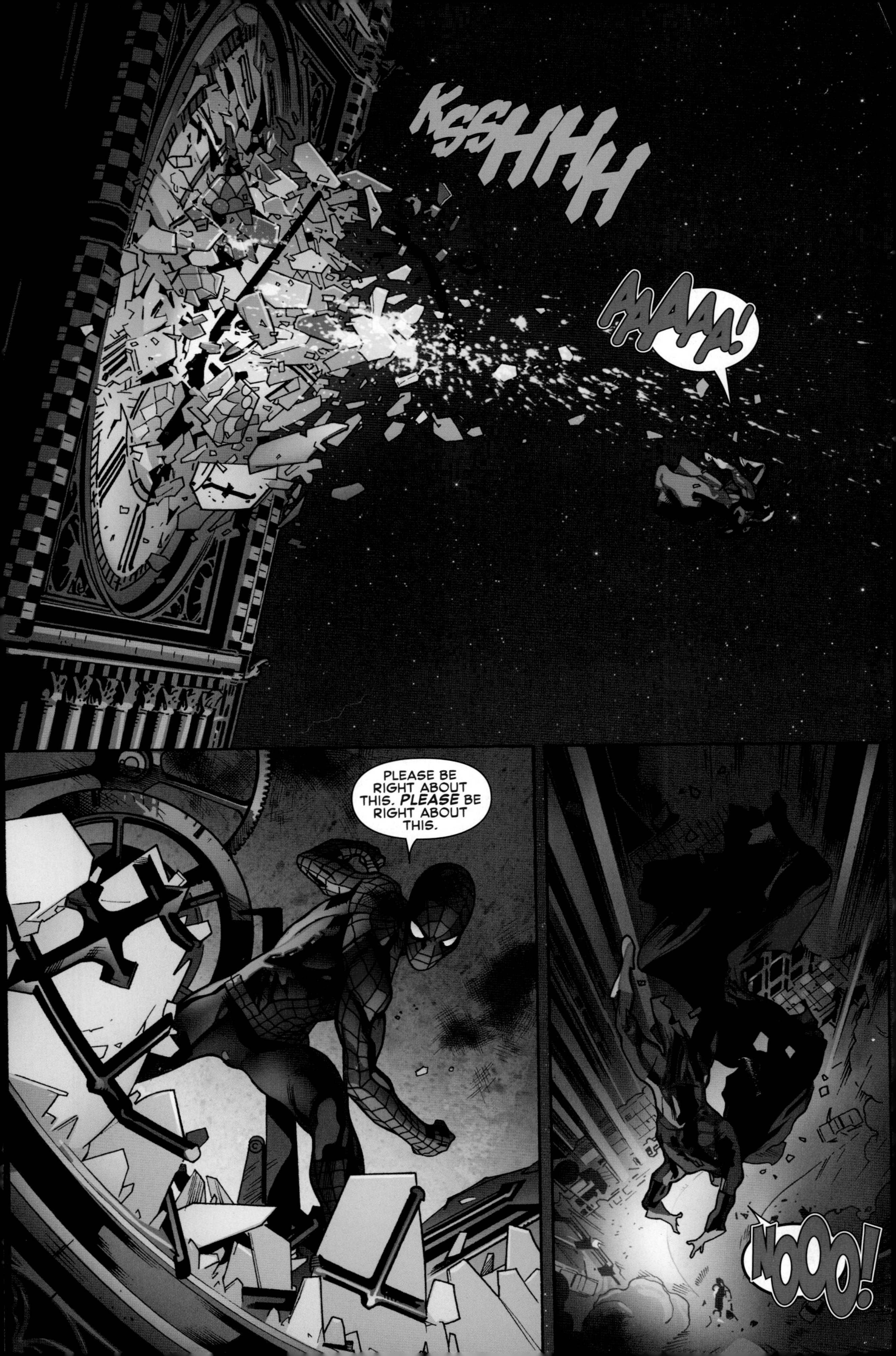
KSSHHH
AAAAA!
PLEASE BE RIGHT ABOUT THIS. *PLEASE* BE RIGHT ABOUT THIS.
NOOO!

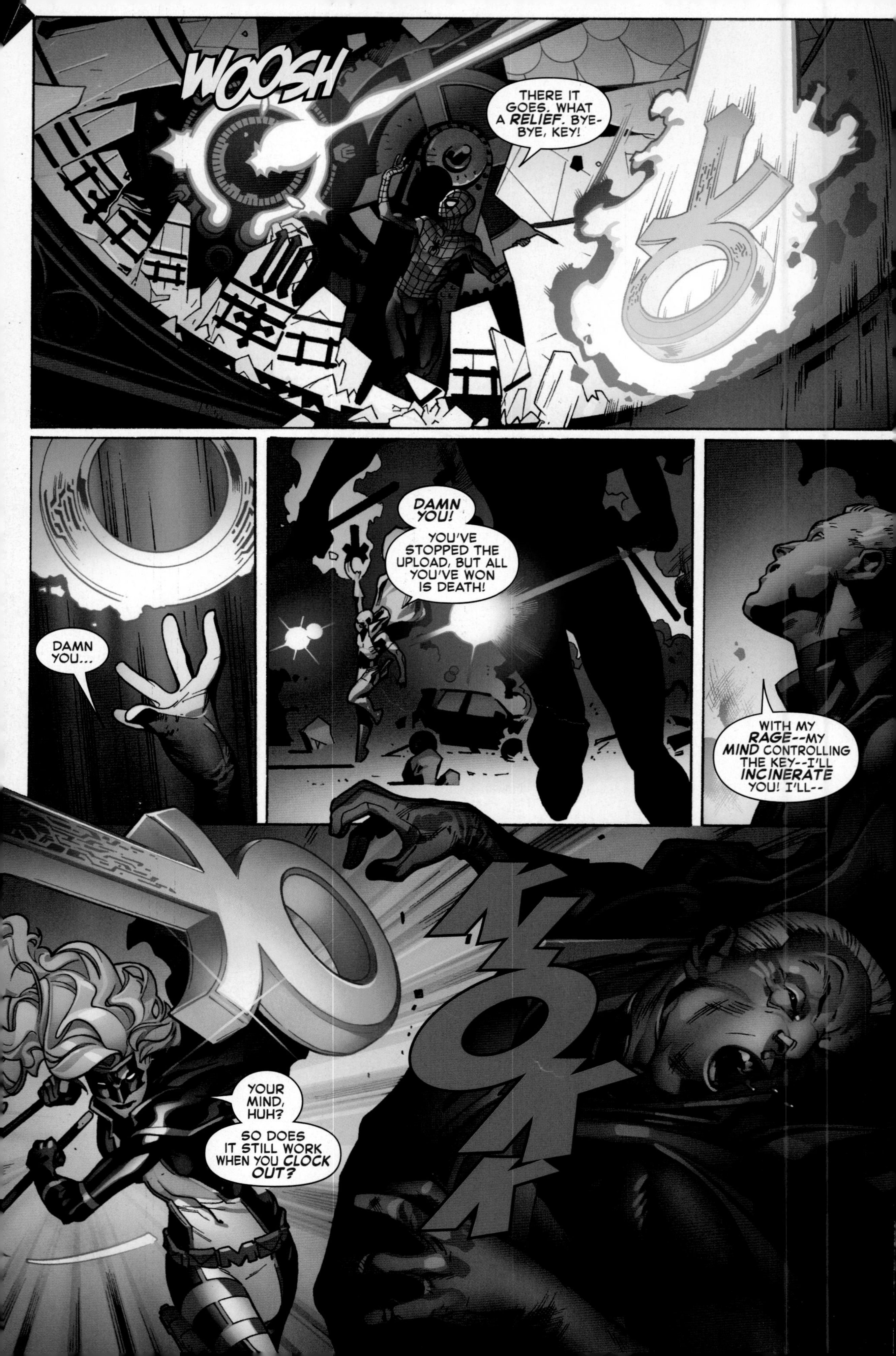

WOOSH
THERE IT GOES. WHAT A RELIEF. BYE-BYE, KEY!
DAMN YOU...
DAMN YOU!
YOU'VE STOPPED THE UPLOAD, BUT ALL YOU'VE WON IS DEATH!
WITH MY RAGE--MY MIND CONTROLLING THE KEY--I'LL INCINERATE YOU! I'LL--
YOUR MIND, HUH?
SO DOES IT STILL WORK WHEN YOU CLOCK OUT?

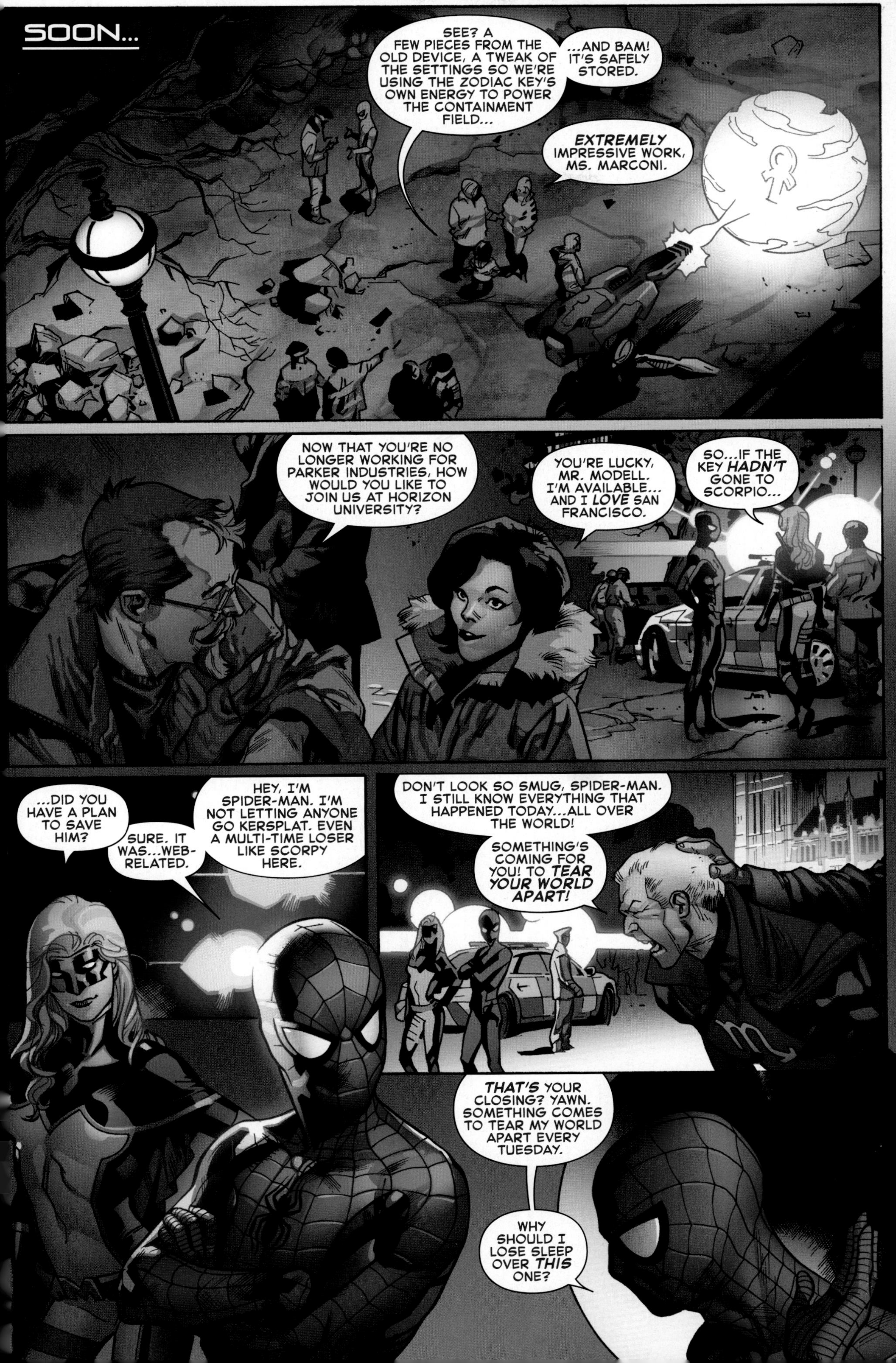
SOON...
SEE? A FEW PIECES FROM THE OLD DEVICE, A TWEAK OF THE SETTINGS SO WE'RE USING THE ZODIAC KEY'S OWN ENERGY TO POWER THE CONTAINMENT FIELD...
...AND BAM! IT'S SAFELY STORED.
EXTREMELY IMPRESSIVE WORK, MS. MARCONI.
NOW THAT YOU'RE NO LONGER WORKING FOR PARKER INDUSTRIES, HOW WOULD YOU LIKE TO JOIN US AT HORIZON UNIVERSITY?
YOU'RE LUCKY, MR. MODELL. I'M AVAILABLE... AND I LOVE SAN FRANCISCO.
SO...IF THE KEY HADN'T GONE TO SCORPIO...
...DID YOU HAVE A PLAN TO SAVE HIM?
SURE. IT WAS...WEB-RELATED.
HEY, I'M SPIDER-MAN. I'M NOT LETTING ANYONE GO KERSPLAT. EVEN A MULTI-TIME LOSER LIKE SCORPY HERE.
DON'T LOOK SO SMUG, SPIDER-MAN. I STILL KNOW EVERYTHING THAT HAPPENED TODAY...ALL OVER THE WORLD!
SOMETHING'S COMING FOR YOU! TO TEAR YOUR WORLD APART!
THAT'S YOUR CLOSING? YAWN. SOMETHING COMES TO TEAR MY WORLD APART EVERY TUESDAY.
WHY SHOULD I LOSE SLEEP OVER THIS ONE?

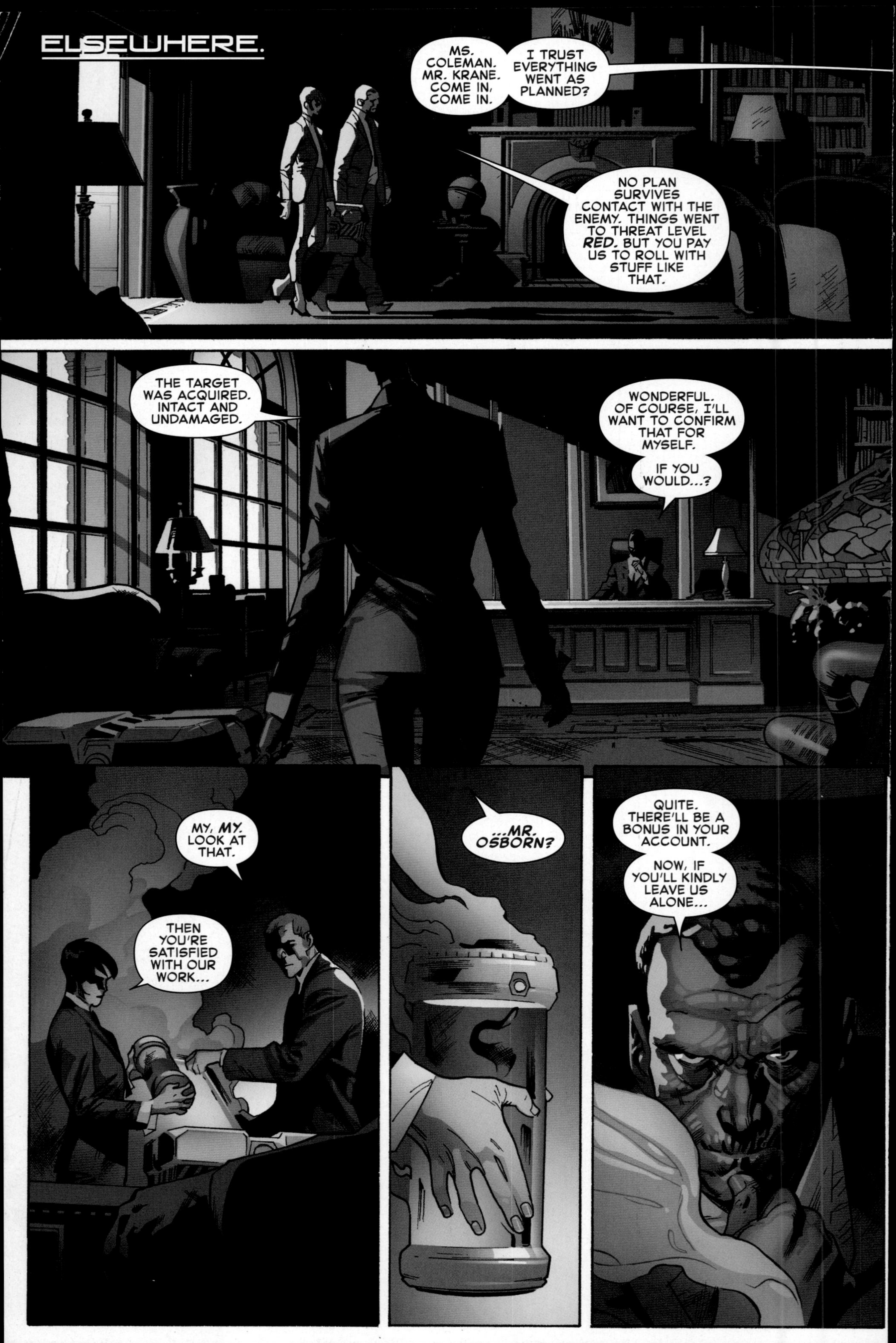
ELSEWHERE.
MS. COLEMAN. MR. KRANE. COME IN, COME IN.
I TRUST EVERYTHING WENT AS PLANNED?
NO PLAN SURVIVES CONTACT WITH THE ENEMY. THINGS WENT TO THREAT LEVEL RED. BUT YOU PAY US TO ROLL WITH STUFF LIKE THAT.
THE TARGET WAS ACQUIRED. INTACT AND UNDAMAGED.
WONDERFUL. OF COURSE, I'LL WANT TO CONFIRM THAT FOR MYSELF.
IF YOU WOULD...?
MY, MY. LOOK AT THAT.
THEN YOU'RE SATISFIED WITH OUR WORK...
...MR. OSBORN?
QUITE. THERE'LL BE A BONUS IN YOUR ACCOUNT.
NOW, IF YOU'LL KINDLY LEAVE US ALONE...

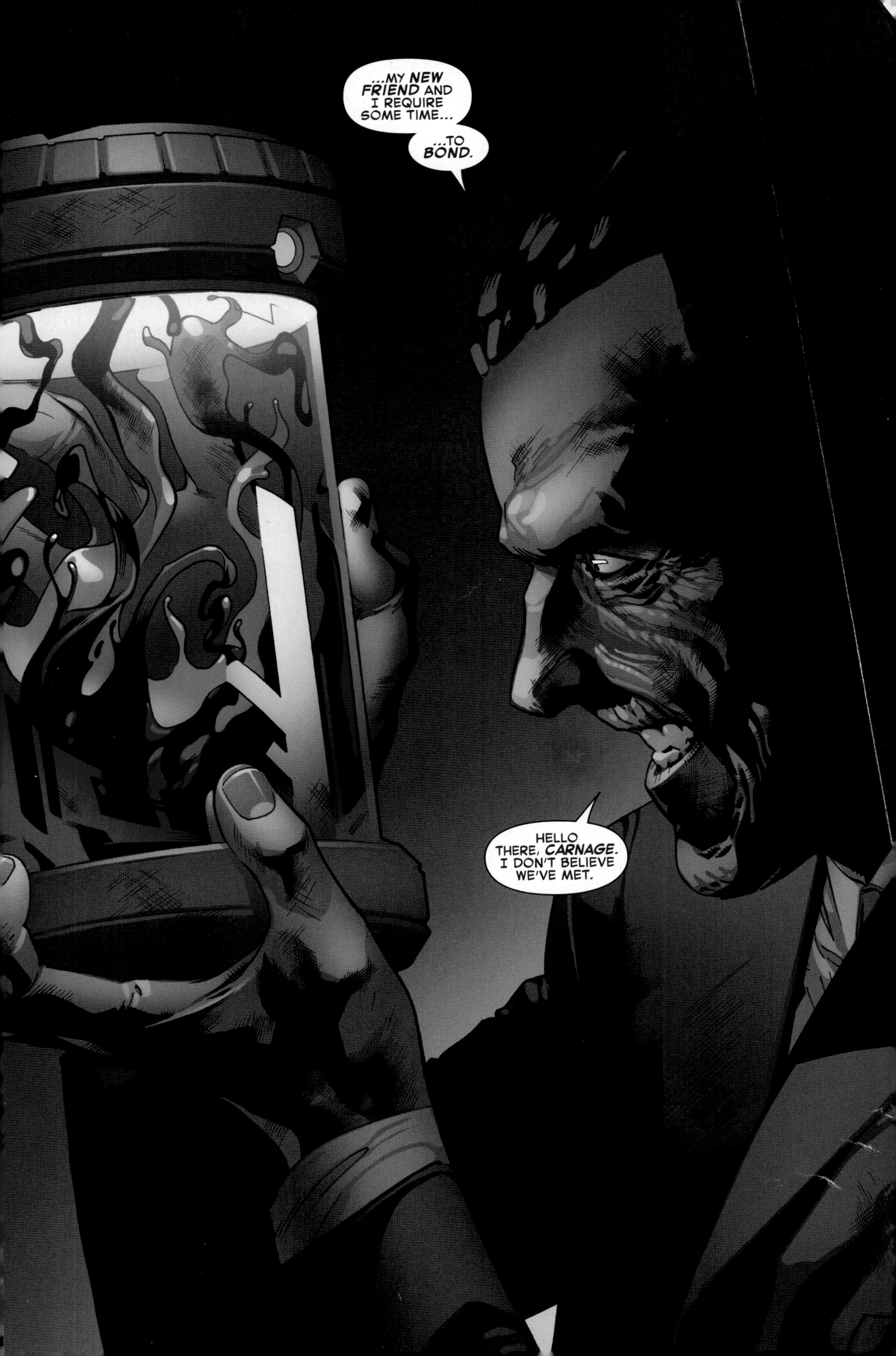
...MY NEW FRIEND AND I REQUIRE SOME TIME...
...TO BOND.
HELLO THERE, CARNAGE. I DON'T BELIEVE WE'VE MET.

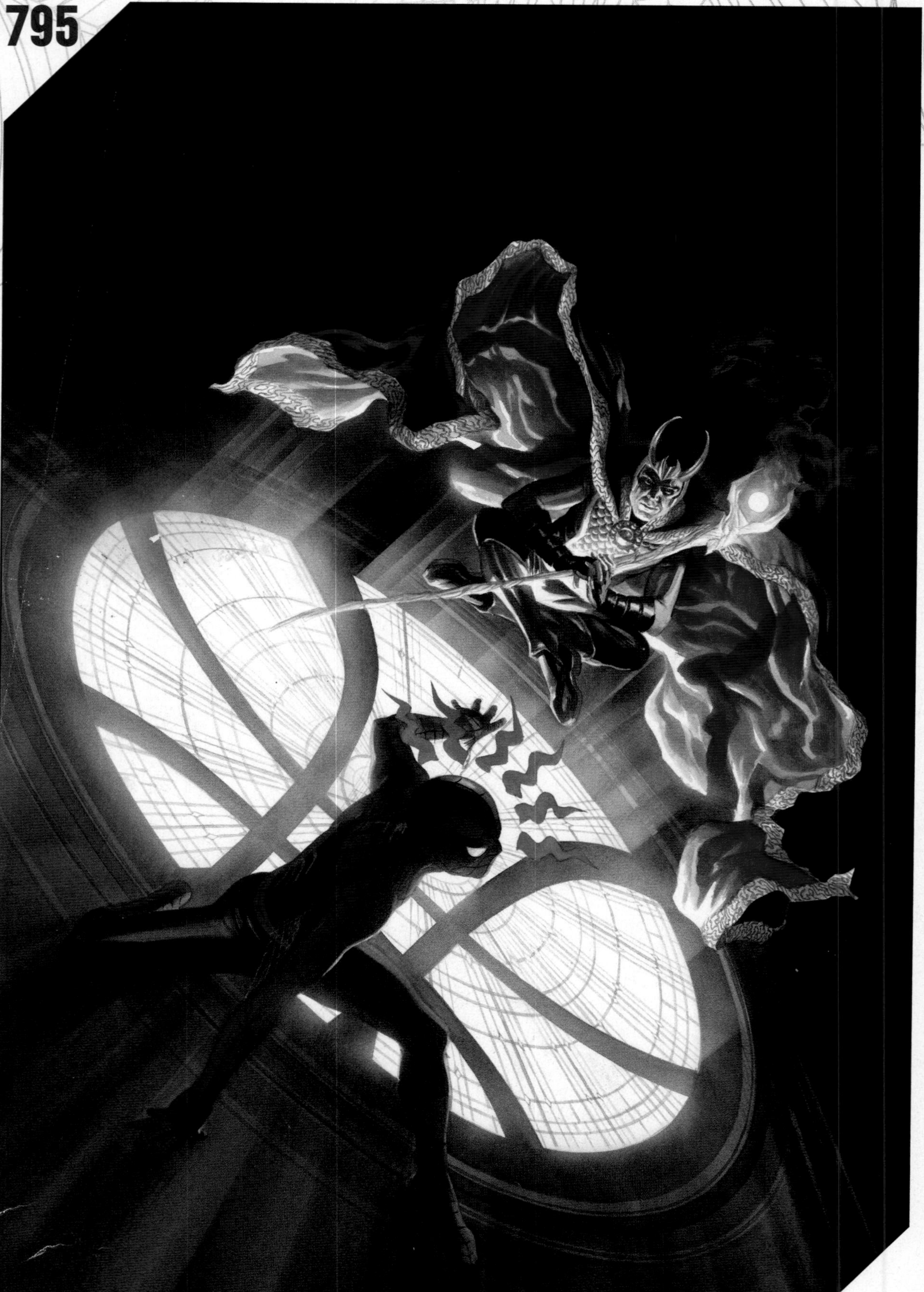

THREAT LEVEL: RED PART TWO "THE FAVOR"

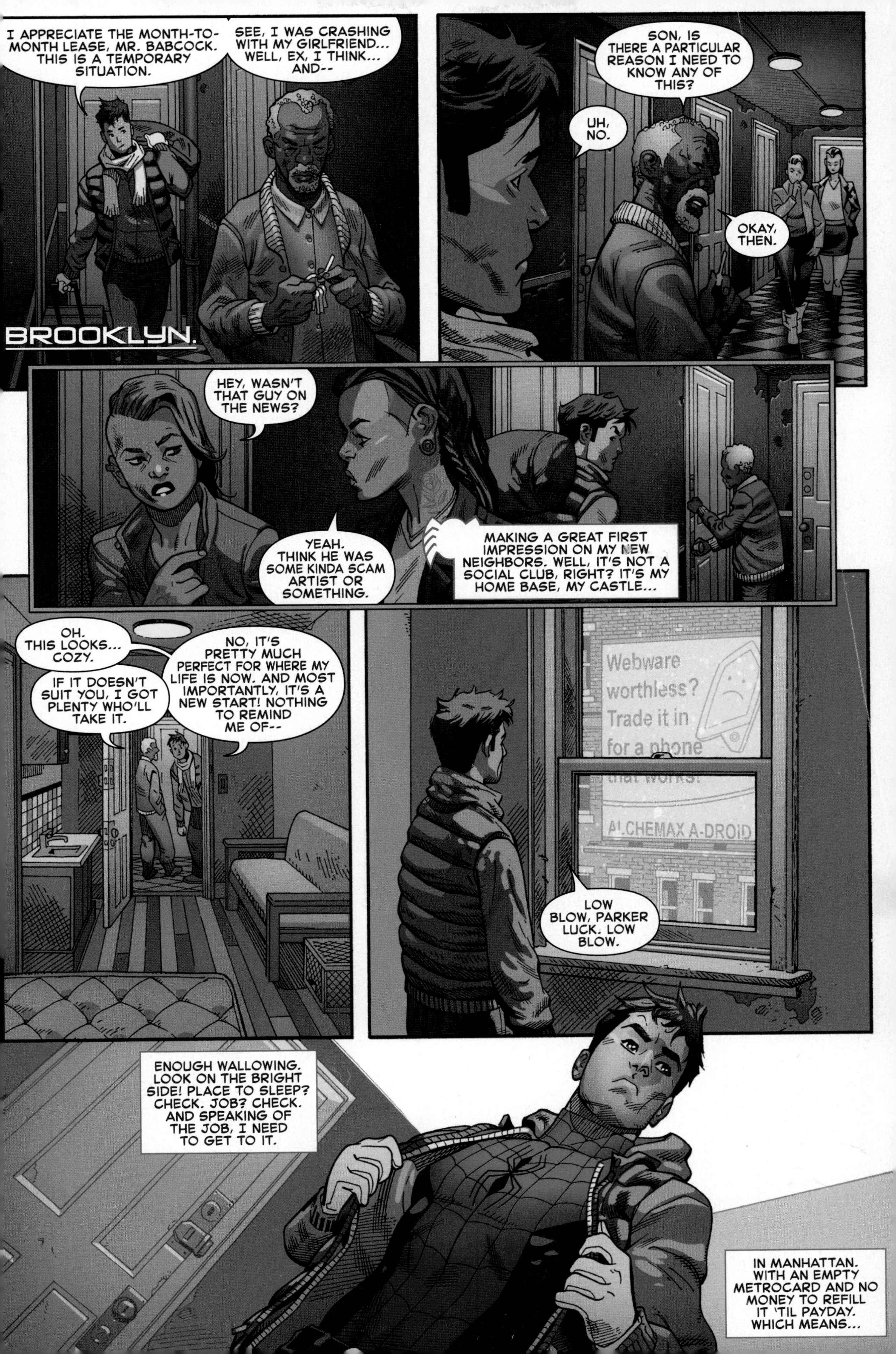
I APPRECIATE THE MONTH-TO-MONTH LEASE, MR. BABCOCK. THIS IS A TEMPORARY SITUATION.
SEE, I WAS CRASHING WITH MY GIRLFRIEND... WELL, EX, I THINK... AND--
BROOKLYN.
SON, IS THERE A PARTICULAR REASON I NEED TO KNOW ANY OF THIS?
UH, NO.
OKAY, THEN.
HEY, WASN'T THAT GUY ON THE NEWS?
YEAH. THINK HE WAS SOME KINDA SCAM ARTIST OR SOMETHING.
MAKING A GREAT FIRST IMPRESSION ON MY NEW NEIGHBORS. WELL, IT'S NOT A SOCIAL CLUB, RIGHT? IT'S MY HOME BASE, MY CASTLE...
OH. THIS LOOKS... COZY.
IF IT DOESN'T SUIT YOU, I GOT PLENTY WHO'LL TAKE IT.
NO, IT'S PRETTY MUCH PERFECT FOR WHERE MY LIFE IS NOW. AND MOST IMPORTANTLY, IT'S A NEW START! NOTHING TO REMIND ME OF--
Webware worthless? Trade it in for a phone that works!
ALCHEMAX A-DROID
LOW BLOW, PARKER LUCK. LOW BLOW.
ENOUGH WALLOWING. LOOK ON THE BRIGHT SIDE! PLACE TO SLEEP? CHECK. JOB? CHECK. AND SPEAKING OF THE JOB, I NEED TO GET TO IT.
IN MANHATTAN. WITH AN EMPTY METROCARD AND NO MONEY TO REFILL IT 'TIL PAYDAY. WHICH MEANS...

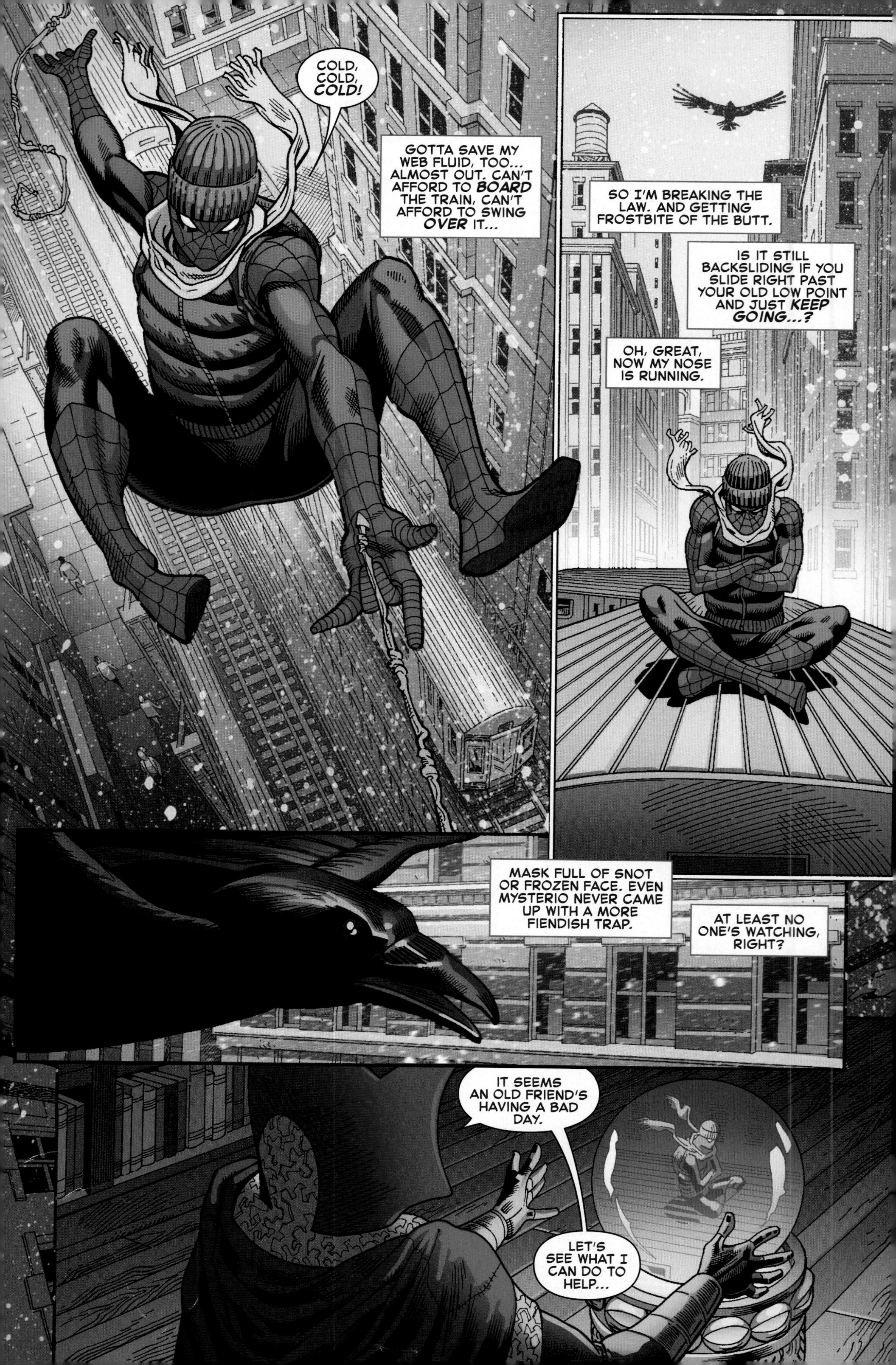
COLD, COLD, COLD!
GOTTA SAVE MY WEB FLUID, TOO... ALMOST OUT. CAN'T AFFORD TO BOARD THE TRAIN, CAN'T AFFORD TO SWING OVER IT...
SO I'M BREAKING THE LAW. AND GETTING FROSTBITE OF THE BUTT.
IS IT STILL BACKSLIDING IF YOU SLIDE RIGHT PAST YOUR OLD LOW POINT AND JUST KEEP GOING...?
OH, GREAT, NOW MY NOSE IS RUNNING.
MASK FULL OF SNOT OR FROZEN FACE. EVEN MYSTERIO NEVER CAME UP WITH A MORE FIENDISH TRAP.
AT LEAST NO ONE'S WATCHING, RIGHT?
IT SEEMS AN OLD FRIEND'S HAVING A BAD DAY.
LET'S SEE WHAT I CAN DO TO HELP...

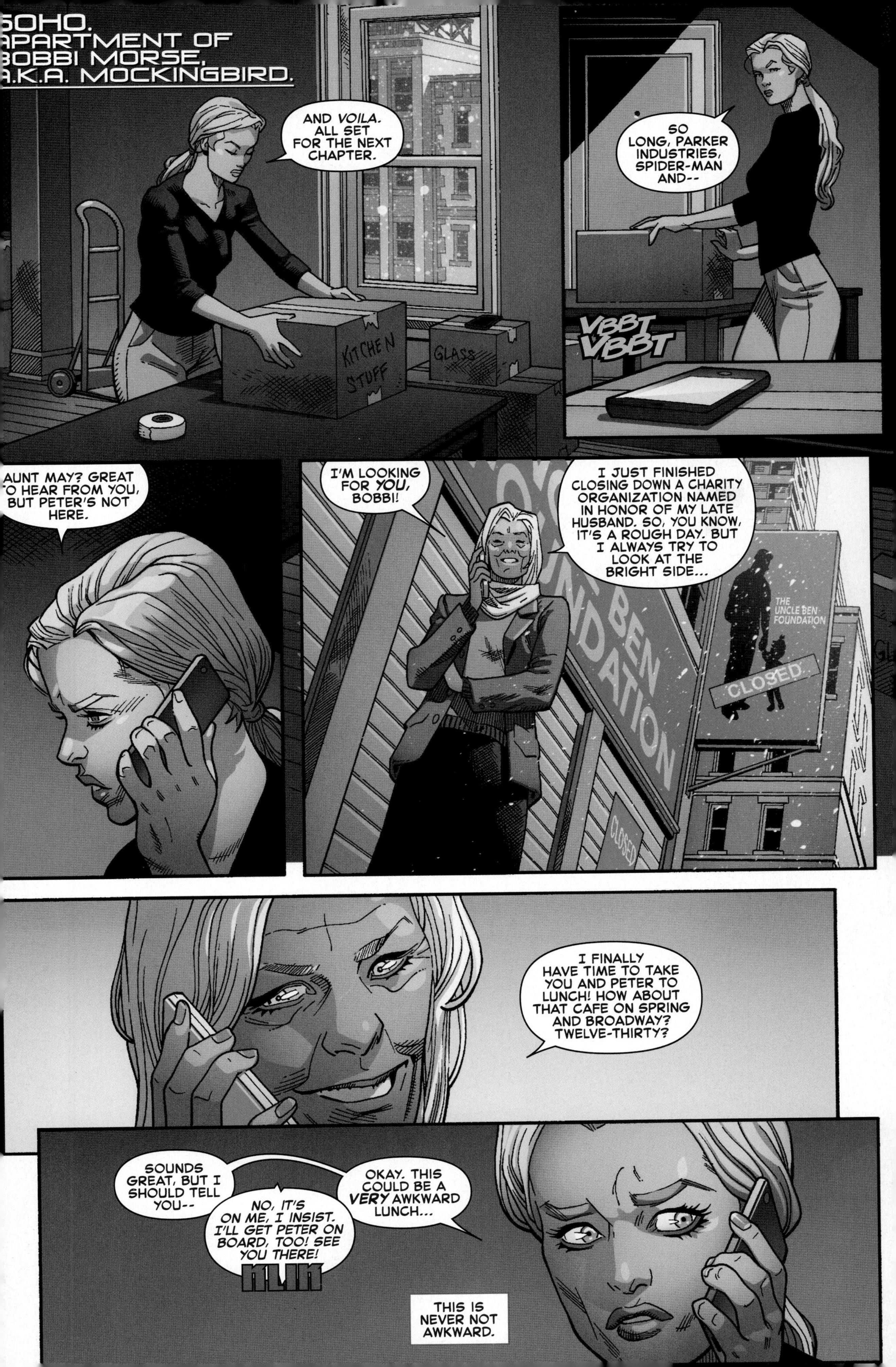

SOHO.
APARTMENT OF BOBBI MORSE, A.K.A. MOCKINGBIRD.
AND VOILA. ALL SET FOR THE NEXT CHAPTER.
KITCHEN STUFF
GLASS
SO LONG, PARKER INDUSTRIES, SPIDER-MAN AND--
VBBT VBBT
AUNT MAY? GREAT TO HEAR FROM YOU, BUT PETER'S NOT HERE.
I'M LOOKING FOR YOU, BOBBI!
I JUST FINISHED CLOSING DOWN A CHARITY ORGANIZATION NAMED IN HONOR OF MY LATE HUSBAND. SO, YOU KNOW, IT'S A ROUGH DAY. BUT I ALWAYS TRY TO LOOK AT THE BRIGHT SIDE...
THE UNCLE BEN FOUNDATION
CLOSED
CLOSED
I FINALLY HAVE TIME TO TAKE YOU AND PETER TO LUNCH! HOW ABOUT THAT CAFE ON SPRING AND BROADWAY? TWELVE-THIRTY?
SOUNDS GREAT, BUT I SHOULD TELL YOU--
NO, IT'S ON ME, I INSIST. I'LL GET PETER ON BOARD, TOO! SEE YOU THERE!
KLIK
OKAY. THIS COULD BE A VERY AWKWARD LUNCH...
THIS IS NEVER NOT AWKWARD.

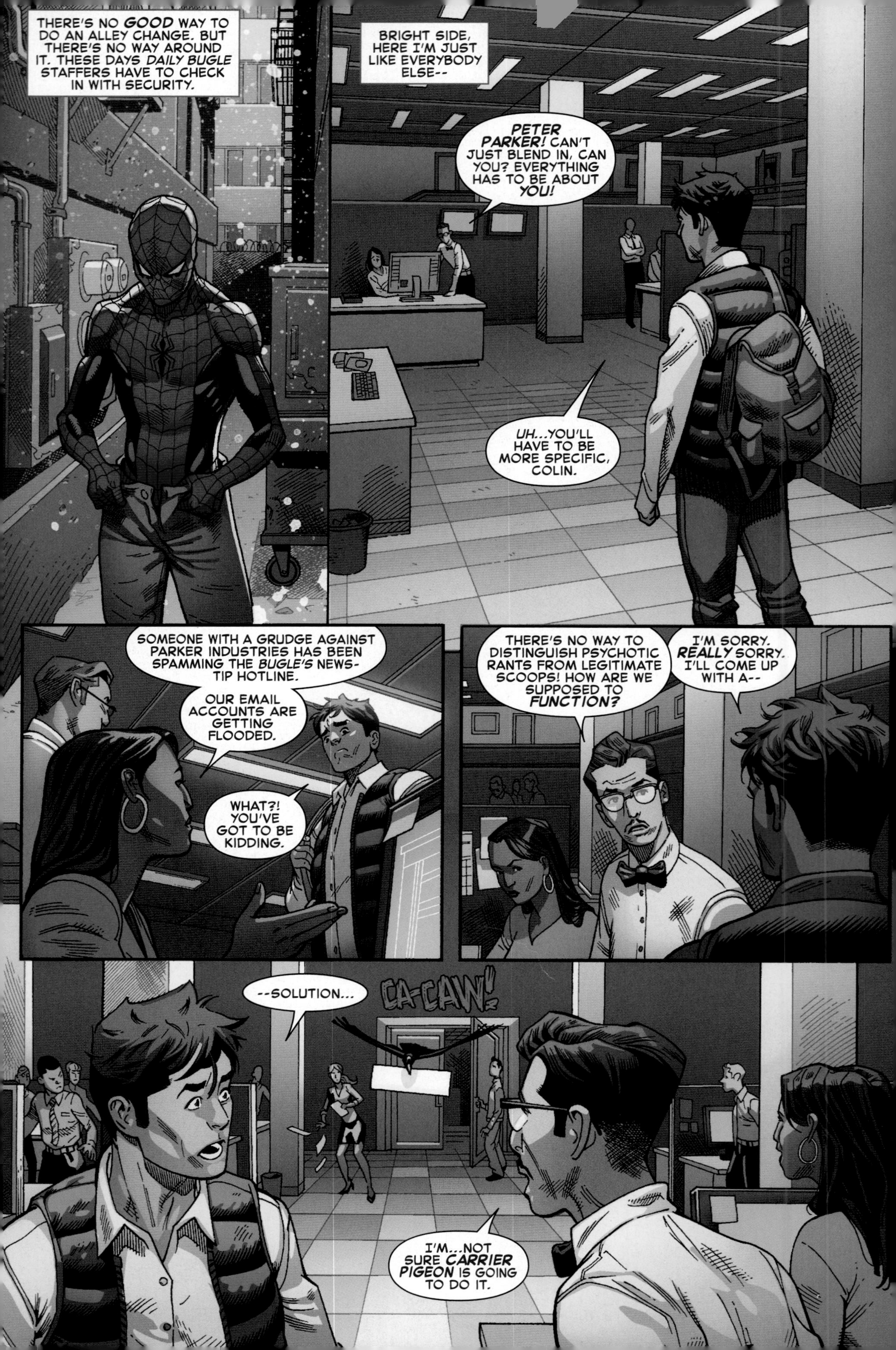
THERE'S NO *GOOD* WAY TO DO AN ALLEY CHANGE. BUT THERE'S NO WAY AROUND IT. THESE DAYS *DAILY BUGLE* STAFFERS HAVE TO CHECK IN WITH SECURITY.
BRIGHT SIDE, HERE I'M JUST LIKE EVERYBODY ELSE--
PETER PARKER! CAN'T JUST BLEND IN, CAN YOU? EVERYTHING HAS TO BE ABOUT *YOU!*
UH...YOU'LL HAVE TO BE MORE SPECIFIC, COLIN.
SOMEONE WITH A GRUDGE AGAINST PARKER INDUSTRIES HAS BEEN SPAMMING THE *BUGLE'S* NEWS-TIP HOTLINE.
OUR EMAIL ACCOUNTS ARE GETTING FLOODED.
WHAT?! YOU'VE GOT TO BE KIDDING.
THERE'S NO WAY TO DISTINGUISH PSYCHOTIC RANTS FROM LEGITIMATE SCOOPS! HOW ARE WE SUPPOSED TO *FUNCTION?*
I'M SORRY. *REALLY* SORRY. I'LL COME UP WITH A--
--SOLUTION...
CA-CAW!
I'M...NOT SURE *CARRIER PIGEON* IS GOING TO DO IT.

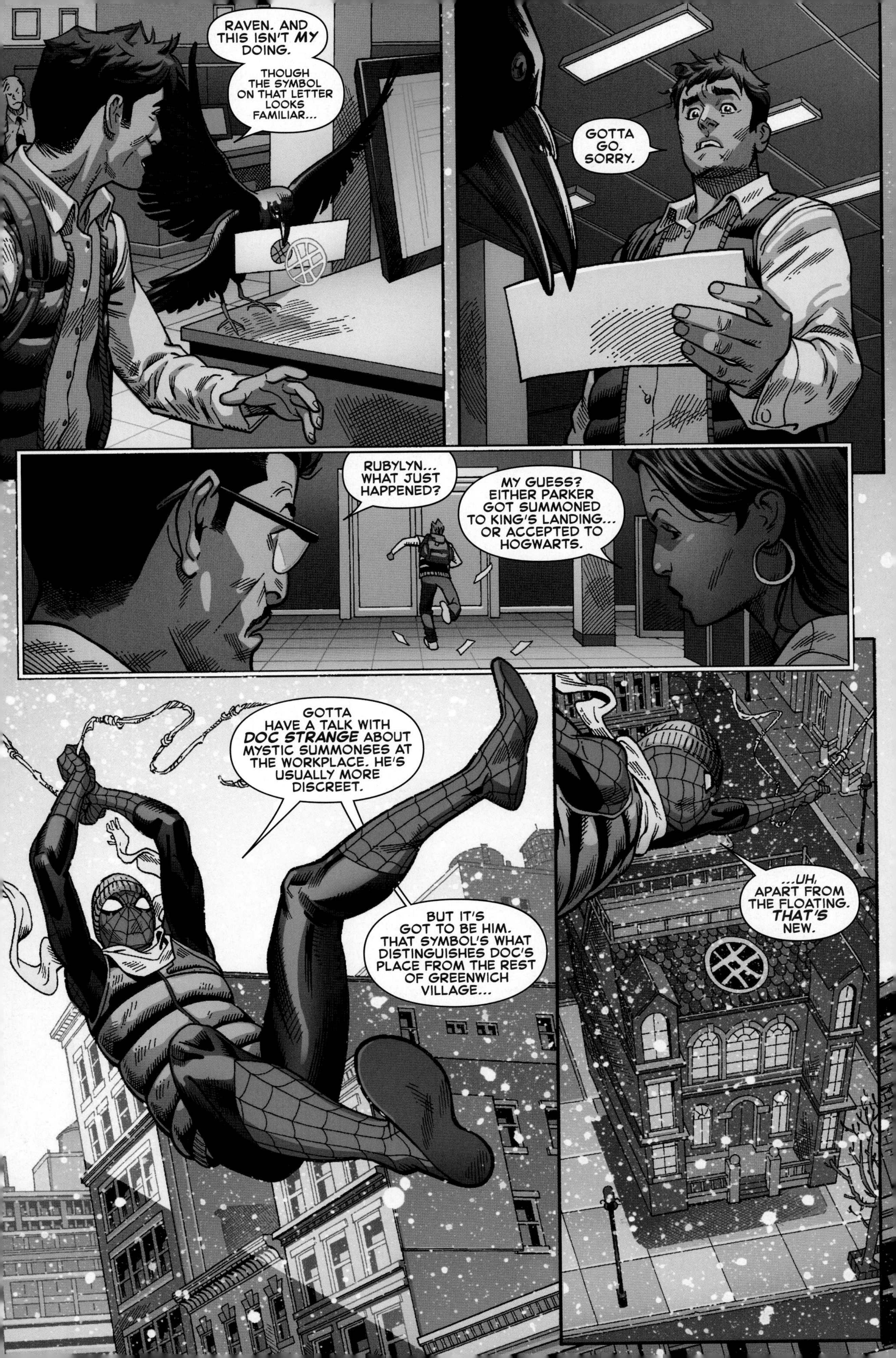
RAVEN. AND THIS ISN'T *MY* DOING.
THOUGH THE SYMBOL ON THAT LETTER LOOKS FAMILIAR...
GOTTA GO. SORRY.
RUBYLYN... WHAT JUST HAPPENED?
MY GUESS? EITHER PARKER GOT SUMMONED TO KING'S LANDING... OR ACCEPTED TO HOGWARTS.
GOTTA HAVE A TALK WITH *DOC STRANGE* ABOUT MYSTIC SUMMONSES AT THE WORKPLACE. HE'S USUALLY MORE DISCREET.
BUT IT'S GOT TO BE HIM. THAT SYMBOL'S WHAT DISTINGUISHES DOC'S PLACE FROM THE REST OF GREENWICH VILLAGE...
...UH, APART FROM THE FLOATING. *THAT'S* NEW.

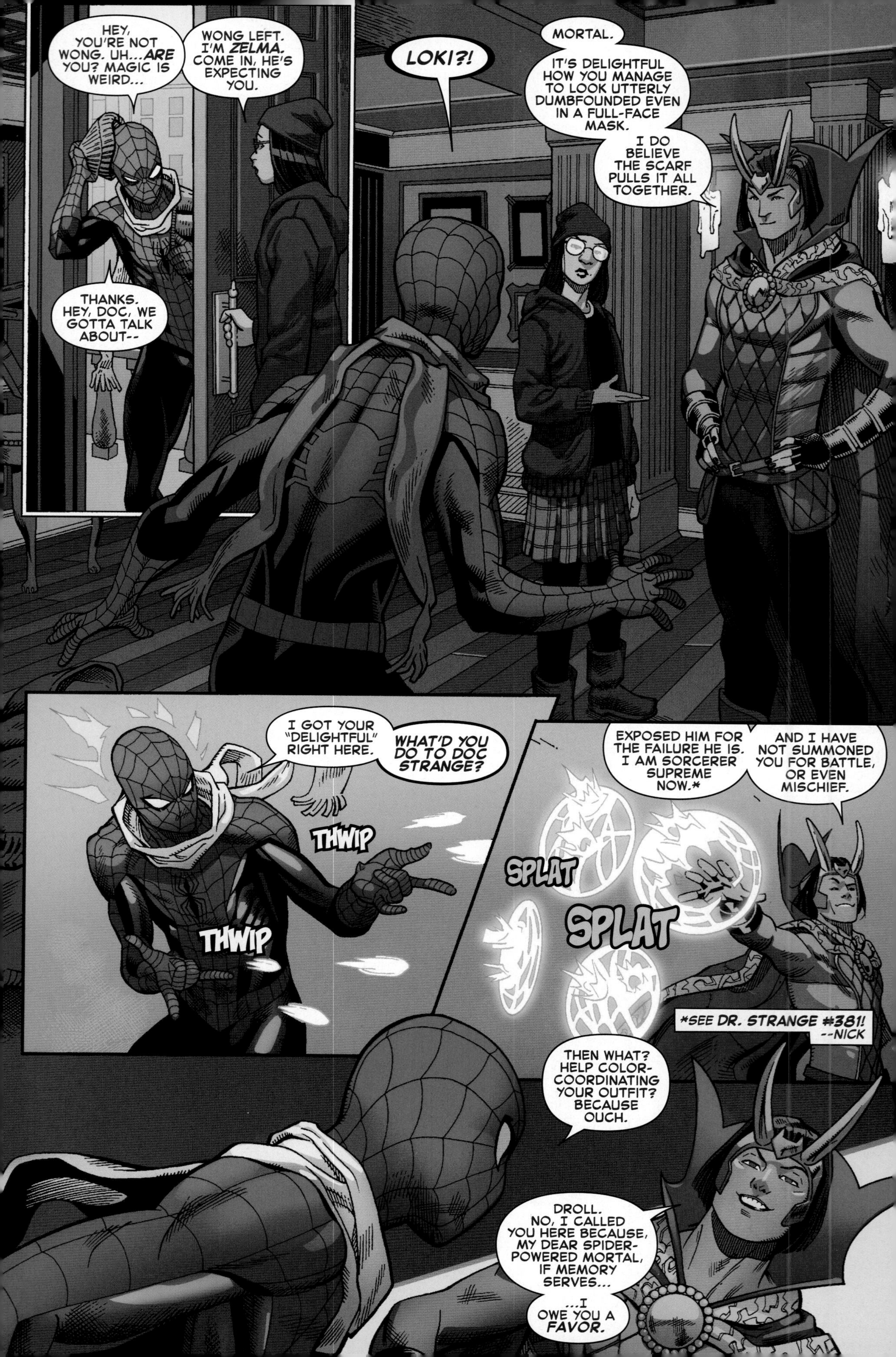
HEY, YOU'RE NOT WONG. UH...ARE YOU? MAGIC IS WEIRD...
WONG LEFT. I'M ZELMA. COME IN, HE'S EXPECTING YOU.
THANKS. HEY, DOC, WE GOTTA TALK ABOUT--
LOKI?!
MORTAL.
IT'S DELIGHTFUL HOW YOU MANAGE TO LOOK UTTERLY DUMBFOUNDED EVEN IN A FULL-FACE MASK.
I DO BELIEVE THE SCARF PULLS IT ALL TOGETHER.
I GOT YOUR "DELIGHTFUL" RIGHT HERE.
WHAT'D YOU DO TO DOC STRANGE?
THWIP
THWIP
EXPOSED HIM FOR THE FAILURE HE IS. I AM SORCERER SUPREME NOW.*
AND I HAVE NOT SUMMONED YOU FOR BATTLE, OR EVEN MISCHIEF.
SPLAT
SPLAT
*SEE DR. STRANGE #381! --NICK
THEN WHAT? HELP COLOR-COORDINATING YOUR OUTFIT? BECAUSE OUCH.
DROLL. NO, I CALLED YOU HERE BECAUSE, MY DEAR SPIDER-POWERED MORTAL, IF MEMORY SERVES...
...I OWE YOU A FAVOR.

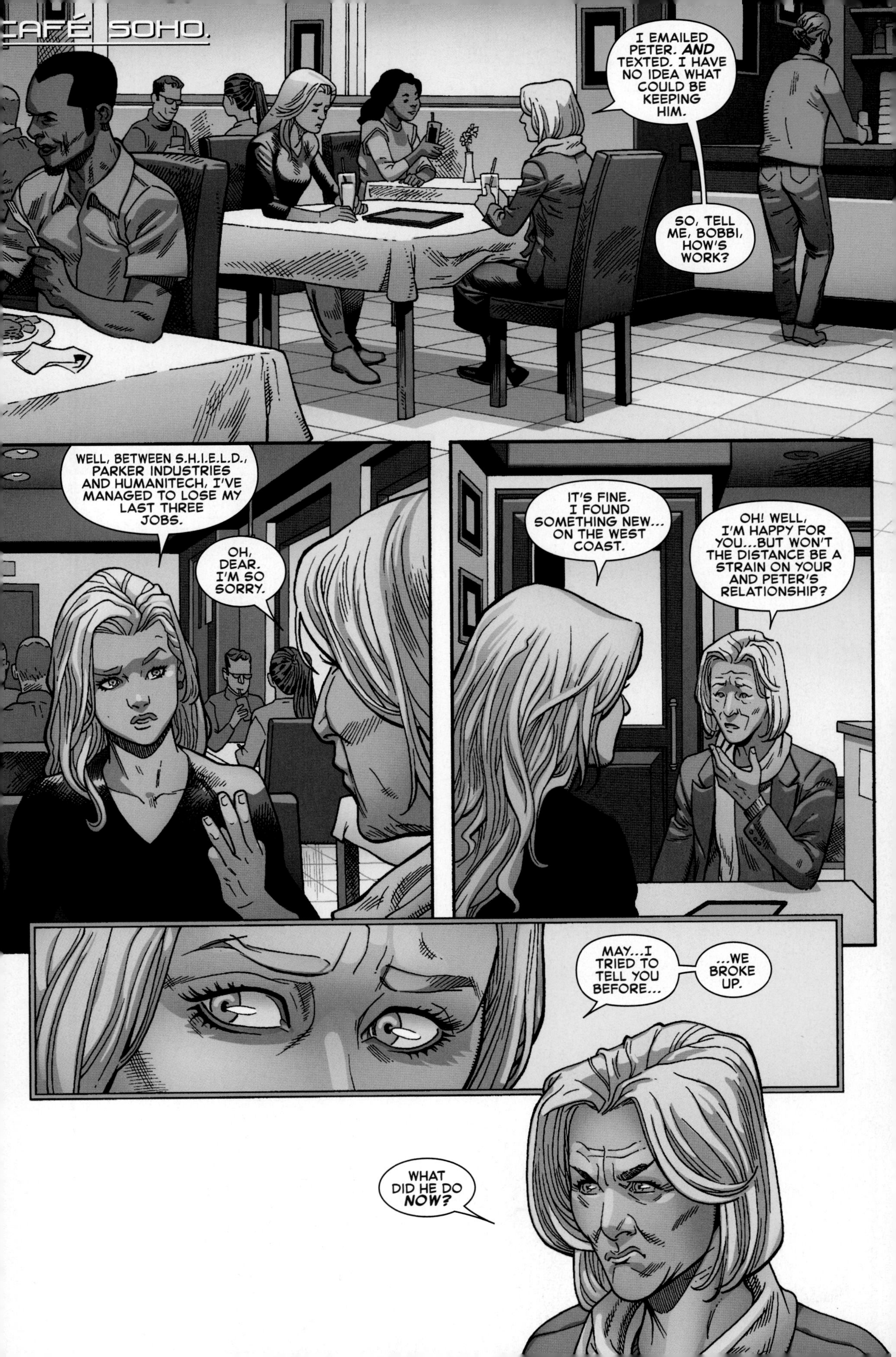
CAFÉ SOHO.
I EMAILED PETER. AND TEXTED. I HAVE NO IDEA WHAT COULD BE KEEPING HIM.
SO, TELL ME, BOBBI, HOW'S WORK?
WELL, BETWEEN S.H.I.E.L.D., PARKER INDUSTRIES AND HUMANITECH, I'VE MANAGED TO LOSE MY LAST THREE JOBS.
OH, DEAR. I'M SO SORRY.
IT'S FINE. I FOUND SOMETHING NEW... ON THE WEST COAST.
OH! WELL, I'M HAPPY FOR YOU...BUT WON'T THE DISTANCE BE A STRAIN ON YOUR AND PETER'S RELATIONSHIP?
MAY...I TRIED TO TELL YOU BEFORE...
...WE BROKE UP.
WHAT DID HE DO NOW?

IT WASN'T JUST HIM.

WHEN WE GOT TOGETHER, IT WAS IN THIS HECTIC, FAST-PACED JOB, GLOBE-HOPPING ON ONE...*PARKER INDUSTRIES VENTURE*...AFTER ANOTHER.

BARELY TIME TO BREATHE. IT WAS *GREAT*.

THEN, RECENTLY, WE WENT TO ENGLAND TO...WRAP UP A LOOSE END...

"...AND ON THE FLIGHT BACK, WE DIDN'T HAVE ANY WORK TO TALK ABOUT...OUR TVs WERE BROKEN...IT WAS JUST US."

"AND AFTER BEING STUCK TOGETHER FOR *SEVEN HOURS*, WE FINALLY REALIZED..."

OUTSIDE OF WORK...

...WE HAVE *ABSOLUTELY NOTHING* IN COMMON.

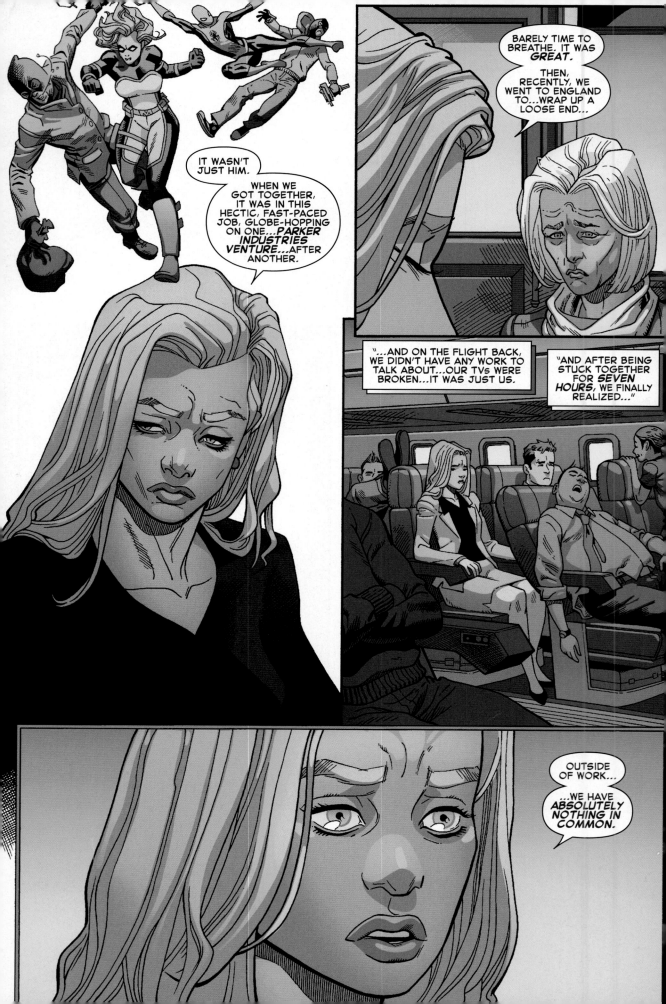

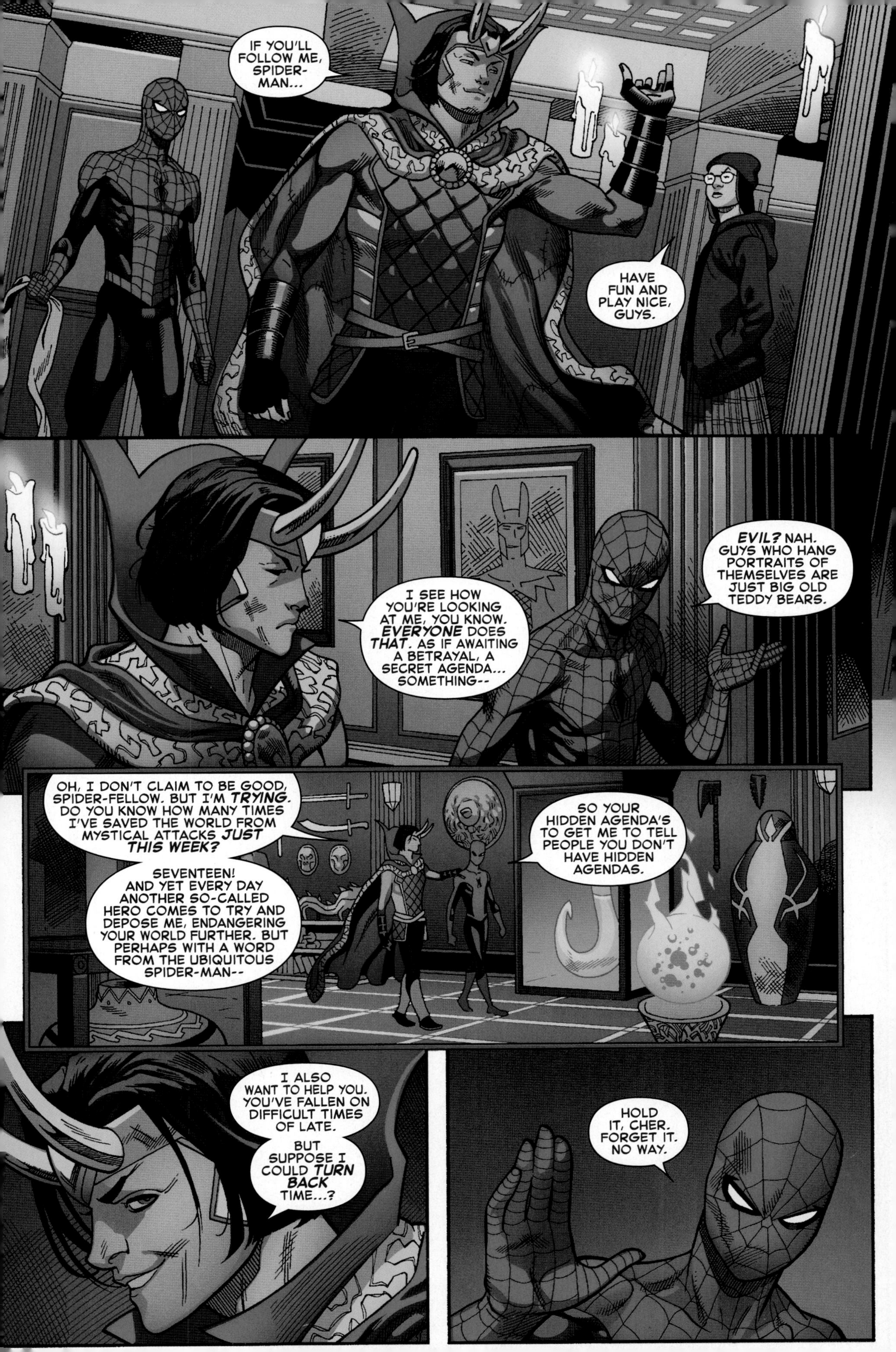
IF YOU'LL FOLLOW ME, SPIDER-MAN...
HAVE FUN AND PLAY NICE, GUYS.
I SEE HOW YOU'RE LOOKING AT ME, YOU KNOW. EVERYONE DOES THAT. AS IF AWAITING A BETRAYAL, A SECRET AGENDA... SOMETHING--
EVIL? NAH. GUYS WHO HANG PORTRAITS OF THEMSELVES ARE JUST BIG OLD TEDDY BEARS.
OH, I DON'T CLAIM TO BE GOOD, SPIDER-FELLOW. BUT I'M TRYING. DO YOU KNOW HOW MANY TIMES I'VE SAVED THE WORLD FROM MYSTICAL ATTACKS JUST THIS WEEK?
SEVENTEEN! AND YET EVERY DAY ANOTHER SO-CALLED HERO COMES TO TRY AND DEPOSE ME, ENDANGERING YOUR WORLD FURTHER. BUT PERHAPS WITH A WORD FROM THE UBIQUITOUS SPIDER-MAN--
SO YOUR HIDDEN AGENDA'S TO GET ME TO TELL PEOPLE YOU DON'T HAVE HIDDEN AGENDAS.
I ALSO WANT TO HELP YOU. YOU'VE FALLEN ON DIFFICULT TIMES OF LATE.
BUT SUPPOSE I COULD TURN BACK TIME...?
HOLD IT, CHER. FORGET IT. NO WAY.

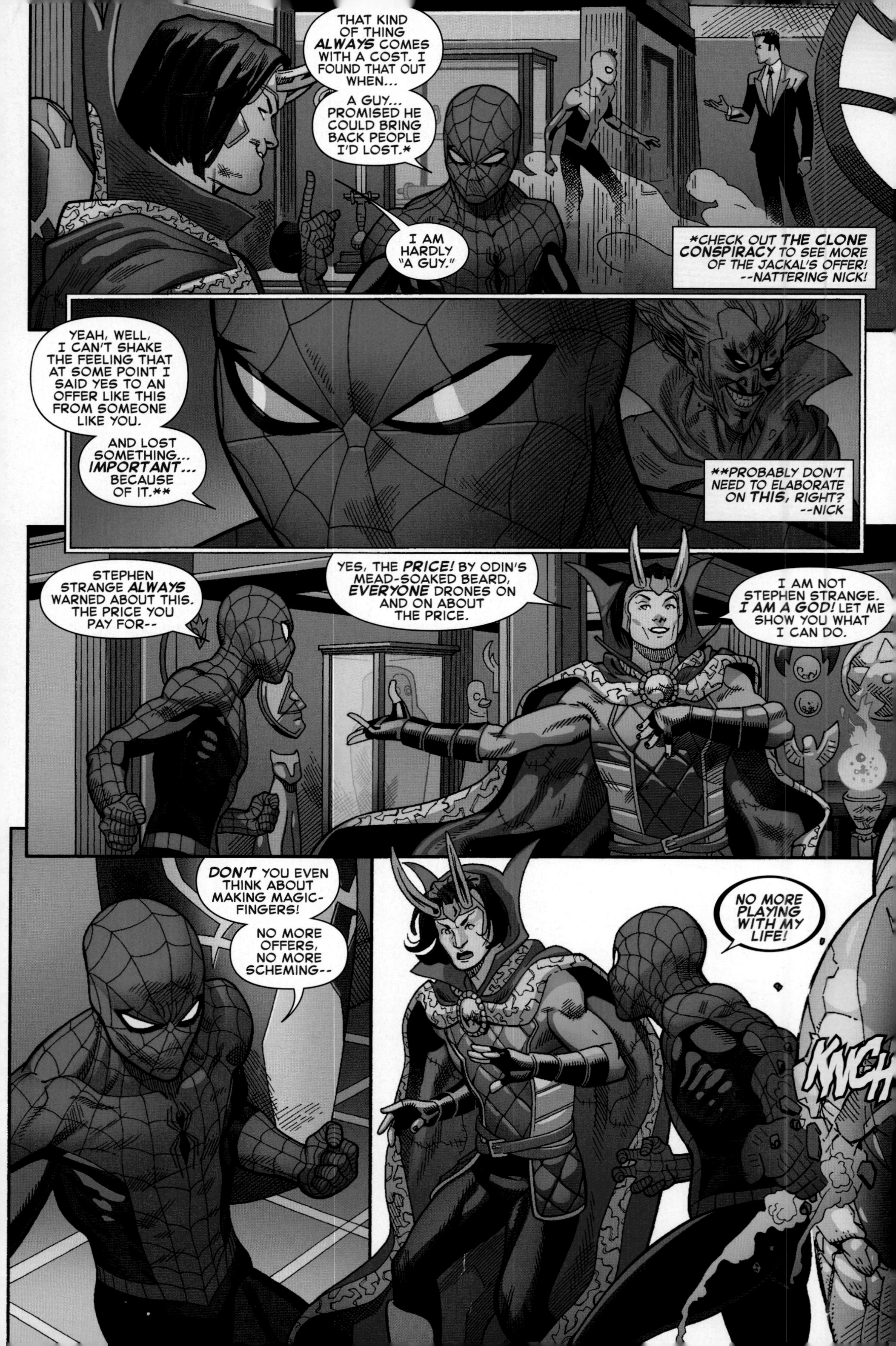
THAT KIND OF THING ALWAYS COMES WITH A COST. I FOUND THAT OUT WHEN...
A GUY... PROMISED HE COULD BRING BACK PEOPLE I'D LOST.*
I AM HARDLY "A GUY."
*CHECK OUT THE CLONE CONSPIRACY TO SEE MORE OF THE JACKAL'S OFFER! --NATTERING NICK!
YEAH, WELL, I CAN'T SHAKE THE FEELING THAT AT SOME POINT I SAID YES TO AN OFFER LIKE THIS FROM SOMEONE LIKE YOU.
AND LOST SOMETHING... IMPORTANT... BECAUSE OF IT.**
**PROBABLY DON'T NEED TO ELABORATE ON THIS, RIGHT? --NICK
STEPHEN STRANGE ALWAYS WARNED ABOUT THIS. THE PRICE YOU PAY FOR--
YES, THE PRICE! BY ODIN'S MEAD-SOAKED BEARD, EVERYONE DRONES ON AND ON ABOUT THE PRICE.
I AM NOT STEPHEN STRANGE. I AM A GOD! LET ME SHOW YOU WHAT I CAN DO.
DON'T YOU EVEN THINK ABOUT MAKING MAGIC-FINGERS!
NO MORE OFFERS, NO MORE SCHEMING--
NO MORE PLAYING WITH MY LIFE!
KNCH

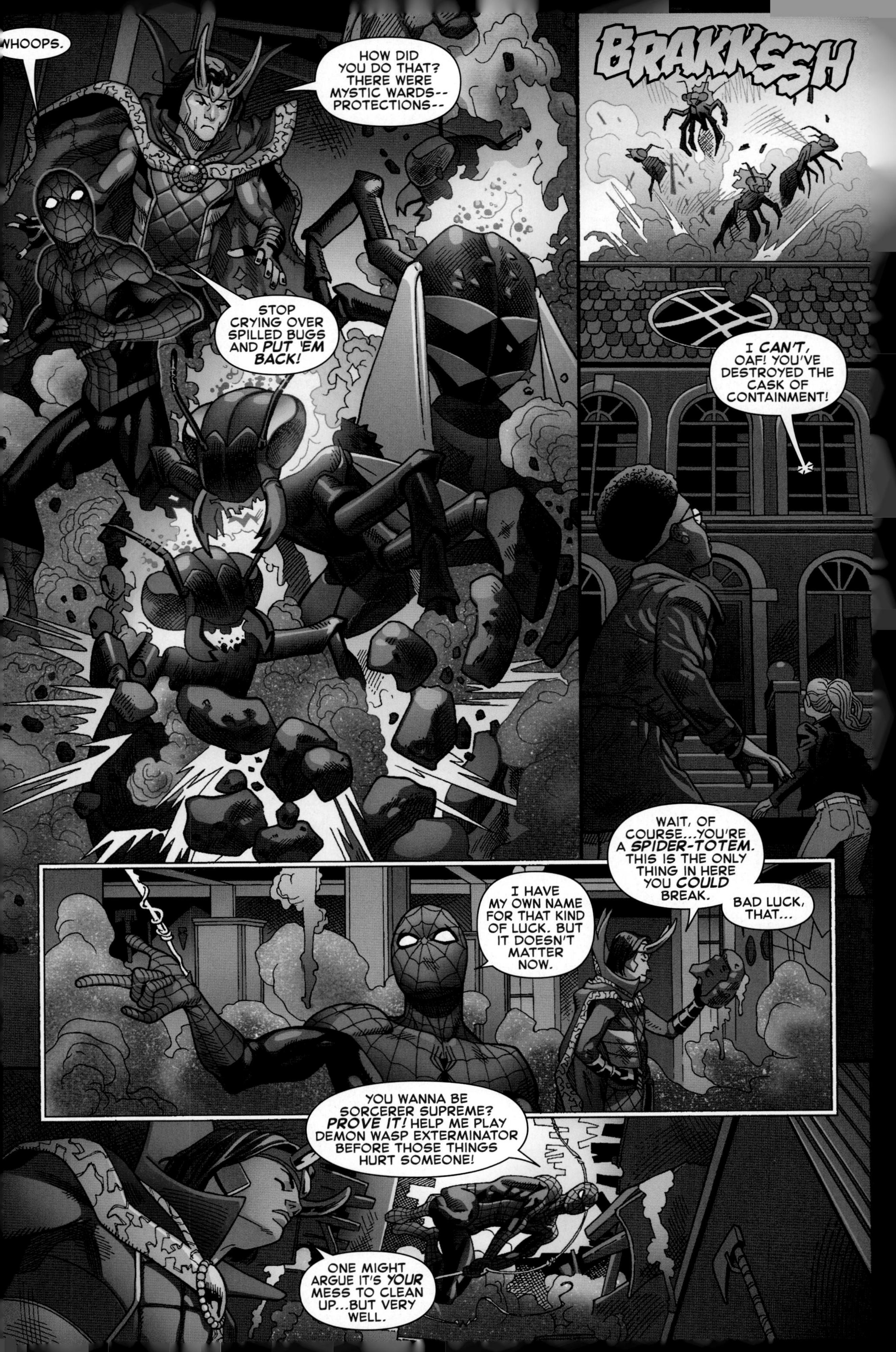
WHOOPS.
HOW DID YOU DO THAT? THERE WERE MYSTIC WARDS-- PROTECTIONS--
STOP CRYING OVER SPILLED BUGS AND PUT 'EM BACK!
BRAKKSSH
I CAN'T, OAF! YOU'VE DESTROYED THE CASK OF CONTAINMENT!
WAIT, OF COURSE...YOU'RE A SPIDER-TOTEM. THIS IS THE ONLY THING IN HERE YOU COULD BREAK.
BAD LUCK, THAT...
I HAVE MY OWN NAME FOR THAT KIND OF LUCK. BUT IT DOESN'T MATTER NOW.
YOU WANNA BE SORCERER SUPREME? PROVE IT! HELP ME PLAY DEMON WASP EXTERMINATOR BEFORE THOSE THINGS HURT SOMEONE!
ONE MIGHT ARGUE IT'S YOUR MESS TO CLEAN UP...BUT VERY WELL.

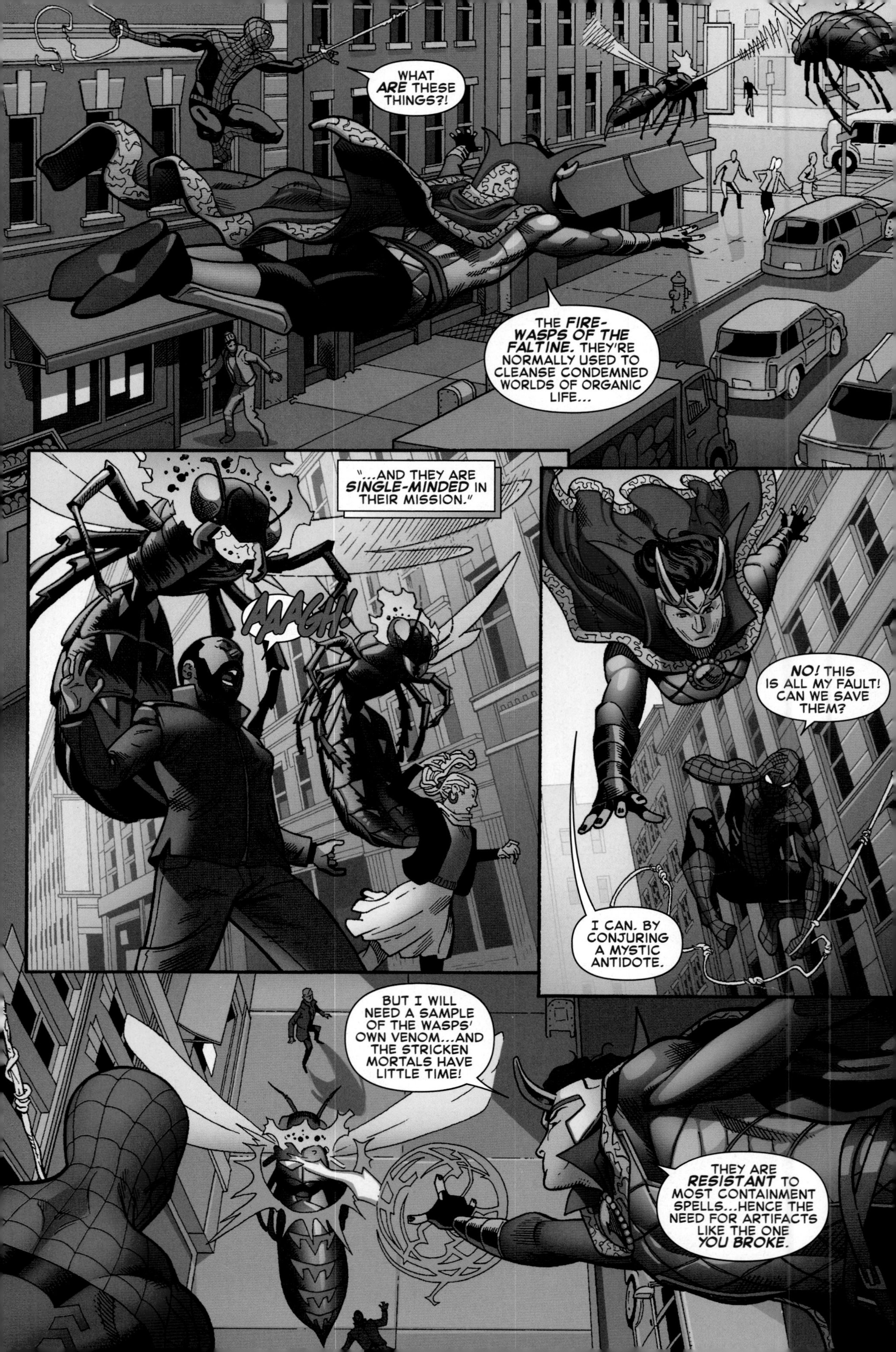
WHAT ARE THESE THINGS?!
THE FIRE-WASPS OF THE FALTINE. THEY'RE NORMALLY USED TO CLEANSE CONDEMNED WORLDS OF ORGANIC LIFE...
"...AND THEY ARE SINGLE-MINDED IN THEIR MISSION."
AAAGH!
NO! THIS IS ALL MY FAULT! CAN WE SAVE THEM?
I CAN. BY CONJURING A MYSTIC ANTIDOTE.
BUT I WILL NEED A SAMPLE OF THE WASPS' OWN VENOM...AND THE STRICKEN MORTALS HAVE LITTLE TIME!
THEY ARE RESISTANT TO MOST CONTAINMENT SPELLS...HENCE THE NEED FOR ARTIFACTS LIKE THE ONE YOU BROKE.

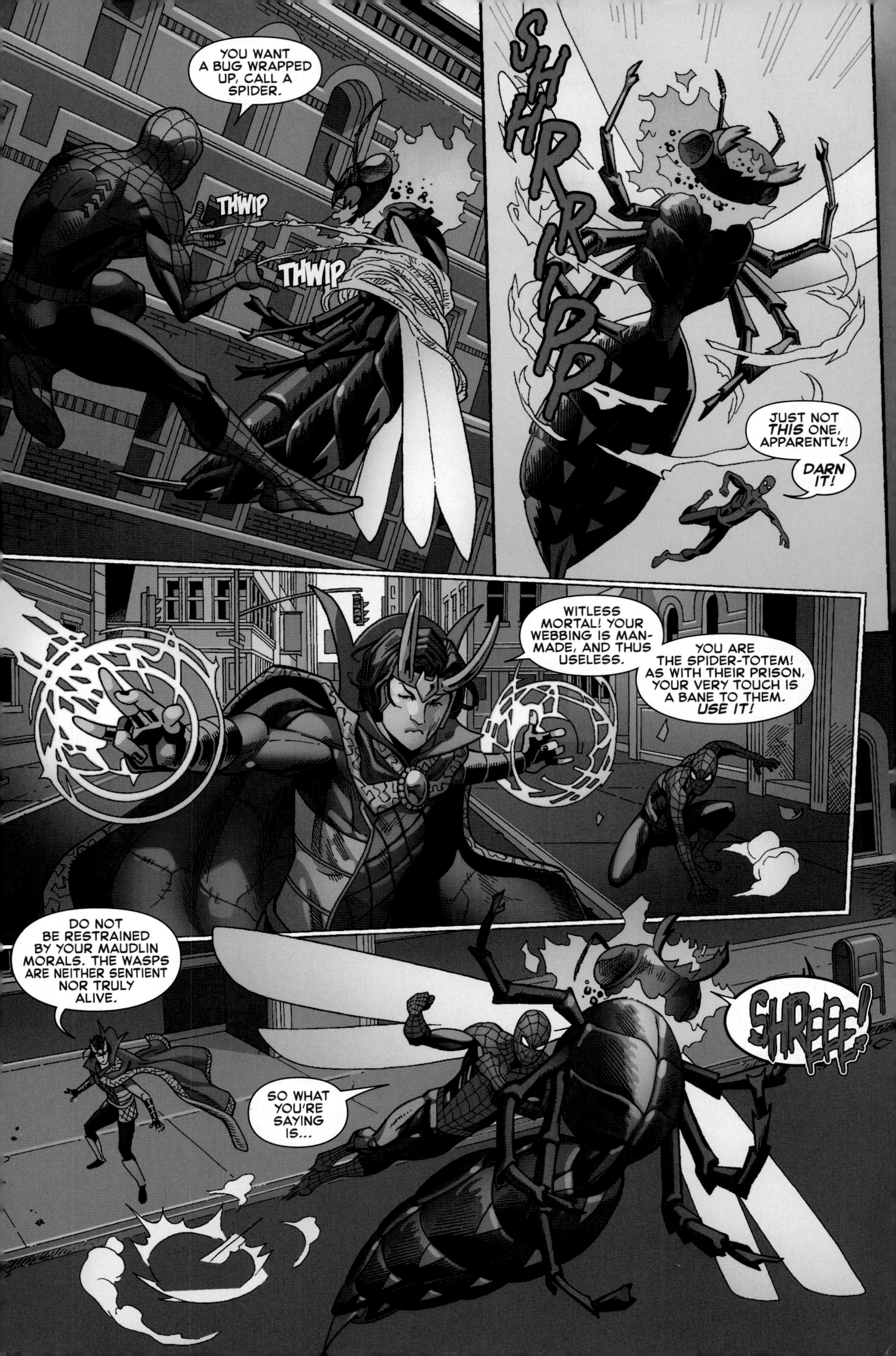
YOU WANT A BUG WRAPPED UP, CALL A SPIDER.
THWIP
THWIP
SHHRRIPP
JUST NOT THIS ONE, APPARENTLY!
DARN IT!
WITLESS MORTAL! YOUR WEBBING IS MAN-MADE, AND THUS USELESS.
YOU ARE THE SPIDER-TOTEM! AS WITH THEIR PRISON, YOUR VERY TOUCH IS A BANE TO THEM. USE IT!
DO NOT BE RESTRAINED BY YOUR MAUDLIN MORALS. THE WASPS ARE NEITHER SENTIENT NOR TRULY ALIVE.
SHREEE!
SO WHAT YOU'RE SAYING IS...

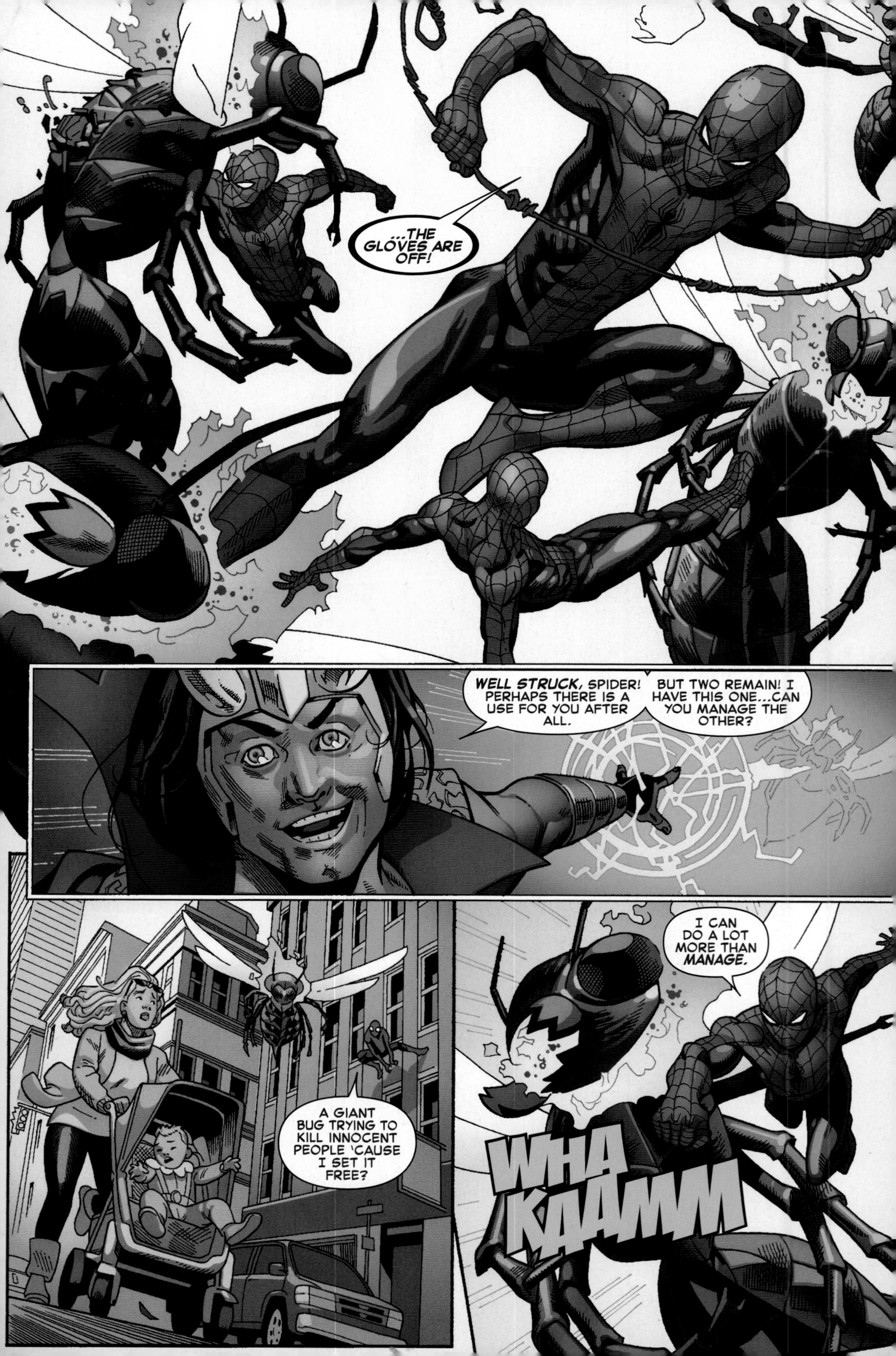
...THE GLOVES ARE OFF!
WELL STRUCK, SPIDER! PERHAPS THERE IS A USE FOR YOU AFTER ALL.
BUT TWO REMAIN! I HAVE THIS ONE...CAN YOU MANAGE THE OTHER?
A GIANT BUG TRYING TO KILL INNOCENT PEOPLE 'CAUSE I SET IT FREE?
I CAN DO A LOT MORE THAN MANAGE.
WHA KAAMM

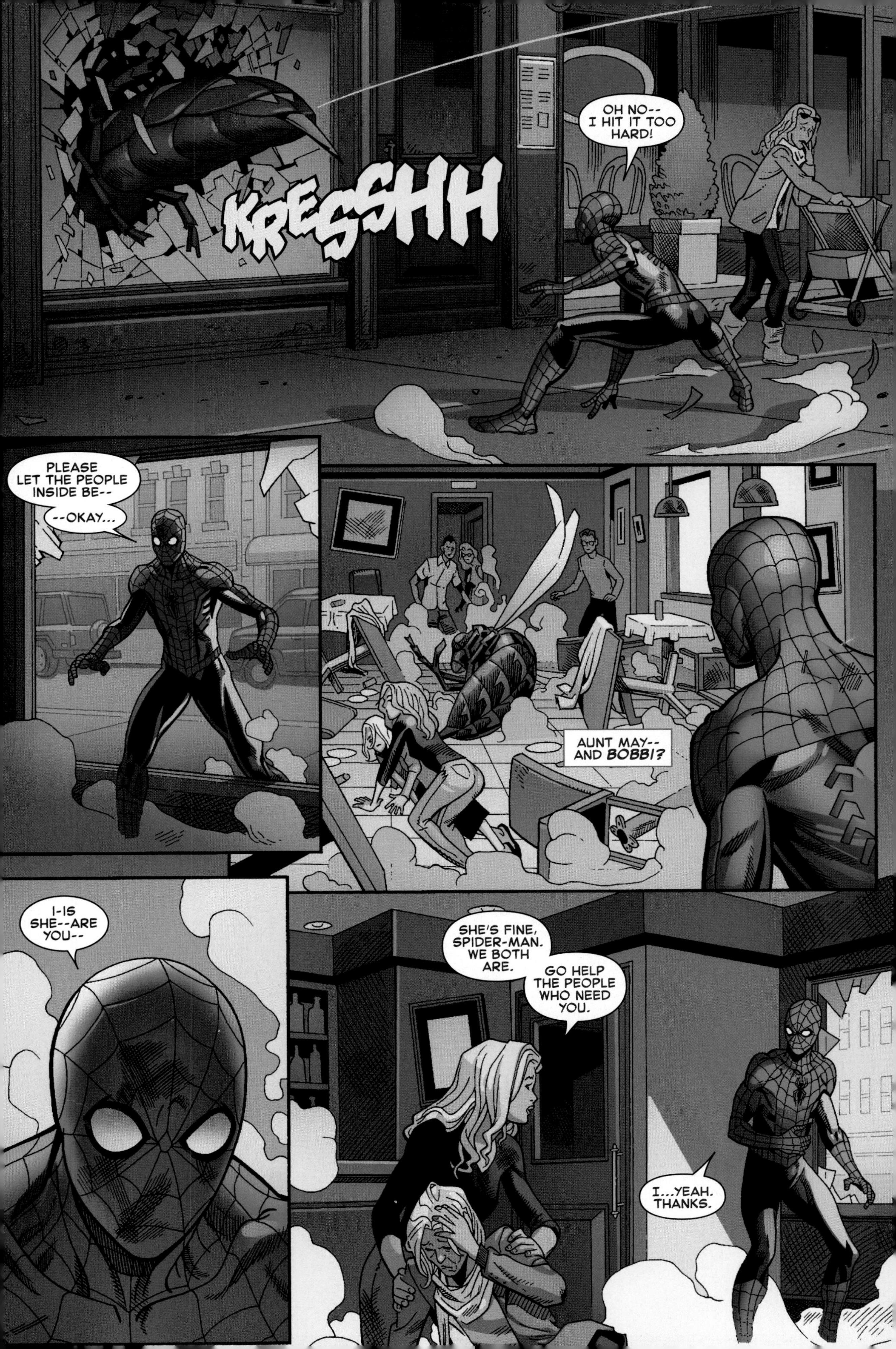
KRESSHH
OH NO-- I HIT IT TOO HARD!
PLEASE LET THE PEOPLE INSIDE BE--
--OKAY...
AUNT MAY-- AND BOBBI?
I-IS SHE--ARE YOU--
SHE'S FINE, SPIDER-MAN. WE BOTH ARE.
GO HELP THE PEOPLE WHO NEED YOU.
I...YEAH. THANKS.

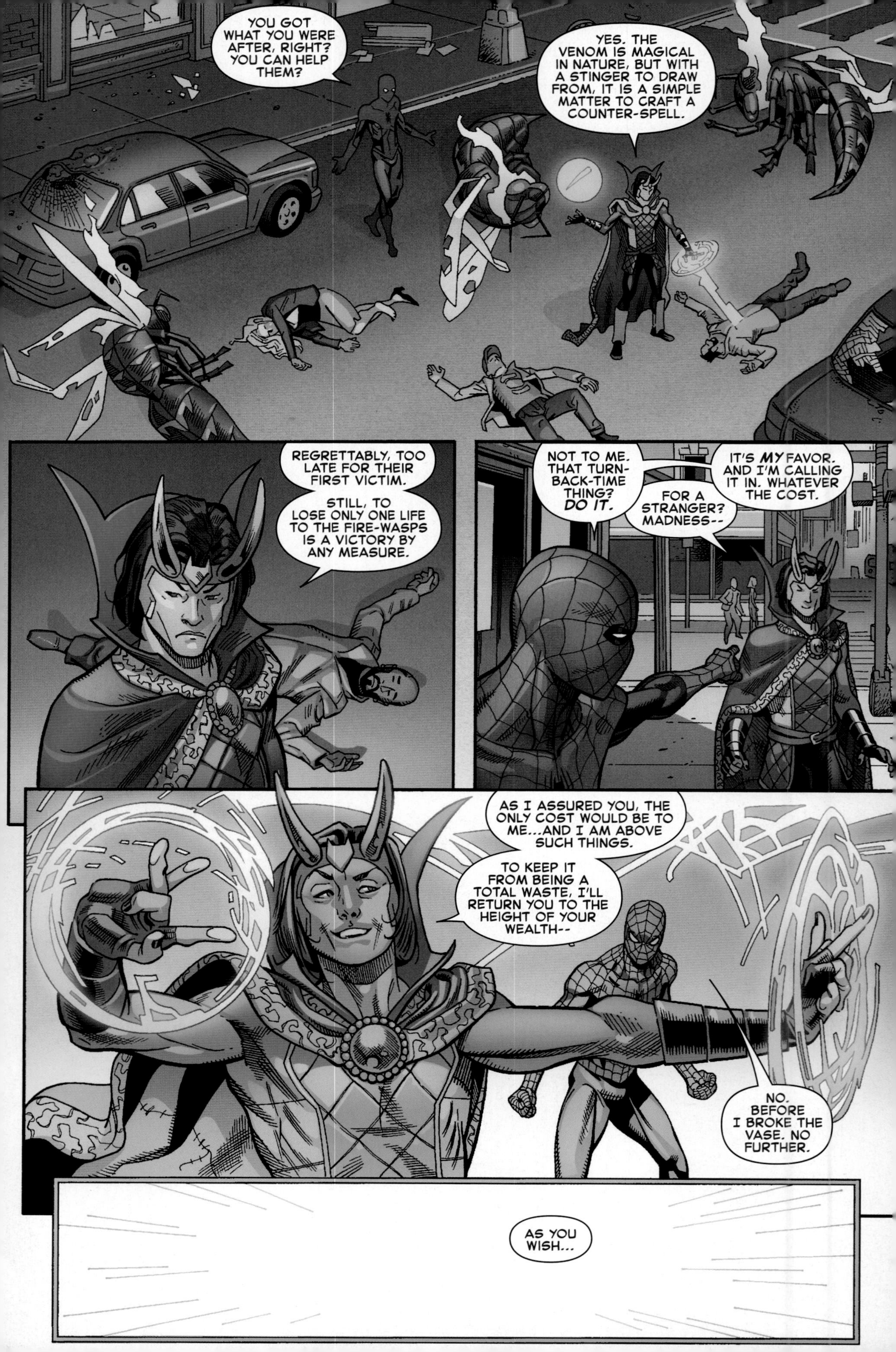

YOU GOT WHAT YOU WERE AFTER, RIGHT? YOU CAN HELP THEM?
YES. THE VENOM IS MAGICAL IN NATURE, BUT WITH A STINGER TO DRAW FROM, IT IS A SIMPLE MATTER TO CRAFT A COUNTER-SPELL.
REGRETTABLY, TOO LATE FOR THEIR FIRST VICTIM.
STILL, TO LOSE ONLY ONE LIFE TO THE FIRE-WASPS IS A VICTORY BY ANY MEASURE.
NOT TO ME. THAT TURN-BACK-TIME THING? DO IT.
FOR A STRANGER? MADNESS--
IT'S MY FAVOR. AND I'M CALLING IT IN. WHATEVER THE COST.
AS I ASSURED YOU, THE ONLY COST WOULD BE TO ME...AND I AM ABOVE SUCH THINGS.
TO KEEP IT FROM BEING A TOTAL WASTE, I'LL RETURN YOU TO THE HEIGHT OF YOUR WEALTH--
NO. BEFORE I BROKE THE VASE. NO FURTHER.
AS YOU WISH...

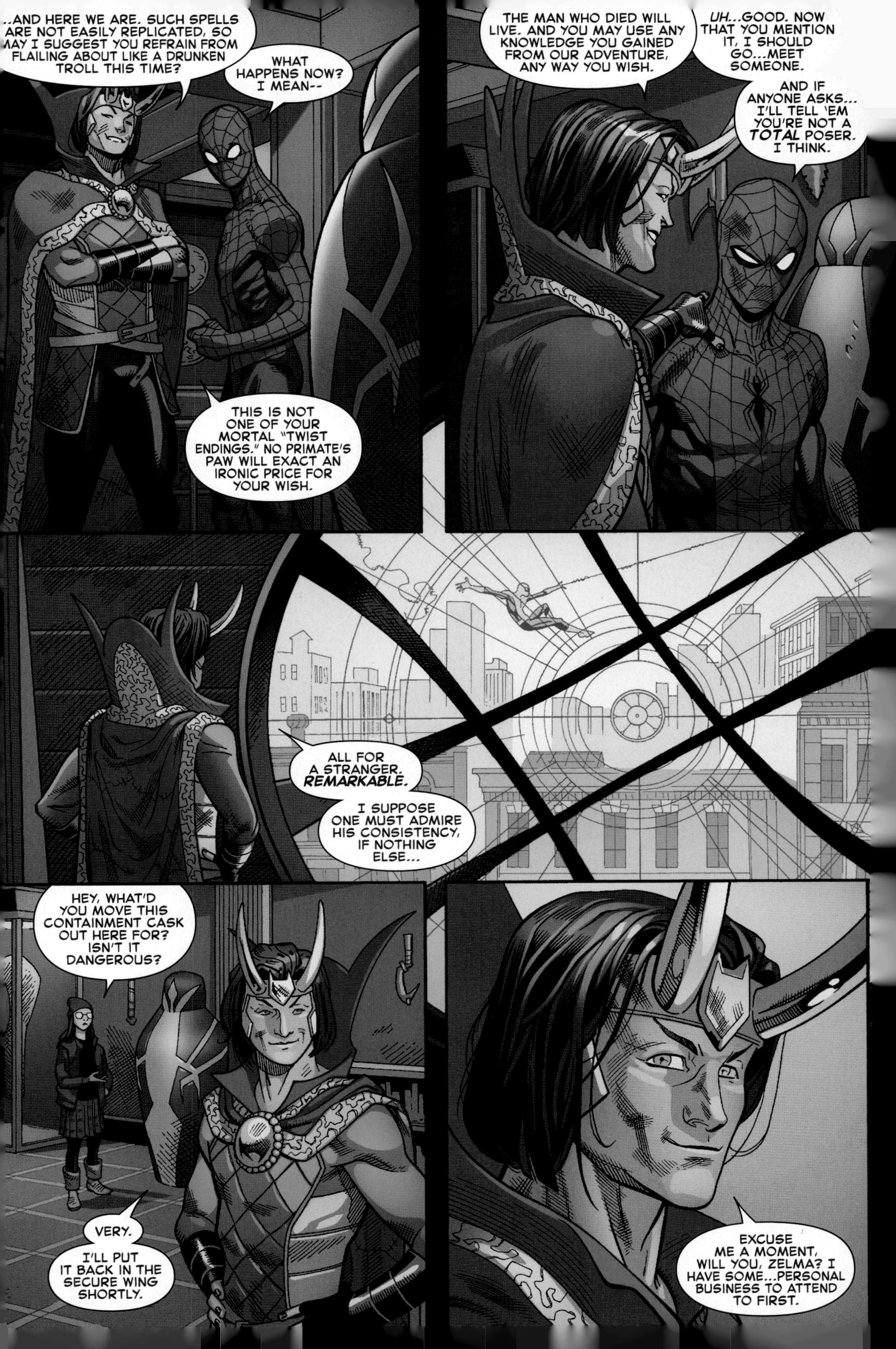
...AND HERE WE ARE. SUCH SPELLS ARE NOT EASILY REPLICATED, SO MAY I SUGGEST YOU REFRAIN FROM FLAILING ABOUT LIKE A DRUNKEN TROLL THIS TIME?
WHAT HAPPENS NOW? I MEAN--
THIS IS NOT ONE OF YOUR MORTAL "TWIST ENDINGS." NO PRIMATE'S PAW WILL EXACT AN IRONIC PRICE FOR YOUR WISH.
THE MAN WHO DIED WILL LIVE. AND YOU MAY USE ANY KNOWLEDGE YOU GAINED FROM OUR ADVENTURE, ANY WAY YOU WISH.
UH...GOOD. NOW THAT YOU MENTION IT, I SHOULD GO...MEET SOMEONE.
AND IF ANYONE ASKS... I'LL TELL 'EM YOU'RE NOT A ***TOTAL*** POSER. I THINK.
ALL FOR A STRANGER. ***REMARKABLE.***
I SUPPOSE ONE MUST ADMIRE HIS CONSISTENCY, IF NOTHING ELSE...
HEY, WHAT'D YOU MOVE THIS CONTAINMENT CASK OUT HERE FOR? ISN'T IT DANGEROUS?
VERY.
I'LL PUT IT BACK IN THE SECURE WING SHORTLY.
EXCUSE ME A MOMENT, WILL YOU, ZELMA? I HAVE SOME...PERSONAL BUSINESS TO ATTEND TO FIRST.

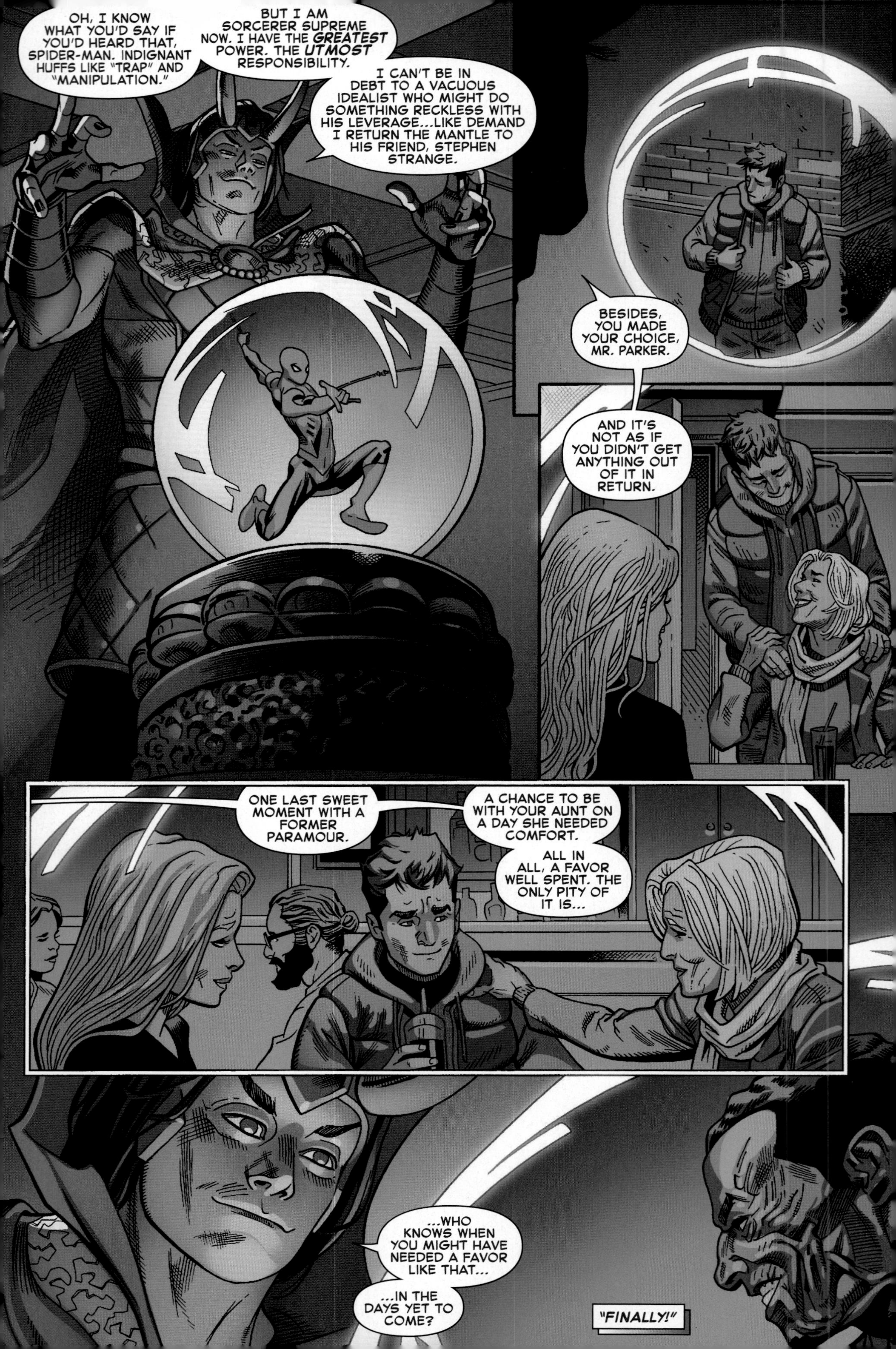
OH, I KNOW WHAT YOU'D SAY IF YOU'D HEARD THAT, SPIDER-MAN. INDIGNANT HUFFS LIKE "TRAP" AND "MANIPULATION."
BUT I AM SORCERER SUPREME NOW. I HAVE THE *GREATEST* POWER. THE *UTMOST* RESPONSIBILITY.
I CAN'T BE IN DEBT TO A VACUOUS IDEALIST WHO MIGHT DO SOMETHING RECKLESS WITH HIS LEVERAGE...LIKE DEMAND I RETURN THE MANTLE TO HIS FRIEND, STEPHEN STRANGE.
BESIDES, YOU MADE YOUR CHOICE, MR. PARKER.
AND IT'S NOT AS IF YOU DIDN'T GET ANYTHING OUT OF IT IN RETURN.
ONE LAST SWEET MOMENT WITH A FORMER PARAMOUR.
A CHANCE TO BE WITH YOUR AUNT ON A DAY SHE NEEDED COMFORT.
ALL IN ALL, A FAVOR WELL SPENT. THE ONLY PITY OF IT IS...
...WHO KNOWS WHEN YOU MIGHT HAVE NEEDED A FAVOR LIKE THAT...
...IN THE DAYS YET TO COME?
"FINALLY!"

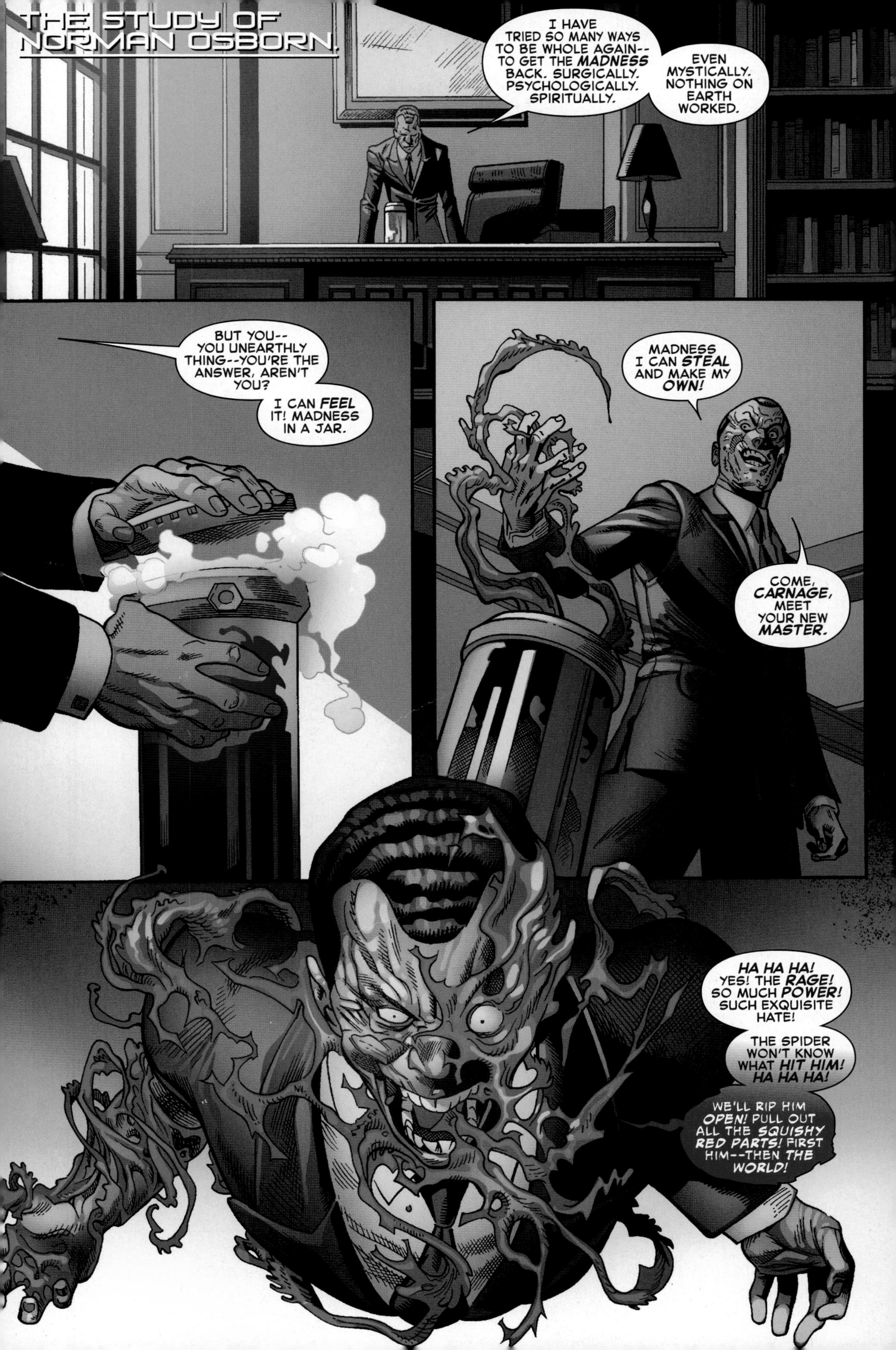
THE STUDY OF NORMAN OSBORN.
I HAVE TRIED SO MANY WAYS TO BE WHOLE AGAIN-- TO GET THE MADNESS BACK. SURGICALLY. PSYCHOLOGICALLY. SPIRITUALLY.
EVEN MYSTICALLY. NOTHING ON EARTH WORKED.
BUT YOU-- YOU UNEARTHLY THING--YOU'RE THE ANSWER, AREN'T YOU?
I CAN FEEL IT! MADNESS IN A JAR.
MADNESS I CAN STEAL AND MAKE MY OWN!
COME, CARNAGE, MEET YOUR NEW MASTER.
HA HA HA! YES! THE RAGE! SO MUCH POWER! SUCH EXQUISITE HATE!
THE SPIDER WON'T KNOW WHAT HIT HIM! HA HA HA!
WE'LL RIP HIM OPEN! PULL OUT ALL THE SQUISHY RED PARTS! FIRST HIM--THEN THE WORLD!

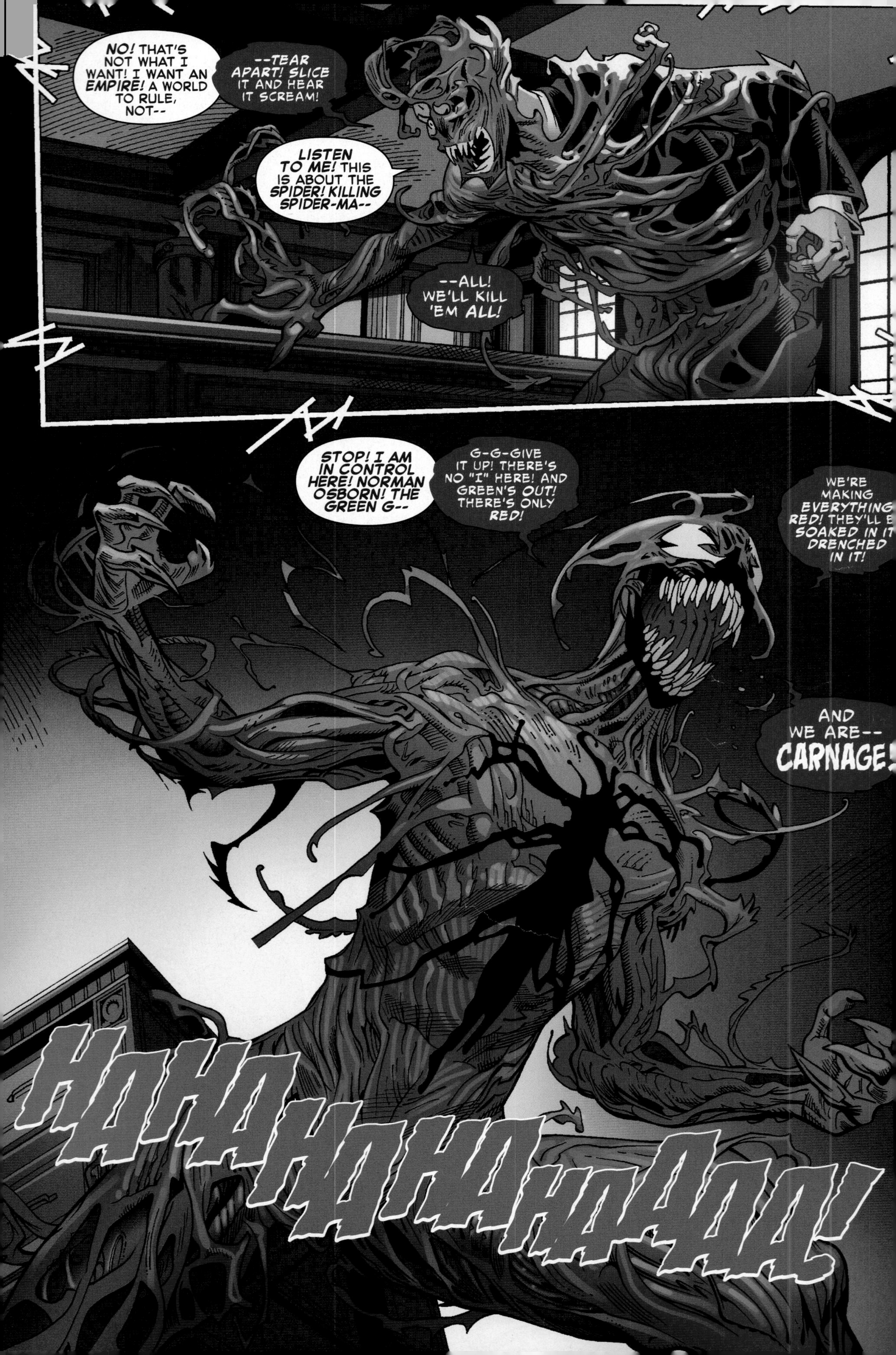
NO! THAT'S NOT WHAT I WANT! I WANT AN EMPIRE! A WORLD TO RULE, NOT--
--TEAR APART! SLICE IT AND HEAR IT SCREAM!
LISTEN TO ME! THIS IS ABOUT THE SPIDER! KILLING SPIDER-MA--
--ALL! WE'LL KILL 'EM ALL!
STOP! I AM IN CONTROL HERE! NORMAN OSBORN! THE GREEN G--
G-G-GIVE IT UP! THERE'S NO "I" HERE! AND GREEN'S OUT! THERE'S ONLY RED!
WE'RE MAKING EVERYTHING RED! THEY'LL B SOAKED IN IT DRENCHED IN IT!
AND WE ARE-- CARNAGE!
HAHAHAHAHAHAAAA!

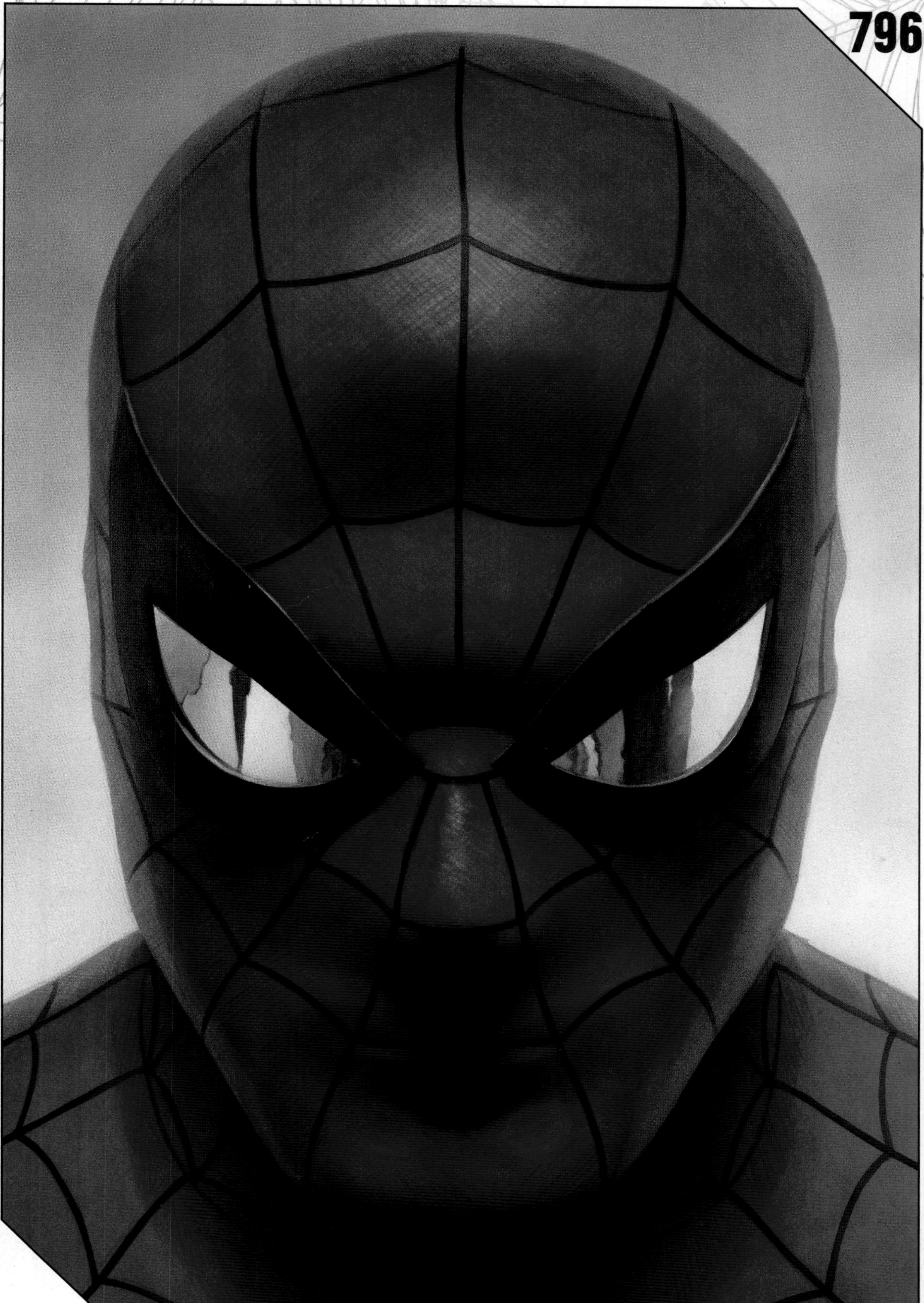
796

THREAT LEVEL: RED PART THREE "HIGHER PRIORITIES"

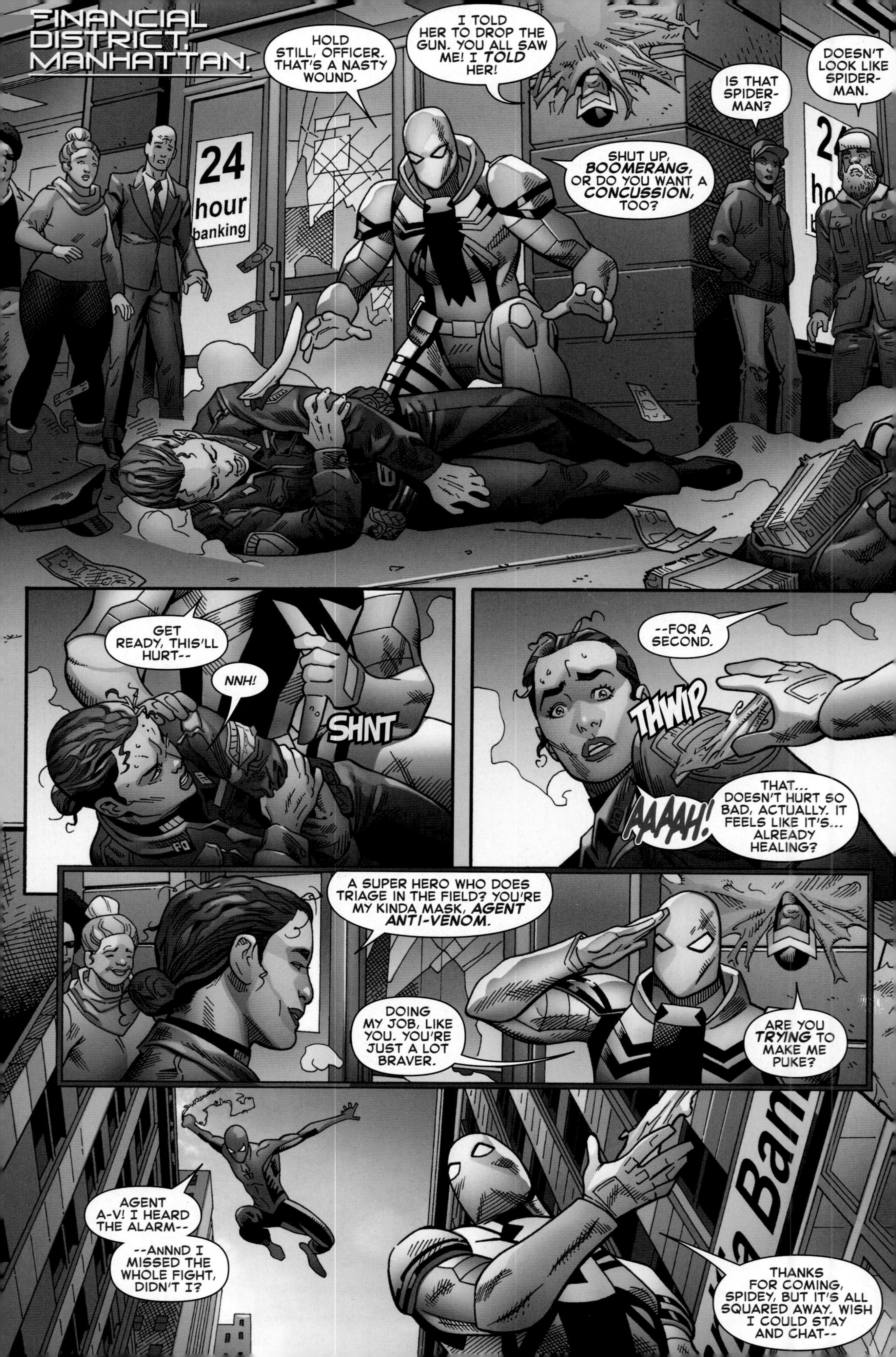
FINANCIAL DISTRICT, MANHATTAN.
HOLD STILL, OFFICER. THAT'S A NASTY WOUND.
I TOLD HER TO DROP THE GUN. YOU ALL SAW ME! I TOLD HER!
SHUT UP, BOOMERANG, OR DO YOU WANT A CONCUSSION, TOO?
IS THAT SPIDER-MAN?
DOESN'T LOOK LIKE SPIDER-MAN.
24 hour banking
GET READY, THIS'LL HURT--
NNH!
SHNT
--FOR A SECOND.
THWIP
AAAAH!
THAT... DOESN'T HURT SO BAD, ACTUALLY. IT FEELS LIKE IT'S... ALREADY HEALING?
A SUPER HERO WHO DOES TRIAGE IN THE FIELD? YOU'RE MY KINDA MASK, AGENT ANTI-VENOM.
DOING MY JOB, LIKE YOU. YOU'RE JUST A LOT BRAVER.
ARE YOU TRYING TO MAKE ME PUKE?
AGENT A-V! I HEARD THE ALARM--
--ANNND I MISSED THE WHOLE FIGHT, DIDN'T I?
THANKS FOR COMING, SPIDEY, BUT IT'S ALL SQUARED AWAY. WISH I COULD STAY AND CHAT--

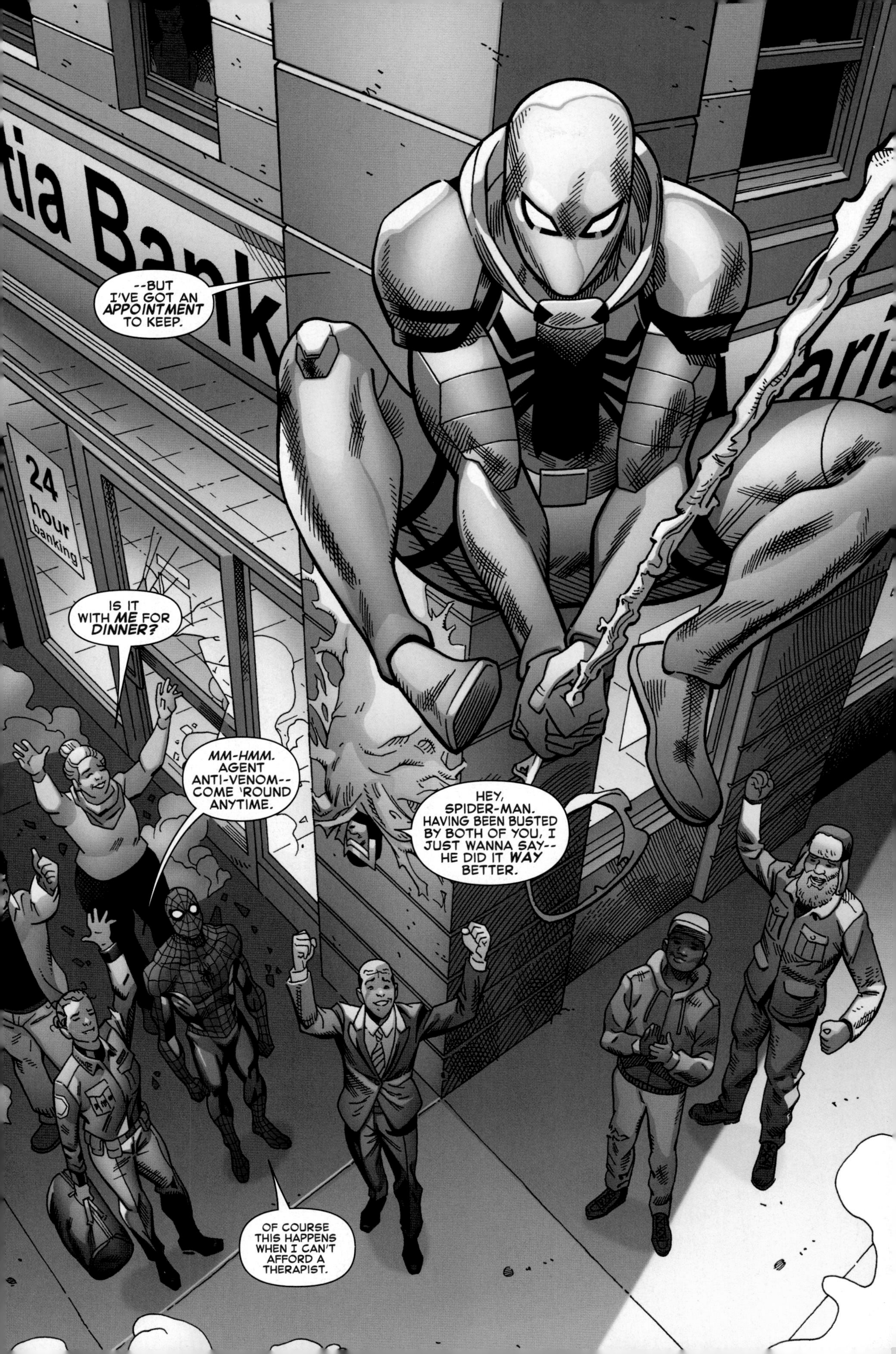
--BUT I'VE GOT AN APPOINTMENT TO KEEP.
IS IT WITH ME FOR DINNER?
MM-HMM. AGENT ANTI-VENOM-- COME 'ROUND ANYTIME.
HEY, SPIDER-MAN. HAVING BEEN BUSTED BY BOTH OF YOU, I JUST WANNA SAY-- HE DID IT WAY BETTER.
OF COURSE THIS HAPPENS WHEN I CAN'T AFFORD A THERAPIST.
24 hour banking
tia Bank

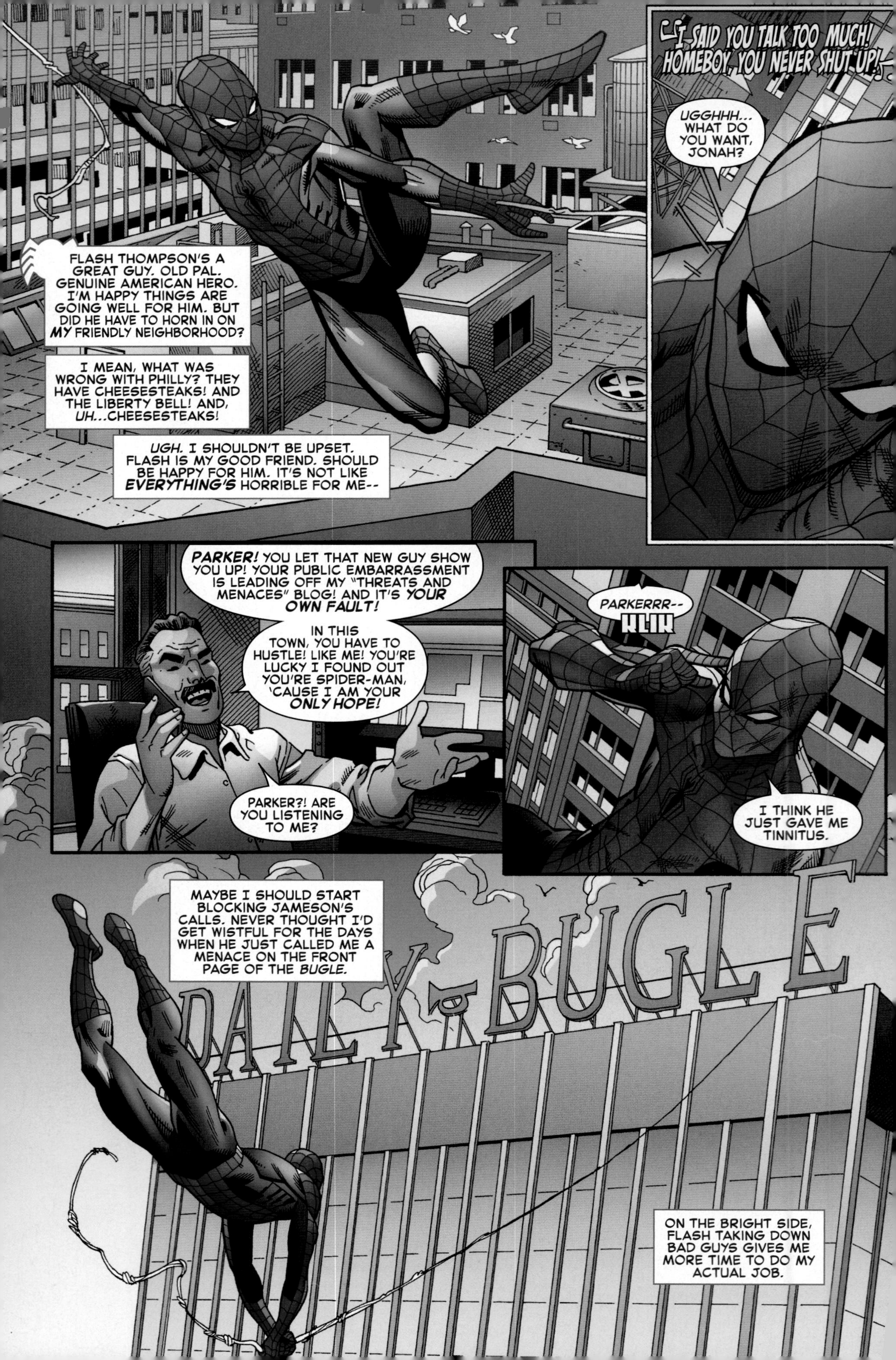
FLASH THOMPSON'S A GREAT GUY. OLD PAL. GENUINE AMERICAN HERO. I'M HAPPY THINGS ARE GOING WELL FOR HIM. BUT DID HE HAVE TO HORN IN ON MY FRIENDLY NEIGHBORHOOD?
I MEAN, WHAT WAS WRONG WITH PHILLY? THEY HAVE CHEESESTEAKS! AND THE LIBERTY BELL! AND, UH...CHEESESTEAKS!
UGH. I SHOULDN'T BE UPSET. FLASH IS MY GOOD FRIEND. SHOULD BE HAPPY FOR HIM. IT'S NOT LIKE EVERYTHING'S HORRIBLE FOR ME--
I SAID YOU TALK TOO MUCH! HOMEBOY, YOU NEVER SHUT UP!
UGGHHH... WHAT DO YOU WANT, JONAH?
PARKER! YOU LET THAT NEW GUY SHOW YOU UP! YOUR PUBLIC EMBARRASSMENT IS LEADING OFF MY "THREATS AND MENACES" BLOG! AND IT'S YOUR OWN FAULT!
IN THIS TOWN, YOU HAVE TO HUSTLE! LIKE ME! YOU'RE LUCKY I FOUND OUT YOU'RE SPIDER-MAN, 'CAUSE I AM YOUR ONLY HOPE!
PARKER?! ARE YOU LISTENING TO ME?
PARKERRR--
KLIK
I THINK HE JUST GAVE ME TINNITUS.
MAYBE I SHOULD START BLOCKING JAMESON'S CALLS. NEVER THOUGHT I'D GET WISTFUL FOR THE DAYS WHEN HE JUST CALLED ME A MENACE ON THE FRONT PAGE OF THE BUGLE.
DAILY BUGLE
ON THE BRIGHT SIDE, FLASH TAKING DOWN BAD GUYS GIVES ME MORE TIME TO DO MY ACTUAL JOB.

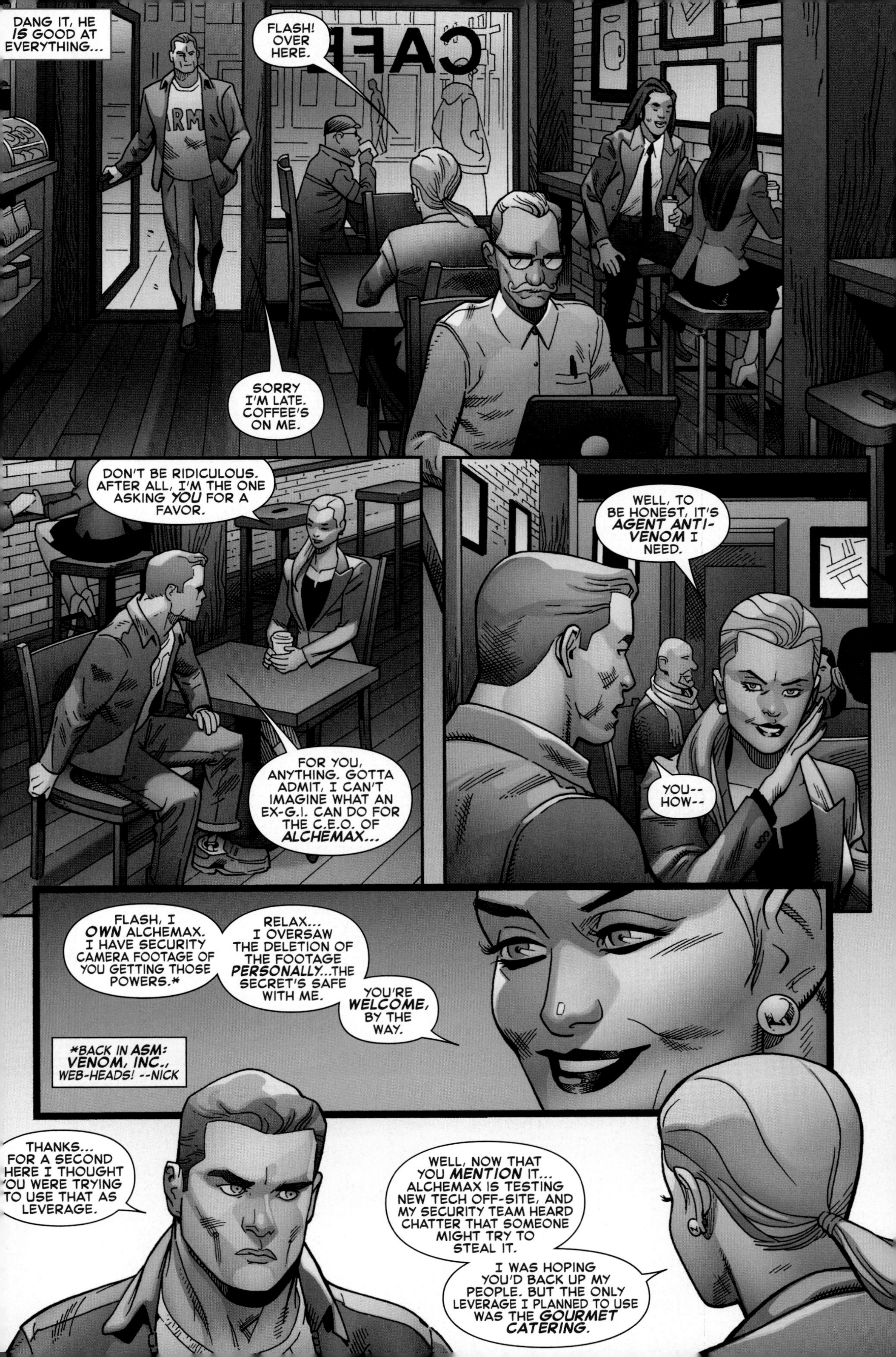
DANG IT, HE IS GOOD AT EVERYTHING...
FLASH! OVER HERE.
CAFE
SORRY I'M LATE. COFFEE'S ON ME.
DON'T BE RIDICULOUS. AFTER ALL, I'M THE ONE ASKING YOU FOR A FAVOR.
FOR YOU, ANYTHING. GOTTA ADMIT, I CAN'T IMAGINE WHAT AN EX-G.I. CAN DO FOR THE C.E.O. OF ALCHEMAX...
WELL, TO BE HONEST, IT'S AGENT ANTI-VENOM I NEED.
YOU-- HOW--
FLASH, I OWN ALCHEMAX. I HAVE SECURITY CAMERA FOOTAGE OF YOU GETTING THOSE POWERS.*
RELAX... I OVERSAW THE DELETION OF THE FOOTAGE PERSONALLY...THE SECRET'S SAFE WITH ME.
YOU'RE WELCOME, BY THE WAY.
*BACK IN ASM: VENOM, INC., WEB-HEADS! --NICK
THANKS... FOR A SECOND HERE I THOUGHT YOU WERE TRYING TO USE THAT AS LEVERAGE.
WELL, NOW THAT YOU MENTION IT... ALCHEMAX IS TESTING NEW TECH OFF-SITE, AND MY SECURITY TEAM HEARD CHATTER THAT SOMEONE MIGHT TRY TO STEAL IT.
I WAS HOPING YOU'D BACK UP MY PEOPLE. BUT THE ONLY LEVERAGE I PLANNED TO USE WAS THE GOURMET CATERING.

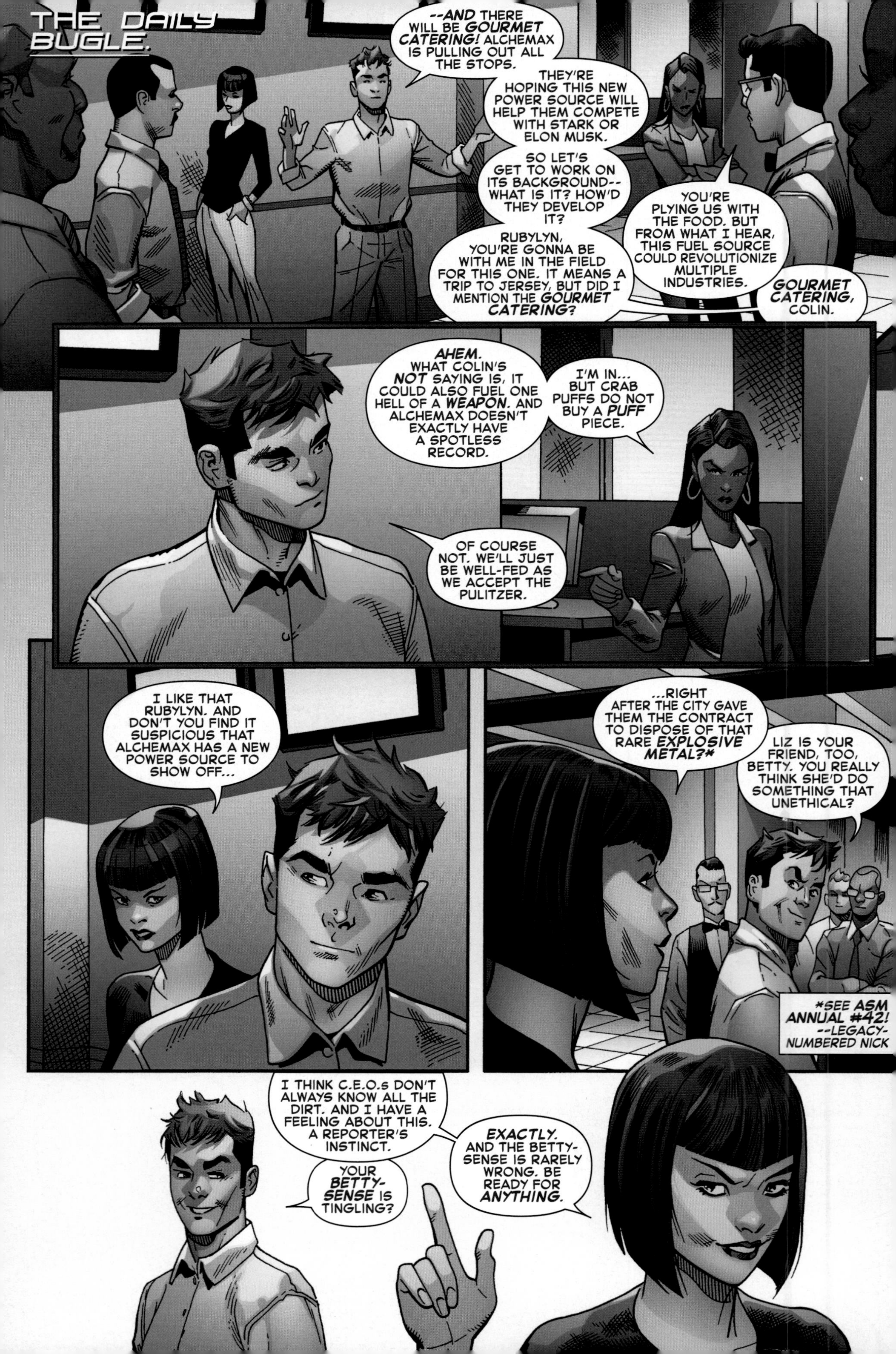
THE DAILY BUGLE.
--AND THERE WILL BE GOURMET CATERING! ALCHEMAX IS PULLING OUT ALL THE STOPS.
THEY'RE HOPING THIS NEW POWER SOURCE WILL HELP THEM COMPETE WITH STARK OR ELON MUSK.
SO LET'S GET TO WORK ON ITS BACKGROUND-- WHAT IS IT? HOW'D THEY DEVELOP IT?
RUBYLYN, YOU'RE GONNA BE WITH ME IN THE FIELD FOR THIS ONE. IT MEANS A TRIP TO JERSEY, BUT DID I MENTION THE GOURMET CATERING?
YOU'RE PLYING US WITH THE FOOD. BUT FROM WHAT I HEAR, THIS FUEL SOURCE COULD REVOLUTIONIZE MULTIPLE INDUSTRIES.
GOURMET CATERING, COLIN.
AHEM. WHAT COLIN'S NOT SAYING IS, IT COULD ALSO FUEL ONE HELL OF A WEAPON. AND ALCHEMAX DOESN'T EXACTLY HAVE A SPOTLESS RECORD.
I'M IN... BUT CRAB PUFFS DO NOT BUY A PUFF PIECE.
OF COURSE NOT. WE'LL JUST BE WELL-FED AS WE ACCEPT THE PULITZER.
I LIKE THAT RUBYLYN. AND DON'T YOU FIND IT SUSPICIOUS THAT ALCHEMAX HAS A NEW POWER SOURCE TO SHOW OFF...
...RIGHT AFTER THE CITY GAVE THEM THE CONTRACT TO DISPOSE OF THAT RARE EXPLOSIVE METAL?*
LIZ IS YOUR FRIEND, TOO, BETTY. YOU REALLY THINK SHE'D DO SOMETHING THAT UNETHICAL?
*SEE ASM ANNUAL #42! --LEGACY-NUMBERED NICK
I THINK C.E.O.s DON'T ALWAYS KNOW ALL THE DIRT. AND I HAVE A FEELING ABOUT THIS. A REPORTER'S INSTINCT.
YOUR BETTY-SENSE IS TINGLING?
EXACTLY. AND THE BETTY-SENSE IS RARELY WRONG. BE READY FOR ANYTHING.

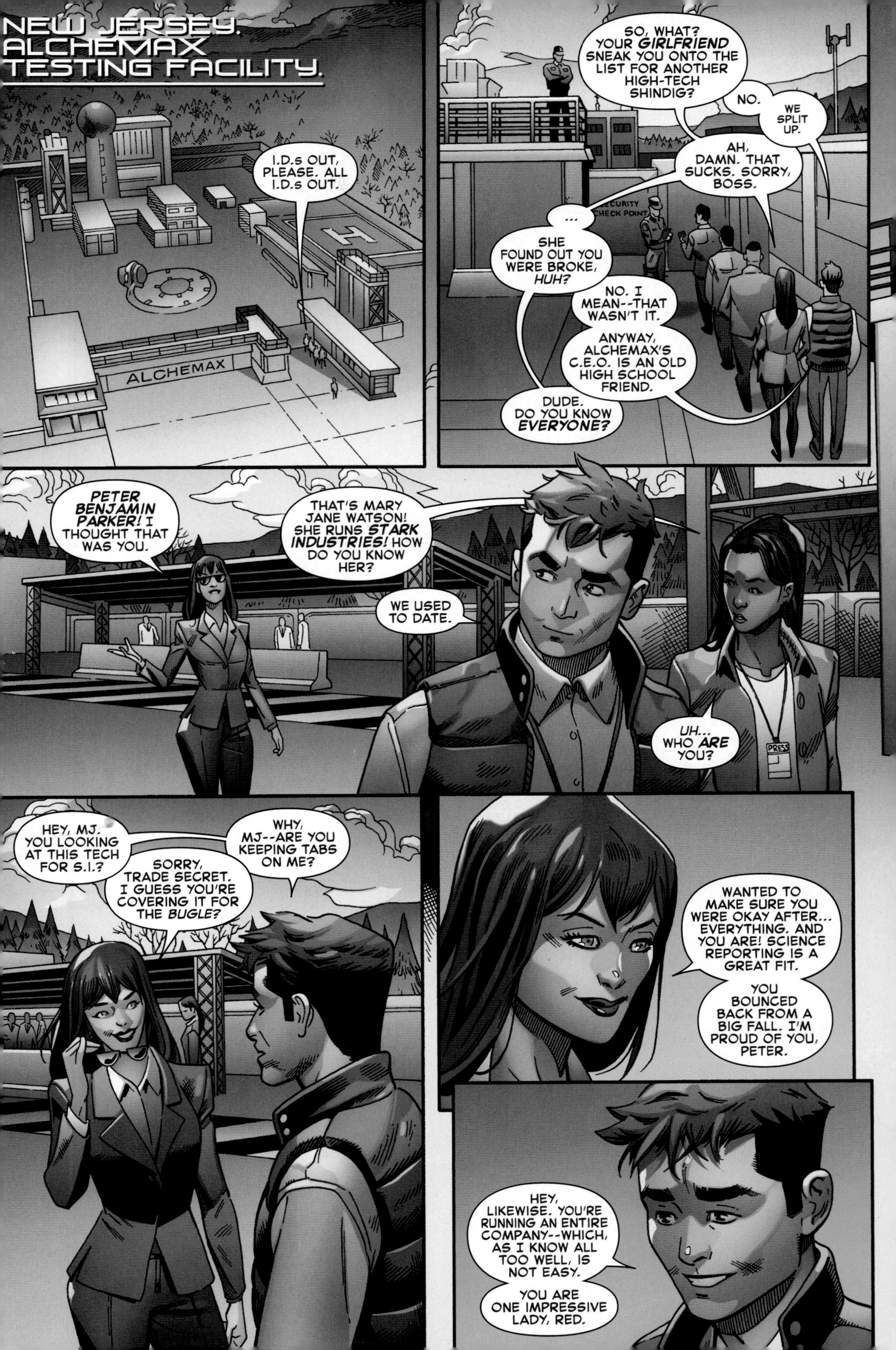
NEW JERSEY. ALCHEMAX TESTING FACILITY.
ALCHEMAX
I.D.s OUT, PLEASE. ALL I.D.s OUT.
SO, WHAT? YOUR GIRLFRIEND SNEAK YOU ONTO THE LIST FOR ANOTHER HIGH-TECH SHINDIG?
NO.
WE SPLIT UP.
AH, DAMN. THAT SUCKS. SORRY, BOSS.
...
SHE FOUND OUT YOU WERE BROKE, HUH?
NO. I MEAN--THAT WASN'T IT.
ANYWAY, ALCHEMAX'S C.E.O. IS AN OLD HIGH SCHOOL FRIEND.
DUDE. DO YOU KNOW EVERYONE?
PETER BENJAMIN PARKER! I THOUGHT THAT WAS YOU.
THAT'S MARY JANE WATSON! SHE RUNS STARK INDUSTRIES! HOW DO YOU KNOW HER?
WE USED TO DATE.
UH... WHO ARE YOU?
PRESS
HEY, MJ. YOU LOOKING AT THIS TECH FOR S.I.?
SORRY, TRADE SECRET. I GUESS YOU'RE COVERING IT FOR THE BUGLE?
WHY, MJ--ARE YOU KEEPING TABS ON ME?
WANTED TO MAKE SURE YOU WERE OKAY AFTER... EVERYTHING. AND YOU ARE! SCIENCE REPORTING IS A GREAT FIT.
YOU BOUNCED BACK FROM A BIG FALL. I'M PROUD OF YOU, PETER.
HEY, LIKEWISE. YOU'RE RUNNING AN ENTIRE COMPANY--WHICH, AS I KNOW ALL TOO WELL, IS NOT EASY.
YOU ARE ONE IMPRESSIVE LADY, RED.

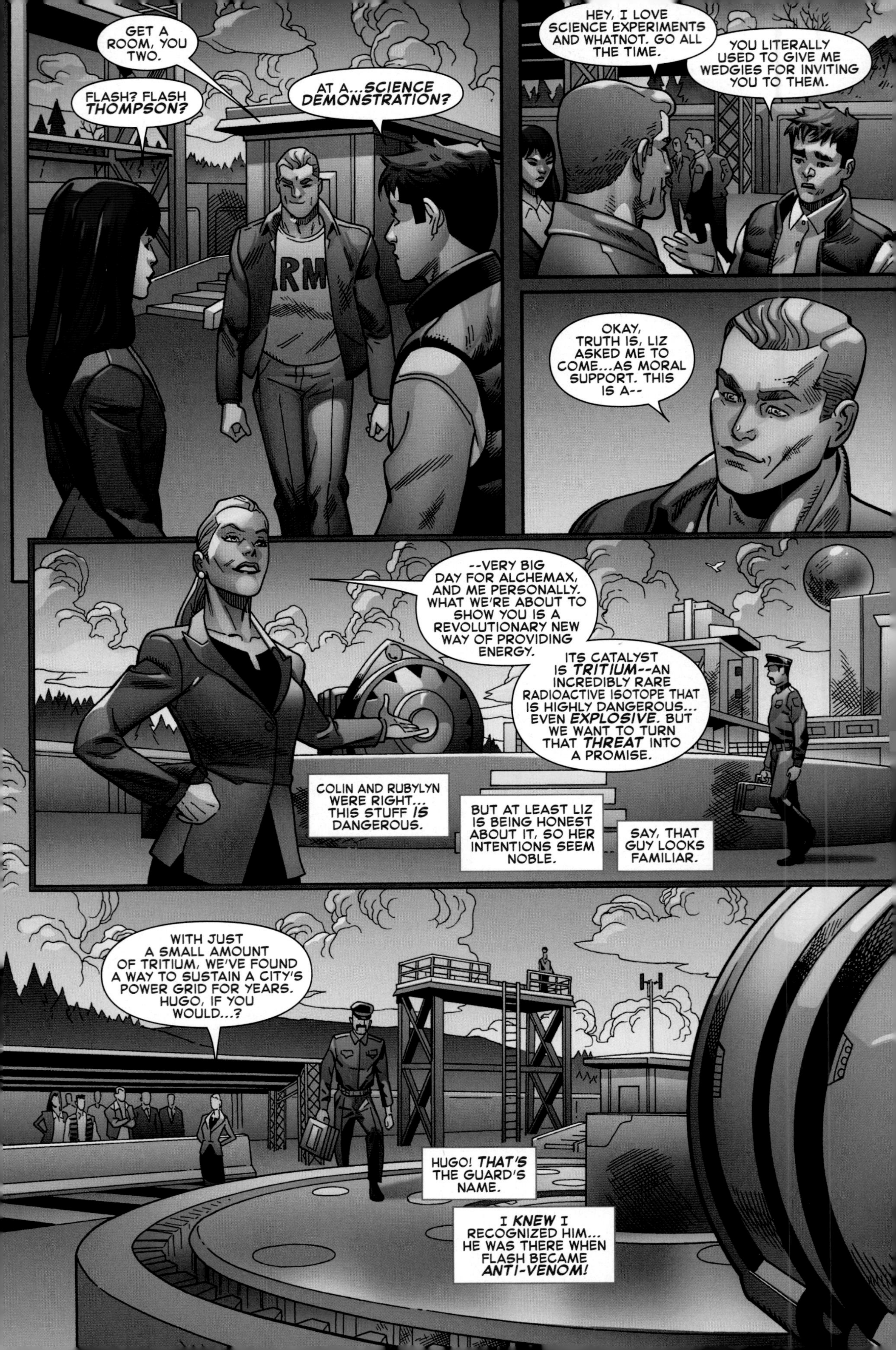
GET A ROOM, YOU TWO.
FLASH? FLASH THOMPSON?
AT A...SCIENCE DEMONSTRATION?
HEY, I LOVE SCIENCE EXPERIMENTS AND WHATNOT. GO ALL THE TIME.
YOU LITERALLY USED TO GIVE ME WEDGIES FOR INVITING YOU TO THEM.
OKAY, TRUTH IS, LIZ ASKED ME TO COME...AS MORAL SUPPORT. THIS IS A--
--VERY BIG DAY FOR ALCHEMAX, AND ME PERSONALLY. WHAT WE'RE ABOUT TO SHOW YOU IS A REVOLUTIONARY NEW WAY OF PROVIDING ENERGY.
ITS CATALYST IS TRITIUM--AN INCREDIBLY RARE RADIOACTIVE ISOTOPE THAT IS HIGHLY DANGEROUS... EVEN EXPLOSIVE. BUT WE WANT TO TURN THAT THREAT INTO A PROMISE.
COLIN AND RUBYLYN WERE RIGHT... THIS STUFF IS DANGEROUS.
BUT AT LEAST LIZ IS BEING HONEST ABOUT IT, SO HER INTENTIONS SEEM NOBLE.
SAY, THAT GUY LOOKS FAMILIAR.
WITH JUST A SMALL AMOUNT OF TRITIUM, WE'VE FOUND A WAY TO SUSTAIN A CITY'S POWER GRID FOR YEARS. HUGO, IF YOU WOULD...?
HUGO! THAT'S THE GUARD'S NAME.
I KNEW I RECOGNIZED HIM... HE WAS THERE WHEN FLASH BECAME ANTI-VENOM!

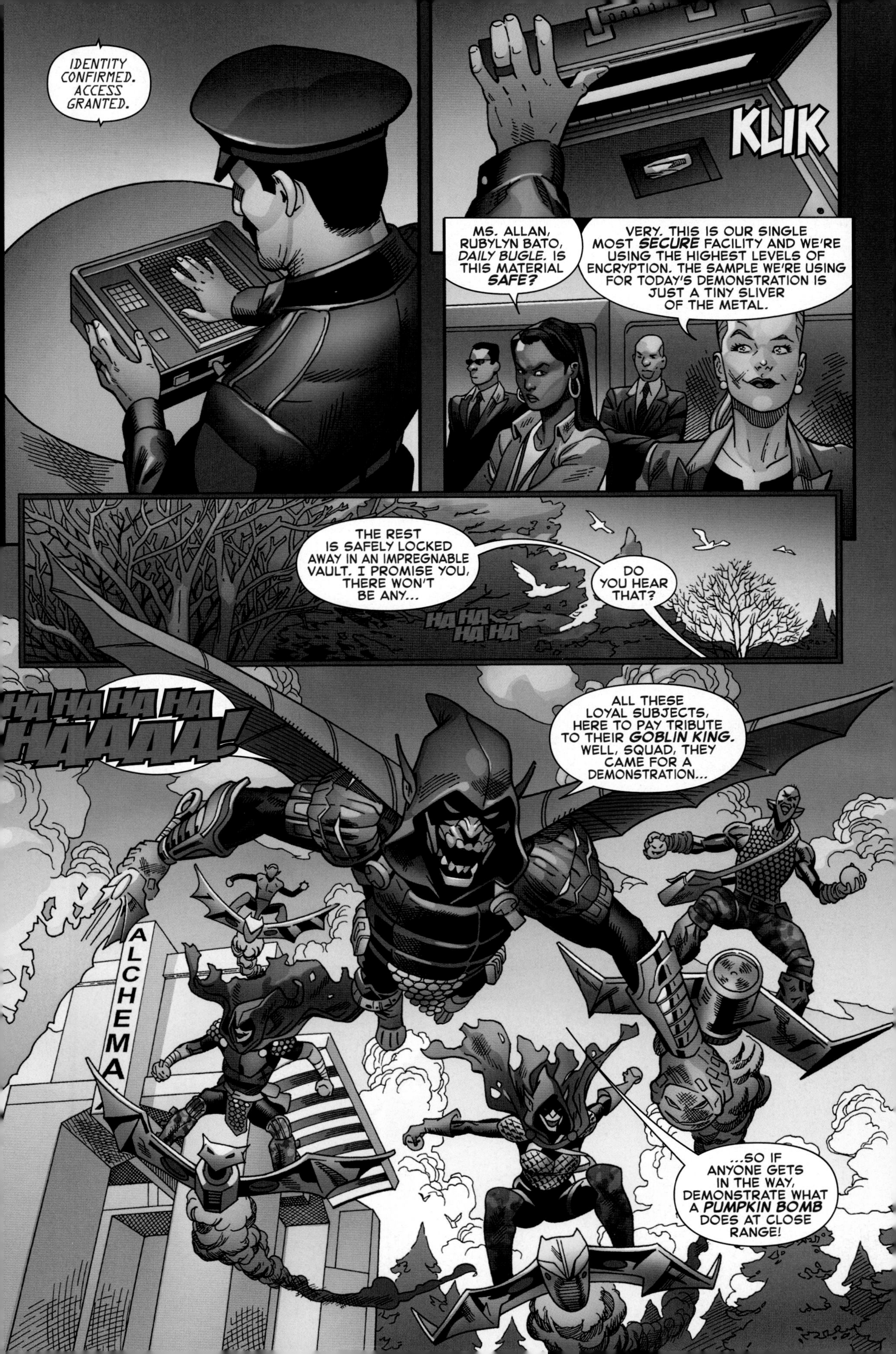
IDENTITY CONFIRMED. ACCESS GRANTED.
KLIK
MS. ALLAN, RUBYLYN BATO, DAILY BUGLE. IS THIS MATERIAL SAFE?
VERY. THIS IS OUR SINGLE MOST SECURE FACILITY AND WE'RE USING THE HIGHEST LEVELS OF ENCRYPTION. THE SAMPLE WE'RE USING FOR TODAY'S DEMONSTRATION IS JUST A TINY SLIVER OF THE METAL.
THE REST IS SAFELY LOCKED AWAY IN AN IMPREGNABLE VAULT. I PROMISE YOU, THERE WON'T BE ANY...
HA HA HA HA
DO YOU HEAR THAT?
HA HA HA HA HAAAAA!
ALL THESE LOYAL SUBJECTS, HERE TO PAY TRIBUTE TO THEIR GOBLIN KING. WELL, SQUAD, THEY CAME FOR A DEMONSTRATION...
ALCHEMA
...SO IF ANYONE GETS IN THE WAY, DEMONSTRATE WHAT A PUMPKIN BOMB DOES AT CLOSE RANGE!

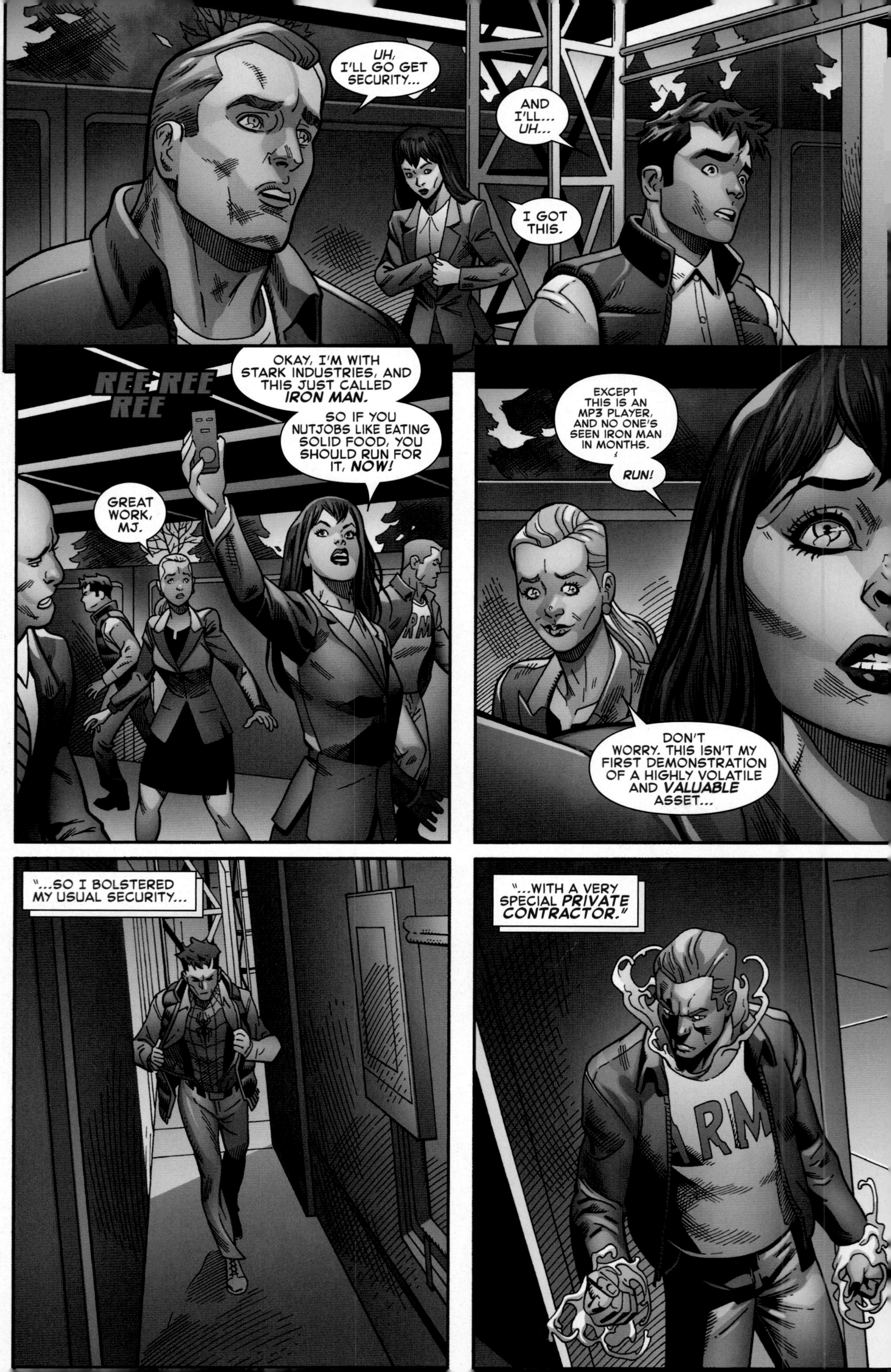
UH, I'LL GO GET SECURITY...
AND I'LL... UH...
I GOT THIS.
REE REE REE
OKAY, I'M WITH STARK INDUSTRIES, AND THIS JUST CALLED IRON MAN.
SO IF YOU NUTJOBS LIKE EATING SOLID FOOD, YOU SHOULD RUN FOR IT, NOW!
GREAT WORK, MJ.
EXCEPT THIS IS AN MP3 PLAYER, AND NO ONE'S SEEN IRON MAN IN MONTHS.
RUN!
DON'T WORRY. THIS ISN'T MY FIRST DEMONSTRATION OF A HIGHLY VOLATILE AND VALUABLE ASSET...
"...SO I BOLSTERED MY USUAL SECURITY...
"...WITH A VERY SPECIAL PRIVATE CONTRACTOR."

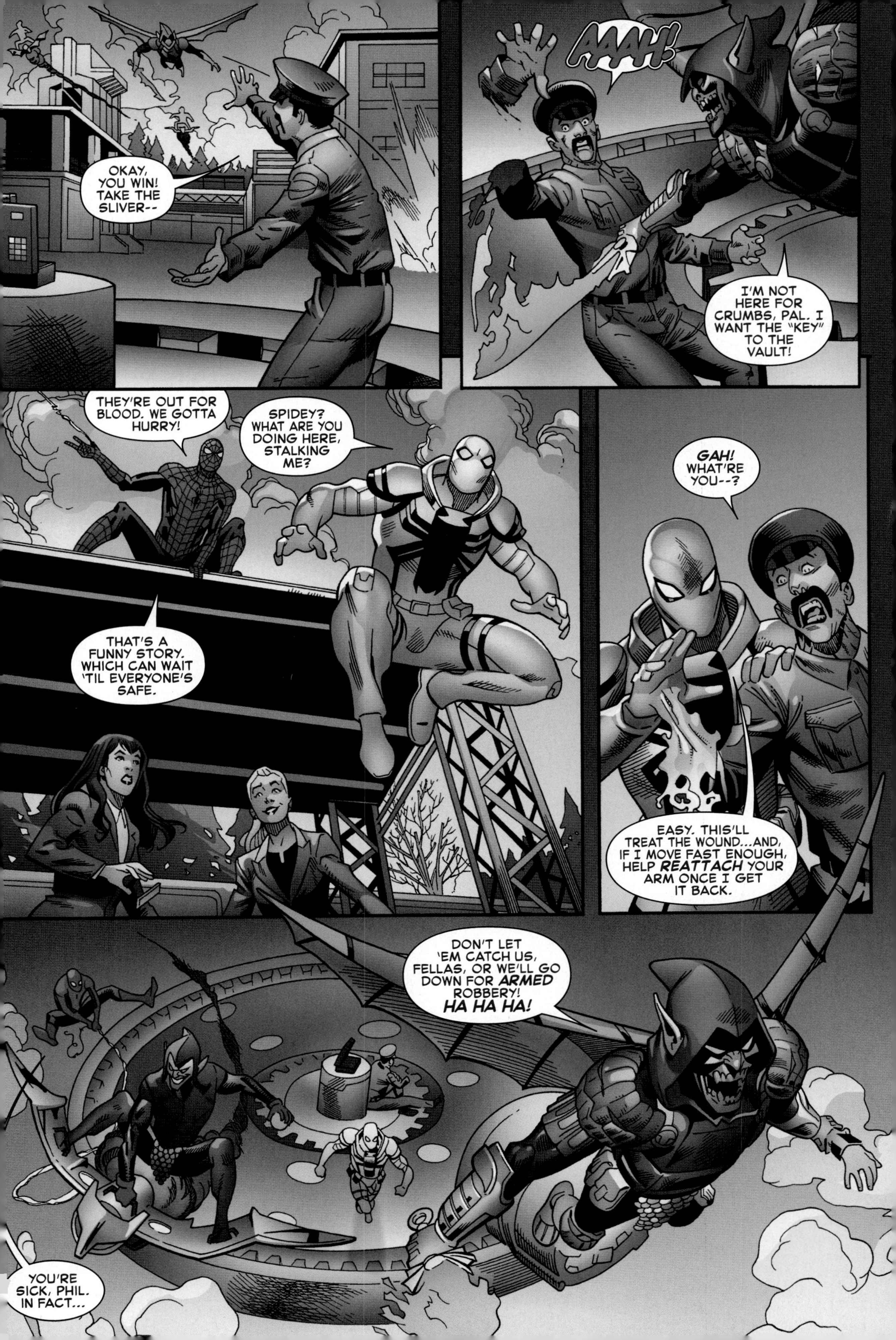

OKAY, YOU WIN! TAKE THE SLIVER--
AAAH!
I'M NOT HERE FOR CRUMBS, PAL. I WANT THE "KEY" TO THE VAULT!
THEY'RE OUT FOR BLOOD. WE GOTTA HURRY!
SPIDEY? WHAT ARE YOU DOING HERE, STALKING ME?
THAT'S A FUNNY STORY. WHICH CAN WAIT 'TIL EVERYONE'S SAFE.
GAH! WHAT'RE YOU--?
EASY. THIS'LL TREAT THE WOUND...AND, IF I MOVE FAST ENOUGH, HELP *REATTACH* YOUR ARM ONCE I GET IT BACK.
DON'T LET 'EM CATCH US, FELLAS, OR WE'LL GO DOWN FOR *ARMED* ROBBERY! *HA HA HA!*
YOU'RE SICK, PHIL. IN FACT...

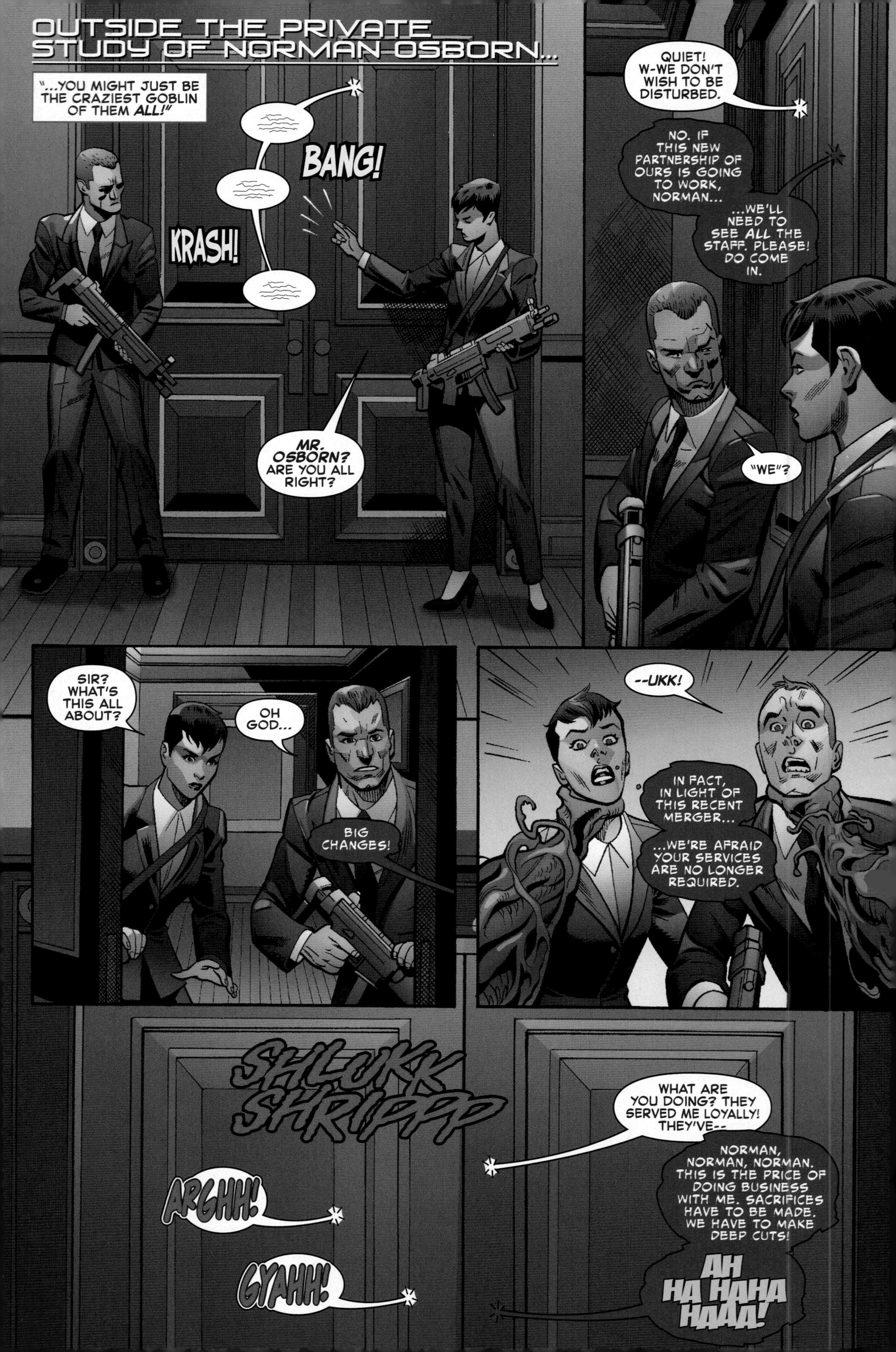
OUTSIDE THE PRIVATE STUDY OF NORMAN OSBORN...
"...YOU MIGHT JUST BE THE CRAZIEST GOBLIN OF THEM ALL!"
BANG!
KRASH!
MR. OSBORN? ARE YOU ALL RIGHT?
QUIET! W-WE DON'T WISH TO BE DISTURBED.
NO. IF THIS NEW PARTNERSHIP OF OURS IS GOING TO WORK, NORMAN...
...WE'LL NEED TO SEE ALL THE STAFF. PLEASE! DO COME IN.
"WE"?
SIR? WHAT'S THIS ALL ABOUT?
OH GOD...
BIG CHANGES!
--UKK!
IN FACT, IN LIGHT OF THIS RECENT MERGER...
...WE'RE AFRAID YOUR SERVICES ARE NO LONGER REQUIRED.
SHLUKK SHRIPPP
WHAT ARE YOU DOING? THEY SERVED ME LOYALLY! THEY'VE--
NORMAN, NORMAN, NORMAN. THIS IS THE PRICE OF DOING BUSINESS WITH ME. SACRIFICES HAVE TO BE MADE. WE HAVE TO MAKE DEEP CUTS!
ARGHH!
GYAHH!
AH HA HAHA HAAA!

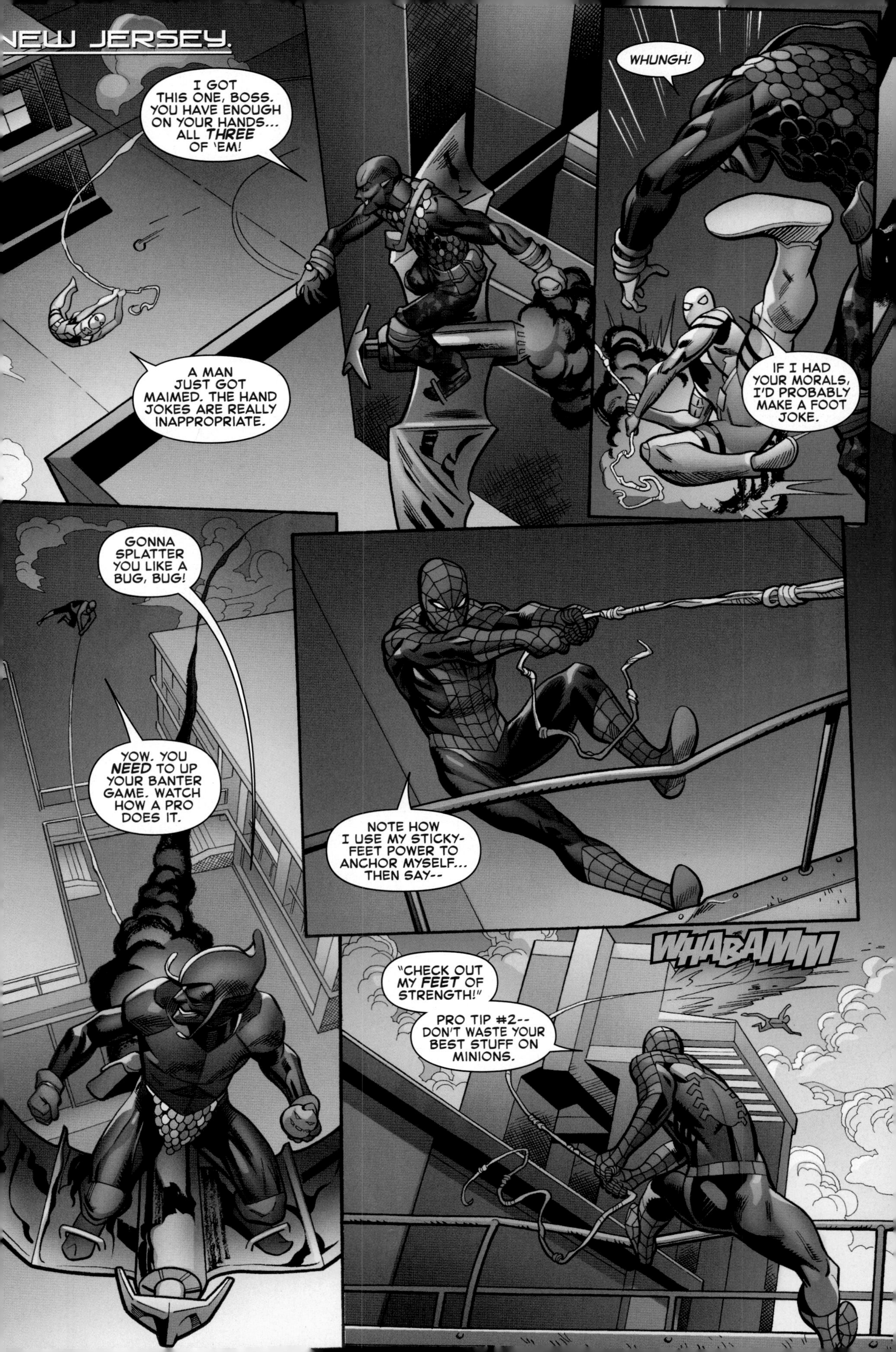
NEW JERSEY.
I GOT THIS ONE, BOSS. YOU HAVE ENOUGH ON YOUR HANDS... ALL THREE OF 'EM!
A MAN JUST GOT MAIMED. THE HAND JOKES ARE REALLY INAPPROPRIATE.
WHUNGH!
IF I HAD YOUR MORALS, I'D PROBABLY MAKE A FOOT JOKE.
GONNA SPLATTER YOU LIKE A BUG, BUG!
YOW. YOU NEED TO UP YOUR BANTER GAME. WATCH HOW A PRO DOES IT.
NOTE HOW I USE MY STICKY-FEET POWER TO ANCHOR MYSELF... THEN SAY--
WHABAMM
"CHECK OUT MY FEET OF STRENGTH!"
PRO TIP #2-- DON'T WASTE YOUR BEST STUFF ON MINIONS.

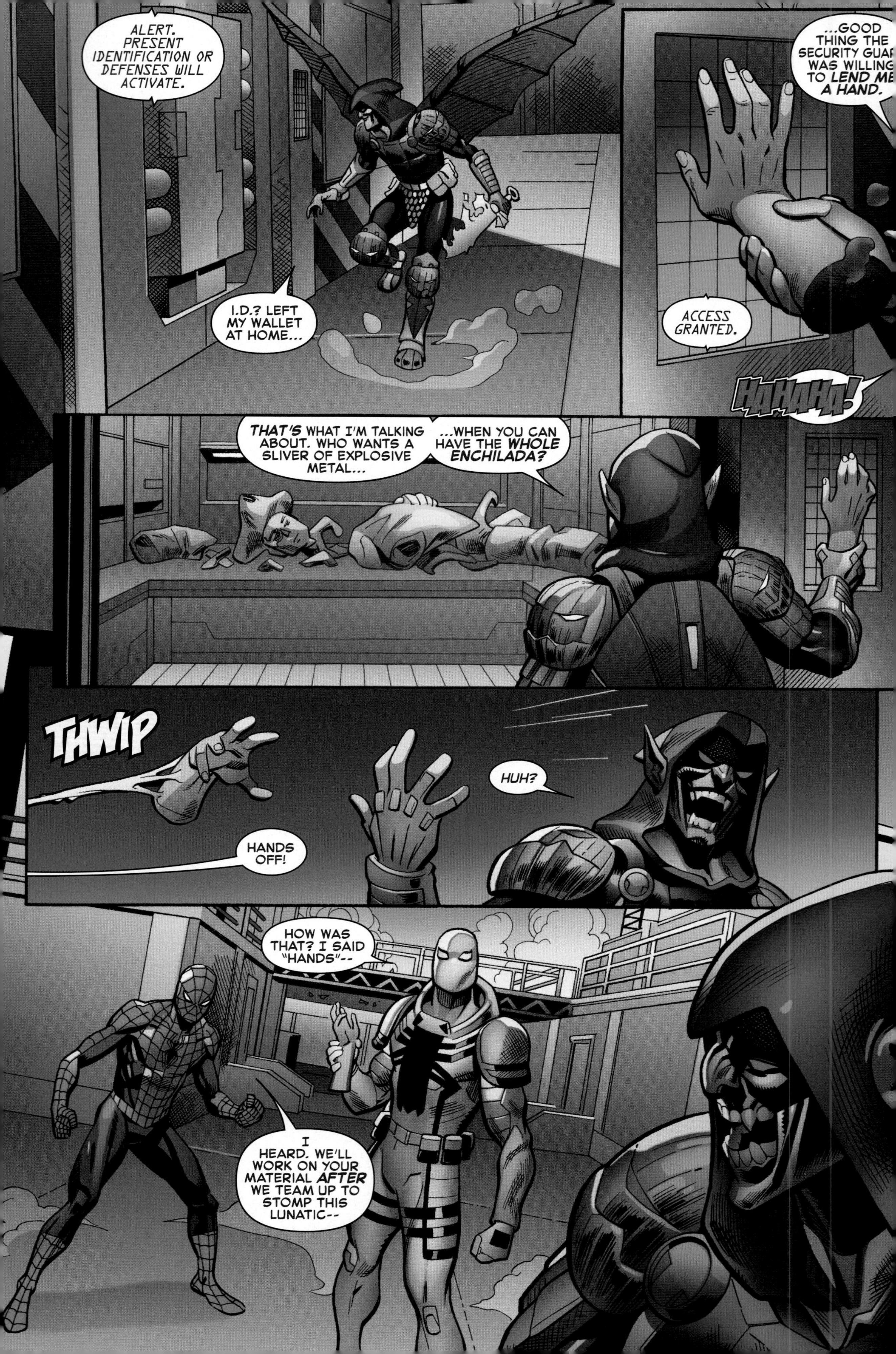
ALERT. PRESENT IDENTIFICATION OR DEFENSES WILL ACTIVATE.
I.D.? LEFT MY WALLET AT HOME...
...GOOD THING THE SECURITY GUAR WAS WILLING TO LEND ME A HAND.
ACCESS GRANTED.
HAHAHA!
THAT'S WHAT I'M TALKING ABOUT. WHO WANTS A SLIVER OF EXPLOSIVE METAL...
...WHEN YOU CAN HAVE THE WHOLE ENCHILADA?
THWIP
HUH?
HANDS OFF!
HOW WAS THAT? I SAID "HANDS"--
I HEARD. WE'LL WORK ON YOUR MATERIAL AFTER WE TEAM UP TO STOMP THIS LUNATIC--

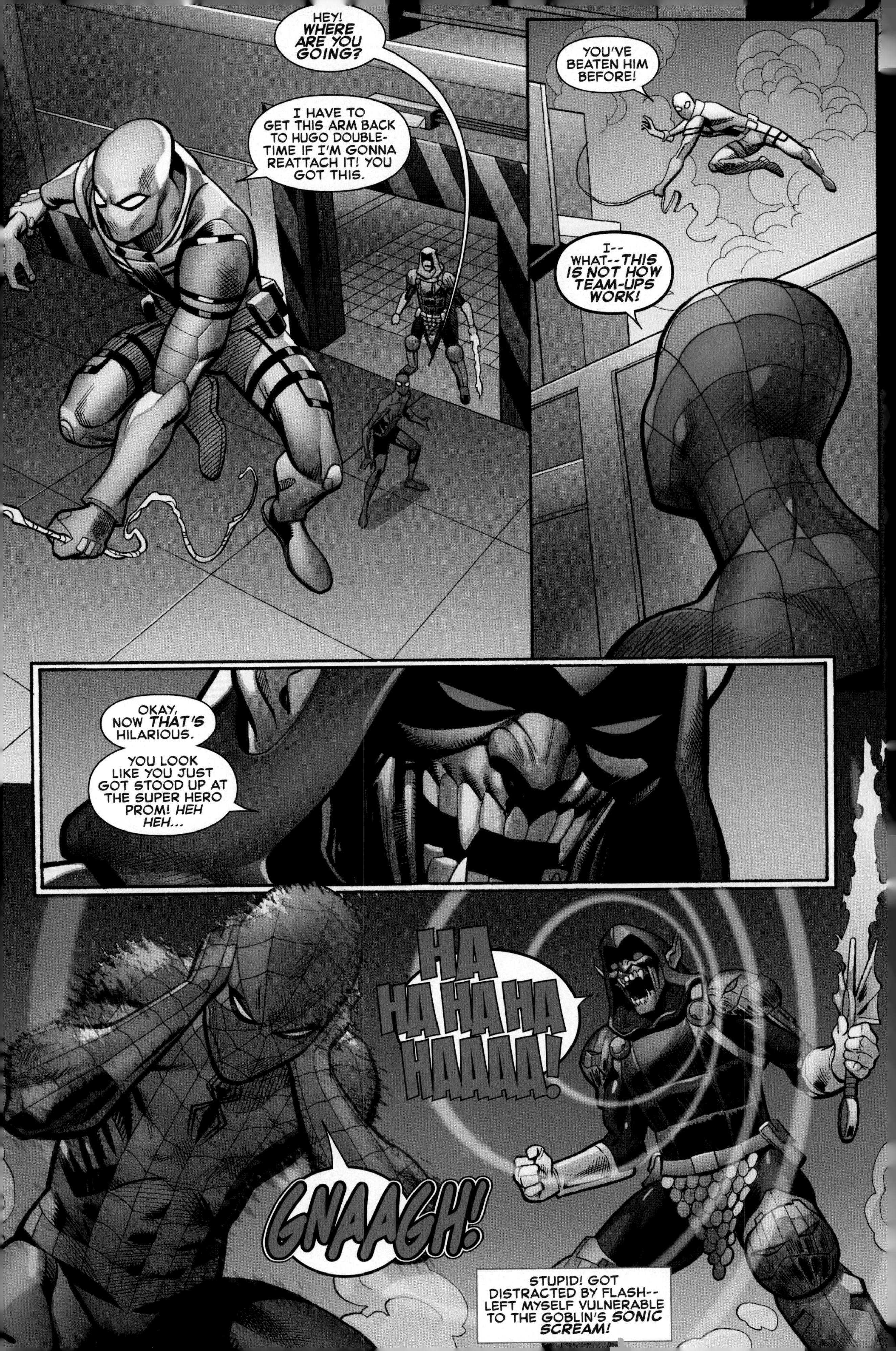
HEY! WHERE ARE YOU GOING?
I HAVE TO GET THIS ARM BACK TO HUGO DOUBLE-TIME IF I'M GONNA REATTACH IT! YOU GOT THIS.
YOU'VE BEATEN HIM BEFORE!
I-- WHAT--THIS IS NOT HOW TEAM-UPS WORK!
OKAY, NOW THAT'S HILARIOUS.
YOU LOOK LIKE YOU JUST GOT STOOD UP AT THE SUPER HERO PROM! HEH HEH...
HA HA HA HA HAAAA!
GNAAGH!
STUPID! GOT DISTRACTED BY FLASH-- LEFT MYSELF VULNERABLE TO THE GOBLIN'S SONIC SCREAM!

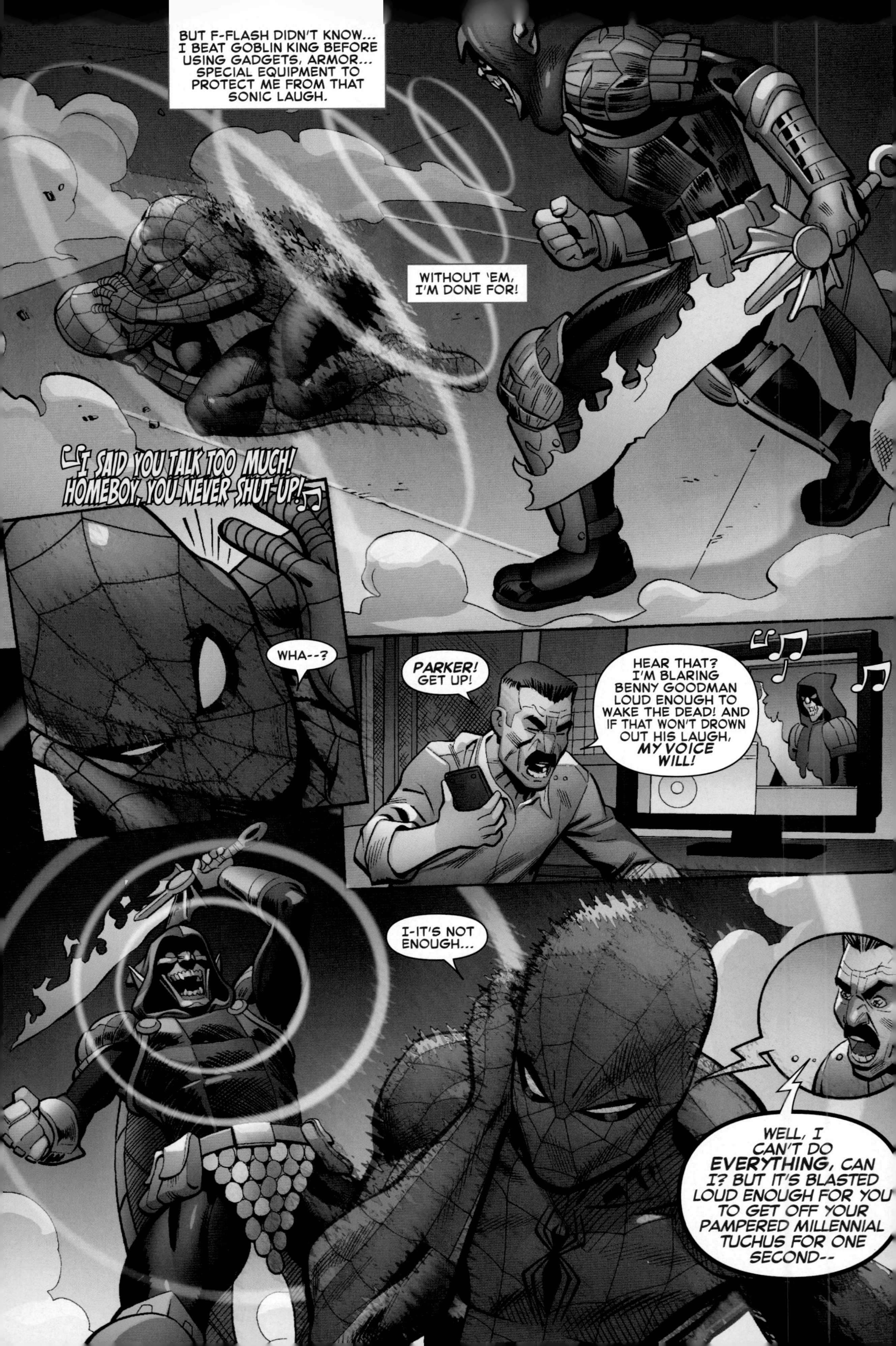
BUT F-FLASH DIDN'T KNOW... I BEAT GOBLIN KING BEFORE USING GADGETS, ARMOR... SPECIAL EQUIPMENT TO PROTECT ME FROM THAT SONIC LAUGH.
WITHOUT 'EM, I'M DONE FOR!
I SAID YOU TALK TOO MUCH! HOMEBOY, YOU NEVER SHUT UP!
WHA--?
PARKER! GET UP!
HEAR THAT? I'M BLARING BENNY GOODMAN LOUD ENOUGH TO WAKE THE DEAD! AND IF THAT WON'T DROWN OUT HIS LAUGH, MY VOICE WILL!
I-IT'S NOT ENOUGH...
WELL, I CAN'T DO EVERYTHING, CAN I? BUT IT'S BLASTED LOUD ENOUGH FOR YOU TO GET OFF YOUR PAMPERED MILLENNIAL TUCHUS FOR ONE SECOND--

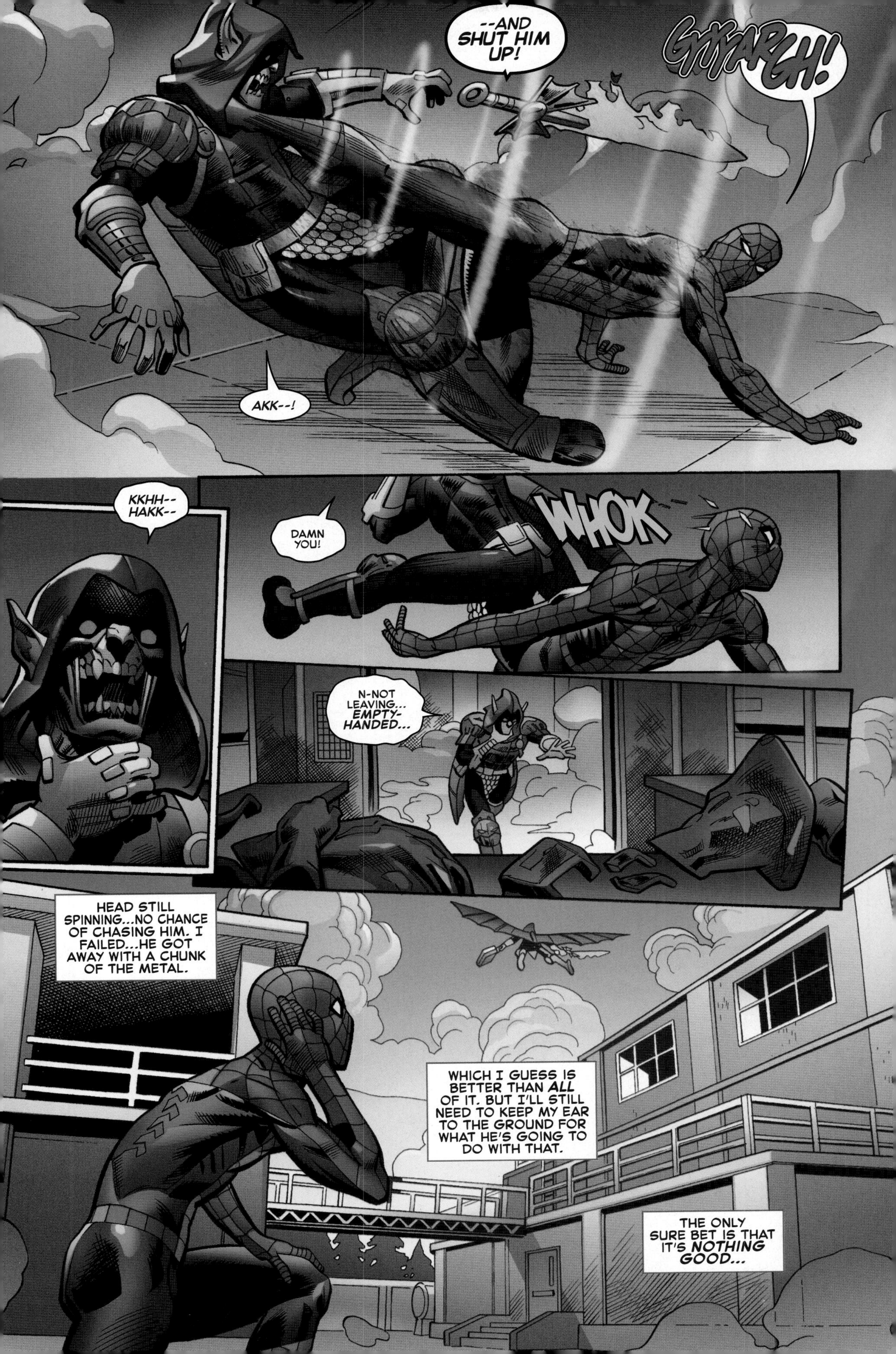
--AND SHUT HIM UP!
GYYARGH!
AKK--!
KKHH-- HAKK--
DAMN YOU!
WHOK
N-NOT LEAVING... EMPTY-HANDED...
HEAD STILL SPINNING...NO CHANCE OF CHASING HIM. I FAILED...HE GOT AWAY WITH A CHUNK OF THE METAL.
WHICH I GUESS IS BETTER THAN ALL OF IT. BUT I'LL STILL NEED TO KEEP MY EAR TO THE GROUND FOR WHAT HE'S GOING TO DO WITH THAT.
THE ONLY SURE BET IS THAT IT'S NOTHING GOOD...

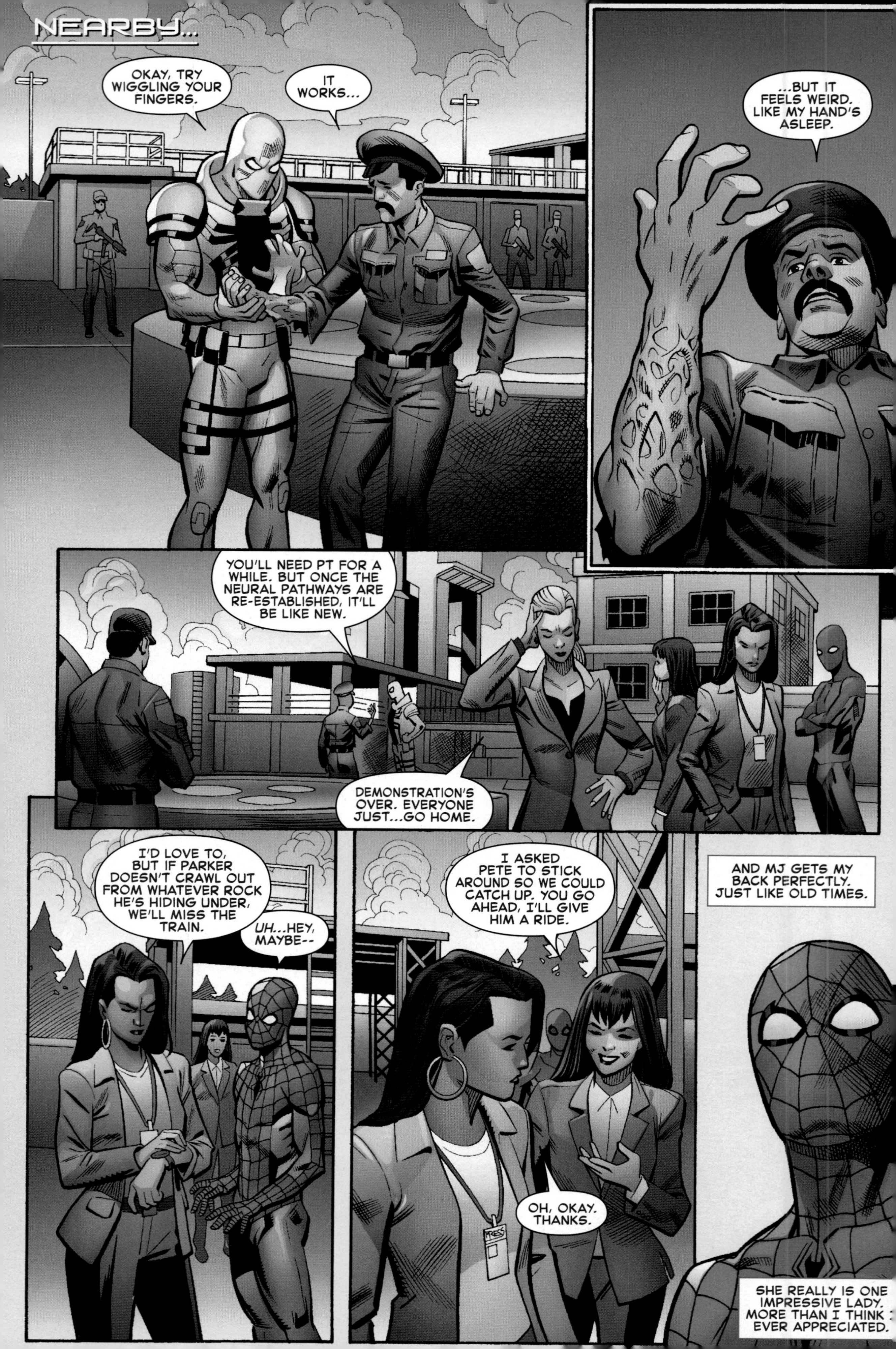
NEARBY...
OKAY, TRY WIGGLING YOUR FINGERS.
IT WORKS...
...BUT IT FEELS WEIRD. LIKE MY HAND'S ASLEEP.
YOU'LL NEED PT FOR A WHILE. BUT ONCE THE NEURAL PATHWAYS ARE RE-ESTABLISHED, IT'LL BE LIKE NEW.
DEMONSTRATION'S OVER. EVERYONE JUST...GO HOME.
I'D LOVE TO, BUT IF PARKER DOESN'T CRAWL OUT FROM WHATEVER ROCK HE'S HIDING UNDER, WE'LL MISS THE TRAIN.
UH...HEY, MAYBE--
I ASKED PETE TO STICK AROUND SO WE COULD CATCH UP. YOU GO AHEAD, I'LL GIVE HIM A RIDE.
OH, OKAY. THANKS.
PRESS
AND MJ GETS MY BACK PERFECTLY. JUST LIKE OLD TIMES.
SHE REALLY IS ONE IMPRESSIVE LADY. MORE THAN I THINK I EVER APPRECIATED.

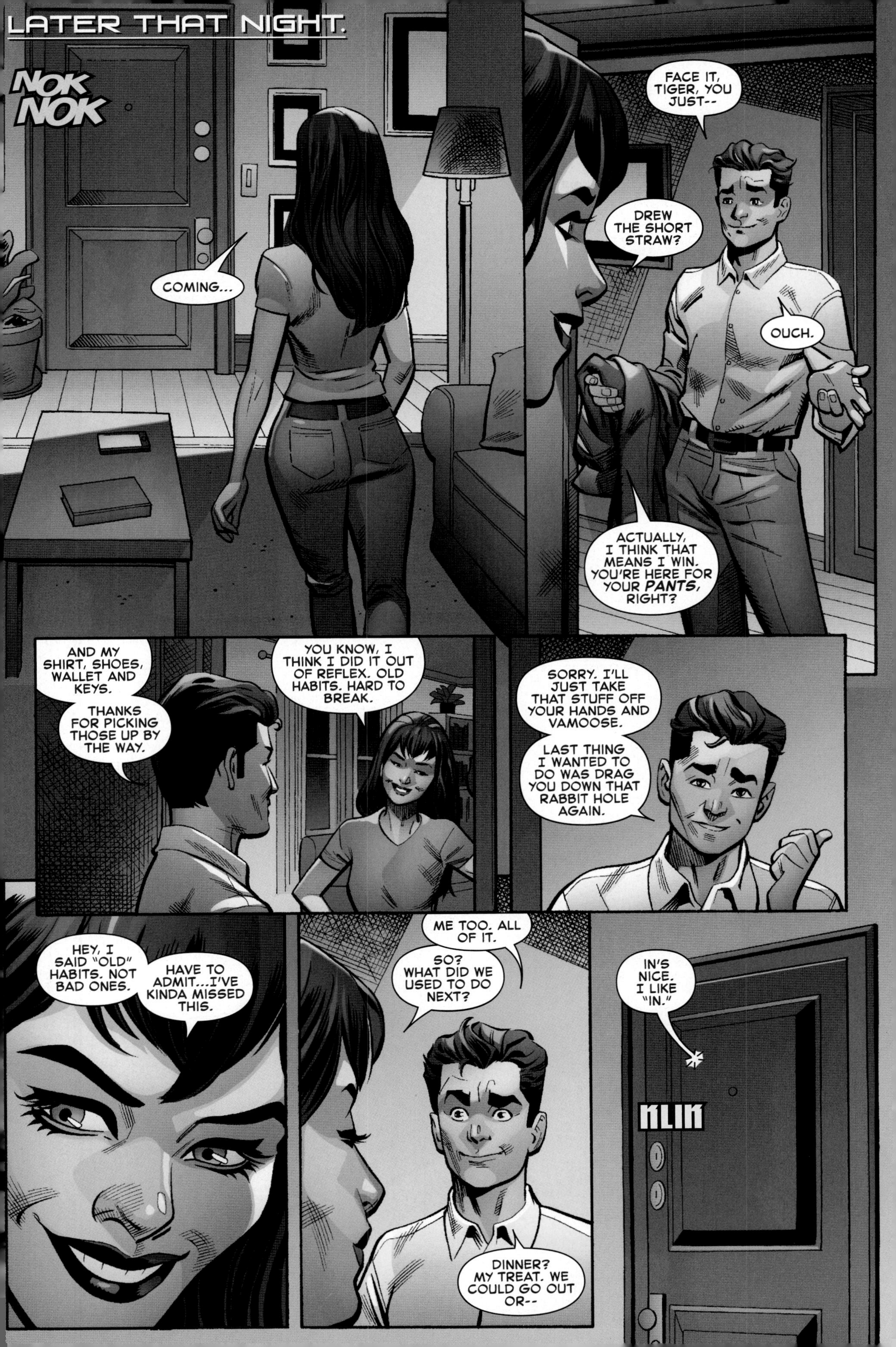
LATER THAT NIGHT.
NOK NOK
COMING...
FACE IT, TIGER, YOU JUST--
DREW THE SHORT STRAW?
OUCH.
ACTUALLY, I THINK THAT MEANS I WIN. YOU'RE HERE FOR YOUR *PANTS*, RIGHT?
AND MY SHIRT, SHOES, WALLET AND KEYS.
THANKS FOR PICKING THOSE UP BY THE WAY.
YOU KNOW, I THINK I DID IT OUT OF REFLEX. OLD HABITS. HARD TO BREAK.
SORRY. I'LL JUST TAKE THAT STUFF OFF YOUR HANDS AND VAMOOSE.
LAST THING I WANTED TO DO WAS DRAG YOU DOWN THAT RABBIT HOLE AGAIN.
HEY, I SAID "OLD" HABITS. NOT BAD ONES.
HAVE TO ADMIT...I'VE KINDA MISSED THIS.
ME TOO. ALL OF IT.
SO? WHAT DID WE USED TO DO NEXT?
DINNER? MY TREAT. WE COULD GO OUT OR--
IN'S NICE. I LIKE "IN."
KLIK

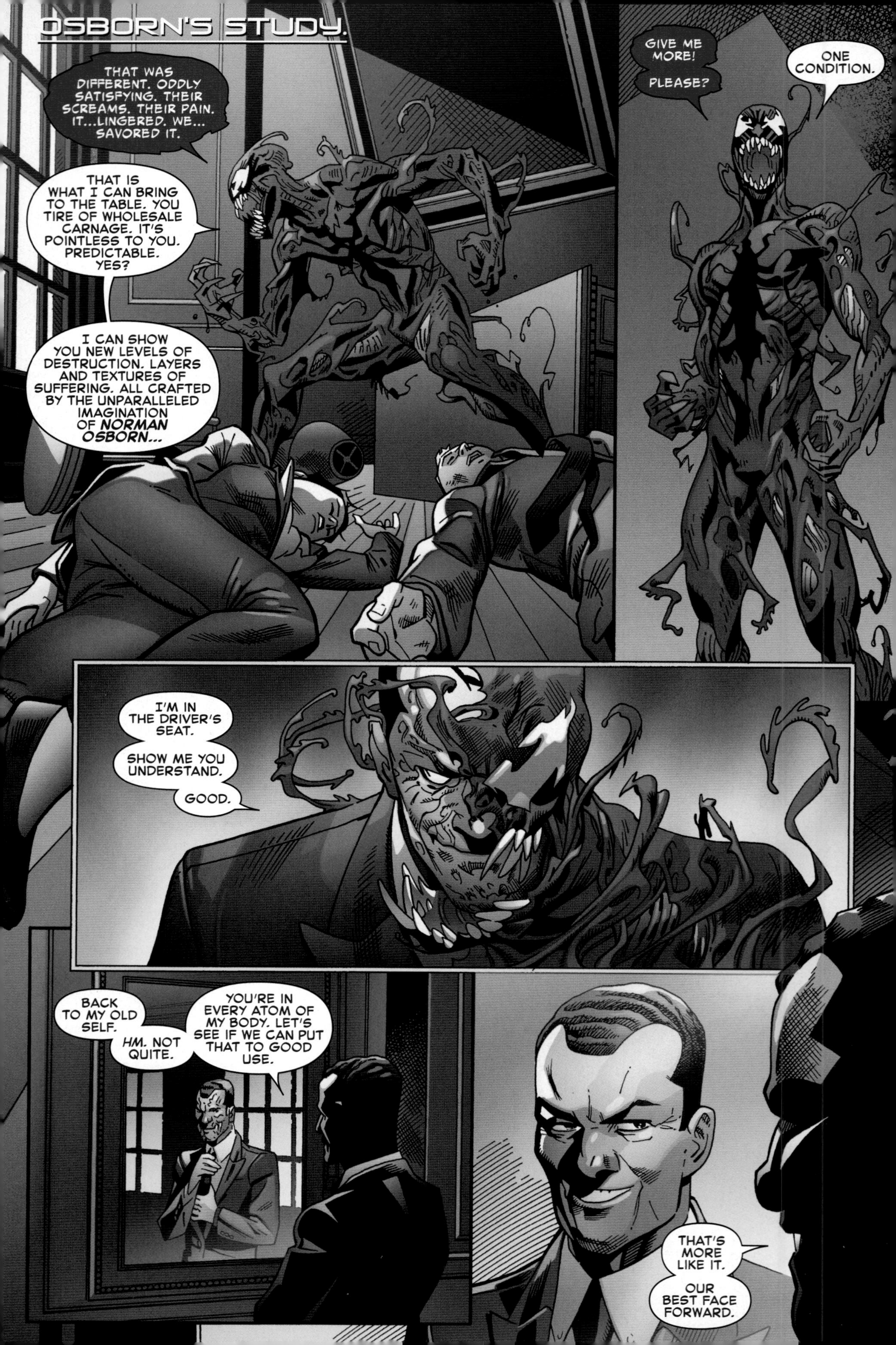
OSBORN'S STUDY.
THAT WAS DIFFERENT. ODDLY SATISFYING. THEIR SCREAMS. THEIR PAIN. IT...LINGERED. WE... SAVORED IT.
THAT IS WHAT I CAN BRING TO THE TABLE. YOU TIRE OF WHOLESALE CARNAGE. IT'S POINTLESS TO YOU. PREDICTABLE. YES?
I CAN SHOW YOU NEW LEVELS OF DESTRUCTION. LAYERS AND TEXTURES OF SUFFERING. ALL CRAFTED BY THE UNPARALLELED IMAGINATION OF NORMAN OSBORN...
GIVE ME MORE!
PLEASE?
ONE CONDITION.
I'M IN THE DRIVER'S SEAT.
SHOW ME YOU UNDERSTAND.
GOOD.
BACK TO MY OLD SELF.
HM. NOT QUITE.
YOU'RE IN EVERY ATOM OF MY BODY. LET'S SEE IF WE CAN PUT THAT TO GOOD USE.
THAT'S MORE LIKE IT.
OUR BEST FACE FORWARD.

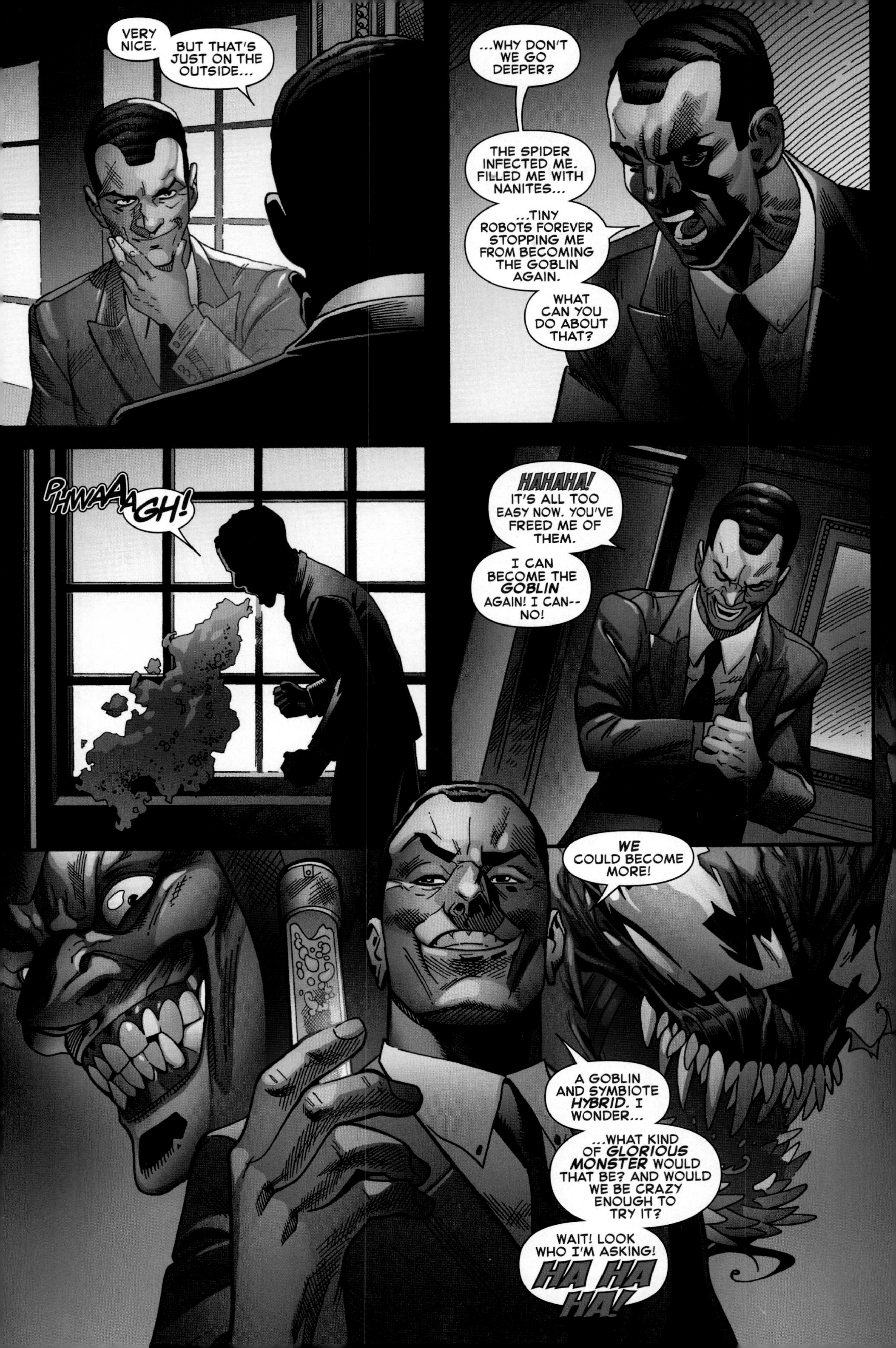

VERY NICE.
BUT THAT'S JUST ON THE OUTSIDE...
...WHY DON'T WE GO DEEPER?
THE SPIDER INFECTED ME. FILLED ME WITH NANITES...
...TINY ROBOTS FOREVER STOPPING ME FROM BECOMING THE GOBLIN AGAIN.
WHAT CAN YOU DO ABOUT THAT?
PHWAAAAGH!
HAHAHA! IT'S ALL TOO EASY NOW. YOU'VE FREED ME OF THEM.
I CAN BECOME THE GOBLIN AGAIN! I CAN-- NO!
WE COULD BECOME MORE!
A GOBLIN AND SYMBIOTE HYBRID. I WONDER...
...WHAT KIND OF GLORIOUS MONSTER WOULD THAT BE? AND WOULD WE BE CRAZY ENOUGH TO TRY IT?
WAIT! LOOK WHO I'M ASKING!
HA HA HA!

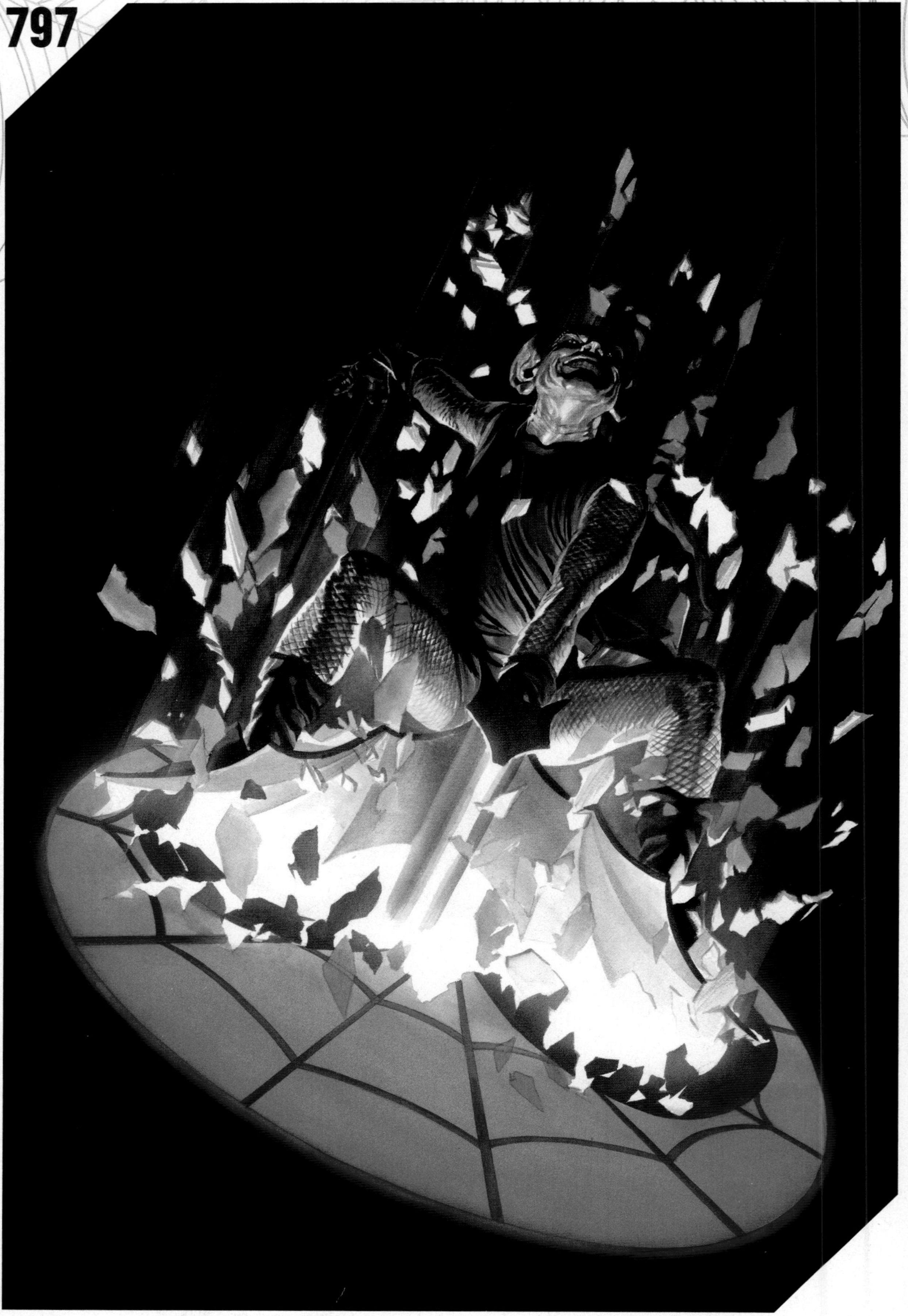

GO DOWN SWINGING PART ONE "THE LOOSE THREAD"

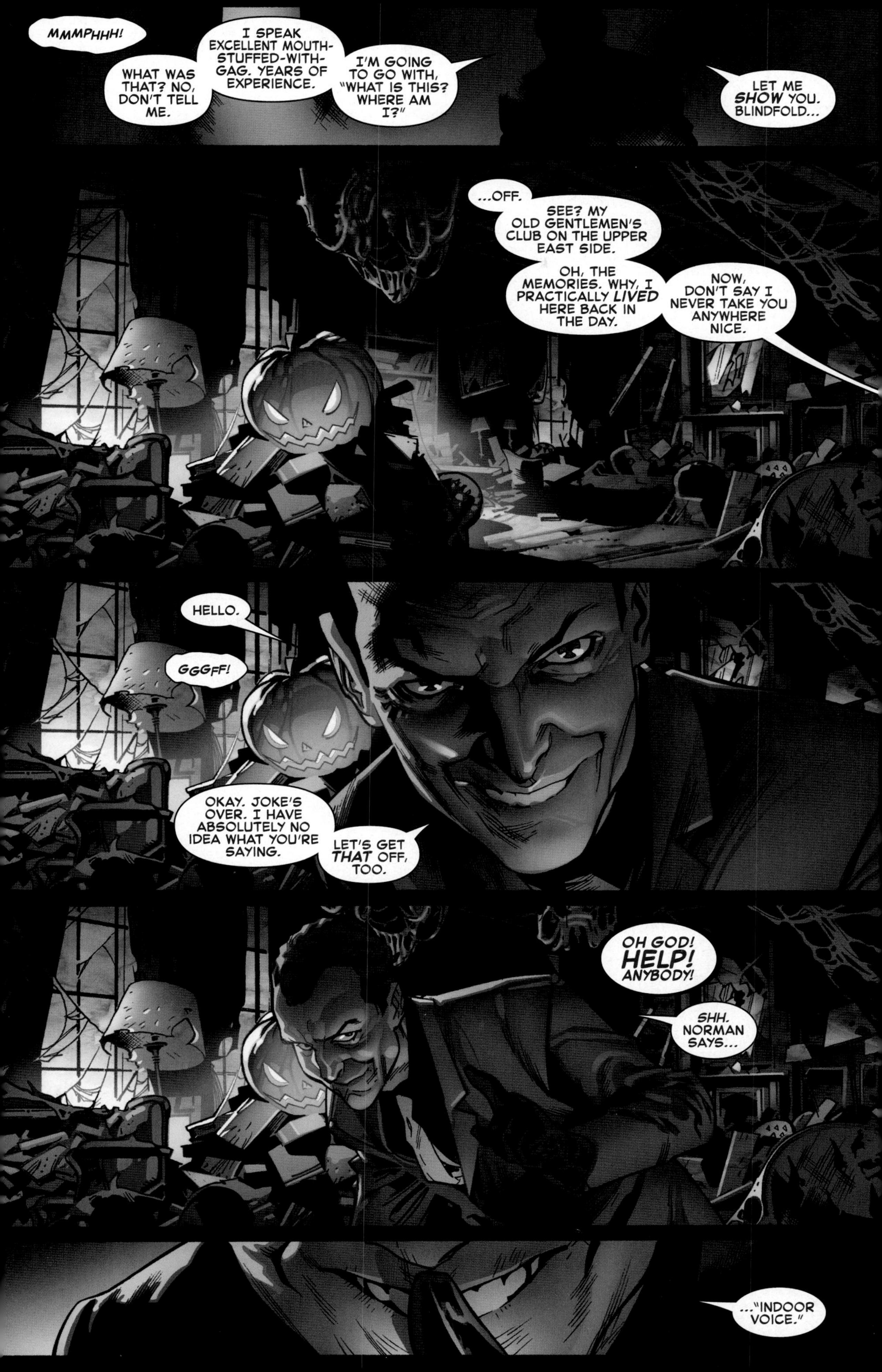
MMMPHHH!
WHAT WAS THAT? NO, DON'T TELL ME.
I SPEAK EXCELLENT MOUTH-STUFFED-WITH-GAG. YEARS OF EXPERIENCE.
I'M GOING TO GO WITH, "WHAT IS THIS? WHERE AM I?"
LET ME SHOW YOU. BLINDFOLD...
...OFF.
SEE? MY OLD GENTLEMEN'S CLUB ON THE UPPER EAST SIDE.
OH, THE MEMORIES. WHY, I PRACTICALLY LIVED HERE BACK IN THE DAY.
NOW, DON'T SAY I NEVER TAKE YOU ANYWHERE NICE.
HELLO.
GGGFF!
OKAY. JOKE'S OVER. I HAVE ABSOLUTELY NO IDEA WHAT YOU'RE SAYING.
LET'S GET THAT OFF, TOO.
OH GOD! HELP! ANYBODY!
SHH. NORMAN SAYS...
..."INDOOR VOICE."

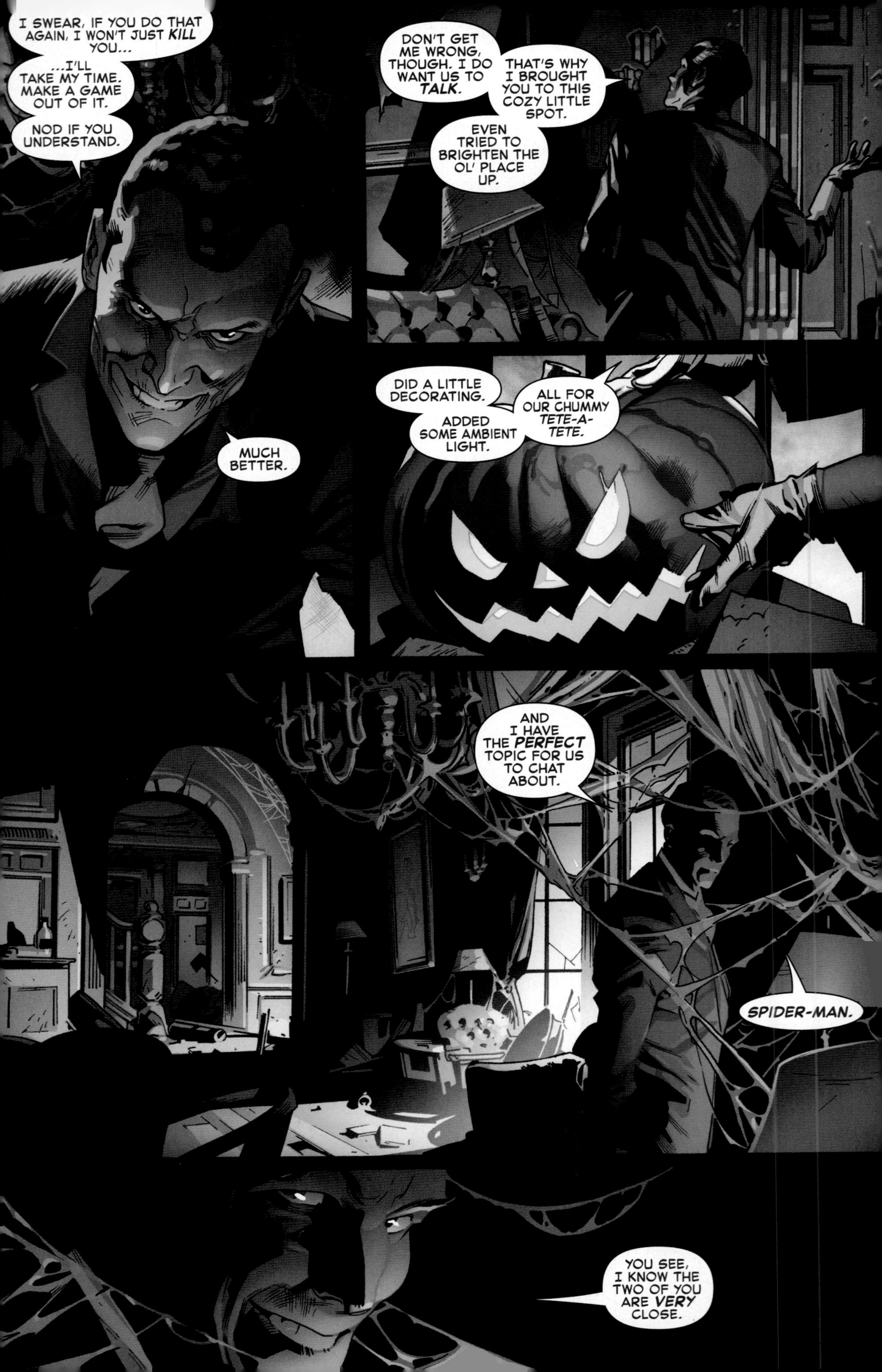
I SWEAR, IF YOU DO THAT AGAIN, I WON'T JUST KILL YOU...
...I'LL TAKE MY TIME. MAKE A GAME OUT OF IT.
NOD IF YOU UNDERSTAND.
MUCH BETTER.
DON'T GET ME WRONG, THOUGH. I DO WANT US TO TALK.
THAT'S WHY I BROUGHT YOU TO THIS COZY LITTLE SPOT.
EVEN TRIED TO BRIGHTEN THE OL' PLACE UP.
DID A LITTLE DECORATING.
ADDED SOME AMBIENT LIGHT.
ALL FOR OUR CHUMMY TETE-A-TETE.
AND I HAVE THE PERFECT TOPIC FOR US TO CHAT ABOUT.
SPIDER-MAN.
YOU SEE, I KNOW THE TWO OF YOU ARE VERY CLOSE.

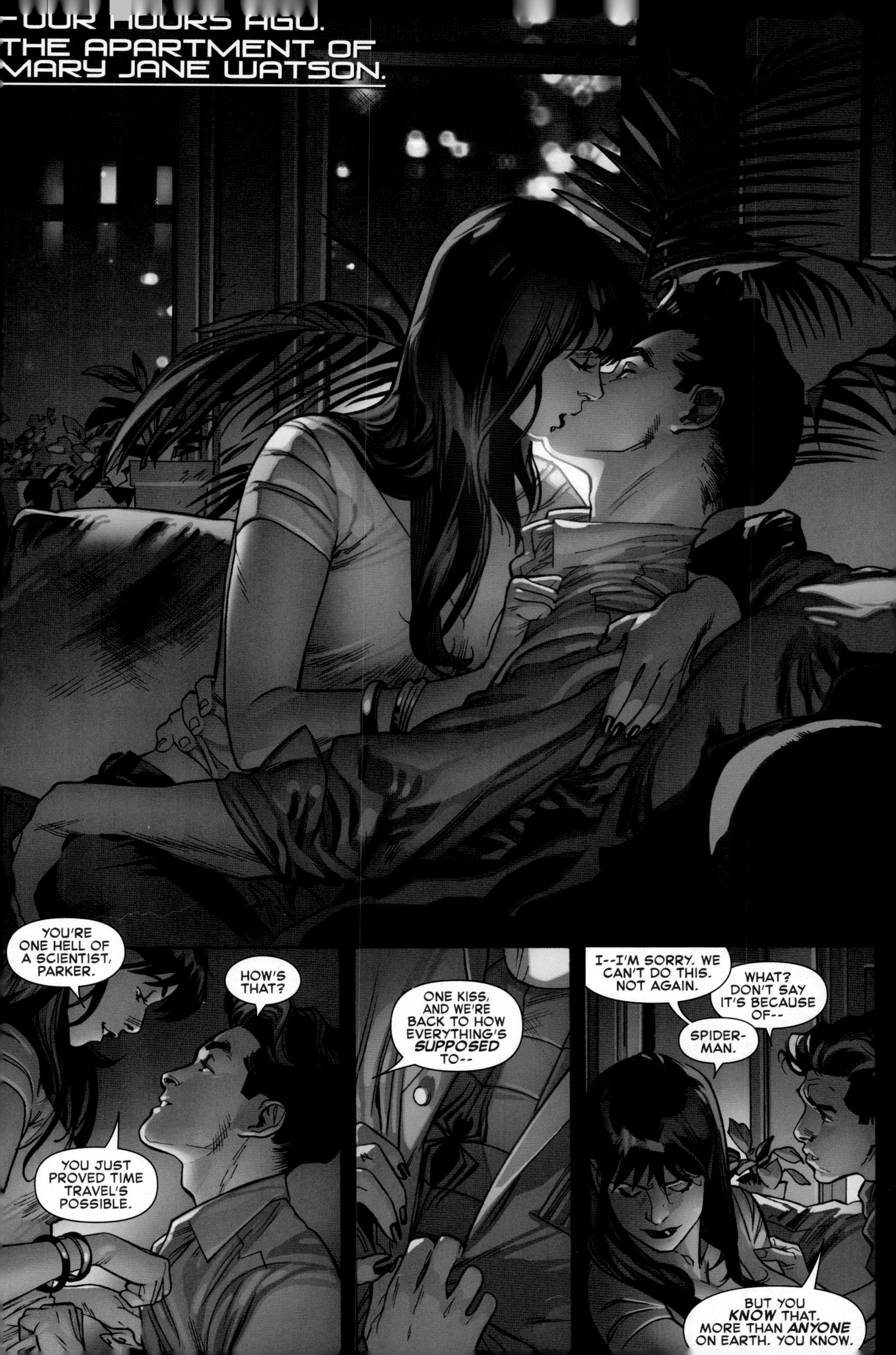
OUR HOURS AGO. THE APARTMENT OF MARY JANE WATSON.
YOU'RE ONE HELL OF A SCIENTIST, PARKER.
HOW'S THAT?
YOU JUST PROVED TIME TRAVEL'S POSSIBLE.
ONE KISS, AND WE'RE BACK TO HOW EVERYTHING'S *SUPPOSED* TO--
I--I'M SORRY. WE CAN'T DO THIS. NOT AGAIN.
WHAT? DON'T SAY IT'S BECAUSE OF--
SPIDER-MAN.
BUT YOU *KNOW* THAT. MORE THAN *ANYONE* ON EARTH. YOU KNOW.

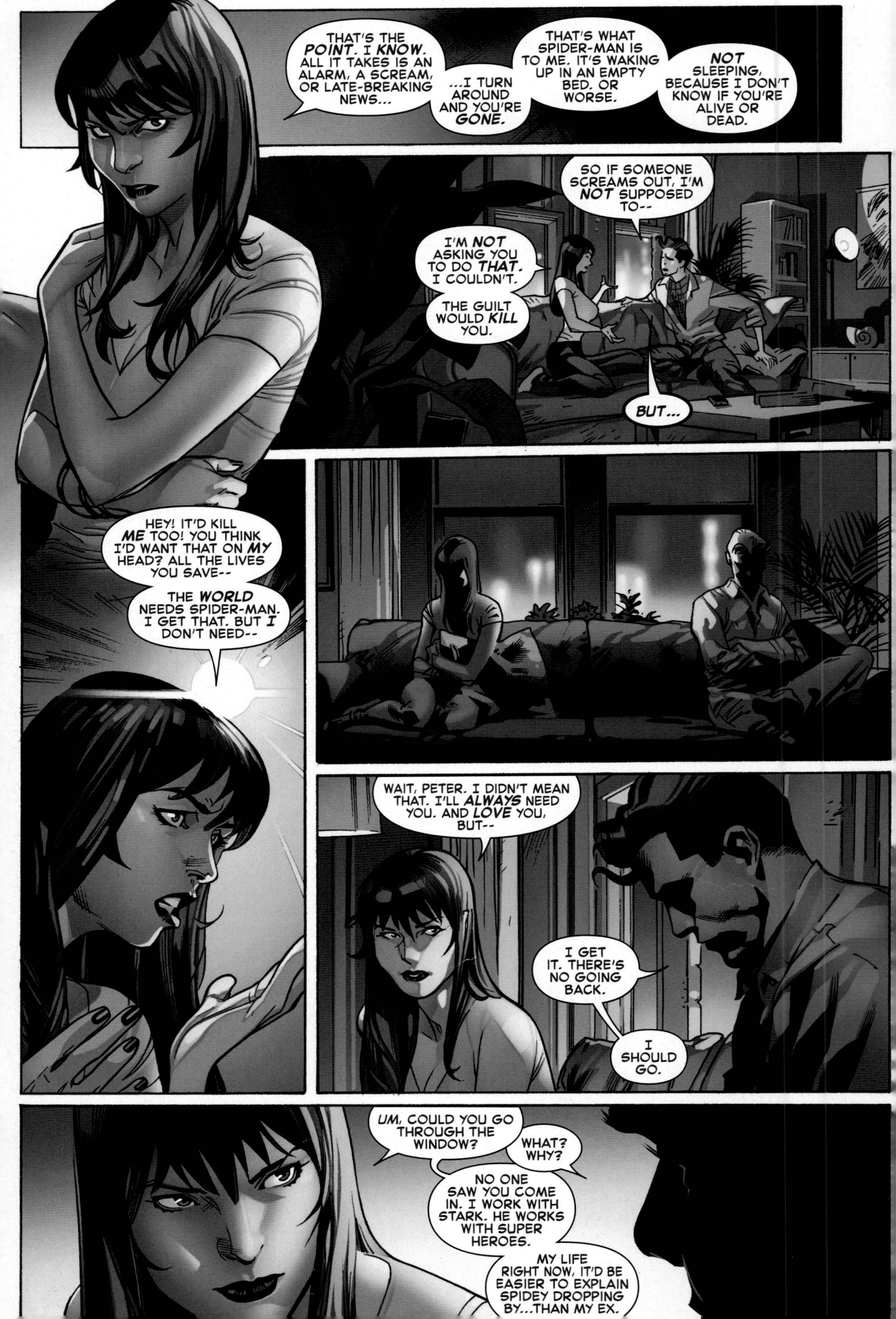
THAT'S THE POINT. I KNOW. ALL IT TAKES IS AN ALARM, A SCREAM, OR LATE-BREAKING NEWS...
...I TURN AROUND AND YOU'RE GONE.
THAT'S WHAT SPIDER-MAN IS TO ME. IT'S WAKING UP IN AN EMPTY BED. OR WORSE.
NOT SLEEPING, BECAUSE I DON'T KNOW IF YOU'RE ALIVE OR DEAD.
SO IF SOMEONE SCREAMS OUT, I'M NOT SUPPOSED TO--
I'M NOT ASKING YOU TO DO THAT. I COULDN'T.
THE GUILT WOULD KILL YOU.
BUT...
HEY! IT'D KILL ME TOO! YOU THINK I'D WANT THAT ON MY HEAD? ALL THE LIVES YOU SAVE--
THE WORLD NEEDS SPIDER-MAN. I GET THAT. BUT I DON'T NEED--
WAIT, PETER. I DIDN'T MEAN THAT. I'LL ALWAYS NEED YOU. AND LOVE YOU, BUT--
I GET IT. THERE'S NO GOING BACK.
I SHOULD GO.
UM, COULD YOU GO THROUGH THE WINDOW?
WHAT? WHY?
NO ONE SAW YOU COME IN. I WORK WITH STARK. HE WORKS WITH SUPER HEROES.
MY LIFE RIGHT NOW, IT'D BE EASIER TO EXPLAIN SPIDEY DROPPING BY...THAN MY EX.

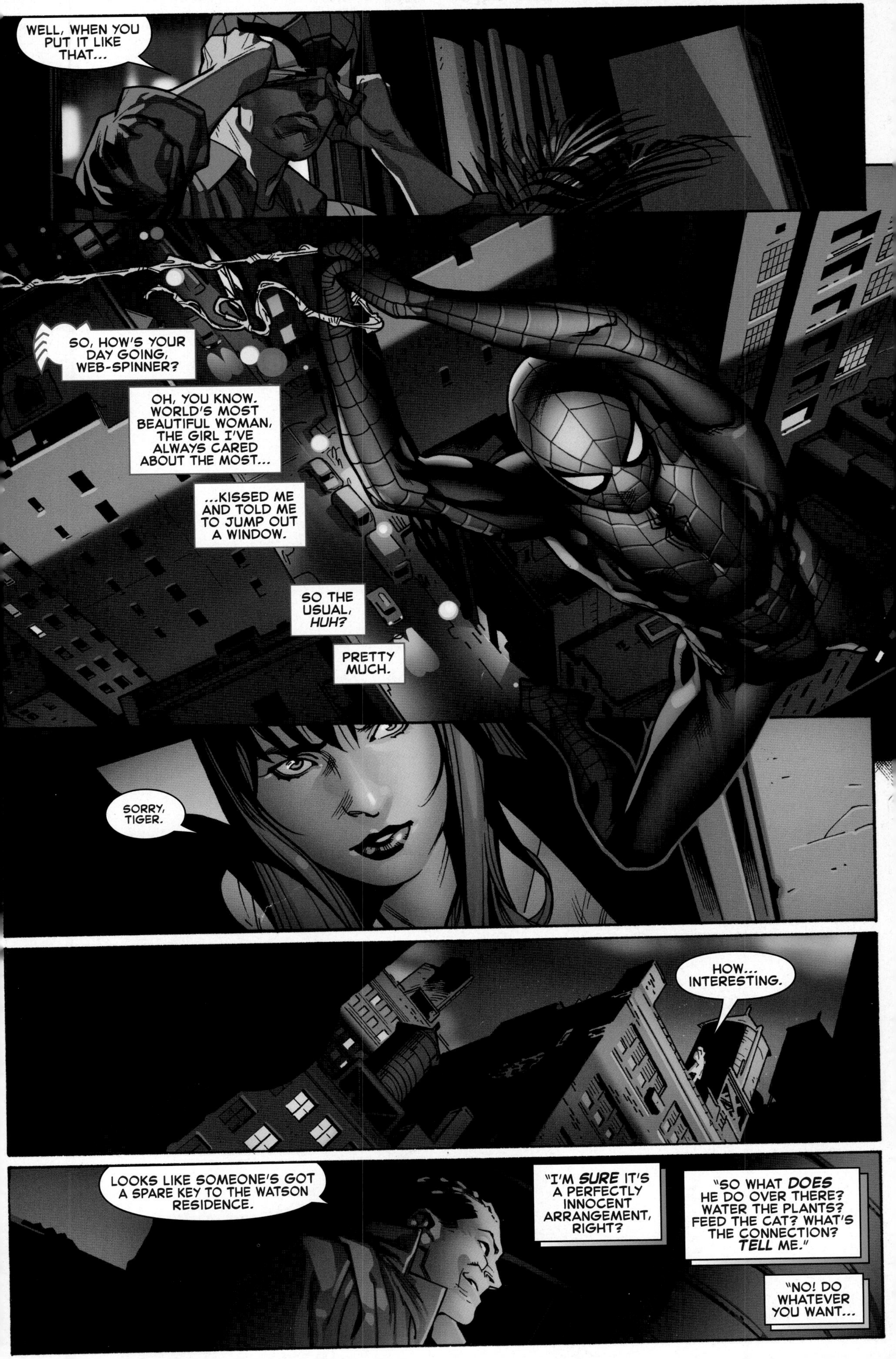
WELL, WHEN YOU PUT IT LIKE THAT...
SO, HOW'S YOUR DAY GOING, WEB-SPINNER?
OH, YOU KNOW. WORLD'S MOST BEAUTIFUL WOMAN, THE GIRL I'VE ALWAYS CARED ABOUT THE MOST...
...KISSED ME AND TOLD ME TO JUMP OUT A WINDOW.
SO THE USUAL, *HUH?*
PRETTY MUCH.
SORRY, TIGER.
HOW... INTERESTING.
LOOKS LIKE SOMEONE'S GOT A SPARE KEY TO THE WATSON RESIDENCE.
"I'M *SURE* IT'S A PERFECTLY INNOCENT ARRANGEMENT, RIGHT?
"SO WHAT *DOES* HE DO OVER THERE? WATER THE PLANTS? FEED THE CAT? WHAT'S THE CONNECTION? *TELL* ME."
"NO! DO WHATEVER YOU WANT...

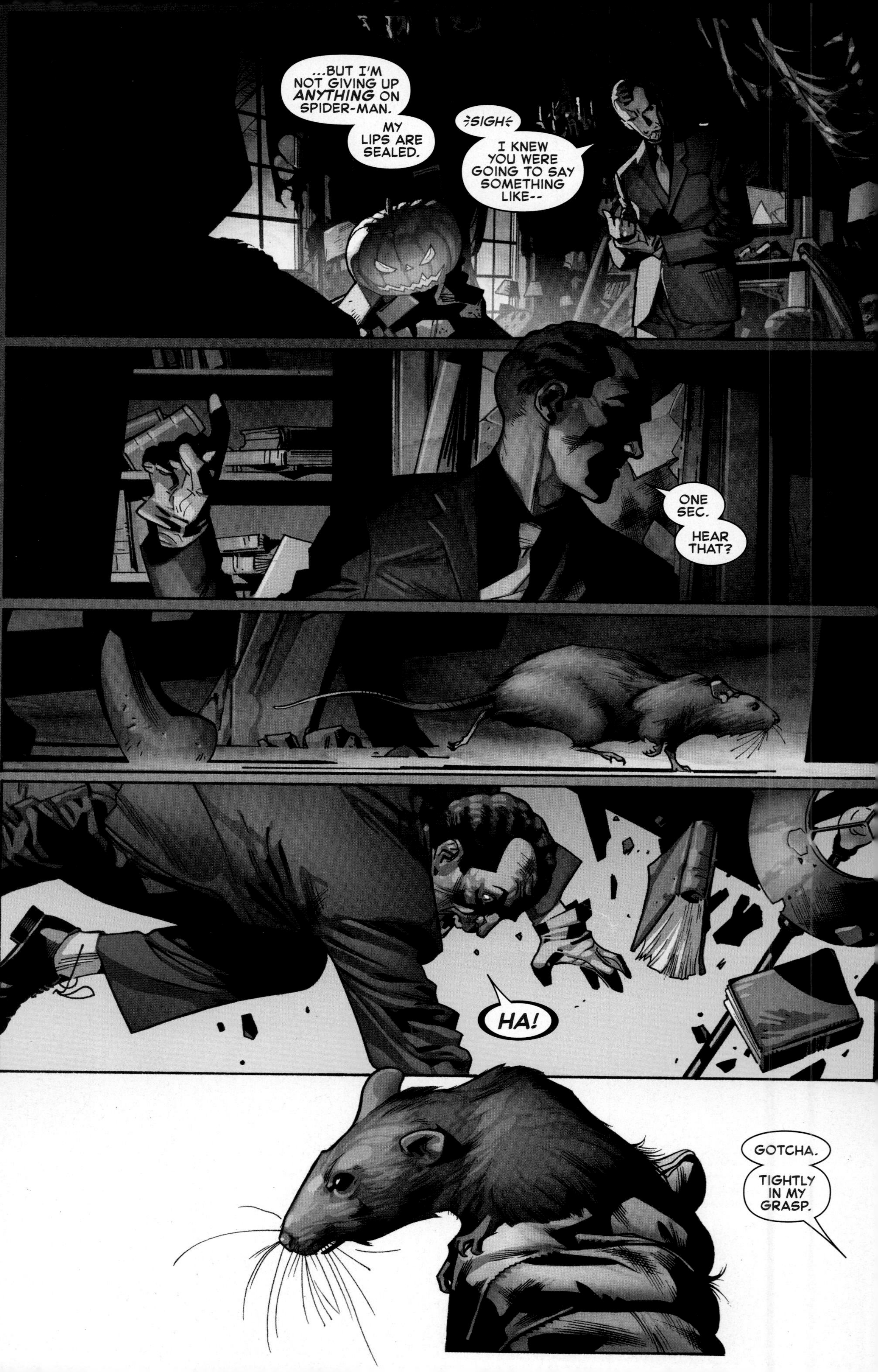
...BUT I'M NOT GIVING UP *ANYTHING* ON SPIDER-MAN.
MY LIPS ARE SEALED.
SIGH
I KNEW YOU WERE GOING TO SAY SOMETHING LIKE--
ONE SEC.
HEAR THAT?
HA!
GOTCHA.
TIGHTLY IN MY GRASP.

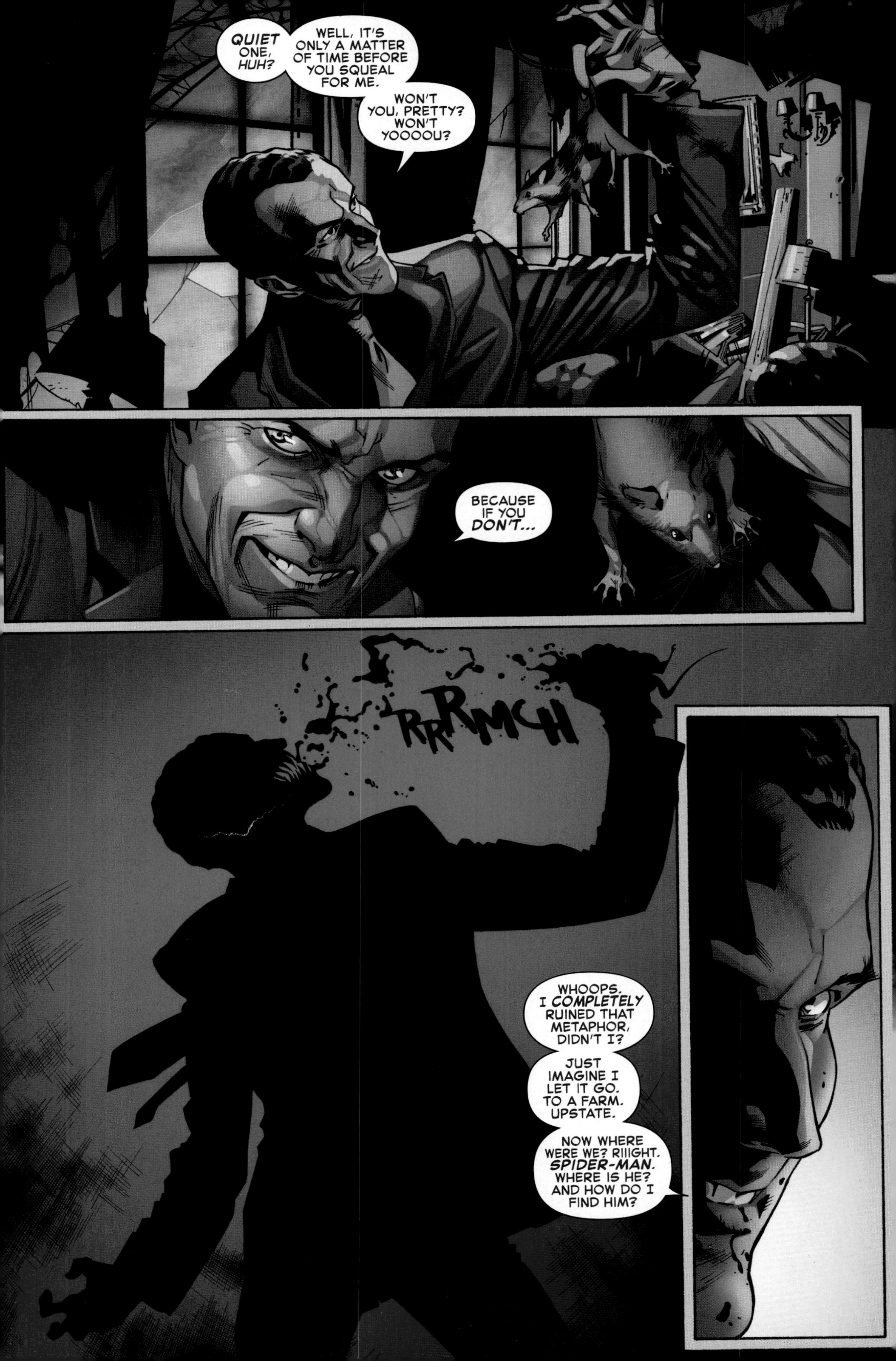
QUIET ONE, HUH?
WELL, IT'S ONLY A MATTER OF TIME BEFORE YOU SQUEAL FOR ME.
WON'T YOU, PRETTY? WON'T YOOOOU?
BECAUSE IF YOU DON'T...
RRRRMCH
WHOOPS. I COMPLETELY RUINED THAT METAPHOR, DIDN'T I?
JUST IMAGINE I LET IT GO. TO A FARM. UPSTATE.
NOW WHERE WERE WE? RIIIGHT. SPIDER-MAN. WHERE IS HE? AND HOW DO I FIND HIM?

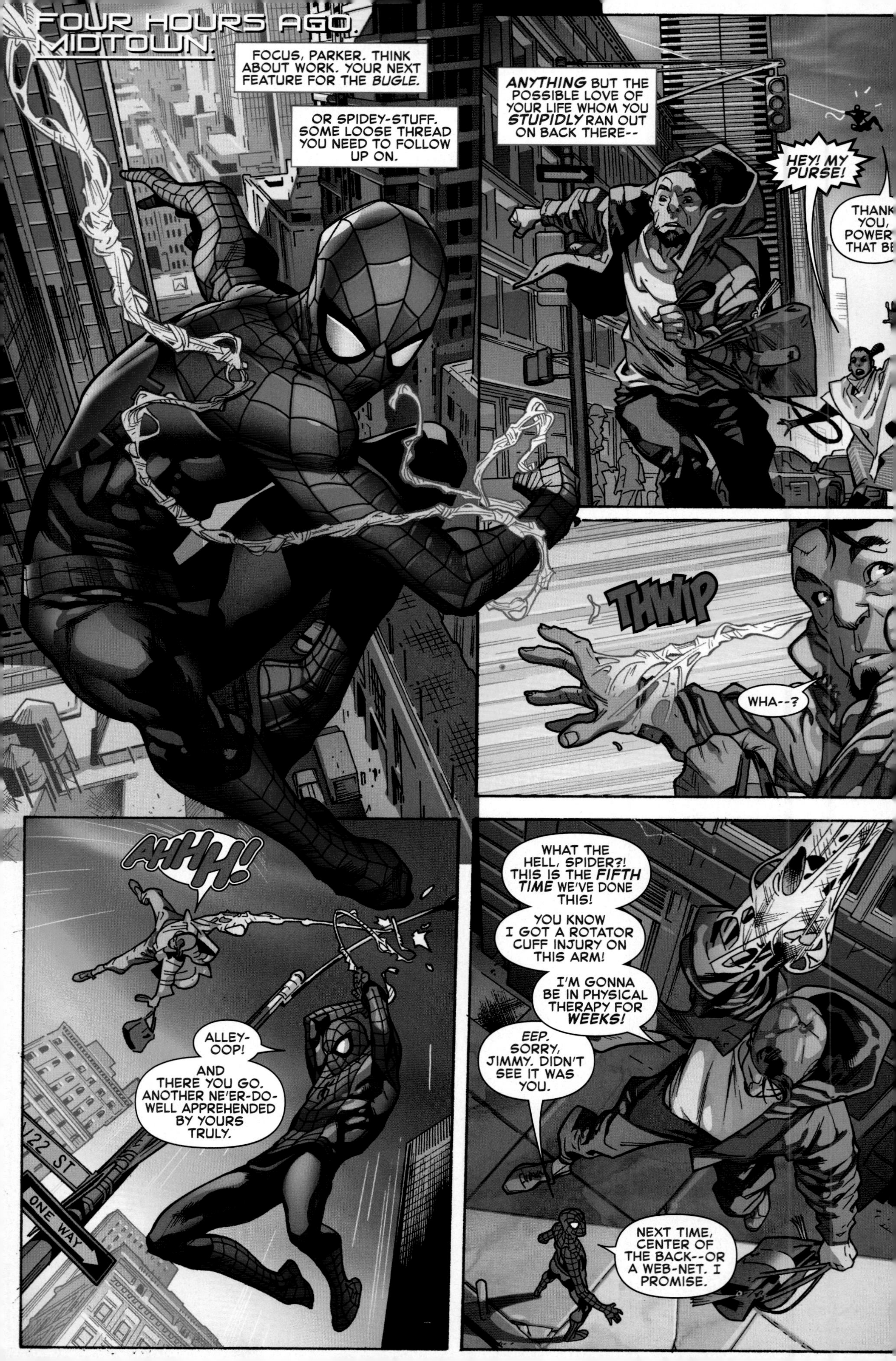

FOUR HOURS AGO. MIDTOWN.
FOCUS, PARKER. THINK ABOUT WORK. YOUR NEXT FEATURE FOR THE *BUGLE*.
OR SPIDEY-STUFF. SOME LOOSE THREAD YOU NEED TO FOLLOW UP ON.
ANYTHING BUT THE POSSIBLE LOVE OF YOUR LIFE WHOM YOU *STUPIDLY* RAN OUT ON BACK THERE--
HEY! MY PURSE!
THANK YOU, POWER THAT BE
THWIP
WHA--?
AHHH!
ALLEY-OOP!
AND THERE YOU GO. ANOTHER NE'ER-DO-WELL APPREHENDED BY YOURS TRULY.
WHAT THE HELL, SPIDER?! THIS IS THE *FIFTH TIME* WE'VE DONE THIS!
YOU KNOW I GOT A ROTATOR CUFF INJURY ON THIS ARM!
I'M GONNA BE IN PHYSICAL THERAPY FOR *WEEKS!*
EEP. SORRY, JIMMY. DIDN'T SEE IT WAS YOU.
NEXT TIME, CENTER OF THE BACK--OR A WEB-NET. I PROMISE.
ONE WAY

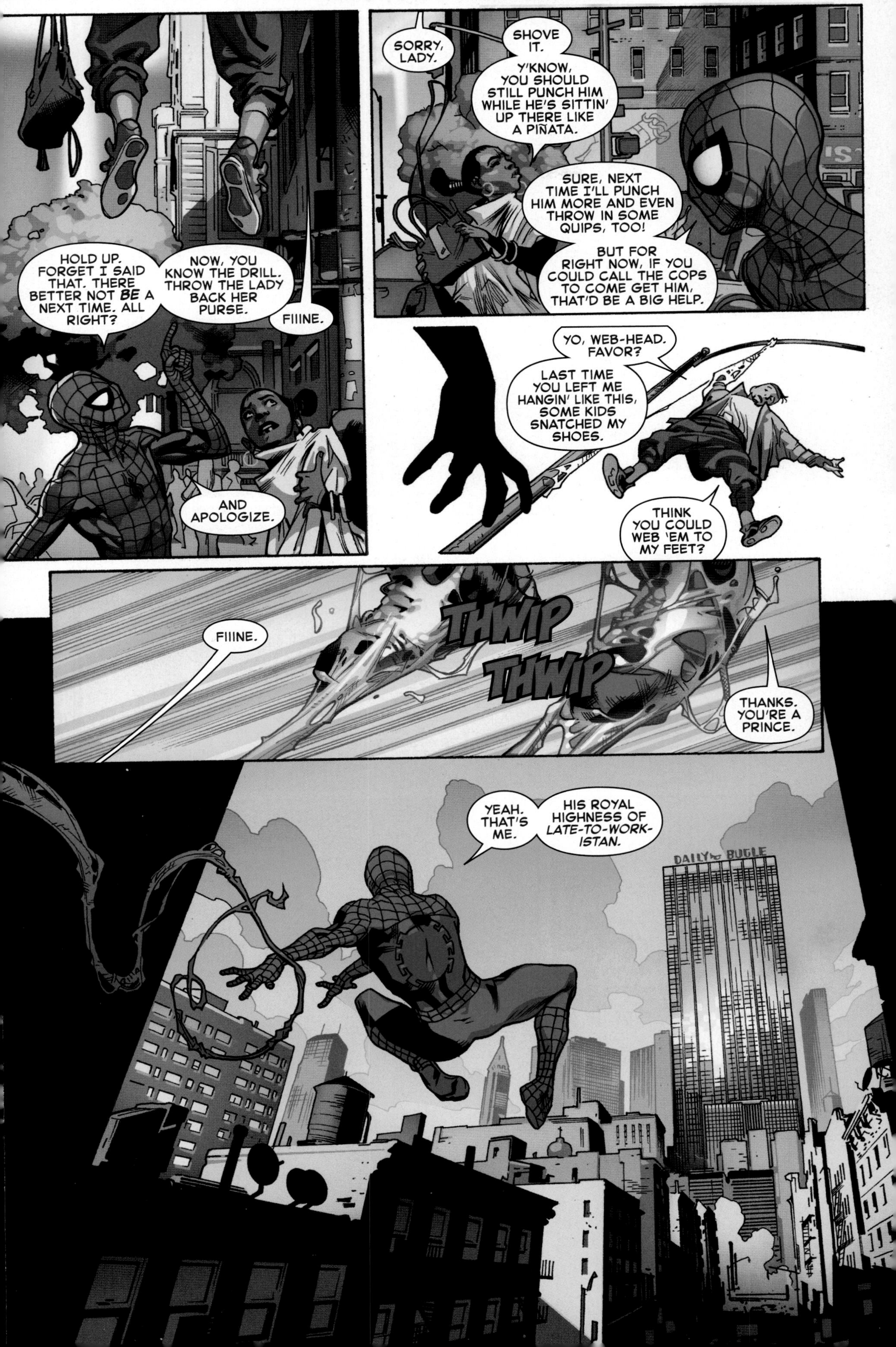
HOLD UP. FORGET I SAID THAT. THERE BETTER NOT BE A NEXT TIME. ALL RIGHT?
NOW, YOU KNOW THE DRILL. THROW THE LADY BACK HER PURSE.
FIIINE.
AND APOLOGIZE.
SORRY, LADY.
SHOVE IT.
Y'KNOW, YOU SHOULD STILL PUNCH HIM WHILE HE'S SITTIN' UP THERE LIKE A PIÑATA.
SURE, NEXT TIME I'LL PUNCH HIM MORE AND EVEN THROW IN SOME QUIPS, TOO!
BUT FOR RIGHT NOW, IF YOU COULD CALL THE COPS TO COME GET HIM, THAT'D BE A BIG HELP.
YO, WEB-HEAD. FAVOR?
LAST TIME YOU LEFT ME HANGIN' LIKE THIS, SOME KIDS SNATCHED MY SHOES.
THINK YOU COULD WEB 'EM TO MY FEET?
FIIINE.
THWIP
THWIP
THANKS. YOU'RE A PRINCE.
YEAH. THAT'S ME.
HIS ROYAL HIGHNESS OF LATE-TO-WORK-ISTAN.
DAILY BUGLE

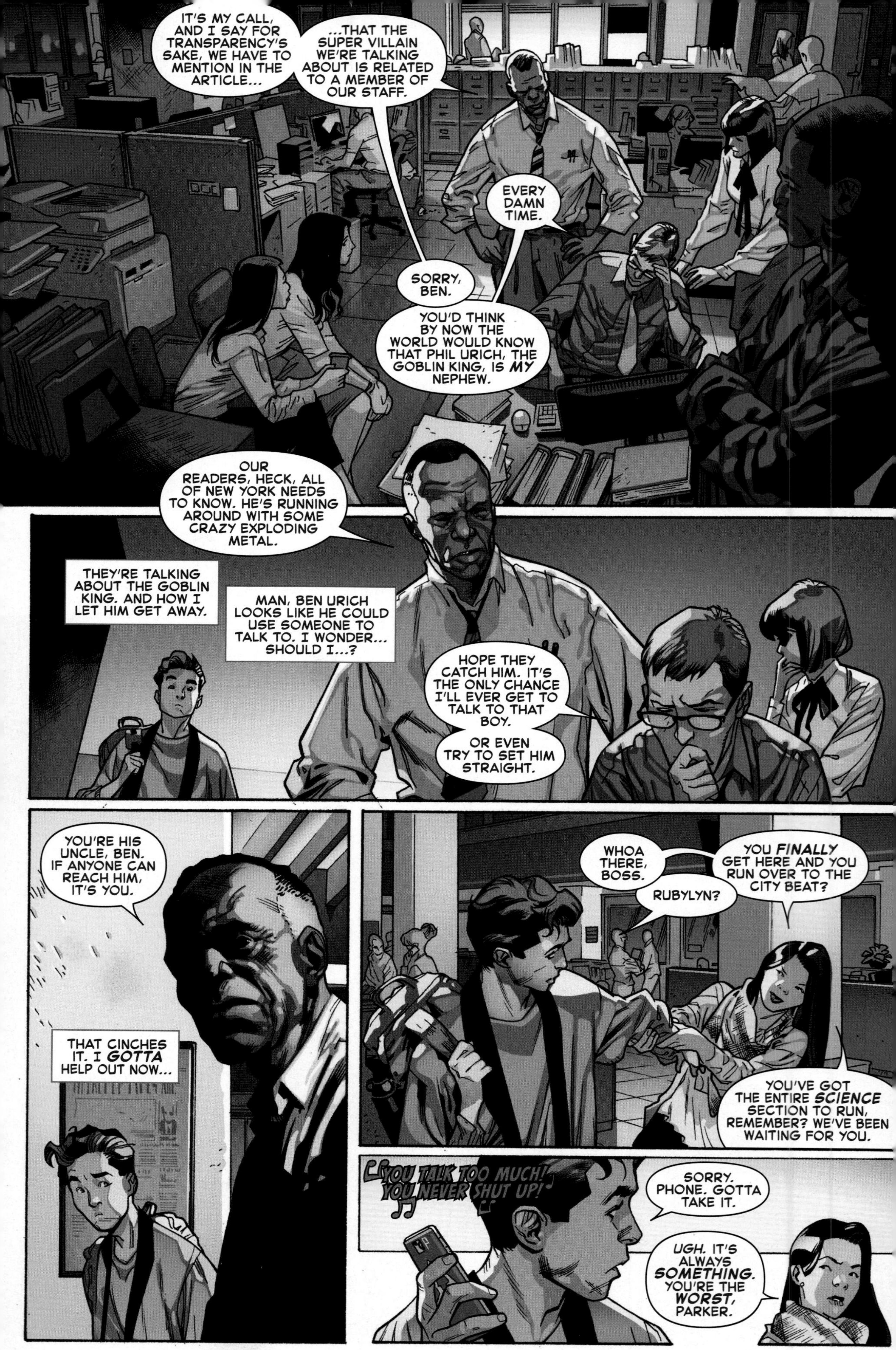
IT'S MY CALL, AND I SAY FOR TRANSPARENCY'S SAKE, WE HAVE TO MENTION IN THE ARTICLE...
...THAT THE SUPER VILLAIN WE'RE TALKING ABOUT IS RELATED TO A MEMBER OF OUR STAFF.
EVERY DAMN TIME.
SORRY, BEN.
YOU'D THINK BY NOW THE WORLD WOULD KNOW THAT PHIL URICH, THE GOBLIN KING, IS MY NEPHEW.
OUR READERS, HECK, ALL OF NEW YORK NEEDS TO KNOW. HE'S RUNNING AROUND WITH SOME CRAZY EXPLODING METAL.
THEY'RE TALKING ABOUT THE GOBLIN KING. AND HOW I LET HIM GET AWAY.
MAN, BEN URICH LOOKS LIKE HE COULD USE SOMEONE TO TALK TO. I WONDER... SHOULD I...?
HOPE THEY CATCH HIM. IT'S THE ONLY CHANCE I'LL EVER GET TO TALK TO THAT BOY.
OR EVEN TRY TO SET HIM STRAIGHT.
YOU'RE HIS UNCLE, BEN. IF ANYONE CAN REACH HIM, IT'S YOU.
THAT CINCHES IT. I GOTTA HELP OUT NOW...
WHOA THERE, BOSS.
RUBYLYN?
YOU FINALLY GET HERE AND YOU RUN OVER TO THE CITY BEAT?
YOU'VE GOT THE ENTIRE SCIENCE SECTION TO RUN, REMEMBER? WE'VE BEEN WAITING FOR YOU.
YOU TALK TOO MUCH! YOU NEVER SHUT UP!
SORRY. PHONE. GOTTA TAKE IT.
UGH. IT'S ALWAYS SOMETHING. YOU'RE THE WORST, PARKER.

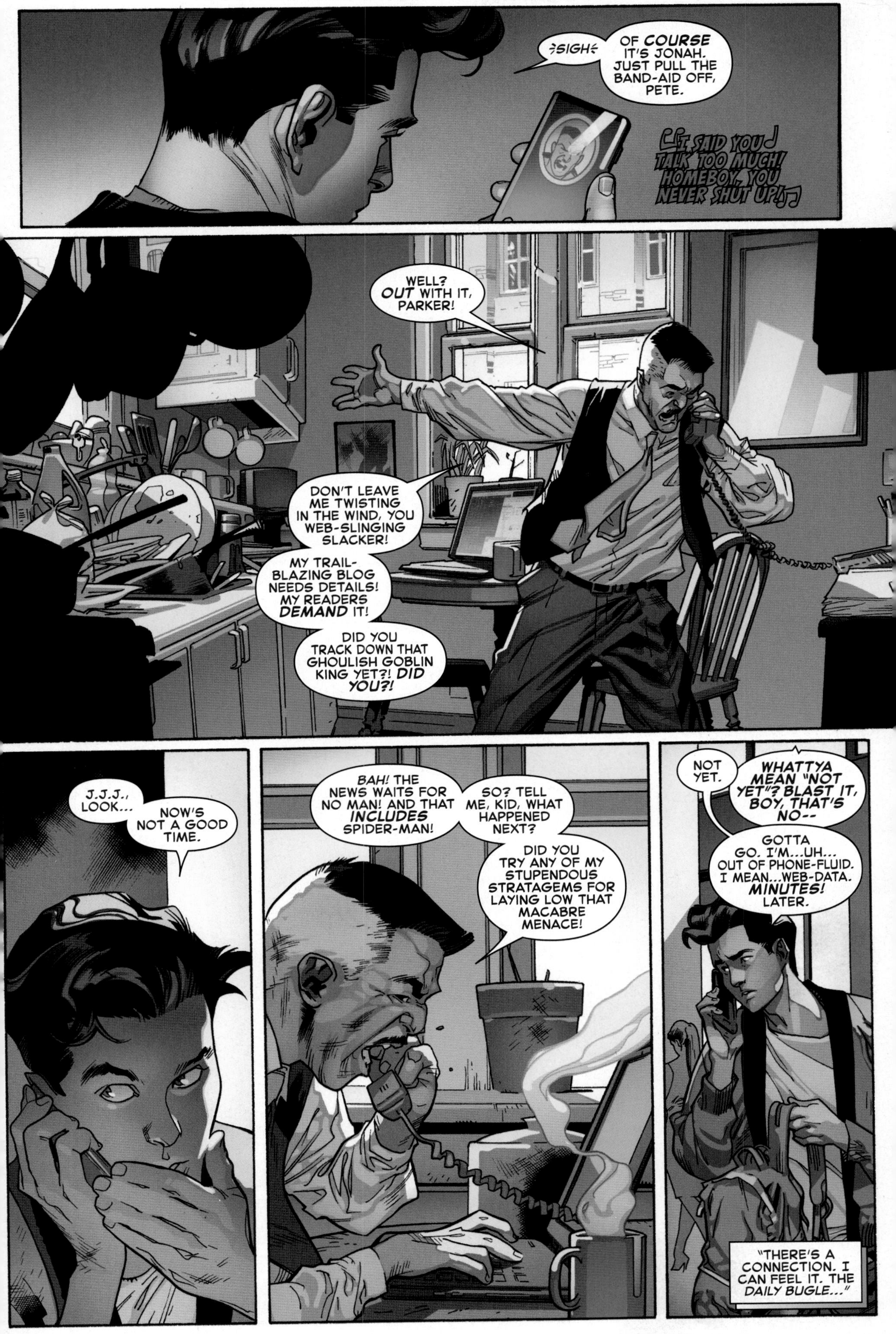

⸗SIGH⸗
OF COURSE IT'S JONAH. JUST PULL THE BAND-AID OFF, PETE.
♩I SAID YOU♩ TALK TOO MUCH! HOMEBOY, YOU NEVER SHUT UP!♫
WELL? OUT WITH IT, PARKER!
DON'T LEAVE ME TWISTING IN THE WIND, YOU WEB-SLINGING SLACKER!
MY TRAIL-BLAZING BLOG NEEDS DETAILS! MY READERS DEMAND IT!
DID YOU TRACK DOWN THAT GHOULISH GOBLIN KING YET?! DID YOU?!
J.J.J., LOOK...
NOW'S NOT A GOOD TIME.
BAH! THE NEWS WAITS FOR NO MAN! AND THAT INCLUDES SPIDER-MAN!
SO? TELL ME, KID, WHAT HAPPENED NEXT?
DID YOU TRY ANY OF MY STUPENDOUS STRATAGEMS FOR LAYING LOW THAT MACABRE MENACE!
NOT YET.
WHATTYA MEAN "NOT YET"? BLAST IT, BOY, THAT'S NO--
GOTTA GO. I'M...UH... OUT OF PHONE-FLUID. I MEAN...WEB-DATA. MINUTES! LATER.
"THERE'S A CONNECTION. I CAN FEEL IT. THE DAILY BUGLE..."

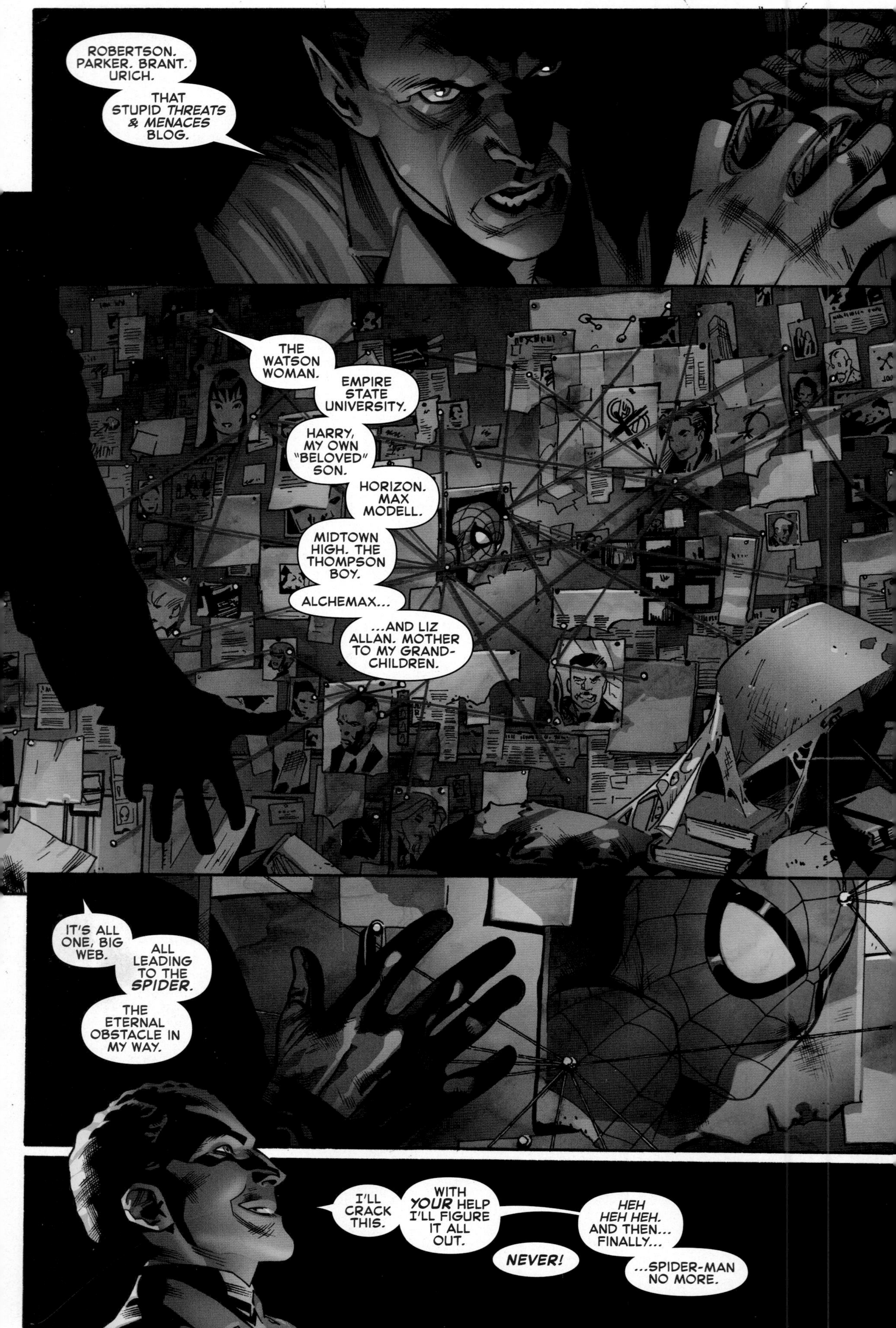
ROBERTSON. PARKER. BRANT. URICH.
THAT STUPID *THREATS & MENACES* BLOG.
THE WATSON WOMAN.
EMPIRE STATE UNIVERSITY.
HARRY, MY OWN "BELOVED" SON.
HORIZON. MAX MODELL.
MIDTOWN HIGH. THE THOMPSON BOY.
ALCHEMAX...
...AND LIZ ALLAN. MOTHER TO MY GRAND-CHILDREN.
IT'S ALL ONE, BIG WEB.
ALL LEADING TO THE *SPIDER*.
THE ETERNAL OBSTACLE IN MY WAY.
I'LL CRACK THIS.
WITH ***YOUR*** HELP I'LL FIGURE IT ALL OUT.
HEH HEH HEH. THEN... FINALLY...
NEVER!
...SPIDER-MAN NO MORE.

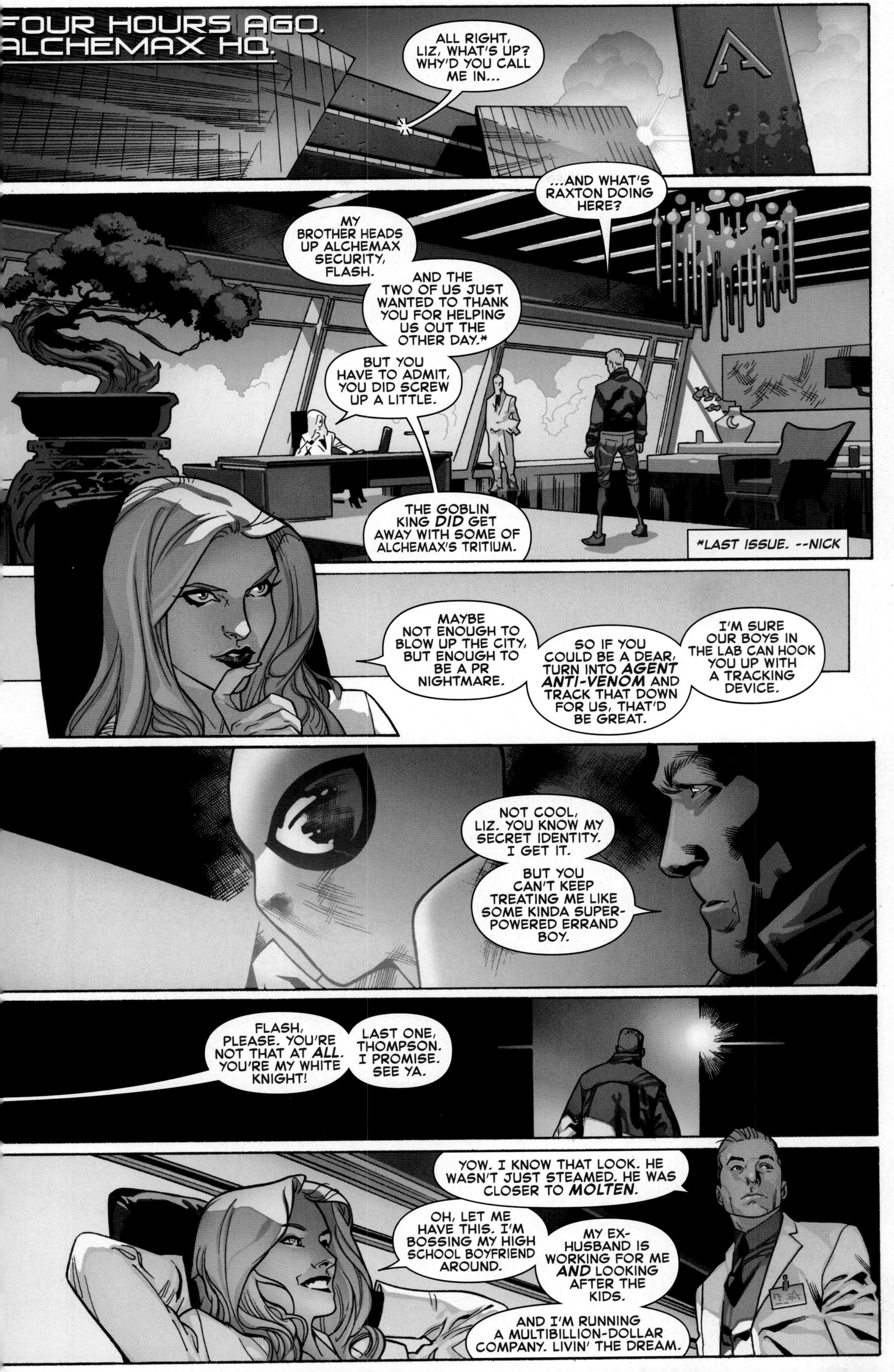
FOUR HOURS AGO. ALCHEMAX HQ.
ALL RIGHT, LIZ, WHAT'S UP? WHY'D YOU CALL ME IN...
...AND WHAT'S RAXTON DOING HERE?
MY BROTHER HEADS UP ALCHEMAX SECURITY, FLASH.
AND THE TWO OF US JUST WANTED TO THANK YOU FOR HELPING US OUT THE OTHER DAY.*
BUT YOU HAVE TO ADMIT, YOU DID SCREW UP A LITTLE.
THE GOBLIN KING DID GET AWAY WITH SOME OF ALCHEMAX'S TRITIUM.
*LAST ISSUE. --NICK
MAYBE NOT ENOUGH TO BLOW UP THE CITY, BUT ENOUGH TO BE A PR NIGHTMARE.
SO IF YOU COULD BE A DEAR, TURN INTO AGENT ANTI-VENOM AND TRACK THAT DOWN FOR US, THAT'D BE GREAT.
I'M SURE OUR BOYS IN THE LAB CAN HOOK YOU UP WITH A TRACKING DEVICE.
NOT COOL, LIZ. YOU KNOW MY SECRET IDENTITY. I GET IT.
BUT YOU CAN'T KEEP TREATING ME LIKE SOME KINDA SUPER-POWERED ERRAND BOY.
FLASH, PLEASE. YOU'RE NOT THAT AT ALL. YOU'RE MY WHITE KNIGHT!
LAST ONE, THOMPSON. I PROMISE. SEE YA.
YOW. I KNOW THAT LOOK. HE WASN'T JUST STEAMED. HE WAS CLOSER TO MOLTEN.
OH, LET ME HAVE THIS. I'M BOSSING MY HIGH SCHOOL BOYFRIEND AROUND.
MY EX-HUSBAND IS WORKING FOR ME AND LOOKING AFTER THE KIDS.
AND I'M RUNNING A MULTIBILLION-DOLLAR COMPANY. LIVIN' THE DREAM.

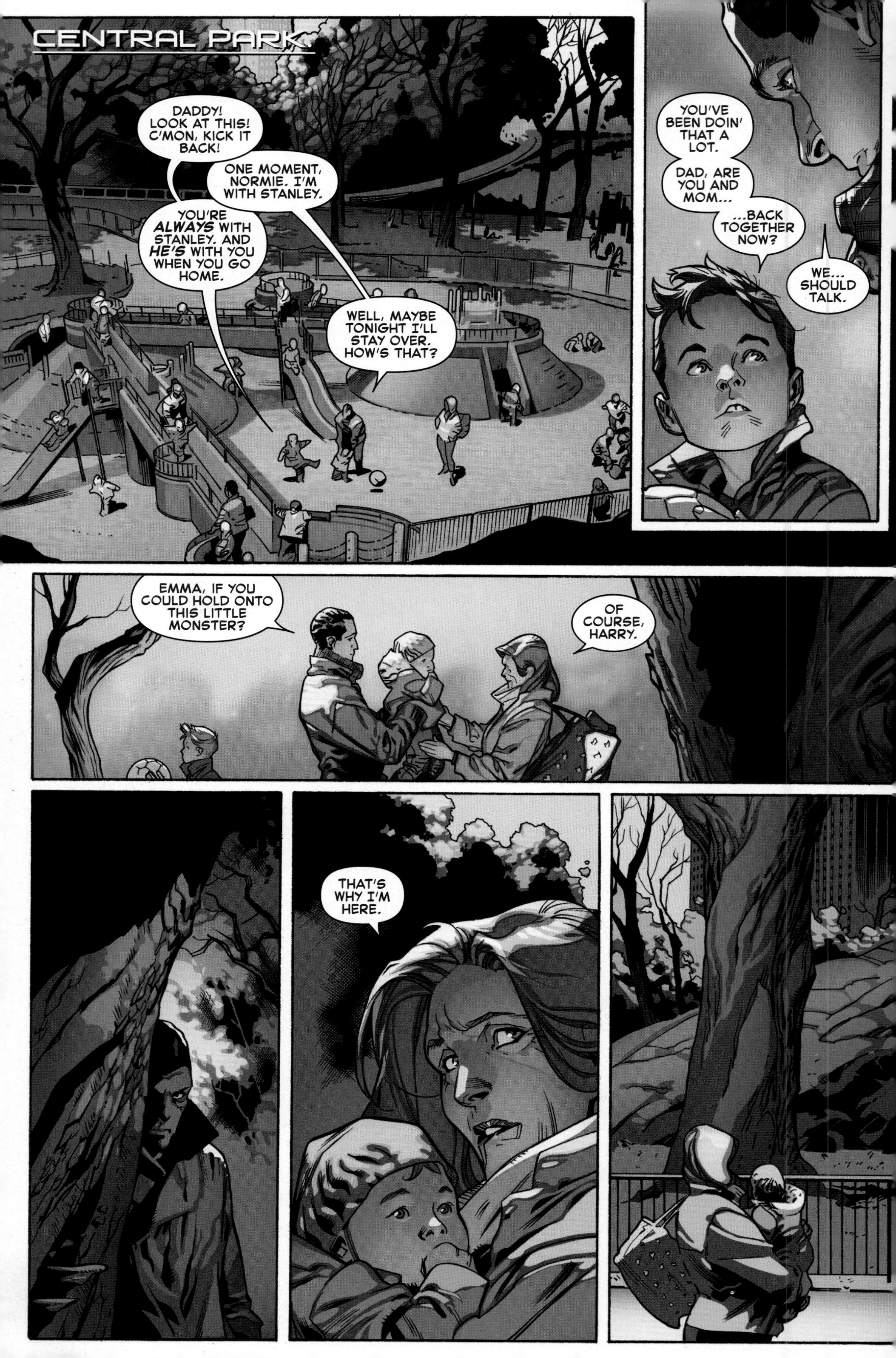
CENTRAL PARK
DADDY! LOOK AT THIS! C'MON, KICK IT BACK!
ONE MOMENT, NORMIE. I'M WITH STANLEY.
YOU'RE ALWAYS WITH STANLEY. AND HE'S WITH YOU WHEN YOU GO HOME.
WELL, MAYBE TONIGHT I'LL STAY OVER. HOW'S THAT?
YOU'VE BEEN DOIN' THAT A LOT.
DAD, ARE YOU AND MOM...
...BACK TOGETHER NOW?
WE... SHOULD TALK.
EMMA, IF YOU COULD HOLD ONTO THIS LITTLE MONSTER?
OF COURSE, HARRY.
THAT'S WHY I'M HERE.

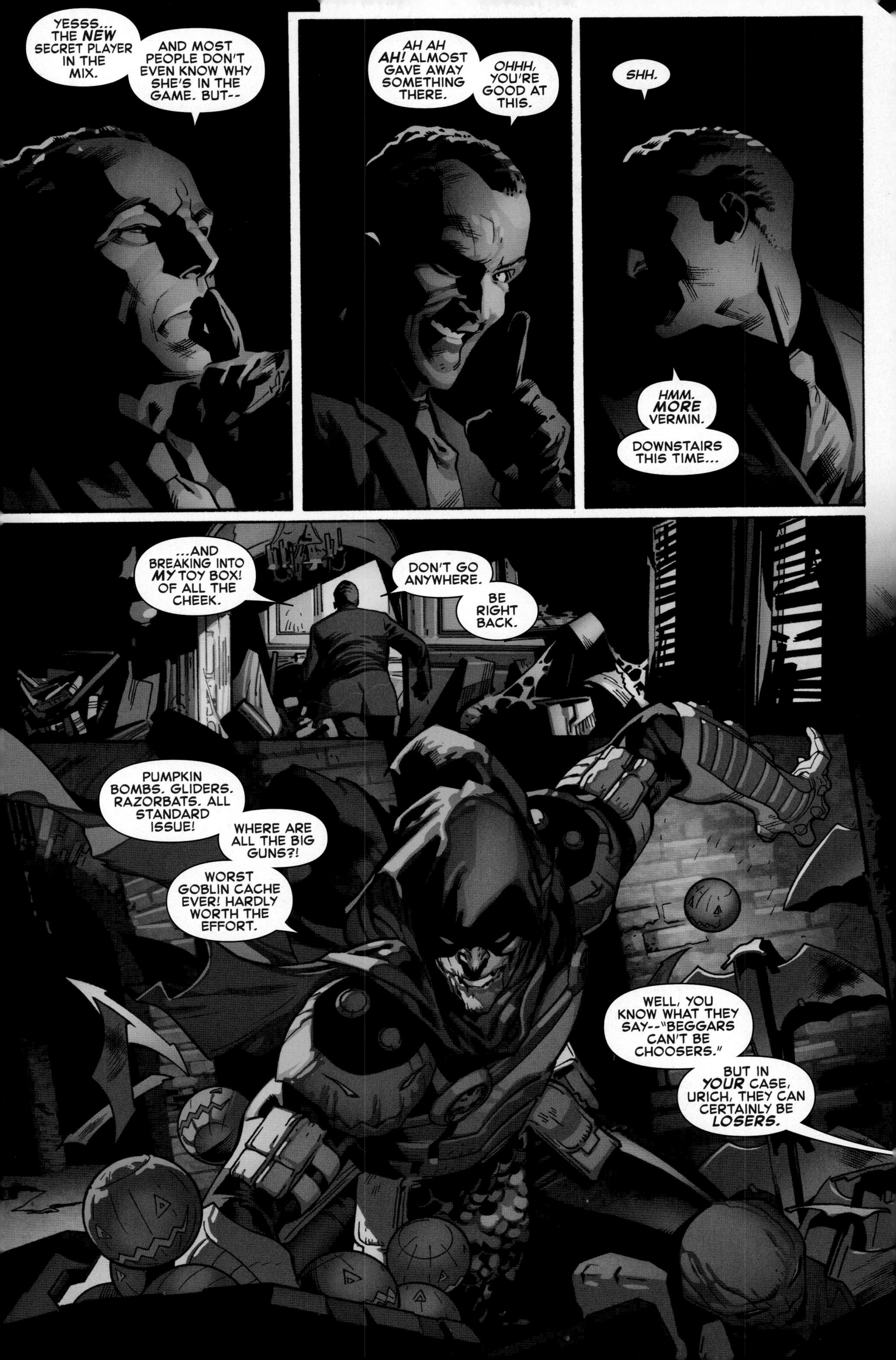
YESSS... THE NEW SECRET PLAYER IN THE MIX.
AND MOST PEOPLE DON'T EVEN KNOW WHY SHE'S IN THE GAME. BUT--
AH AH AH! ALMOST GAVE AWAY SOMETHING THERE.
OHHH, YOU'RE GOOD AT THIS.
SHH.
HMM. MORE VERMIN.
DOWNSTAIRS THIS TIME...
...AND BREAKING INTO MY TOY BOX! OF ALL THE CHEEK.
DON'T GO ANYWHERE.
BE RIGHT BACK.
PUMPKIN BOMBS. GLIDERS. RAZORBATS. ALL STANDARD ISSUE!
WHERE ARE ALL THE BIG GUNS?!
WORST GOBLIN CACHE EVER! HARDLY WORTH THE EFFORT.
WELL, YOU KNOW WHAT THEY SAY--"BEGGARS CAN'T BE CHOOSERS."
BUT IN YOUR CASE, URICH, THEY CAN CERTAINLY BE LOSERS.

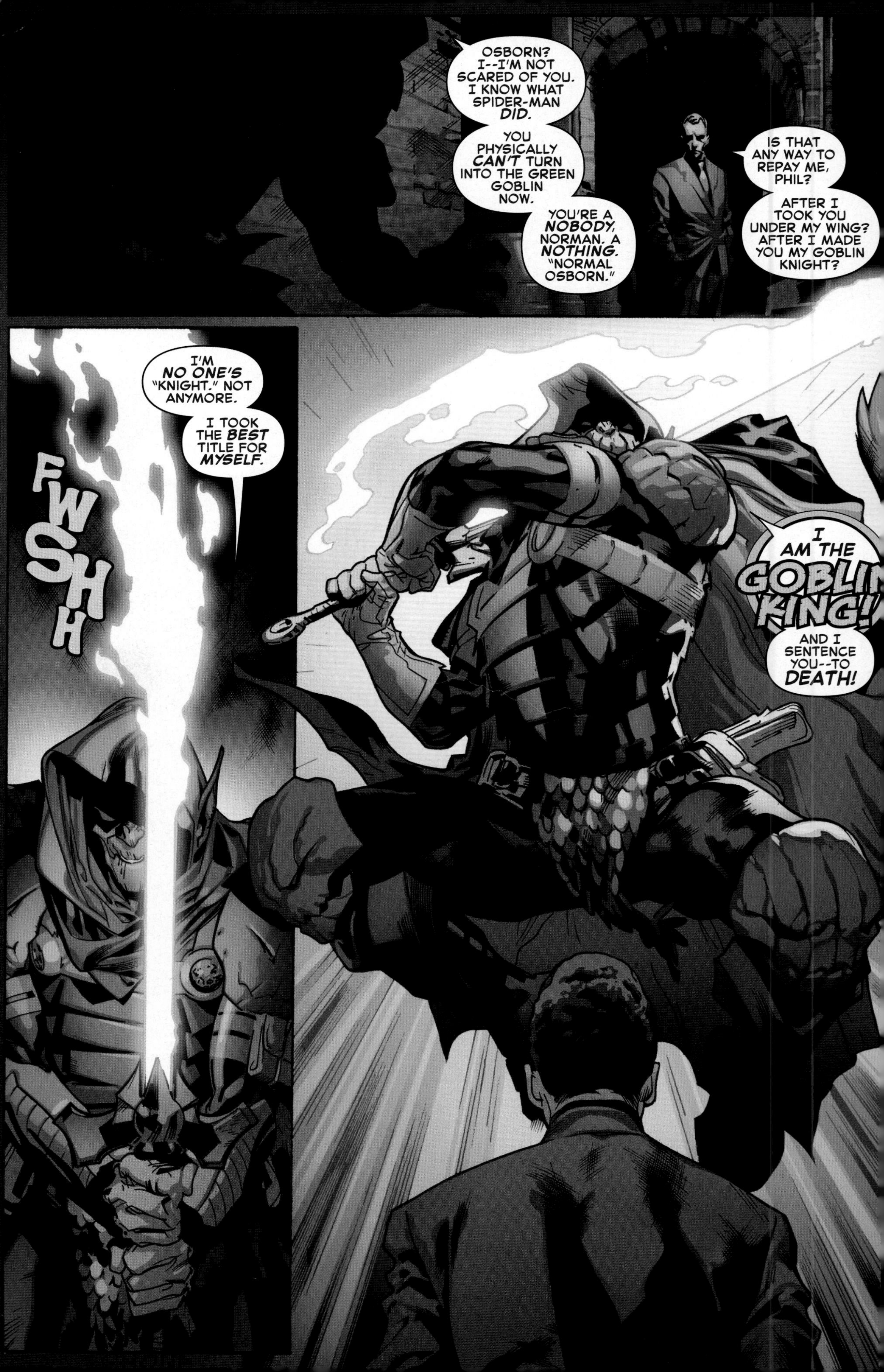
OSBORN? I--I'M NOT SCARED OF YOU. I KNOW WHAT SPIDER-MAN DID.
YOU PHYSICALLY CAN'T TURN INTO THE GREEN GOBLIN NOW.
YOU'RE A NOBODY, NORMAN. A NOTHING. "NORMAL OSBORN."
IS THAT ANY WAY TO REPAY ME, PHIL?
AFTER I TOOK YOU UNDER MY WING? AFTER I MADE YOU MY GOBLIN KNIGHT?
I'M NO ONE'S "KNIGHT." NOT ANYMORE.
I TOOK THE BEST TITLE FOR MYSELF.
FWSHH
I AM THE GOBLIN KING!
AND I SENTENCE YOU--TO DEATH!

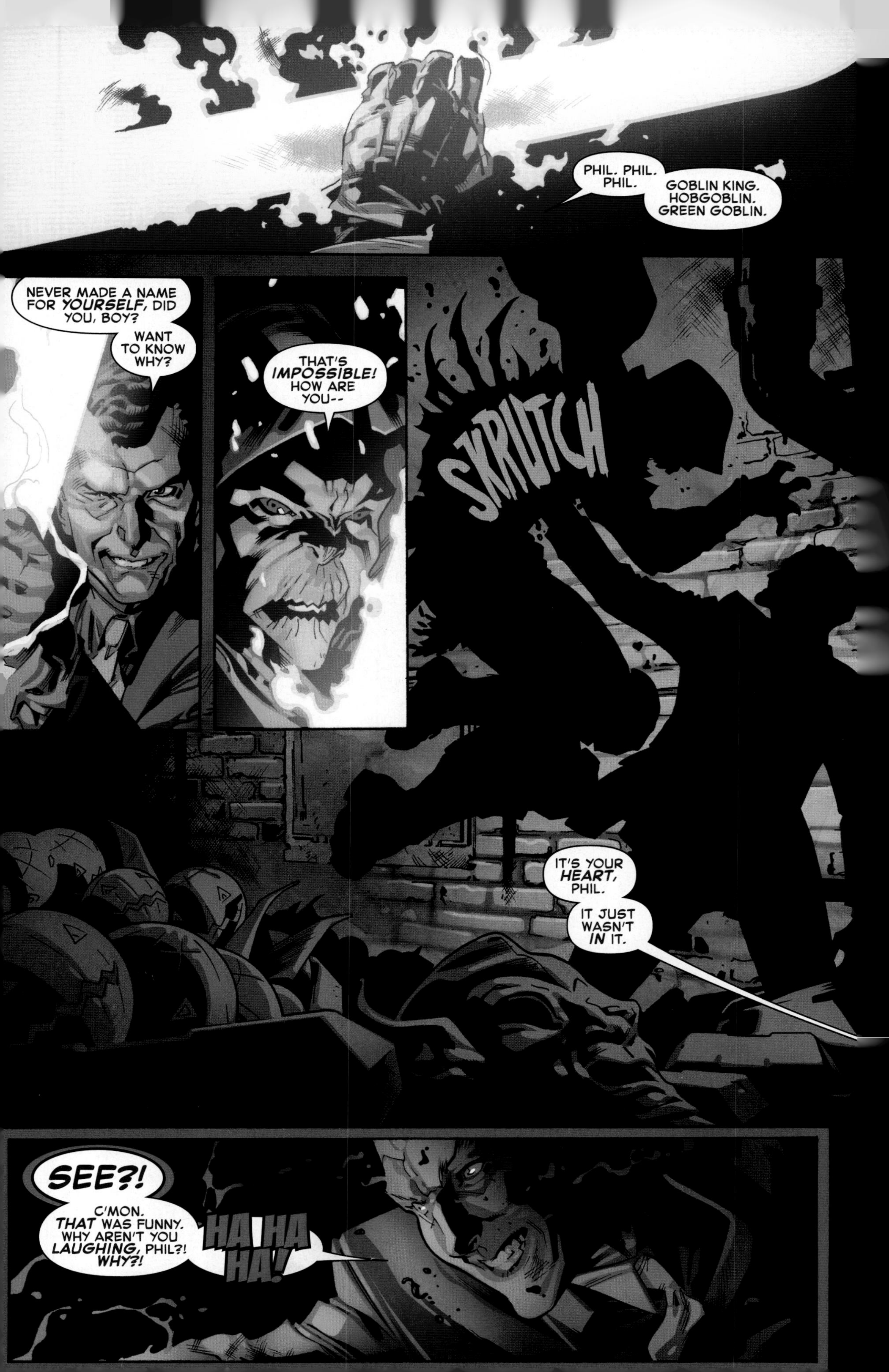
PHIL. PHIL. PHIL.
GOBLIN KING. HOBGOBLIN. GREEN GOBLIN.
NEVER MADE A NAME FOR YOURSELF, DID YOU, BOY?
WANT TO KNOW WHY?
THAT'S IMPOSSIBLE! HOW ARE YOU--
SKRUTCH
IT'S YOUR HEART, PHIL.
IT JUST WASN'T IN IT.
SEE?!
C'MON. THAT WAS FUNNY. WHY AREN'T YOU LAUGHING, PHIL?! WHY?!
HA HA HA!

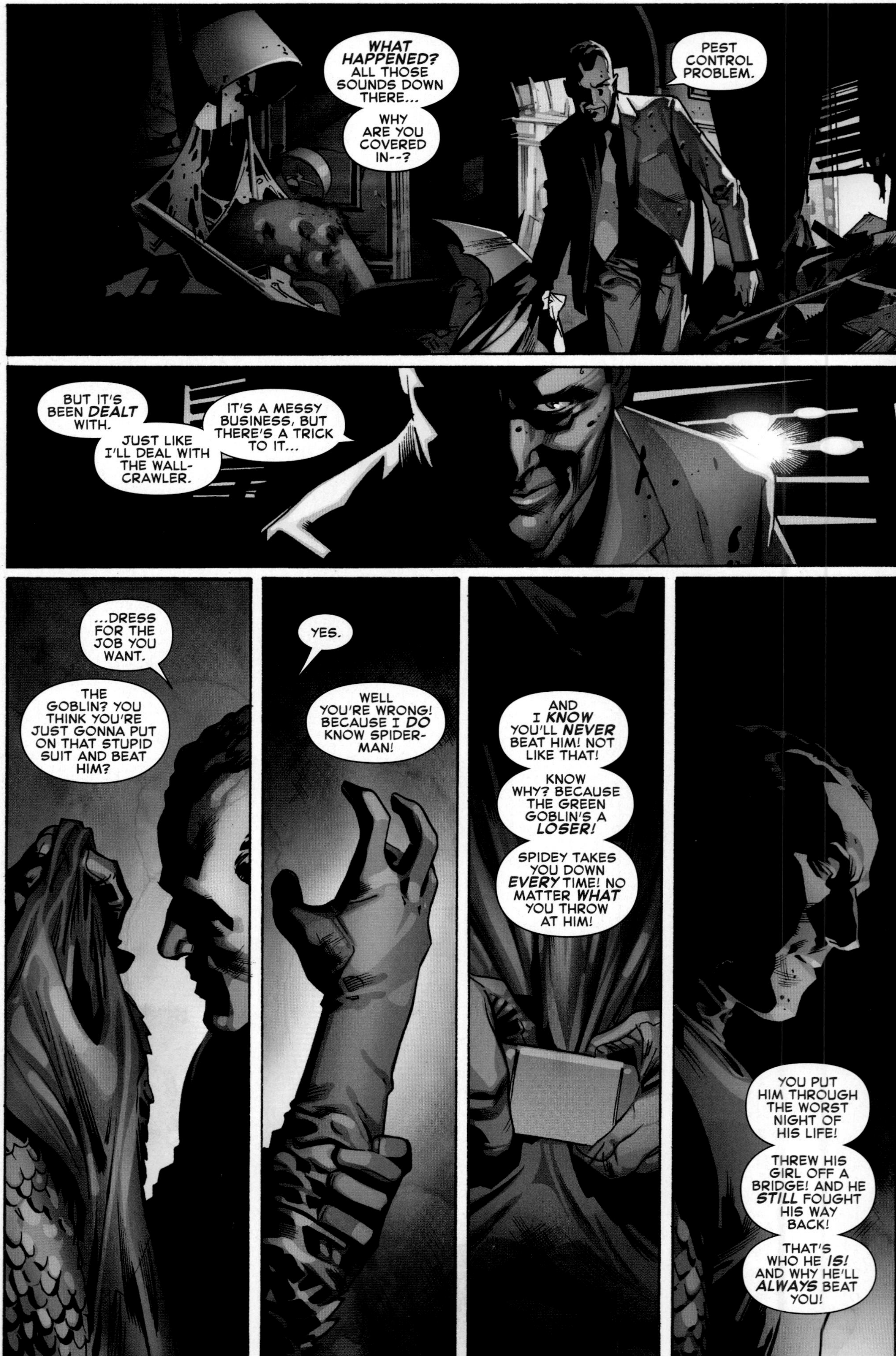
WHAT HAPPENED? ALL THOSE SOUNDS DOWN THERE...
WHY ARE YOU COVERED IN--?
PEST CONTROL PROBLEM.
BUT IT'S BEEN DEALT WITH.
JUST LIKE I'LL DEAL WITH THE WALL-CRAWLER.
IT'S A MESSY BUSINESS, BUT THERE'S A TRICK TO IT...
...DRESS FOR THE JOB YOU WANT.
THE GOBLIN? YOU THINK YOU'RE JUST GONNA PUT ON THAT STUPID SUIT AND BEAT HIM?
YES.
WELL YOU'RE WRONG! BECAUSE I DO KNOW SPIDER-MAN!
AND I KNOW YOU'LL NEVER BEAT HIM! NOT LIKE THAT!
KNOW WHY? BECAUSE THE GREEN GOBLIN'S A LOSER!
SPIDEY TAKES YOU DOWN EVERY TIME! NO MATTER WHAT YOU THROW AT HIM!
YOU PUT HIM THROUGH THE WORST NIGHT OF HIS LIFE!
THREW HIS GIRL OFF A BRIDGE! AND HE STILL FOUGHT HIS WAY BACK!
THAT'S WHO HE IS! AND WHY HE'LL ALWAYS BEAT YOU!

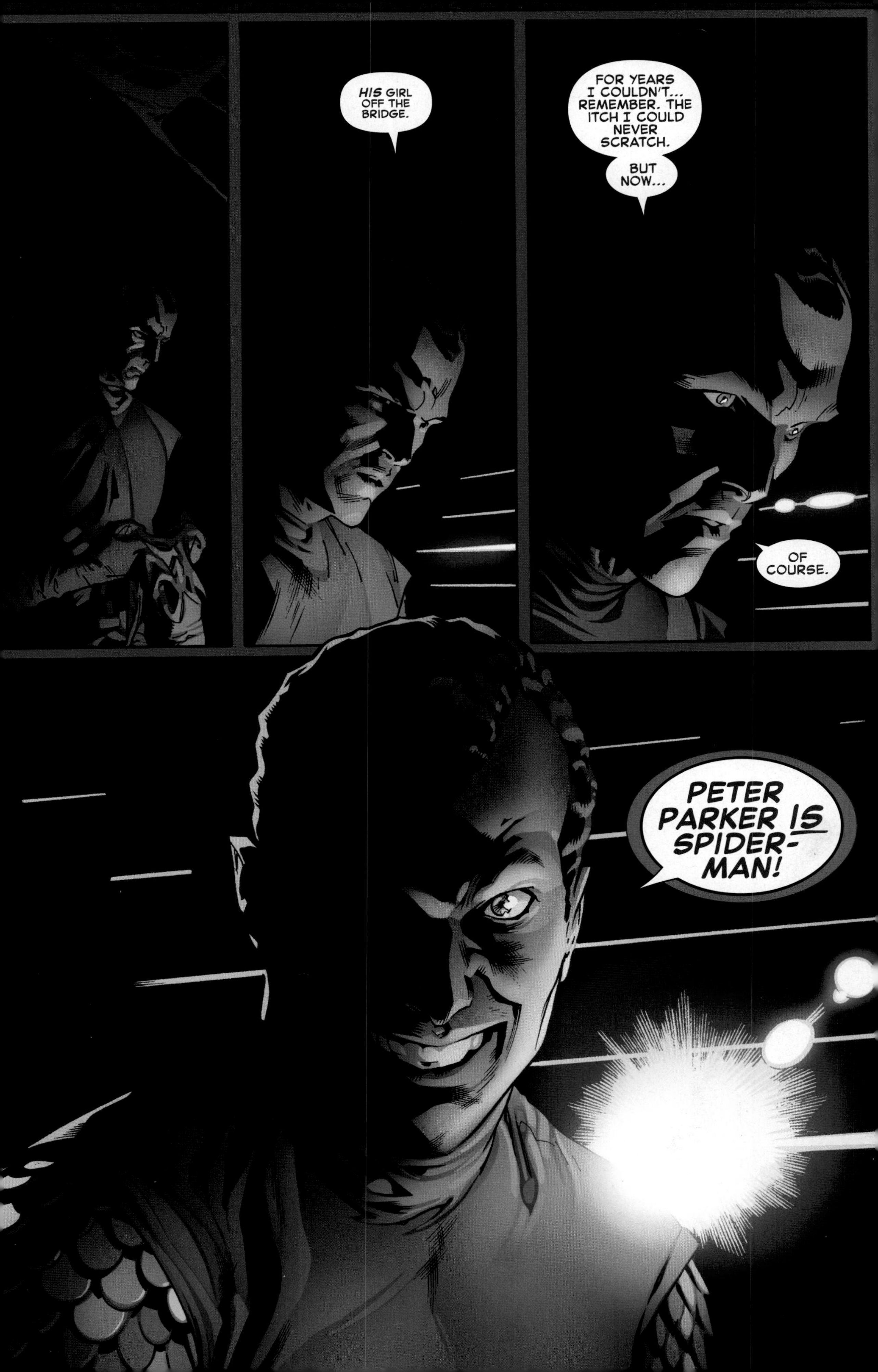
HIS GIRL OFF THE BRIDGE.
FOR YEARS I COULDN'T... REMEMBER. THE ITCH I COULD NEVER SCRATCH.
BUT NOW...
OF COURSE.
PETER PARKER IS SPIDER-MAN!

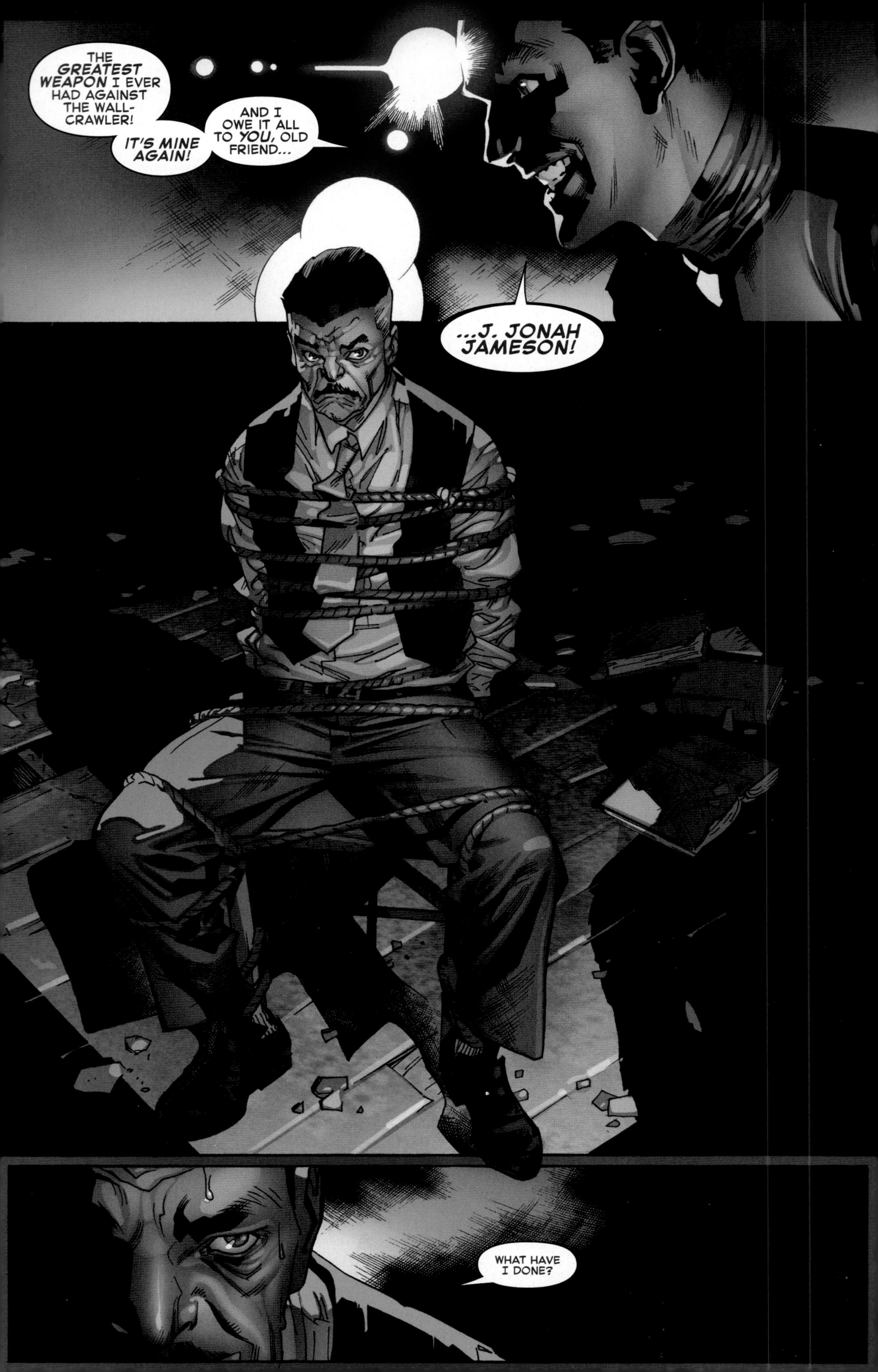
THE *GREATEST WEAPON* I EVER HAD AGAINST THE WALL-CRAWLER!
IT'S MINE AGAIN!
AND I OWE IT ALL TO *YOU*, OLD FRIEND...
...J. JONAH JAMESON!
WHAT HAVE I DONE?

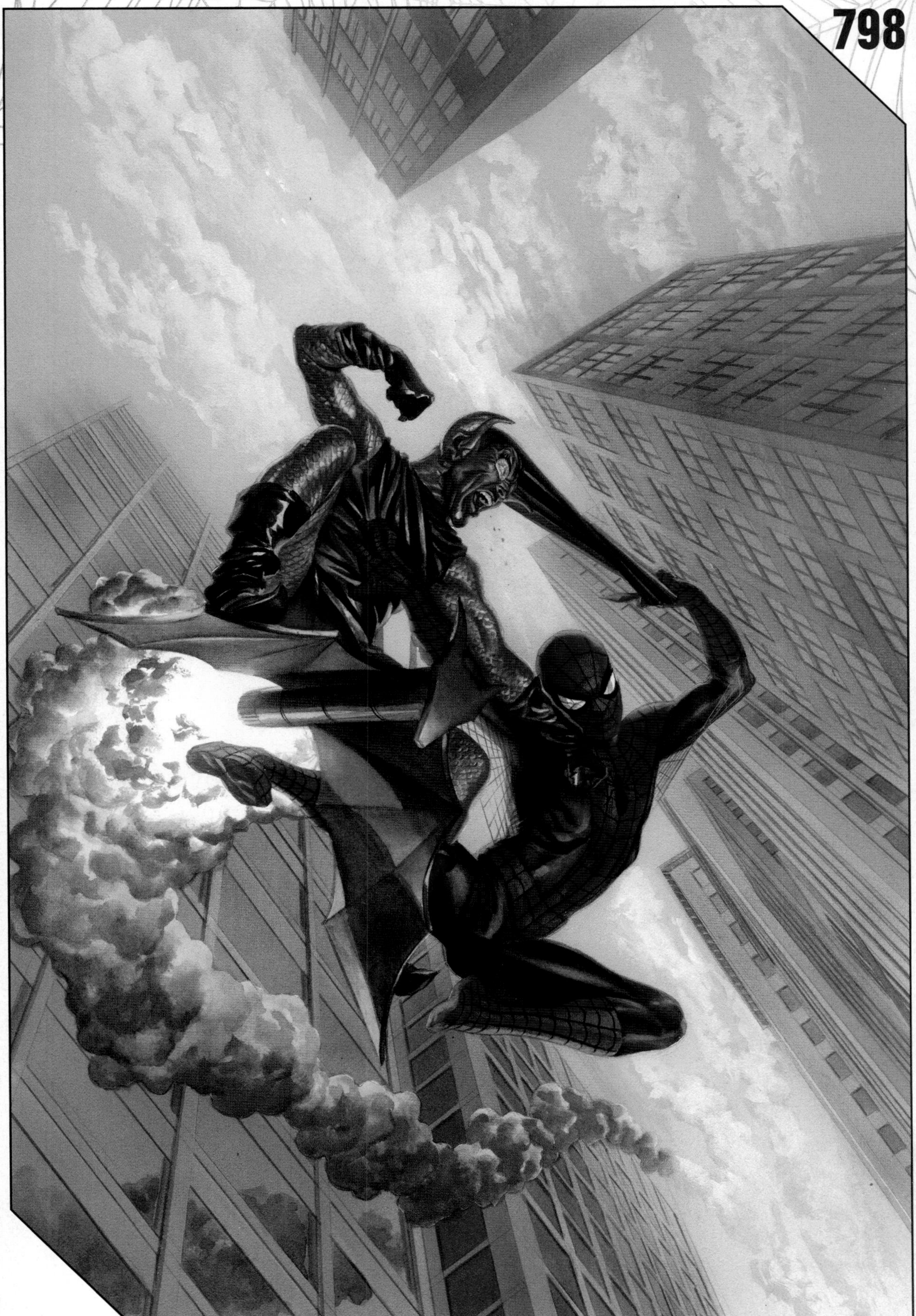
798

GO DOWN SWINGING PART TWO "THE ROPE-A-DOPE"

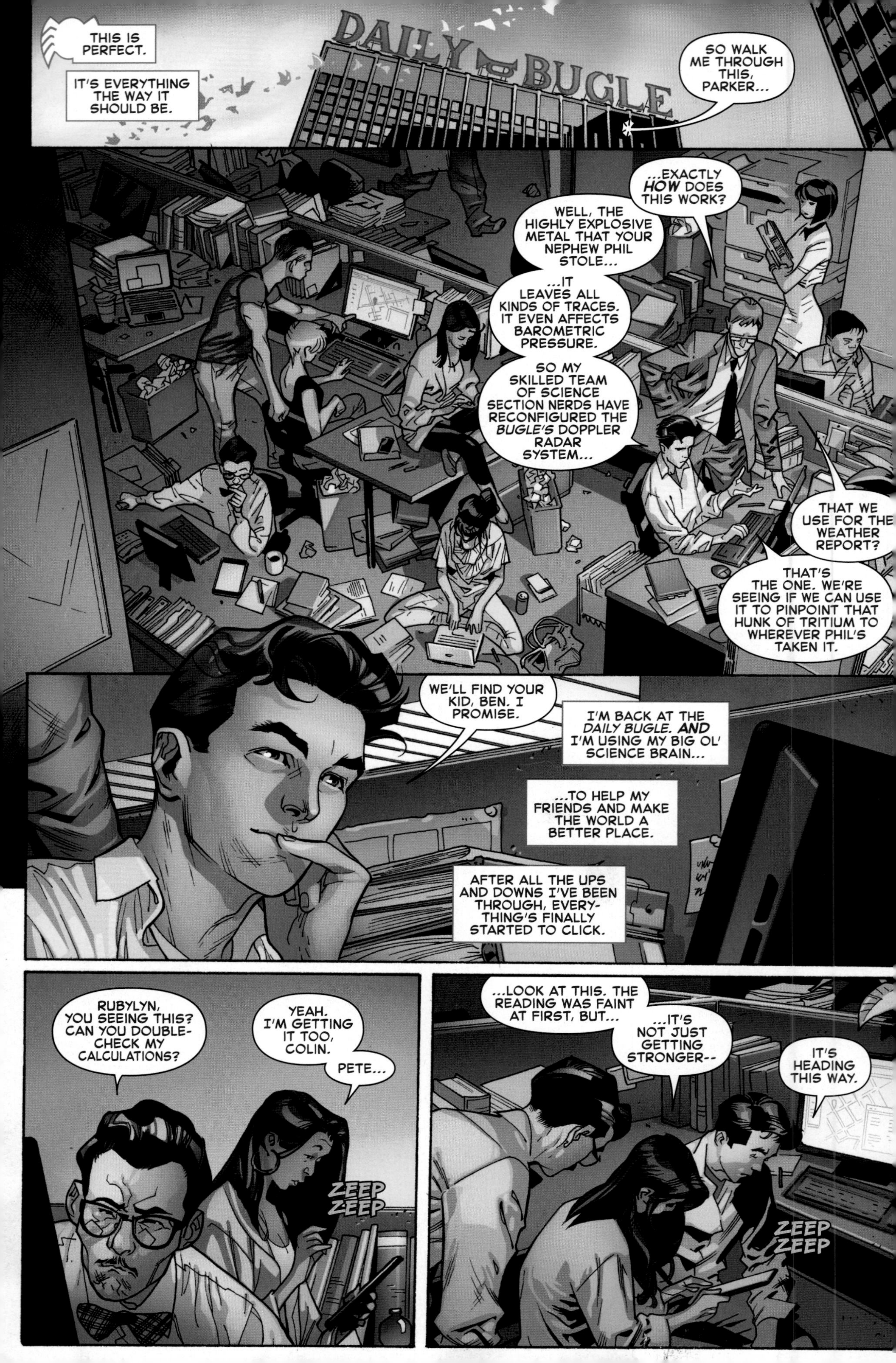
DAILY BUGLE
THIS IS PERFECT.
IT'S EVERYTHING THE WAY IT SHOULD BE.
SO WALK ME THROUGH THIS, PARKER...
...EXACTLY HOW DOES THIS WORK?
WELL, THE HIGHLY EXPLOSIVE METAL THAT YOUR NEPHEW PHIL STOLE...
...IT LEAVES ALL KINDS OF TRACES. IT EVEN AFFECTS BAROMETRIC PRESSURE.
SO MY SKILLED TEAM OF SCIENCE SECTION NERDS HAVE RECONFIGURED THE BUGLE'S DOPPLER RADAR SYSTEM...
THAT WE USE FOR THE WEATHER REPORT?
THAT'S THE ONE. WE'RE SEEING IF WE CAN USE IT TO PINPOINT THAT HUNK OF TRITIUM TO WHEREVER PHIL'S TAKEN IT.
WE'LL FIND YOUR KID, BEN. I PROMISE.
I'M BACK AT THE DAILY BUGLE. AND I'M USING MY BIG OL' SCIENCE BRAIN...
...TO HELP MY FRIENDS AND MAKE THE WORLD A BETTER PLACE.
AFTER ALL THE UPS AND DOWNS I'VE BEEN THROUGH, EVERYTHING'S FINALLY STARTED TO CLICK.
RUBYLYN, YOU SEEING THIS? CAN YOU DOUBLE-CHECK MY CALCULATIONS?
YEAH. I'M GETTING IT TOO, COLIN.
PETE...
ZEEP ZEEP
...LOOK AT THIS. THE READING WAS FAINT AT FIRST, BUT...
...IT'S NOT JUST GETTING STRONGER--
IT'S HEADING THIS WAY.
ZEEP ZEEP

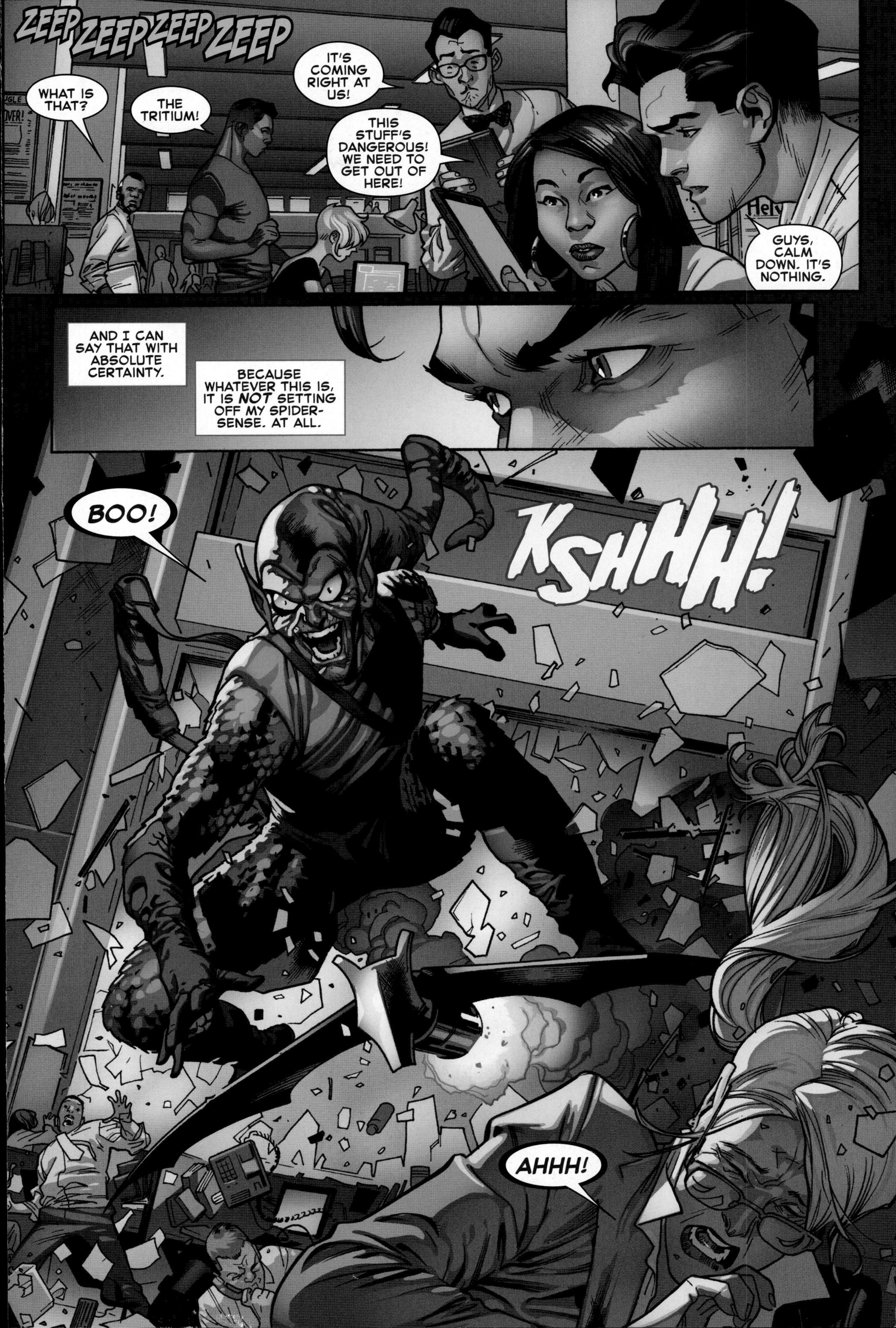
ZEEP ZEEP ZEEP ZEEP
WHAT IS THAT?
THE TRITIUM!
IT'S COMING RIGHT AT US!
THIS STUFF'S DANGEROUS! WE NEED TO GET OUT OF HERE!
GUYS, CALM DOWN. IT'S NOTHING.
AND I CAN SAY THAT WITH ABSOLUTE CERTAINTY.
BECAUSE WHATEVER THIS IS, IT IS NOT SETTING OFF MY SPIDER-SENSE. AT ALL.
BOO!
KSHHH!
AHHH!

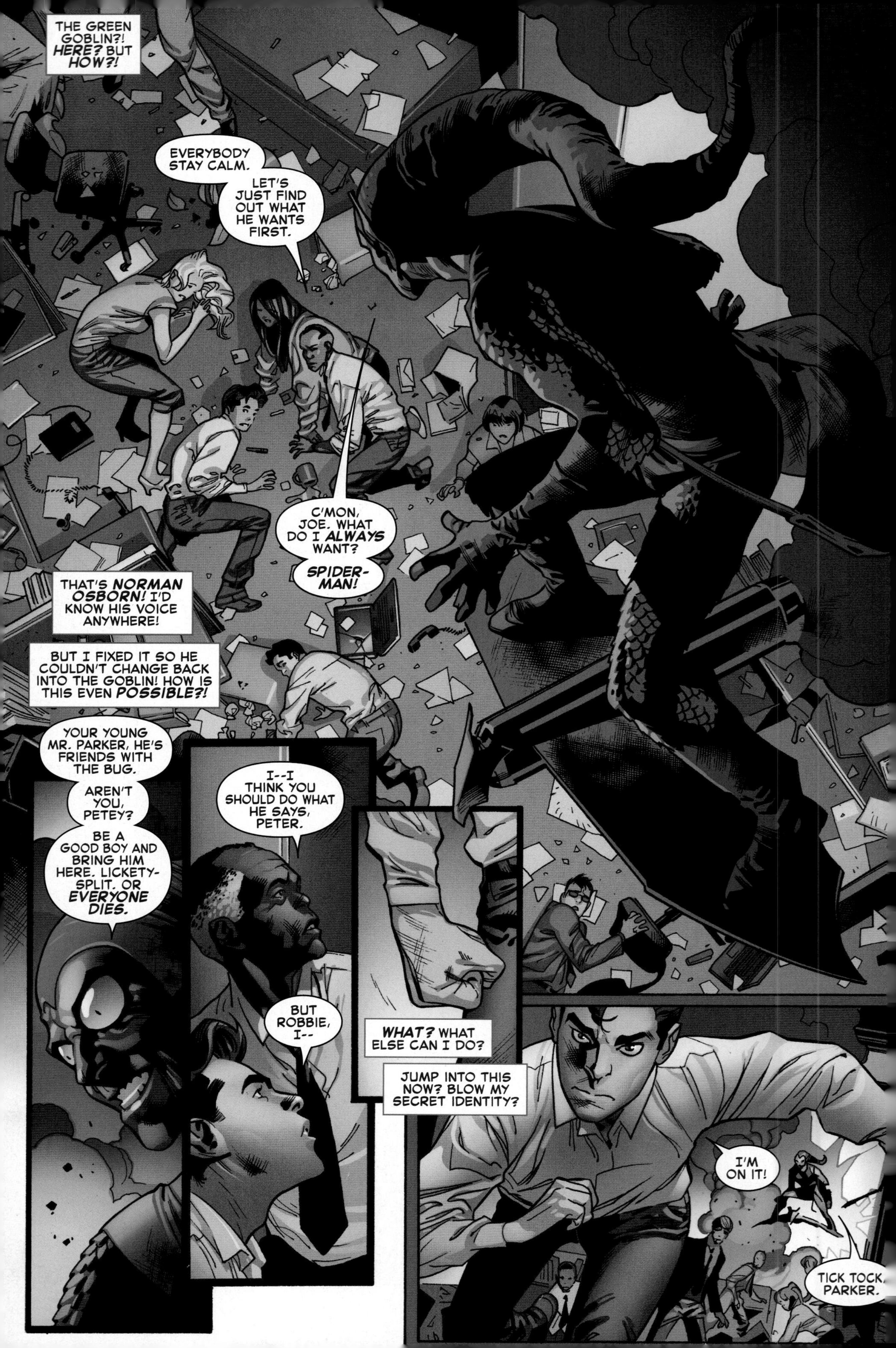
THE GREEN GOBLIN?! HERE? BUT HOW?!
EVERYBODY STAY CALM.
LET'S JUST FIND OUT WHAT HE WANTS FIRST.
C'MON, JOE. WHAT DO I ALWAYS WANT?
SPIDER-MAN!
THAT'S NORMAN OSBORN! I'D KNOW HIS VOICE ANYWHERE!
BUT I FIXED IT SO HE COULDN'T CHANGE BACK INTO THE GOBLIN! HOW IS THIS EVEN POSSIBLE?!
YOUR YOUNG MR. PARKER, HE'S FRIENDS WITH THE BUG.
AREN'T YOU, PETEY?
BE A GOOD BOY AND BRING HIM HERE. LICKETY-SPLIT. OR EVERYONE DIES.
I--I THINK YOU SHOULD DO WHAT HE SAYS, PETER.
BUT ROBBIE, I--
WHAT? WHAT ELSE CAN I DO?
JUMP INTO THIS NOW? BLOW MY SECRET IDENTITY?
I'M ON IT!
TICK TOCK, PARKER.

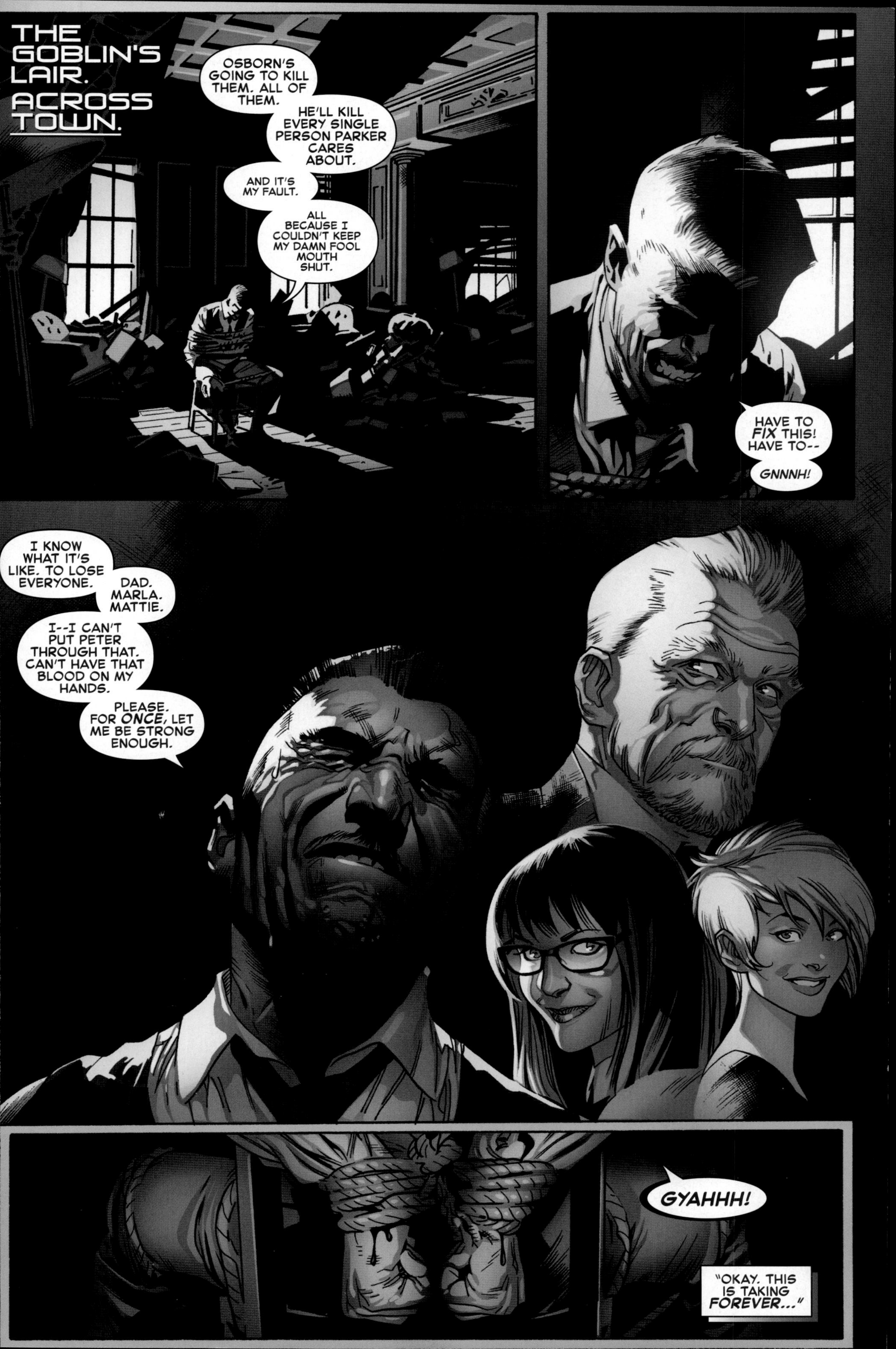
THE GOBLIN'S LAIR.
ACROSS TOWN.
OSBORN'S GOING TO KILL THEM. ALL OF THEM.
HE'LL KILL EVERY SINGLE PERSON PARKER CARES ABOUT.
AND IT'S MY FAULT.
ALL BECAUSE I COULDN'T KEEP MY DAMN FOOL MOUTH SHUT.
HAVE TO FIX THIS! HAVE TO--
GNNNH!
I KNOW WHAT IT'S LIKE. TO LOSE EVERYONE.
DAD. MARLA. MATTIE.
I--I CAN'T PUT PETER THROUGH THAT. CAN'T HAVE THAT BLOOD ON MY HANDS.
PLEASE. FOR ONCE, LET ME BE STRONG ENOUGH.
GYAHHH!
"OKAY. THIS IS TAKING FOREVER..."

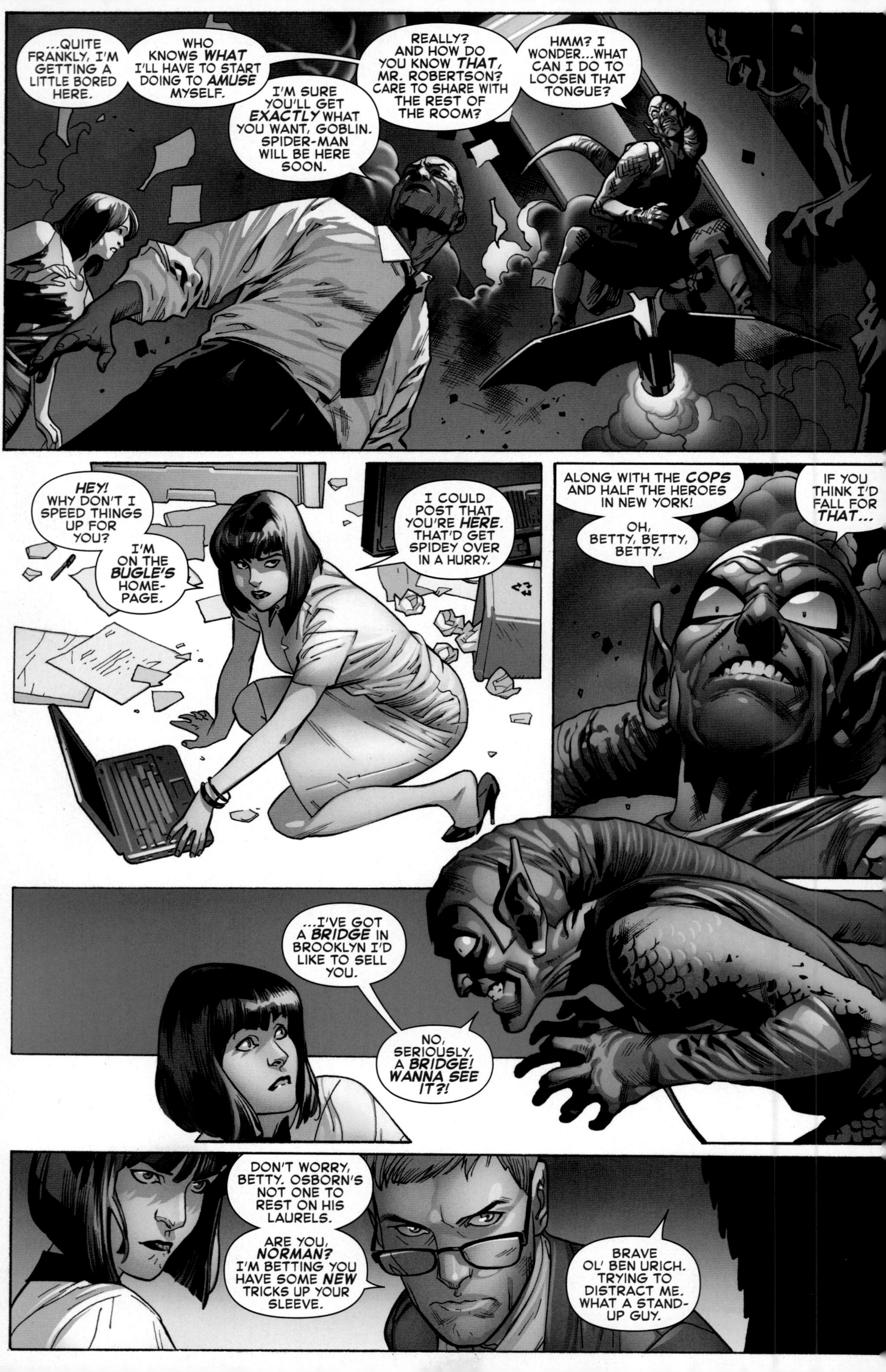

...QUITE FRANKLY, I'M GETTING A LITTLE BORED HERE.
WHO KNOWS WHAT I'LL HAVE TO START DOING TO AMUSE MYSELF.
I'M SURE YOU'LL GET EXACTLY WHAT YOU WANT, GOBLIN. SPIDER-MAN WILL BE HERE SOON.
REALLY? AND HOW DO YOU KNOW THAT, MR. ROBERTSON? CARE TO SHARE WITH THE REST OF THE ROOM?
HMM? I WONDER...WHAT CAN I DO TO LOOSEN THAT TONGUE?
HEY! WHY DON'T I SPEED THINGS UP FOR YOU?
I'M ON THE BUGLE'S HOME-PAGE.
I COULD POST THAT YOU'RE HERE. THAT'D GET SPIDEY OVER IN A HURRY.
ALONG WITH THE COPS AND HALF THE HEROES IN NEW YORK!
OH, BETTY, BETTY, BETTY.
IF YOU THINK I'D FALL FOR THAT...
...I'VE GOT A BRIDGE IN BROOKLYN I'D LIKE TO SELL YOU.
NO, SERIOUSLY. A BRIDGE! WANNA SEE IT?!
DON'T WORRY, BETTY. OSBORN'S NOT ONE TO REST ON HIS LAURELS.
ARE YOU, NORMAN? I'M BETTING YOU HAVE SOME NEW TRICKS UP YOUR SLEEVE.
BRAVE OL' BEN URICH. TRYING TO DISTRACT ME. WHAT A STAND-UP GUY.

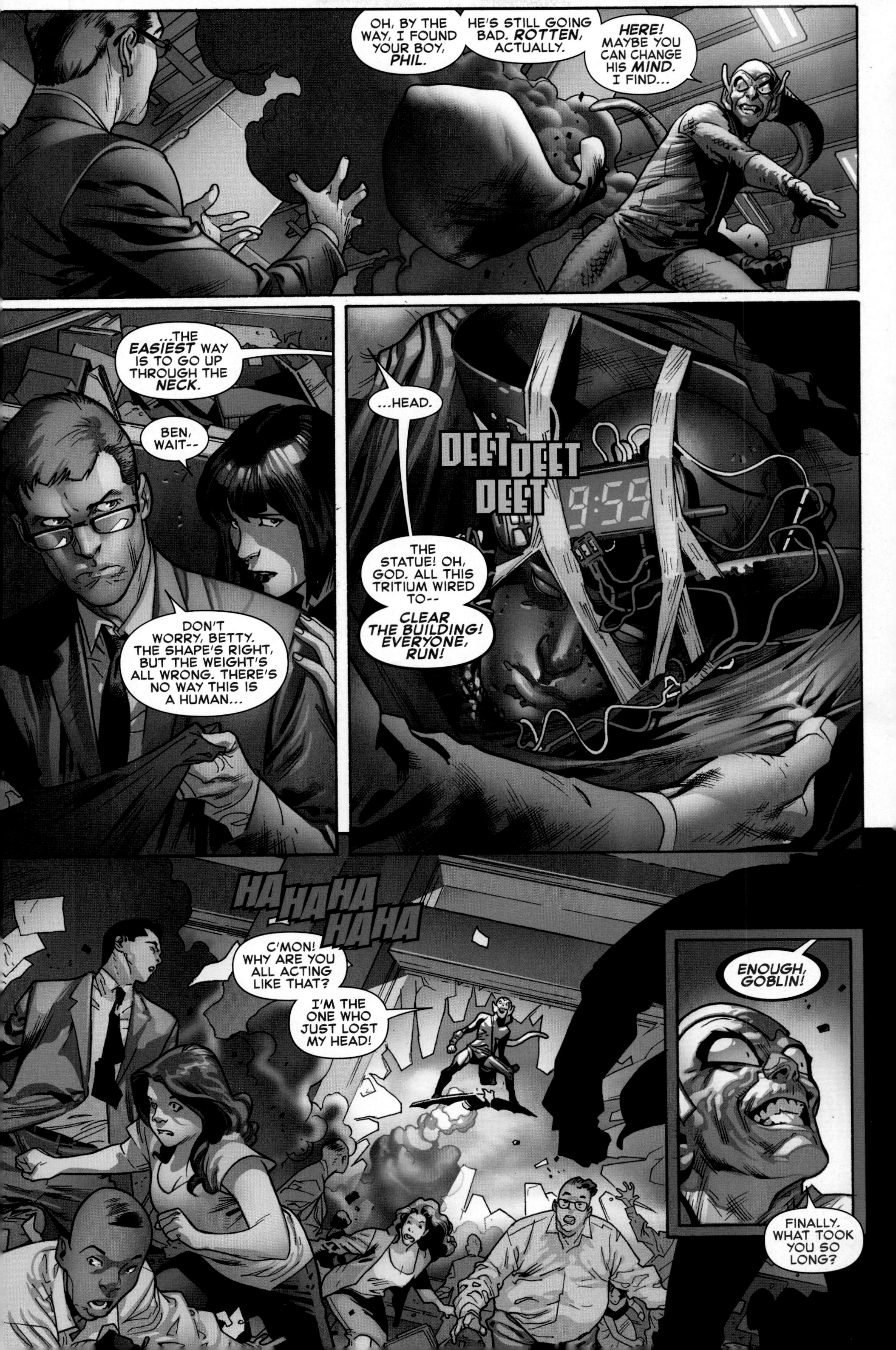
OH, BY THE WAY, I FOUND YOUR BOY, PHIL.
HE'S STILL GOING BAD. ROTTEN, ACTUALLY.
HERE! MAYBE YOU CAN CHANGE HIS MIND. I FIND...
...THE EASIEST WAY IS TO GO UP THROUGH THE NECK.
BEN, WAIT--
DON'T WORRY, BETTY. THE SHAPE'S RIGHT, BUT THE WEIGHT'S ALL WRONG. THERE'S NO WAY THIS IS A HUMAN...
...HEAD.
DEET DEET DEET
9:59
THE STATUE! OH, GOD. ALL THIS TRITIUM WIRED TO--
CLEAR THE BUILDING! EVERYONE, RUN!
HA HA HA HAHA
C'MON! WHY ARE YOU ALL ACTING LIKE THAT?
I'M THE ONE WHO JUST LOST MY HEAD!
ENOUGH, GOBLIN!
FINALLY. WHAT TOOK YOU SO LONG?

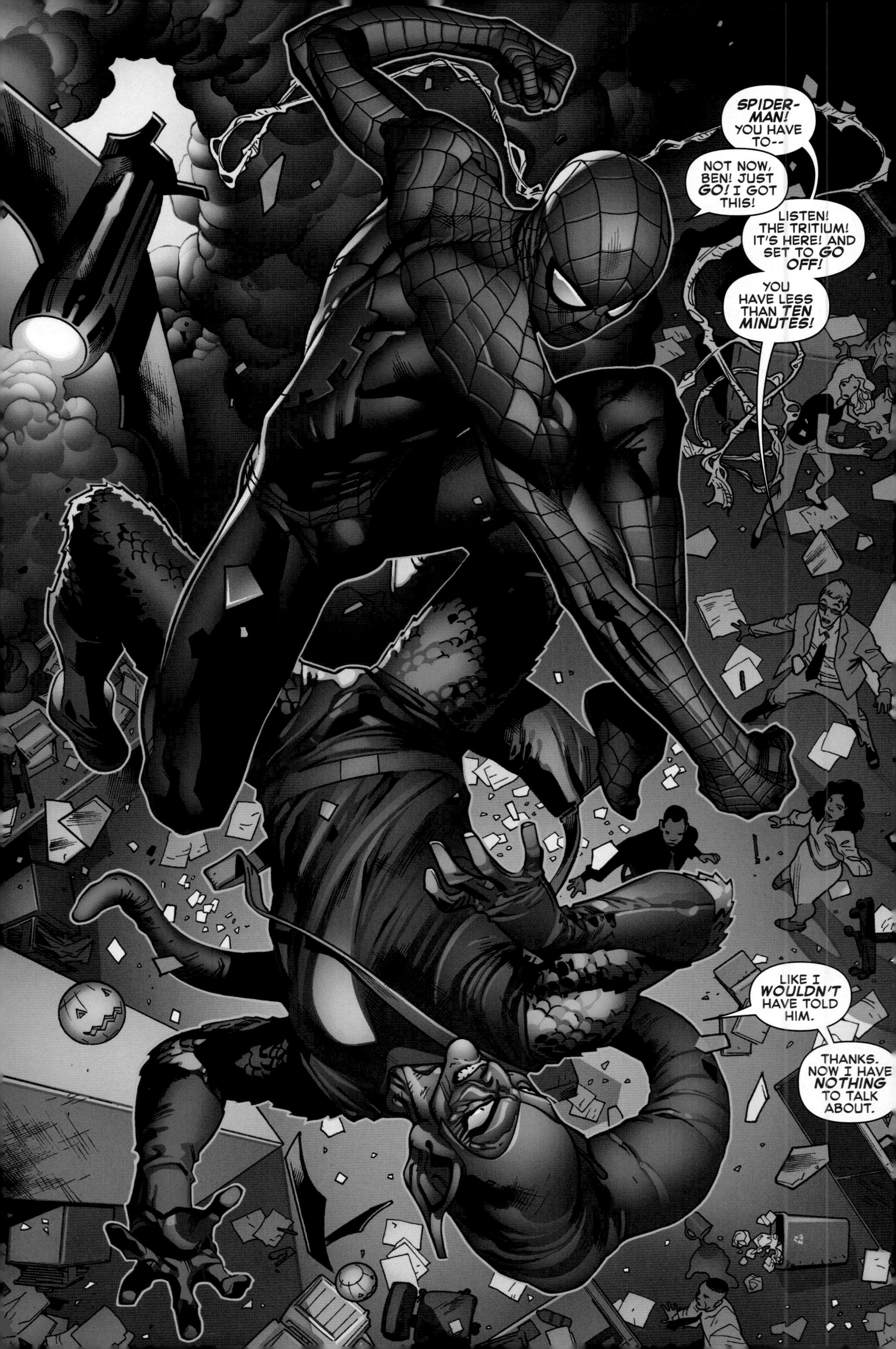
SPIDER-MAN! YOU HAVE TO--
NOT NOW, BEN! JUST GO! I GOT THIS!
LISTEN! THE TRITIUM! IT'S HERE! AND SET TO GO OFF!
YOU HAVE LESS THAN TEN MINUTES!
LIKE I WOULDN'T HAVE TOLD HIM.
THANKS. NOW I HAVE NOTHING TO TALK ABOUT.

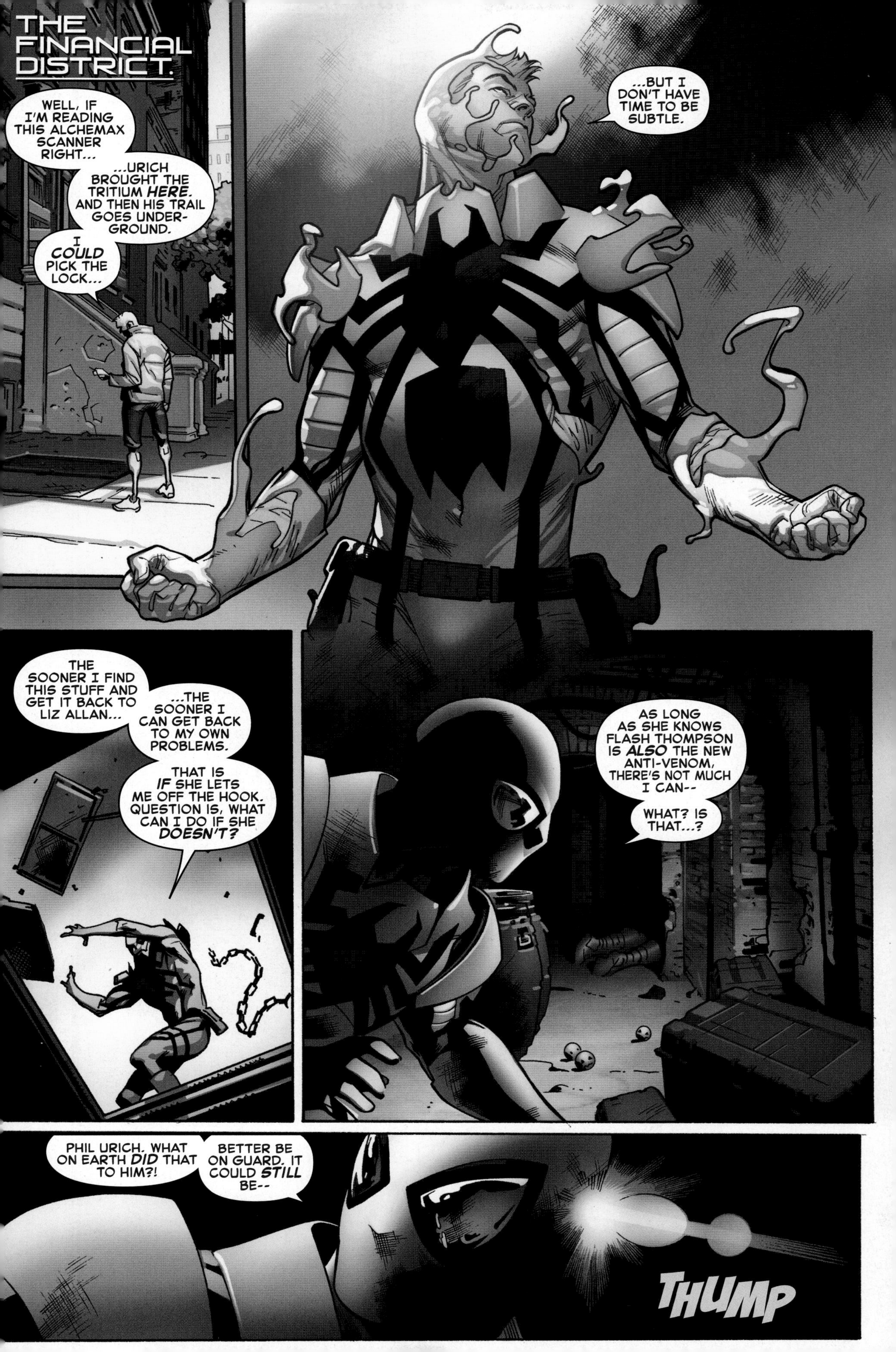
THE FINANCIAL DISTRICT.
WELL, IF I'M READING THIS ALCHEMAX SCANNER RIGHT...
...URICH BROUGHT THE TRITIUM HERE. AND THEN HIS TRAIL GOES UNDER-GROUND.
I COULD PICK THE LOCK...
...BUT I DON'T HAVE TIME TO BE SUBTLE.
THE SOONER I FIND THIS STUFF AND GET IT BACK TO LIZ ALLAN...
...THE SOONER I CAN GET BACK TO MY OWN PROBLEMS.
THAT IS IF SHE LETS ME OFF THE HOOK. QUESTION IS, WHAT CAN I DO IF SHE DOESN'T?
AS LONG AS SHE KNOWS FLASH THOMPSON IS ALSO THE NEW ANTI-VENOM, THERE'S NOT MUCH I CAN--
WHAT? IS THAT...?
PHIL URICH. WHAT ON EARTH DID THAT TO HIM?!
BETTER BE ON GUARD. IT COULD STILL BE--
THUMP

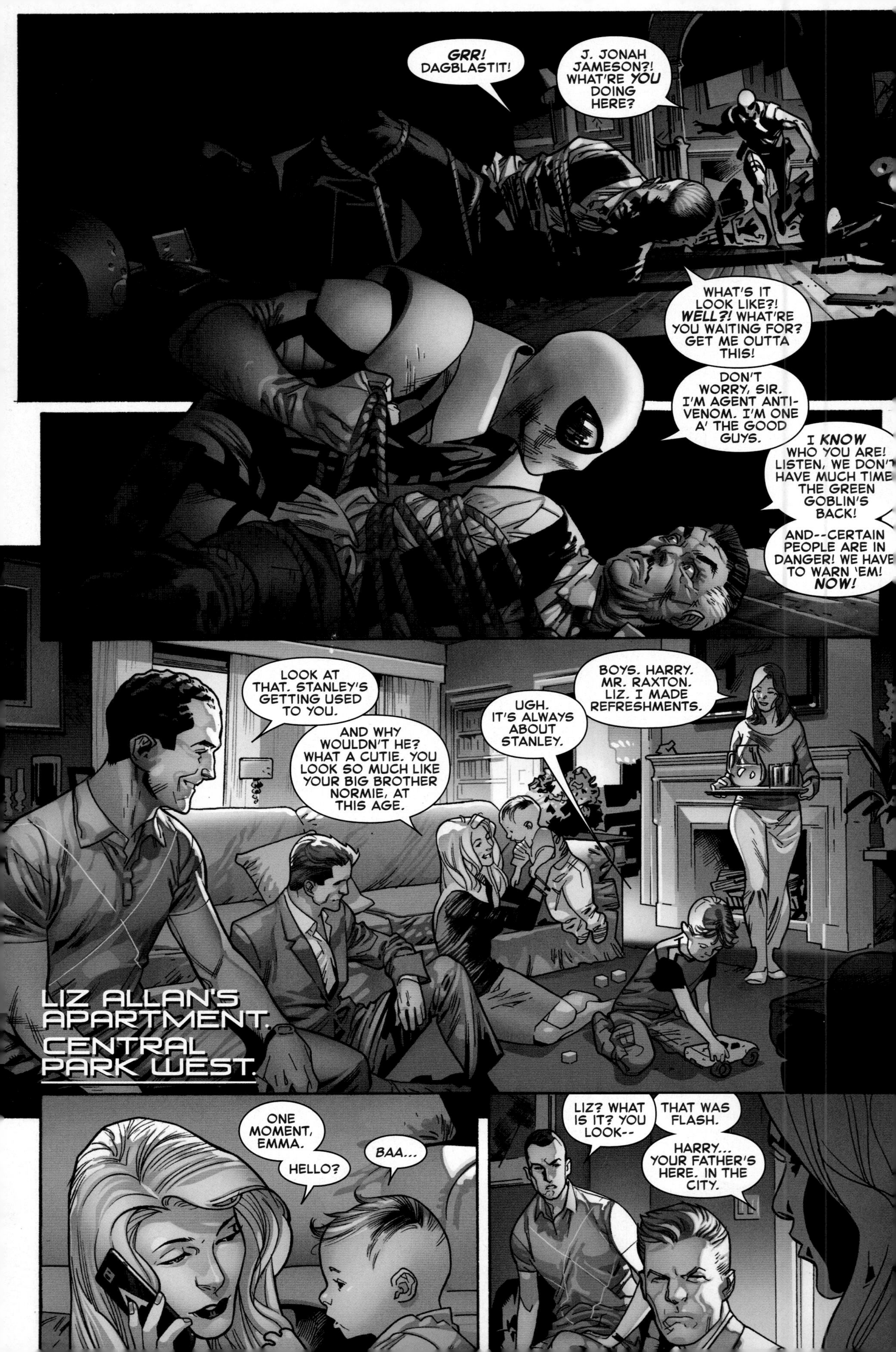
GRR! DAGBLASTIT!
J. JONAH JAMESON?! WHAT'RE YOU DOING HERE?
WHAT'S IT LOOK LIKE?! WELL?! WHAT'RE YOU WAITING FOR? GET ME OUTTA THIS!
DON'T WORRY, SIR. I'M AGENT ANTI-VENOM. I'M ONE A' THE GOOD GUYS.
I KNOW WHO YOU ARE! LISTEN, WE DON'T HAVE MUCH TIME. THE GREEN GOBLIN'S BACK!
AND--CERTAIN PEOPLE ARE IN DANGER! WE HAVE TO WARN 'EM! NOW!
LIZ ALLAN'S APARTMENT. CENTRAL PARK WEST.
LOOK AT THAT. STANLEY'S GETTING USED TO YOU.
AND WHY WOULDN'T HE? WHAT A CUTIE. YOU LOOK SO MUCH LIKE YOUR BIG BROTHER NORMIE, AT THIS AGE.
UGH. IT'S ALWAYS ABOUT STANLEY.
BOYS. HARRY. MR. RAXTON. LIZ. I MADE REFRESHMENTS.
ONE MOMENT, EMMA.
HELLO?
BAA...
LIZ? WHAT IS IT? YOU LOOK--
THAT WAS FLASH.
HARRY... YOUR FATHER'S HERE. IN THE CITY.

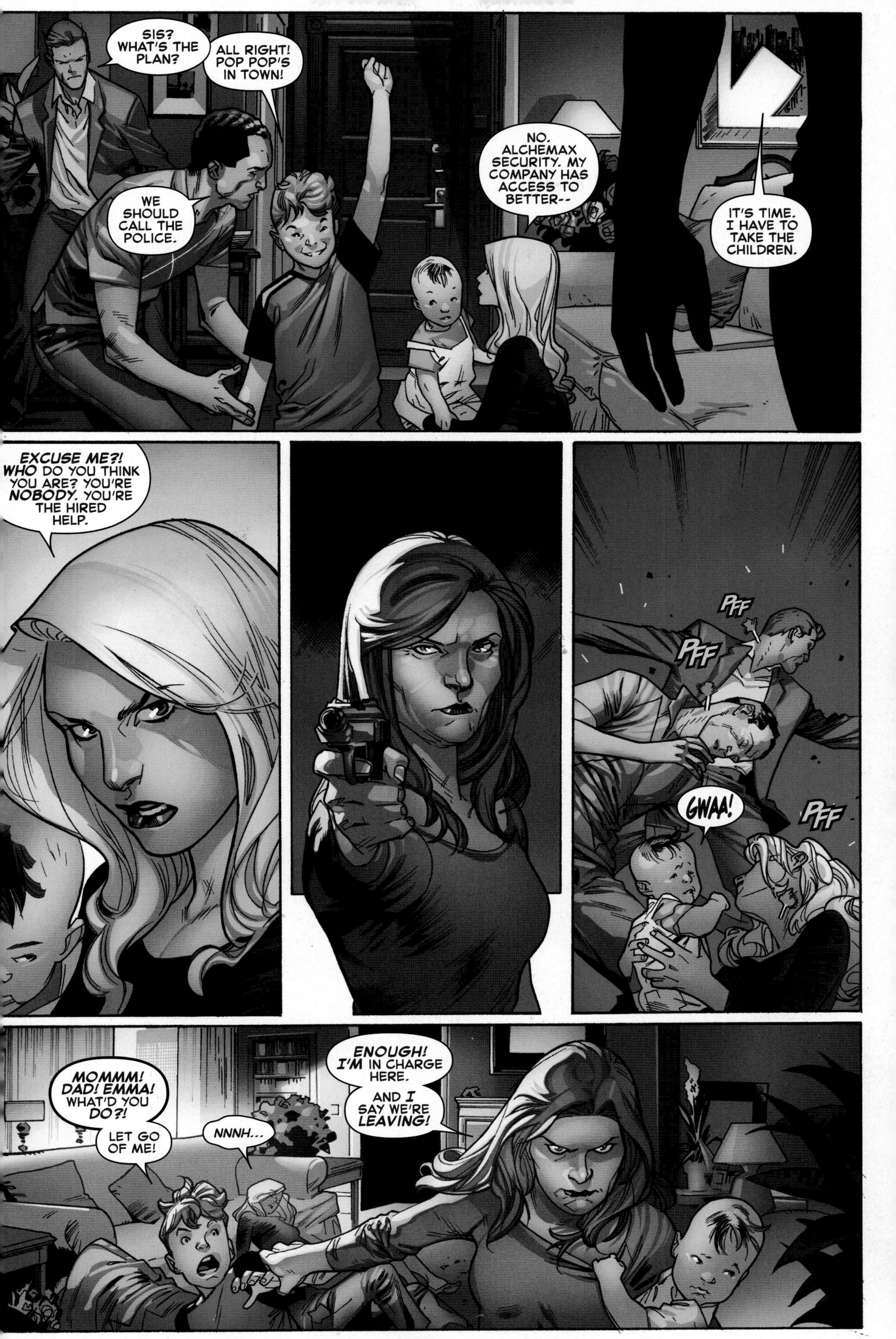
SIS? WHAT'S THE PLAN?
ALL RIGHT! POP POP'S IN TOWN!
WE SHOULD CALL THE POLICE.
NO. ALCHEMAX SECURITY. MY COMPANY HAS ACCESS TO BETTER--
IT'S TIME. I HAVE TO TAKE THE CHILDREN.
EXCUSE ME?! WHO DO YOU THINK YOU ARE? YOU'RE NOBODY. YOU'RE THE HIRED HELP.
PFF
PFF
GWAA!
PFF
MOMMM! DAD! EMMA! WHAT'D YOU DO?!
LET GO OF ME!
NNNH...
ENOUGH! I'M IN CHARGE HERE.
AND I SAY WE'RE LEAVING!

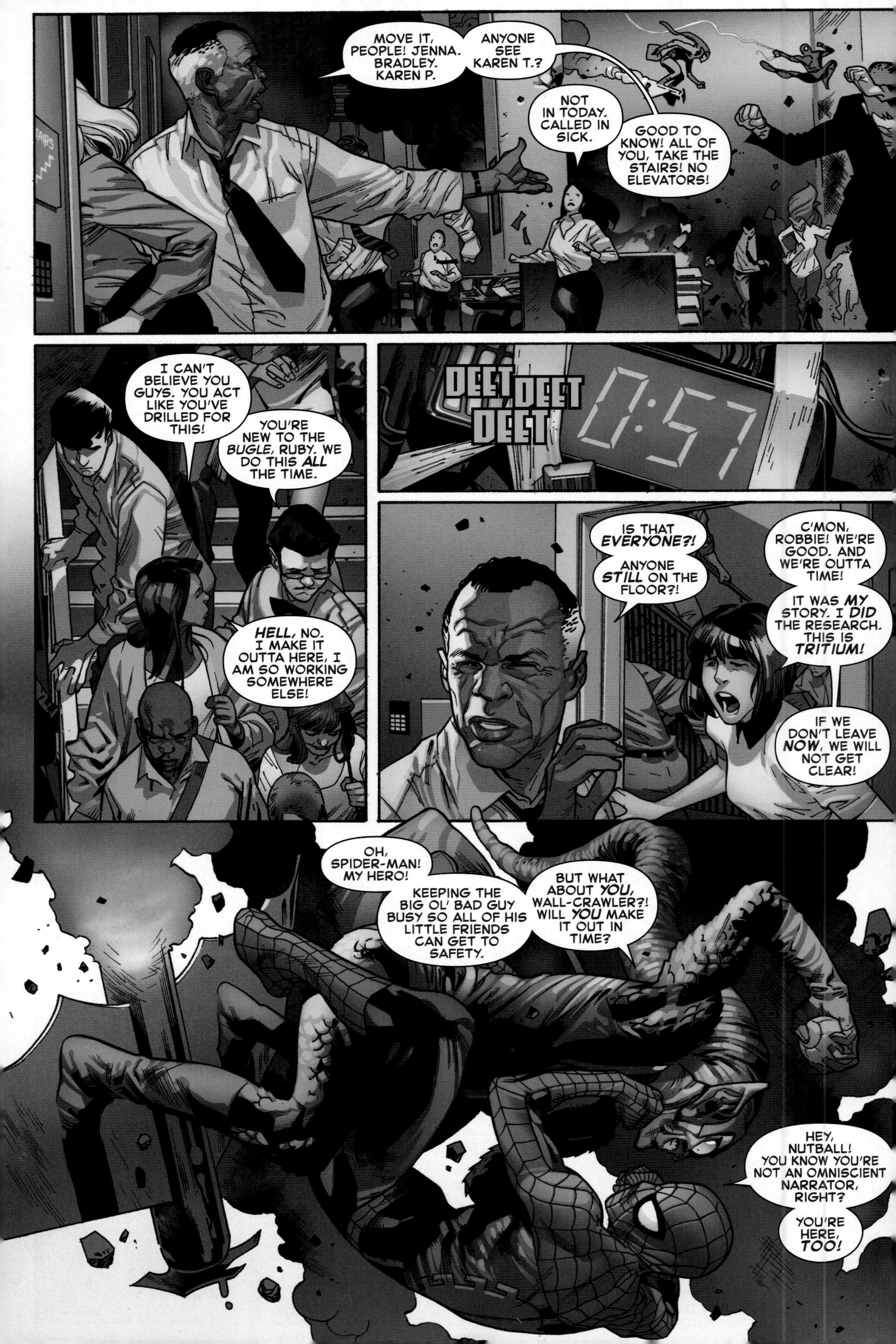

MOVE IT, PEOPLE! JENNA. BRADLEY. KAREN P.
ANYONE SEE KAREN T.?
NOT IN TODAY. CALLED IN SICK.
GOOD TO KNOW! ALL OF YOU, TAKE THE STAIRS! NO ELEVATORS!
STAIRS
I CAN'T BELIEVE YOU GUYS. YOU ACT LIKE YOU'VE DRILLED FOR THIS!
YOU'RE NEW TO THE BUGLE, RUBY. WE DO THIS ALL THE TIME.
HELL, NO. I MAKE IT OUTTA HERE, I AM SO WORKING SOMEWHERE ELSE!
DEET DEET DEET
0:57
IS THAT EVERYONE?!
ANYONE STILL ON THE FLOOR?!
C'MON, ROBBIE! WE'RE GOOD. AND WE'RE OUTTA TIME!
IT WAS MY STORY. I DID THE RESEARCH. THIS IS TRITIUM!
IF WE DON'T LEAVE NOW, WE WILL NOT GET CLEAR!
OH, SPIDER-MAN! MY HERO!
KEEPING THE BIG OL' BAD GUY BUSY SO ALL OF HIS LITTLE FRIENDS CAN GET TO SAFETY.
BUT WHAT ABOUT YOU, WALL-CRAWLER?! WILL YOU MAKE IT OUT IN TIME?
HEY, NUTBALL! YOU KNOW YOU'RE NOT AN OMNISCIENT NARRATOR, RIGHT?
YOU'RE HERE, TOO!

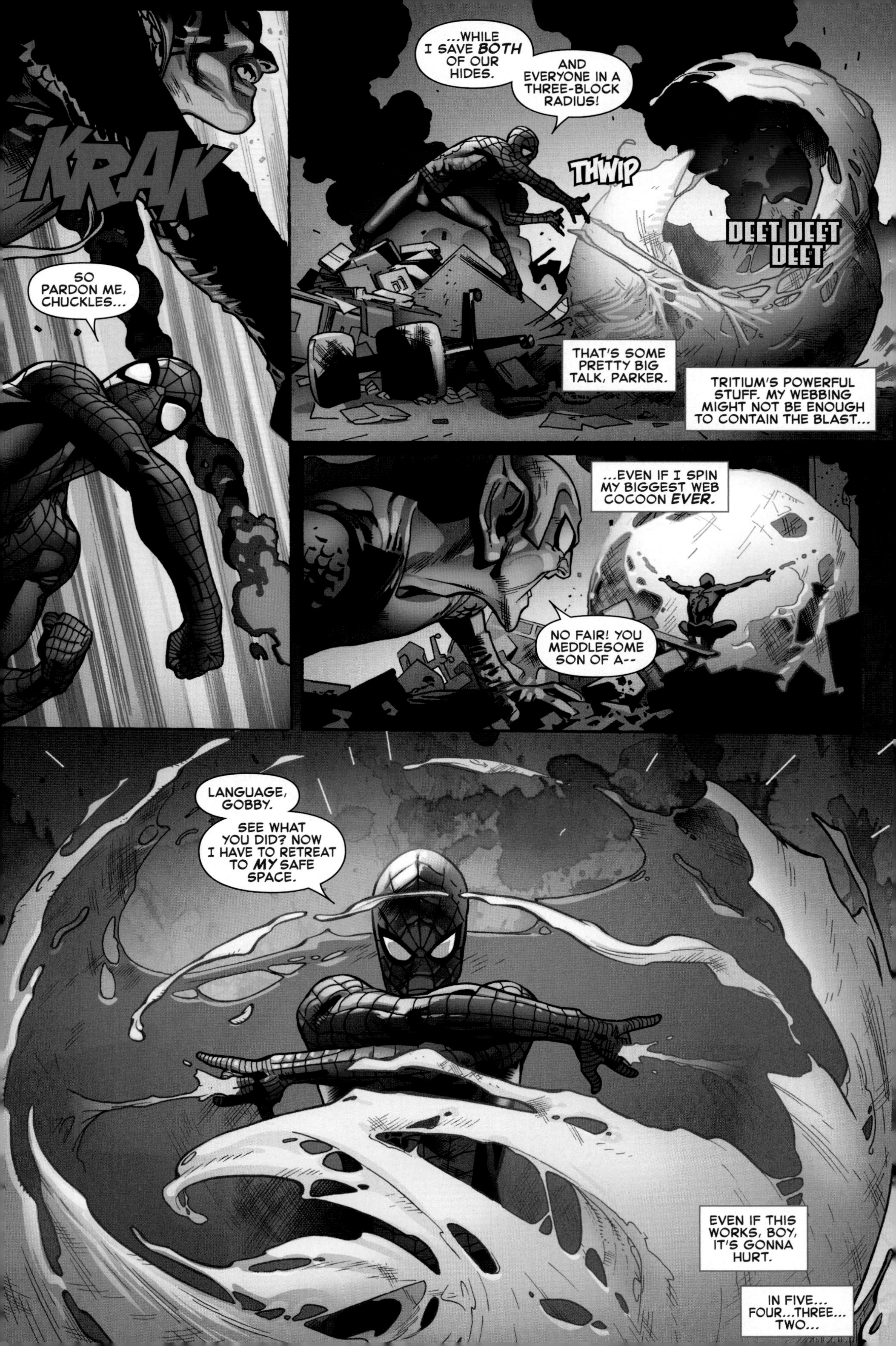

KRAK
SO PARDON ME, CHUCKLES...
...WHILE I SAVE BOTH OF OUR HIDES.
AND EVERYONE IN A THREE-BLOCK RADIUS!
THWIP
DEET DEET DEET
THAT'S SOME PRETTY BIG TALK, PARKER.
TRITIUM'S POWERFUL STUFF. MY WEBBING MIGHT NOT BE ENOUGH TO CONTAIN THE BLAST...
...EVEN IF I SPIN MY BIGGEST WEB COCOON EVER.
NO FAIR! YOU MEDDLESOME SON OF A--
LANGUAGE, GOBBY.
SEE WHAT YOU DID? NOW I HAVE TO RETREAT TO MY SAFE SPACE.
EVEN IF THIS WORKS, BOY, IT'S GONNA HURT.
IN FIVE... FOUR...THREE... TWO...

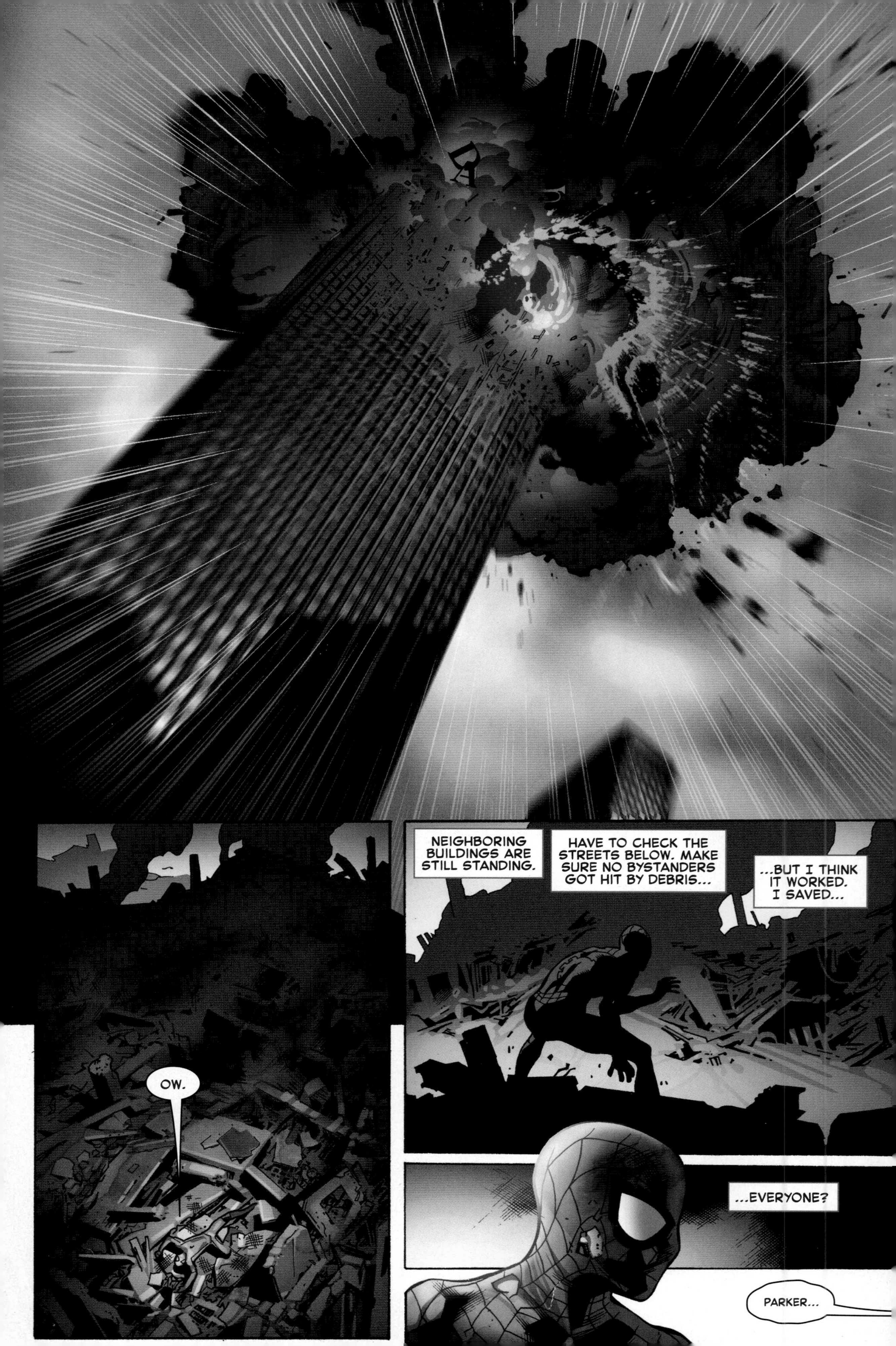

NEIGHBORING BUILDINGS ARE STILL STANDING.
HAVE TO CHECK THE STREETS BELOW. MAKE SURE NO BYSTANDERS GOT HIT BY DEBRIS...
...BUT I THINK IT WORKED. I SAVED...
OW.
...EVERYONE?
PARKER...

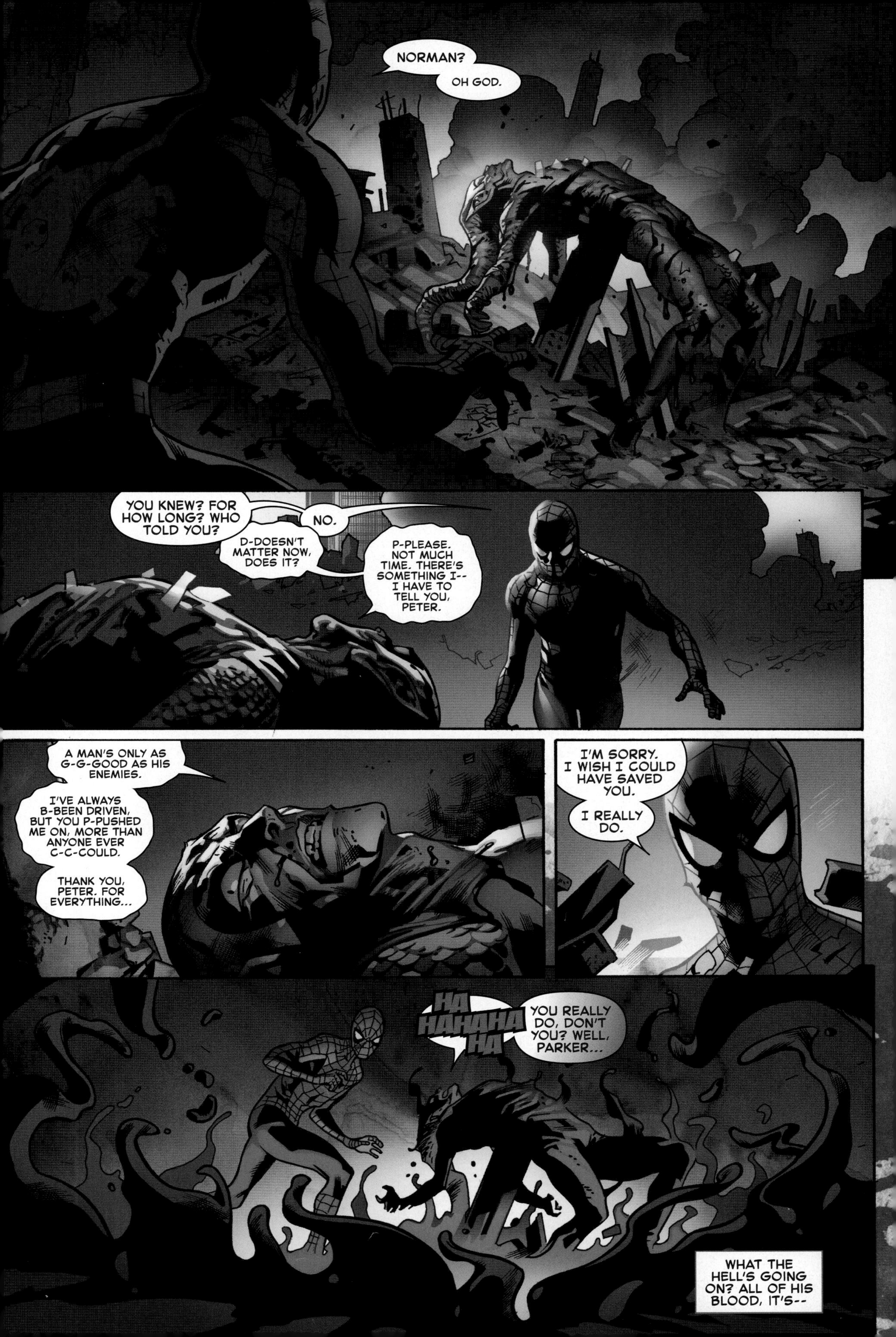
NORMAN?
OH GOD.
YOU KNEW? FOR HOW LONG? WHO TOLD YOU?
NO.
D-DOESN'T MATTER NOW, DOES IT?
P-PLEASE. NOT MUCH TIME. THERE'S SOMETHING I-- I HAVE TO TELL YOU, PETER.
A MAN'S ONLY AS G-G-GOOD AS HIS ENEMIES.
I'VE ALWAYS B-BEEN DRIVEN, BUT YOU P-PUSHED ME ON, MORE THAN ANYONE EVER C-C-COULD.
THANK YOU, PETER. FOR EVERYTHING...
I'M SORRY. I WISH I COULD HAVE SAVED YOU.
I REALLY DO.
HA HAHAHA HA
YOU REALLY DO, DON'T YOU? WELL, PARKER...
WHAT THE HELL'S GOING ON? ALL OF HIS BLOOD, IT'S--

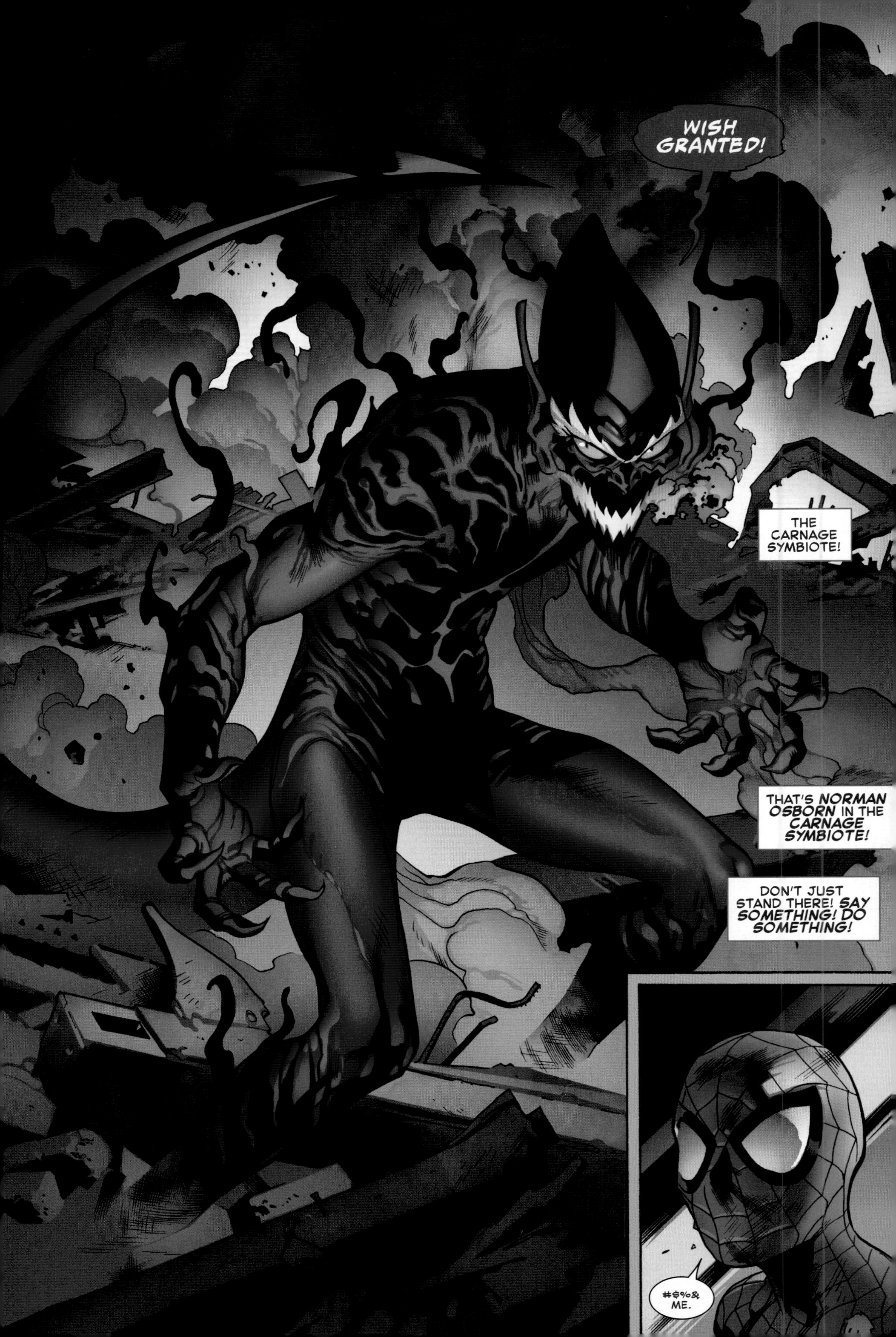
WISH GRANTED!
THE CARNAGE SYMBIOTE!
THAT'S NORMAN OSBORN IN THE CARNAGE SYMBIOTE!
DON'T JUST STAND THERE! SAY SOMETHING! DO SOMETHING!
#$%& ME.

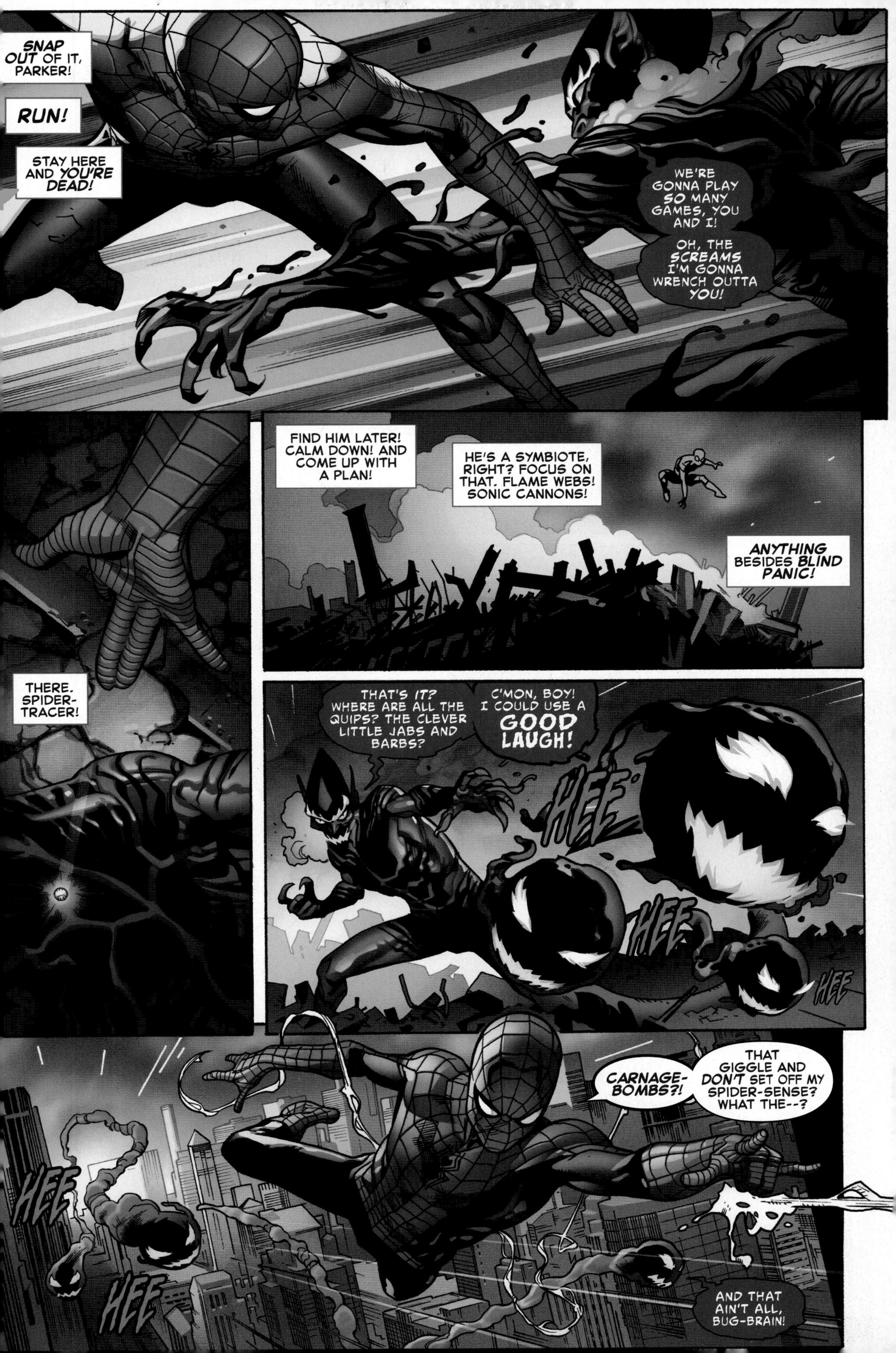
SNAP OUT OF IT, PARKER!
RUN!
STAY HERE AND YOU'RE DEAD!
WE'RE GONNA PLAY SO MANY GAMES, YOU AND I!
OH, THE SCREAMS I'M GONNA WRENCH OUTTA YOU!
FIND HIM LATER! CALM DOWN! AND COME UP WITH A PLAN!
HE'S A SYMBIOTE, RIGHT? FOCUS ON THAT. FLAME WEBS! SONIC CANNONS!
ANYTHING BESIDES BLIND PANIC!
THERE. SPIDER-TRACER!
THAT'S IT? WHERE ARE ALL THE QUIPS? THE CLEVER LITTLE JABS AND BARBS?
C'MON, BOY! I COULD USE A GOOD LAUGH!
HEE
HEE
HEE
CARNAGE-BOMBS?!
THAT GIGGLE AND DON'T SET OFF MY SPIDER-SENSE? WHAT THE--?
HEE
HEE
AND THAT AIN'T ALL, BUG-BRAIN!

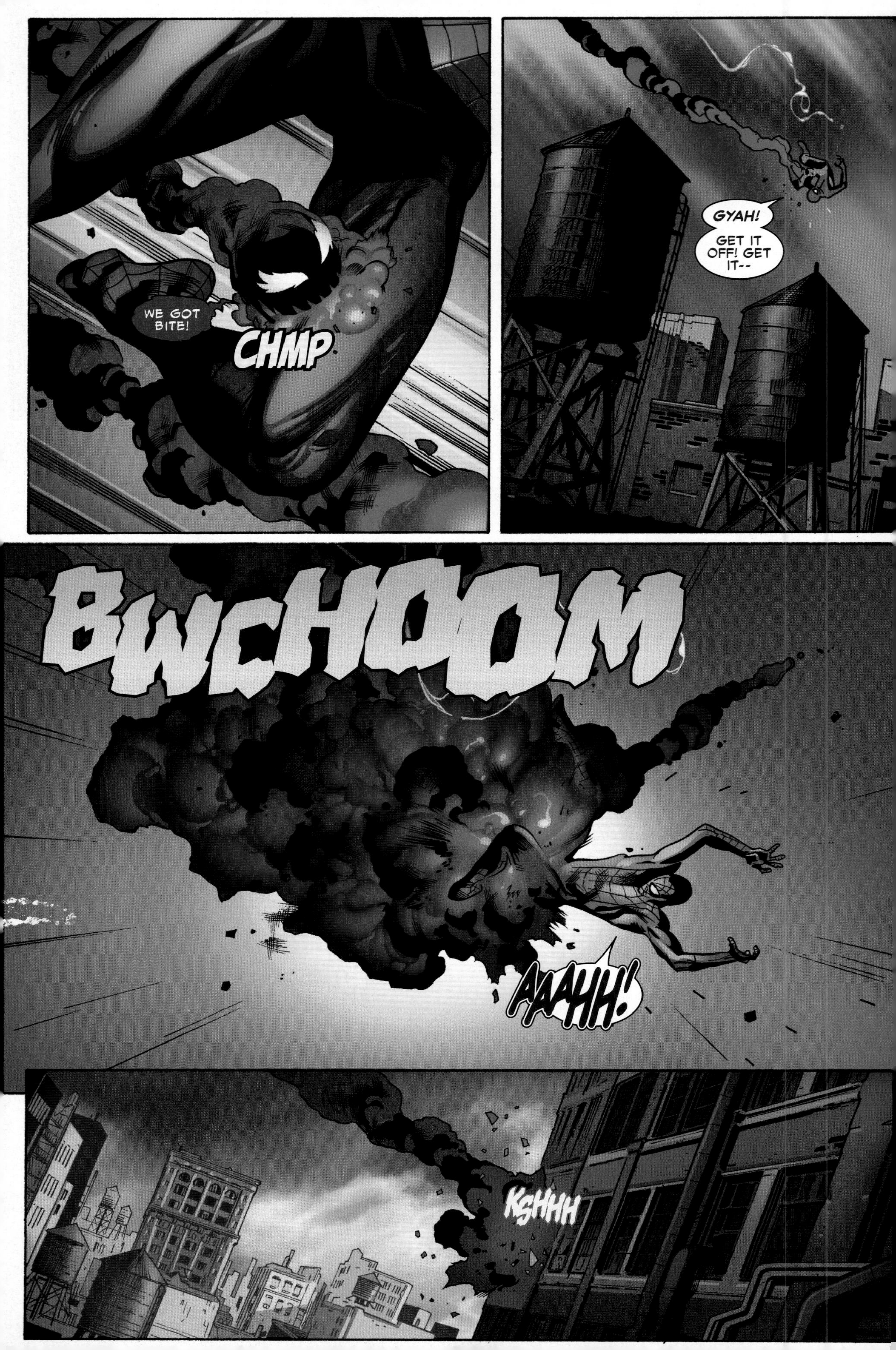
WE GOT BITE!
CHMP
GYAH!
GET IT OFF! GET IT--
BWCHOOM
AAAHH!
KSHHH

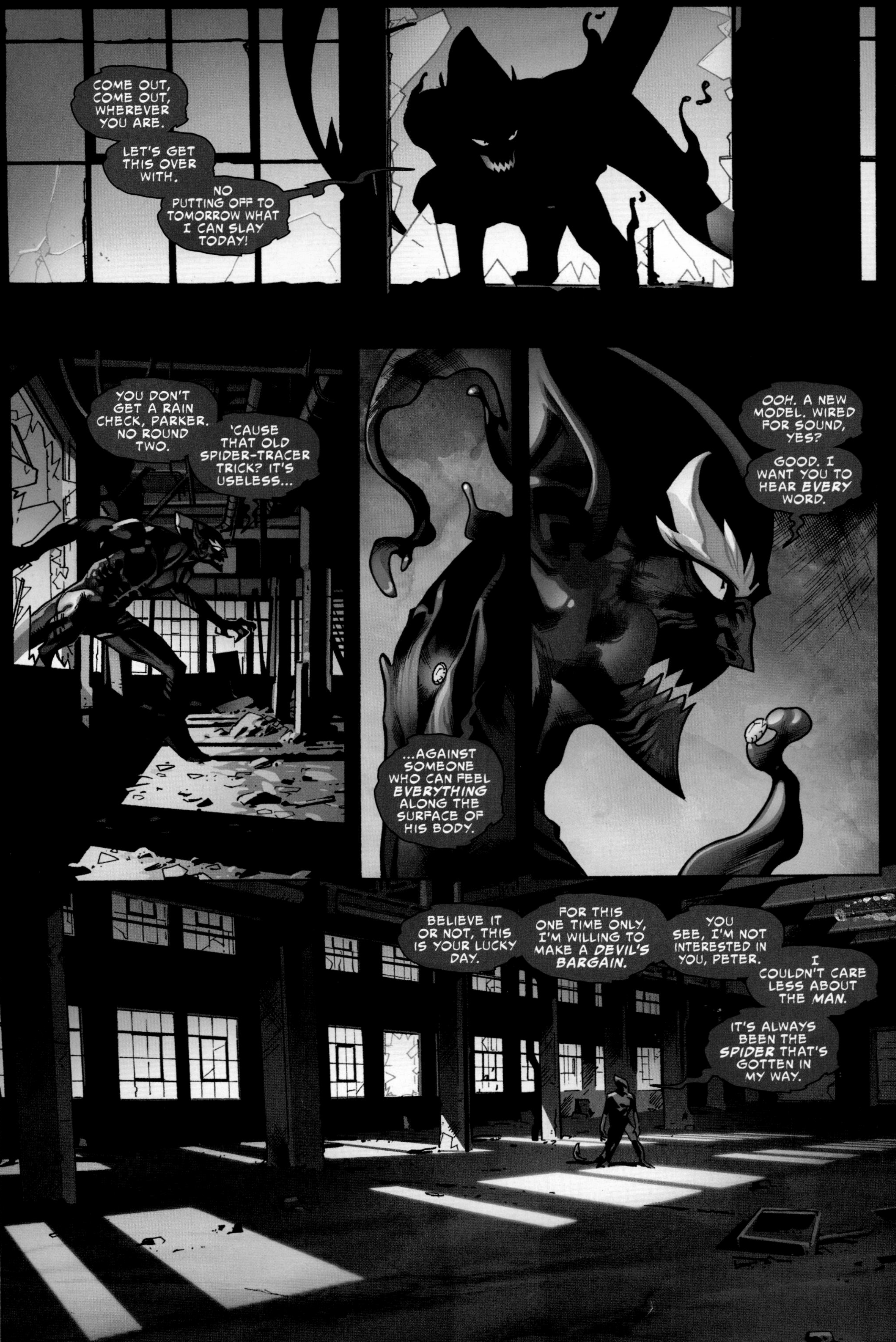
COME OUT, COME OUT, WHEREVER YOU ARE.
LET'S GET THIS OVER WITH.
NO PUTTING OFF TO TOMORROW WHAT I CAN SLAY TODAY!
YOU DON'T GET A RAIN CHECK, PARKER. NO ROUND TWO.
'CAUSE THAT OLD SPIDER-TRACER TRICK? IT'S USELESS...
...AGAINST SOMEONE WHO CAN FEEL EVERYTHING ALONG THE SURFACE OF HIS BODY.
OOH. A NEW MODEL. WIRED FOR SOUND, YES?
GOOD. I WANT YOU TO HEAR EVERY WORD.
BELIEVE IT OR NOT, THIS IS YOUR LUCKY DAY.
FOR THIS ONE TIME ONLY, I'M WILLING TO MAKE A DEVIL'S BARGAIN.
YOU SEE, I'M NOT INTERESTED IN YOU, PETER.
I COULDN'T CARE LESS ABOUT THE MAN.
IT'S ALWAYS BEEN THE SPIDER THAT'S GOTTEN IN MY WAY.

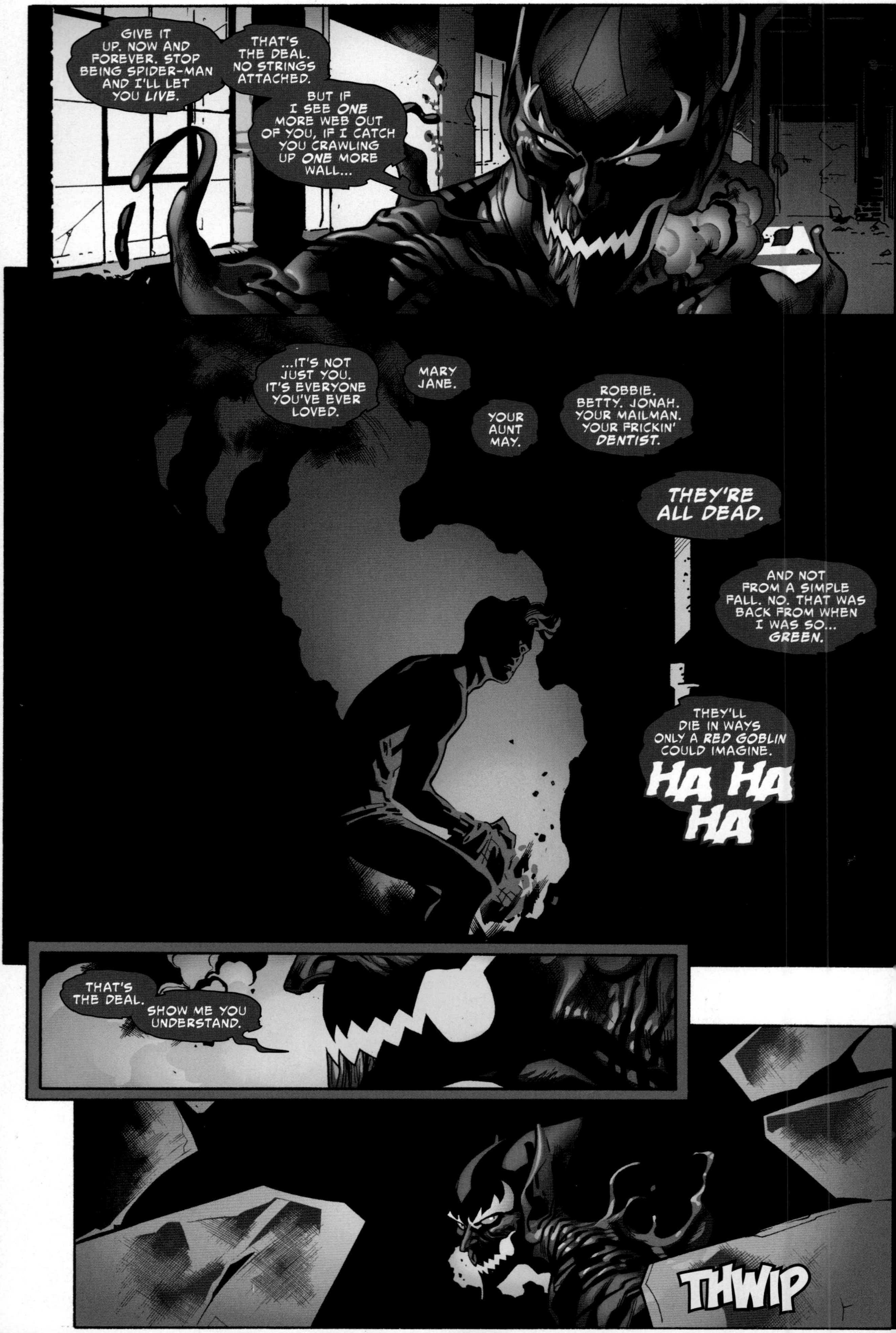
GIVE IT UP. NOW AND FOREVER. STOP BEING SPIDER-MAN AND I'LL LET YOU LIVE.
THAT'S THE DEAL. NO STRINGS ATTACHED.
BUT IF I SEE ONE MORE WEB OUT OF YOU, IF I CATCH YOU CRAWLING UP ONE MORE WALL...
...IT'S NOT JUST YOU. IT'S EVERYONE YOU'VE EVER LOVED.
MARY JANE.
YOUR AUNT MAY.
ROBBIE. BETTY. JONAH. YOUR MAILMAN. YOUR FRICKIN' DENTIST.
THEY'RE ALL DEAD.
AND NOT FROM A SIMPLE FALL. NO. THAT WAS BACK FROM WHEN I WAS SO... GREEN.
THEY'LL DIE IN WAYS ONLY A RED GOBLIN COULD IMAGINE.
HA HA HA
THAT'S THE DEAL.
SHOW ME YOU UNDERSTAND.
THWIP

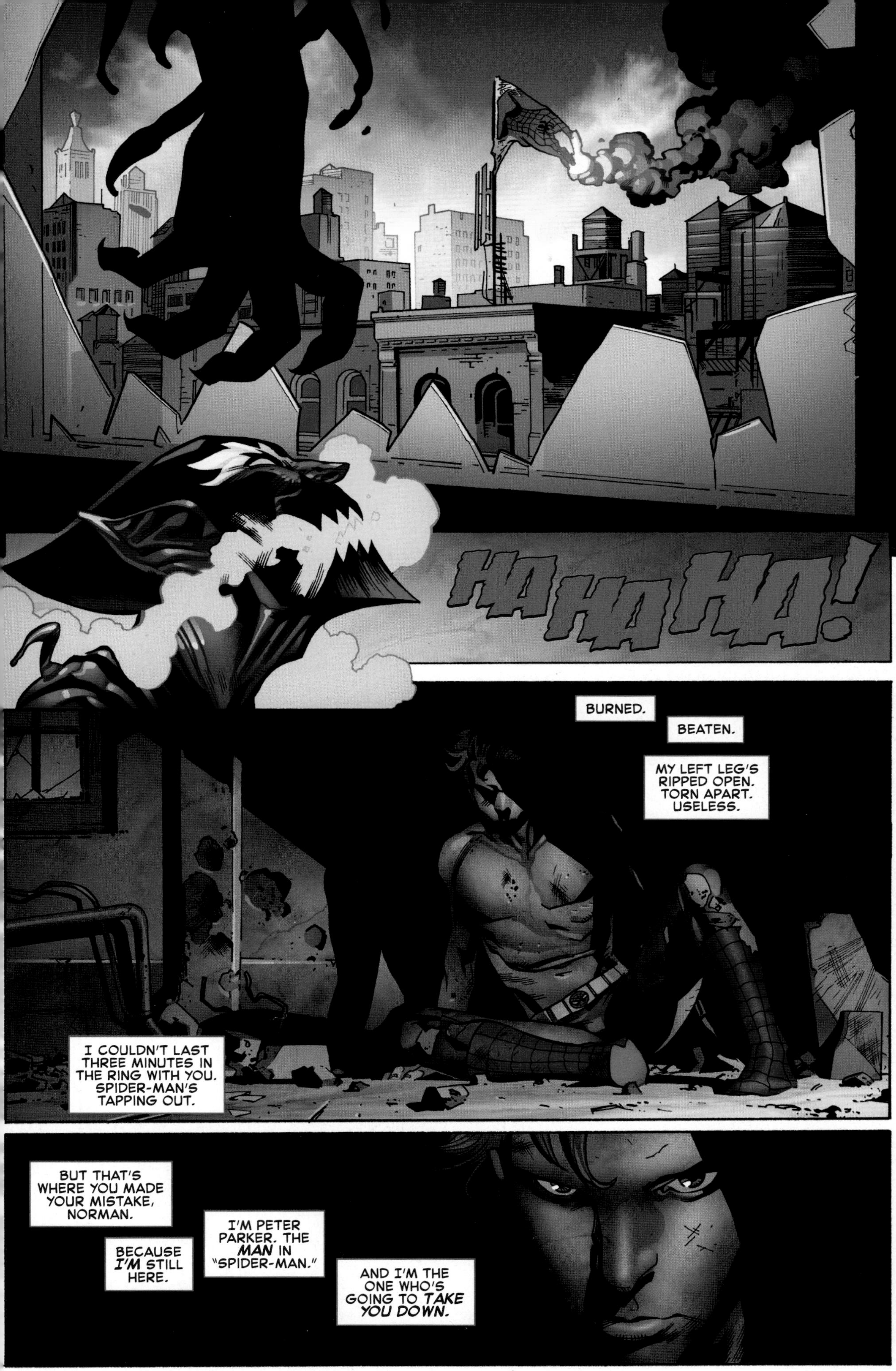
HA HA HA!
BURNED.
BEATEN.
MY LEFT LEG'S RIPPED OPEN. TORN APART. USELESS.
I COULDN'T LAST THREE MINUTES IN THE RING WITH YOU. SPIDER-MAN'S TAPPING OUT.
BUT THAT'S WHERE YOU MADE YOUR MISTAKE, NORMAN.
BECAUSE I'M STILL HERE.
I'M PETER PARKER. THE MAN IN "SPIDER-MAN."
AND I'M THE ONE WHO'S GOING TO TAKE YOU DOWN.

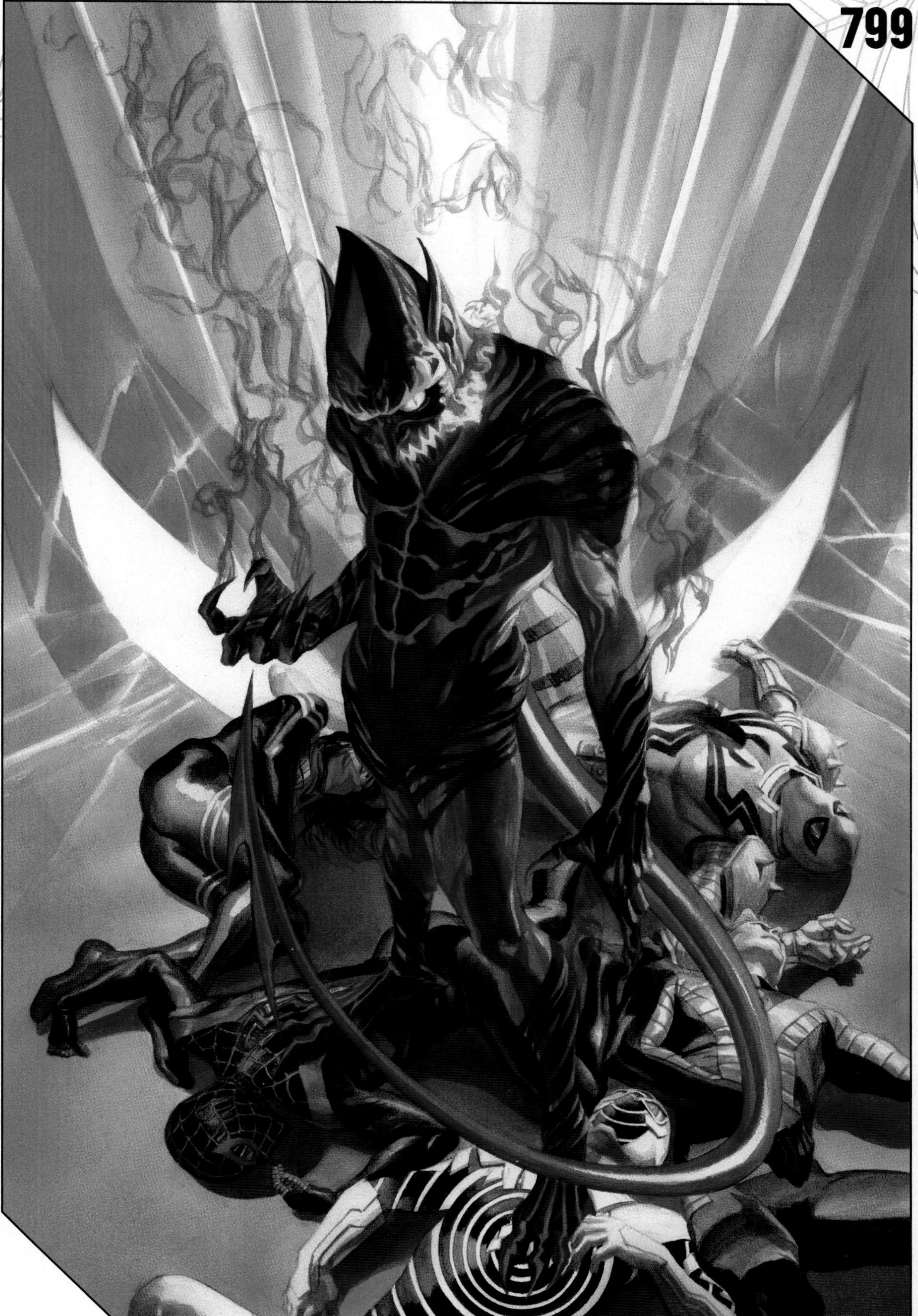
799

GO DOWN SWINGING PART THREE "THE TIES THAT BIND"

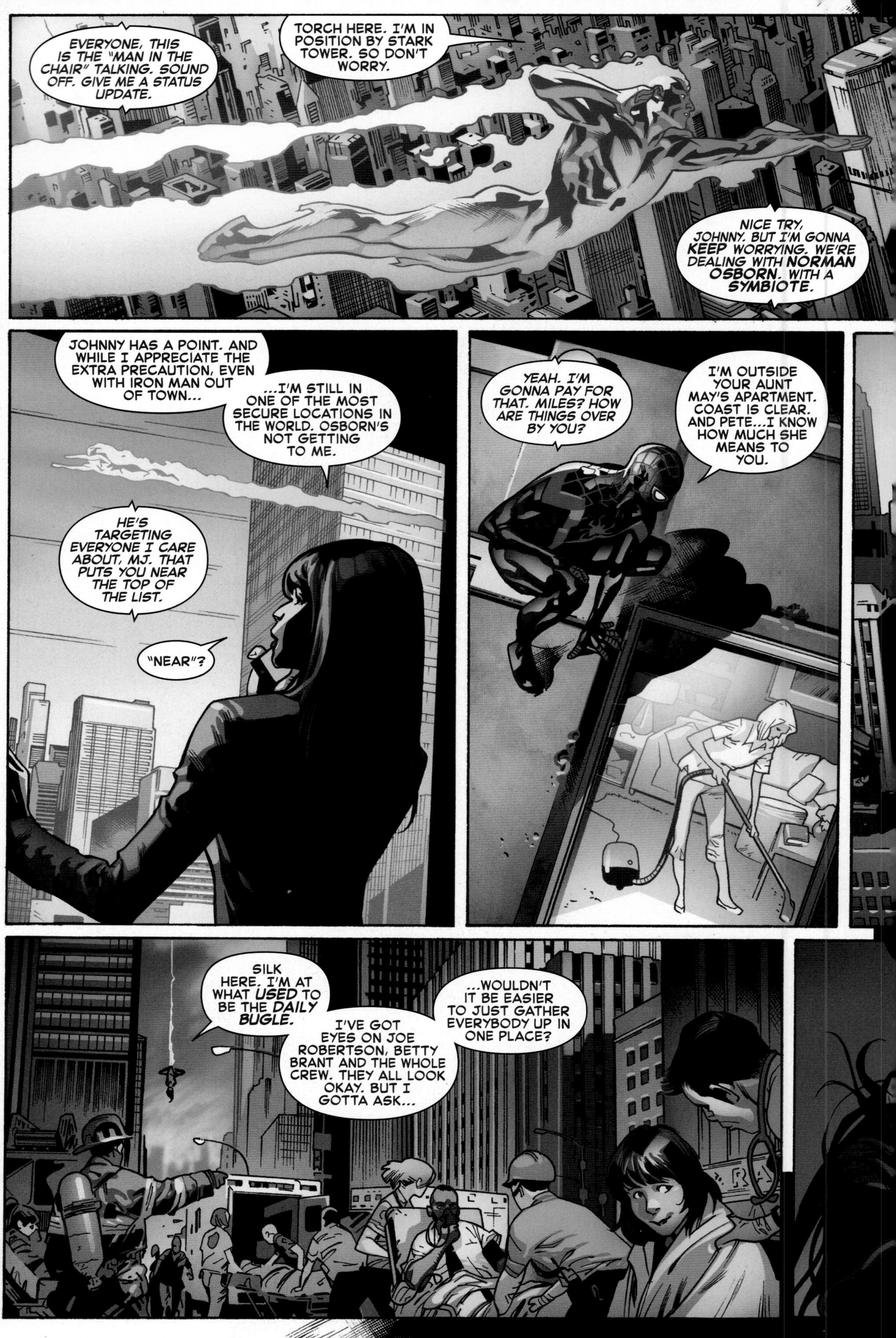
EVERYONE, THIS IS THE "MAN IN THE CHAIR" TALKING. SOUND OFF. GIVE ME A STATUS UPDATE.
TORCH HERE. I'M IN POSITION BY STARK TOWER. SO DON'T WORRY.
NICE TRY, JOHNNY. BUT I'M GONNA **KEEP** WORRYING. WE'RE DEALING WITH **NORMAN OSBORN**. WITH A ***SYMBIOTE***.
JOHNNY HAS A POINT. AND WHILE I APPRECIATE THE EXTRA PRECAUTION, EVEN WITH IRON MAN OUT OF TOWN...
...I'M STILL IN ONE OF THE MOST SECURE LOCATIONS IN THE WORLD. OSBORN'S NOT GETTING TO ME.
HE'S TARGETING EVERYONE I CARE ABOUT, MJ. THAT PUTS YOU NEAR THE TOP OF THE LIST.
"NEAR"?
YEAH. I'M GONNA PAY FOR THAT. MILES? HOW ARE THINGS OVER BY YOU?
I'M OUTSIDE YOUR AUNT MAY'S APARTMENT. COAST IS CLEAR. AND PETE...I KNOW HOW MUCH SHE MEANS TO YOU.
SILK HERE. I'M AT WHAT *USED* TO BE THE ***DAILY BUGLE***.
I'VE GOT EYES ON JOE ROBERTSON, BETTY BRANT AND THE WHOLE CREW. THEY ALL LOOK OKAY. BUT I GOTTA ASK...
...WOULDN'T IT BE EASIER TO JUST GATHER EVERYBODY UP IN ONE PLACE?

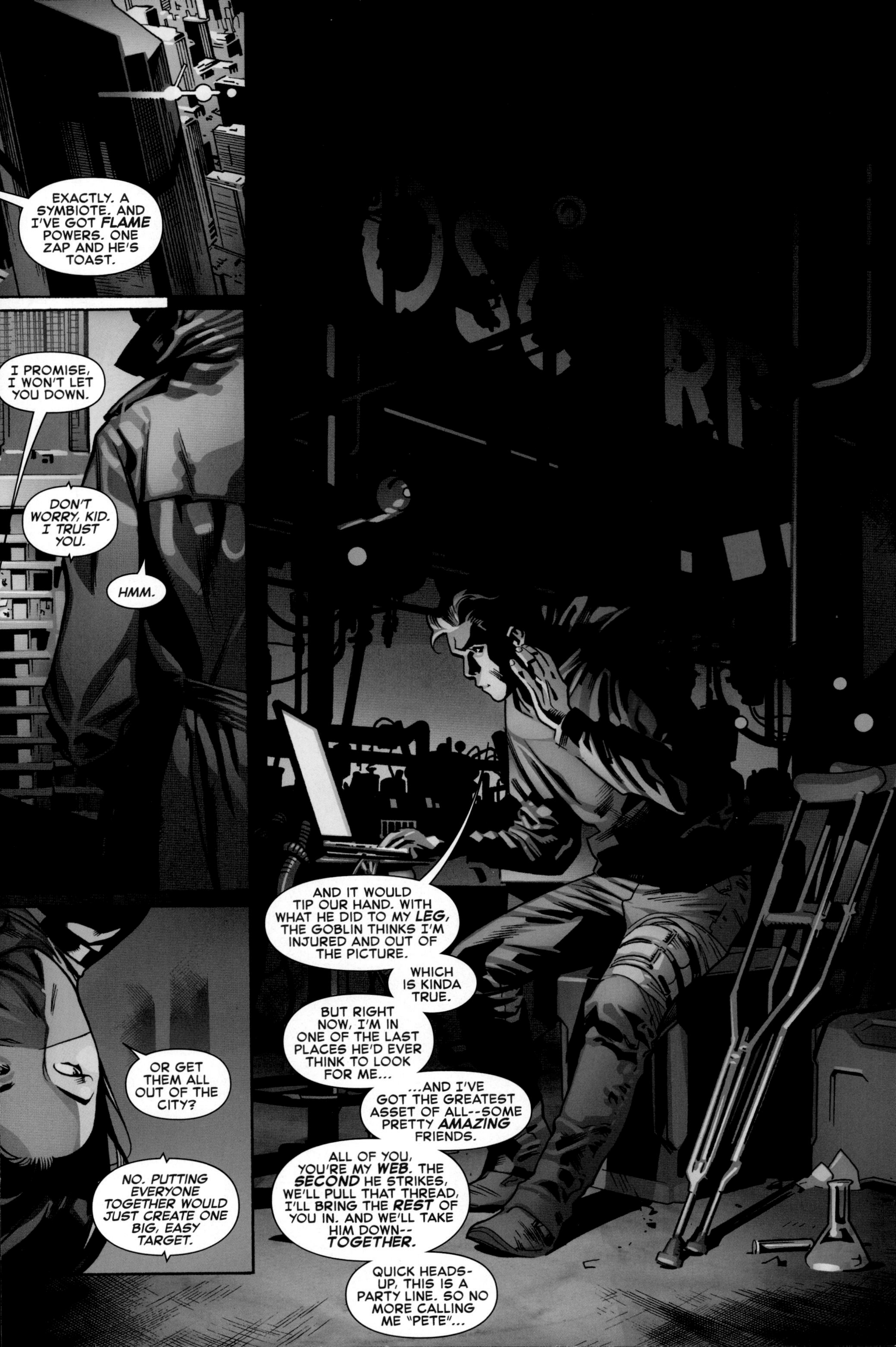
EXACTLY. A SYMBIOTE. AND I'VE GOT FLAME POWERS. ONE ZAP AND HE'S TOAST.
I PROMISE, I WON'T LET YOU DOWN.
DON'T WORRY, KID. I TRUST YOU.
HMM.
AND IT WOULD TIP OUR HAND. WITH WHAT HE DID TO MY LEG, THE GOBLIN THINKS I'M INJURED AND OUT OF THE PICTURE.
WHICH IS KINDA TRUE.
BUT RIGHT NOW, I'M IN ONE OF THE LAST PLACES HE'D EVER THINK TO LOOK FOR ME...
...AND I'VE GOT THE GREATEST ASSET OF ALL--SOME PRETTY AMAZING FRIENDS.
OR GET THEM ALL OUT OF THE CITY?
NO. PUTTING EVERYONE TOGETHER WOULD JUST CREATE ONE BIG, EASY TARGET.
ALL OF YOU, YOU'RE MY WEB. THE SECOND HE STRIKES, WE'LL PULL THAT THREAD, I'LL BRING THE REST OF YOU IN. AND WE'LL TAKE HIM DOWN--TOGETHER.
QUICK HEADS-UP, THIS IS A PARTY LINE. SO NO MORE CALLING ME "PETE"...

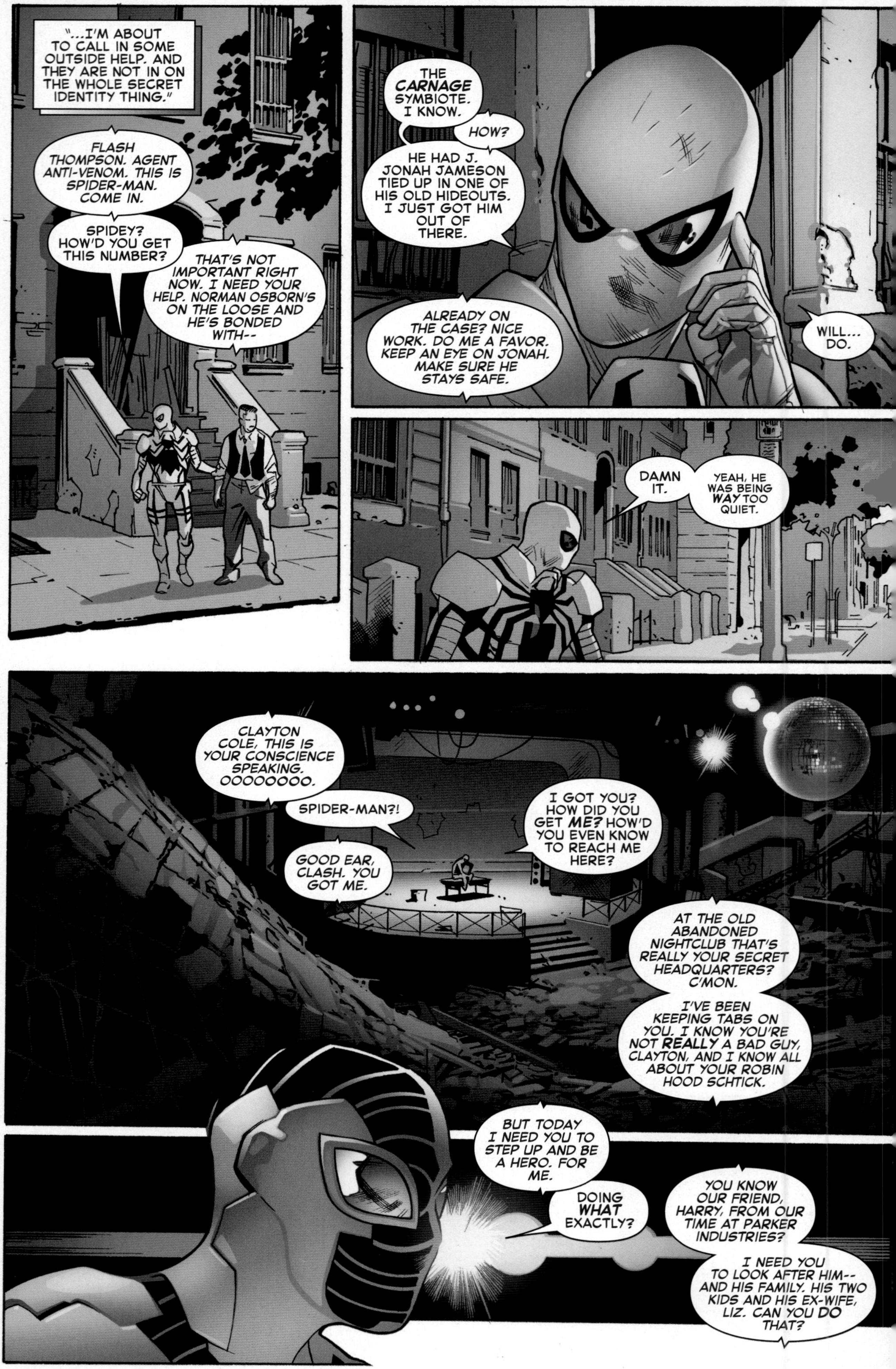
"...I'M ABOUT TO CALL IN SOME OUTSIDE HELP. AND THEY ARE NOT IN ON THE WHOLE SECRET IDENTITY THING."
FLASH THOMPSON. AGENT ANTI-VENOM. THIS IS SPIDER-MAN. COME IN.
SPIDEY? HOW'D YOU GET THIS NUMBER?
THAT'S NOT IMPORTANT RIGHT NOW. I NEED YOUR HELP. NORMAN OSBORN'S ON THE LOOSE AND HE'S BONDED WITH--
THE CARNAGE SYMBIOTE. I KNOW.
HOW?
HE HAD J. JONAH JAMESON TIED UP IN ONE OF HIS OLD HIDEOUTS. I JUST GOT HIM OUT OF THERE.
ALREADY ON THE CASE? NICE WORK. DO ME A FAVOR. KEEP AN EYE ON JONAH. MAKE SURE HE STAYS SAFE.
WILL... DO.
DAMN IT.
YEAH, HE WAS BEING WAY TOO QUIET.
CLAYTON COLE, THIS IS YOUR CONSCIENCE SPEAKING. OOOOOOOO.
SPIDER-MAN?!
GOOD EAR, CLASH. YOU GOT ME.
I GOT YOU? HOW DID YOU GET ME? HOW'D YOU EVEN KNOW TO REACH ME HERE?
AT THE OLD ABANDONED NIGHTCLUB THAT'S REALLY YOUR SECRET HEADQUARTERS? C'MON.
I'VE BEEN KEEPING TABS ON YOU. I KNOW YOU'RE NOT REALLY A BAD GUY, CLAYTON, AND I KNOW ALL ABOUT YOUR ROBIN HOOD SCHTICK.
BUT TODAY I NEED YOU TO STEP UP AND BE A HERO. FOR ME.
DOING WHAT EXACTLY?
YOU KNOW OUR FRIEND, HARRY, FROM OUR TIME AT PARKER INDUSTRIES?
I NEED YOU TO LOOK AFTER HIM--AND HIS FAMILY. HIS TWO KIDS AND HIS EX-WIFE, LIZ. CAN YOU DO THAT?

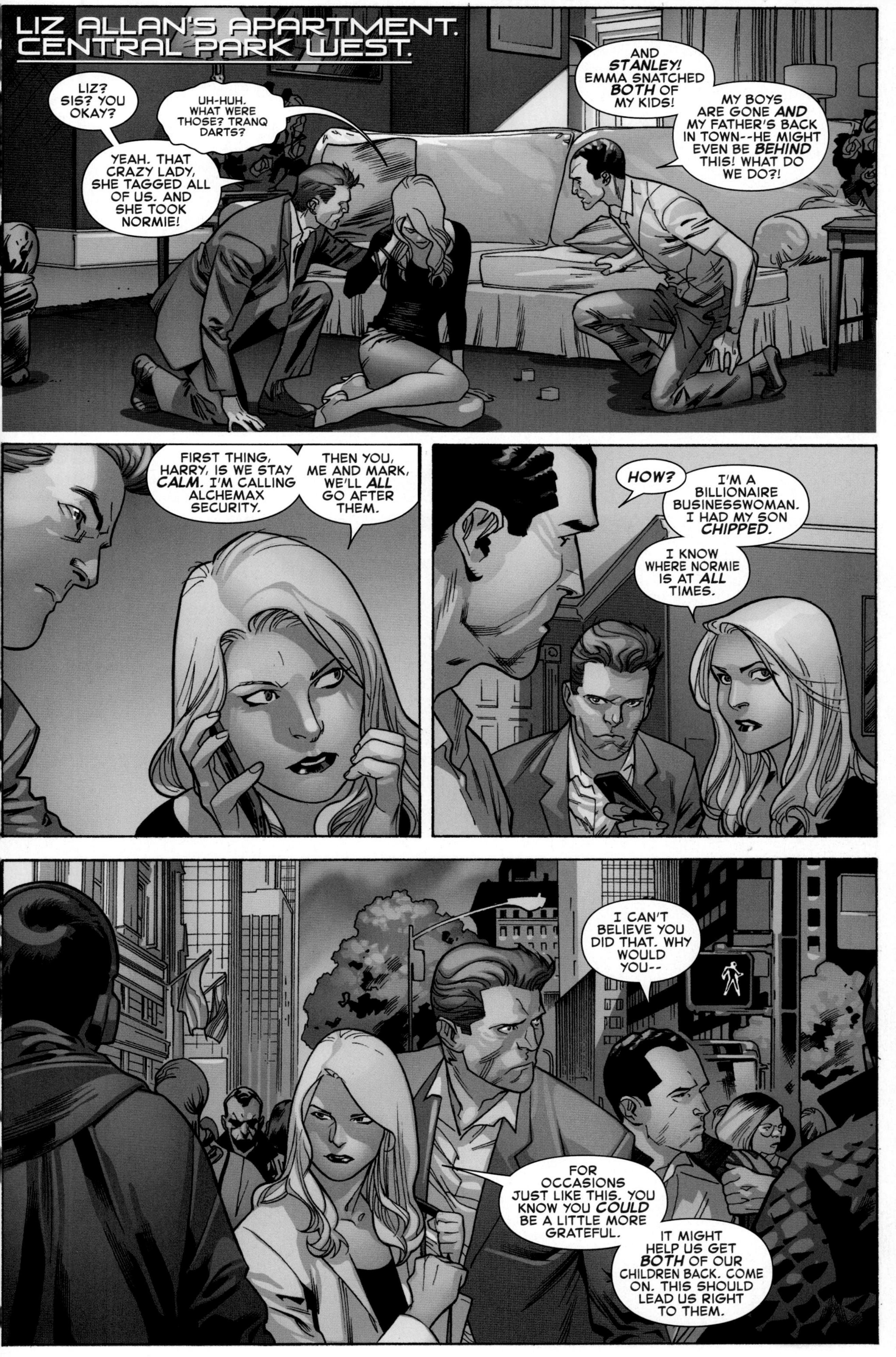
LIZ ALLAN'S APARTMENT. CENTRAL PARK WEST.
LIZ? SIS? YOU OKAY?
UH-HUH. WHAT WERE THOSE? TRANQ DARTS?
YEAH. THAT CRAZY LADY, SHE TAGGED ALL OF US. AND SHE TOOK NORMIE!
AND STANLEY! EMMA SNATCHED BOTH OF MY KIDS!
MY BOYS ARE GONE AND MY FATHER'S BACK IN TOWN--HE MIGHT EVEN BE BEHIND THIS! WHAT DO WE DO?!
FIRST THING, HARRY, IS WE STAY CALM. I'M CALLING ALCHEMAX SECURITY.
THEN YOU, ME AND MARK, WE'LL ALL GO AFTER THEM.
HOW?
I'M A BILLIONAIRE BUSINESSWOMAN. I HAD MY SON CHIPPED.
I KNOW WHERE NORMIE IS AT ALL TIMES.
I CAN'T BELIEVE YOU DID THAT. WHY WOULD YOU--
FOR OCCASIONS JUST LIKE THIS. YOU KNOW YOU COULD BE A LITTLE MORE GRATEFUL.
IT MIGHT HELP US GET BOTH OF OUR CHILDREN BACK. COME ON. THIS SHOULD LEAD US RIGHT TO THEM.

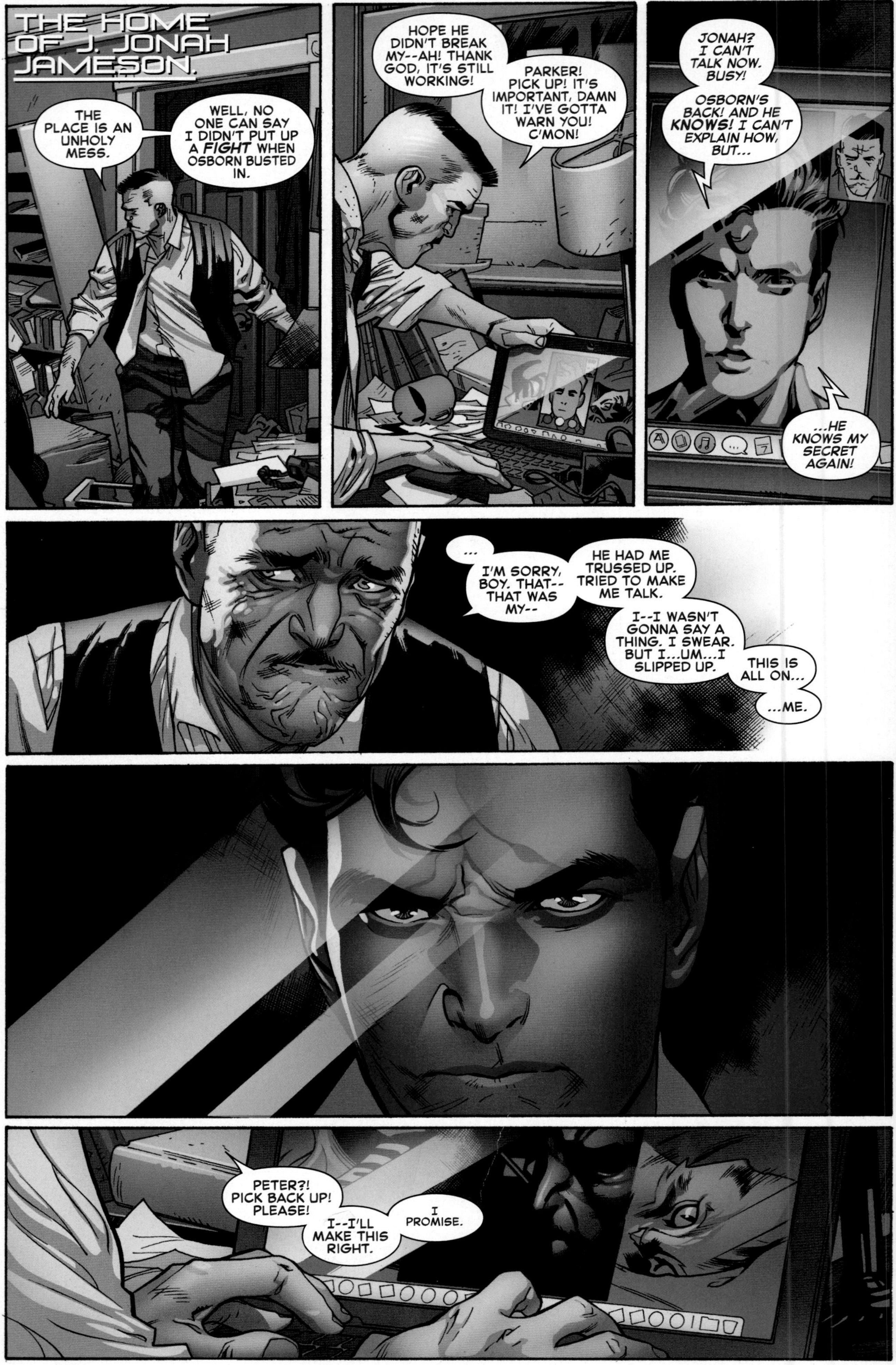
THE HOME OF J. JONAH JAMESON.
THE PLACE IS AN UNHOLY MESS.
WELL, NO ONE CAN SAY I DIDN'T PUT UP A FIGHT WHEN OSBORN BUSTED IN.
HOPE HE DIDN'T BREAK MY--AH! THANK GOD, IT'S STILL WORKING!
PARKER! PICK UP! IT'S IMPORTANT, DAMN IT! I'VE GOTTA WARN YOU! C'MON!
JONAH? I CAN'T TALK NOW. BUSY!
OSBORN'S BACK! AND HE KNOWS! I CAN'T EXPLAIN HOW, BUT...
...HE KNOWS MY SECRET AGAIN!
...
I'M SORRY, BOY. THAT--THAT WAS MY--
HE HAD ME TRUSSED UP. TRIED TO MAKE ME TALK.
I--I WASN'T GONNA SAY A THING. I SWEAR. BUT I...UM...I SLIPPED UP.
THIS IS ALL ON...
...ME.
PETER?! PICK BACK UP! PLEASE!
I--I'LL MAKE THIS RIGHT.
I PROMISE.

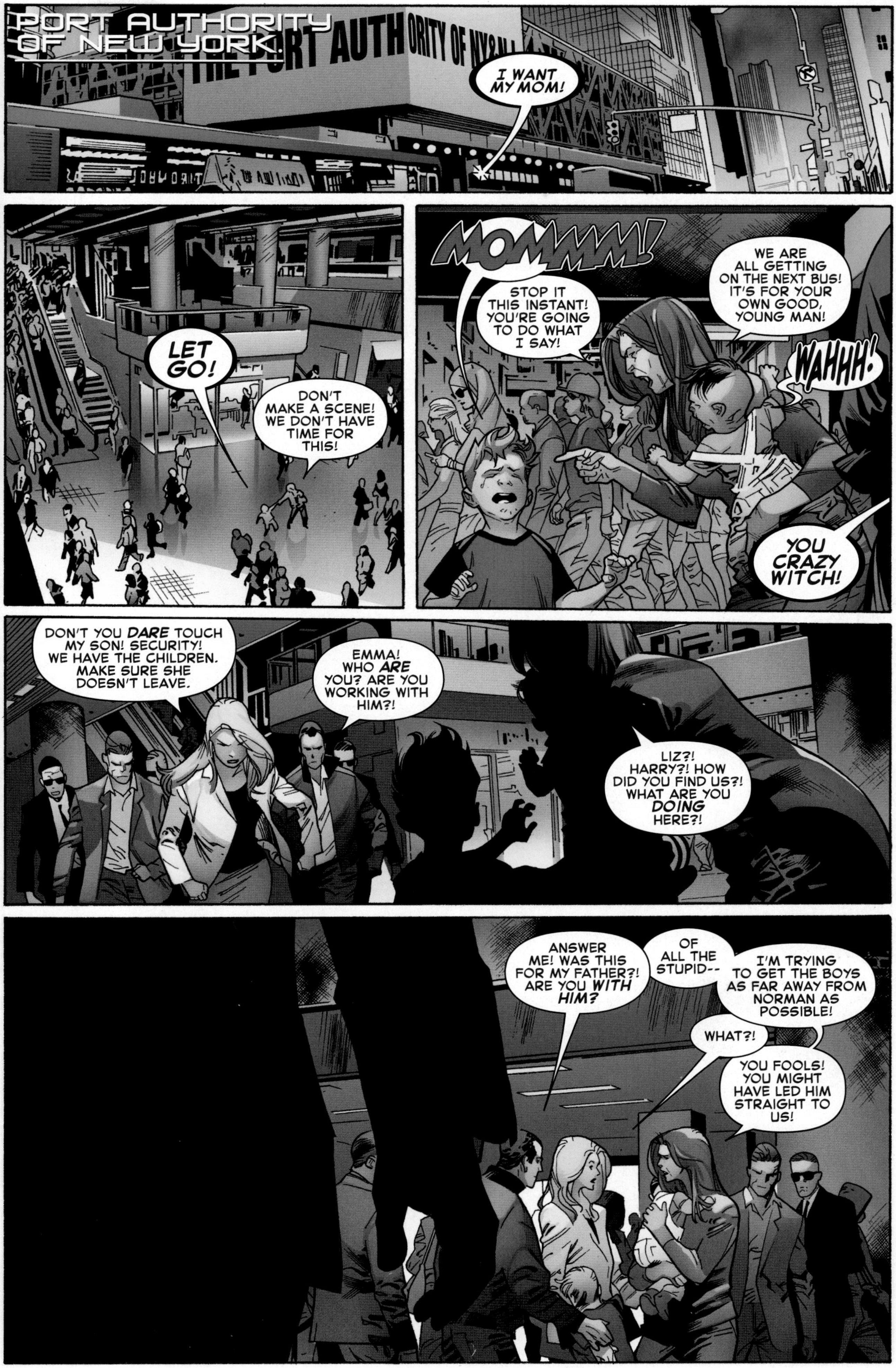
PORT AUTHORITY OF NEW YORK.
THE PORT AUTHORITY OF NY&NJ
I WANT MY MOM!
LET GO!
DON'T MAKE A SCENE! WE DON'T HAVE TIME FOR THIS!
MOMMM!
STOP IT THIS INSTANT! YOU'RE GOING TO DO WHAT I SAY!
WE ARE ALL GETTING ON THE NEXT BUS! IT'S FOR YOUR OWN GOOD, YOUNG MAN!
WAHHH!
YOU CRAZY WITCH!
DON'T YOU DARE TOUCH MY SON! SECURITY! WE HAVE THE CHILDREN. MAKE SURE SHE DOESN'T LEAVE.
EMMA! WHO ARE YOU? ARE YOU WORKING WITH HIM?!
LIZ?! HARRY?! HOW DID YOU FIND US?! WHAT ARE YOU DOING HERE?!
ANSWER ME! WAS THIS FOR MY FATHER?! ARE YOU WITH HIM?
OF ALL THE STUPID--
I'M TRYING TO GET THE BOYS AS FAR AWAY FROM NORMAN AS POSSIBLE!
WHAT?!
YOU FOOLS! YOU MIGHT HAVE LED HIM STRAIGHT TO US!

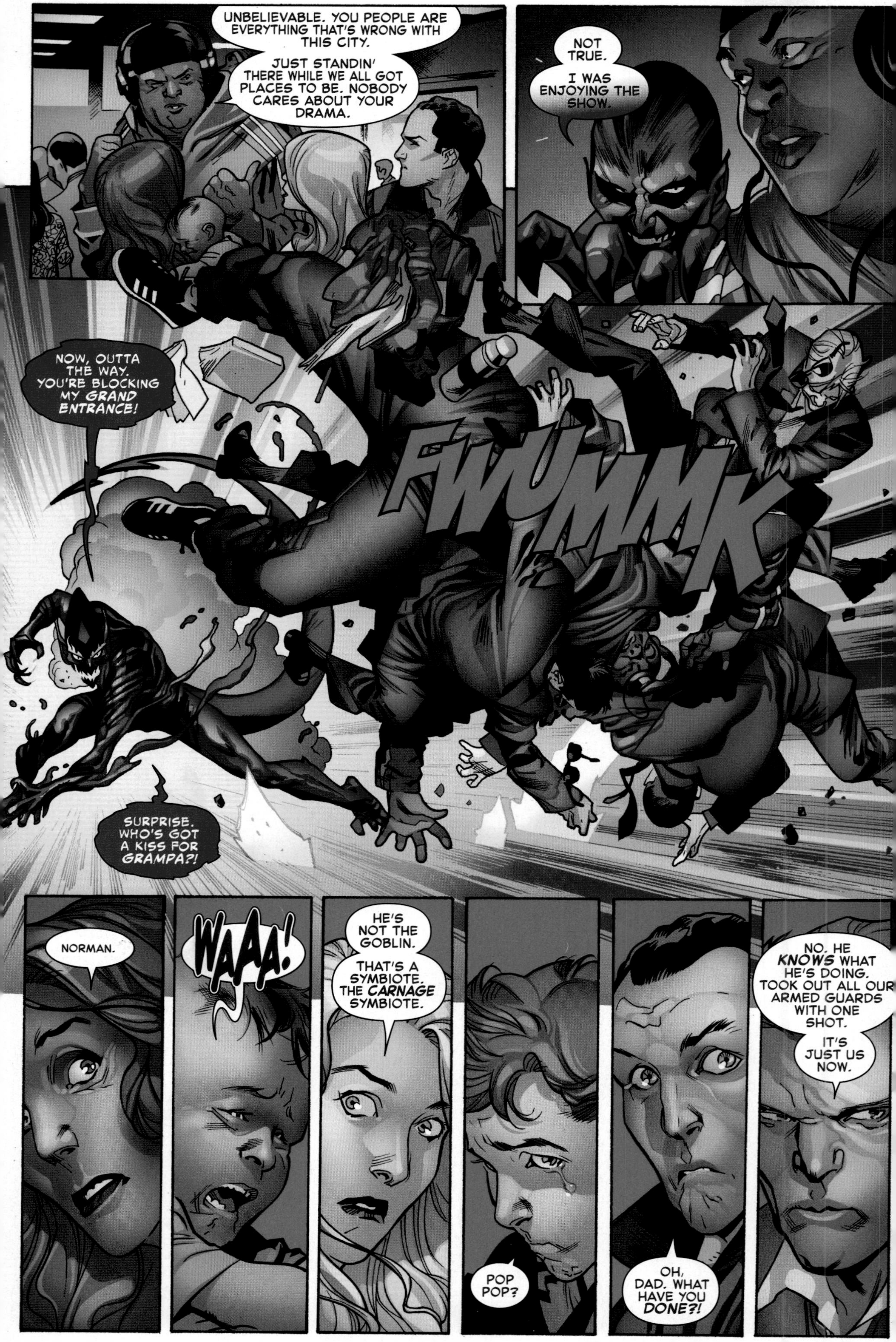
UNBELIEVABLE. YOU PEOPLE ARE EVERYTHING THAT'S WRONG WITH THIS CITY.
JUST STANDIN' THERE WHILE WE ALL GOT PLACES TO BE. NOBODY CARES ABOUT YOUR DRAMA.
NOT TRUE.
I WAS ENJOYING THE SHOW.
NOW, OUTTA THE WAY. YOU'RE BLOCKING MY GRAND ENTRANCE!
FWUMMK
SURPRISE. WHO'S GOT A KISS FOR GRAMPA?!
NORMAN.
WAAA!
HE'S NOT THE GOBLIN.
THAT'S A SYMBIOTE. THE CARNAGE SYMBIOTE.
POP POP?
OH, DAD. WHAT HAVE YOU DONE?!
NO. HE KNOWS WHAT HE'S DOING. TOOK OUT ALL OUR ARMED GUARDS WITH ONE SHOT.
IT'S JUST US NOW.

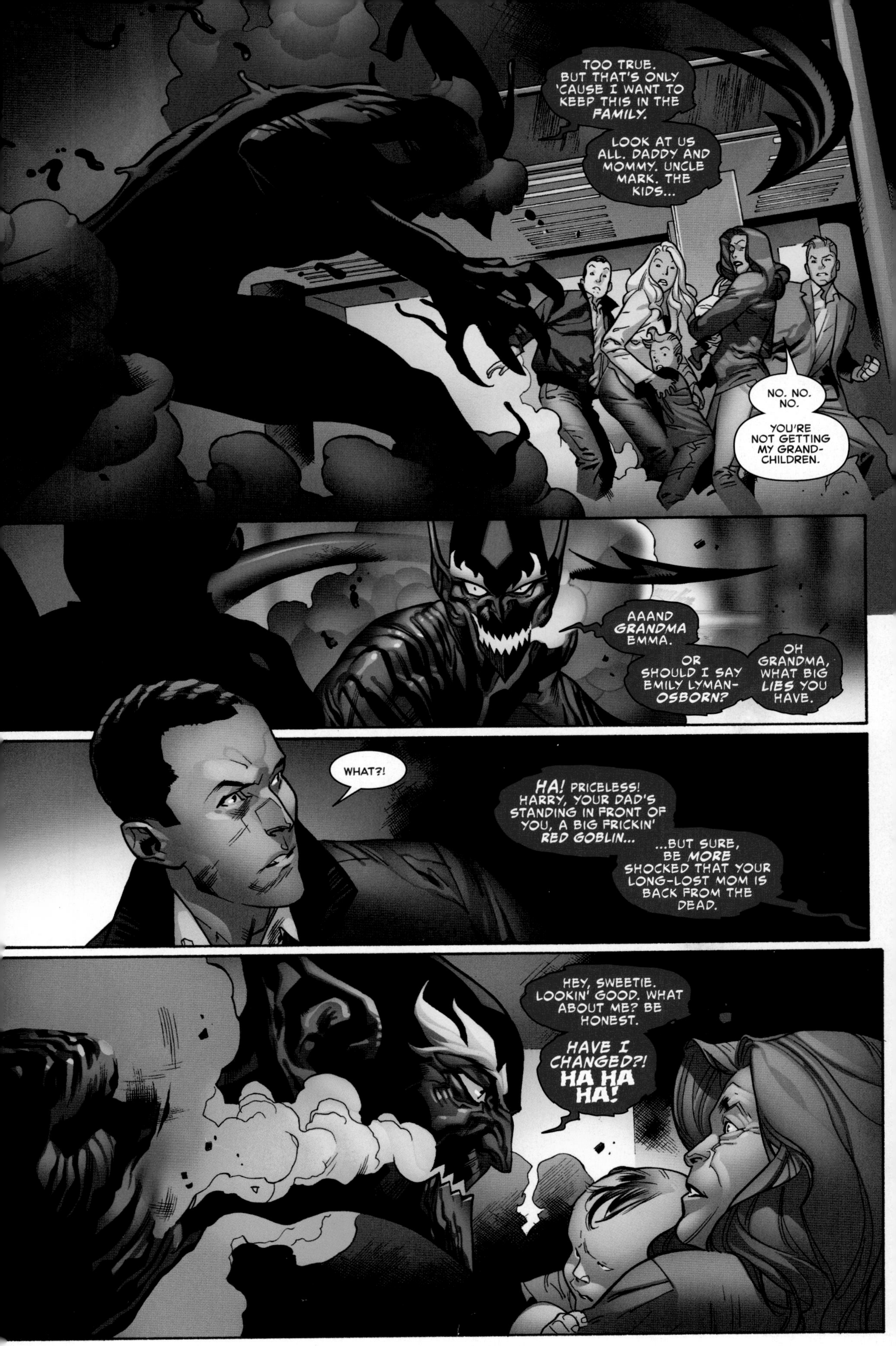
TOO TRUE. BUT THAT'S ONLY 'CAUSE I WANT TO KEEP THIS IN THE FAMILY.
LOOK AT US ALL. DADDY AND MOMMY. UNCLE MARK. THE KIDS...
NO. NO. NO.
YOU'RE NOT GETTING MY GRAND-CHILDREN.
AAAND GRANDMA EMMA.
OR SHOULD I SAY EMILY LYMAN-OSBORN?
OH GRANDMA, WHAT BIG LIES YOU HAVE.
WHAT?!
HA! PRICELESS! HARRY, YOUR DAD'S STANDING IN FRONT OF YOU, A BIG FRICKIN' RED GOBLIN...
...BUT SURE, BE MORE SHOCKED THAT YOUR LONG-LOST MOM IS BACK FROM THE DEAD.
HEY, SWEETIE. LOOKIN' GOOD. WHAT ABOUT ME? BE HONEST.
HAVE I CHANGED?! HA HA HA!

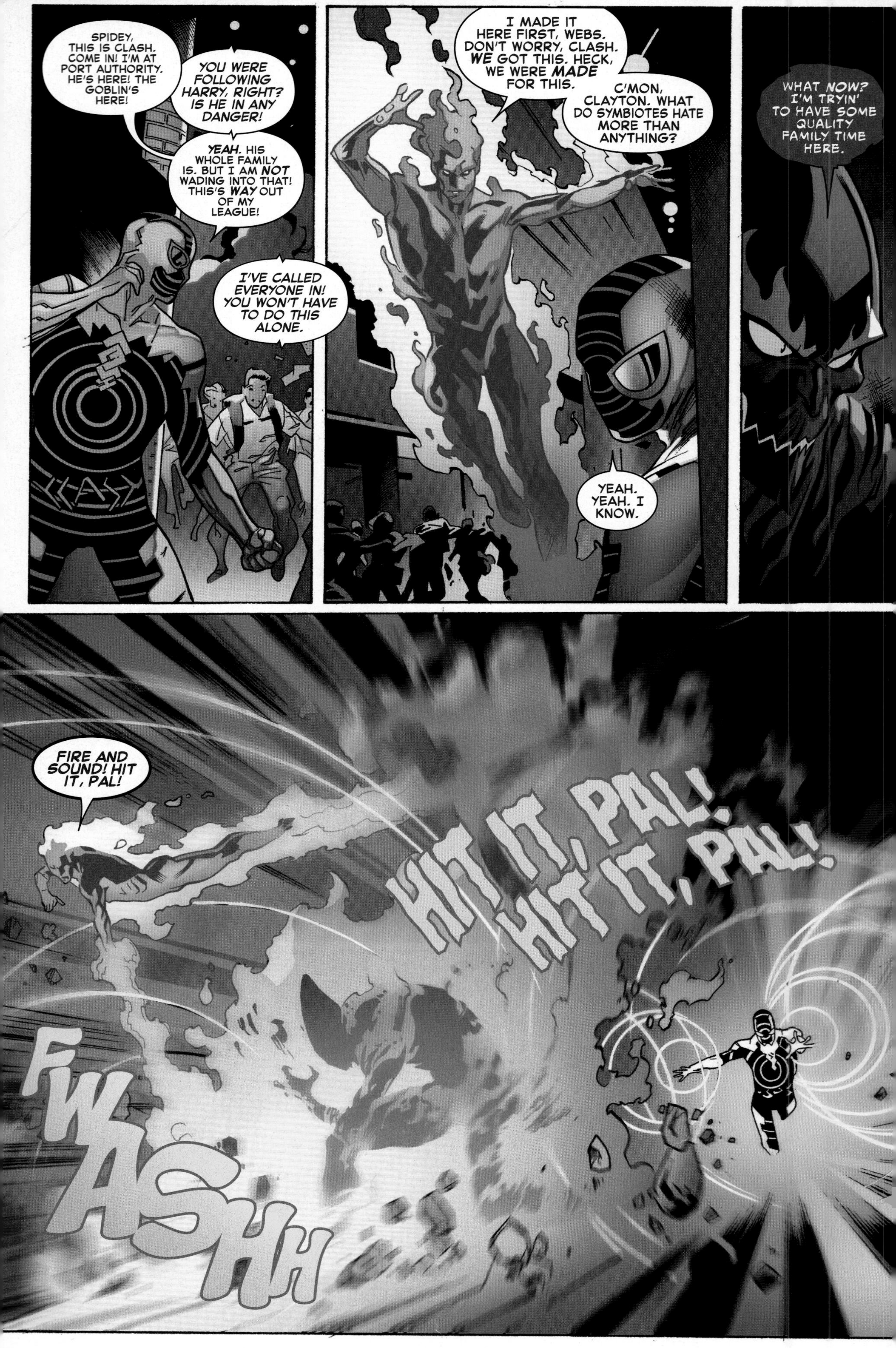
SPIDEY, THIS IS CLASH. COME IN! I'M AT PORT AUTHORITY. HE'S HERE! THE GOBLIN'S HERE!
YOU WERE FOLLOWING HARRY, RIGHT? IS HE IN ANY DANGER!
YEAH. HIS WHOLE FAMILY IS. BUT I AM NOT WADING INTO THAT! THIS'S WAY OUT OF MY LEAGUE!
I'VE CALLED EVERYONE IN! YOU WON'T HAVE TO DO THIS ALONE.
I MADE IT HERE FIRST, WEBS. DON'T WORRY, CLASH. WE GOT THIS. HECK, WE WERE MADE FOR THIS.
C'MON, CLAYTON. WHAT DO SYMBIOTES HATE MORE THAN ANYTHING?
YEAH. YEAH. I KNOW.
WHAT NOW? I'M TRYIN' TO HAVE SOME QUALITY FAMILY TIME HERE.
FIRE AND SOUND! HIT IT, PAL!
HIT IT, PAL!
HIT IT, PAL!
FWASHH

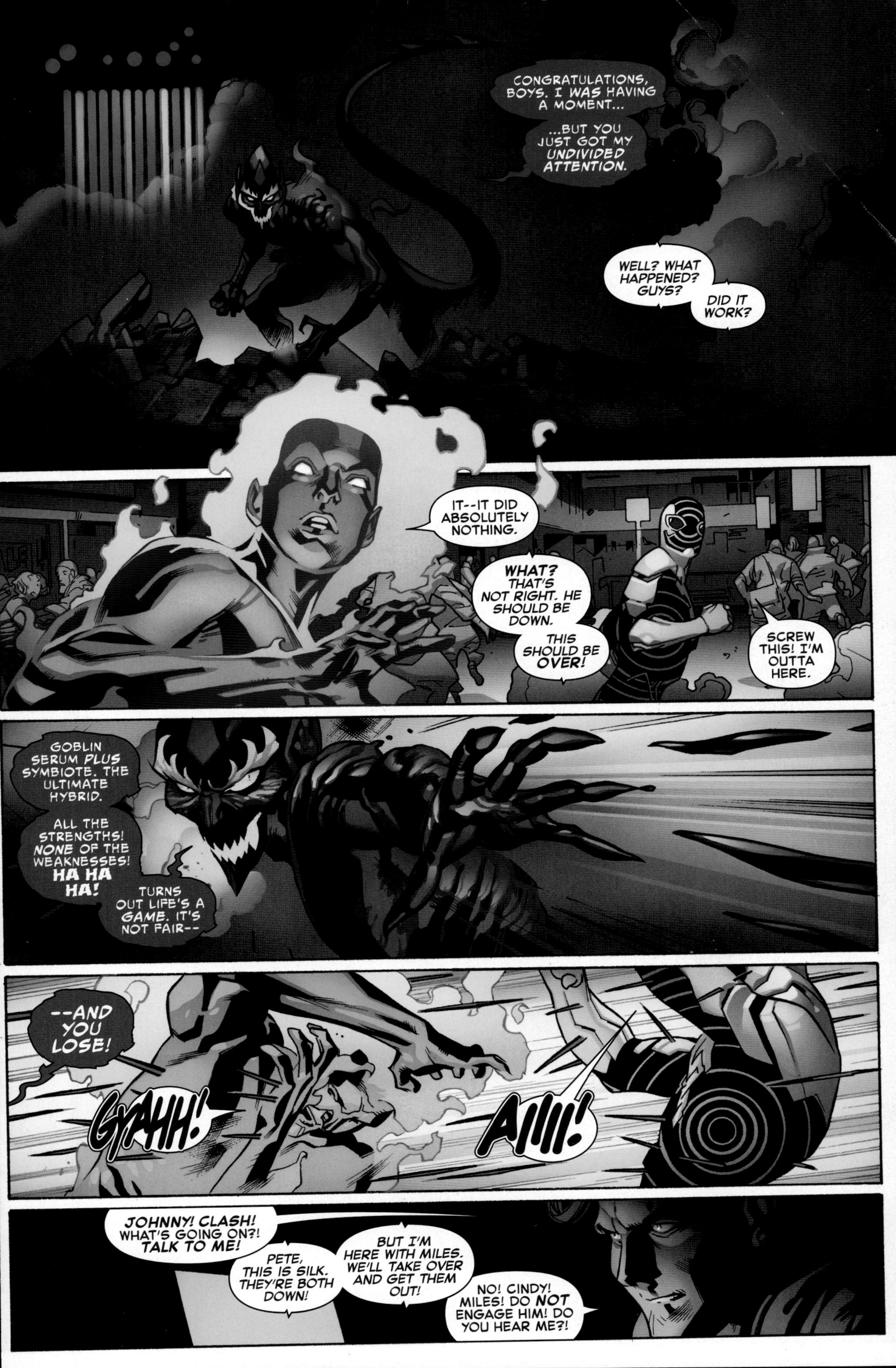
CONGRATULATIONS, BOYS. I WAS HAVING A MOMENT...
...BUT YOU JUST GOT MY UNDIVIDED ATTENTION.
WELL? WHAT HAPPENED? GUYS?
DID IT WORK?
IT--IT DID ABSOLUTELY NOTHING.
WHAT? THAT'S NOT RIGHT. HE SHOULD BE DOWN.
THIS SHOULD BE OVER!
SCREW THIS! I'M OUTTA HERE.
GOBLIN SERUM PLUS SYMBIOTE. THE ULTIMATE HYBRID.
ALL THE STRENGTHS! NONE OF THE WEAKNESSES! HA HA HA!
TURNS OUT LIFE'S A GAME. IT'S NOT FAIR--
--AND YOU LOSE!
GYAHH!
AIIII!
JOHNNY! CLASH! WHAT'S GOING ON?! TALK TO ME!
PETE, THIS IS SILK. THEY'RE BOTH DOWN!
BUT I'M HERE WITH MILES. WE'LL TAKE OVER AND GET THEM OUT!
NO! CINDY! MILES! DO NOT ENGAGE HIM! DO YOU HEAR ME?!

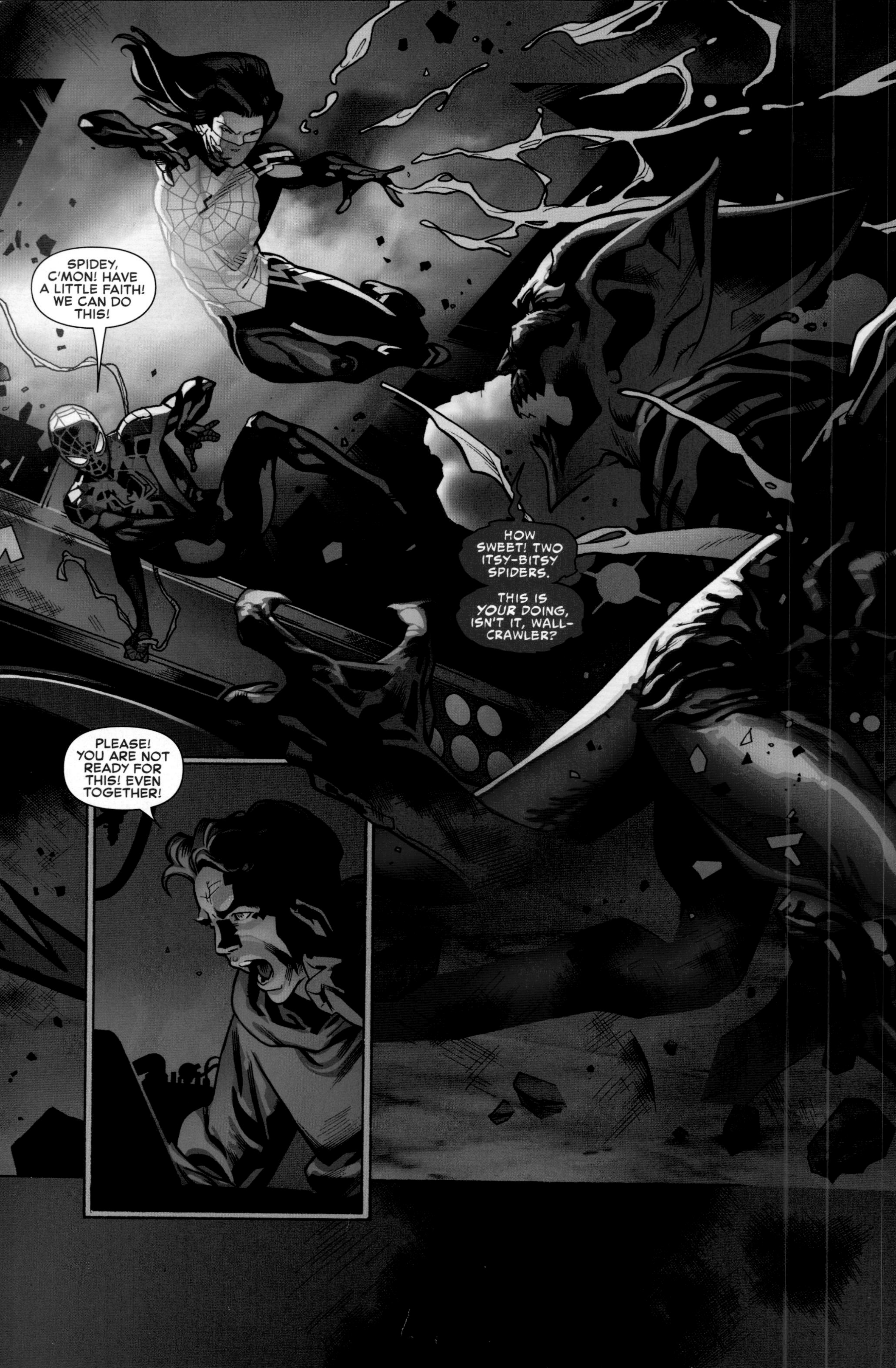
SPIDEY, C'MON! HAVE A LITTLE FAITH! WE CAN DO THIS!
HOW SWEET! TWO ITSY-BITSY SPIDERS.
THIS IS *YOUR* DOING, ISN'T IT, WALL-CRAWLER?
PLEASE! YOU ARE NOT READY FOR THIS! EVEN TOGETHER!

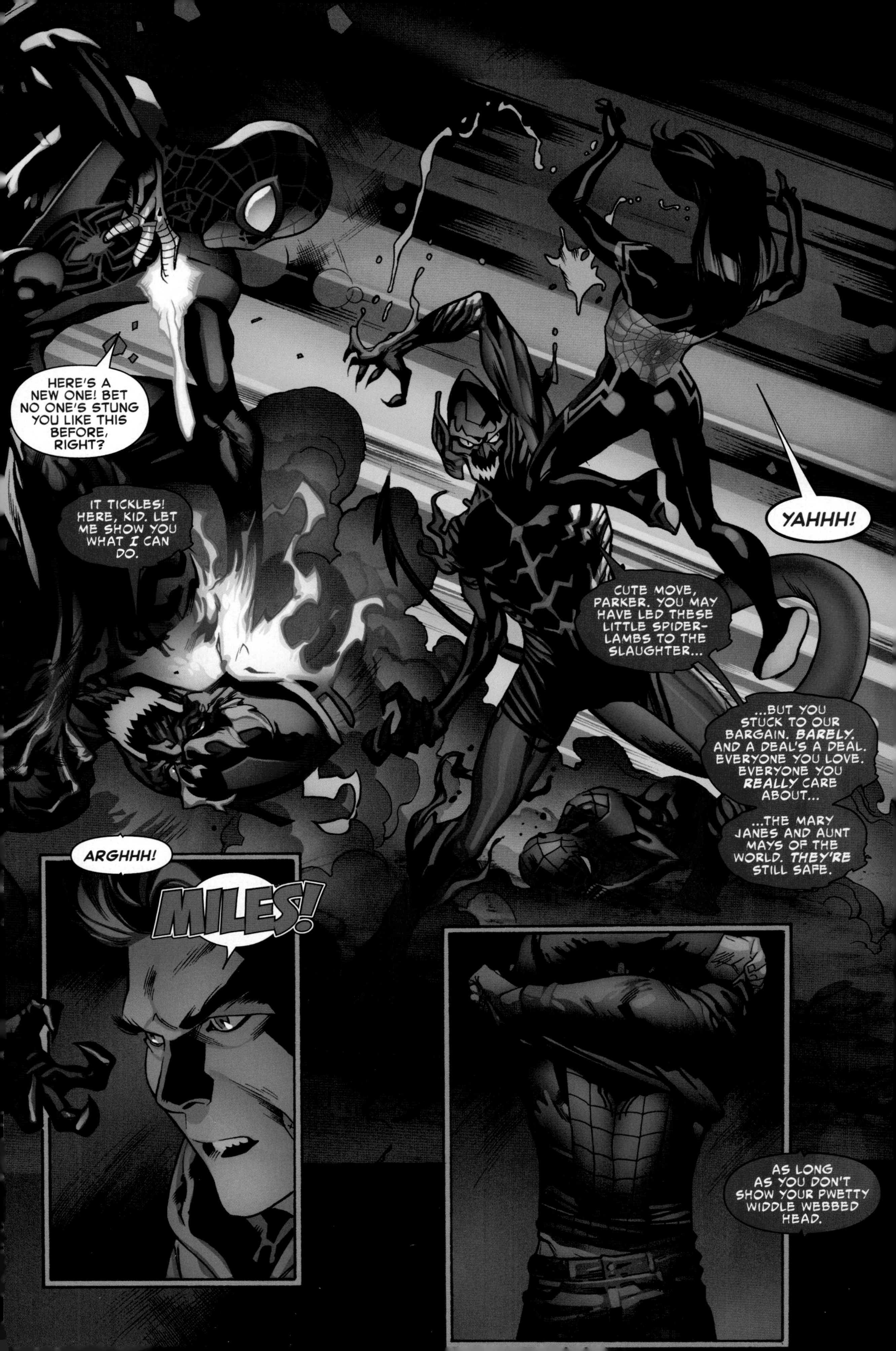
HERE'S A NEW ONE! BET NO ONE'S STUNG YOU LIKE THIS BEFORE, RIGHT?
IT TICKLES! HERE, KID. LET ME SHOW YOU WHAT I CAN DO.
YAHHH!
CUTE MOVE, PARKER. YOU MAY HAVE LED THESE LITTLE SPIDER-LAMBS TO THE SLAUGHTER...
...BUT YOU STUCK TO OUR BARGAIN. BARELY. AND A DEAL'S A DEAL. EVERYONE YOU LOVE. EVERYONE YOU REALLY CARE ABOUT...
...THE MARY JANES AND AUNT MAYS OF THE WORLD. THEY'RE STILL SAFE.
ARGHHH!
MILES!
AS LONG AS YOU DON'T SHOW YOUR PWETTY WIDDLE WEBBED HEAD.

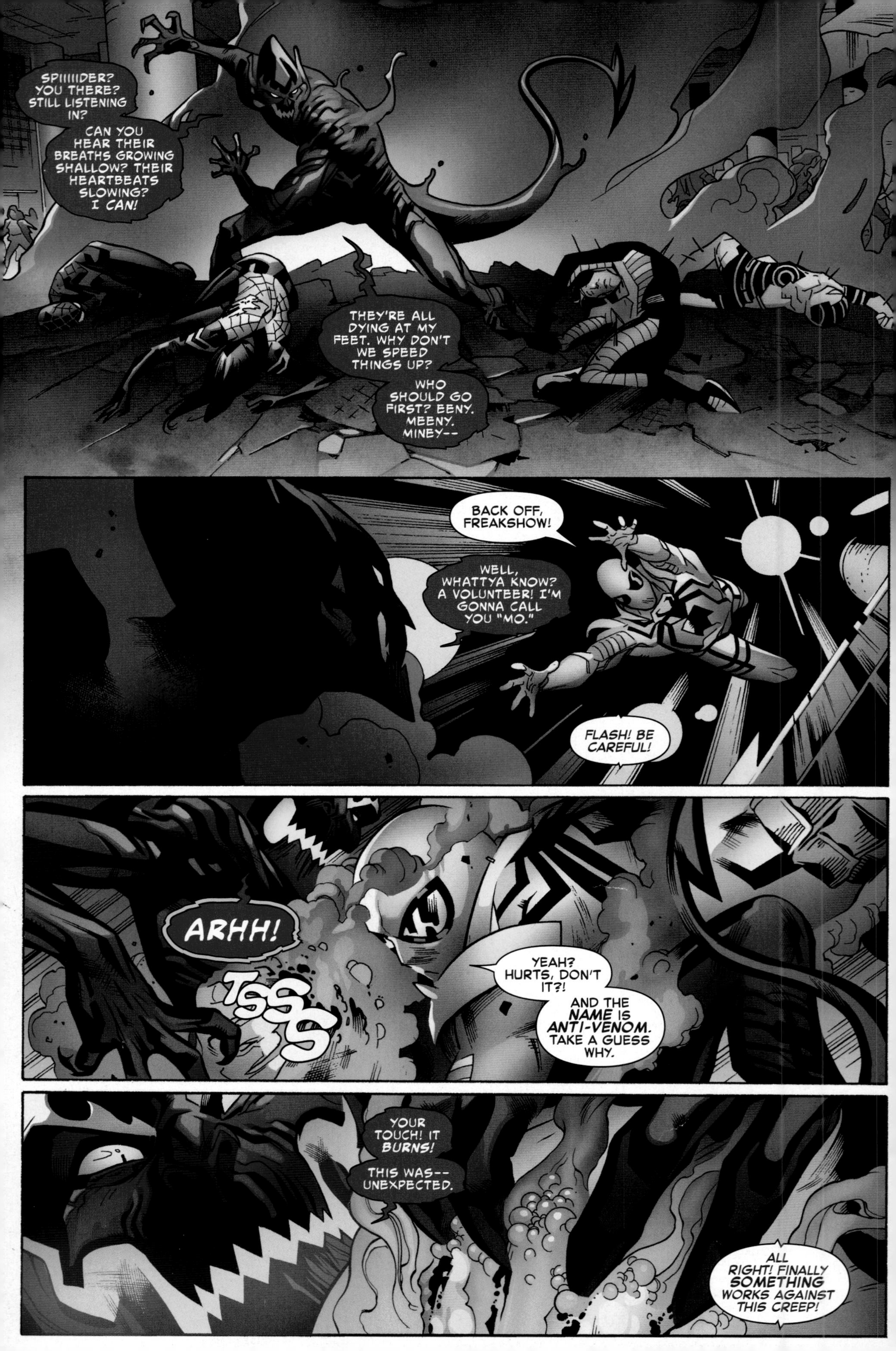
SPIIIIIDER? YOU THERE? STILL LISTENING IN?
CAN YOU HEAR THEIR BREATHS GROWING SHALLOW? THEIR HEARTBEATS SLOWING? I CAN!
THEY'RE ALL DYING AT MY FEET. WHY DON'T WE SPEED THINGS UP?
WHO SHOULD GO FIRST? EENY. MEENY. MINEY--
BACK OFF, FREAKSHOW!
WELL, WHATTYA KNOW? A VOLUNTEER! I'M GONNA CALL YOU "MO."
FLASH! BE CAREFUL!
ARHH!
TSSS
YEAH? HURTS, DON'T IT?!
AND THE NAME IS ANTI-VENOM. TAKE A GUESS WHY.
YOUR TOUCH! IT BURNS!
THIS WAS-- UNEXPECTED.
ALL RIGHT! FINALLY SOMETHING WORKS AGAINST THIS CREEP!

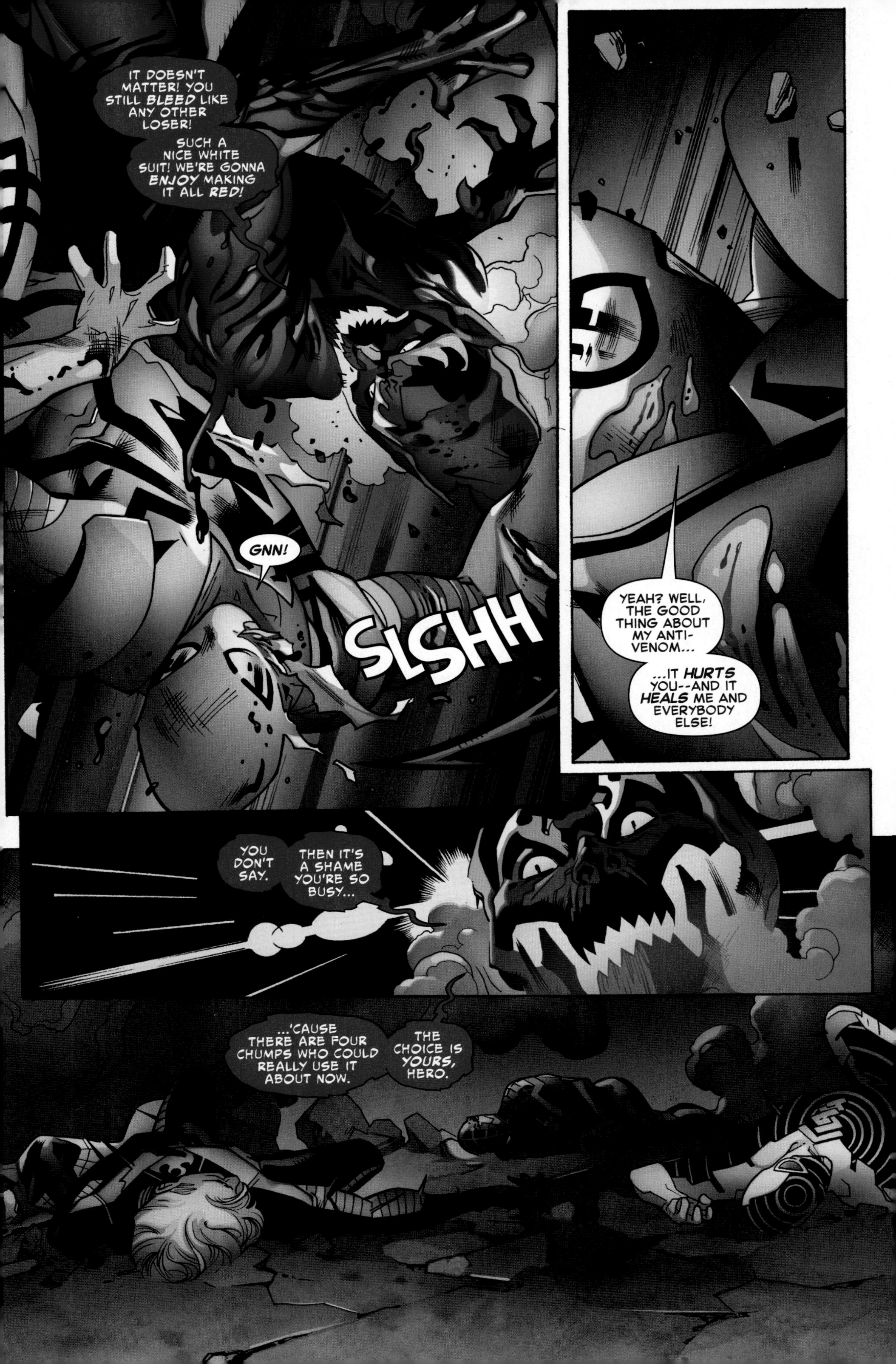
IT DOESN'T MATTER! YOU STILL BLEED LIKE ANY OTHER LOSER!
SUCH A NICE WHITE SUIT! WE'RE GONNA ENJOY MAKING IT ALL RED!
GNN!
SLSHH
YEAH? WELL, THE GOOD THING ABOUT MY ANTI-VENOM...
...IT HURTS YOU--AND IT HEALS ME AND EVERYBODY ELSE!
YOU DON'T SAY.
THEN IT'S A SHAME YOU'RE SO BUSY...
...'CAUSE THERE ARE FOUR CHUMPS WHO COULD REALLY USE IT ABOUT NOW.
THE CHOICE IS YOURS, HERO.

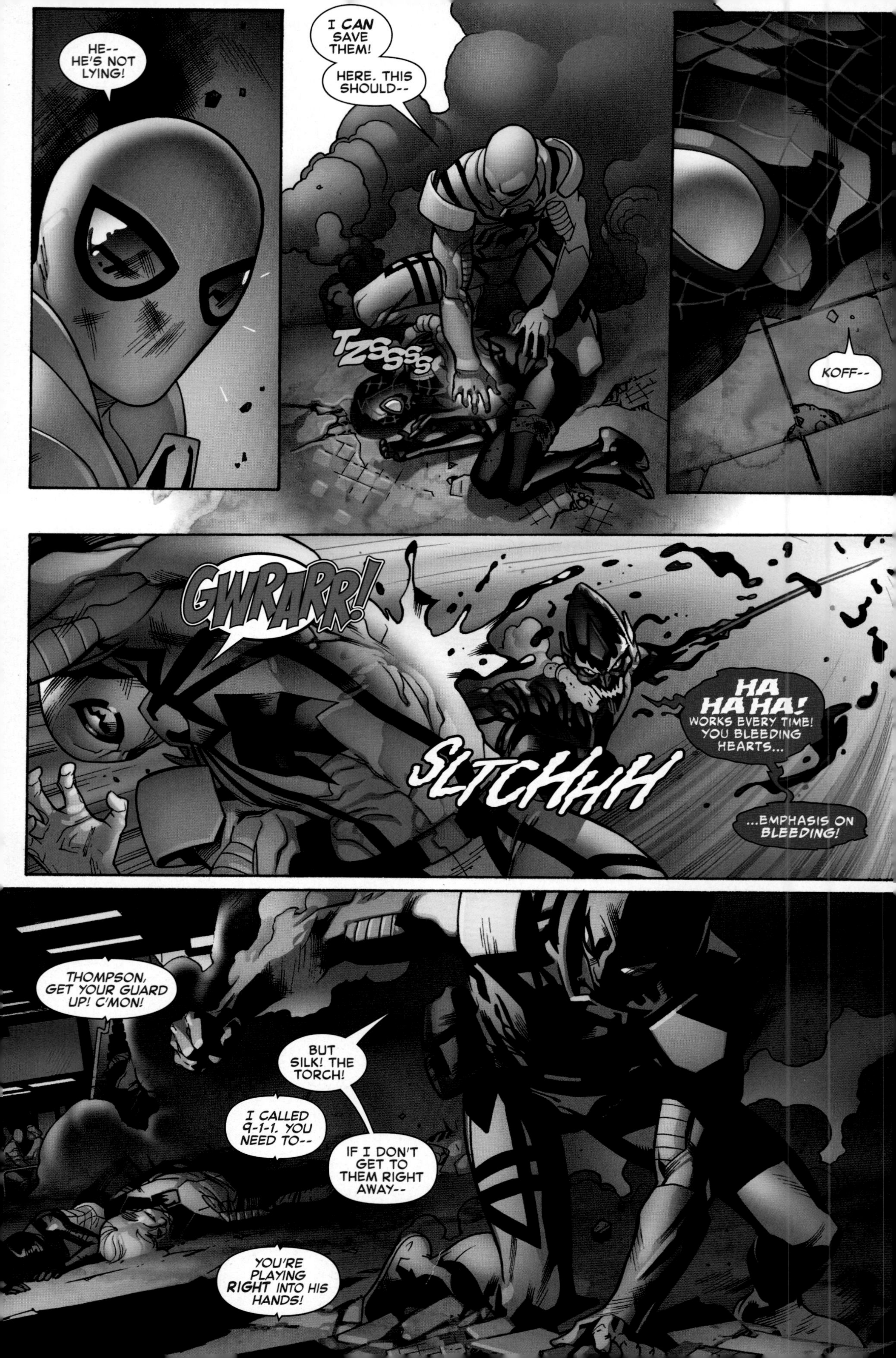
HE-- HE'S NOT LYING!
I CAN SAVE THEM!
HERE. THIS SHOULD--
TZSSSS
KOFF--
GWRARR!
SLTCHHH
HA HA HA! WORKS EVERY TIME! YOU BLEEDING HEARTS...
...EMPHASIS ON BLEEDING!
THOMPSON, GET YOUR GUARD UP! C'MON!
BUT SILK! THE TORCH!
I CALLED 9-1-1. YOU NEED TO--
IF I DON'T GET TO THEM RIGHT AWAY--
YOU'RE PLAYING RIGHT INTO HIS HANDS!

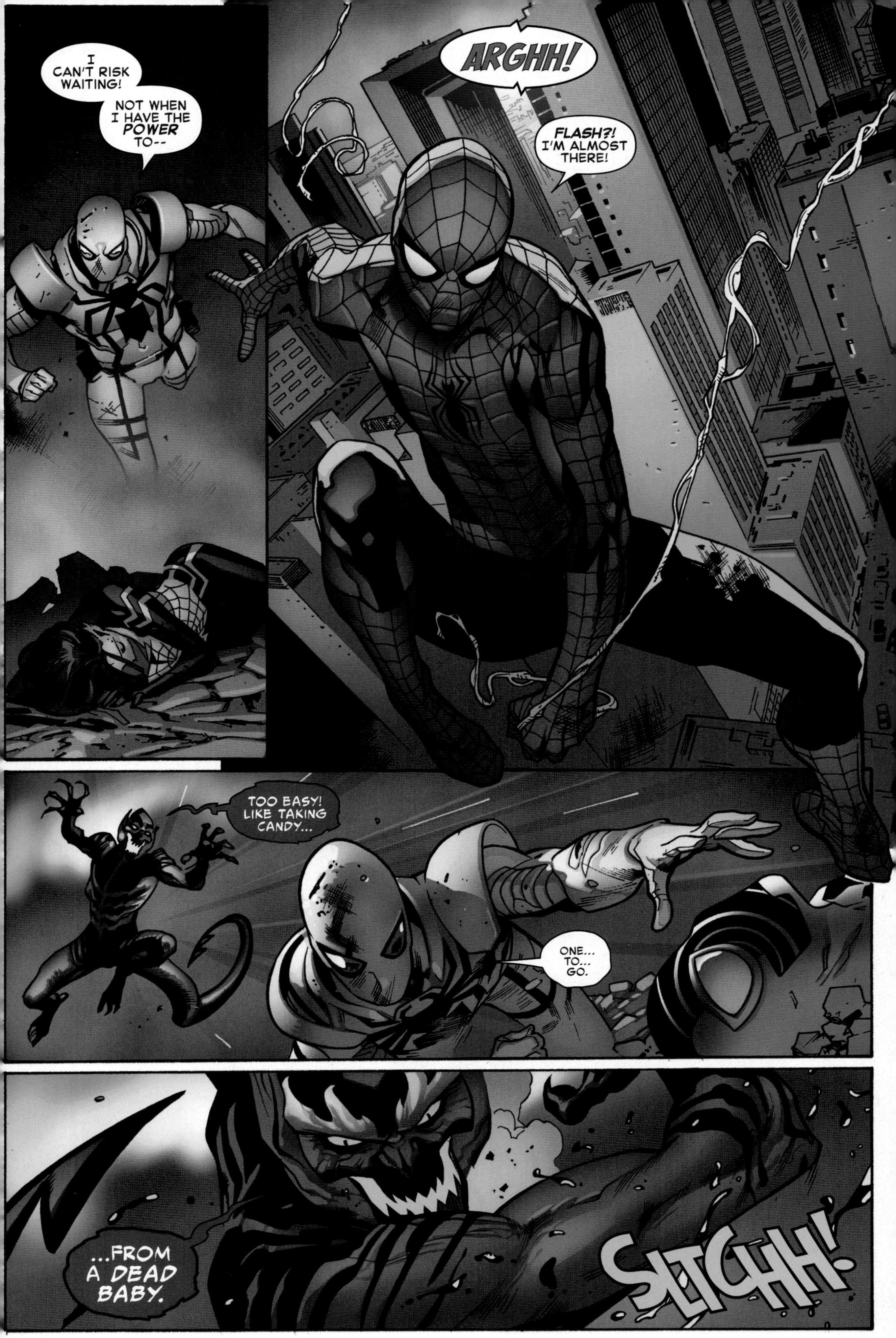
I CAN'T RISK WAITING!
NOT WHEN I HAVE THE *POWER* TO--
ARGHH!
FLASH?! I'M ALMOST THERE!
TOO EASY! LIKE TAKING CANDY...
ONE... TO... GO.
...FROM A *DEAD* BABY.
SLTCHH!

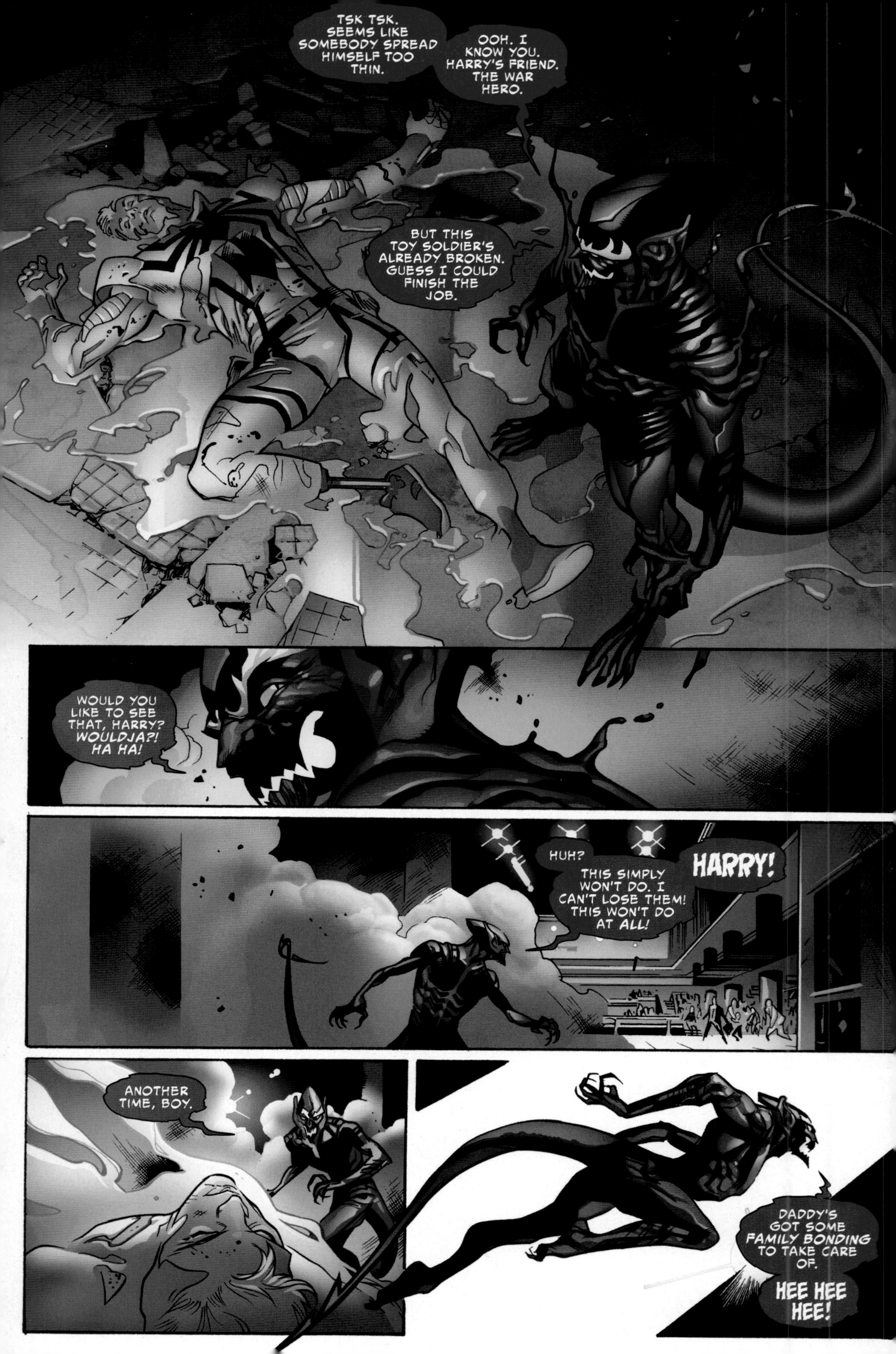
TSK TSK. SEEMS LIKE SOMEBODY SPREAD HIMSELF TOO THIN.
OOH. I KNOW YOU. HARRY'S FRIEND. THE WAR HERO.
BUT THIS TOY SOLDIER'S ALREADY BROKEN. GUESS I COULD FINISH THE JOB.
WOULD YOU LIKE TO SEE THAT, HARRY? WOULDJA?! HA HA!
HUH?
THIS SIMPLY WON'T DO. I CAN'T LOSE THEM! THIS WON'T DO AT ALL!
HARRY!
ANOTHER TIME, BOY.
DADDY'S GOT SOME FAMILY BONDING TO TAKE CARE OF.
HEE HEE HEE!

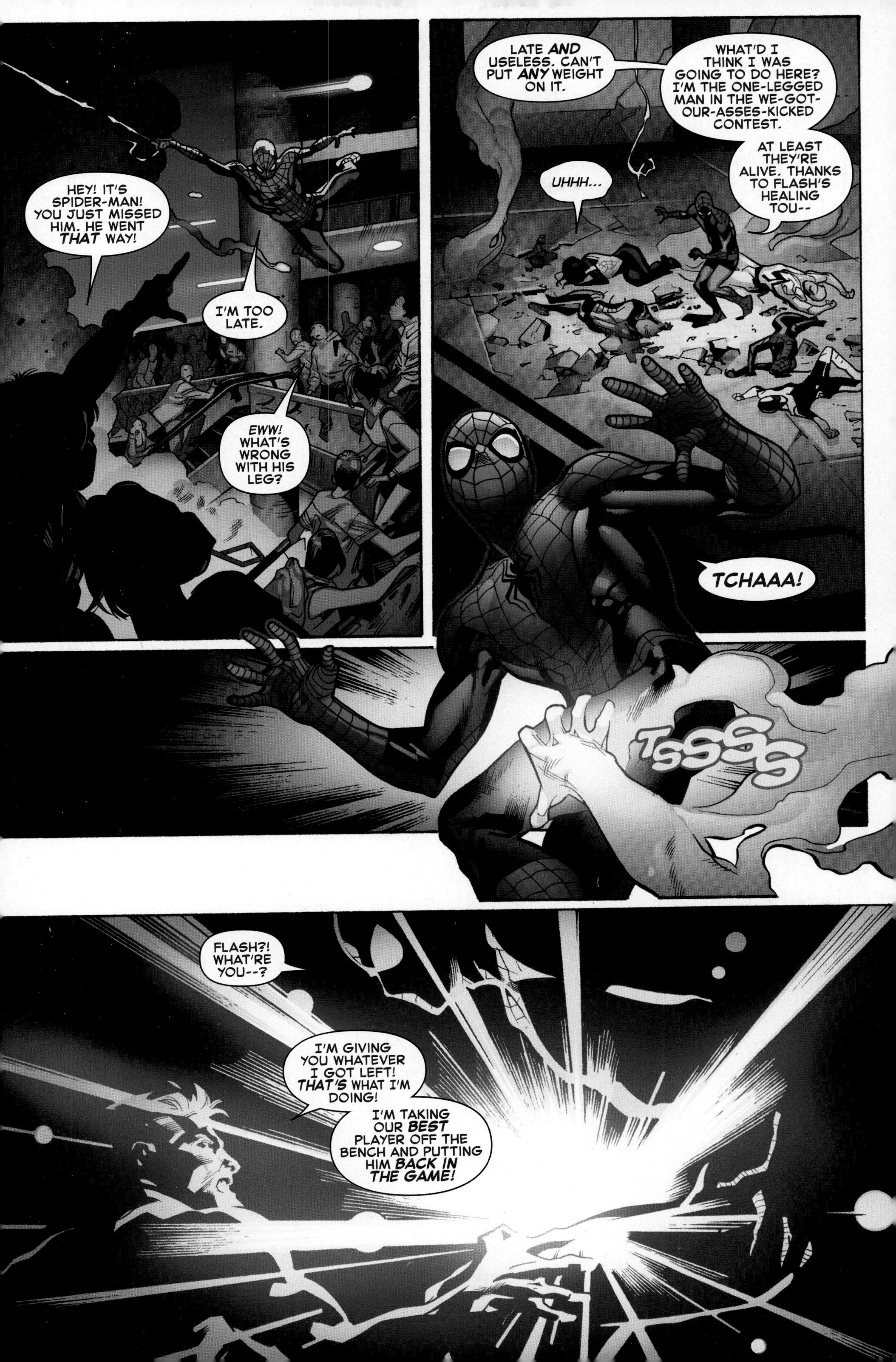
HEY! IT'S SPIDER-MAN! YOU JUST MISSED HIM. HE WENT THAT WAY!
I'M TOO LATE.
EWW! WHAT'S WRONG WITH HIS LEG?
LATE AND USELESS. CAN'T PUT ANY WEIGHT ON IT.
WHAT'D I THINK I WAS GOING TO DO HERE? I'M THE ONE-LEGGED MAN IN THE WE-GOT-OUR-ASSES-KICKED CONTEST.
UHHH...
AT LEAST THEY'RE ALIVE. THANKS TO FLASH'S HEALING TOU--
TCHAAA!
TSSSS
FLASH?! WHAT'RE YOU--?
I'M GIVING YOU WHATEVER I GOT LEFT! THAT'S WHAT I'M DOING!
I'M TAKING OUR BEST PLAYER OFF THE BENCH AND PUTTING HIM BACK IN THE GAME!

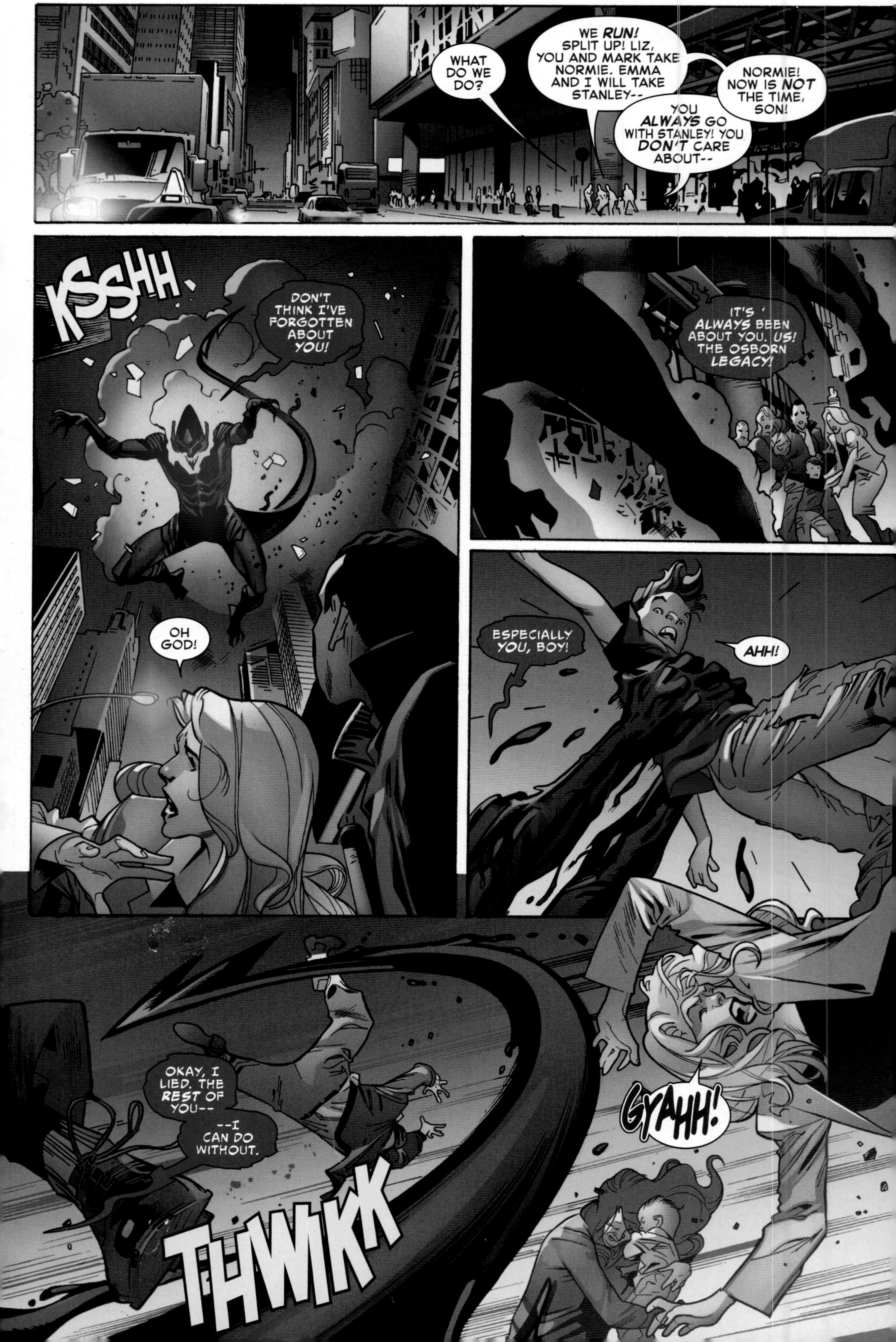

WHAT DO WE DO?
WE RUN! SPLIT UP! LIZ, YOU AND MARK TAKE NORMIE. EMMA AND I WILL TAKE STANLEY--
YOU ALWAYS GO WITH STANLEY! YOU DON'T CARE ABOUT--
NORMIE! NOW IS NOT THE TIME, SON!
KSSHH
DON'T THINK I'VE FORGOTTEN ABOUT YOU!
OH GOD!
IT'S ALWAYS BEEN ABOUT YOU. US! THE OSBORN LEGACY!
ESPECIALLY YOU, BOY!
AHH!
OKAY, I LIED. THE REST OF YOU--
--I CAN DO WITHOUT.
GYAHH!
THWKK

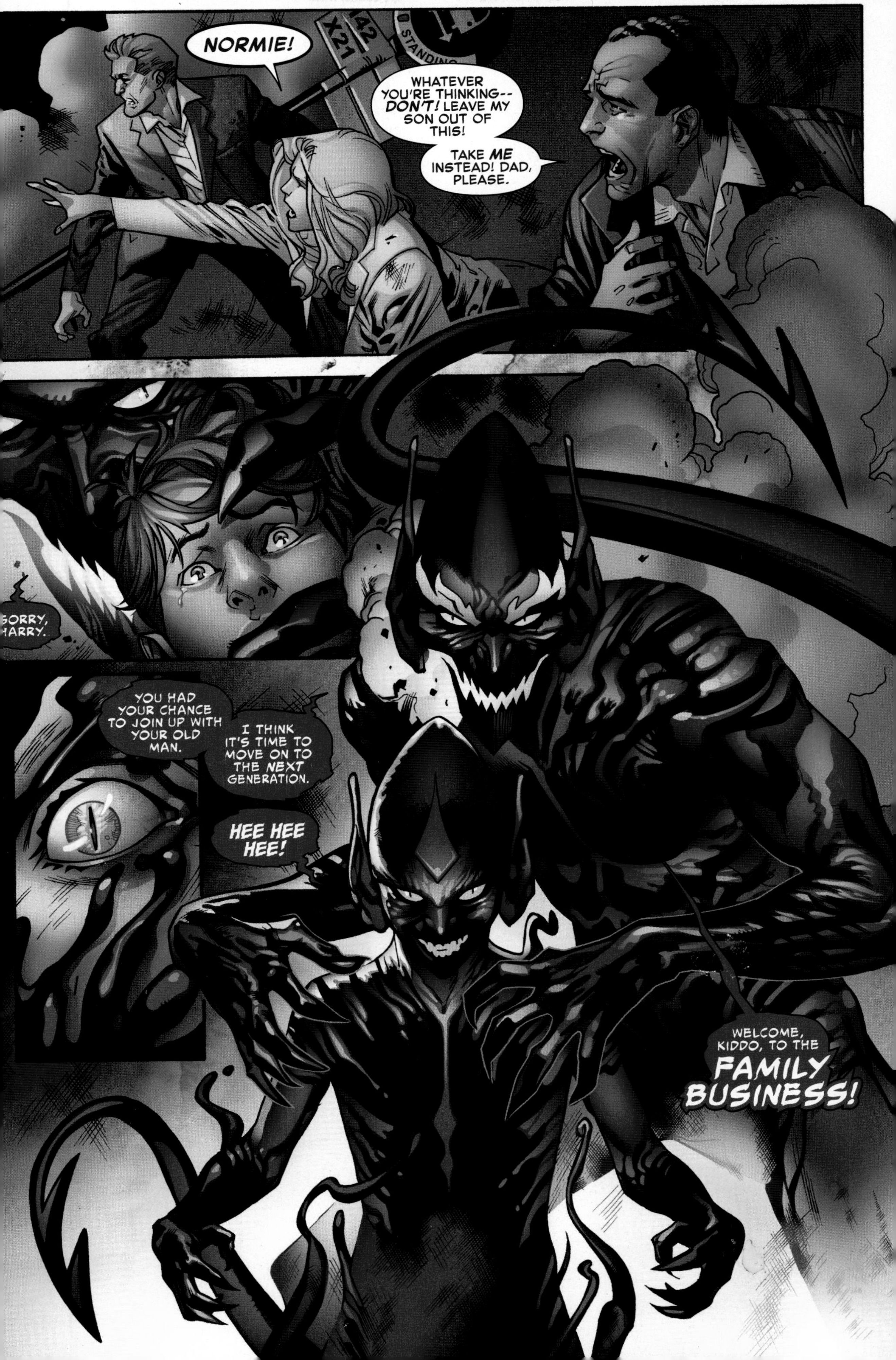
NORMIE!
WHATEVER YOU'RE THINKING-- DON'T! LEAVE MY SON OUT OF THIS!
TAKE ME INSTEAD! DAD, PLEASE.
SORRY, HARRY.
YOU HAD YOUR CHANCE TO JOIN UP WITH YOUR OLD MAN.
I THINK IT'S TIME TO MOVE ON TO THE NEXT GENERATION.
HEE HEE HEE!
WELCOME, KIDDO, TO THE FAMILY BUSINESS!

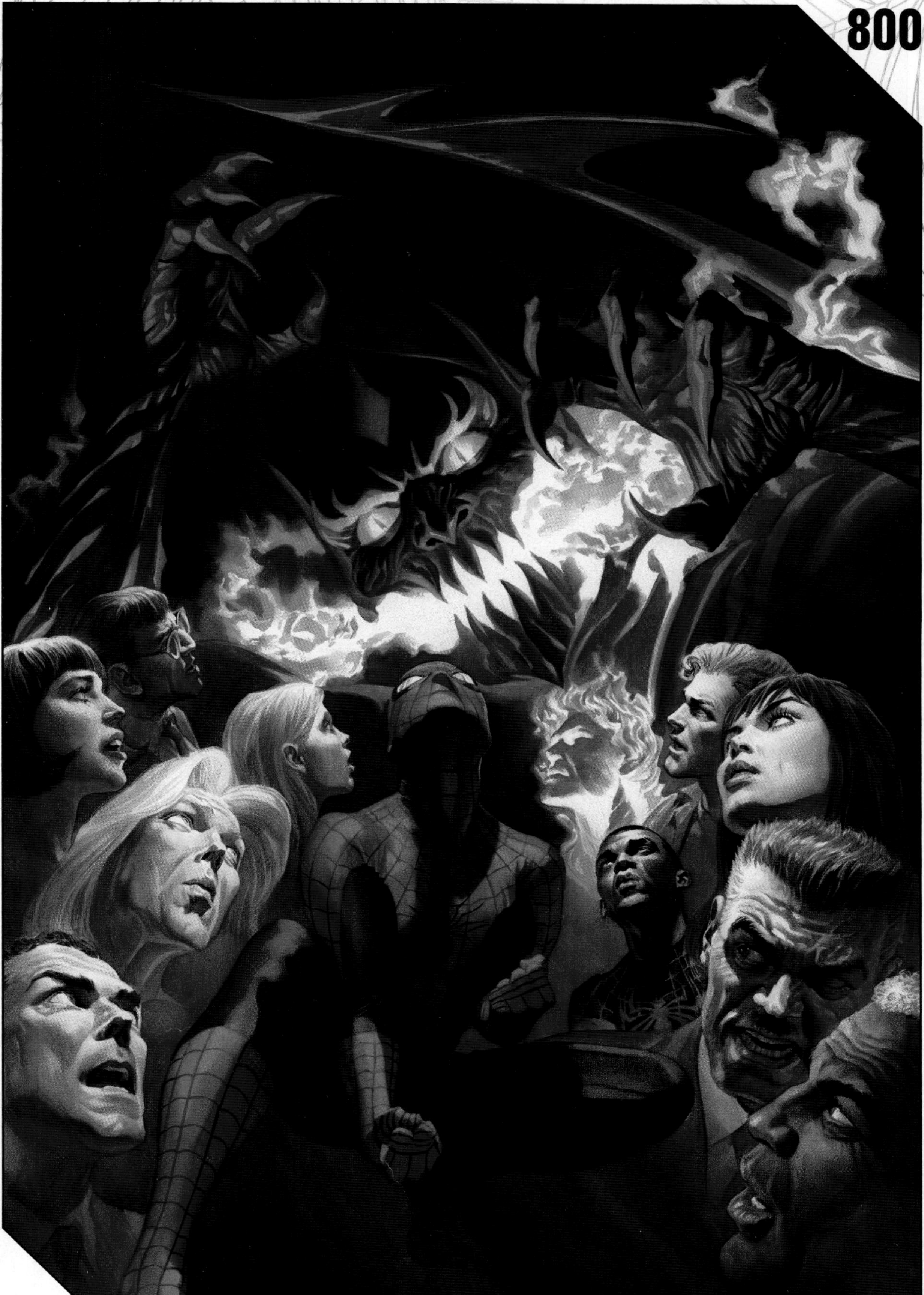
800

GO DOWN SWINGING CONCLUSION

Chapter 1
Crawling Through the Wreckage

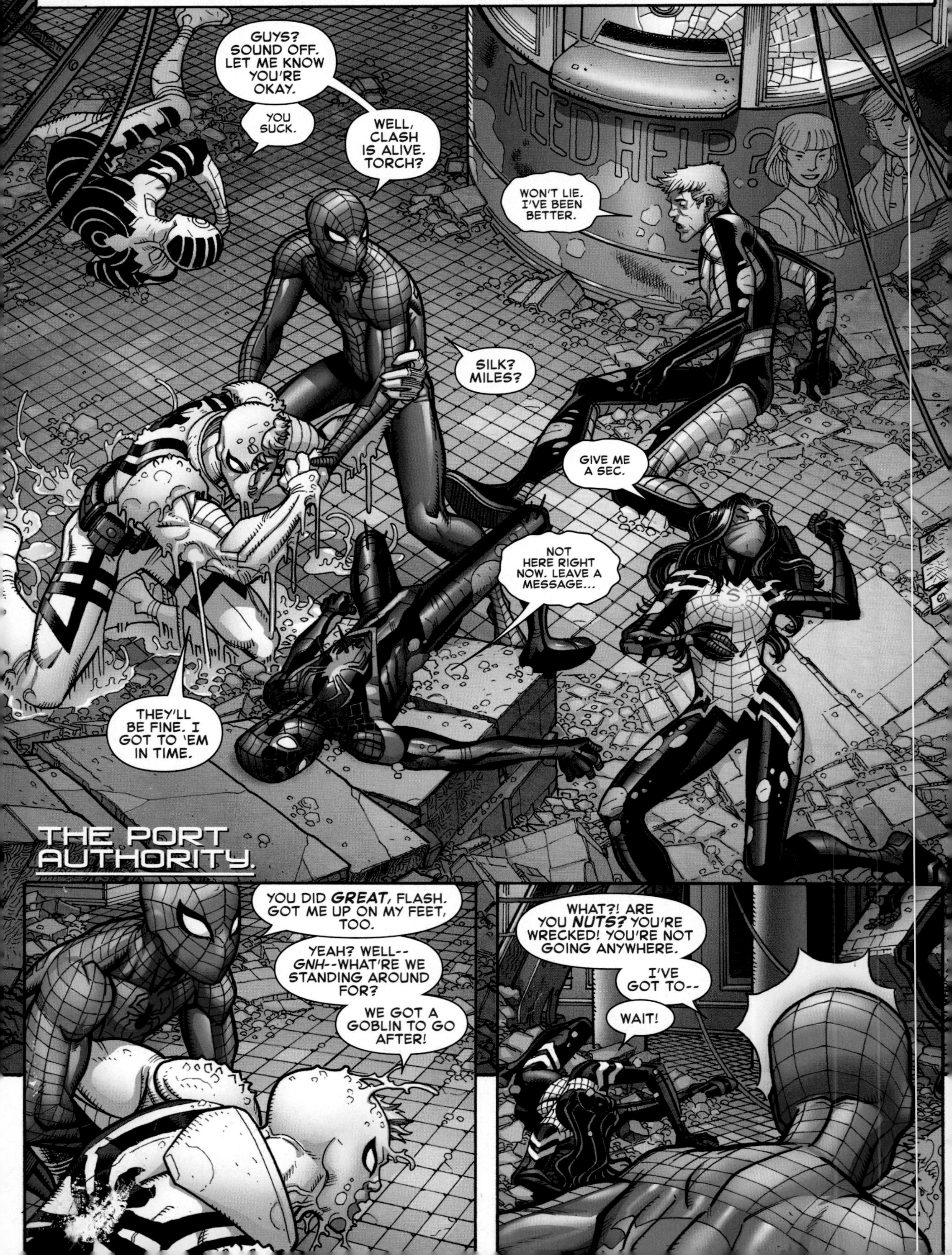
GUYS? SOUND OFF. LET ME KNOW YOU'RE OKAY.
YOU SUCK.
WELL, CLASH IS ALIVE. TORCH?
WON'T LIE. I'VE BEEN BETTER.
SILK? MILES?
GIVE ME A SEC.
NOT HERE RIGHT NOW. LEAVE A MESSAGE...
THEY'LL BE FINE. I GOT TO 'EM IN TIME.
THE PORT AUTHORITY.
YOU DID *GREAT,* FLASH. GOT ME UP ON MY FEET, TOO.
YEAH? WELL-- *GNH*--WHAT'RE WE STANDING AROUND FOR?
WE GOT A GOBLIN TO GO AFTER!
WHAT?! ARE YOU *NUTS?* YOU'RE WRECKED! YOU'RE NOT GOING ANYWHERE.
I'VE GOT TO--
WAIT!

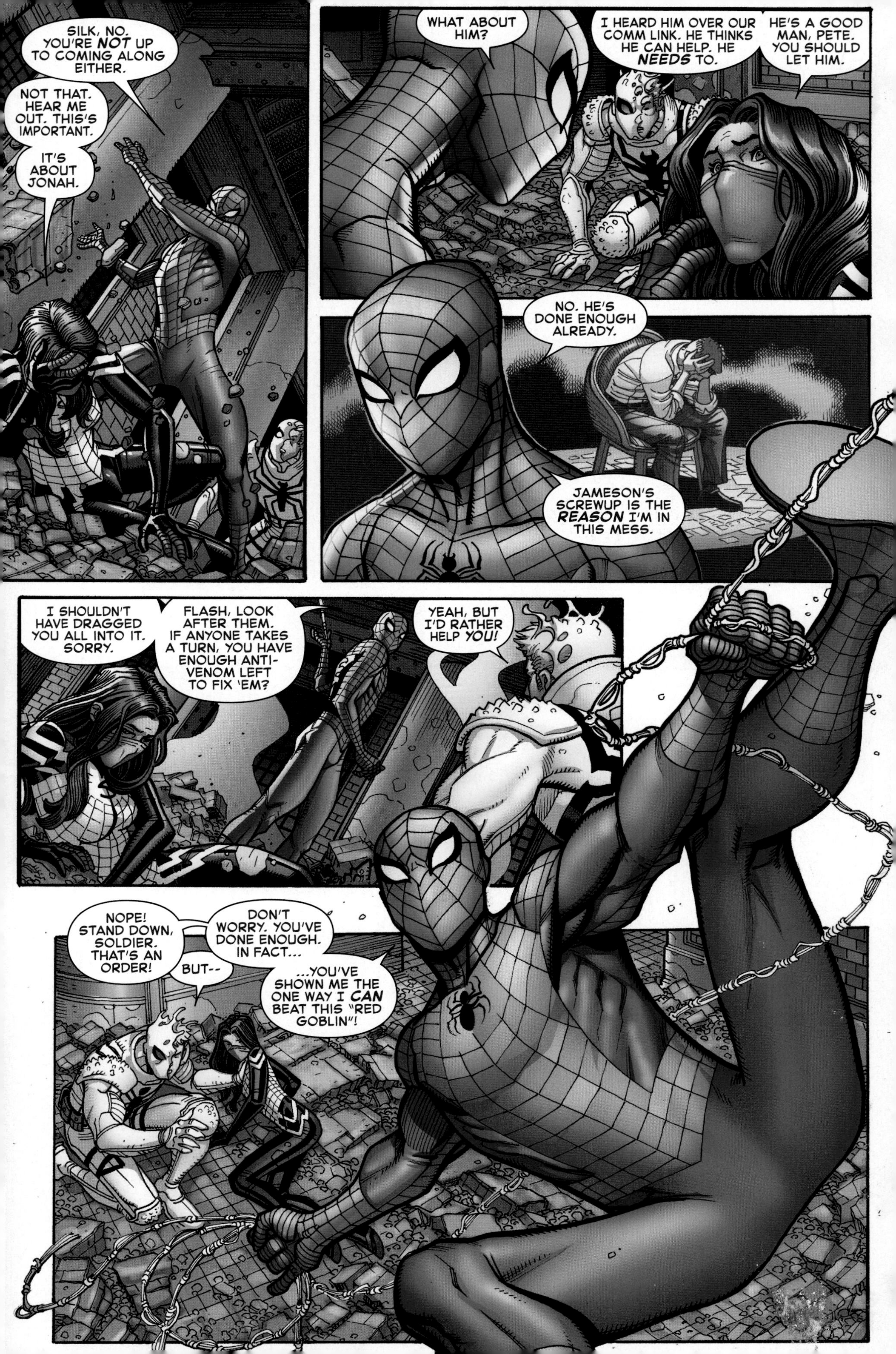
SILK, NO. YOU'RE *NOT* UP TO COMING ALONG EITHER.
NOT THAT. HEAR ME OUT. THIS'S IMPORTANT.
IT'S ABOUT JONAH.
WHAT ABOUT HIM?
I HEARD HIM OVER OUR COMM LINK. HE THINKS HE CAN HELP. HE *NEEDS* TO.
HE'S A GOOD MAN, PETE. YOU SHOULD LET HIM.
NO. HE'S DONE ENOUGH ALREADY.
JAMESON'S SCREWUP IS THE *REASON* I'M IN THIS MESS.
I SHOULDN'T HAVE DRAGGED YOU ALL INTO IT. SORRY.
FLASH, LOOK AFTER THEM. IF ANYONE TAKES A TURN, YOU HAVE ENOUGH ANTI-VENOM LEFT TO FIX 'EM?
YEAH, BUT I'D RATHER HELP *YOU*!
NOPE! STAND DOWN, SOLDIER. THAT'S AN ORDER!
BUT--
DON'T WORRY. YOU'VE DONE ENOUGH. IN FACT...
...YOU'VE SHOWN ME THE ONE WAY I *CAN* BEAT THIS "RED GOBLIN"!

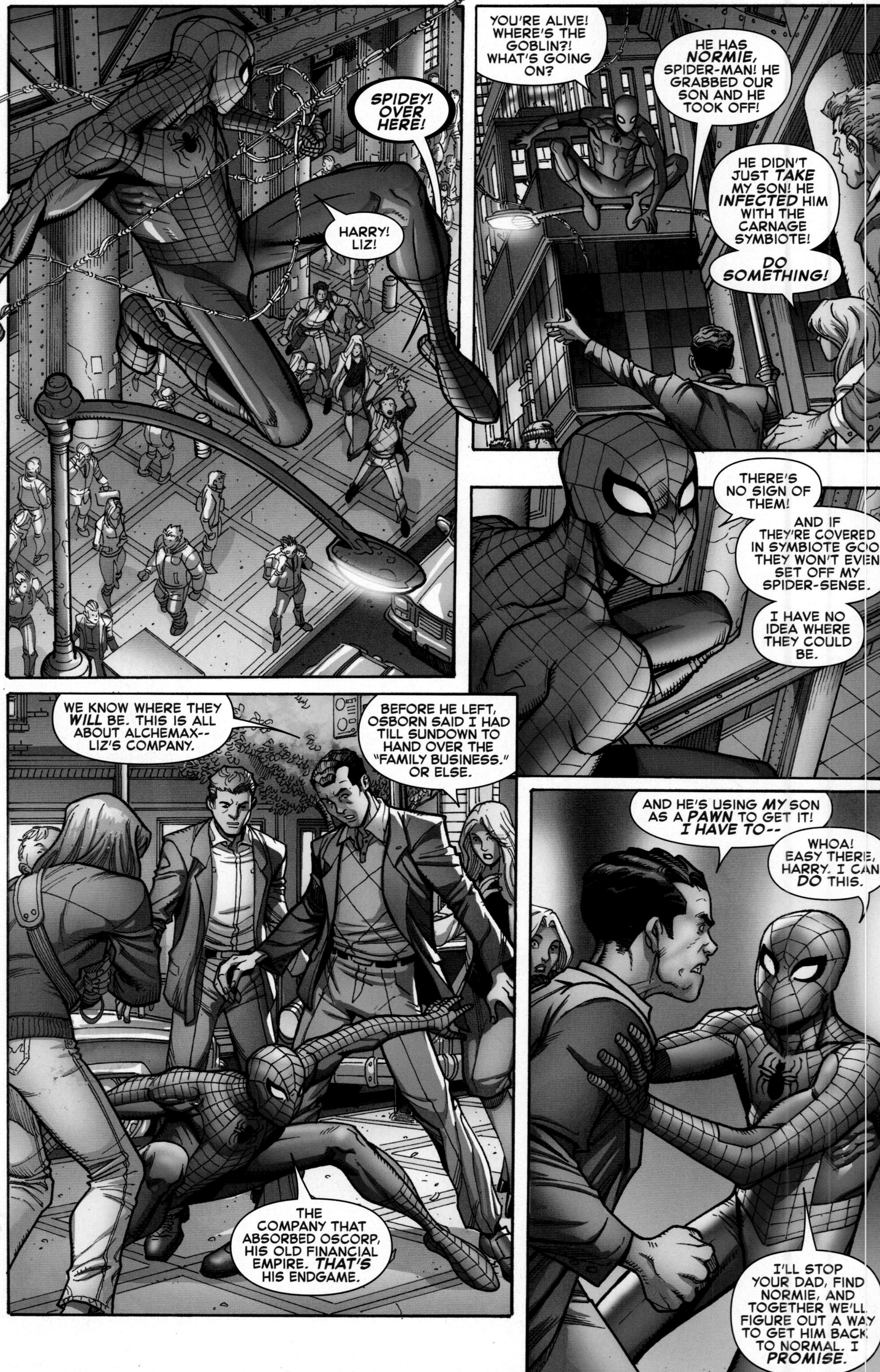
SPIDEY! OVER HERE!
HARRY! LIZ!
YOU'RE ALIVE! WHERE'S THE GOBLIN?! WHAT'S GOING ON?
HE HAS NORMIE, SPIDER-MAN! HE GRABBED OUR SON AND HE TOOK OFF!
HE DIDN'T JUST TAKE MY SON! HE INFECTED HIM WITH THE CARNAGE SYMBIOTE!
DO SOMETHING!
THERE'S NO SIGN OF THEM!
AND IF THEY'RE COVERED IN SYMBIOTE GOO, THEY WON'T EVEN SET OFF MY SPIDER-SENSE.
I HAVE NO IDEA WHERE THEY COULD BE.
WE KNOW WHERE THEY WILL BE. THIS IS ALL ABOUT ALCHEMAX-- LIZ'S COMPANY.
BEFORE HE LEFT, OSBORN SAID I HAD TILL SUNDOWN TO HAND OVER THE "FAMILY BUSINESS." OR ELSE.
THE COMPANY THAT ABSORBED OSCORP, HIS OLD FINANCIAL EMPIRE. THAT'S HIS ENDGAME.
AND HE'S USING MY SON AS A PAWN TO GET IT! I HAVE TO--
WHOA! EASY THERE, HARRY. I CAN DO THIS.
I'LL STOP YOUR DAD, FIND NORMIE, AND TOGETHER WE'LL FIGURE OUT A WAY TO GET HIM BACK TO NORMAL. I PROMISE.

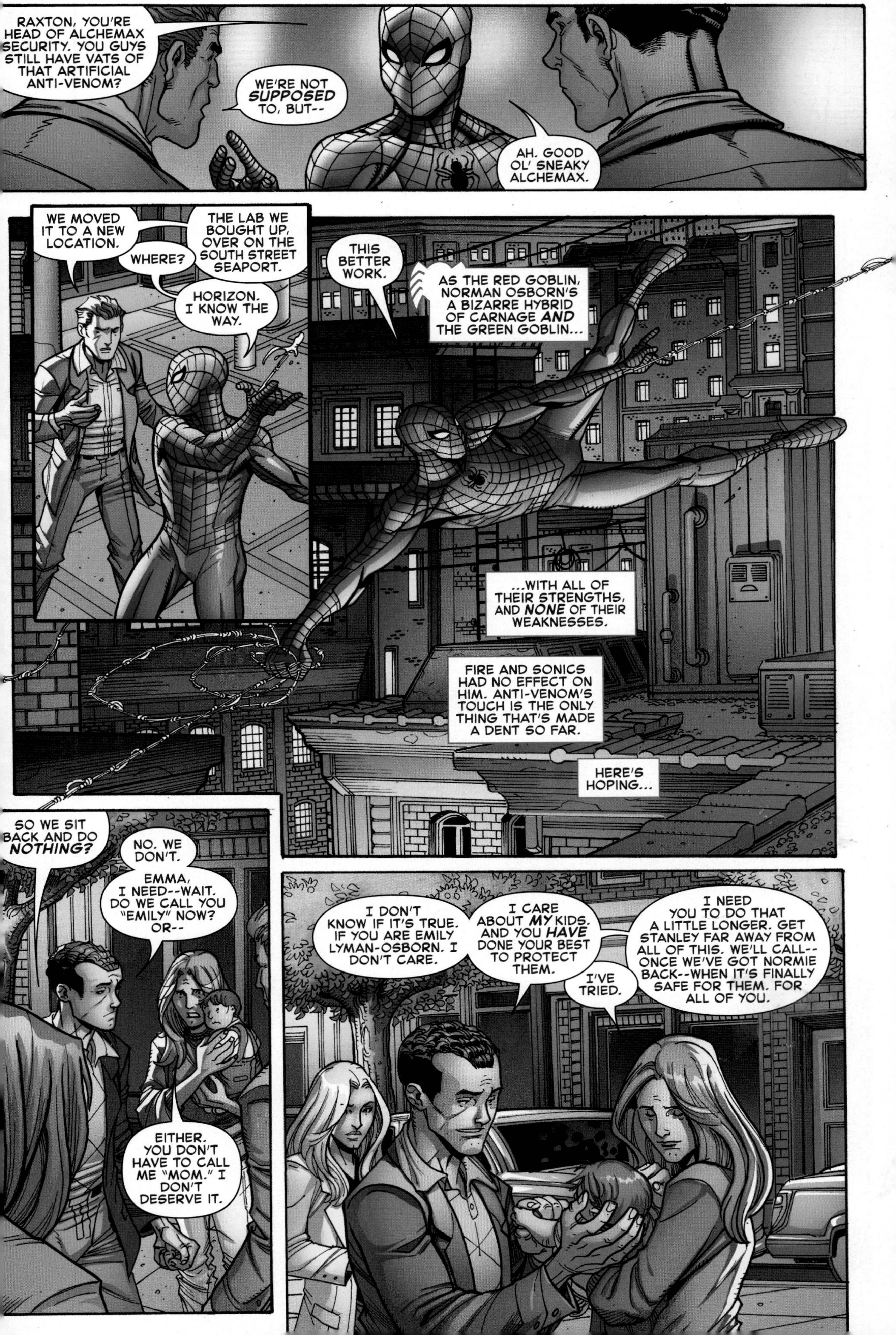
RAXTON, YOU'RE HEAD OF ALCHEMAX SECURITY. YOU GUYS STILL HAVE VATS OF THAT ARTIFICIAL ANTI-VENOM?
WE'RE NOT SUPPOSED TO, BUT--
AH. GOOD OL' SNEAKY ALCHEMAX.
WE MOVED IT TO A NEW LOCATION.
THE LAB WE BOUGHT UP, OVER ON THE SOUTH STREET SEAPORT.
WHERE?
HORIZON. I KNOW THE WAY.
THIS BETTER WORK.
AS THE RED GOBLIN, NORMAN OSBORN'S A BIZARRE HYBRID OF CARNAGE AND THE GREEN GOBLIN...
...WITH ALL OF THEIR STRENGTHS, AND NONE OF THEIR WEAKNESSES.
FIRE AND SONICS HAD NO EFFECT ON HIM. ANTI-VENOM'S TOUCH IS THE ONLY THING THAT'S MADE A DENT SO FAR.
HERE'S HOPING...
SO WE SIT BACK AND DO NOTHING?
NO. WE DON'T.
EMMA, I NEED--WAIT. DO WE CALL YOU "EMILY" NOW? OR--
EITHER. YOU DON'T HAVE TO CALL ME "MOM." I DON'T DESERVE IT.
I DON'T KNOW IF IT'S TRUE. IF YOU ARE EMILY LYMAN-OSBORN. I DON'T CARE.
I CARE ABOUT MY KIDS. AND YOU HAVE DONE YOUR BEST TO PROTECT THEM.
I'VE TRIED.
I NEED YOU TO DO THAT A LITTLE LONGER. GET STANLEY FAR AWAY FROM ALL OF THIS. WE'LL CALL--ONCE WE'VE GOT NORMIE BACK--WHEN IT'S FINALLY SAFE FOR THEM. FOR ALL OF YOU.

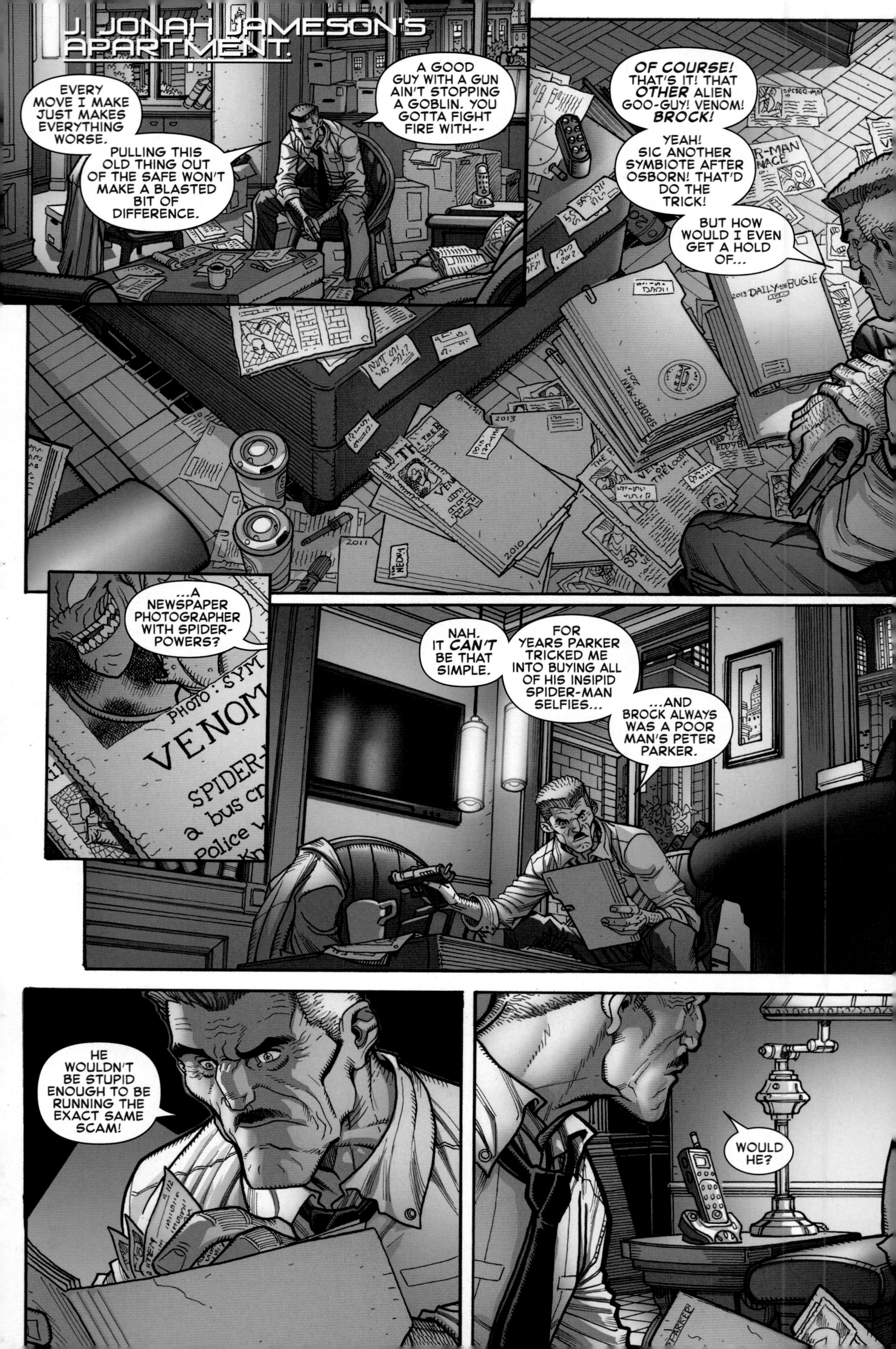
J. JONAH JAMESON'S APARTMENT.
EVERY MOVE I MAKE JUST MAKES EVERYTHING WORSE.
PULLING THIS OLD THING OUT OF THE SAFE WON'T MAKE A BLASTED BIT OF DIFFERENCE.
A GOOD GUY WITH A GUN AIN'T STOPPING A GOBLIN. YOU GOTTA FIGHT FIRE WITH--
OF COURSE! THAT'S IT! THAT OTHER ALIEN GOO-GUY! VENOM! BROCK!
YEAH! SIC ANOTHER SYMBIOTE AFTER OSBORN! THAT'D DO THE TRICK!
BUT HOW WOULD I EVEN GET A HOLD OF...
...A NEWSPAPER PHOTOGRAPHER WITH SPIDER-POWERS?
NAH. IT CAN'T BE THAT SIMPLE.
FOR YEARS PARKER TRICKED ME INTO BUYING ALL OF HIS INSIPID SPIDER-MAN SELFIES...
...AND BROCK ALWAYS WAS A POOR MAN'S PETER PARKER.
HE WOULDN'T BE STUPID ENOUGH TO BE RUNNING THE EXACT SAME SCAM!
WOULD HE?

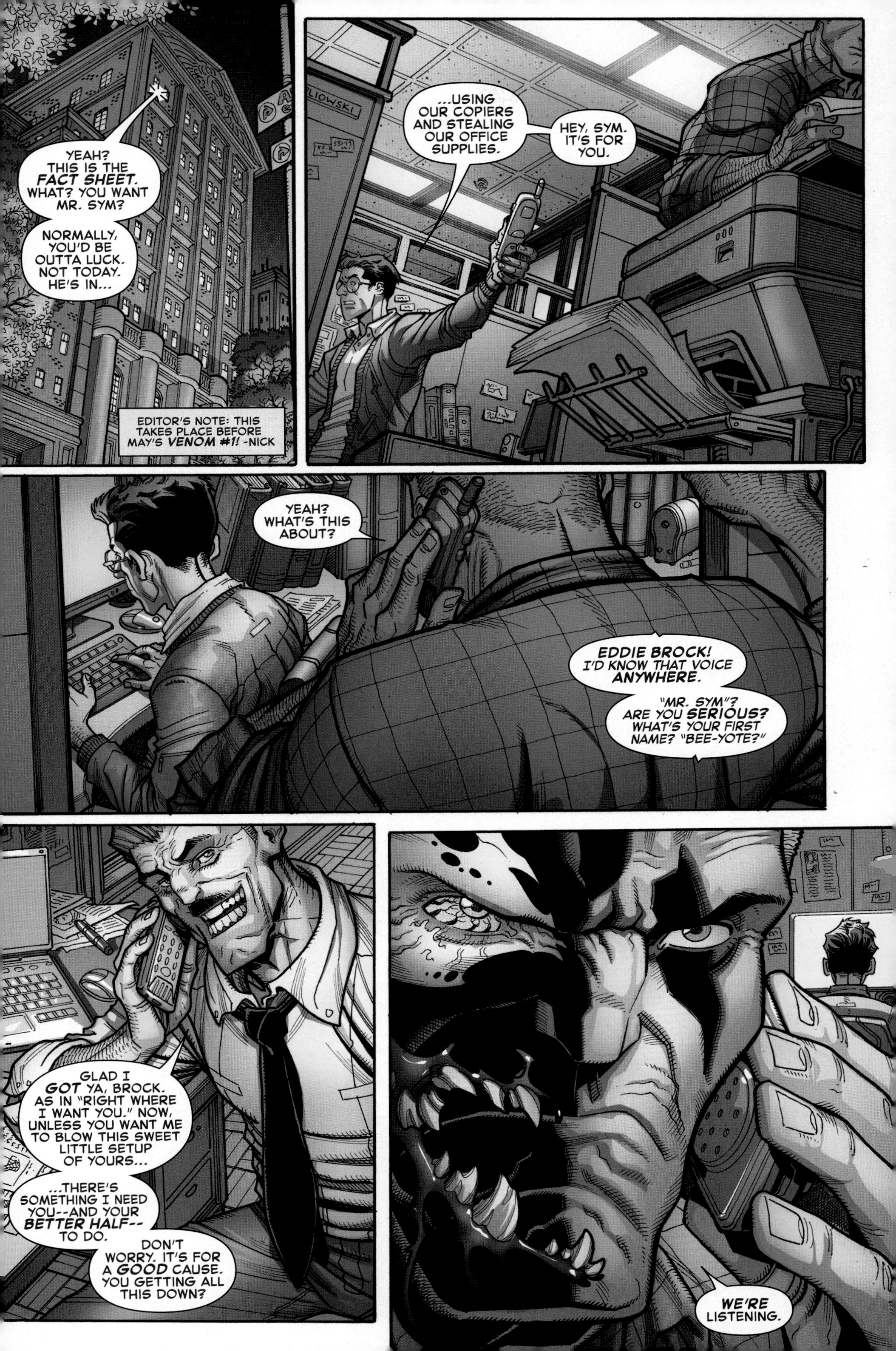
YEAH? THIS IS THE FACT SHEET. WHAT? YOU WANT MR. SYM?
NORMALLY, YOU'D BE OUTTA LUCK. NOT TODAY. HE'S IN...
EDITOR'S NOTE: THIS TAKES PLACE BEFORE MAY'S VENOM #1! -NICK
...USING OUR COPIERS AND STEALING OUR OFFICE SUPPLIES.
HEY, SYM. IT'S FOR YOU.
YEAH? WHAT'S THIS ABOUT?
EDDIE BROCK! I'D KNOW THAT VOICE ANYWHERE.
"MR. SYM"? ARE YOU SERIOUS? WHAT'S YOUR FIRST NAME? "BEE-YOTE?"
GLAD I GOT YA, BROCK. AS IN "RIGHT WHERE I WANT YOU." NOW, UNLESS YOU WANT ME TO BLOW THIS SWEET LITTLE SETUP OF YOURS...
...THERE'S SOMETHING I NEED YOU--AND YOUR BETTER HALF--TO DO.
DON'T WORRY. IT'S FOR A GOOD CAUSE. YOU GETTING ALL THIS DOWN?
WE'RE LISTENING.

Chapter 2
Too Many Targets

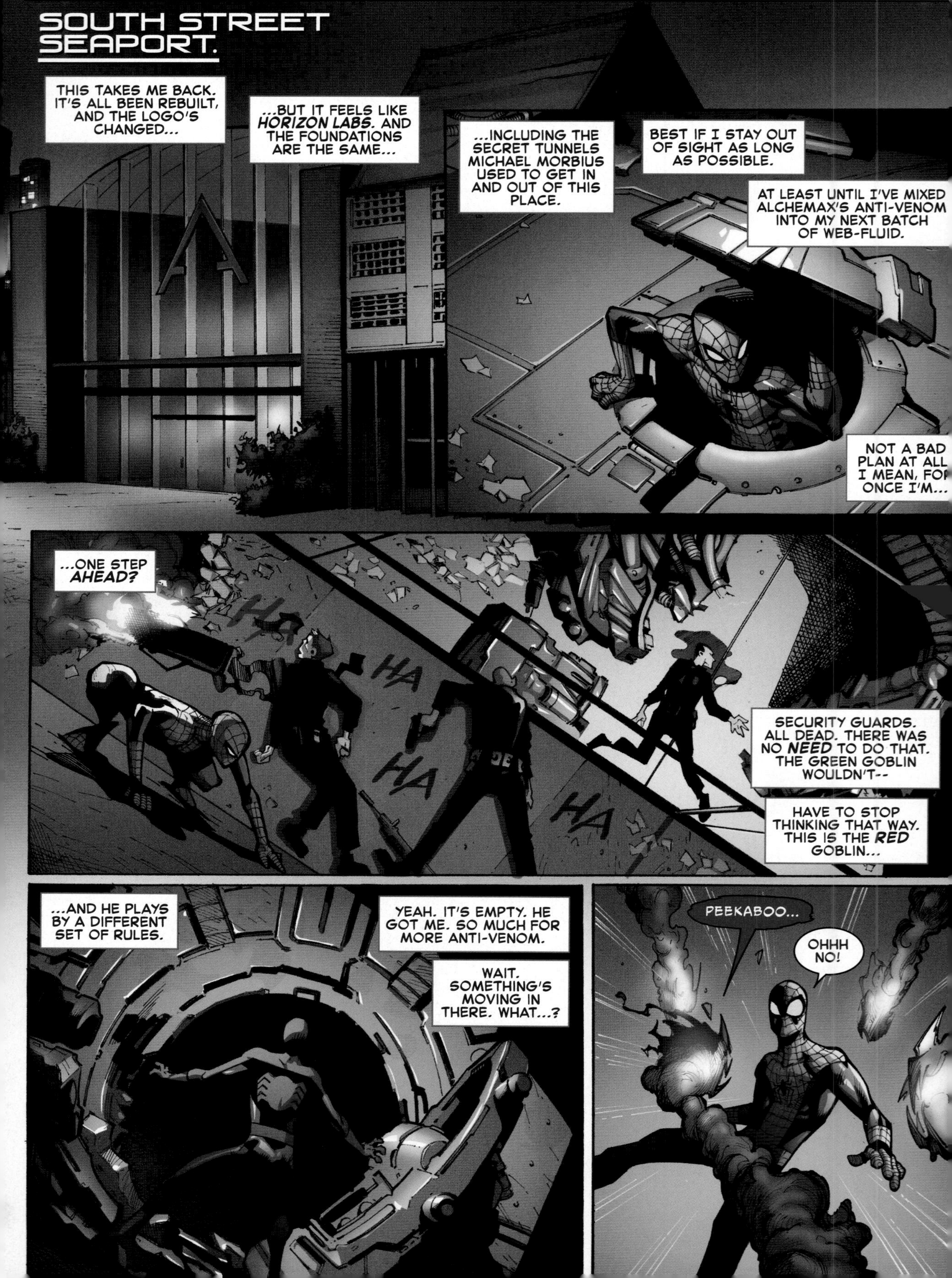
SOUTH STREET SEAPORT.
THIS TAKES ME BACK. IT'S ALL BEEN REBUILT, AND THE LOGO'S CHANGED...
...BUT IT FEELS LIKE HORIZON LABS. AND THE FOUNDATIONS ARE THE SAME...
...INCLUDING THE SECRET TUNNELS MICHAEL MORBIUS USED TO GET IN AND OUT OF THIS PLACE.
BEST IF I STAY OUT OF SIGHT AS LONG AS POSSIBLE.
AT LEAST UNTIL I'VE MIXED ALCHEMAX'S ANTI-VENOM INTO MY NEXT BATCH OF WEB-FLUID.
NOT A BAD PLAN AT ALL I MEAN, FOR ONCE I'M...
...ONE STEP AHEAD?
HA
HA
HA
HA
SECURITY GUARDS. ALL DEAD. THERE WAS NO NEED TO DO THAT. THE GREEN GOBLIN WOULDN'T--
HAVE TO STOP THINKING THAT WAY. THIS IS THE RED GOBLIN...
...AND HE PLAYS BY A DIFFERENT SET OF RULES.
YEAH. IT'S EMPTY. HE GOT ME. SO MUCH FOR MORE ANTI-VENOM.
WAIT. SOMETHING'S MOVING IN THERE. WHAT...?
PEEKABOO...
OHHH NO!

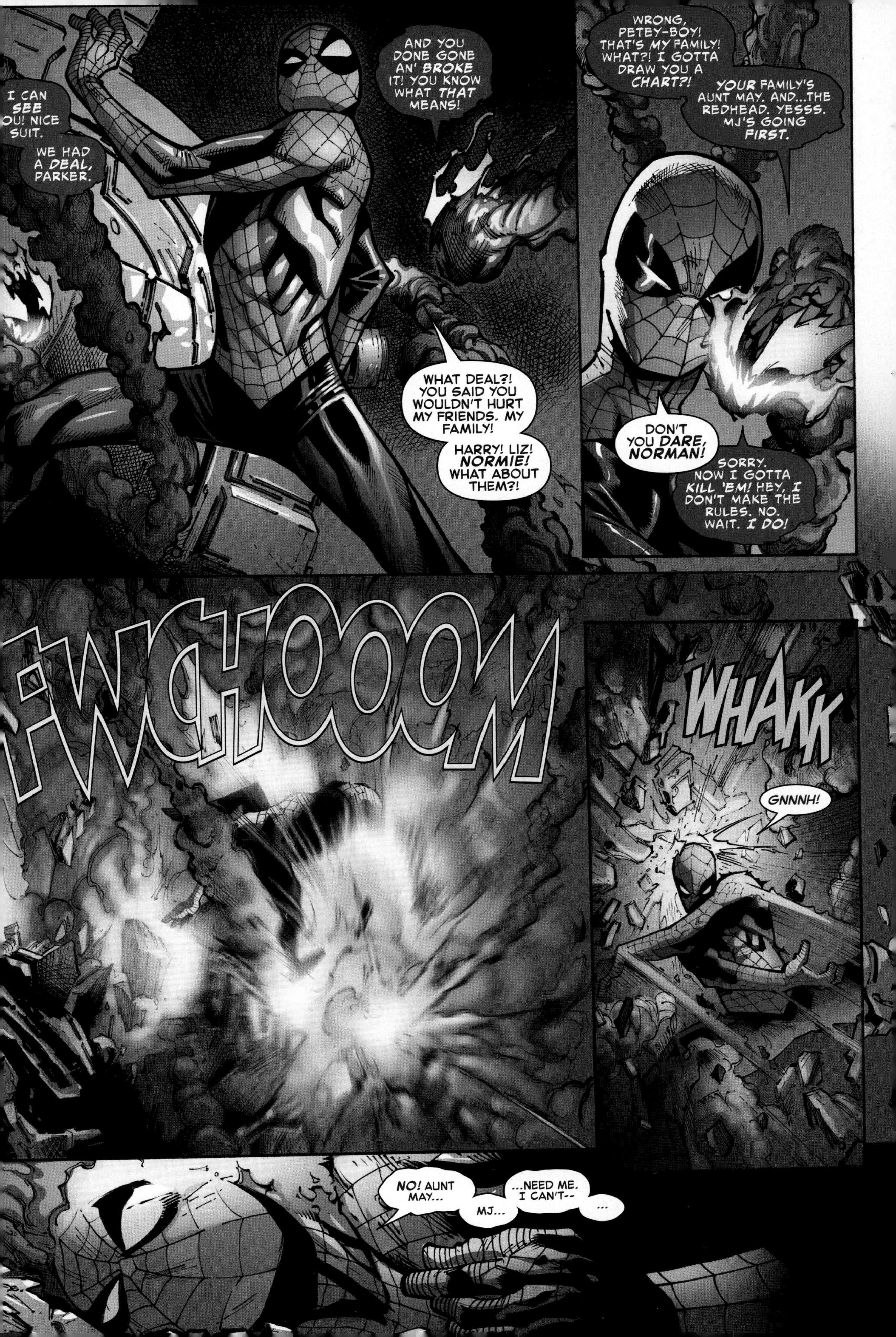
I CAN SEE OU! NICE SUIT.
WE HAD A DEAL, PARKER.
AND YOU DONE GONE AN' BROKE IT! YOU KNOW WHAT THAT MEANS!
WHAT DEAL?! YOU SAID YOU WOULDN'T HURT MY FRIENDS. MY FAMILY!
HARRY! LIZ! NORMIE! WHAT ABOUT THEM?!
WRONG, PETEY-BOY! THAT'S MY FAMILY! WHAT?! I GOTTA DRAW YOU A CHART?!
YOUR FAMILY'S AUNT MAY. AND...THE REDHEAD. YESSS. MJ'S GOING FIRST.
DON'T YOU DARE, NORMAN!
SORRY. NOW I GOTTA KILL 'EM! HEY, I DON'T MAKE THE RULES. NO. WAIT. I DO!
FWCHOOOM
WHAKK
GNNNH!
NO! AUNT MAY...
MJ...
...NEED ME. I CAN'T--
...

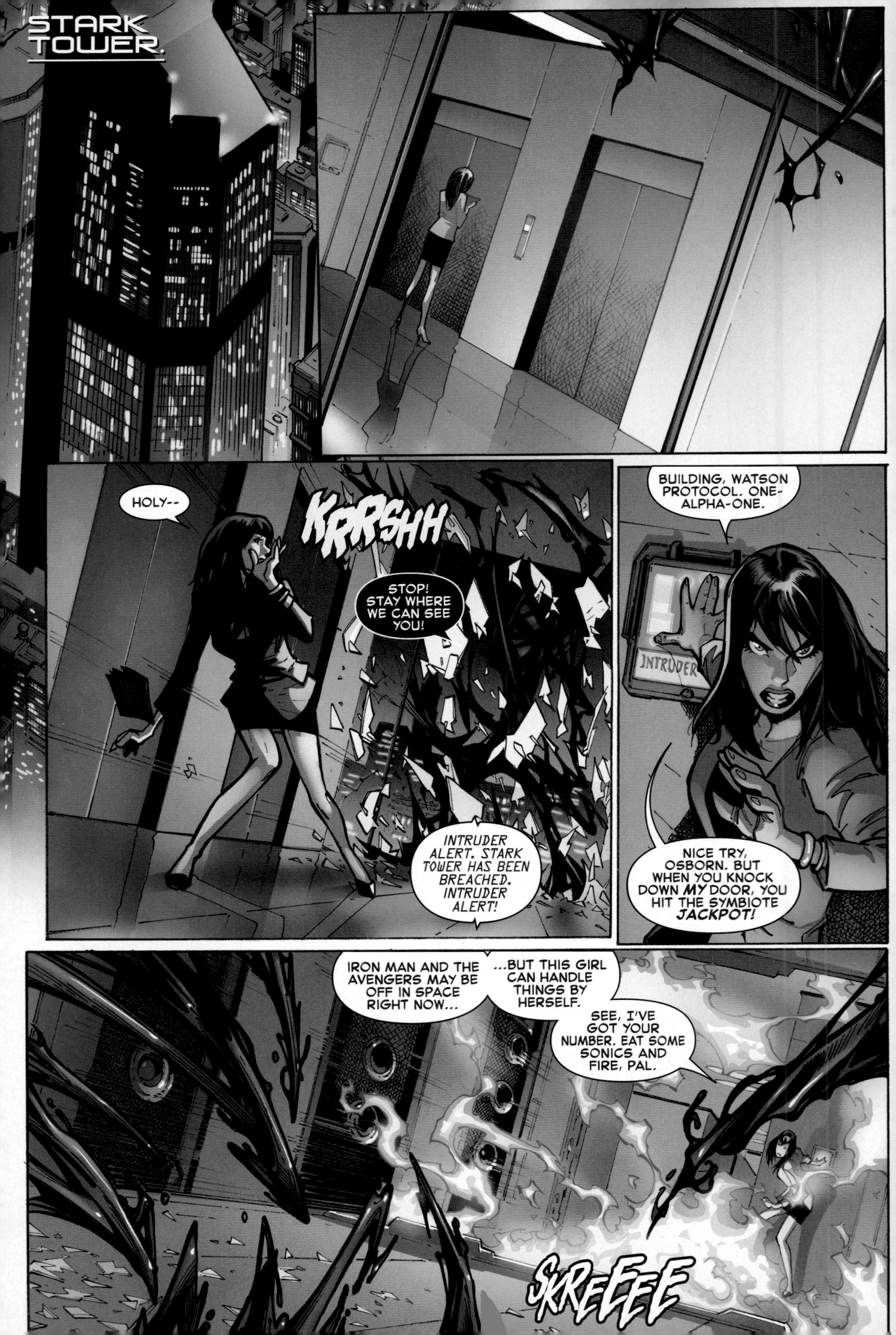
STARK TOWER.
HOLY--
KRRSHH
STOP! STAY WHERE WE CAN SEE YOU!
INTRUDER ALERT. STARK TOWER HAS BEEN BREACHED. INTRUDER ALERT!
BUILDING, WATSON PROTOCOL. ONE-ALPHA-ONE.
INTRUDER
NICE TRY, OSBORN. BUT WHEN YOU KNOCK DOWN MY DOOR, YOU HIT THE SYMBIOTE JACKPOT!
IRON MAN AND THE AVENGERS MAY BE OFF IN SPACE RIGHT NOW...
...BUT THIS GIRL CAN HANDLE THINGS BY HERSELF.
SEE, I'VE GOT YOUR NUMBER. EAT SOME SONICS AND FIRE, PAL.
SKREEEEE

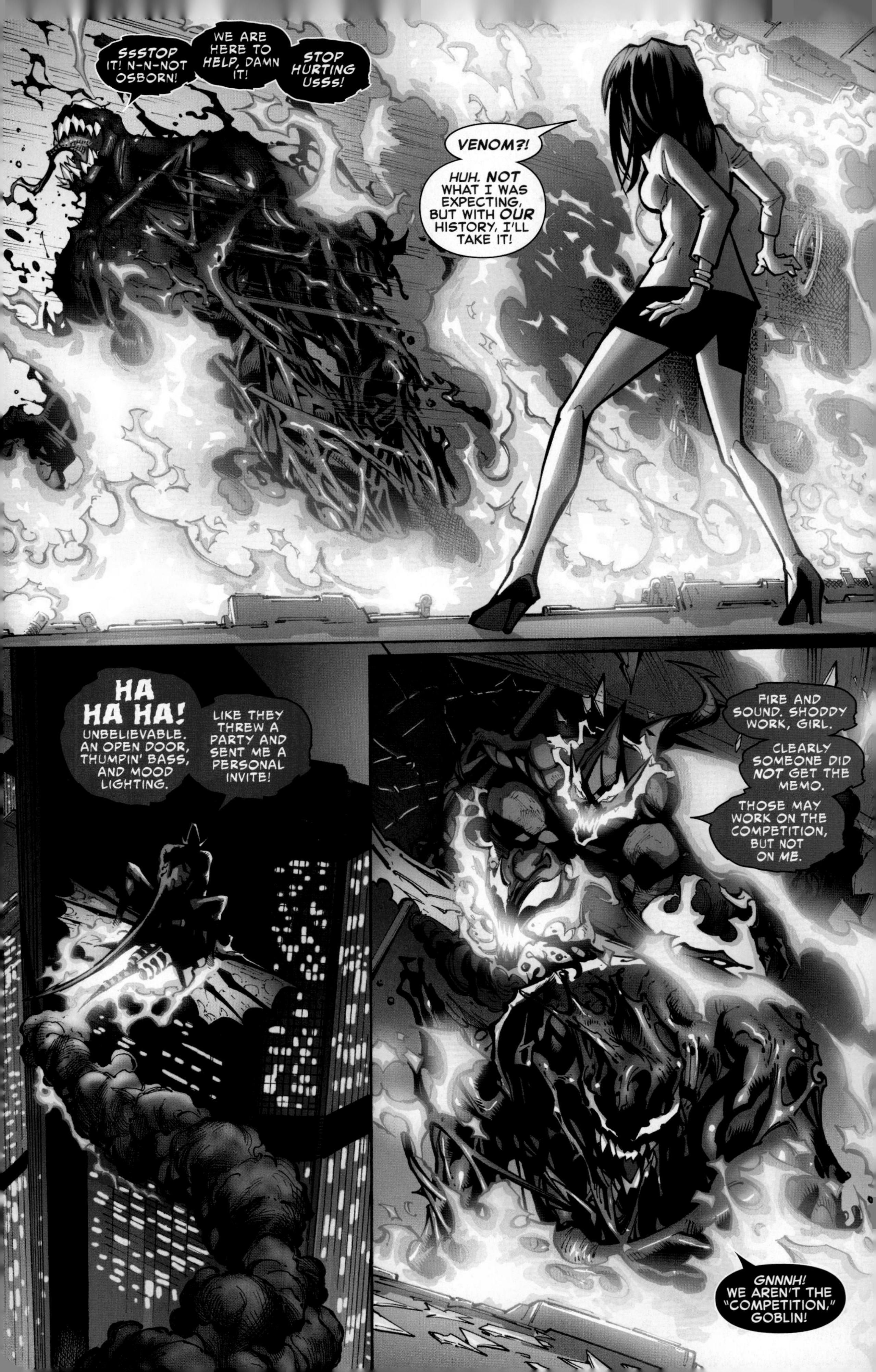
SSSTOP IT! N-N-NOT OSBORN!
WE ARE HERE TO HELP, DAMN IT!
STOP HURTING USSS!
VENOM?!
HUH. NOT WHAT I WAS EXPECTING, BUT WITH OUR HISTORY, I'LL TAKE IT!
HA HA HA! UNBELIEVABLE. AN OPEN DOOR, THUMPIN' BASS, AND MOOD LIGHTING.
LIKE THEY THREW A PARTY AND SENT ME A PERSONAL INVITE!
FIRE AND SOUND. SHODDY WORK, GIRL.
CLEARLY SOMEONE DID NOT GET THE MEMO.
THOSE MAY WORK ON THE COMPETITION, BUT NOT ON ME.
GNNNH! WE AREN'T THE "COMPETITION," GOBLIN!

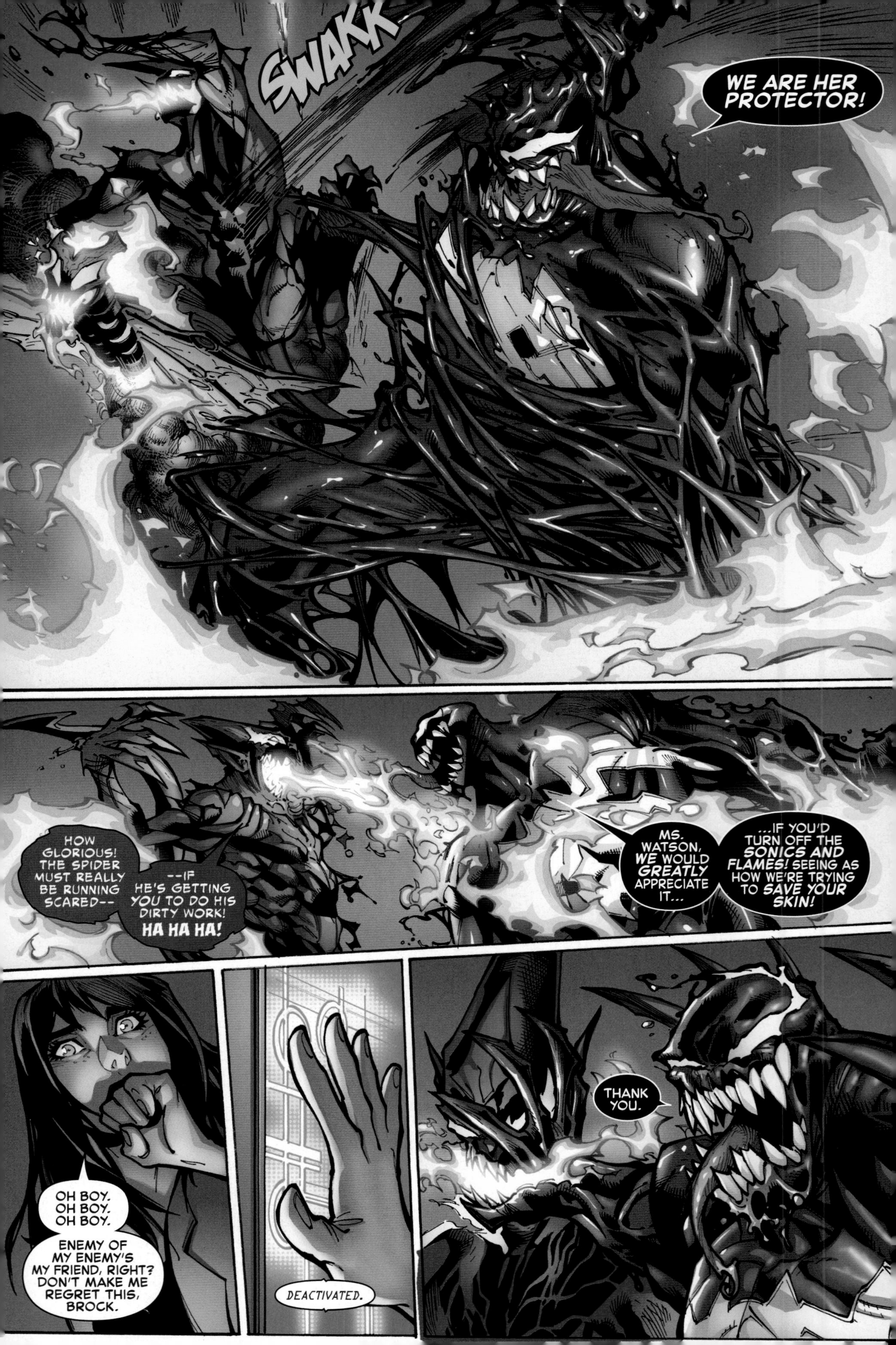
SWAKK
WE ARE HER PROTECTOR!
HOW GLORIOUS! THE SPIDER MUST REALLY BE RUNNING SCARED--
--IF HE'S GETTING YOU TO DO HIS DIRTY WORK! HA HA HA!
MS. WATSON, WE WOULD GREATLY APPRECIATE IT...
...IF YOU'D TURN OFF THE SONICS AND FLAMES! SEEING AS HOW WE'RE TRYING TO SAVE YOUR SKIN!
OH BOY. OH BOY. OH BOY.
ENEMY OF MY ENEMY'S MY FRIEND, RIGHT? DON'T MAKE ME REGRET THIS, BROCK.
DEACTIVATED.
THANK YOU.

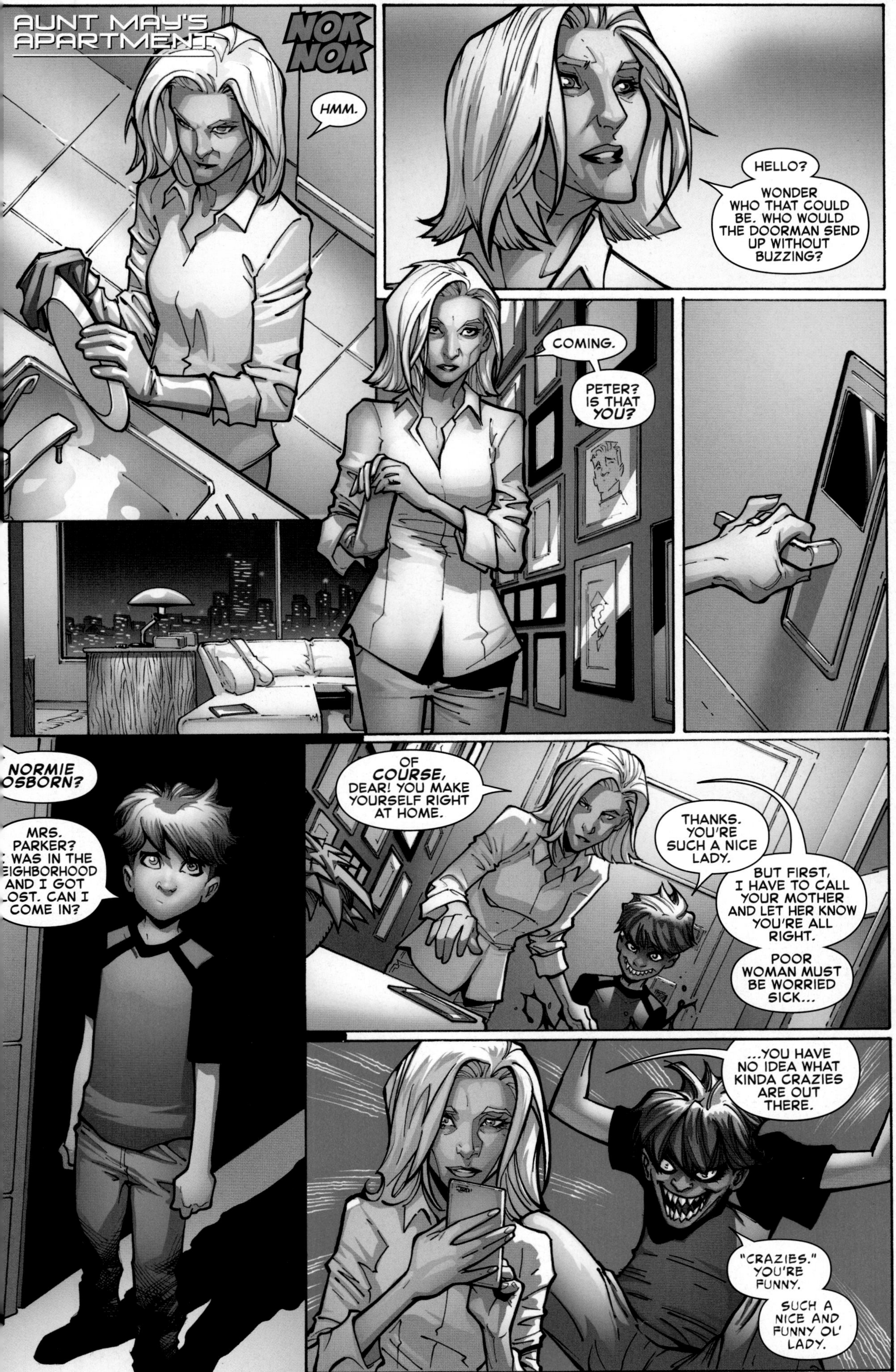
AUNT MAY'S APARTMENT.
NOK NOK
HMM.
HELLO?
WONDER WHO THAT COULD BE. WHO WOULD THE DOORMAN SEND UP WITHOUT BUZZING?
COMING.
PETER? IS THAT *YOU?*
NORMIE OSBORN?
MRS. PARKER? I WAS IN THE NEIGHBORHOOD AND I GOT LOST. CAN I COME IN?
OF *COURSE,* DEAR! YOU MAKE YOURSELF RIGHT AT HOME.
THANKS. YOU'RE SUCH A NICE LADY.
BUT FIRST, I HAVE TO CALL YOUR MOTHER AND LET HER KNOW YOU'RE ALL RIGHT.
POOR WOMAN MUST BE WORRIED SICK...
...YOU HAVE NO IDEA WHAT KINDA CRAZIES ARE OUT THERE.
"CRAZIES." YOU'RE FUNNY.
SUCH A NICE AND FUNNY OL' LADY.

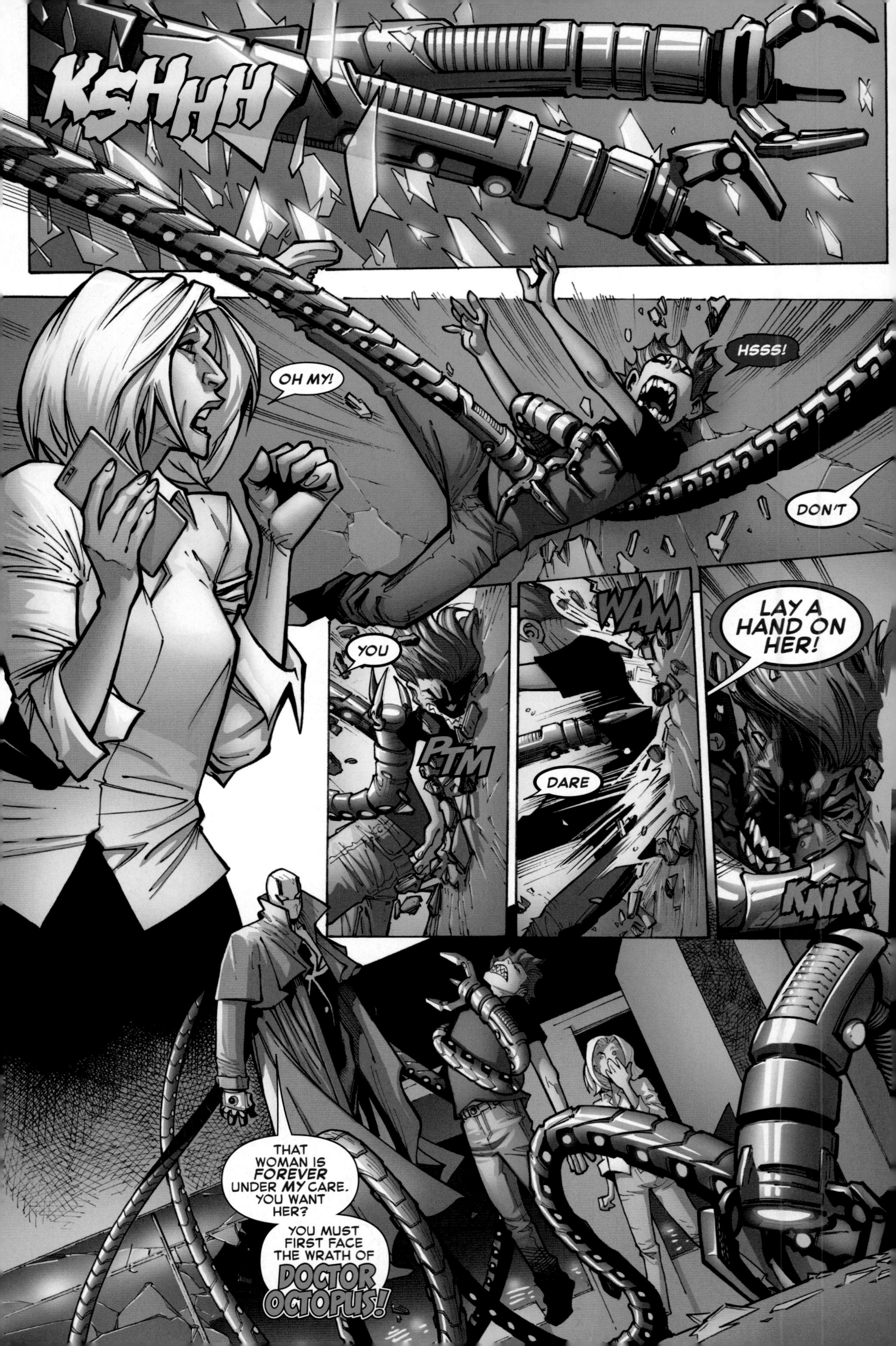
KSHHH
OH MY!
HSSS!
DON'T
YOU
PTM
WAM
DARE
LAY A HAND ON HER!
KNK
THAT WOMAN IS FOREVER UNDER MY CARE. YOU WANT HER?
YOU MUST FIRST FACE THE WRATH OF DOCTOR OCTOPUS!

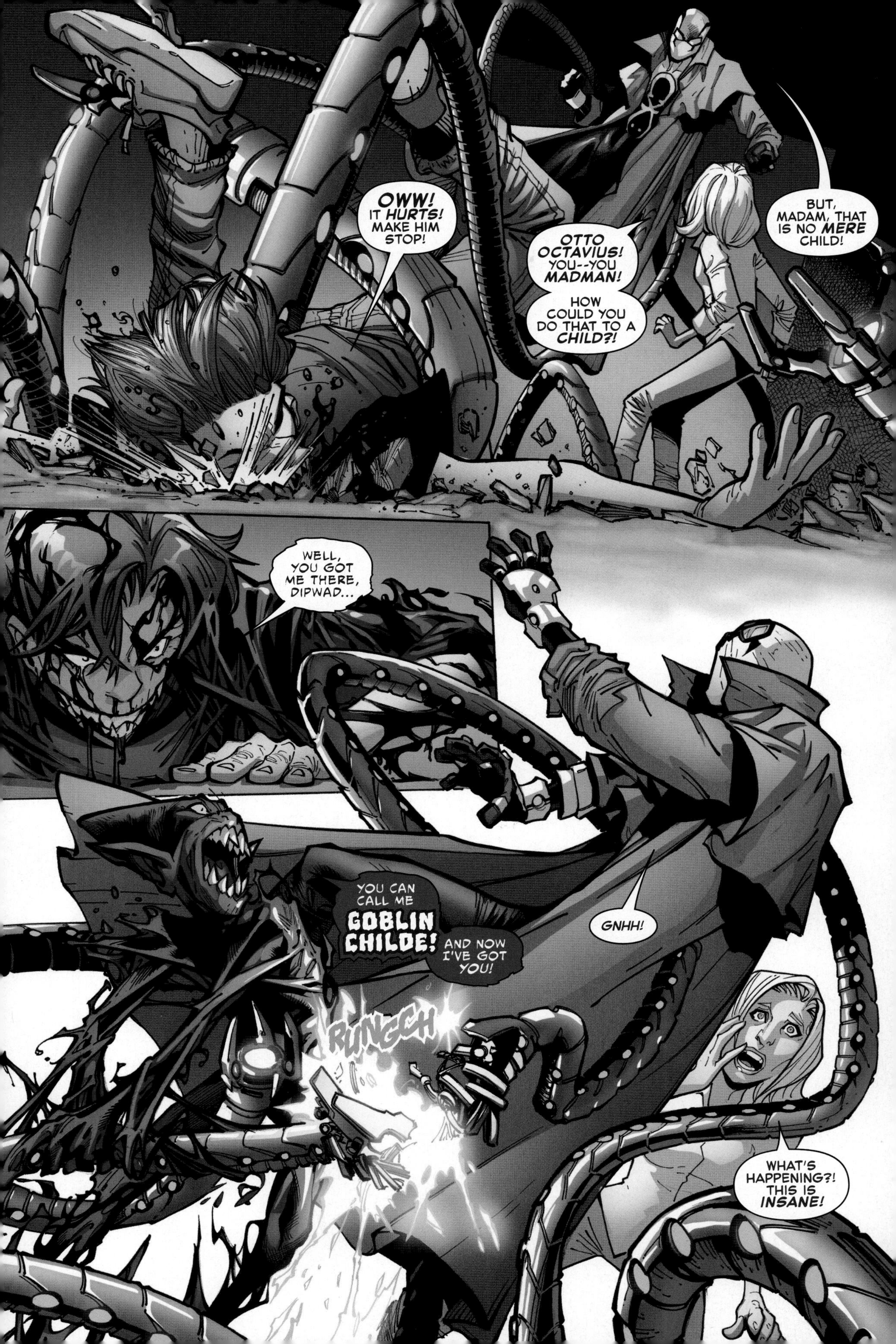
OWW! IT HURTS! MAKE HIM STOP!
OTTO OCTAVIUS! YOU--YOU MADMAN!
HOW COULD YOU DO THAT TO A CHILD?!
BUT, MADAM, THAT IS NO MERE CHILD!
WELL, YOU GOT ME THERE, DIPWAD...
YOU CAN CALL ME GOBLIN CHILDE!
AND NOW I'VE GOT YOU!
GNHH!
KRUNCH
WHAT'S HAPPENING?! THIS IS INSANE!

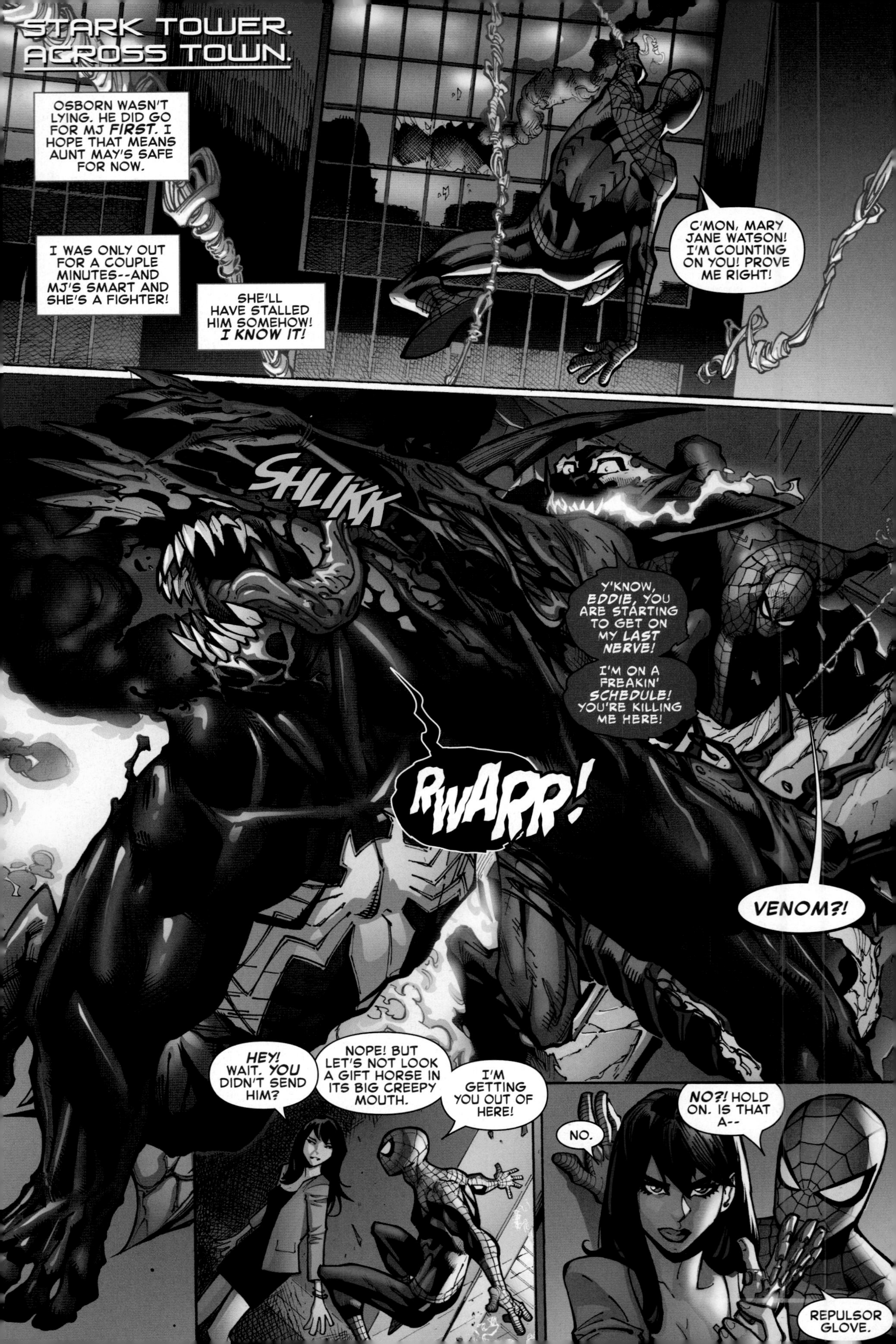
STARK TOWER. ACROSS TOWN.
OSBORN WASN'T LYING. HE DID GO FOR MJ *FIRST*. I HOPE THAT MEANS AUNT MAY'S SAFE FOR NOW.
I WAS ONLY OUT FOR A COUPLE MINUTES--AND MJ'S SMART AND SHE'S A FIGHTER!
SHE'LL HAVE STALLED HIM SOMEHOW! *I KNOW IT!*
C'MON, MARY JANE WATSON! I'M COUNTING ON YOU! PROVE ME RIGHT!
SHLIKK
Y'KNOW, *EDDIE*, YOU ARE STARTING TO GET ON MY *LAST NERVE!*
I'M ON A FREAKIN' *SCHEDULE!* YOU'RE KILLING ME HERE!
RWARR!
VENOM?!
HEY! WAIT. *YOU* DIDN'T SEND HIM?
NOPE! BUT LET'S NOT LOOK A GIFT HORSE IN ITS BIG CREEPY MOUTH.
I'M GETTING YOU OUT OF HERE!
NO.
NO?! HOLD ON. IS THAT A--
REPULSOR GLOVE.

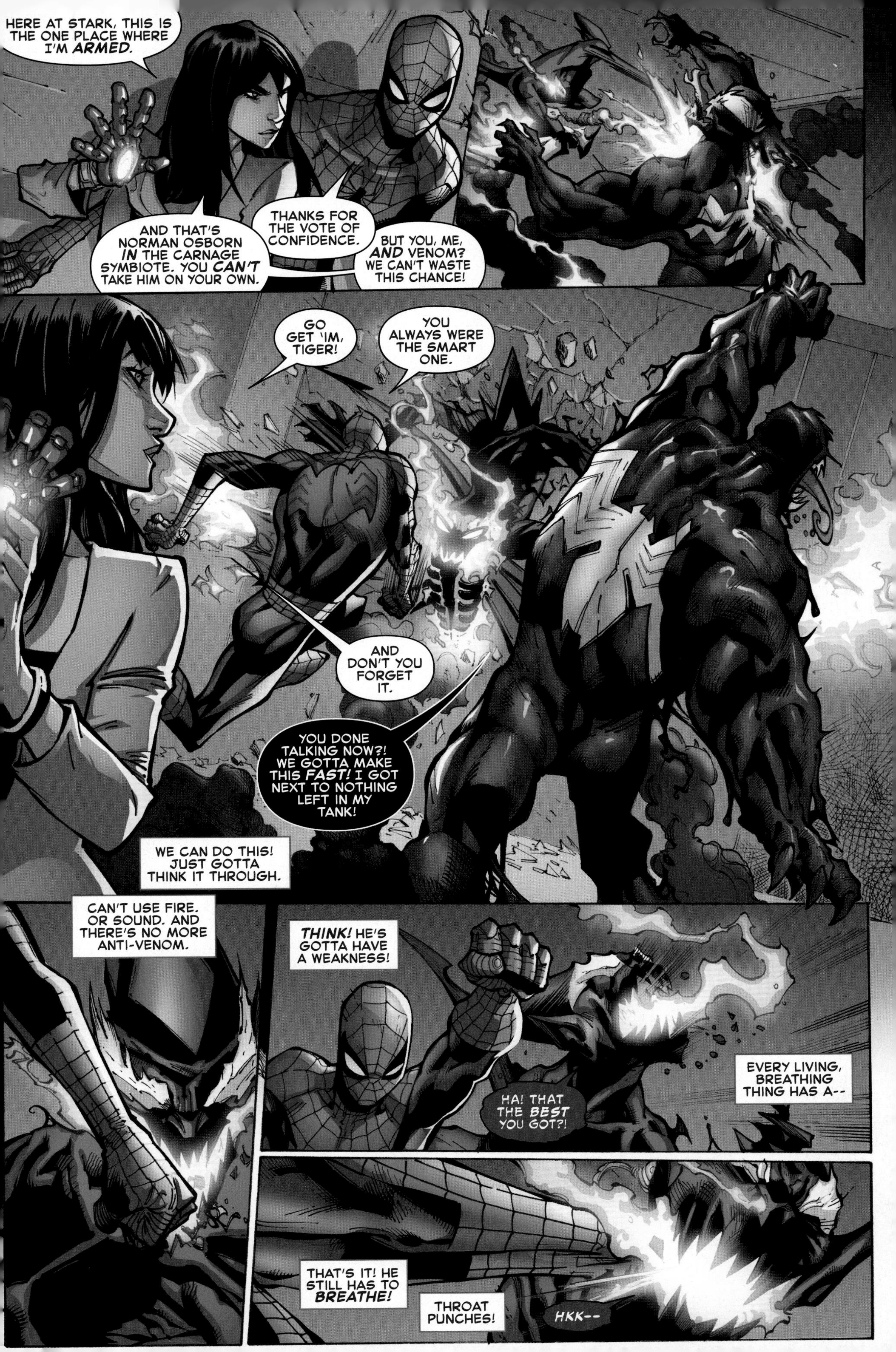
HERE AT STARK, THIS IS THE ONE PLACE WHERE I'M ARMED.
AND THAT'S NORMAN OSBORN IN THE CARNAGE SYMBIOTE. YOU CAN'T TAKE HIM ON YOUR OWN.
THANKS FOR THE VOTE OF CONFIDENCE.
BUT YOU, ME, AND VENOM? WE CAN'T WASTE THIS CHANCE!
GO GET 'IM, TIGER!
YOU ALWAYS WERE THE SMART ONE.
AND DON'T YOU FORGET IT.
YOU DONE TALKING NOW?! WE GOTTA MAKE THIS FAST! I GOT NEXT TO NOTHING LEFT IN MY TANK!
WE CAN DO THIS! JUST GOTTA THINK IT THROUGH.
CAN'T USE FIRE. OR SOUND. AND THERE'S NO MORE ANTI-VENOM.
THINK! HE'S GOTTA HAVE A WEAKNESS!
HA! THAT THE BEST YOU GOT?!
EVERY LIVING, BREATHING THING HAS A--
THAT'S IT! HE STILL HAS TO BREATHE!
THROAT PUNCHES!
HKK--

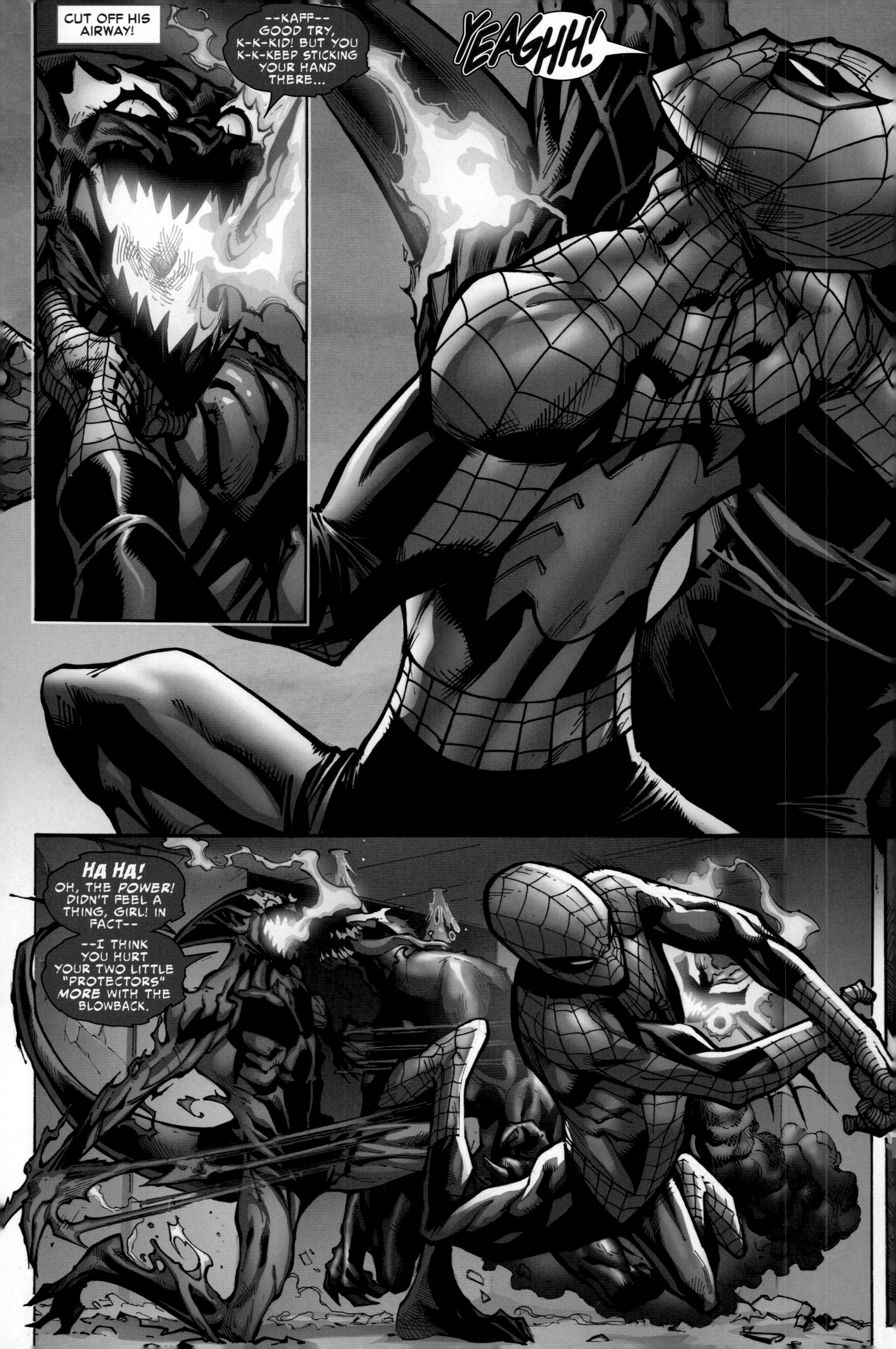
CUT OFF HIS AIRWAY!
--KAFF-- GOOD TRY, K-K-KID! BUT YOU K-K-KEEP STICKING YOUR HAND THERE...
YEAGHH!
HA HA! OH, THE POWER! DIDN'T FEEL A THING, GIRL! IN FACT--
--I THINK YOU HURT YOUR TWO LITTLE "PROTECTORS" MORE WITH THE BLOWBACK.

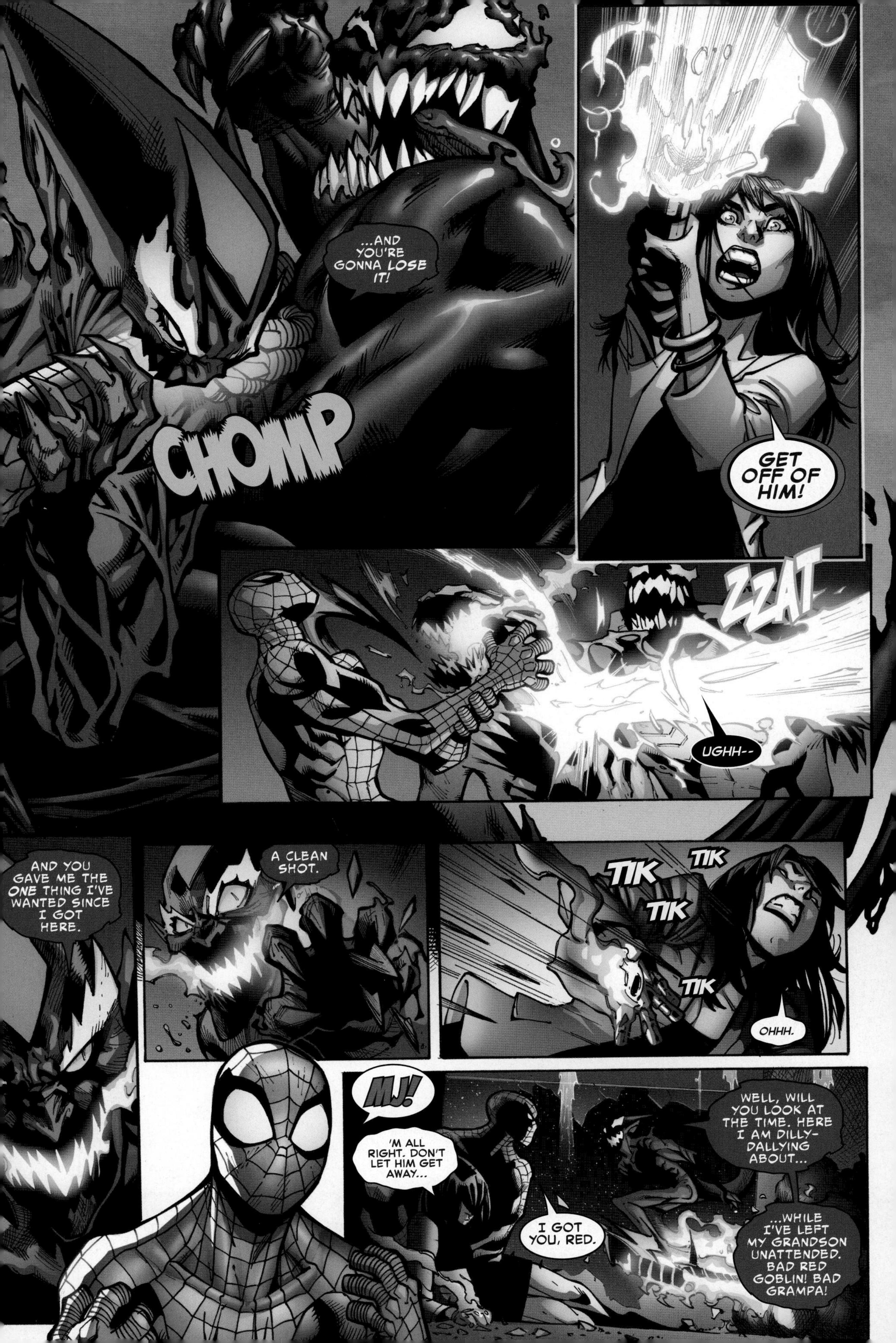
...AND YOU'RE GONNA LOSE IT!
CHOMP
GET OFF OF HIM!
ZZAT
UGHH--
AND YOU GAVE ME THE ONE THING I'VE WANTED SINCE I GOT HERE.
A CLEAN SHOT.
TIK
TIK
TIK
TIK
OHHH.
MJ!
'M ALL RIGHT. DON'T LET HIM GET AWAY...
I GOT YOU, RED.
WELL, WILL YOU LOOK AT THE TIME. HERE I AM DILLY-DALLYING ABOUT...
...WHILE I'VE LEFT MY GRANDSON UNATTENDED. BAD RED GOBLIN! BAD GRAMPA!

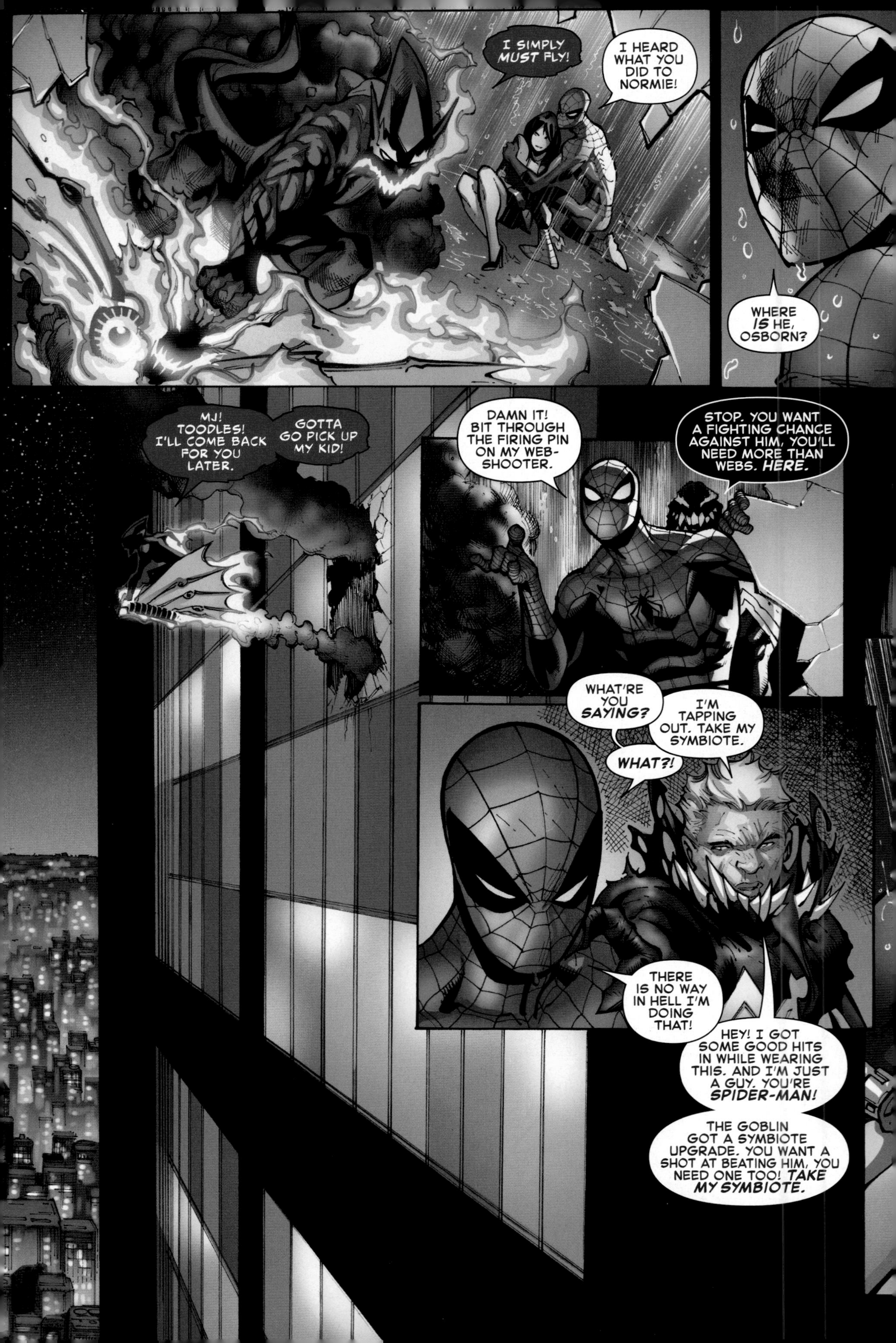

I SIMPLY MUST FLY!
I HEARD WHAT YOU DID TO NORMIE!
WHERE IS HE, OSBORN?
MJ! TOODLES! I'LL COME BACK FOR YOU LATER.
GOTTA GO PICK UP MY KID!
DAMN IT! BIT THROUGH THE FIRING PIN ON MY WEB-SHOOTER.
STOP. YOU WANT A FIGHTING CHANCE AGAINST HIM, YOU'LL NEED MORE THAN WEBS. HERE.
WHAT'RE YOU SAYING?
I'M TAPPING OUT. TAKE MY SYMBIOTE.
WHAT?!
THERE IS NO WAY IN HELL I'M DOING THAT!
HEY! I GOT SOME GOOD HITS IN WHILE WEARING THIS. AND I'M JUST A GUY. YOU'RE SPIDER-MAN!
THE GOBLIN GOT A SYMBIOTE UPGRADE. YOU WANT A SHOT AT BEATING HIM, YOU NEED ONE TOO! TAKE MY SYMBIOTE.

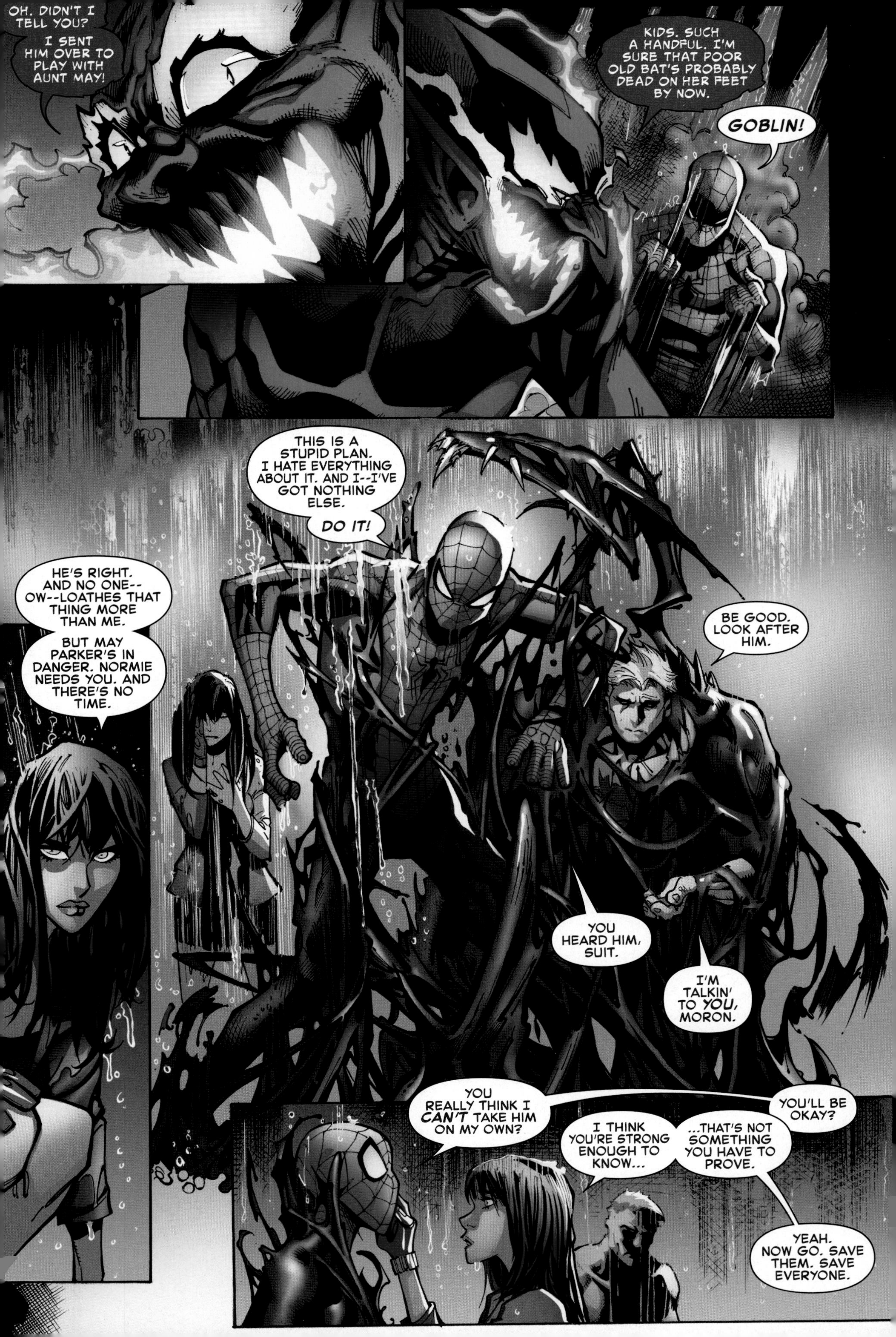
OH. DIDN'T I TELL YOU?
I SENT HIM OVER TO PLAY WITH AUNT MAY!
KIDS. SUCH A HANDFUL. I'M SURE THAT POOR OLD BAT'S PROBABLY DEAD ON HER FEET BY NOW.
GOBLIN!
THIS IS A STUPID PLAN. I HATE EVERYTHING ABOUT IT. AND I--I'VE GOT NOTHING ELSE.
DO IT!
HE'S RIGHT. AND NO ONE--OW--LOATHES THAT THING MORE THAN ME.
BUT MAY PARKER'S IN DANGER. NORMIE NEEDS YOU. AND THERE'S NO TIME.
BE GOOD. LOOK AFTER HIM.
YOU HEARD HIM, SUIT.
I'M TALKIN' TO YOU, MORON.
YOU REALLY THINK I CAN'T TAKE HIM ON MY OWN?
YOU'LL BE OKAY?
I THINK YOU'RE STRONG ENOUGH TO KNOW...
...THAT'S NOT SOMETHING YOU HAVE TO PROVE.
YEAH. NOW GO. SAVE THEM. SAVE EVERYONE.

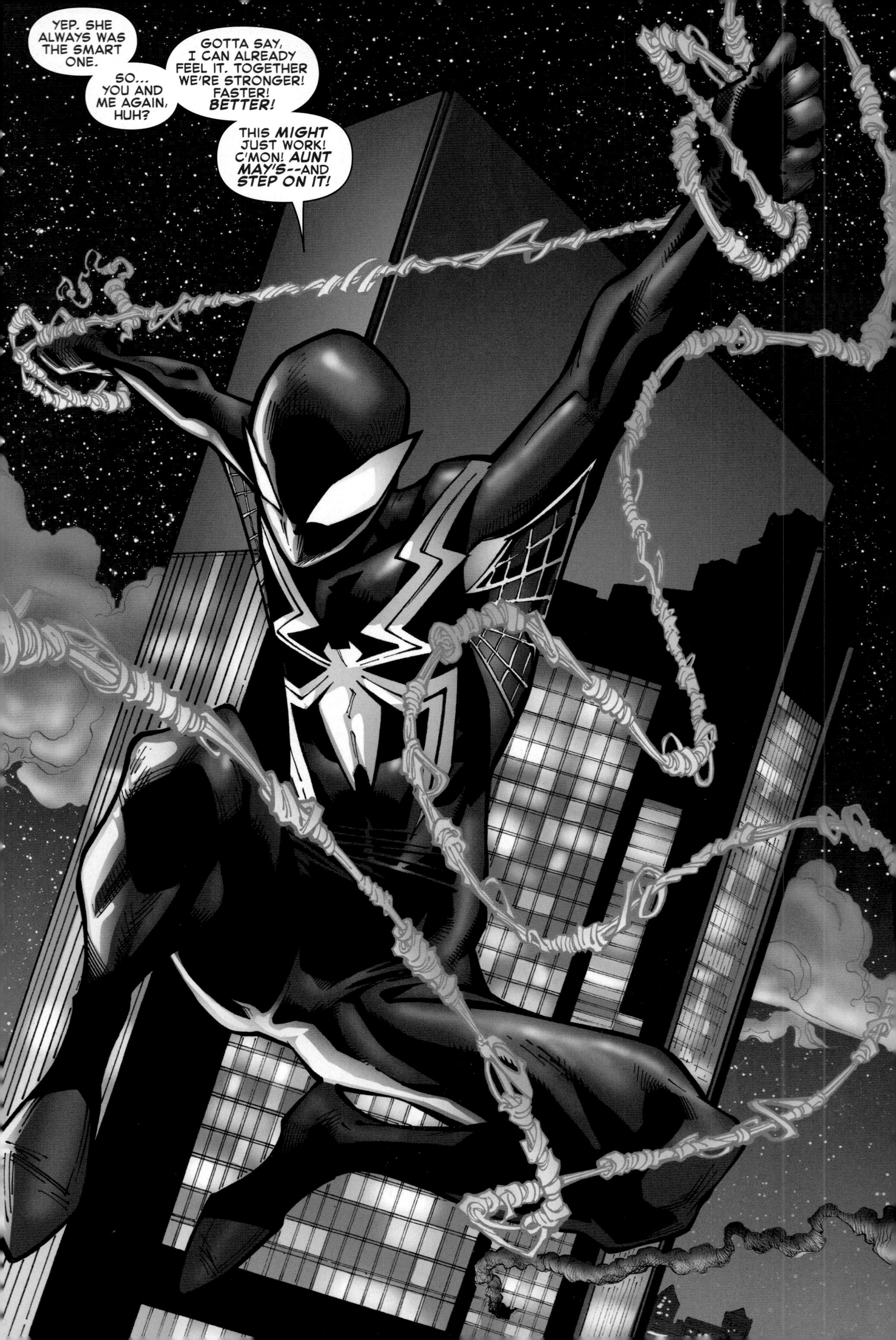
YEP. SHE ALWAYS WAS THE SMART ONE.
SO... YOU AND ME AGAIN, HUH?
GOTTA SAY, I CAN ALREADY FEEL IT. TOGETHER WE'RE STRONGER! FASTER! BETTER!
THIS MIGHT JUST WORK! C'MON! AUNT MAY'S--AND STEP ON IT!

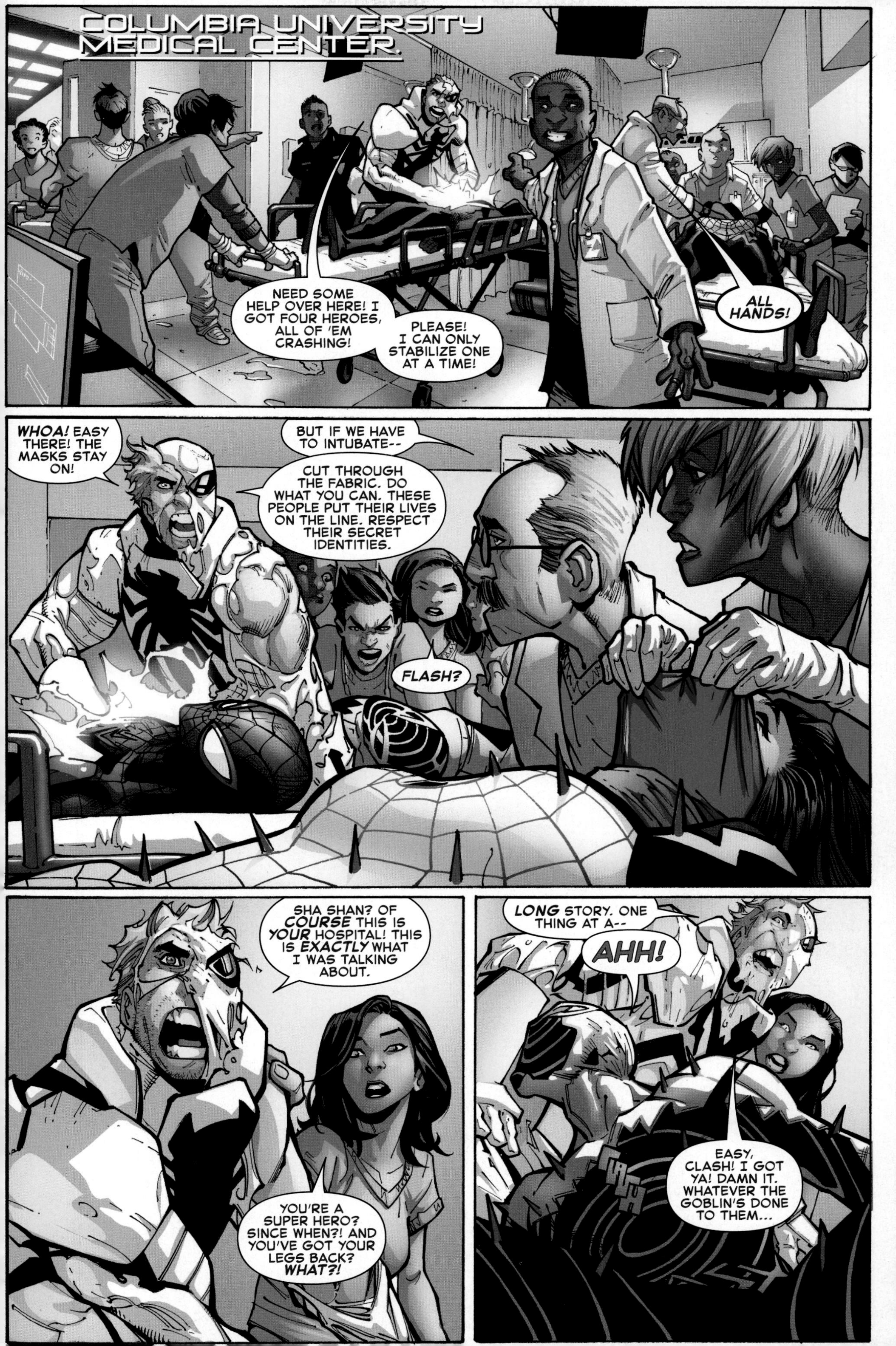

COLUMBIA UNIVERSITY MEDICAL CENTER.
NEED SOME HELP OVER HERE! I GOT FOUR HEROES, ALL OF 'EM CRASHING!
PLEASE! I CAN ONLY STABILIZE ONE AT A TIME!
ALL HANDS!
WHOA! EASY THERE! THE MASKS STAY ON!
BUT IF WE HAVE TO INTUBATE--
CUT THROUGH THE FABRIC. DO WHAT YOU CAN. THESE PEOPLE PUT THEIR LIVES ON THE LINE. RESPECT THEIR SECRET IDENTITIES.
FLASH?
SHA SHAN? OF COURSE THIS IS YOUR HOSPITAL! THIS IS EXACTLY WHAT I WAS TALKING ABOUT.
YOU'RE A SUPER HERO? SINCE WHEN?! AND YOU'VE GOT YOUR LEGS BACK? WHAT?!
LONG STORY. ONE THING AT A--
AHH!
EASY, CLASH! I GOT YA! DAMN IT. WHATEVER THE GOBLIN'S DONE TO THEM...

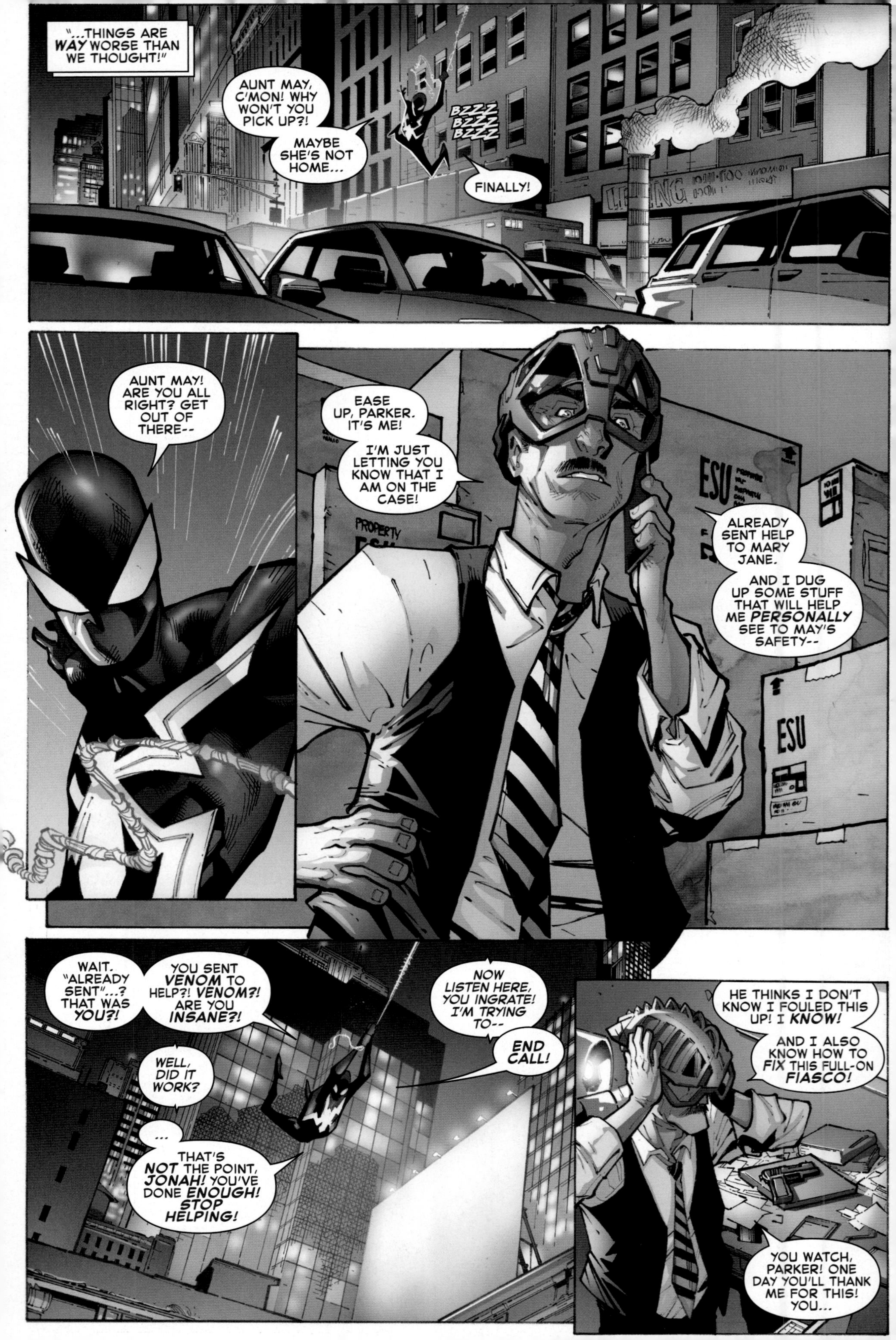
"...THINGS ARE WAY WORSE THAN WE THOUGHT!"
AUNT MAY, C'MON! WHY WON'T YOU PICK UP?!
MAYBE SHE'S NOT HOME...
BZZZ BZZZ BZZZ
FINALLY!
AUNT MAY! ARE YOU ALL RIGHT? GET OUT OF THERE--
EASE UP, PARKER. IT'S ME!
I'M JUST LETTING YOU KNOW THAT I AM ON THE CASE!
ALREADY SENT HELP TO MARY JANE.
AND I DUG UP SOME STUFF THAT WILL HELP ME PERSONALLY SEE TO MAY'S SAFETY--
WAIT. "ALREADY SENT"...? THAT WAS YOU?!
YOU SENT VENOM TO HELP?! VENOM?! ARE YOU INSANE?!
WELL, DID IT WORK?
...
THAT'S NOT THE POINT, JONAH! YOU'VE DONE ENOUGH! STOP HELPING!
NOW LISTEN HERE, YOU INGRATE! I'M TRYING TO--
END CALL!
HE THINKS I DON'T KNOW I FOULED THIS UP! I KNOW!
AND I ALSO KNOW HOW TO FIX THIS FULL-ON FIASCO!
YOU WATCH, PARKER! ONE DAY YOU'LL THANK ME FOR THIS! YOU...

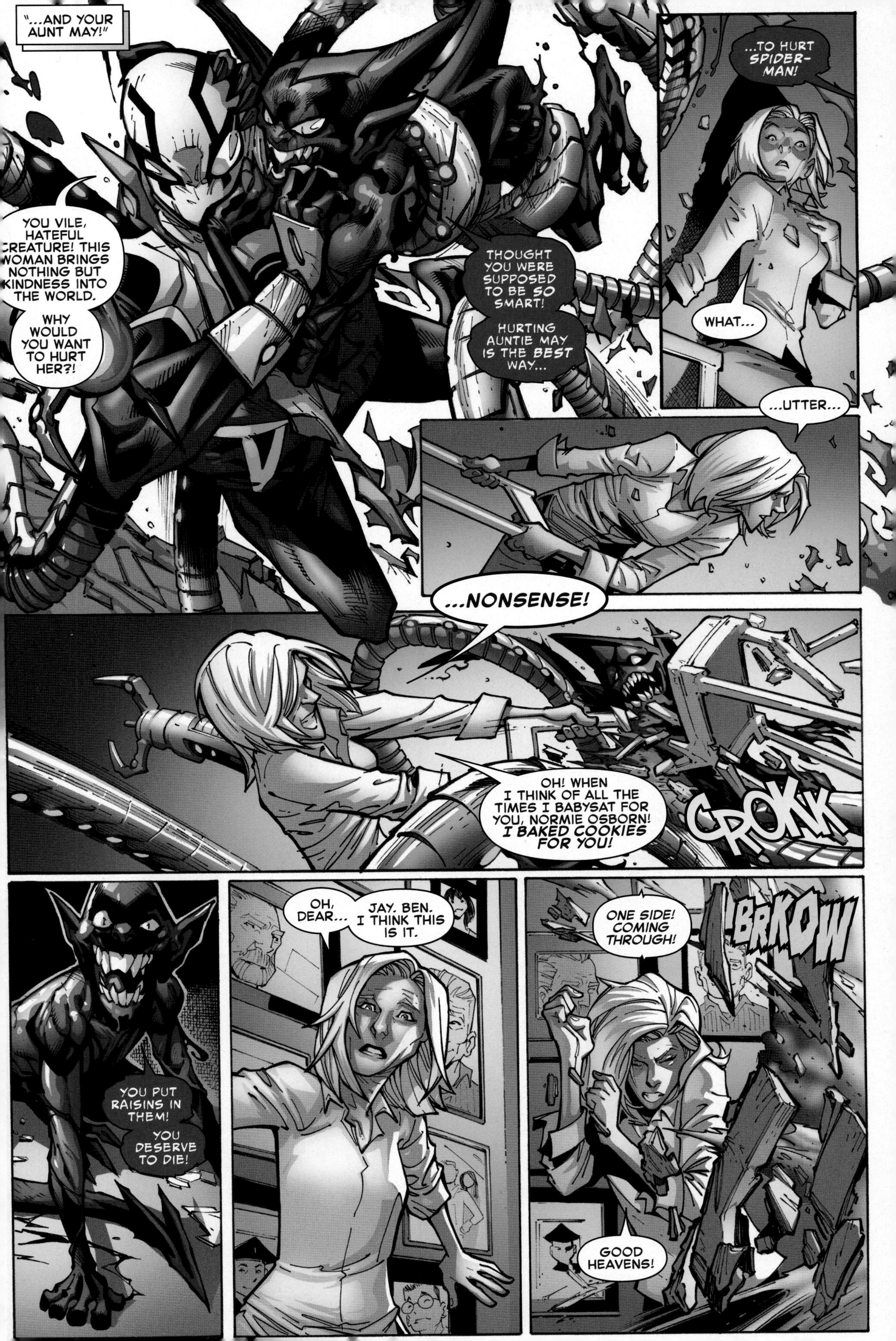
"...AND YOUR AUNT MAY!"
YOU VILE, HATEFUL CREATURE! THIS WOMAN BRINGS NOTHING BUT KINDNESS INTO THE WORLD.
WHY WOULD YOU WANT TO HURT HER?!
THOUGHT YOU WERE SUPPOSED TO BE SO SMART!
HURTING AUNTIE MAY IS THE BEST WAY...
...TO HURT SPIDER-MAN!
WHAT...
...UTTER...
...NONSENSE!
OH! WHEN I THINK OF ALL THE TIMES I BABYSAT FOR YOU, NORMIE OSBORN! I BAKED COOKIES FOR YOU!
CROKK
YOU PUT RAISINS IN THEM!
YOU DESERVE TO DIE!
OH, DEAR...
JAY. BEN. I THINK THIS IS IT.
ONE SIDE! COMING THROUGH!
BRKOW
GOOD HEAVENS!

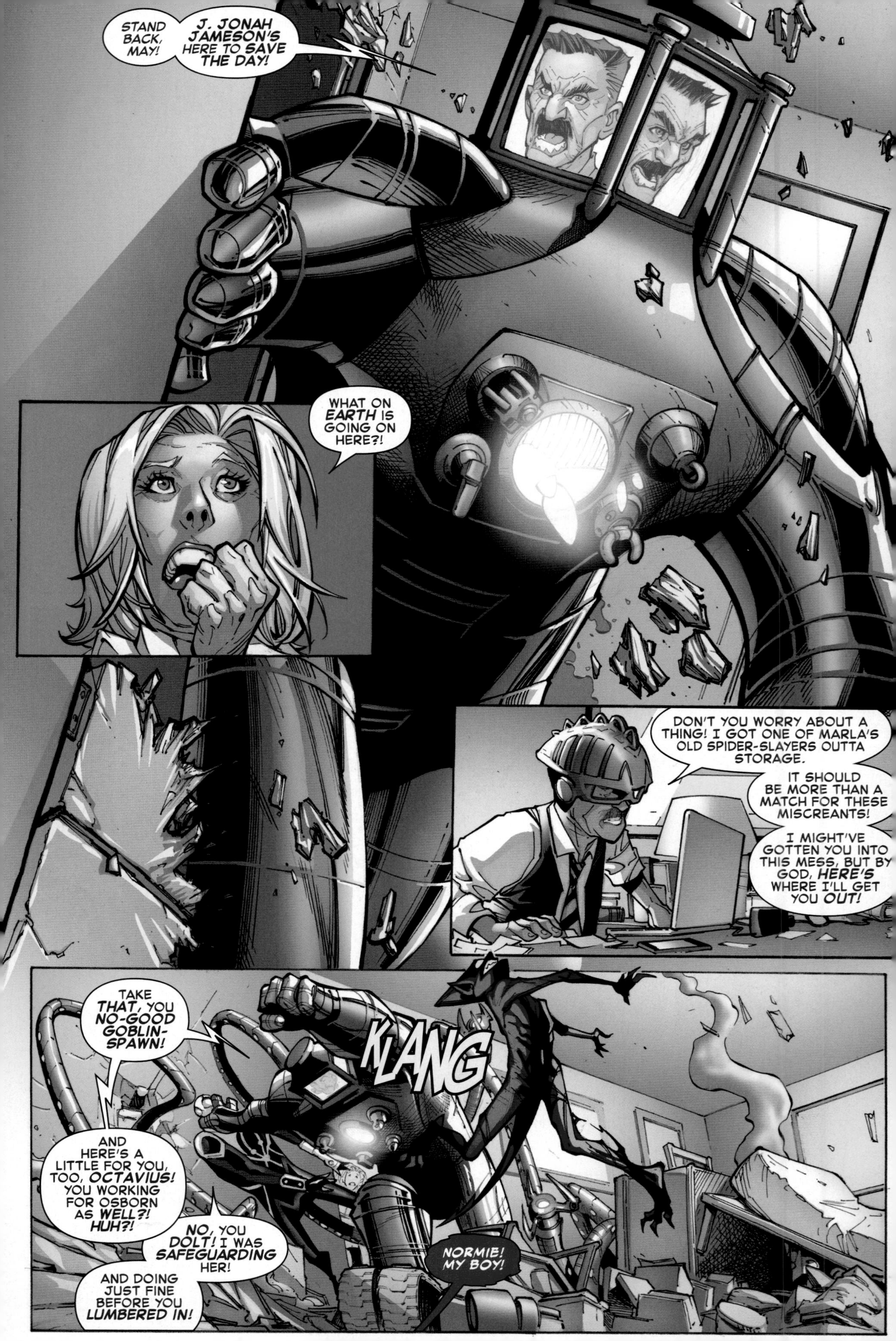
STAND BACK, MAY!
J. JONAH JAMESON'S HERE TO SAVE THE DAY!
WHAT ON EARTH IS GOING ON HERE?!
DON'T YOU WORRY ABOUT A THING! I GOT ONE OF MARLA'S OLD SPIDER-SLAYERS OUTTA STORAGE.
IT SHOULD BE MORE THAN A MATCH FOR THESE MISCREANTS!
I MIGHT'VE GOTTEN YOU INTO THIS MESS, BUT BY GOD, HERE'S WHERE I'LL GET YOU OUT!
TAKE THAT, YOU NO-GOOD GOBLIN-SPAWN!
KLANG
AND HERE'S A LITTLE FOR YOU, TOO, OCTAVIUS! YOU WORKING FOR OSBORN AS WELL?! HUH?!
NO, YOU DOLT! I WAS SAFEGUARDING HER!
AND DOING JUST FINE BEFORE YOU LUMBERED IN!
NORMIE! MY BOY!

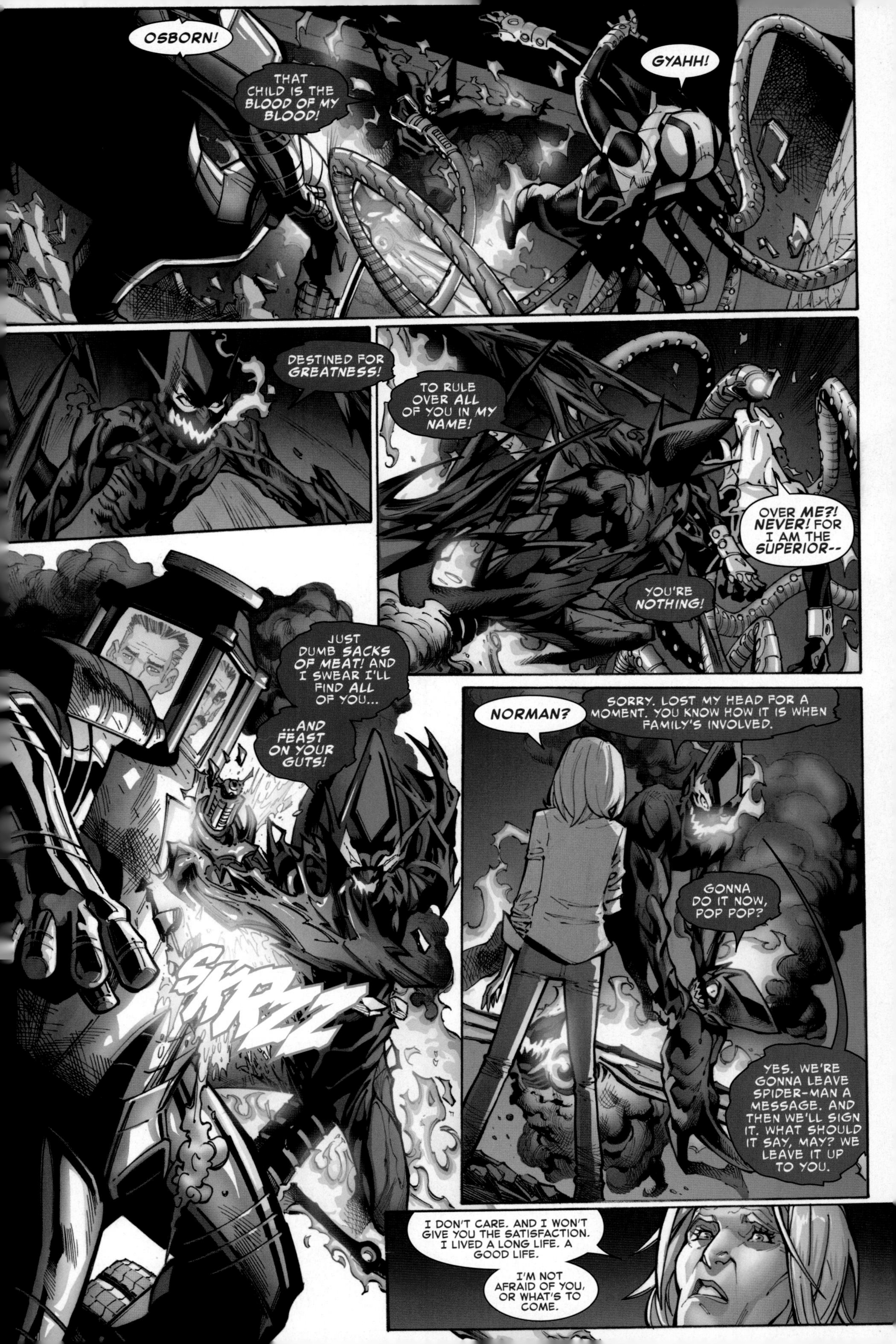
OSBORN!
THAT CHILD IS THE BLOOD OF MY BLOOD!
GYAHH!
DESTINED FOR GREATNESS!
TO RULE OVER ALL OF YOU IN MY NAME!
OVER ME?! NEVER! FOR I AM THE SUPERIOR--
YOU'RE NOTHING!
JUST DUMB SACKS OF MEAT! AND I SWEAR I'LL FIND ALL OF YOU...
...AND FEAST ON YOUR GUTS!
SKRZZ
NORMAN?
SORRY. LOST MY HEAD FOR A MOMENT. YOU KNOW HOW IT IS WHEN FAMILY'S INVOLVED.
GONNA DO IT NOW, POP POP?
YES. WE'RE GONNA LEAVE SPIDER-MAN A MESSAGE. AND THEN WE'LL SIGN IT. WHAT SHOULD IT SAY, MAY? WE LEAVE IT UP TO YOU.
I DON'T CARE. AND I WON'T GIVE YOU THE SATISFACTION. I LIVED A LONG LIFE. A GOOD LIFE.
I'M NOT AFRAID OF YOU, OR WHAT'S TO COME.

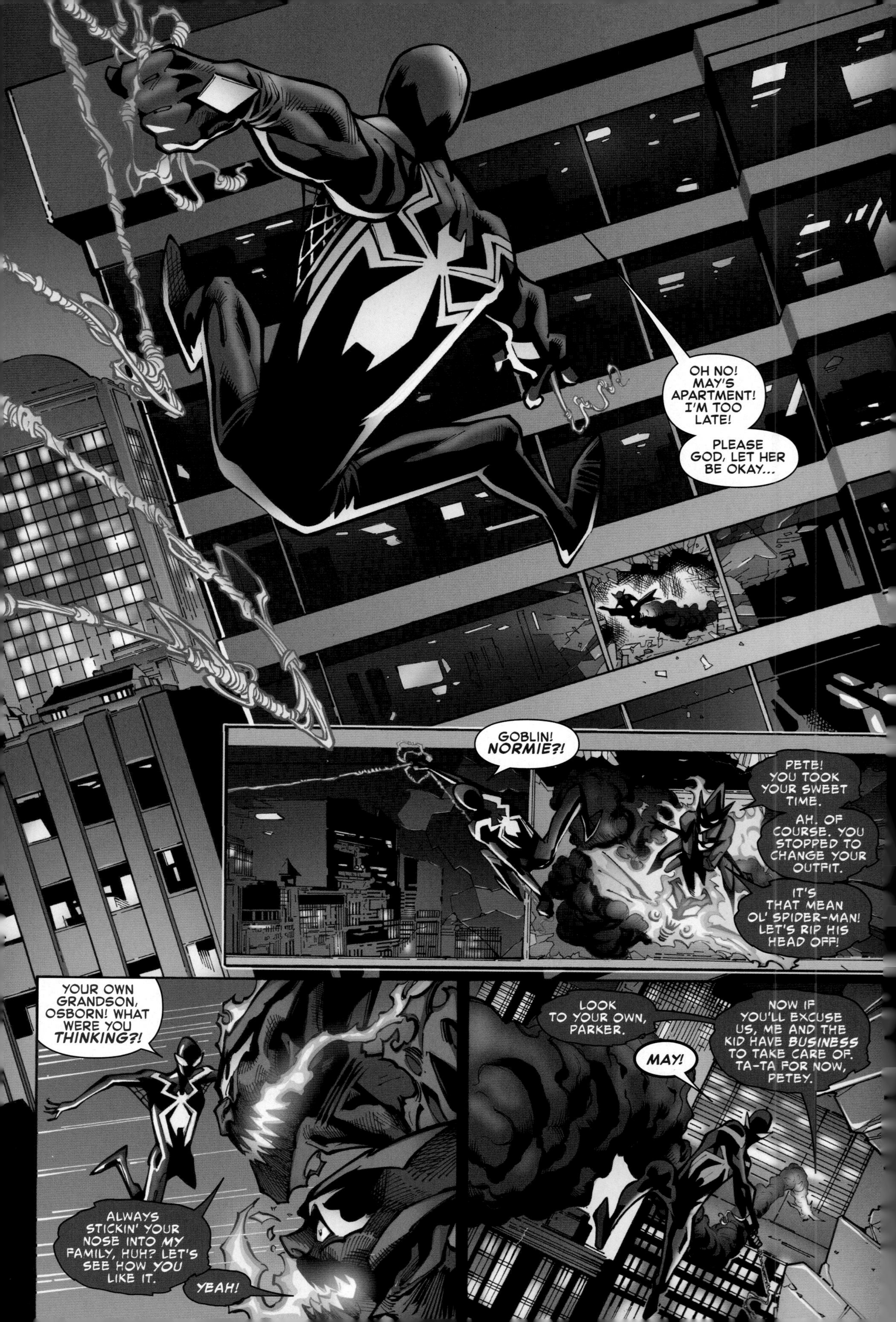
OH NO! MAY'S APARTMENT! I'M TOO LATE!
PLEASE GOD, LET HER BE OKAY...
GOBLIN! NORMIE?!
PETE! YOU TOOK YOUR SWEET TIME.
AH. OF COURSE. YOU STOPPED TO CHANGE YOUR OUTFIT.
IT'S THAT MEAN OL' SPIDER-MAN! LET'S RIP HIS HEAD OFF!
YOUR OWN GRANDSON, OSBORN! WHAT WERE YOU THINKING?!
ALWAYS STICKIN' YOUR NOSE INTO MY FAMILY, HUH? LET'S SEE HOW YOU LIKE IT.
YEAH!
LOOK TO YOUR OWN, PARKER.
NOW IF YOU'LL EXCUSE US, ME AND THE KID HAVE BUSINESS TO TAKE CARE OF. TA-TA FOR NOW, PETEY.
MAY!

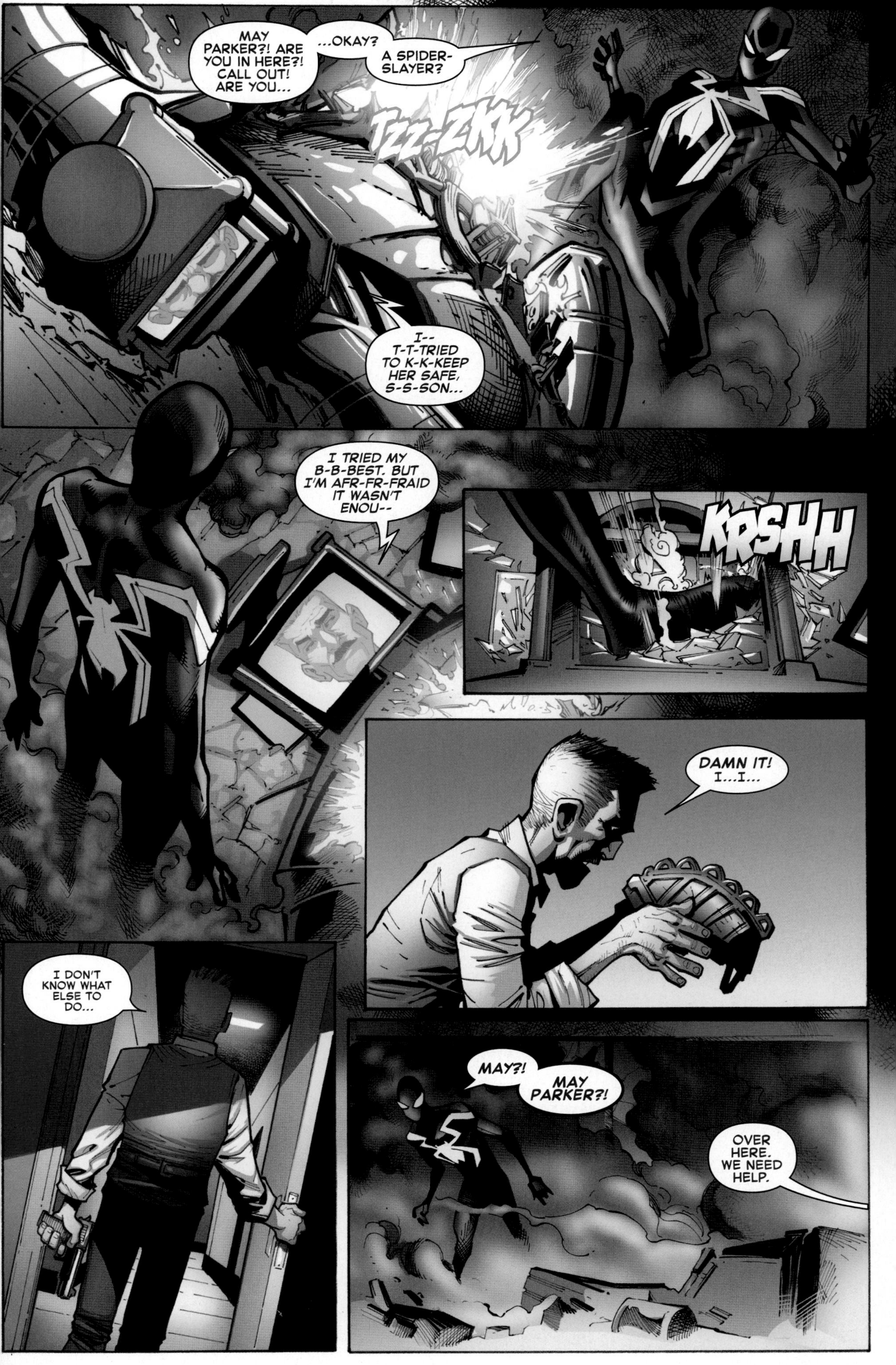
MAY PARKER?! ARE YOU IN HERE?! CALL OUT! ARE YOU...
...OKAY?
A SPIDER-SLAYER?
TZZ-ZKK
I-- T-T-TRIED TO K-K-KEEP HER SAFE, S-S-SON...
I TRIED MY B-B-BEST. BUT I'M AFR-FR-FRAID IT WASN'T ENOU--
KRSHH
DAMN IT! I...I...
I DON'T KNOW WHAT ELSE TO DO...
MAY?!
MAY PARKER?!
OVER HERE. WE NEED HELP.

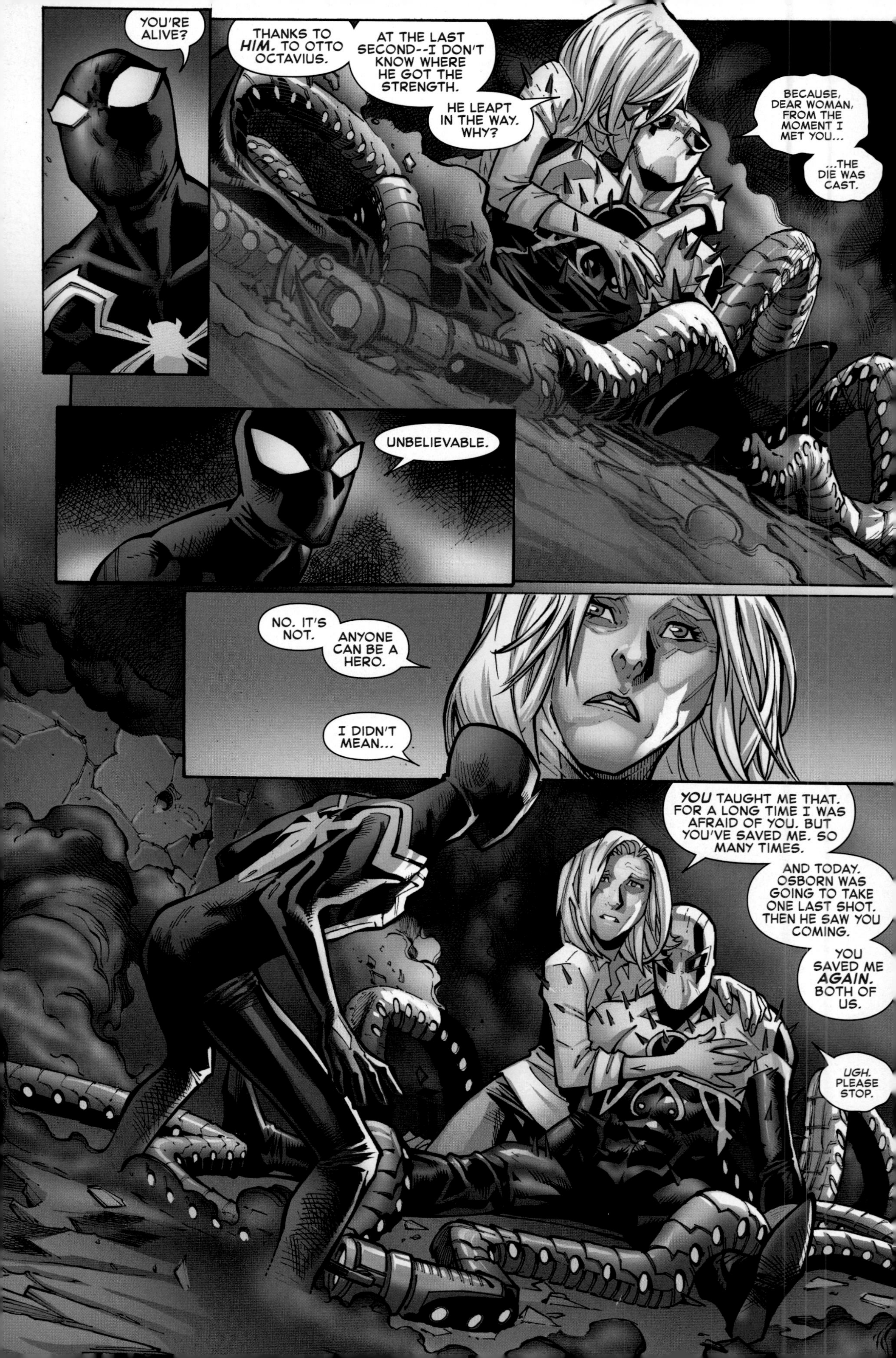
YOU'RE ALIVE?
THANKS TO *HIM*. TO OTTO OCTAVIUS.
AT THE LAST SECOND--I DON'T KNOW WHERE HE GOT THE STRENGTH.
HE LEAPT IN THE WAY. WHY?
BECAUSE, DEAR WOMAN, FROM THE MOMENT I MET YOU...
...THE DIE WAS CAST.
UNBELIEVABLE.
NO. IT'S NOT.
ANYONE CAN BE A HERO.
I DIDN'T MEAN...
YOU TAUGHT ME THAT. FOR A LONG TIME I WAS AFRAID OF YOU. BUT YOU'VE SAVED ME. SO MANY TIMES.
AND TODAY. OSBORN WAS GOING TO TAKE ONE LAST SHOT. THEN HE SAW YOU COMING.
YOU SAVED ME *AGAIN*. BOTH OF US.
UGH. PLEASE STOP.

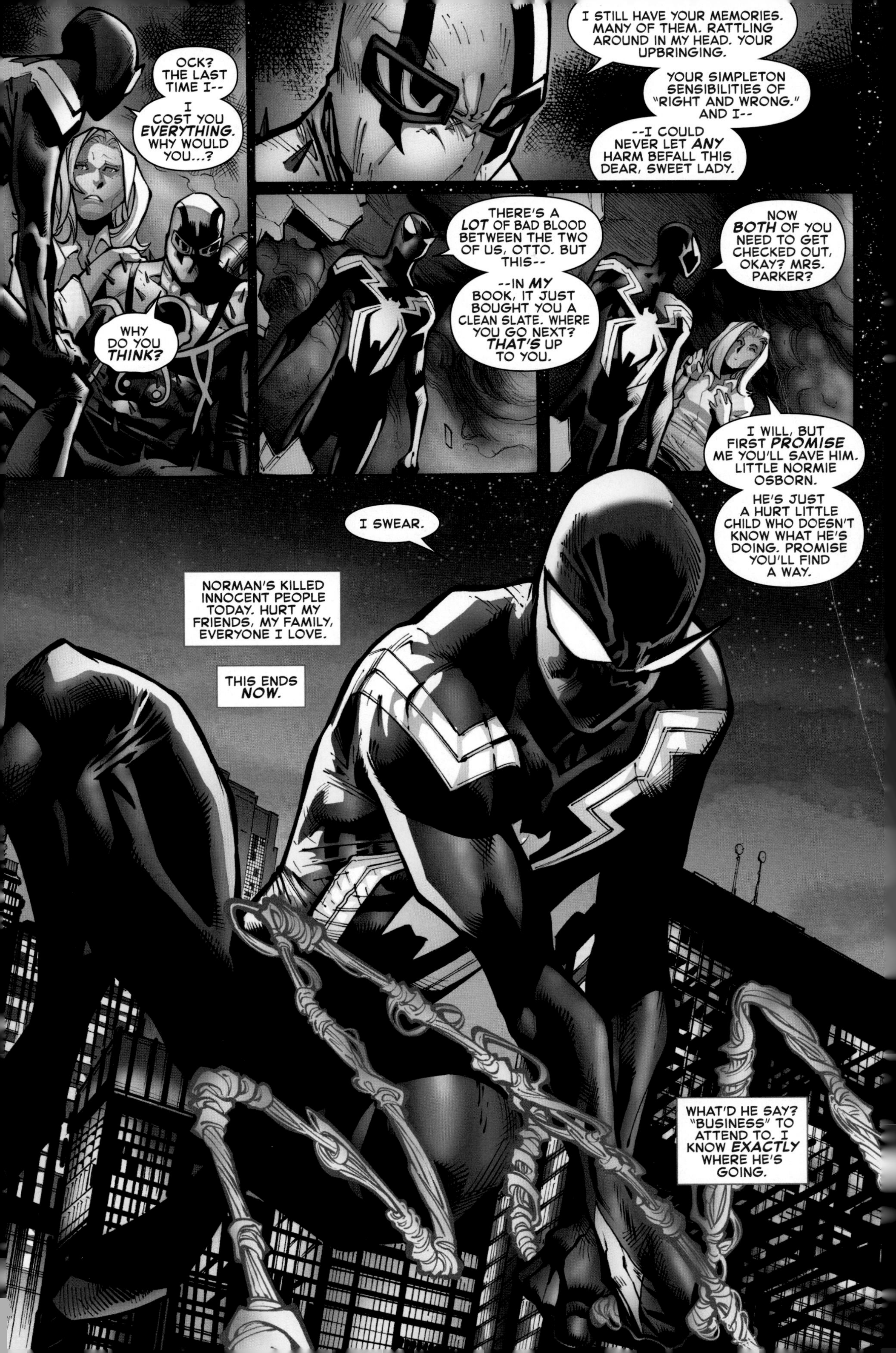
OCK? THE LAST TIME I--
I COST YOU EVERYTHING. WHY WOULD YOU...?
WHY DO YOU THINK?
I STILL HAVE YOUR MEMORIES. MANY OF THEM. RATTLING AROUND IN MY HEAD. YOUR UPBRINGING.
YOUR SIMPLETON SENSIBILITIES OF "RIGHT AND WRONG." AND I--
--I COULD NEVER LET ANY HARM BEFALL THIS DEAR, SWEET LADY.
THERE'S A LOT OF BAD BLOOD BETWEEN THE TWO OF US, OTTO. BUT THIS--
--IN MY BOOK, IT JUST BOUGHT YOU A CLEAN SLATE. WHERE YOU GO NEXT? THAT'S UP TO YOU.
NOW BOTH OF YOU NEED TO GET CHECKED OUT, OKAY? MRS. PARKER?
I WILL, BUT FIRST PROMISE ME YOU'LL SAVE HIM. LITTLE NORMIE OSBORN.
HE'S JUST A HURT LITTLE CHILD WHO DOESN'T KNOW WHAT HE'S DOING. PROMISE YOU'LL FIND A WAY.
I SWEAR.
NORMAN'S KILLED INNOCENT PEOPLE TODAY. HURT MY FRIENDS, MY FAMILY, EVERYONE I LOVE.
THIS ENDS NOW.
WHAT'D HE SAY? "BUSINESS" TO ATTEND TO. I KNOW EXACTLY WHERE HE'S GOING.

Chapter 3
Family Infighting

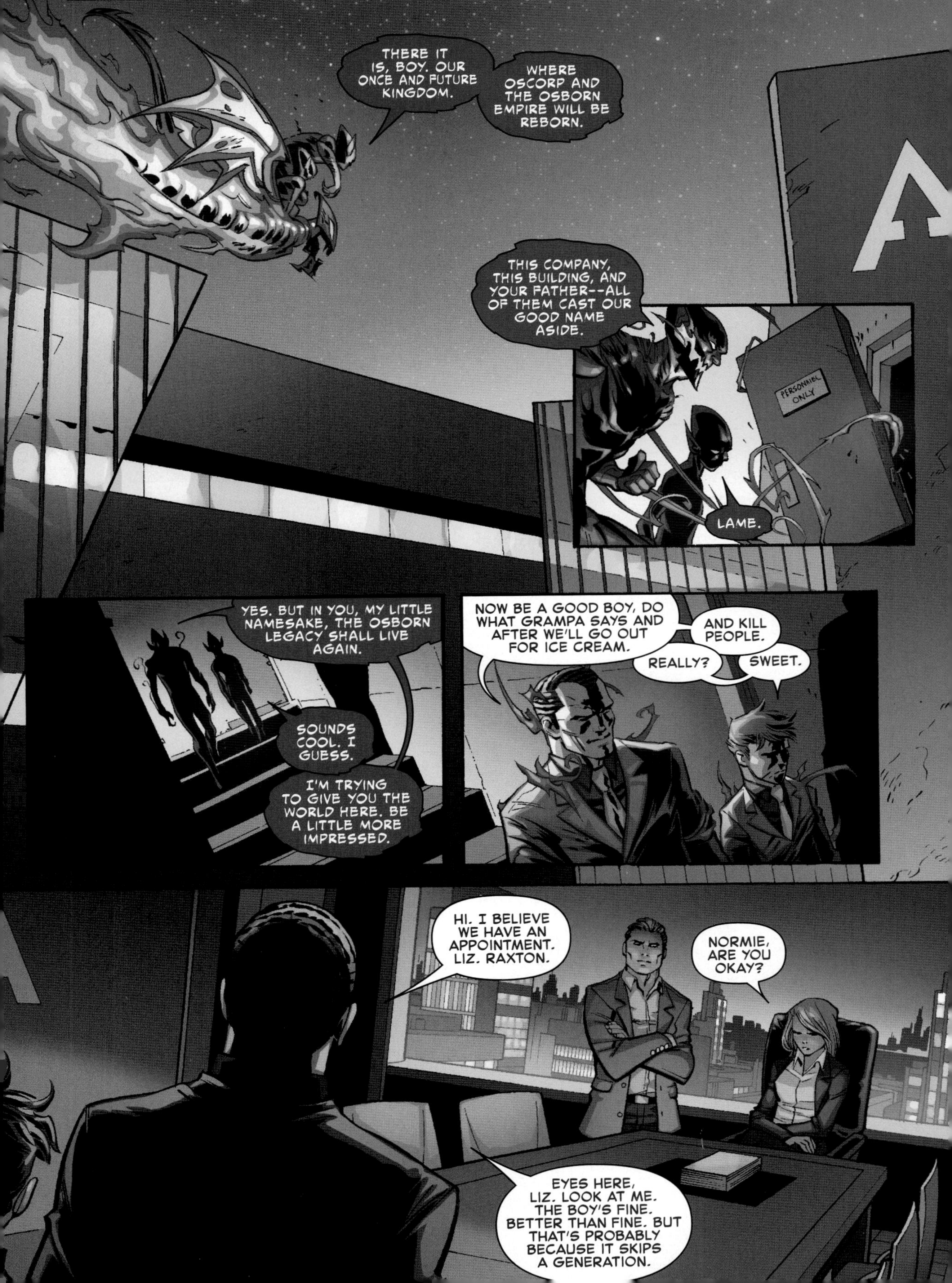
THERE IT IS, BOY. OUR ONCE AND FUTURE KINGDOM.
WHERE OSCORP AND THE OSBORN EMPIRE WILL BE REBORN.
THIS COMPANY, THIS BUILDING, AND YOUR FATHER--ALL OF THEM CAST OUR GOOD NAME ASIDE.
PERSONNEL ONLY
LAME.
YES. BUT IN YOU, MY LITTLE NAMESAKE, THE OSBORN LEGACY SHALL LIVE AGAIN.
SOUNDS COOL. I GUESS.
I'M TRYING TO GIVE YOU THE WORLD HERE. BE A LITTLE MORE IMPRESSED.
NOW BE A GOOD BOY, DO WHAT GRAMPA SAYS AND AFTER WE'LL GO OUT FOR ICE CREAM.
REALLY?
AND KILL PEOPLE.
SWEET.
HI. I BELIEVE WE HAVE AN APPOINTMENT. LIZ. RAXTON.
NORMIE, ARE YOU OKAY?
EYES HERE, LIZ. LOOK AT ME. THE BOY'S FINE. BETTER THAN FINE. BUT THAT'S PROBABLY BECAUSE IT SKIPS A GENERATION.

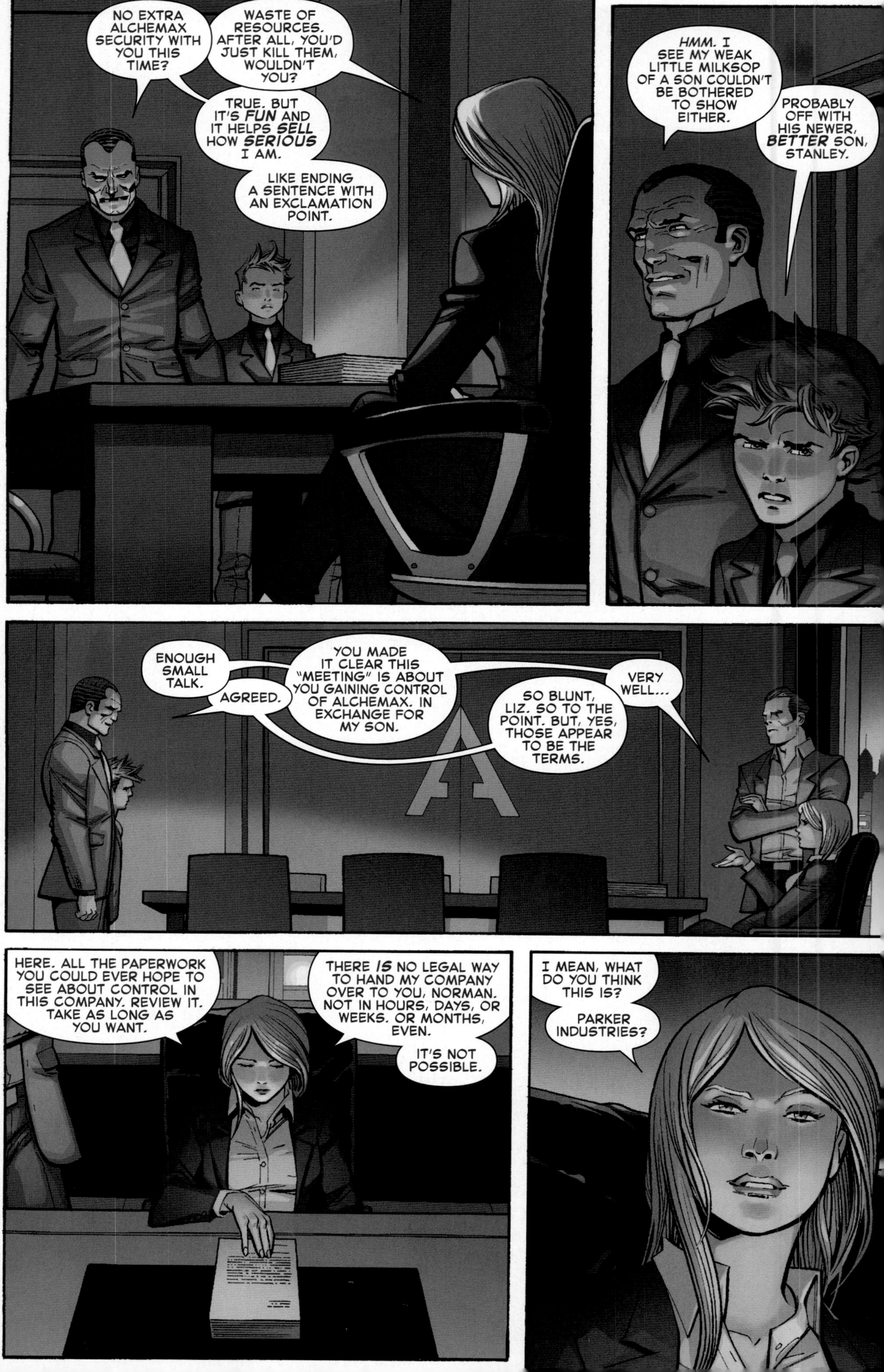
NO EXTRA ALCHEMAX SECURITY WITH YOU THIS TIME?
WASTE OF RESOURCES. AFTER ALL, YOU'D JUST KILL THEM, WOULDN'T YOU?
TRUE. BUT IT'S FUN AND IT HELPS SELL HOW SERIOUS I AM.
LIKE ENDING A SENTENCE WITH AN EXCLAMATION POINT.
HMM. I SEE MY WEAK LITTLE MILKSOP OF A SON COULDN'T BE BOTHERED TO SHOW EITHER.
PROBABLY OFF WITH HIS NEWER, BETTER SON, STANLEY.
ENOUGH SMALL TALK.
AGREED.
YOU MADE IT CLEAR THIS "MEETING" IS ABOUT YOU GAINING CONTROL OF ALCHEMAX. IN EXCHANGE FOR MY SON.
SO BLUNT, LIZ. SO TO THE POINT. BUT, YES, THOSE APPEAR TO BE THE TERMS.
VERY WELL...
HERE. ALL THE PAPERWORK YOU COULD EVER HOPE TO SEE ABOUT CONTROL IN THIS COMPANY. REVIEW IT. TAKE AS LONG AS YOU WANT.
THERE IS NO LEGAL WAY TO HAND MY COMPANY OVER TO YOU, NORMAN. NOT IN HOURS, DAYS, OR WEEKS. OR MONTHS, EVEN.
IT'S NOT POSSIBLE.
I MEAN, WHAT DO YOU THINK THIS IS?
PARKER INDUSTRIES?

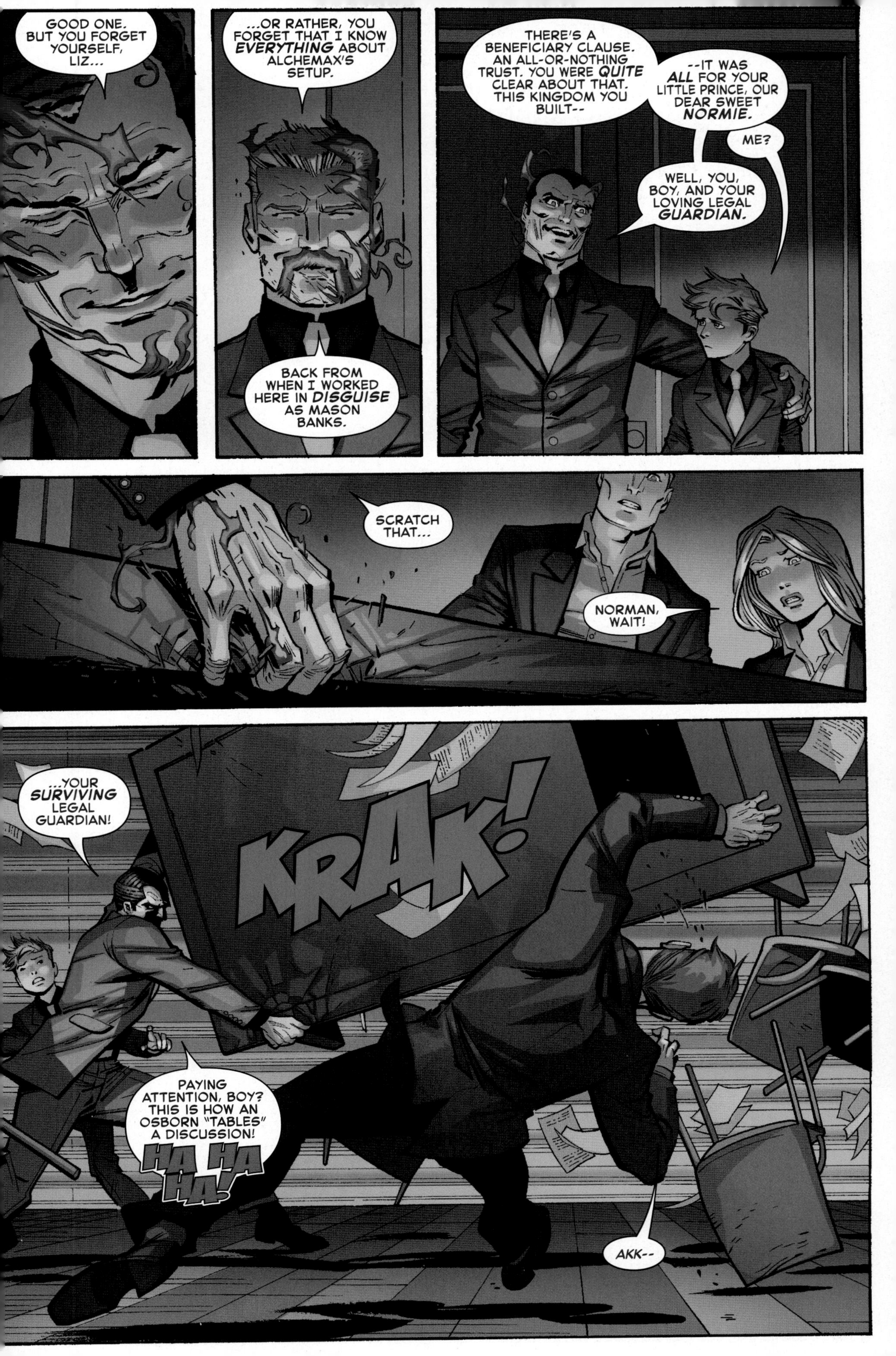
GOOD ONE. BUT YOU FORGET YOURSELF, LIZ...
...OR RATHER, YOU FORGET THAT I KNOW EVERYTHING ABOUT ALCHEMAX'S SETUP.
BACK FROM WHEN I WORKED HERE IN DISGUISE AS MASON BANKS.
THERE'S A BENEFICIARY CLAUSE. AN ALL-OR-NOTHING TRUST. YOU WERE QUITE CLEAR ABOUT THAT. THIS KINGDOM YOU BUILT--
--IT WAS ALL FOR YOUR LITTLE PRINCE, OUR DEAR SWEET NORMIE.
ME?
WELL, YOU, BOY, AND YOUR LOVING LEGAL GUARDIAN.
SCRATCH THAT...
NORMAN, WAIT!
...YOUR SURVIVING LEGAL GUARDIAN!
KRAK!
PAYING ATTENTION, BOY? THIS IS HOW AN OSBORN "TABLES" A DISCUSSION!
HA HA HA!
AKK--

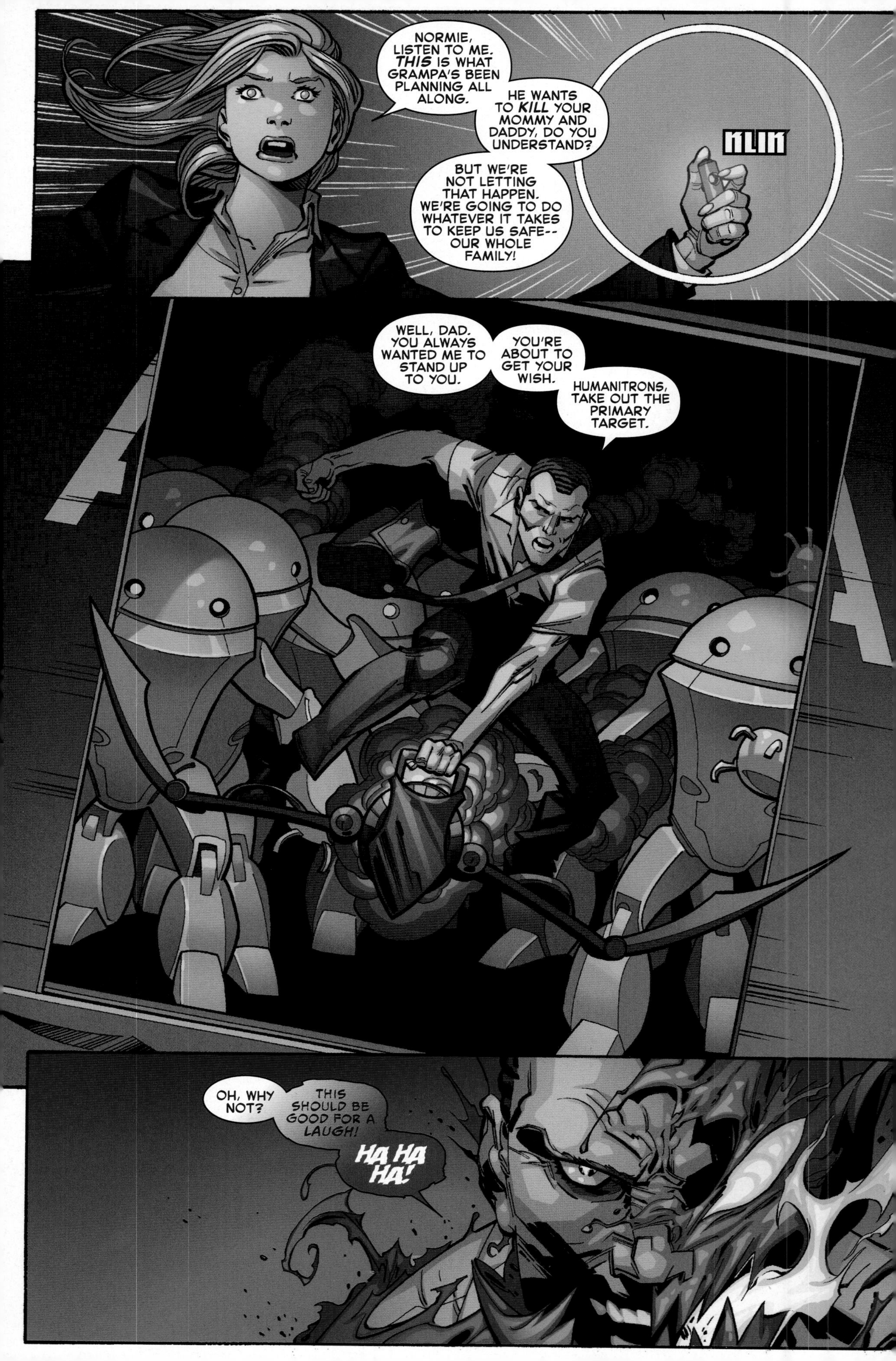
NORMIE, LISTEN TO ME. THIS IS WHAT GRAMPA'S BEEN PLANNING ALL ALONG.
HE WANTS TO KILL YOUR MOMMY AND DADDY, DO YOU UNDERSTAND?
BUT WE'RE NOT LETTING THAT HAPPEN. WE'RE GOING TO DO WHATEVER IT TAKES TO KEEP US SAFE-- OUR WHOLE FAMILY!
KLIK
WELL, DAD. YOU ALWAYS WANTED ME TO STAND UP TO YOU.
YOU'RE ABOUT TO GET YOUR WISH.
HUMANITRONS, TAKE OUT THE PRIMARY TARGET.
OH, WHY NOT?
THIS SHOULD BE GOOD FOR A LAUGH!
HA HA HA!

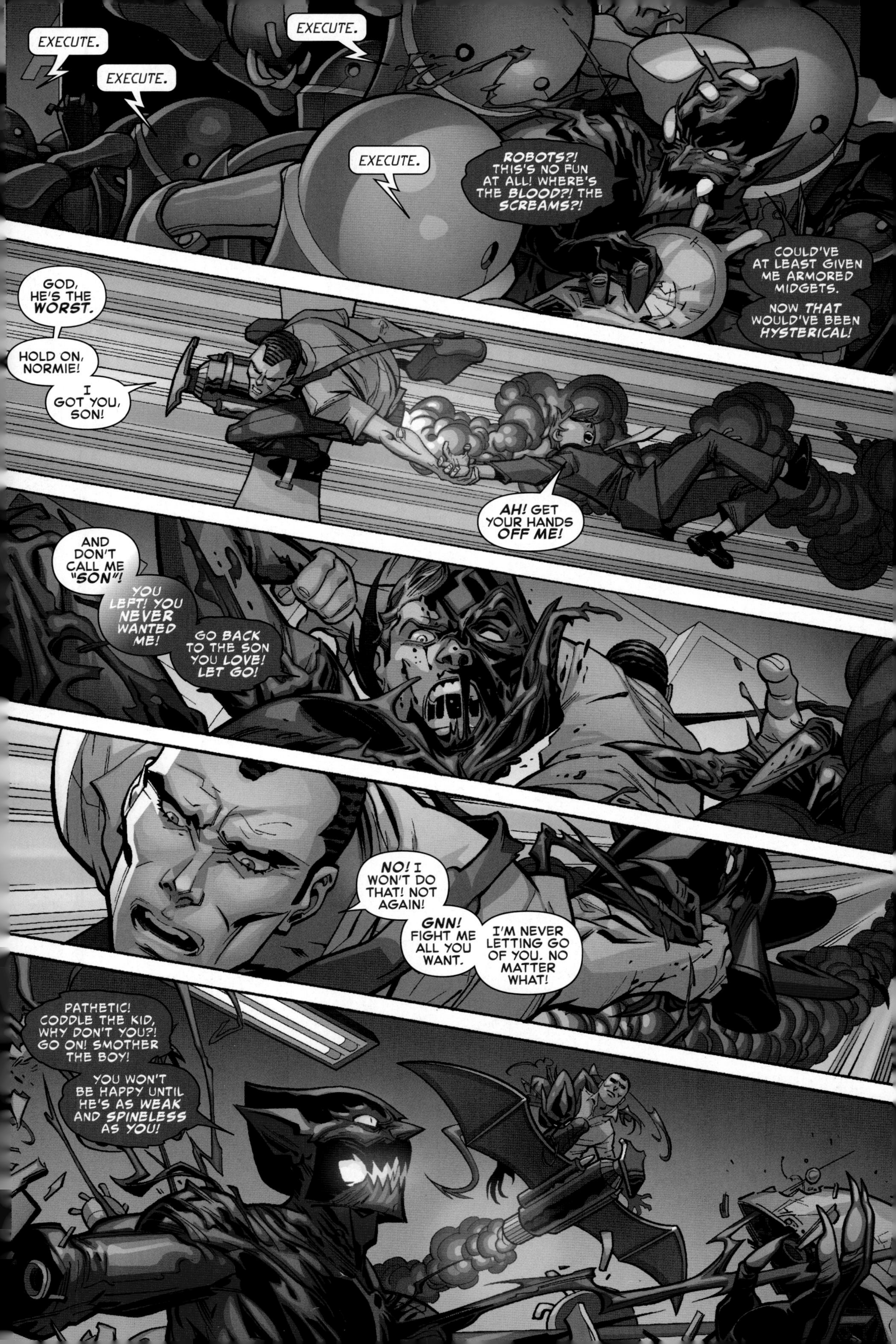
EXECUTE.
EXECUTE.
EXECUTE.
EXECUTE.
ROBOTS?! THIS'S NO FUN AT ALL! WHERE'S THE BLOOD?! THE SCREAMS?!
COULD'VE AT LEAST GIVEN ME ARMORED MIDGETS.
NOW THAT WOULD'VE BEEN HYSTERICAL!
GOD, HE'S THE WORST.
HOLD ON, NORMIE!
I GOT YOU, SON!
AH! GET YOUR HANDS OFF ME!
AND DON'T CALL ME "SON"!
YOU LEFT! YOU NEVER WANTED ME!
GO BACK TO THE SON YOU LOVE! LET GO!
NO! I WON'T DO THAT! NOT AGAIN!
GNN! FIGHT ME ALL YOU WANT.
I'M NEVER LETTING GO OF YOU. NO MATTER WHAT!
PATHETIC! CODDLE THE KID, WHY DON'T YOU?! GO ON! SMOTHER THE BOY!
YOU WON'T BE HAPPY UNTIL HE'S AS WEAK AND SPINELESS AS YOU!

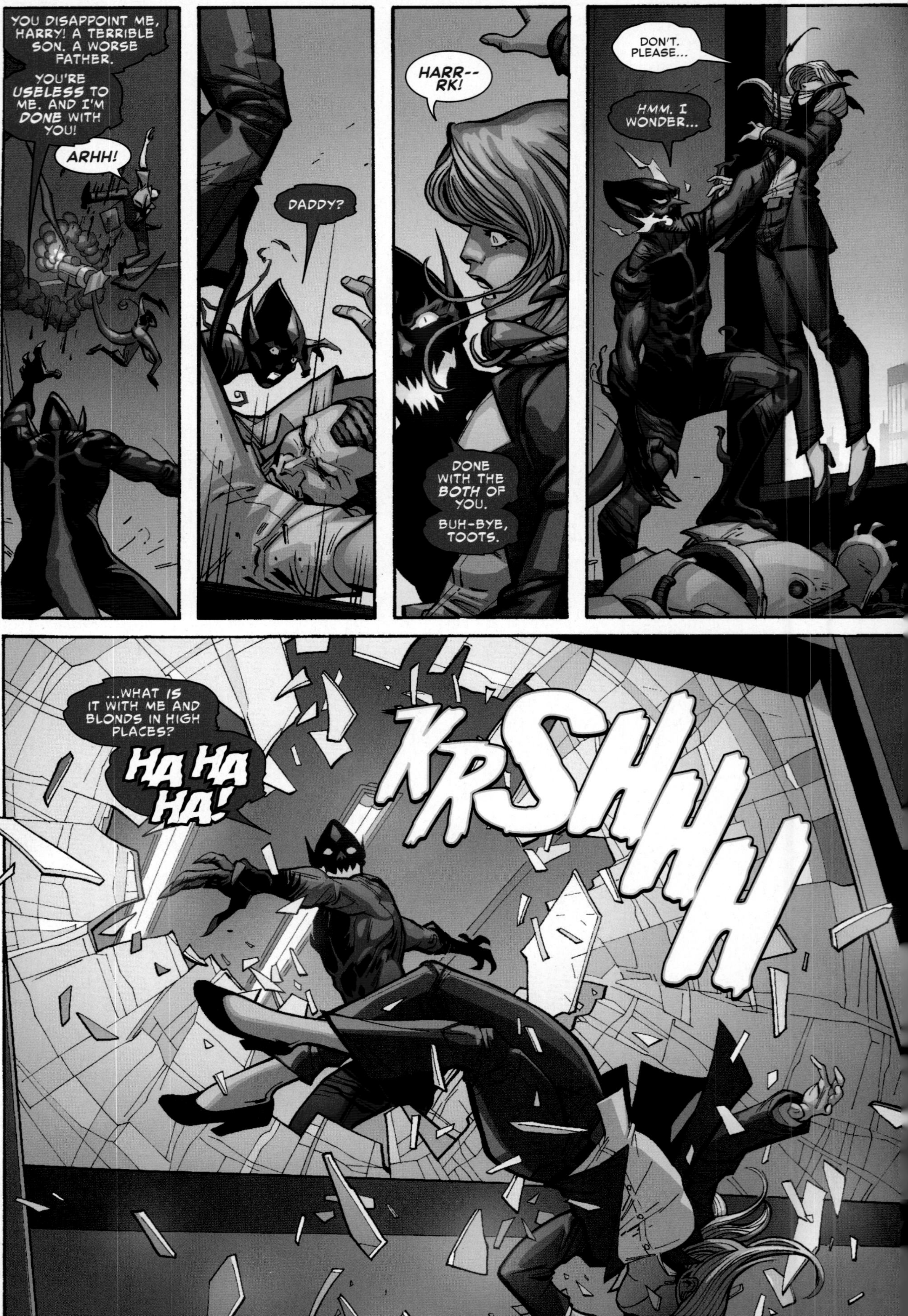
YOU DISAPPOINT ME, HARRY! A TERRIBLE SON. A WORSE FATHER.
YOU'RE USELESS TO ME. AND I'M DONE WITH YOU!
ARHH!
DADDY?
HARR--RK!
DONE WITH THE BOTH OF YOU.
BUH-BYE, TOOTS.
DON'T. PLEASE...
HMM. I WONDER...
...WHAT IS IT WITH ME AND BLONDS IN HIGH PLACES?
HA HA HA!
KRSHHHH

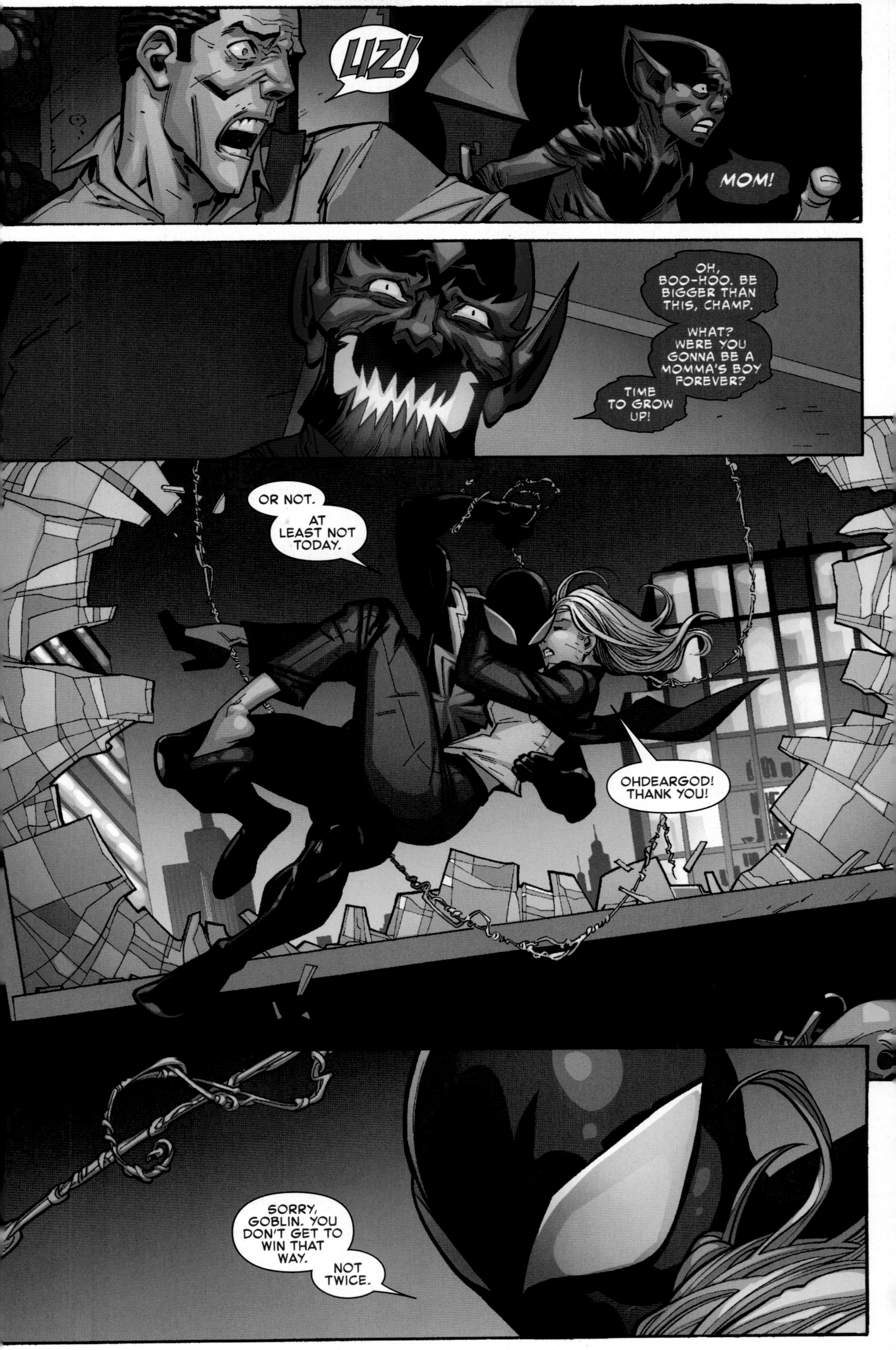
LIZ!
MOM!
OH, BOO-HOO. BE BIGGER THAN THIS, CHAMP.
WHAT? WERE YOU GONNA BE A MOMMA'S BOY FOREVER?
TIME TO GROW UP!
OR NOT.
AT LEAST NOT TODAY.
OHDEARGOD! THANK YOU!
SORRY, GOBLIN. YOU DON'T GET TO WIN THAT WAY.
NOT TWICE.

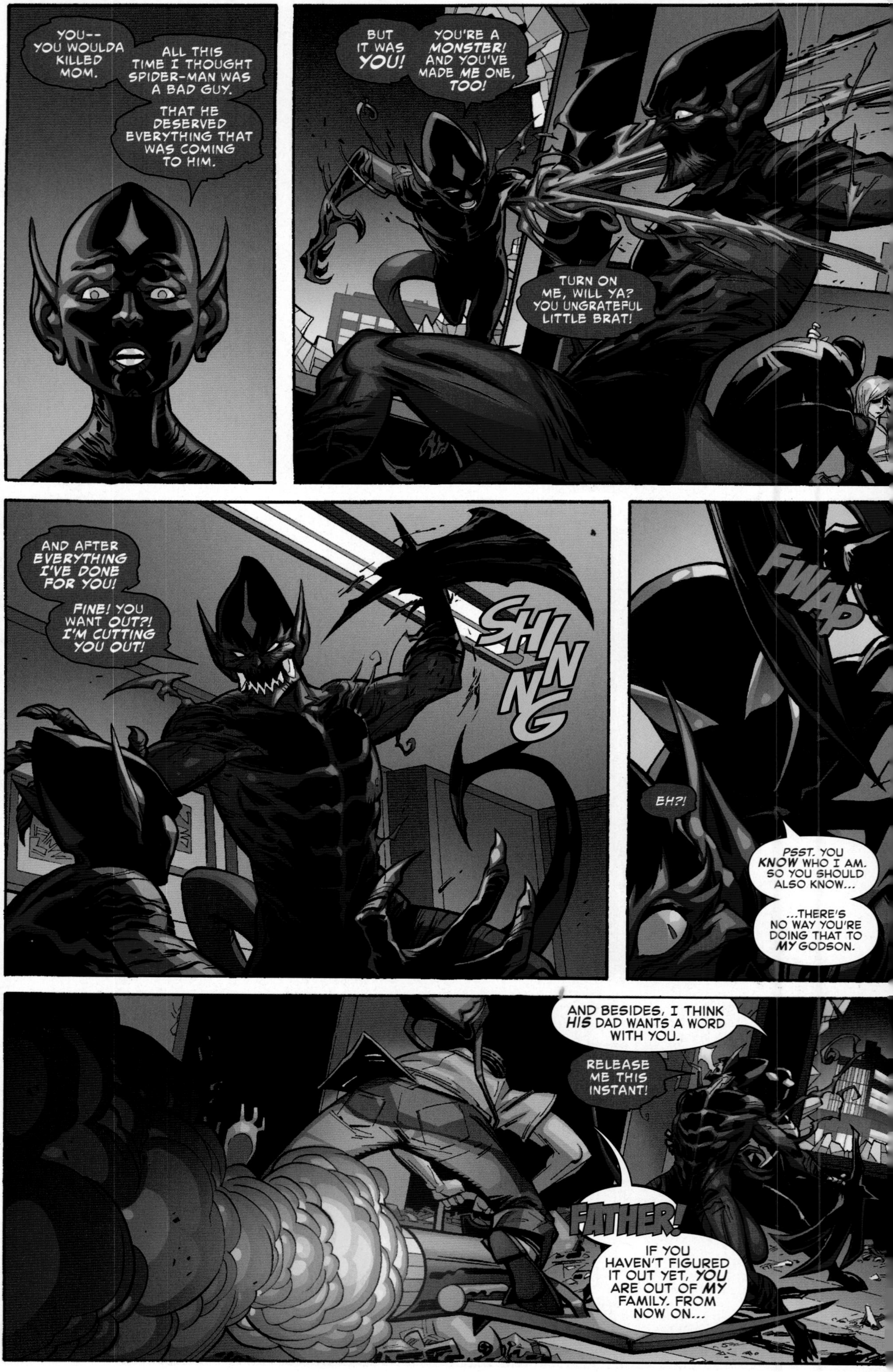
YOU-- YOU WOULDA KILLED MOM.
ALL THIS TIME I THOUGHT SPIDER-MAN WAS A BAD GUY.
THAT HE DESERVED EVERYTHING THAT WAS COMING TO HIM.
BUT IT WAS YOU!
YOU'RE A MONSTER! AND YOU'VE MADE ME ONE, TOO!
TURN ON ME, WILL YA? YOU UNGRATEFUL LITTLE BRAT!
AND AFTER EVERYTHING I'VE DONE FOR YOU!
FINE! YOU WANT OUT?! I'M CUTTING YOU OUT!
SHIIINNG
FWAP
EH?!
PSST. YOU KNOW WHO I AM. SO YOU SHOULD ALSO KNOW...
...THERE'S NO WAY YOU'RE DOING THAT TO MY GODSON.
AND BESIDES, I THINK HIS DAD WANTS A WORD WITH YOU.
RELEASE ME THIS INSTANT!
FATHER!
IF YOU HAVEN'T FIGURED IT OUT YET, YOU ARE OUT OF MY FAMILY. FROM NOW ON...

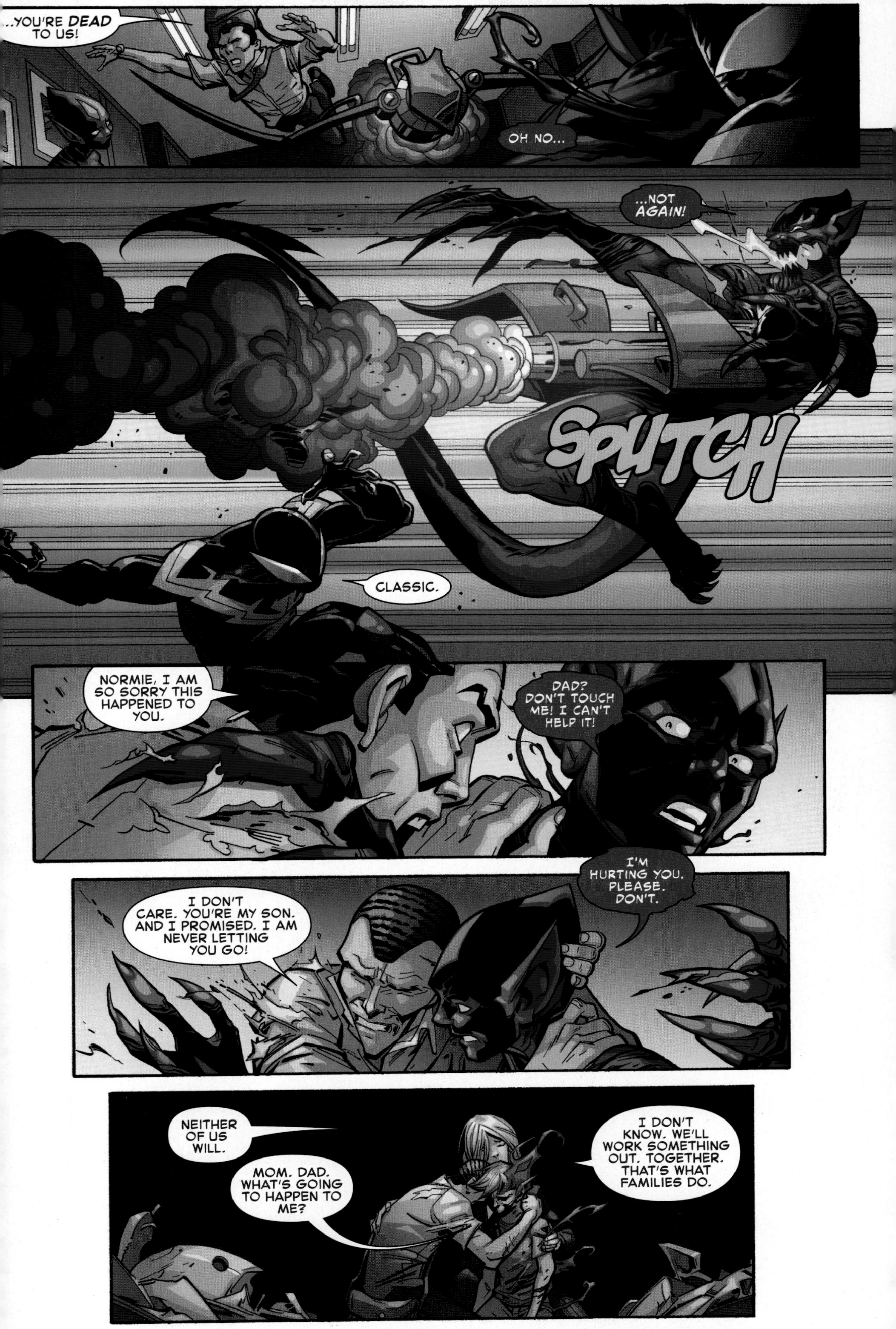
...YOU'RE DEAD TO US!
OH NO...
...NOT AGAIN!
SPUTCH
CLASSIC.
NORMIE, I AM SO SORRY THIS HAPPENED TO YOU.
DAD? DON'T TOUCH ME! I CAN'T HELP IT!
I DON'T CARE. YOU'RE MY SON. AND I PROMISED. I AM NEVER LETTING YOU GO!
I'M HURTING YOU. PLEASE. DON'T.
NEITHER OF US WILL.
MOM. DAD. WHAT'S GOING TO HAPPEN TO ME?
I DON'T KNOW. WE'LL WORK SOMETHING OUT. TOGETHER. THAT'S WHAT FAMILIES DO.

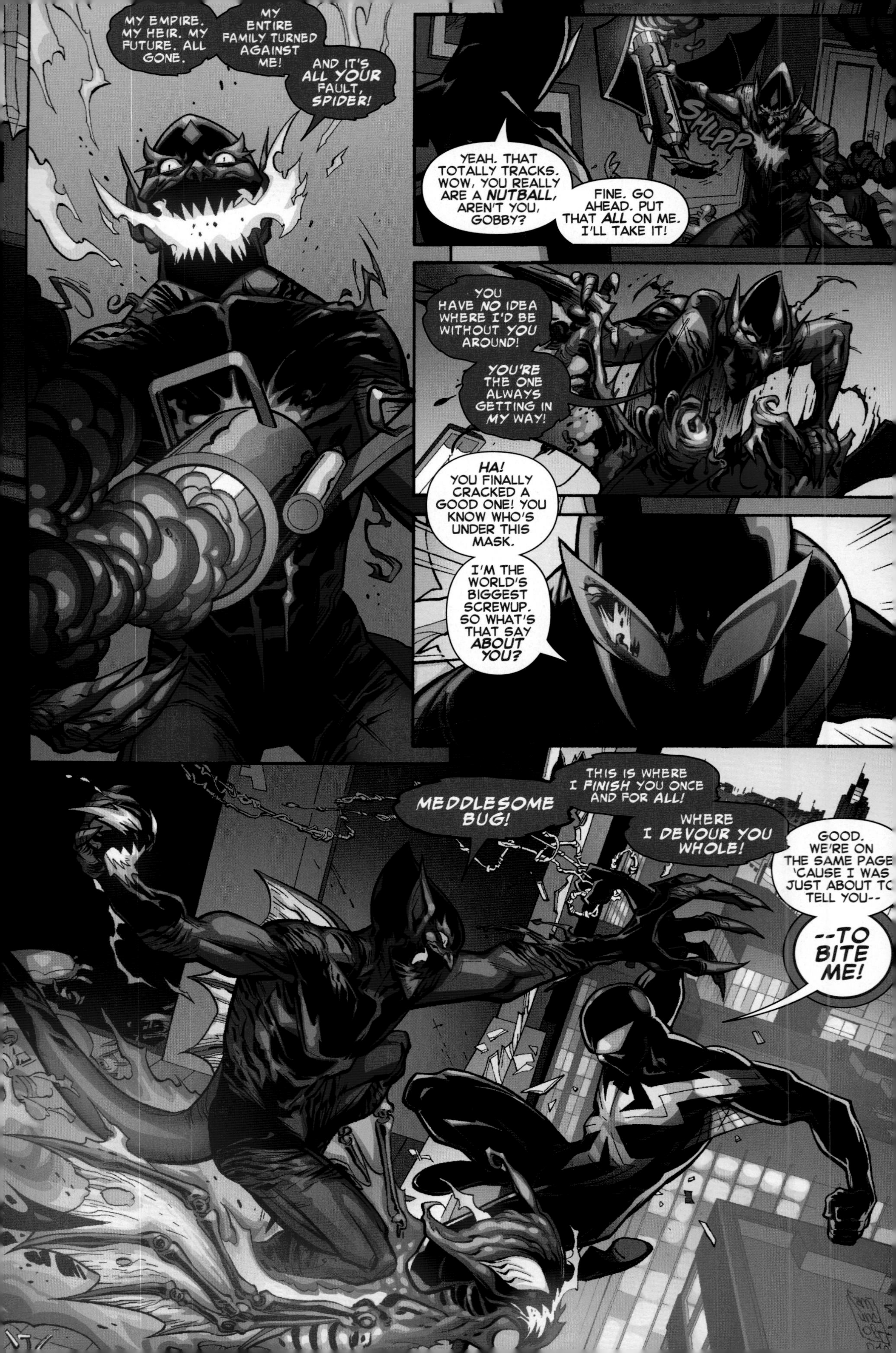
MY EMPIRE. MY HEIR. MY FUTURE. ALL GONE.
MY ENTIRE FAMILY TURNED AGAINST ME!
AND IT'S ALL YOUR FAULT, SPIDER!
SHLPP
YEAH. THAT TOTALLY TRACKS. WOW, YOU REALLY ARE A NUTBALL, AREN'T YOU, GOBBY?
FINE. GO AHEAD. PUT THAT ALL ON ME. I'LL TAKE IT!
YOU HAVE NO IDEA WHERE I'D BE WITHOUT YOU AROUND!
YOU'RE THE ONE ALWAYS GETTING IN MY WAY!
HA! YOU FINALLY CRACKED A GOOD ONE! YOU KNOW WHO'S UNDER THIS MASK.
I'M THE WORLD'S BIGGEST SCREWUP. SO WHAT'S THAT SAY ABOUT YOU?
MEDDLESOME BUG!
THIS IS WHERE I FINISH YOU ONCE AND FOR ALL!
WHERE I DEVOUR YOU WHOLE!
GOOD. WE'RE ON THE SAME PAGE 'CAUSE I WAS JUST ABOUT TO TELL YOU--
--TO BITE ME!

Chapter 4
The Goblin Triumphant

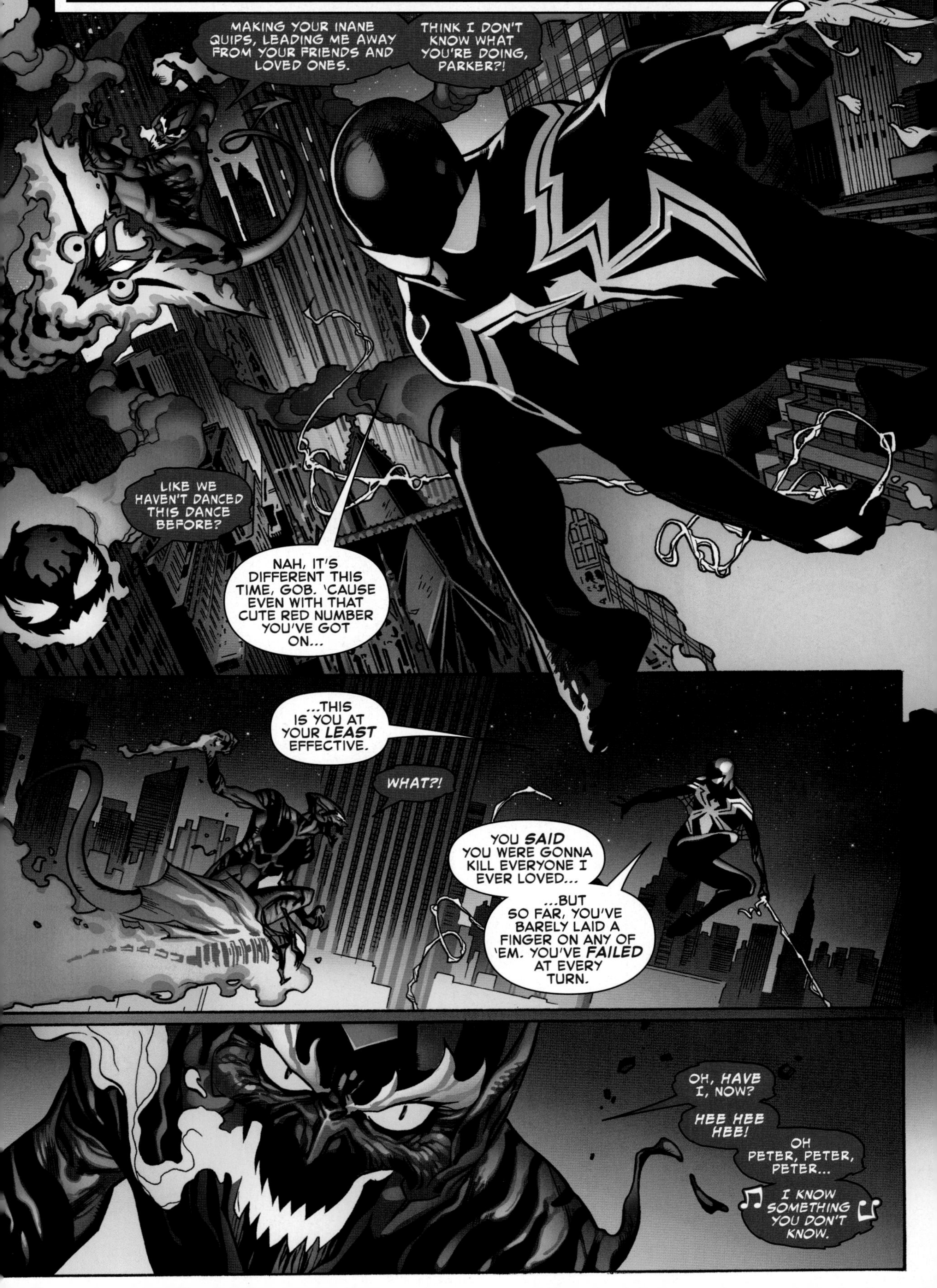
MAKING YOUR INANE QUIPS, LEADING ME AWAY FROM YOUR FRIENDS AND LOVED ONES.
THINK I DON'T KNOW WHAT YOU'RE DOING, PARKER?!
LIKE WE HAVEN'T DANCED THIS DANCE BEFORE?
NAH, IT'S DIFFERENT THIS TIME, GOB. 'CAUSE EVEN WITH THAT CUTE RED NUMBER YOU'VE GOT ON...
...THIS IS YOU AT YOUR *LEAST* EFFECTIVE.
WHAT?!
YOU *SAID* YOU WERE GONNA KILL EVERYONE I EVER LOVED...
...BUT SO FAR, YOU'VE BARELY LAID A FINGER ON ANY OF 'EM. YOU'VE *FAILED* AT EVERY TURN.
OH, *HAVE* I, NOW?
HEE HEE HEE!
OH PETER, PETER, PETER...
♪ *I KNOW SOMETHING YOU DON'T KNOW.* ♪

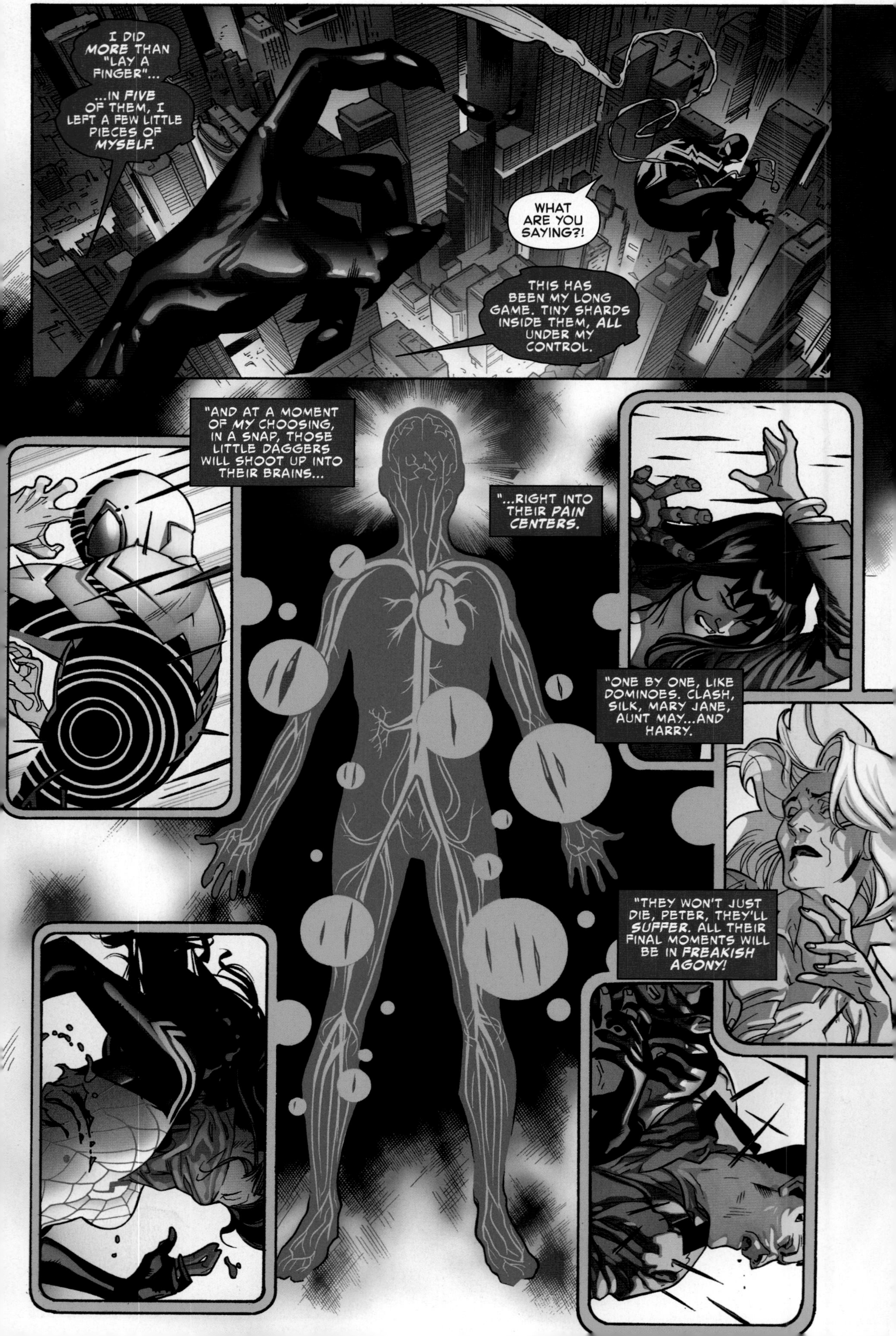
I DID MORE THAN "LAY A FINGER"...
...IN FIVE OF THEM, I LEFT A FEW LITTLE PIECES OF MYSELF.
WHAT ARE YOU SAYING?!
THIS HAS BEEN MY LONG GAME. TINY SHARDS INSIDE THEM, ALL UNDER MY CONTROL.
"AND AT A MOMENT OF MY CHOOSING, IN A SNAP, THOSE LITTLE DAGGERS WILL SHOOT UP INTO THEIR BRAINS...
"...RIGHT INTO THEIR PAIN CENTERS.
"ONE BY ONE, LIKE DOMINOES. CLASH, SILK, MARY JANE, AUNT MAY...AND HARRY.
"THEY WON'T JUST DIE, PETER, THEY'LL SUFFER. ALL THEIR FINAL MOMENTS WILL BE IN FREAKISH AGONY!

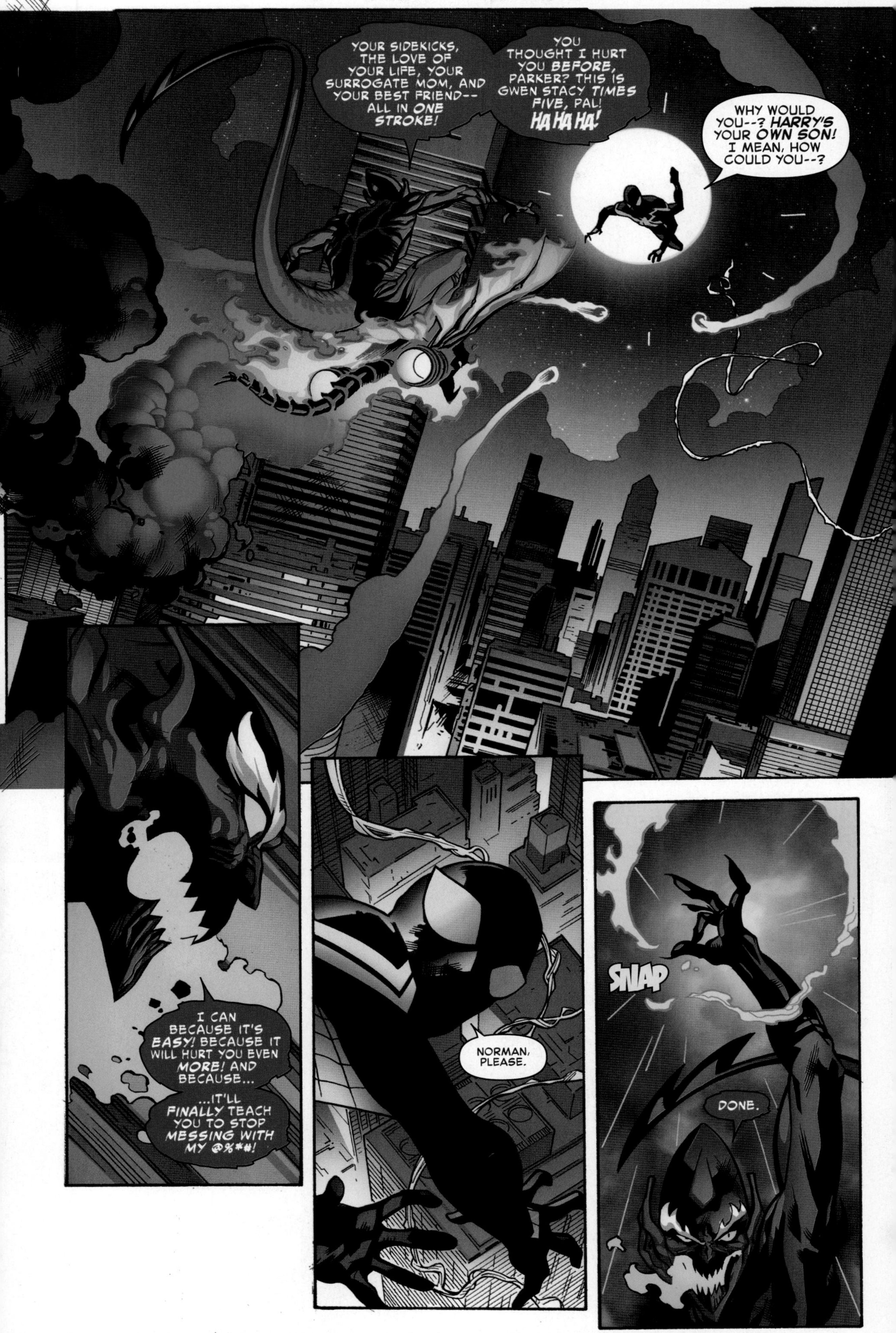

YOUR SIDEKICKS, THE LOVE OF YOUR LIFE, YOUR SURROGATE MOM, AND YOUR BEST FRIEND-- ALL IN ONE STROKE!
YOU THOUGHT I HURT YOU BEFORE, PARKER? THIS IS GWEN STACY TIMES FIVE, PAL! HA HA HA!
WHY WOULD YOU--? HARRY'S YOUR OWN SON! I MEAN, HOW COULD YOU--?
I CAN BECAUSE IT'S EASY! BECAUSE IT WILL HURT YOU EVEN MORE! AND BECAUSE...
...IT'LL FINALLY TEACH YOU TO STOP MESSING WITH MY @%*#!
NORMAN, PLEASE.
SNAP
DONE.

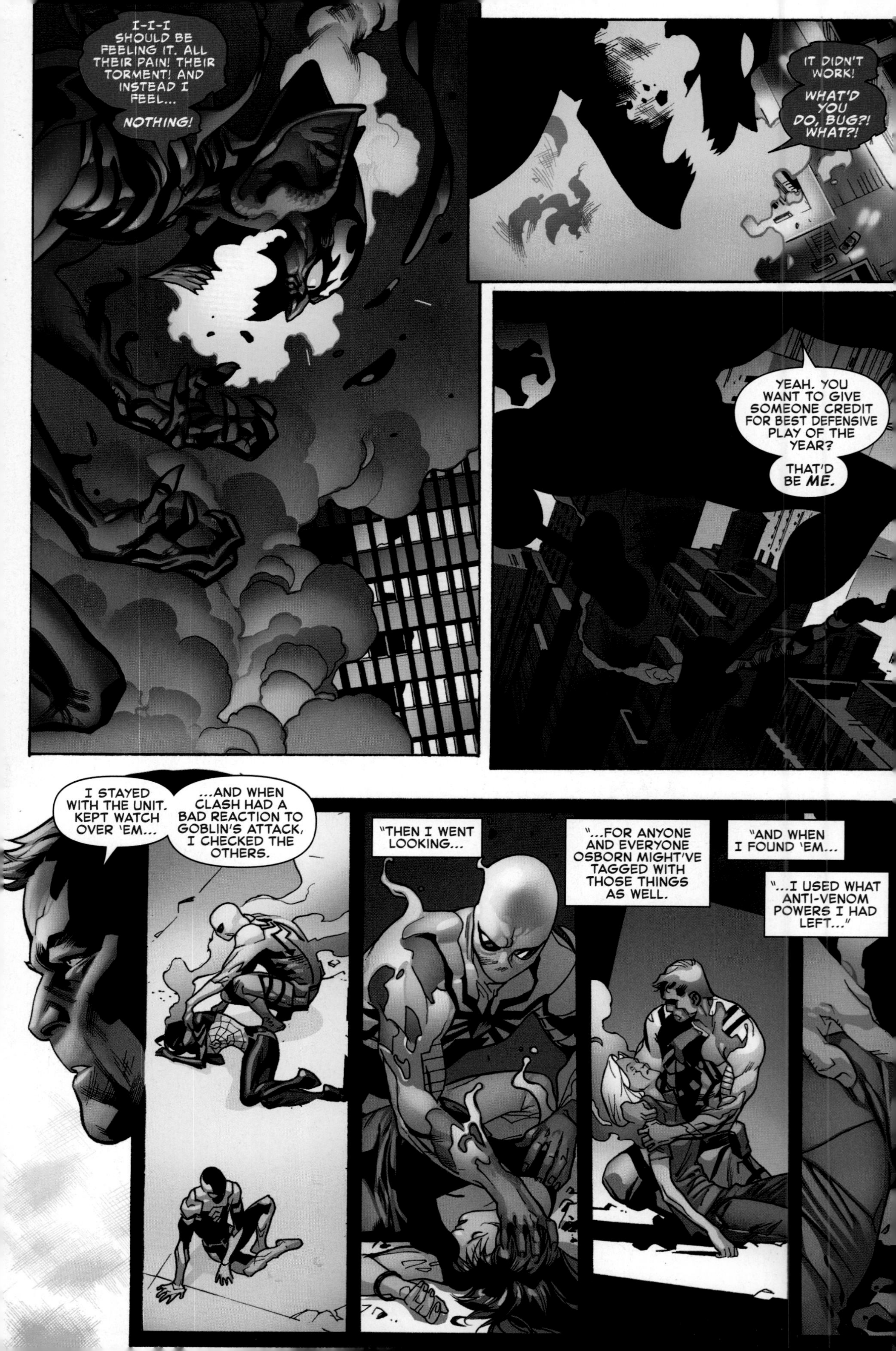
I-I-I SHOULD BE FEELING IT. ALL THEIR PAIN! THEIR TORMENT! AND INSTEAD I FEEL...
NOTHING!
IT DIDN'T WORK!
WHAT'D YOU DO, BUG?! WHAT?!
YEAH. YOU WANT TO GIVE SOMEONE CREDIT FOR BEST DEFENSIVE PLAY OF THE YEAR?
THAT'D BE ME.
I STAYED WITH THE UNIT. KEPT WATCH OVER 'EM...
...AND WHEN CLASH HAD A BAD REACTION TO GOBLIN'S ATTACK, I CHECKED THE OTHERS.
"THEN I WENT LOOKING...
"...FOR ANYONE AND EVERYONE OSBORN MIGHT'VE TAGGED WITH THOSE THINGS AS WELL.
"AND WHEN I FOUND 'EM...
"...I USED WHAT ANTI-VENOM POWERS I HAD LEFT..."

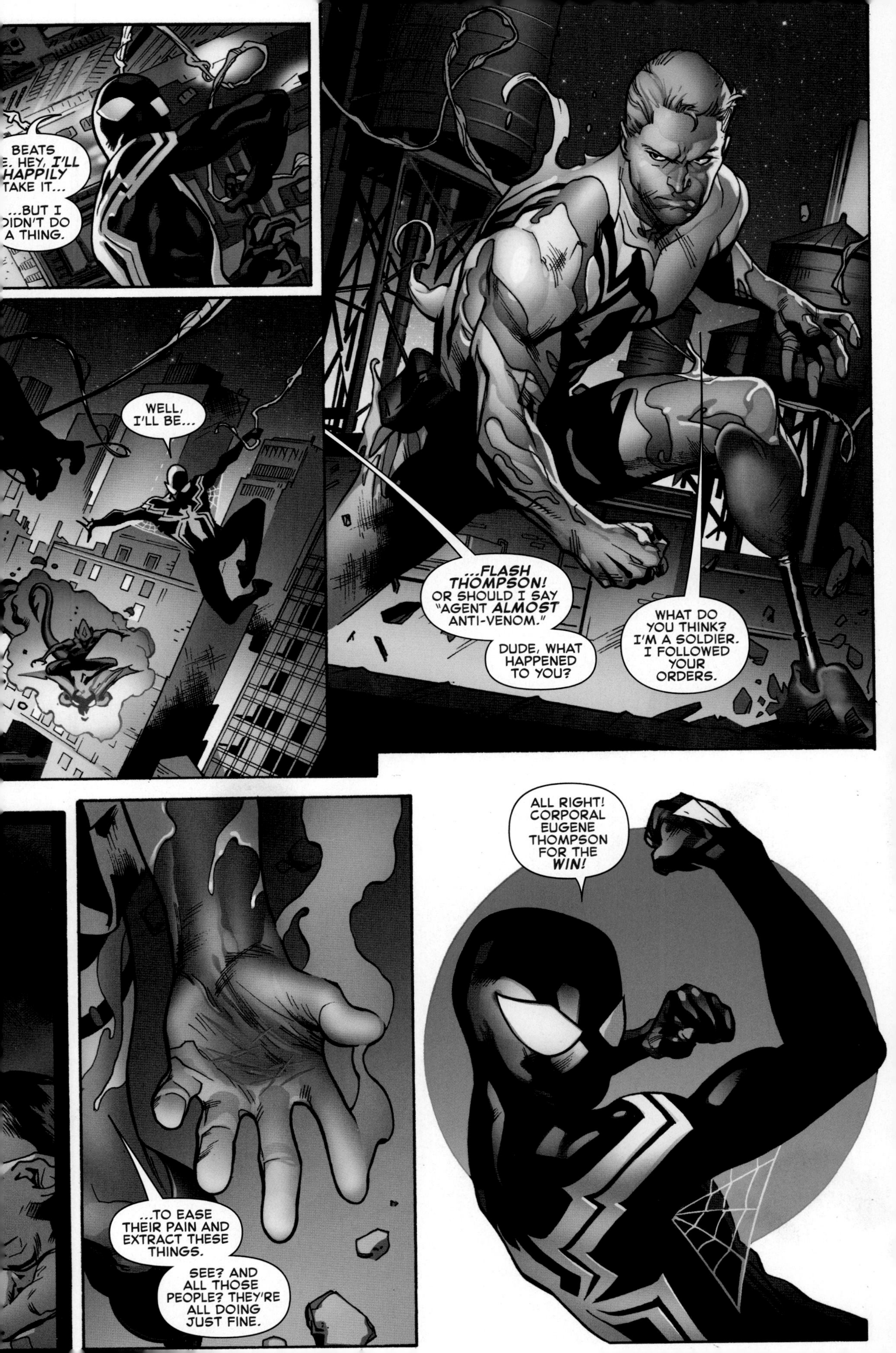

BEATS E. HEY, I'LL HAPPILY TAKE IT...
...BUT I DIDN'T DO A THING.
WELL, I'LL BE...
...FLASH THOMPSON! OR SHOULD I SAY "AGENT ALMOST ANTI-VENOM."
DUDE, WHAT HAPPENED TO YOU?
WHAT DO YOU THINK? I'M A SOLDIER. I FOLLOWED YOUR ORDERS.
...TO EASE THEIR PAIN AND EXTRACT THESE THINGS.
SEE? AND ALL THOSE PEOPLE? THEY'RE ALL DOING JUST FINE.
ALL RIGHT! CORPORAL EUGENE THOMPSON FOR THE WIN!

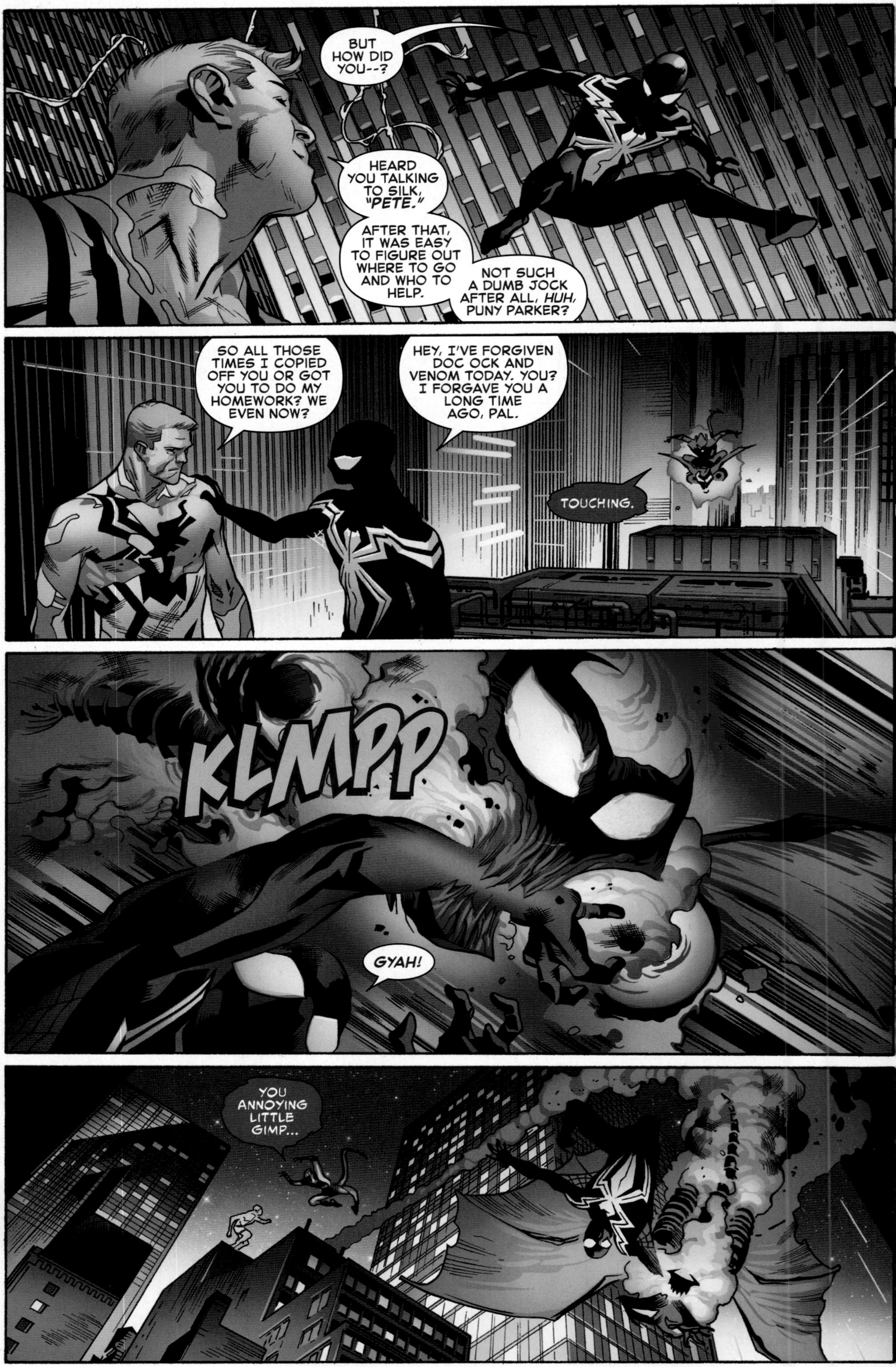
BUT HOW DID YOU--?
HEARD YOU TALKING TO SILK, *"PETE."*
AFTER THAT, IT WAS EASY TO FIGURE OUT WHERE TO GO AND WHO TO HELP.
NOT SUCH A DUMB JOCK AFTER ALL, *HUH,* PUNY PARKER?
SO ALL THOSE TIMES I COPIED OFF YOU OR GOT YOU TO DO MY HOMEWORK? WE EVEN NOW?
HEY, I'VE FORGIVEN DOC OCK AND VENOM TODAY. YOU? I FORGAVE YOU A LONG TIME AGO, PAL.
TOUCHING.
KLMPP
GYAH!
YOU ANNOYING LITTLE GIMP...

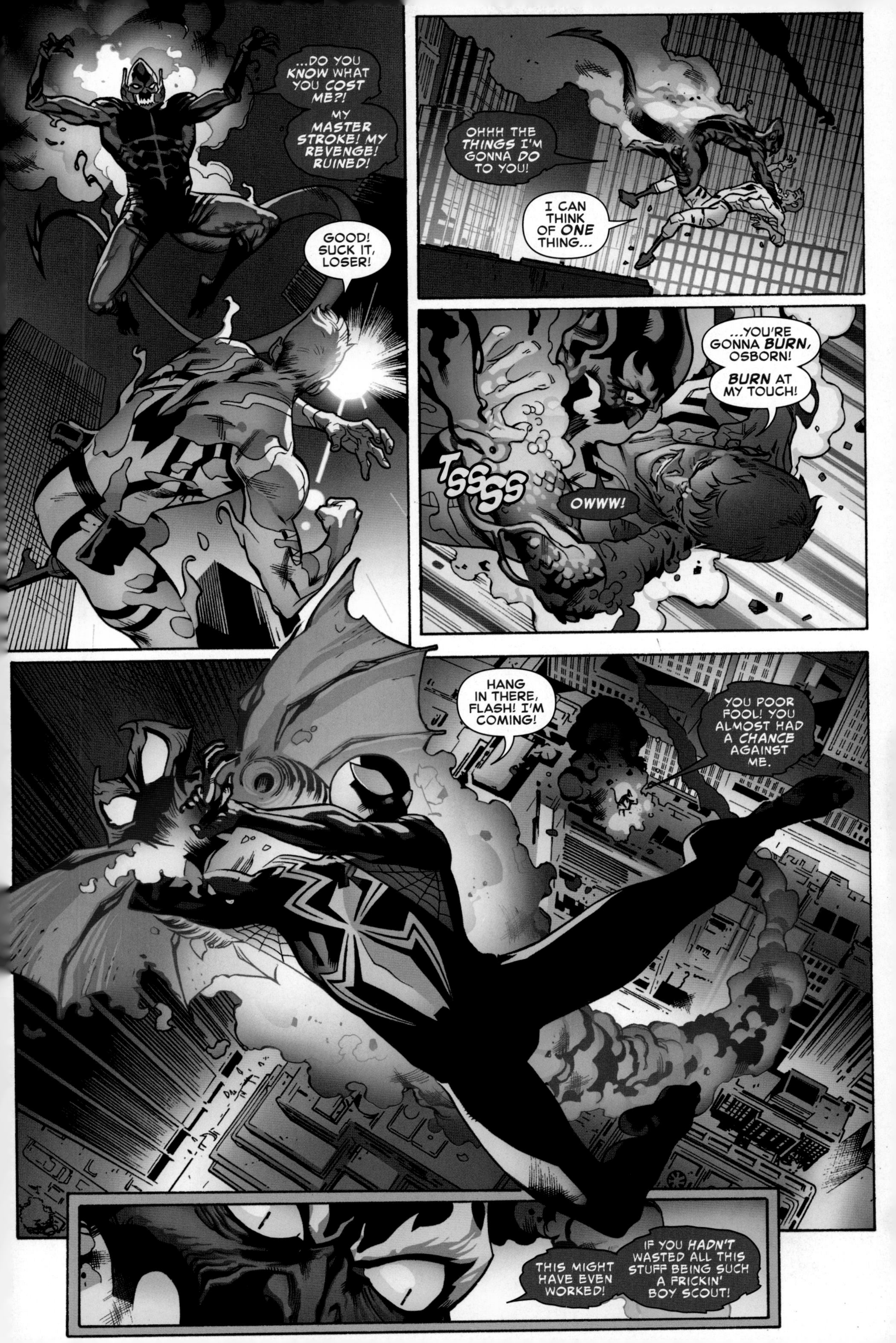

...DO YOU KNOW WHAT YOU COST ME?!
MY MASTER STROKE! MY REVENGE! RUINED!
GOOD! SUCK IT, LOSER!
OHHH THE THINGS I'M GONNA DO TO YOU!
I CAN THINK OF ONE THING...
...YOU'RE GONNA BURN, OSBORN!
BURN AT MY TOUCH!
TSSSS
OWWW!
HANG IN THERE, FLASH! I'M COMING!
YOU POOR FOOL! YOU ALMOST HAD A CHANCE AGAINST ME.
THIS MIGHT HAVE EVEN WORKED!
IF YOU HADN'T WASTED ALL THIS STUFF BEING SUCH A FRICKIN' BOY SCOUT!

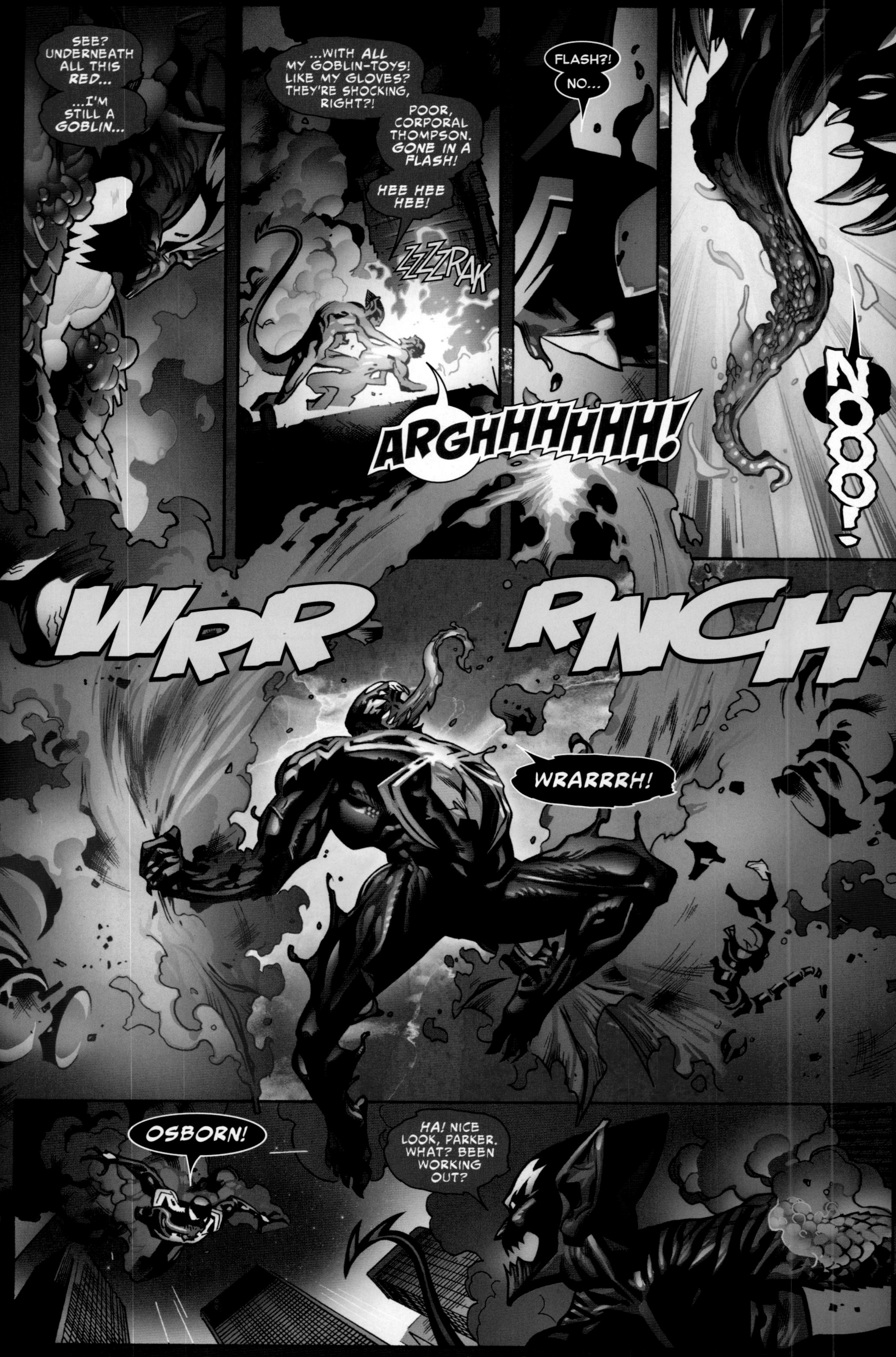
SEE? UNDERNEATH ALL THIS RED...
...I'M STILL A GOBLIN...
...WITH ALL MY GOBLIN-TOYS! LIKE MY GLOVES? THEY'RE SHOCKING, RIGHT?!
POOR, CORPORAL THOMPSON. GONE IN A FLASH!
HEE HEE HEE!
ZZZZRAK
ARGHHHHHH!
FLASH?!
NO...
NOOO!
WRR RNCH
WRARRRH!
OSBORN!
HA! NICE LOOK, PARKER. WHAT? BEEN WORKING OUT?

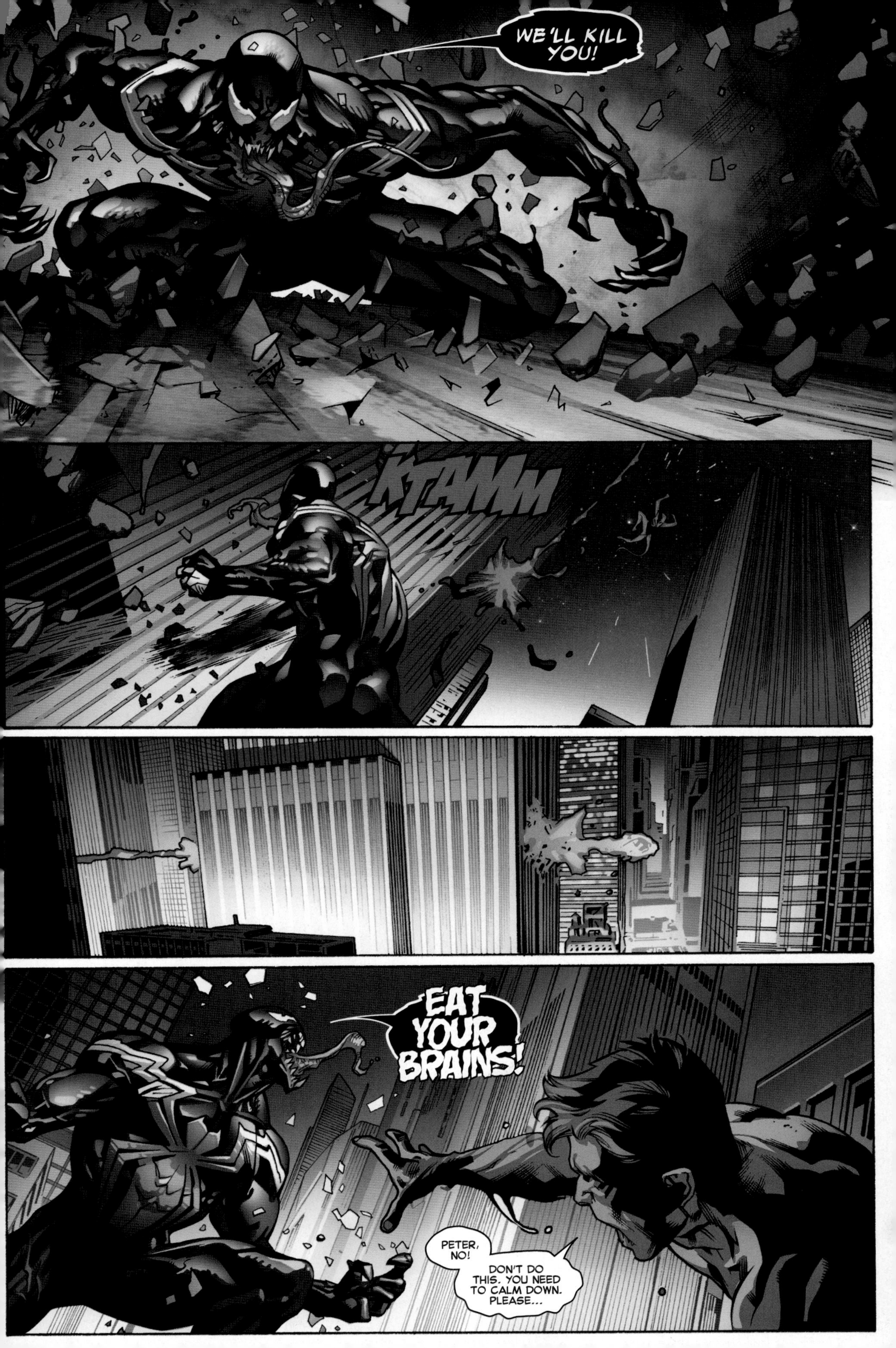
WE'LL KILL YOU!
KTAMM
EAT YOUR BRAINS!
PETER, NO!
DON'T DO THIS. YOU NEED TO CALM DOWN. PLEASE...

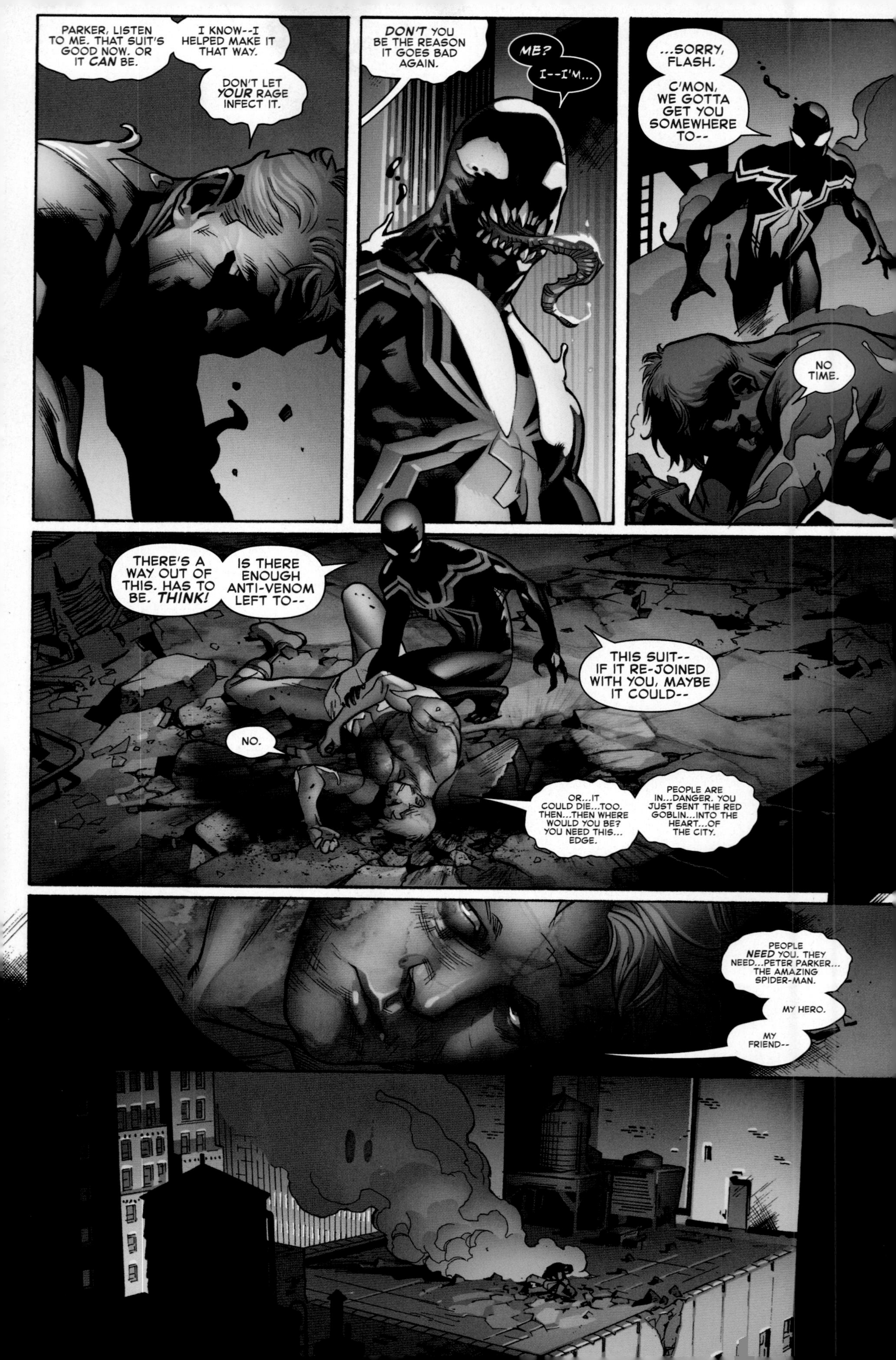
PARKER, LISTEN TO ME. THAT SUIT'S GOOD NOW. OR IT CAN BE.
I KNOW--I HELPED MAKE IT THAT WAY.
DON'T LET YOUR RAGE INFECT IT.
DON'T YOU BE THE REASON IT GOES BAD AGAIN.
ME?
I--I'M...
...SORRY, FLASH.
C'MON, WE GOTTA GET YOU SOMEWHERE TO--
NO TIME.
THERE'S A WAY OUT OF THIS. HAS TO BE. THINK!
IS THERE ENOUGH ANTI-VENOM LEFT TO--
THIS SUIT-- IF IT RE-JOINED WITH YOU, MAYBE IT COULD--
NO.
OR...IT COULD DIE...TOO. THEN...THEN WHERE WOULD YOU BE? YOU NEED THIS... EDGE.
PEOPLE ARE IN...DANGER. YOU JUST SENT THE RED GOBLIN...INTO THE HEART...OF THE CITY.
PEOPLE NEED YOU. THEY NEED...PETER PARKER... THE AMAZING SPIDER-MAN.
MY HERO.
MY FRIEND--

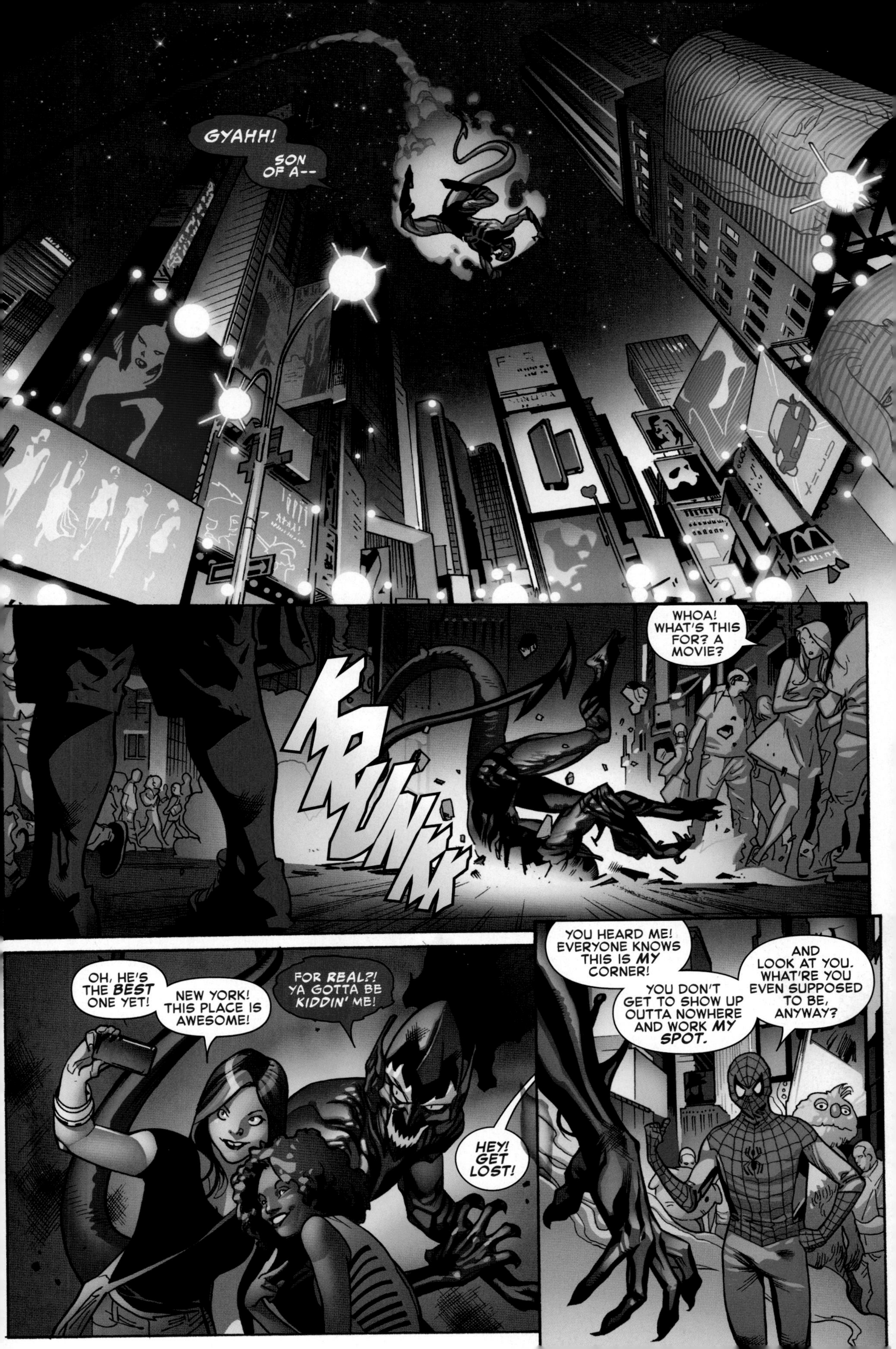
GYAHH!
SON OF A--
WHOA! WHAT'S THIS FOR? A MOVIE?
KRUNKK
OH, HE'S THE BEST ONE YET!
NEW YORK! THIS PLACE IS AWESOME!
FOR REAL?! YA GOTTA BE KIDDIN' ME!
HEY! GET LOST!
YOU HEARD ME! EVERYONE KNOWS THIS IS MY CORNER!
YOU DON'T GET TO SHOW UP OUTTA NOWHERE AND WORK MY SPOT.
AND LOOK AT YOU. WHAT'RE YOU EVEN SUPPOSED TO BE, ANYWAY?

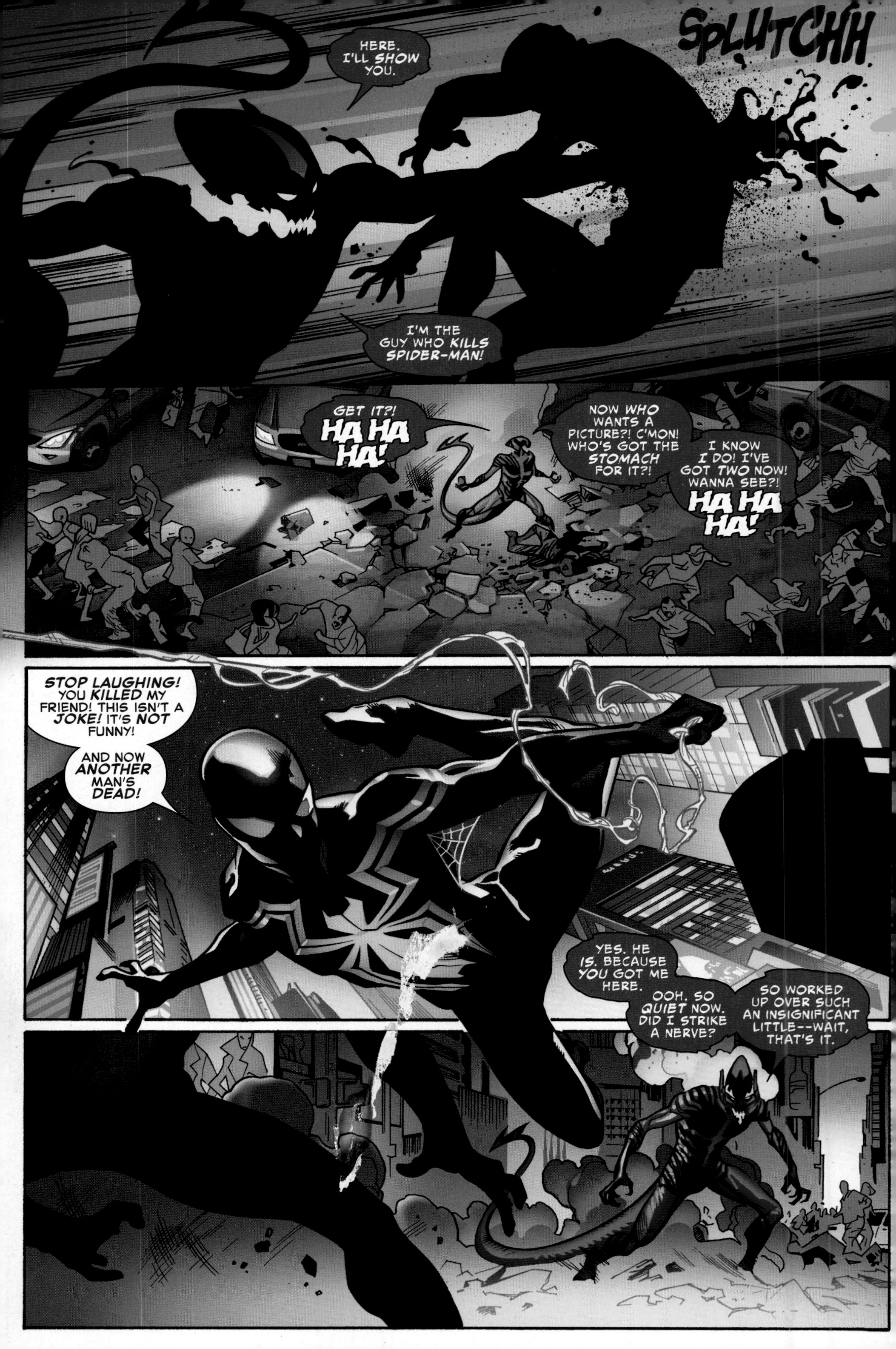
HERE. I'LL SHOW YOU.
SPLUTCHH
I'M THE GUY WHO KILLS SPIDER-MAN!
GET IT?! HA HA HA!
NOW WHO WANTS A PICTURE?! C'MON! WHO'S GOT THE STOMACH FOR IT?!
I KNOW I DO! I'VE GOT TWO NOW! WANNA SEE?! HA HA HA!
STOP LAUGHING! YOU KILLED MY FRIEND! THIS ISN'T A JOKE! IT'S NOT FUNNY!
AND NOW ANOTHER MAN'S DEAD!
YES. HE IS. BECAUSE YOU GOT ME HERE.
OOH. SO QUIET NOW. DID I STRIKE A NERVE?
SO WORKED UP OVER SUCH AN INSIGNIFICANT LITTLE--WAIT, THAT'S IT.

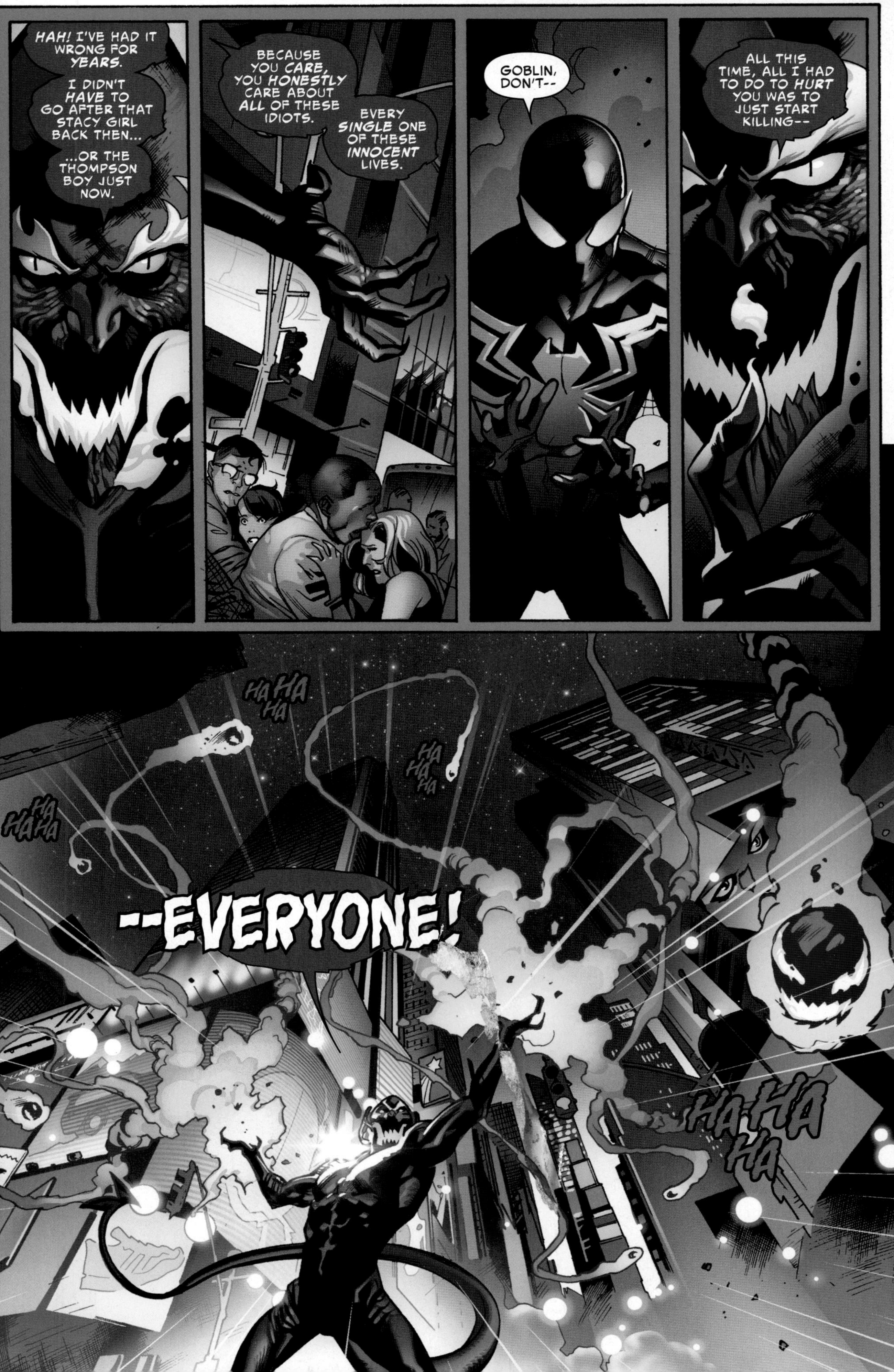

HAH! I'VE HAD IT WRONG FOR YEARS.
I DIDN'T HAVE TO GO AFTER THAT STACY GIRL BACK THEN...
...OR THE THOMPSON BOY JUST NOW.
BECAUSE YOU CARE, YOU HONESTLY CARE ABOUT ALL OF THESE IDIOTS.
EVERY SINGLE ONE OF THESE INNOCENT LIVES.
GOBLIN, DON'T--
ALL THIS TIME, ALL I HAD TO DO TO HURT YOU WAS TO JUST START KILLING--
HA HA HA
HA HA HA
HA HA HA
--EVERYONE!
HA HA HA

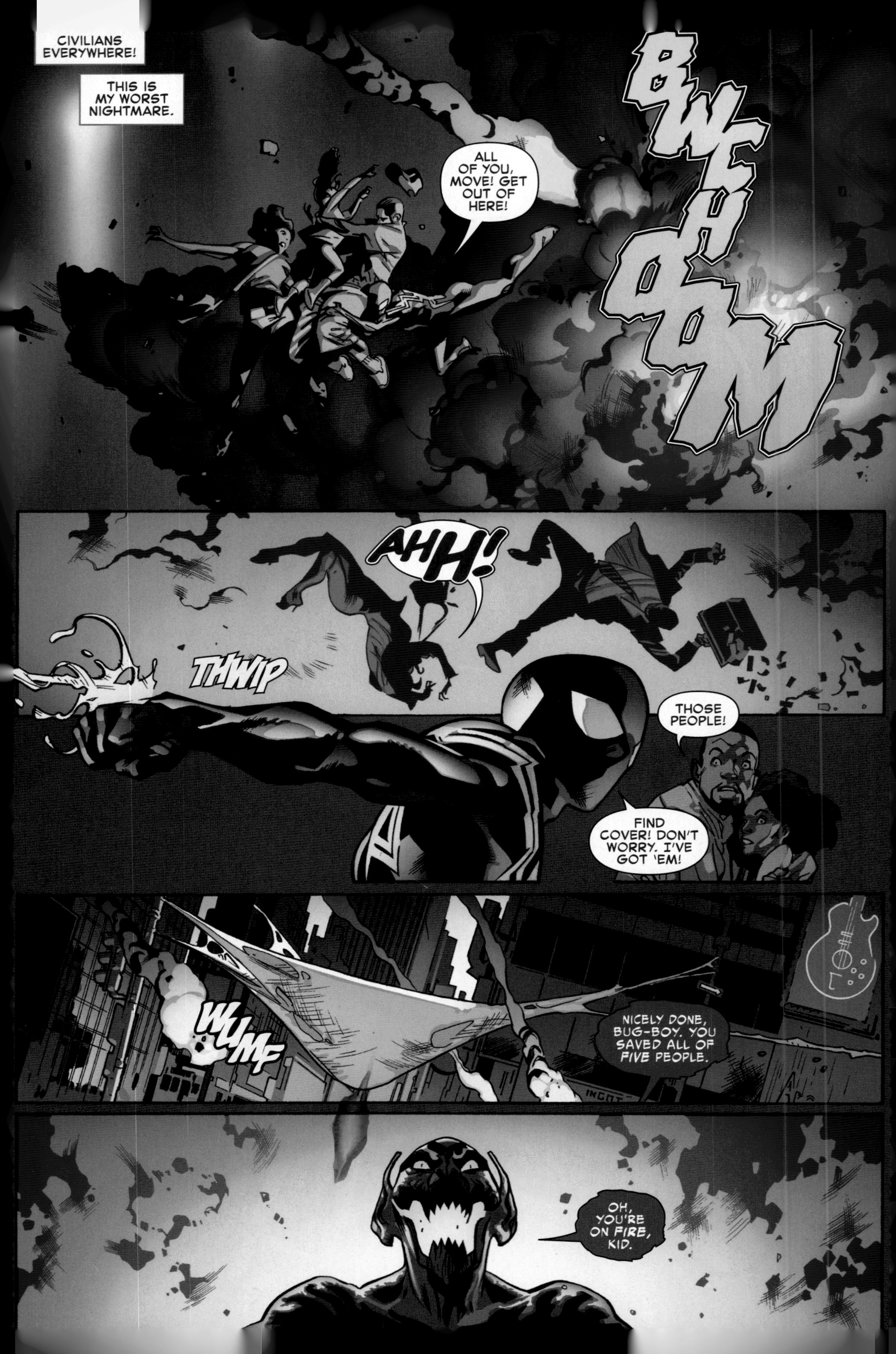
CIVILIANS EVERYWHERE!
THIS IS MY WORST NIGHTMARE.
ALL OF YOU, MOVE! GET OUT OF HERE!
BWHOOM
AHH!
THWIP
THOSE PEOPLE!
FIND COVER! DON'T WORRY. I'VE GOT 'EM!
WUMF
NICELY DONE, BUG-BOY. YOU SAVED ALL OF FIVE PEOPLE.
OH, YOU'RE ON FIRE, KID.

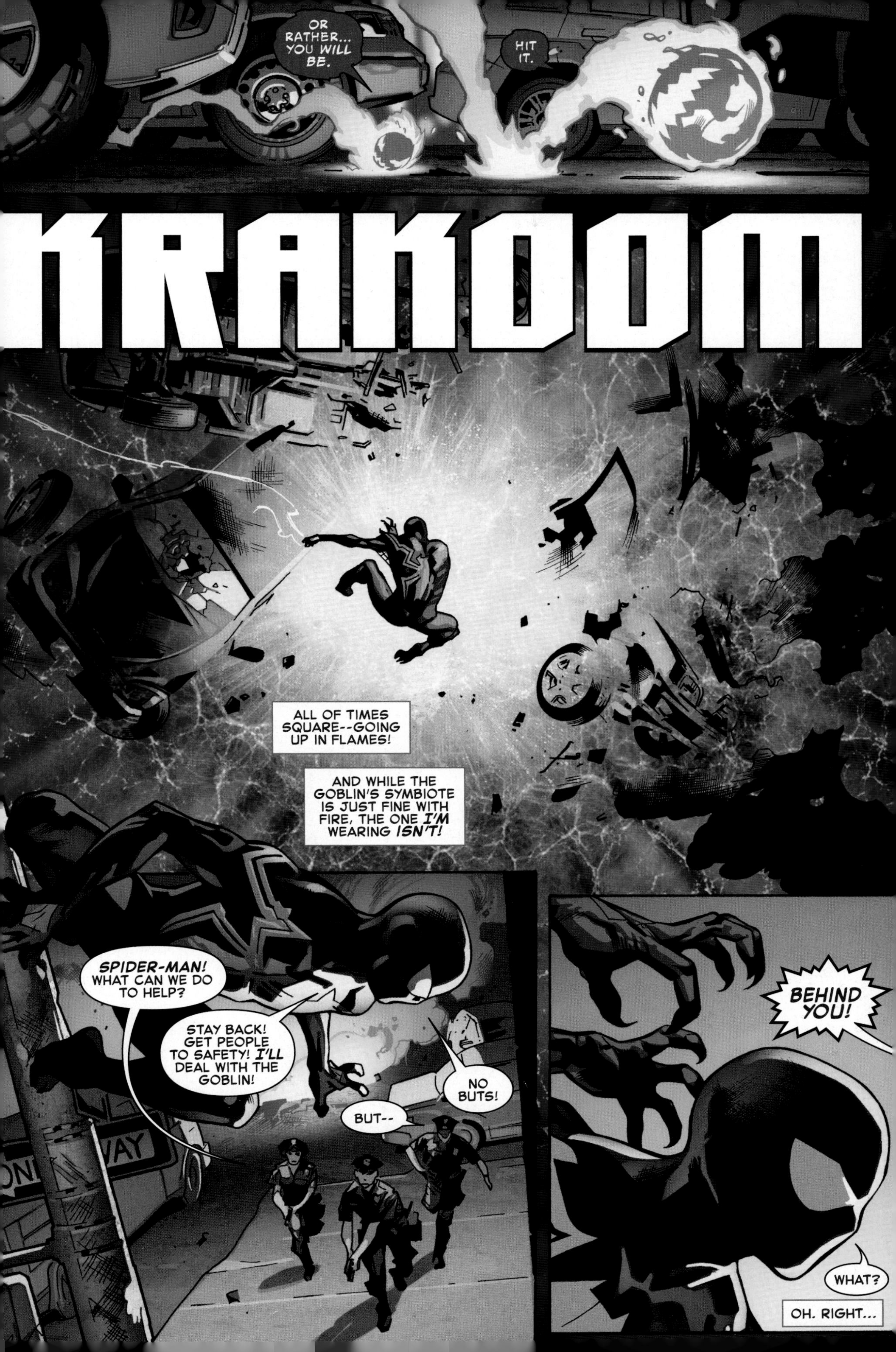
OR RATHER... YOU WILL BE.
HIT IT.
KRAKOOM
ALL OF TIMES SQUARE--GOING UP IN FLAMES!
AND WHILE THE GOBLIN'S SYMBIOTE IS JUST FINE WITH FIRE, THE ONE I'M WEARING ISN'T!
SPIDER-MAN! WHAT CAN WE DO TO HELP?
STAY BACK! GET PEOPLE TO SAFETY! I'LL DEAL WITH THE GOBLIN!
BUT--
NO BUTS!
BEHIND YOU!
WHAT?
OH. RIGHT...

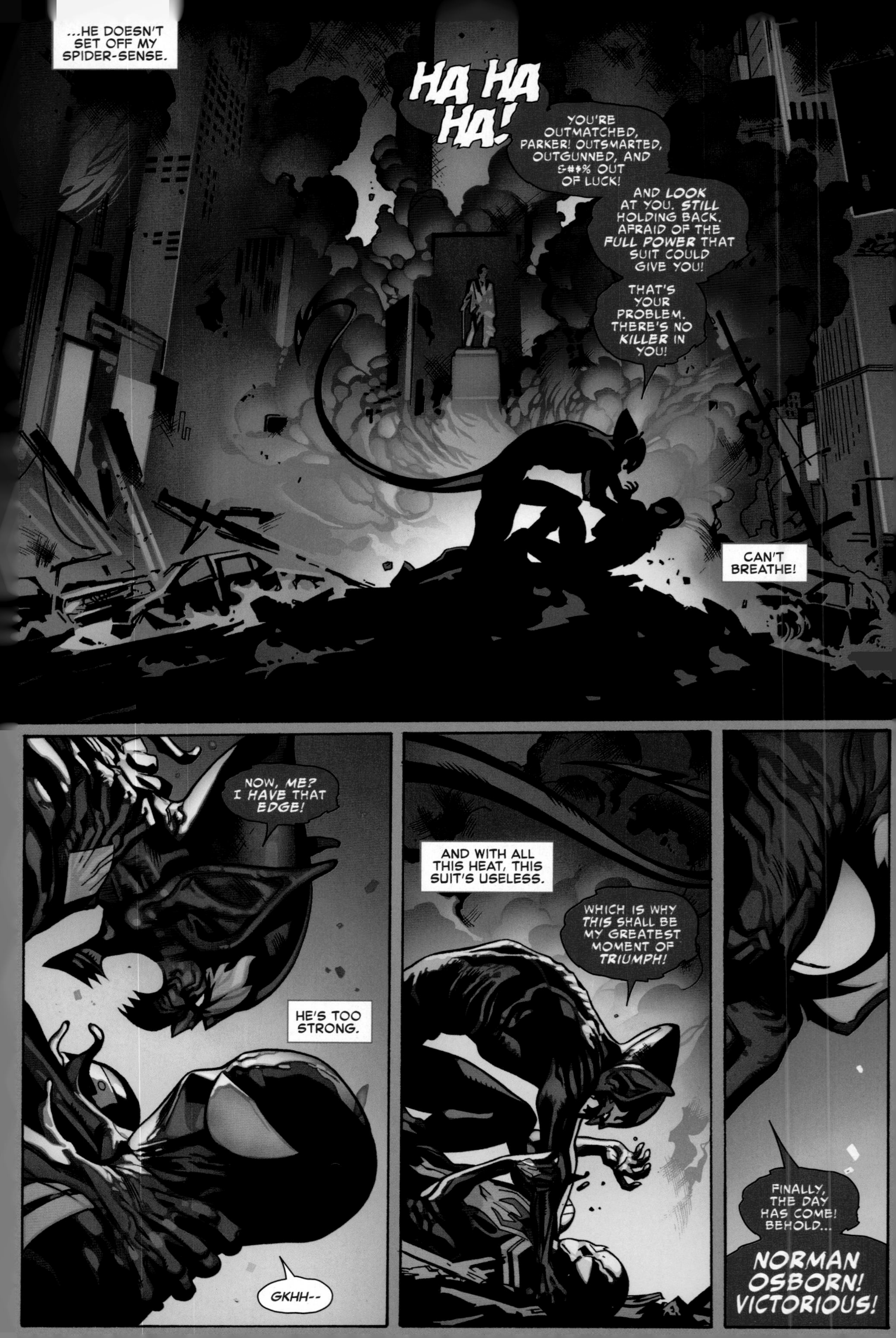

...HE DOESN'T SET OFF MY SPIDER-SENSE.
HA HA HA!
YOU'RE OUTMATCHED, PARKER! OUTSMARTED, OUTGUNNED, AND $#*% OUT OF LUCK!
AND LOOK AT YOU. STILL HOLDING BACK. AFRAID OF THE FULL POWER THAT SUIT COULD GIVE YOU!
THAT'S YOUR PROBLEM. THERE'S NO KILLER IN YOU!
CAN'T BREATHE!
NOW, ME? I HAVE THAT EDGE!
HE'S TOO STRONG.
GKHH--
AND WITH ALL THIS HEAT, THIS SUIT'S USELESS.
WHICH IS WHY THIS SHALL BE MY GREATEST MOMENT OF TRIUMPH!
FINALLY, THE DAY HAS COME! BEHOLD...
NORMAN OSBORN! VICTORIOUS!

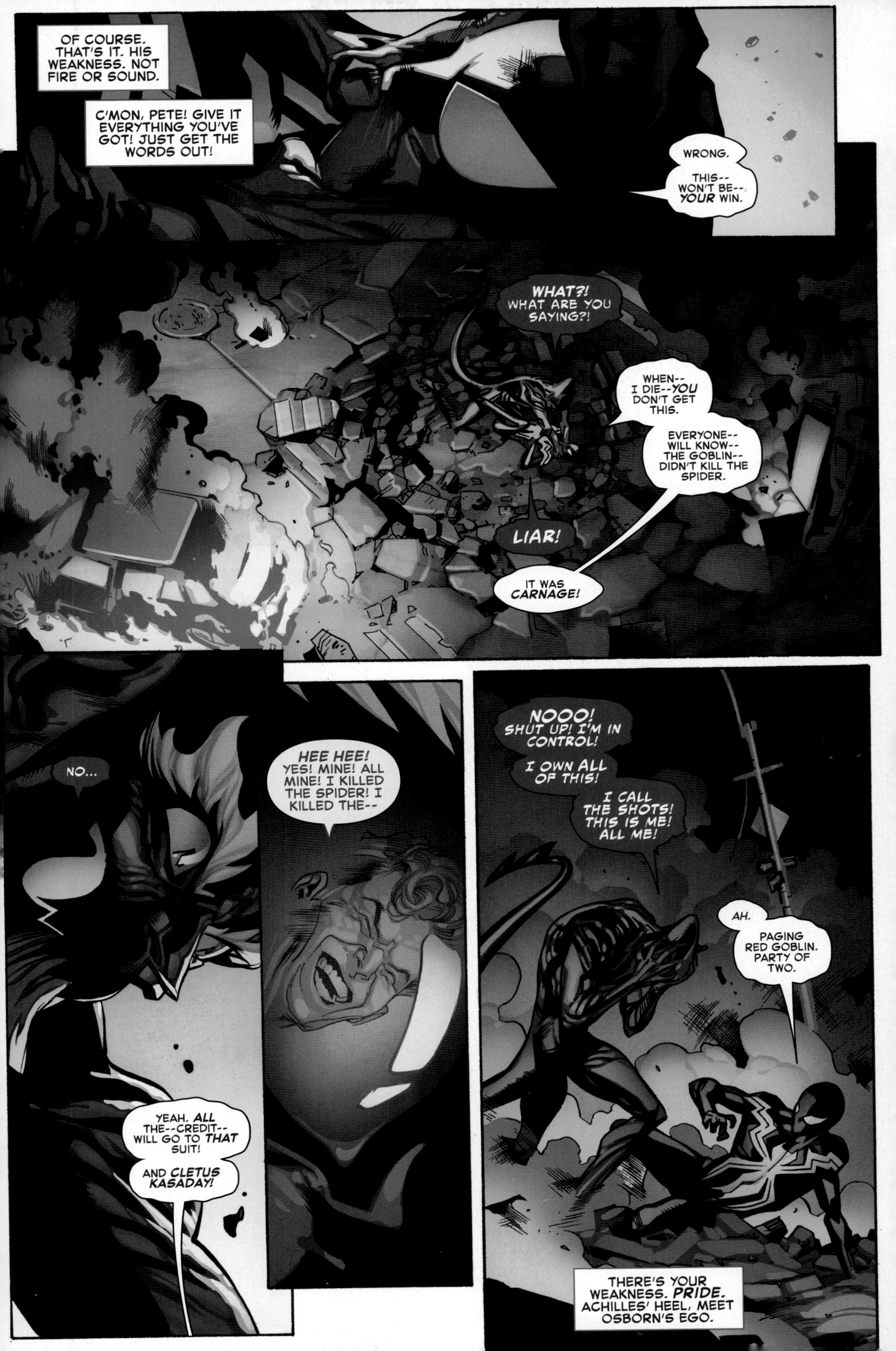

OF COURSE. THAT'S IT. HIS WEAKNESS. NOT FIRE OR SOUND.
C'MON, PETE! GIVE IT EVERYTHING YOU'VE GOT! JUST GET THE WORDS OUT!
WRONG.
THIS-- WON'T BE-- YOUR WIN.
WHAT?! WHAT ARE YOU SAYING?!
WHEN-- I DIE--YOU DON'T GET THIS.
EVERYONE-- WILL KNOW-- THE GOBLIN-- DIDN'T KILL THE SPIDER.
LIAR!
IT WAS CARNAGE!
NO...
HEE HEE! YES! MINE! ALL MINE! I KILLED THE SPIDER! I KILLED THE--
YEAH. ALL THE--CREDIT-- WILL GO TO THAT SUIT!
AND CLETUS KASADAY!
NOOO! SHUT UP! I'M IN CONTROL!
I OWN ALL OF THIS!
I CALL THE SHOTS! THIS IS ME! ALL ME!
AH.
PAGING RED GOBLIN. PARTY OF TWO.
THERE'S YOUR WEAKNESS. PRIDE. ACHILLES' HEEL, MEET OSBORN'S EGO.

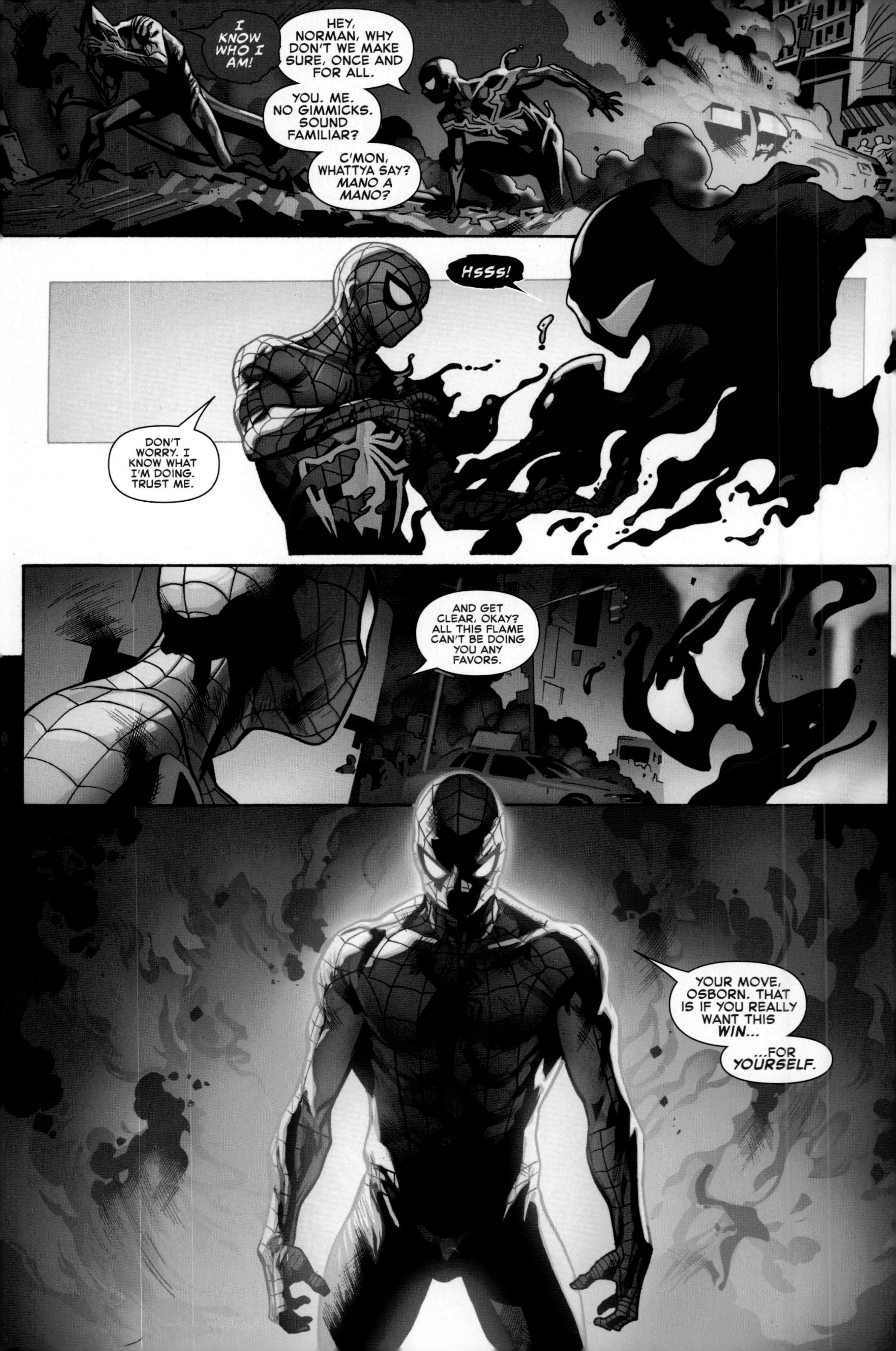

I KNOW WHO I AM!
HEY, NORMAN, WHY DON'T WE MAKE SURE, ONCE AND FOR ALL.
YOU. ME. NO GIMMICKS. SOUND FAMILIAR?
C'MON, WHATTYA SAY? MANO A MANO?
HSSS!
DON'T WORRY. I KNOW WHAT I'M DOING. TRUST ME.
AND GET CLEAR, OKAY? ALL THIS FLAME CAN'T BE DOING YOU ANY FAVORS.
YOUR MOVE, OSBORN. THAT IS IF YOU REALLY WANT THIS WIN...
...FOR YOURSELF.

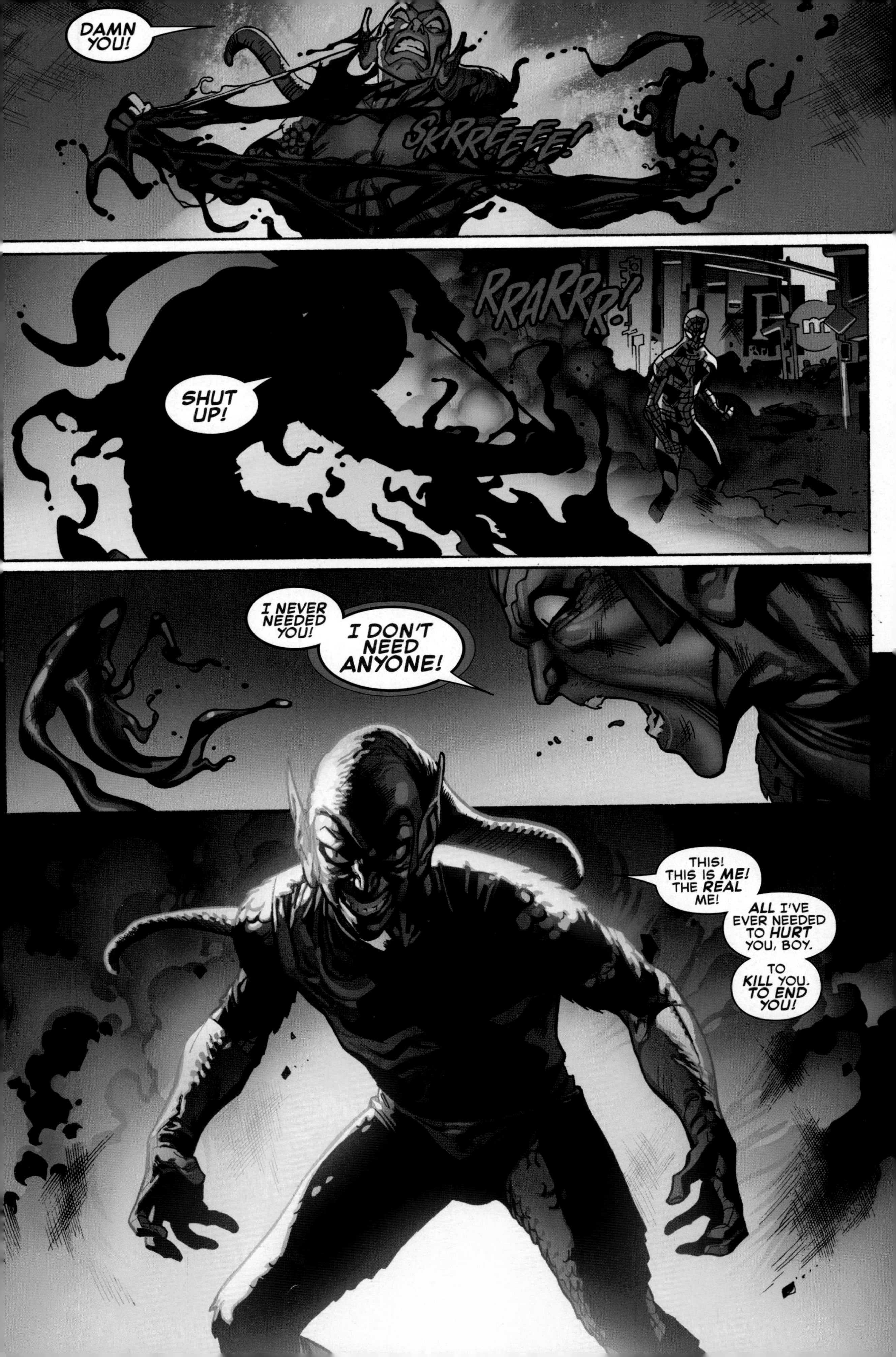
DAMN YOU!
SKRREEEEE!
RRARRRR!
SHUT UP!
I NEVER NEEDED YOU!
I DON'T NEED ANYONE!
THIS! THIS IS ME! THE REAL ME!
ALL I'VE EVER NEEDED TO HURT YOU, BOY.
TO KILL YOU. TO END YOU!

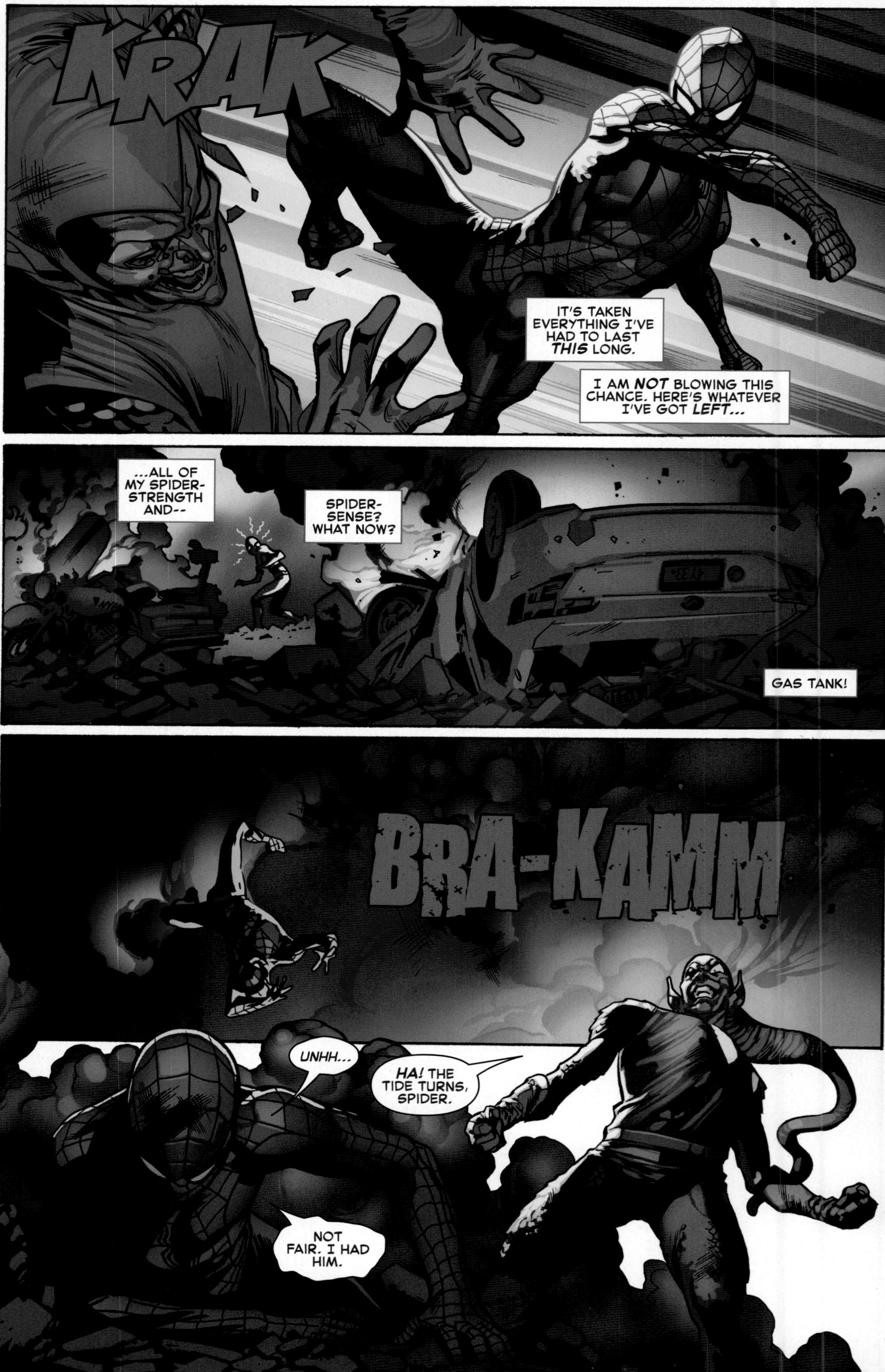
KRAK
IT'S TAKEN EVERYTHING I'VE HAD TO LAST THIS LONG.
I AM NOT BLOWING THIS CHANCE. HERE'S WHATEVER I'VE GOT LEFT...
...ALL OF MY SPIDER-STRENGTH AND--
SPIDER-SENSE? WHAT NOW?
GAS TANK!
BRA-KAMM
UNHH...
HA! THE TIDE TURNS, SPIDER.
NOT FAIR. I HAD HIM.

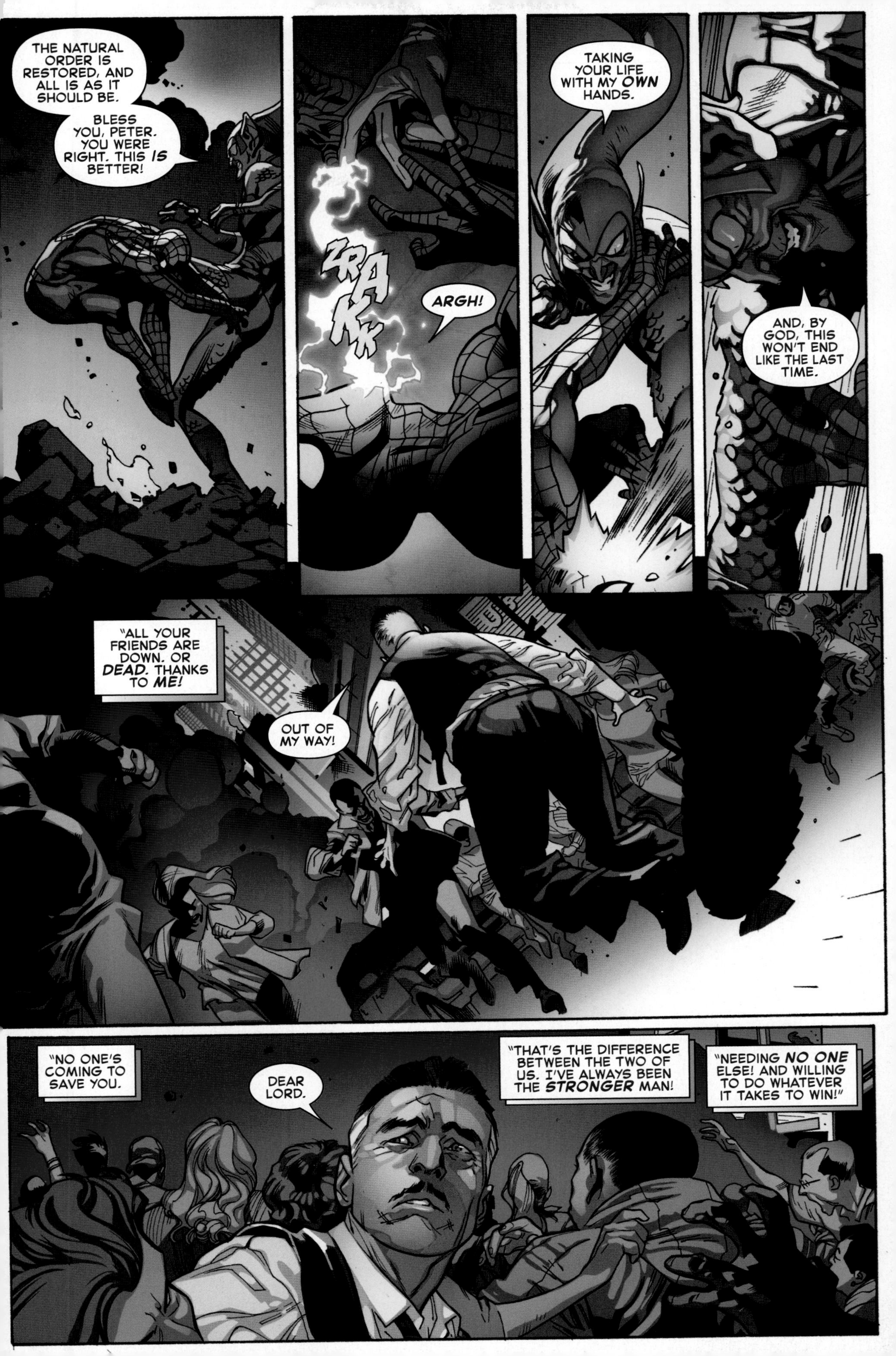

THE NATURAL ORDER IS RESTORED, AND ALL IS AS IT SHOULD BE.
BLESS YOU, PETER. YOU WERE RIGHT. THIS IS BETTER!
ZRAKKK
ARGH!
TAKING YOUR LIFE WITH MY OWN HANDS.
AND, BY GOD, THIS WON'T END LIKE THE LAST TIME.
"ALL YOUR FRIENDS ARE DOWN. OR DEAD. THANKS TO ME!
OUT OF MY WAY!
"NO ONE'S COMING TO SAVE YOU.
DEAR LORD.
"THAT'S THE DIFFERENCE BETWEEN THE TWO OF US. I'VE ALWAYS BEEN THE STRONGER MAN!
"NEEDING NO ONE ELSE! AND WILLING TO DO WHATEVER IT TAKES TO WIN!"

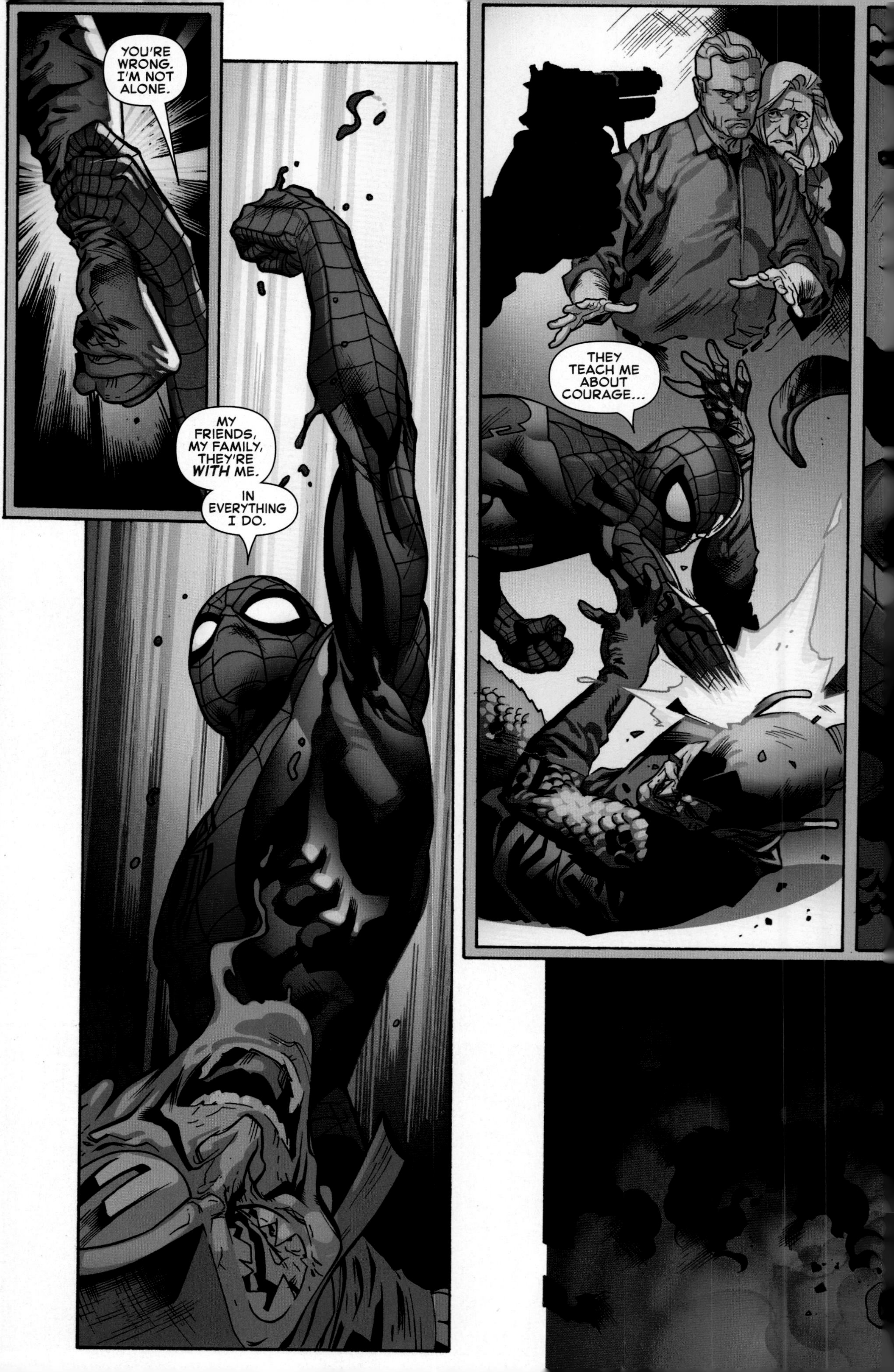
YOU'RE WRONG. I'M NOT ALONE.
MY FRIENDS, MY FAMILY, THEY'RE *WITH* ME.
IN EVERYTHING I DO.
THEY TEACH ME ABOUT COURAGE...

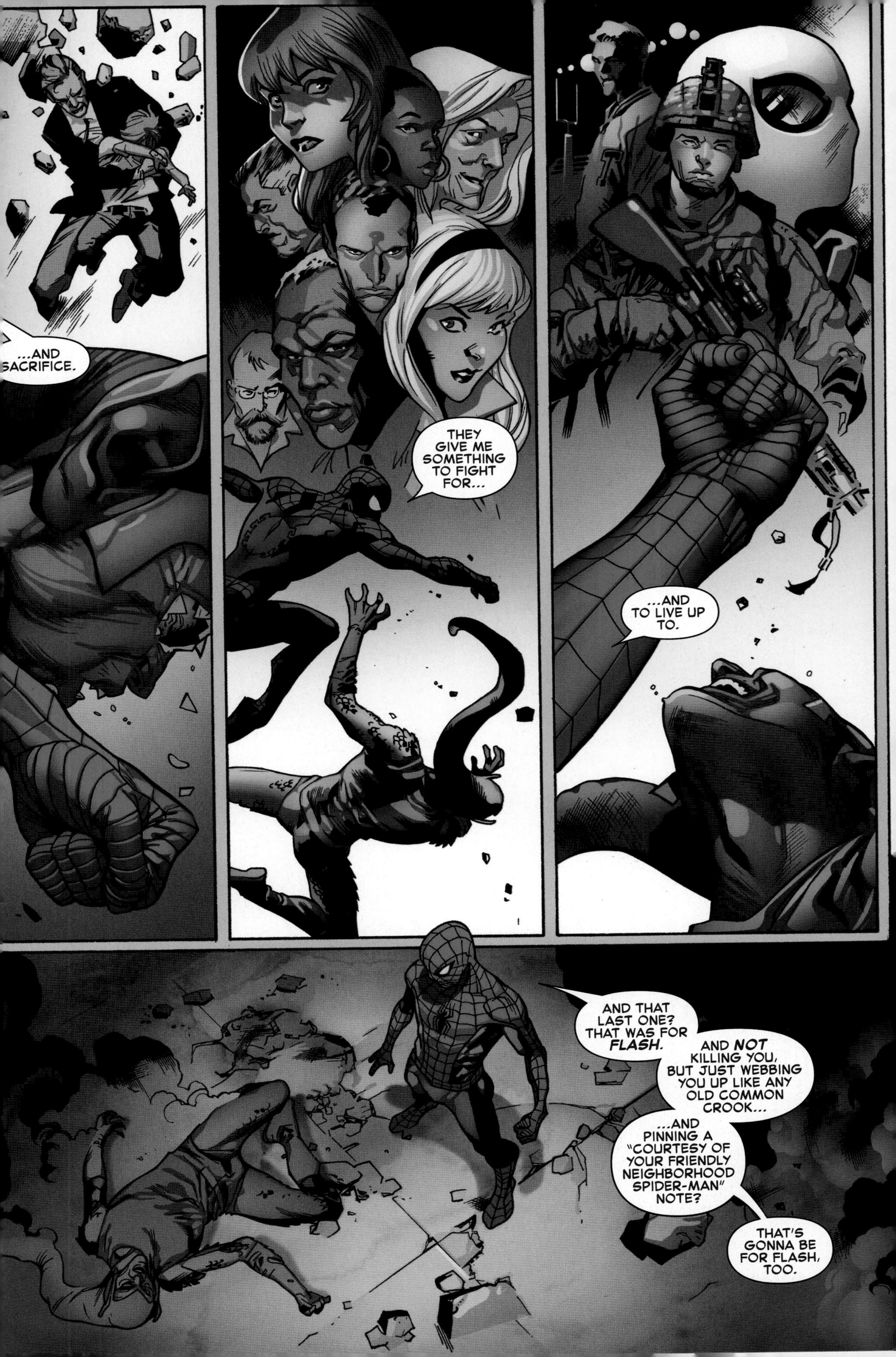
...AND SACRIFICE.
THEY GIVE ME SOMETHING TO FIGHT FOR...
...AND TO LIVE UP TO.
AND THAT LAST ONE? THAT WAS FOR *FLASH.*
AND *NOT* KILLING YOU, BUT JUST WEBBING YOU UP LIKE ANY OLD COMMON CROOK...
...AND PINNING A "COURTESY OF YOUR FRIENDLY NEIGHBORHOOD SPIDER-MAN" NOTE?
THAT'S GONNA BE FOR FLASH, TOO.

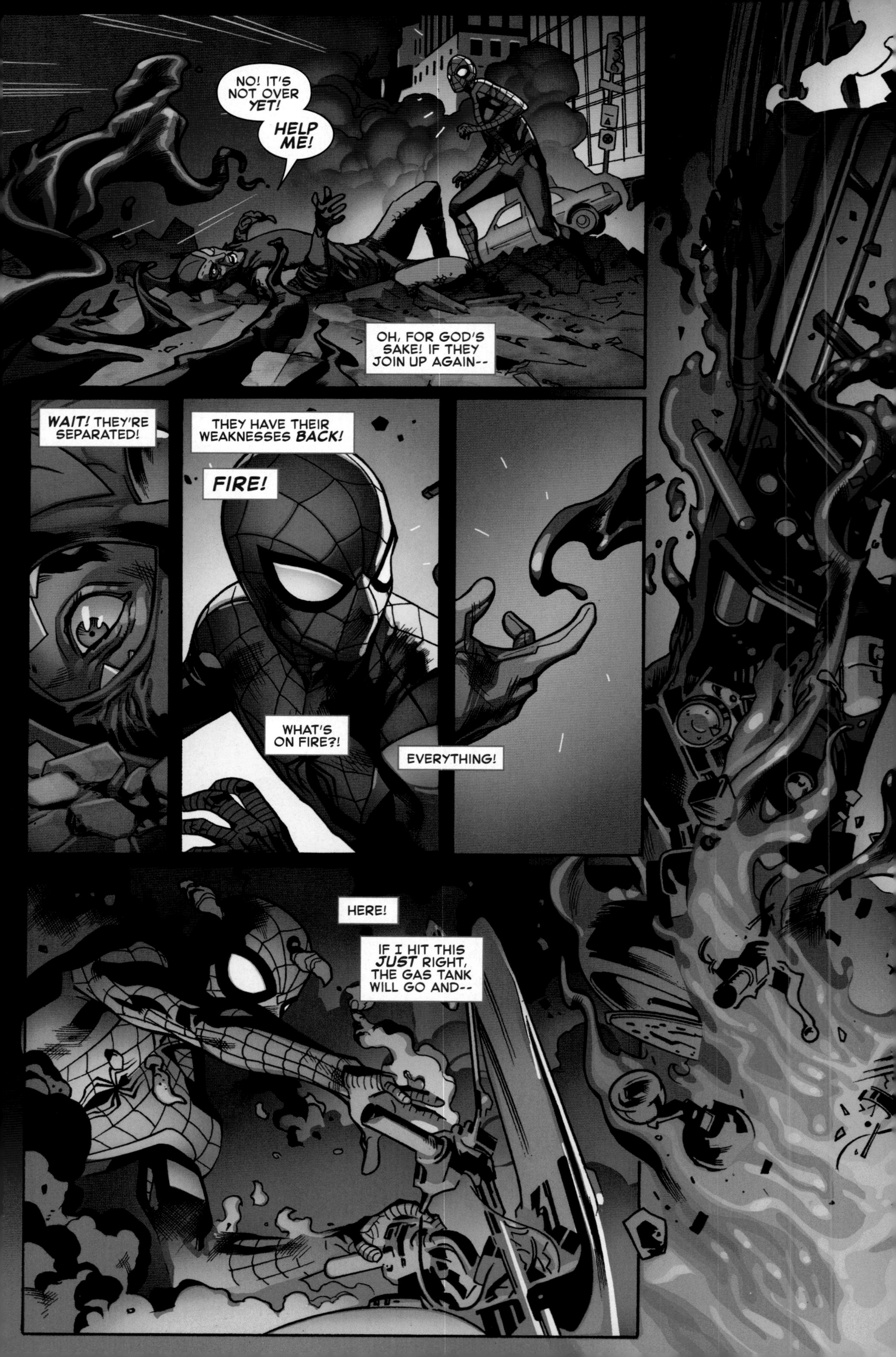

NO! IT'S NOT OVER YET!
HELP ME!
OH, FOR GOD'S SAKE! IF THEY JOIN UP AGAIN--
WAIT! THEY'RE SEPARATED!
THEY HAVE THEIR WEAKNESSES BACK!
FIRE!
WHAT'S ON FIRE?!
EVERYTHING!
HERE!
IF I HIT THIS JUST RIGHT, THE GAS TANK WILL GO AND--

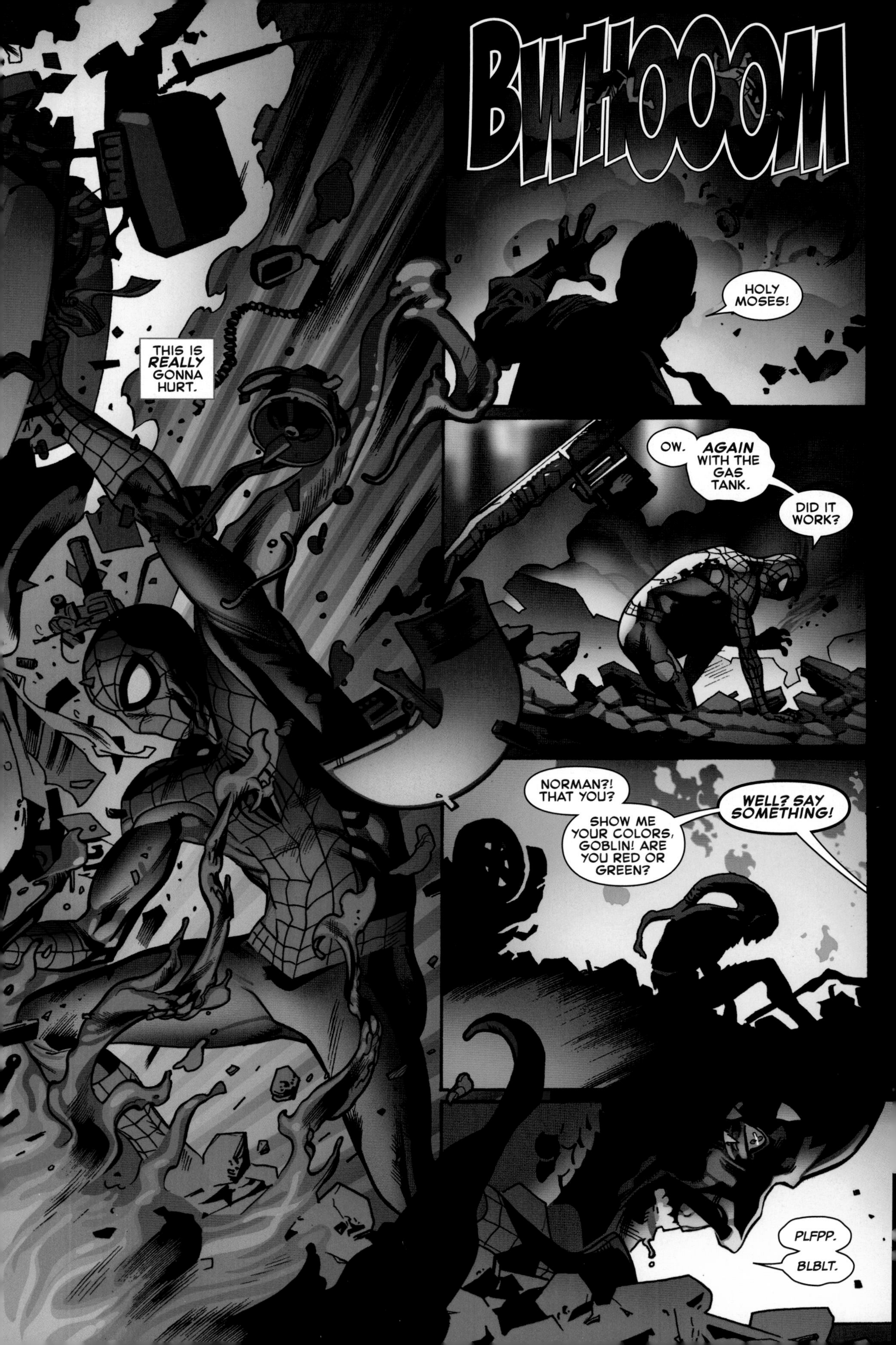
BWHOOOM
THIS IS REALLY GONNA HURT.
HOLY MOSES!
OW. AGAIN WITH THE GAS TANK.
DID IT WORK?
NORMAN?! THAT YOU?
SHOW ME YOUR COLORS, GOBLIN! ARE YOU RED OR GREEN?
WELL? SAY SOMETHING!
PLFPP.
BLBLT.

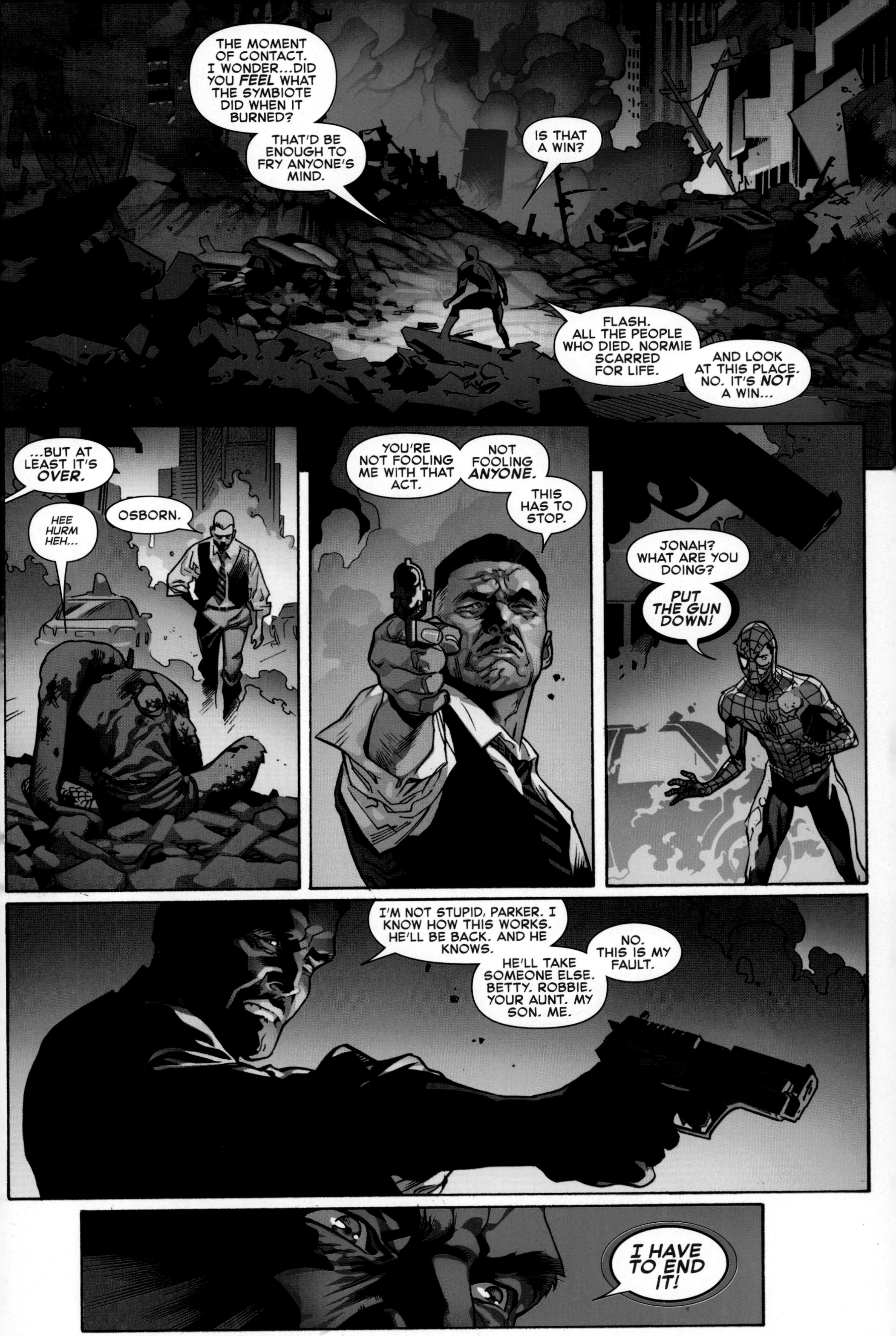
THE MOMENT OF CONTACT. I WONDER...DID YOU FEEL WHAT THE SYMBIOTE DID WHEN IT BURNED?
THAT'D BE ENOUGH TO FRY ANYONE'S MIND.
IS THAT A WIN?
FLASH. ALL THE PEOPLE WHO DIED. NORMIE SCARRED FOR LIFE.
AND LOOK AT THIS PLACE. NO. IT'S NOT A WIN...
...BUT AT LEAST IT'S OVER.
HEE HURM HEH...
OSBORN.
YOU'RE NOT FOOLING ME WITH THAT ACT.
NOT FOOLING ANYONE.
THIS HAS TO STOP.
JONAH? WHAT ARE YOU DOING?
PUT THE GUN DOWN!
I'M NOT STUPID, PARKER. I KNOW HOW THIS WORKS. HE'LL BE BACK. AND HE KNOWS.
HE'LL TAKE SOMEONE ELSE. BETTY. ROBBIE. YOUR AUNT. MY SON. ME.
NO. THIS IS MY FAULT.
I HAVE TO END IT!

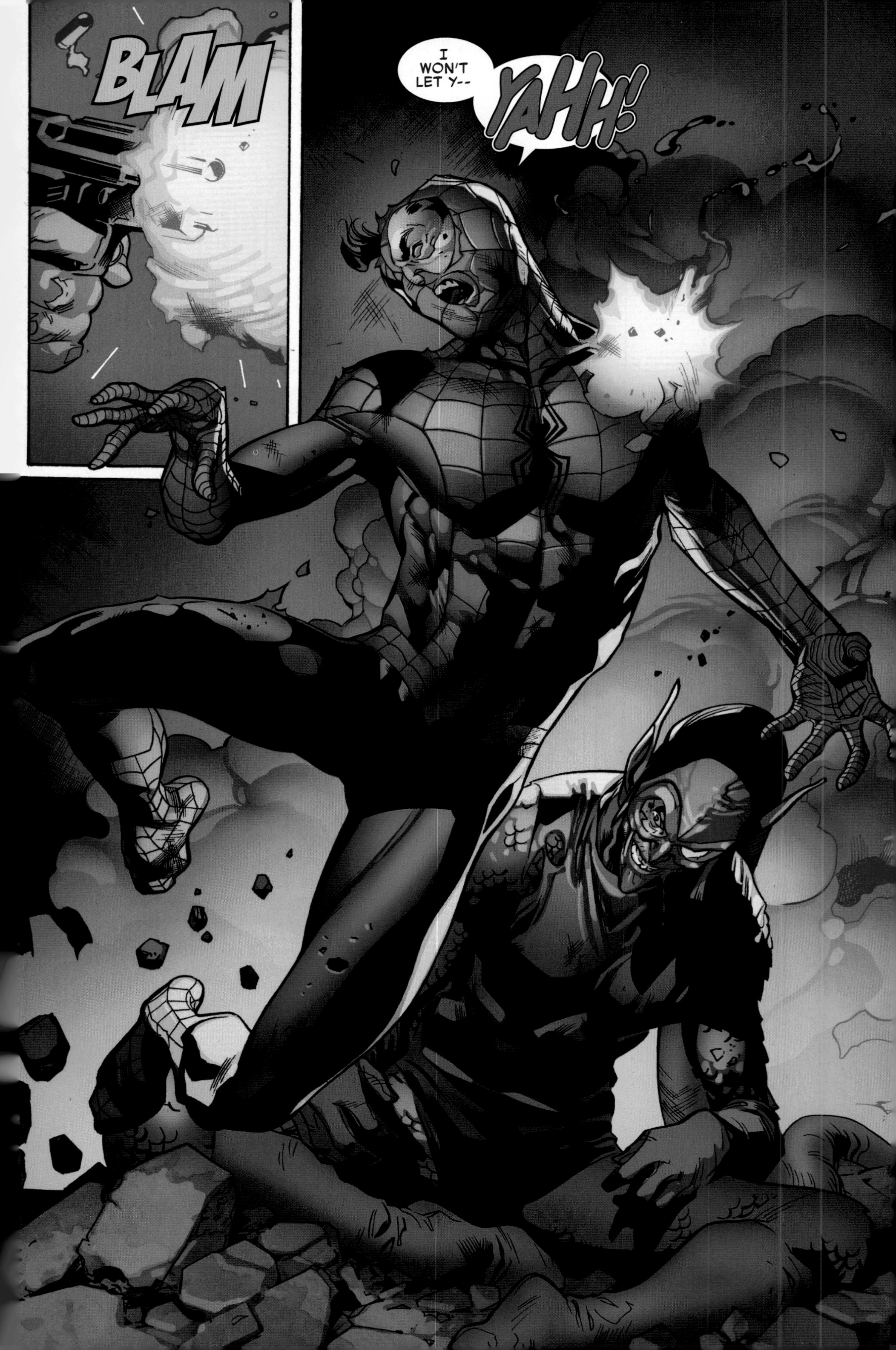
BLAM
I WON'T LET Y--
YAHH!

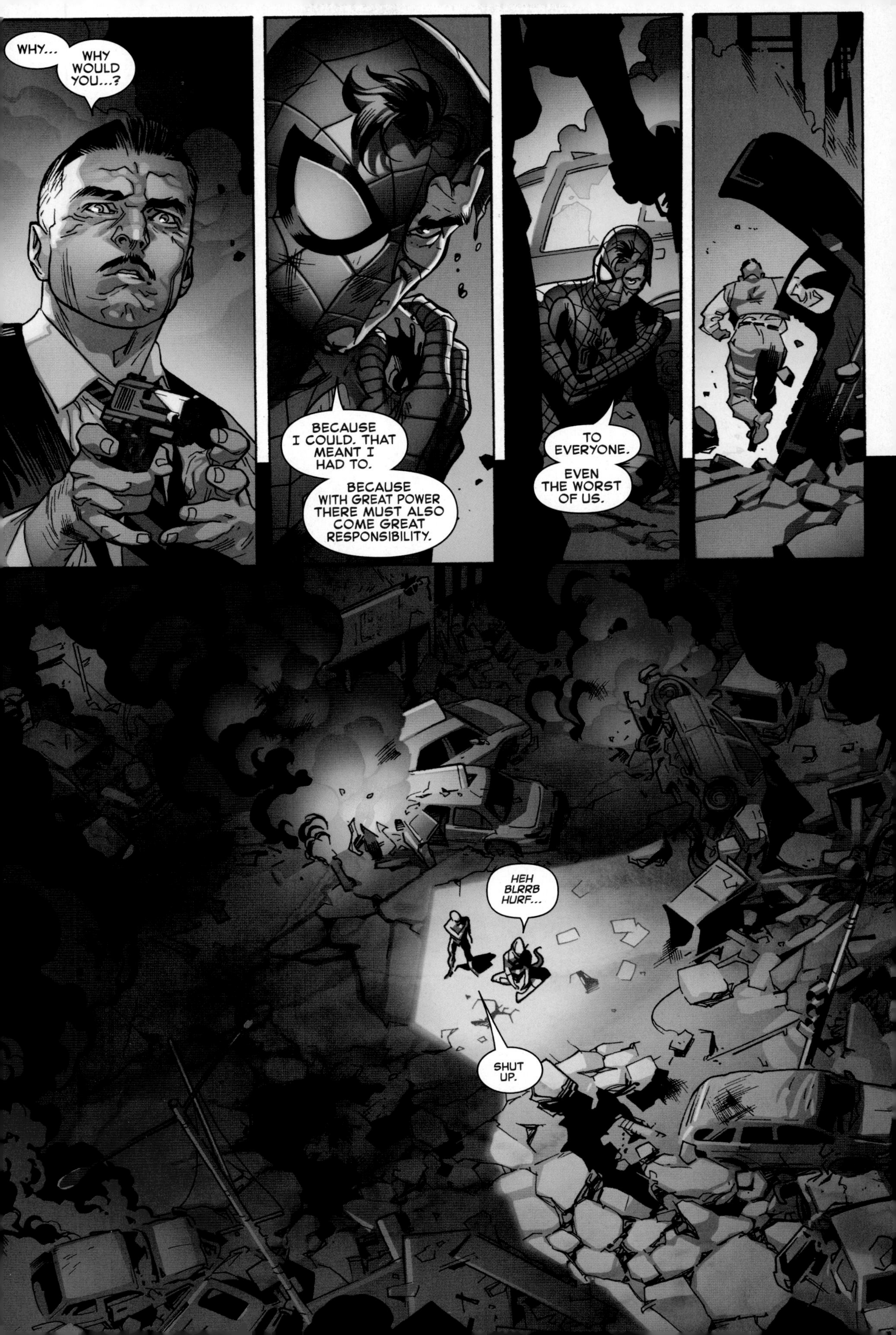
WHY...
WHY WOULD YOU...?
BECAUSE I COULD. THAT MEANT I HAD TO.
BECAUSE WITH GREAT POWER THERE MUST ALSO COME GREAT RESPONSIBILITY.
TO EVERYONE.
EVEN THE WORST OF US.
HEH BLRRB HURF...
SHUT UP.

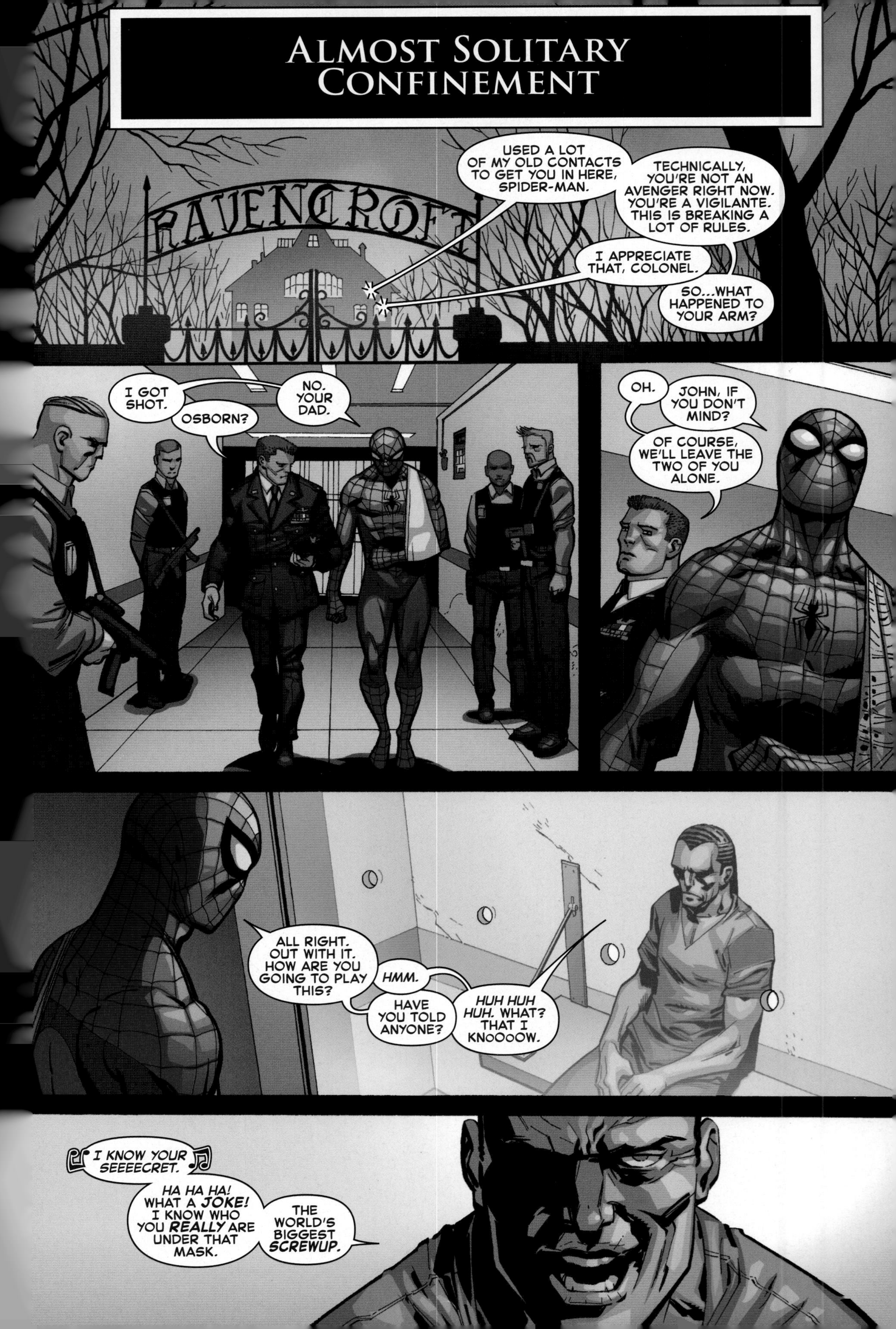
ALMOST SOLITARY CONFINEMENT
RAVENCROFT
USED A LOT OF MY OLD CONTACTS TO GET YOU IN HERE, SPIDER-MAN.
TECHNICALLY, YOU'RE NOT AN AVENGER RIGHT NOW. YOU'RE A VIGILANTE. THIS IS BREAKING A LOT OF RULES.
I APPRECIATE THAT, COLONEL.
SO...WHAT HAPPENED TO YOUR ARM?
I GOT SHOT.
OSBORN?
NO. YOUR DAD.
OH.
JOHN, IF YOU DON'T MIND?
OF COURSE, WE'LL LEAVE THE TWO OF YOU ALONE.
ALL RIGHT. OUT WITH IT. HOW ARE YOU GOING TO PLAY THIS?
HMM.
HAVE YOU TOLD ANYONE?
HUH HUH HUH. WHAT? THAT I KNOOOOW.
I KNOW YOUR SEEEECRET.
HA HA HA! WHAT A JOKE! I KNOW WHO YOU REALLY ARE UNDER THAT MASK.
THE WORLD'S BIGGEST SCREWUP.

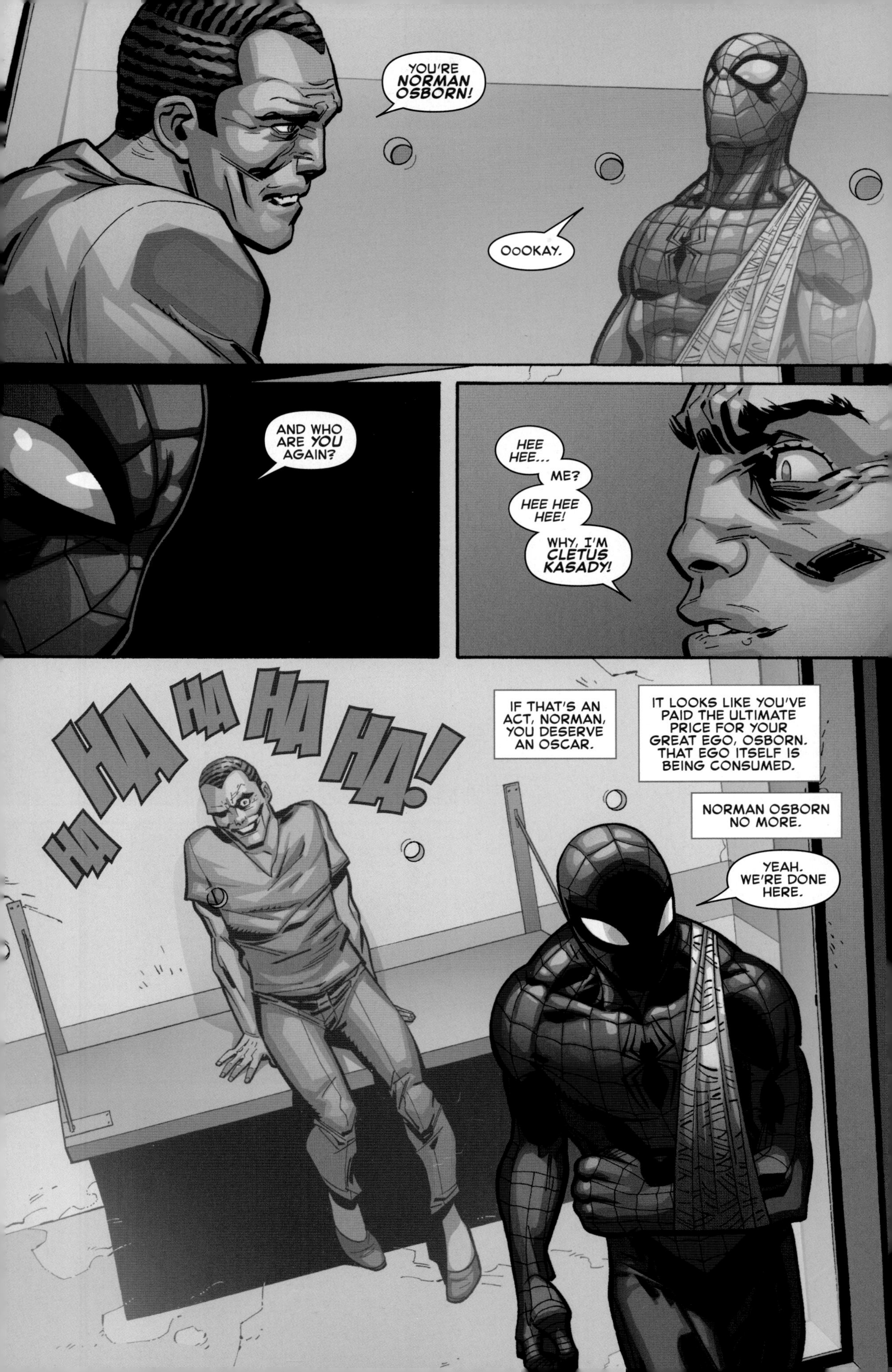
YOU'RE NORMAN OSBORN!
OOOKAY.
AND WHO ARE YOU AGAIN?
HEE HEE...
ME?
HEE HEE HEE!
WHY, I'M CLETUS KASADY!
HA HA HA HA HA HA!
IF THAT'S AN ACT, NORMAN, YOU DESERVE AN OSCAR.
IT LOOKS LIKE YOU'VE PAID THE ULTIMATE PRICE FOR YOUR GREAT EGO, OSBORN. THAT EGO ITSELF IS BEING CONSUMED.
NORMAN OSBORN NO MORE.
YEAH. WE'RE DONE HERE.

THE RETURN OF HARRY OSBORN

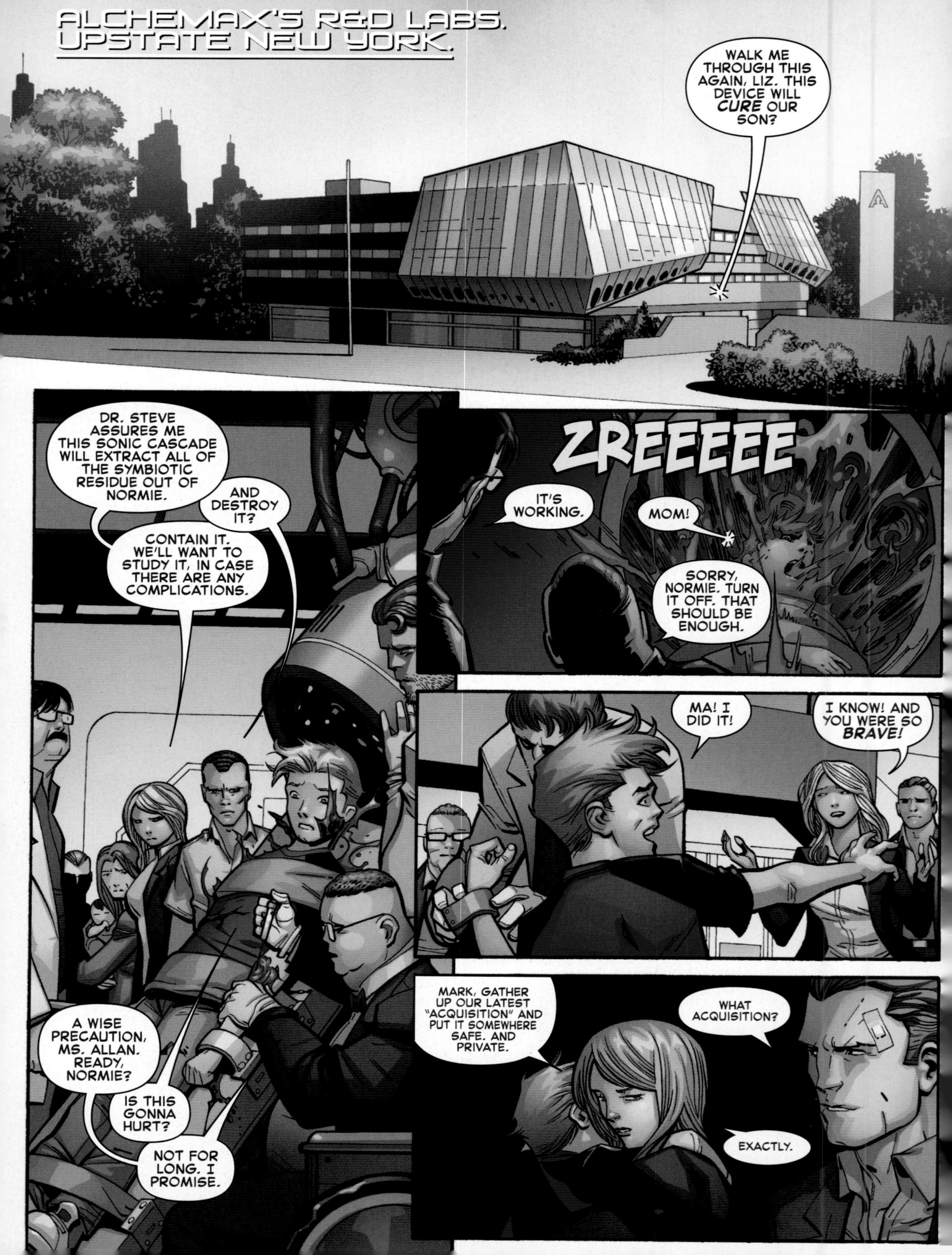
ALCHEMAX'S R&D LABS. UPSTATE NEW YORK.
WALK ME THROUGH THIS AGAIN, LIZ. THIS DEVICE WILL CURE OUR SON?
DR. STEVE ASSURES ME THIS SONIC CASCADE WILL EXTRACT ALL OF THE SYMBIOTIC RESIDUE OUT OF NORMIE.
AND DESTROY IT?
CONTAIN IT. WE'LL WANT TO STUDY IT, IN CASE THERE ARE ANY COMPLICATIONS.
A WISE PRECAUTION, MS. ALLAN. READY, NORMIE?
IS THIS GONNA HURT?
NOT FOR LONG. I PROMISE.
ZREEEEE
IT'S WORKING.
MOM!
SORRY, NORMIE. TURN IT OFF. THAT SHOULD BE ENOUGH.
MA! I DID IT!
I KNOW! AND YOU WERE SO BRAVE!
MARK, GATHER UP OUR LATEST "ACQUISITION" AND PUT IT SOMEWHERE SAFE. AND PRIVATE.
WHAT ACQUISITION?
EXACTLY.

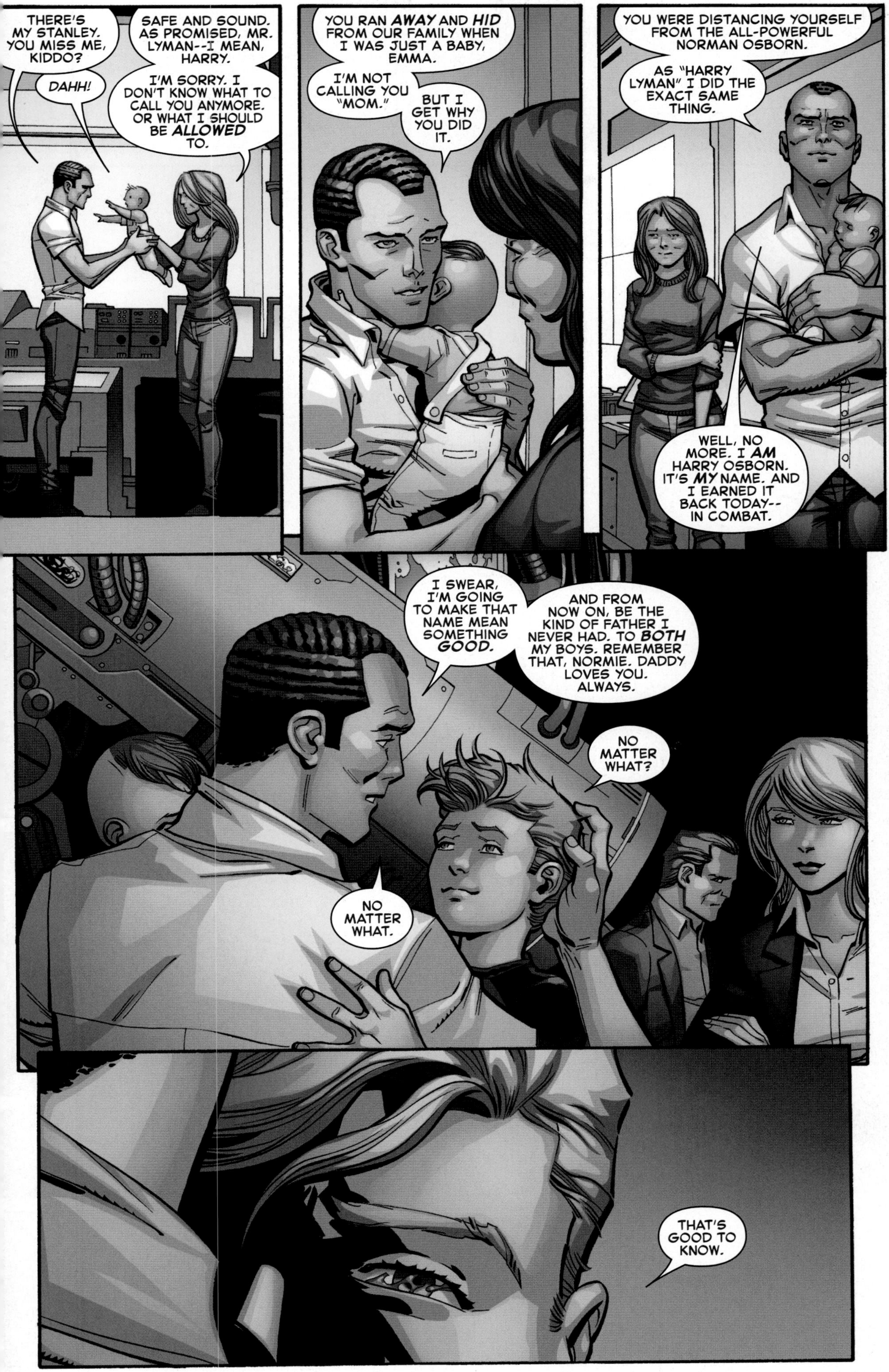
THERE'S MY STANLEY. YOU MISS ME, KIDDO?
DAHH!
SAFE AND SOUND. AS PROMISED, MR. LYMAN--I MEAN, HARRY.
I'M SORRY. I DON'T KNOW WHAT TO CALL YOU ANYMORE. OR WHAT I SHOULD BE ALLOWED TO.
YOU RAN AWAY AND HID FROM OUR FAMILY WHEN I WAS JUST A BABY, EMMA.
I'M NOT CALLING YOU "MOM."
BUT I GET WHY YOU DID IT.
YOU WERE DISTANCING YOURSELF FROM THE ALL-POWERFUL NORMAN OSBORN.
AS "HARRY LYMAN" I DID THE EXACT SAME THING.
WELL, NO MORE. I AM HARRY OSBORN. IT'S MY NAME. AND I EARNED IT BACK TODAY-- IN COMBAT.
I SWEAR, I'M GOING TO MAKE THAT NAME MEAN SOMETHING GOOD.
AND FROM NOW ON, BE THE KIND OF FATHER I NEVER HAD. TO BOTH MY BOYS. REMEMBER THAT, NORMIE. DADDY LOVES YOU. ALWAYS.
NO MATTER WHAT?
NO MATTER WHAT.
THAT'S GOOD TO KNOW.

GOODBYE

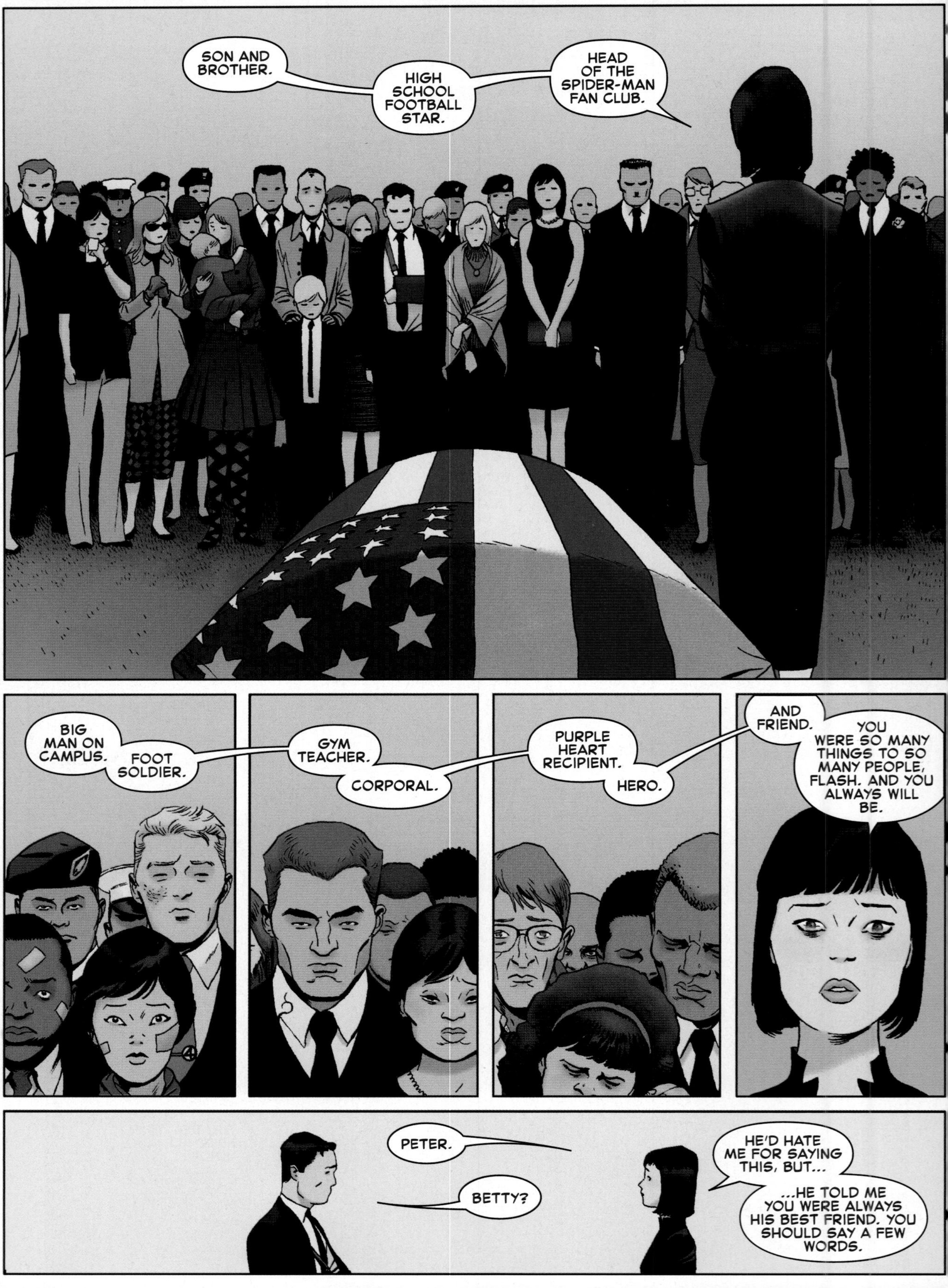
SON AND BROTHER.
HIGH SCHOOL FOOTBALL STAR.
HEAD OF THE SPIDER-MAN FAN CLUB.
BIG MAN ON CAMPUS.
FOOT SOLDIER.
GYM TEACHER.
CORPORAL.
PURPLE HEART RECIPIENT.
HERO.
AND FRIEND.
YOU WERE SO MANY THINGS TO SO MANY PEOPLE, FLASH. AND YOU ALWAYS WILL BE.
PETER.
BETTY?
HE'D HATE ME FOR SAYING THIS, BUT...
...HE TOLD ME YOU WERE ALWAYS HIS BEST FRIEND. YOU SHOULD SAY A FEW WORDS.

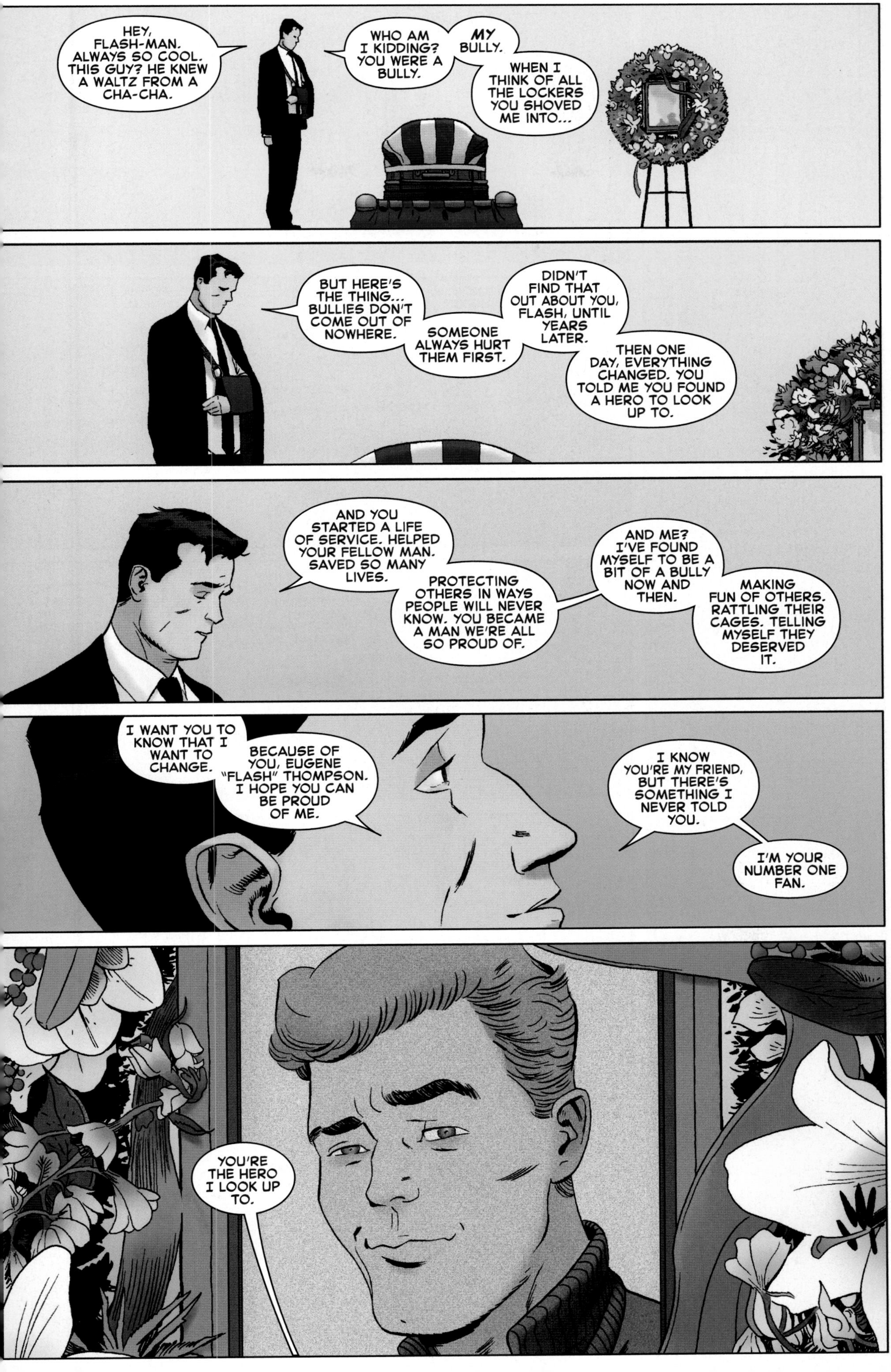

HEY, FLASH-MAN. ALWAYS SO COOL. THIS GUY? HE KNEW A WALTZ FROM A CHA-CHA.
WHO AM I KIDDING? YOU WERE A BULLY.
MY BULLY.
WHEN I THINK OF ALL THE LOCKERS YOU SHOVED ME INTO...
BUT HERE'S THE THING... BULLIES DON'T COME OUT OF NOWHERE.
SOMEONE ALWAYS HURT THEM FIRST.
DIDN'T FIND THAT OUT ABOUT YOU, FLASH, UNTIL YEARS LATER.
THEN ONE DAY, EVERYTHING CHANGED. YOU TOLD ME YOU FOUND A HERO TO LOOK UP TO.
AND YOU STARTED A LIFE OF SERVICE. HELPED YOUR FELLOW MAN. SAVED SO MANY LIVES.
PROTECTING OTHERS IN WAYS PEOPLE WILL NEVER KNOW. YOU BECAME A MAN WE'RE ALL SO PROUD OF.
AND ME? I'VE FOUND MYSELF TO BE A BIT OF A BULLY NOW AND THEN.
MAKING FUN OF OTHERS. RATTLING THEIR CAGES. TELLING MYSELF THEY DESERVED IT.
I WANT YOU TO KNOW THAT I WANT TO CHANGE.
BECAUSE OF YOU, EUGENE "FLASH" THOMPSON. I HOPE YOU CAN BE PROUD OF ME.
I KNOW YOU'RE MY FRIEND, BUT THERE'S SOMETHING I NEVER TOLD YOU.
I'M YOUR NUMBER ONE FAN.
YOU'RE THE HERO I LOOK UP TO.

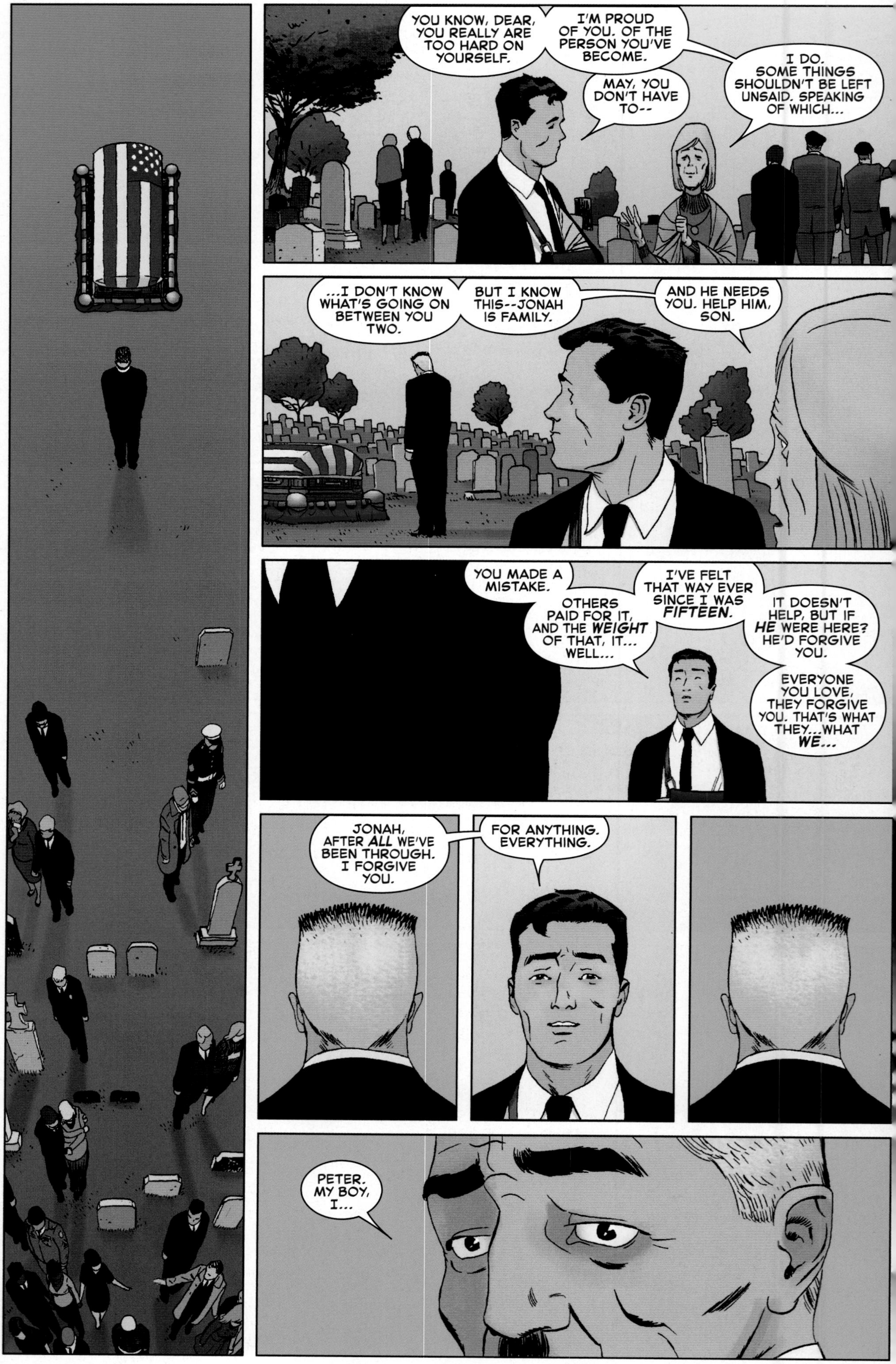
YOU KNOW, DEAR, YOU REALLY ARE TOO HARD ON YOURSELF.
I'M PROUD OF YOU. OF THE PERSON YOU'VE BECOME.
MAY, YOU DON'T HAVE TO--
I DO. SOME THINGS SHOULDN'T BE LEFT UNSAID. SPEAKING OF WHICH...
...I DON'T KNOW WHAT'S GOING ON BETWEEN YOU TWO.
BUT I KNOW THIS--JONAH IS FAMILY.
AND HE NEEDS YOU. HELP HIM, SON.
YOU MADE A MISTAKE.
OTHERS PAID FOR IT, AND THE WEIGHT OF THAT, IT... WELL...
I'VE FELT THAT WAY EVER SINCE I WAS FIFTEEN.
IT DOESN'T HELP, BUT IF HE WERE HERE? HE'D FORGIVE YOU.
EVERYONE YOU LOVE, THEY FORGIVE YOU. THAT'S WHAT THEY...WHAT WE...
JONAH, AFTER ALL WE'VE BEEN THROUGH. I FORGIVE YOU.
FOR ANYTHING. EVERYTHING.
PETER. MY BOY, I...

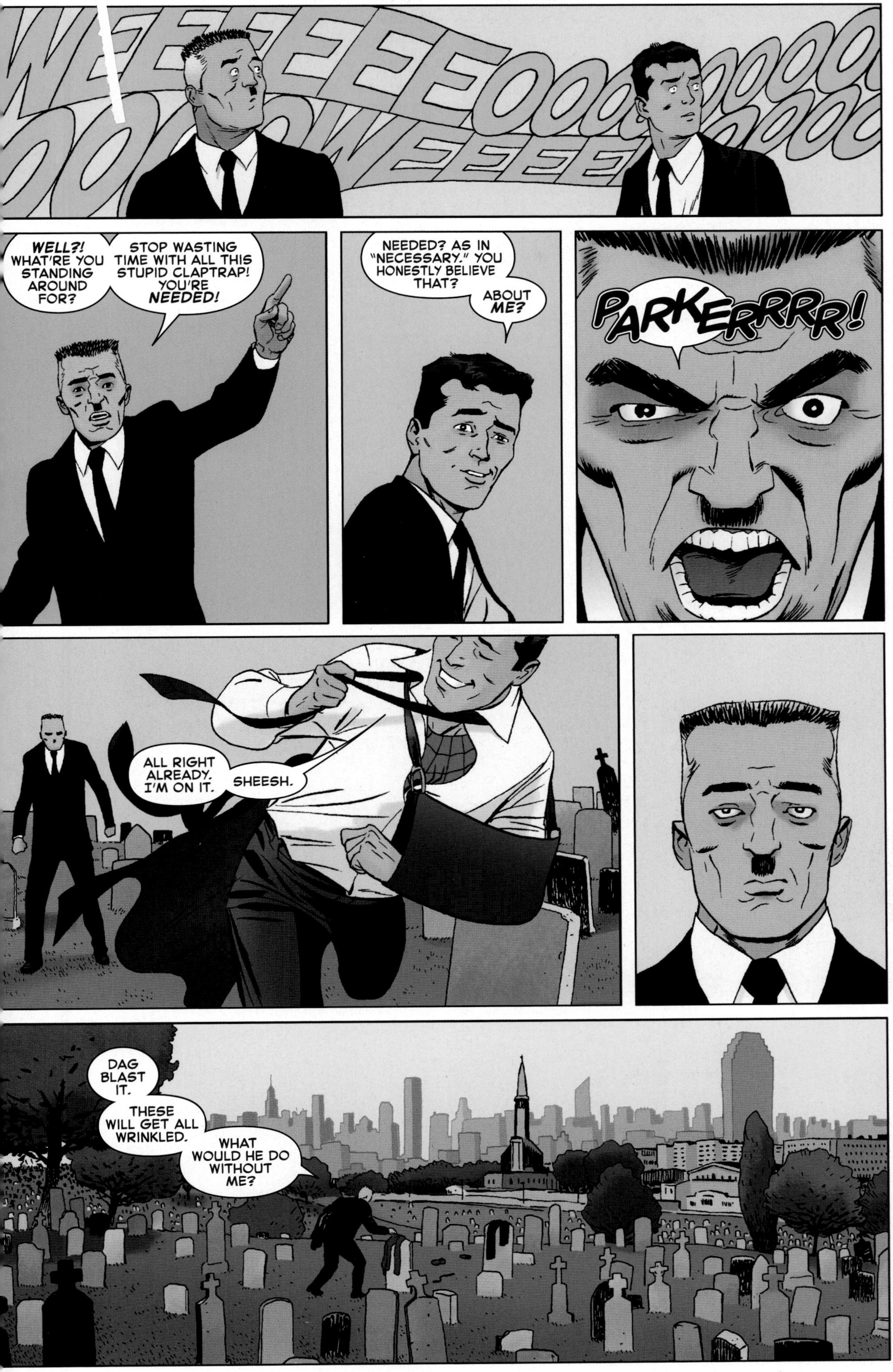
WEEEEEEOOOOOOOOOO
OOOOOWEEEEEOOOOO
WELL?! WHAT'RE YOU STANDING AROUND FOR?
STOP WASTING TIME WITH ALL THIS STUPID CLAPTRAP! YOU'RE NEEDED!
NEEDED? AS IN "NECESSARY." YOU HONESTLY BELIEVE THAT?
ABOUT ME?
PARKERRRR!
ALL RIGHT ALREADY. I'M ON IT.
SHEESH.
DAG BLAST IT.
THESE WILL GET ALL WRINKLED.
WHAT WOULD HE DO WITHOUT ME?

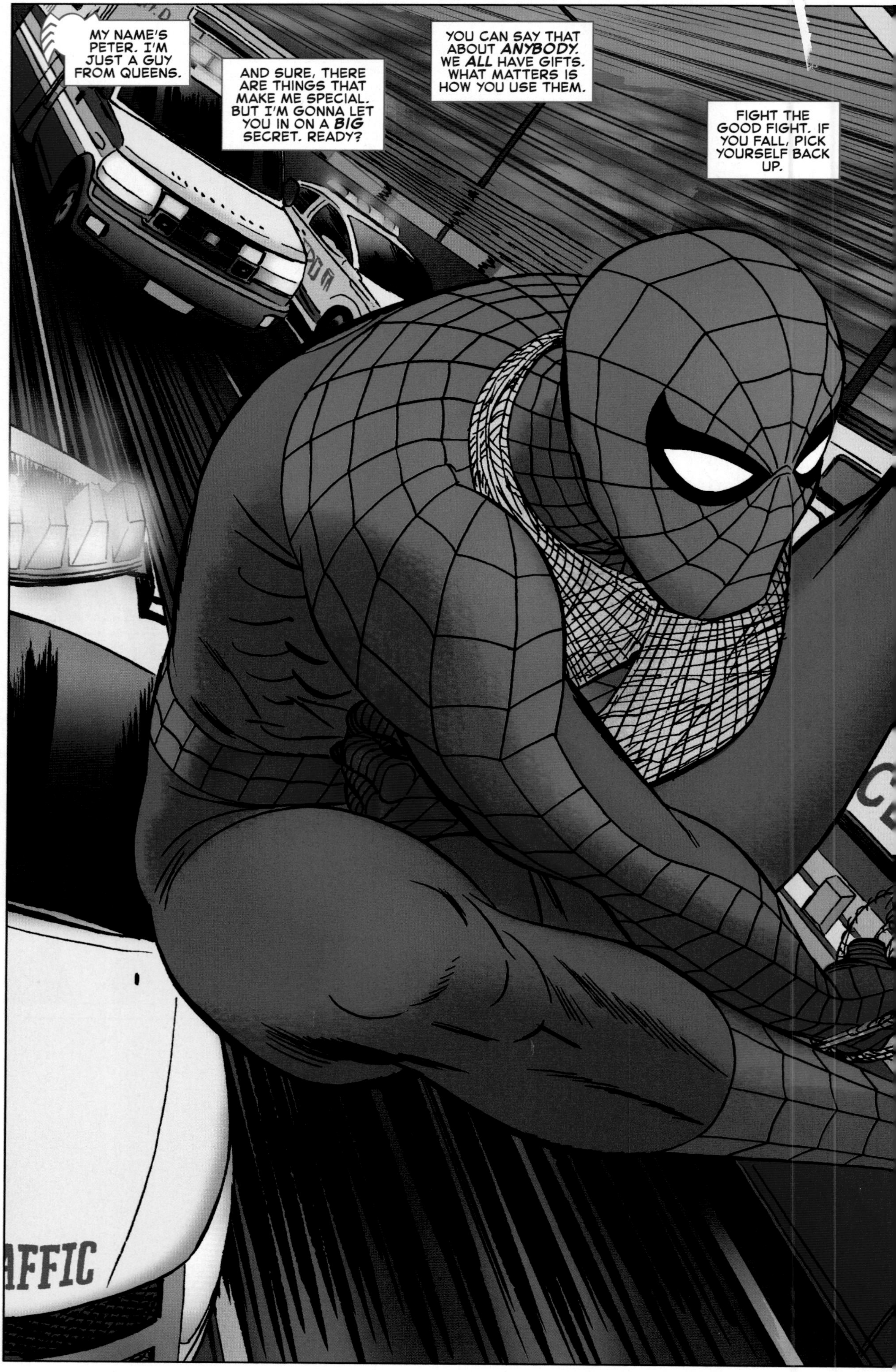
MY NAME'S PETER. I'M JUST A GUY FROM QUEENS.
AND SURE, THERE ARE THINGS THAT MAKE ME SPECIAL. BUT I'M GONNA LET YOU IN ON A BIG SECRET. READY?
YOU CAN SAY THAT ABOUT ANYBODY. WE ALL HAVE GIFTS. WHAT MATTERS IS HOW YOU USE THEM.
FIGHT THE GOOD FIGHT. IF YOU FALL, PICK YOURSELF BACK UP.
AFFIC

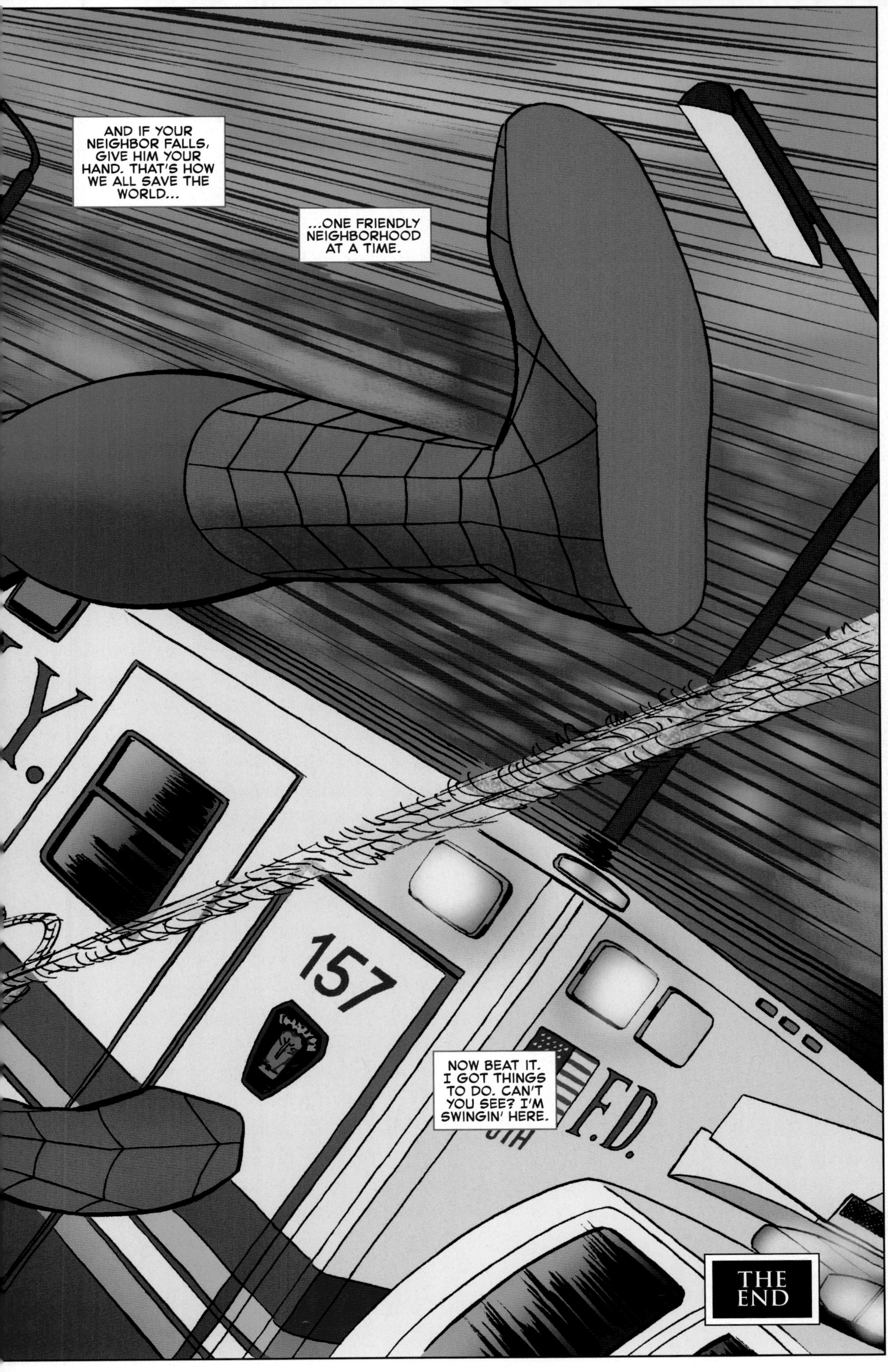
AND IF YOUR NEIGHBOR FALLS, GIVE HIM YOUR HAND. THAT'S HOW WE ALL SAVE THE WORLD...
...ONE FRIENDLY NEIGHBORHOOD AT A TIME.
157
F.D.
NOW BEAT IT. I GOT THINGS TO DO. CAN'T YOU SEE? I'M SWINGIN' HERE.
THE END

the AMAZING SPIDER-MAN

#800

DAN SLOTT writer   VC's **JOE CARAMAGNA** letterer

chapter one: *CRAWLING THROUGH THE WRECKAGE*

NICK BRADSHAW artist   **EDGAR DELGADO** color artist

chapter two: *TOO MANY TARGETS*

HUMBERTO RAMOS
penciler

VICTOR OLAZABA
inker

EDGAR DELGADO
color artist

chapter three: *FAMILY INFIGHTING*

GIUSEPPE CAMUNCOLI
penciler

CAM SMITH
inker

JAVA TARTAGLIA
color artist

chapter four: *THE GOBLIN TRIUMPHANT*

STUART IMMONEN
penciler

WADE von GRAWBADGER
inker

MARTE GRACIA
color artist

ALMOST SOLITARY CONFINEMENT
and *THE RETURN OF HARRY OSBORN*

GIUSEPPE CAMUNCOLI
penciler

CAM SMITH
inker

JAVA TARTAGLIA
color artist

GOODBYE

MARCOS MARTÍN artist   **MUNTSA VICENTE** color artist

ANTHONY GAMBINO production designer   **KATHLEEN WISNESKI** assistant editor   **NICK LOWE** with **DEVIN LEWIS** editors

C.B. CEBULSKI editor in chief   **JOE QUESADA** chief creative officer   **DAN BUCKLEY** president   **ALAN FINE** executive producer

Spider-Man created by **STAN LEE** and **STEVE DITKO**

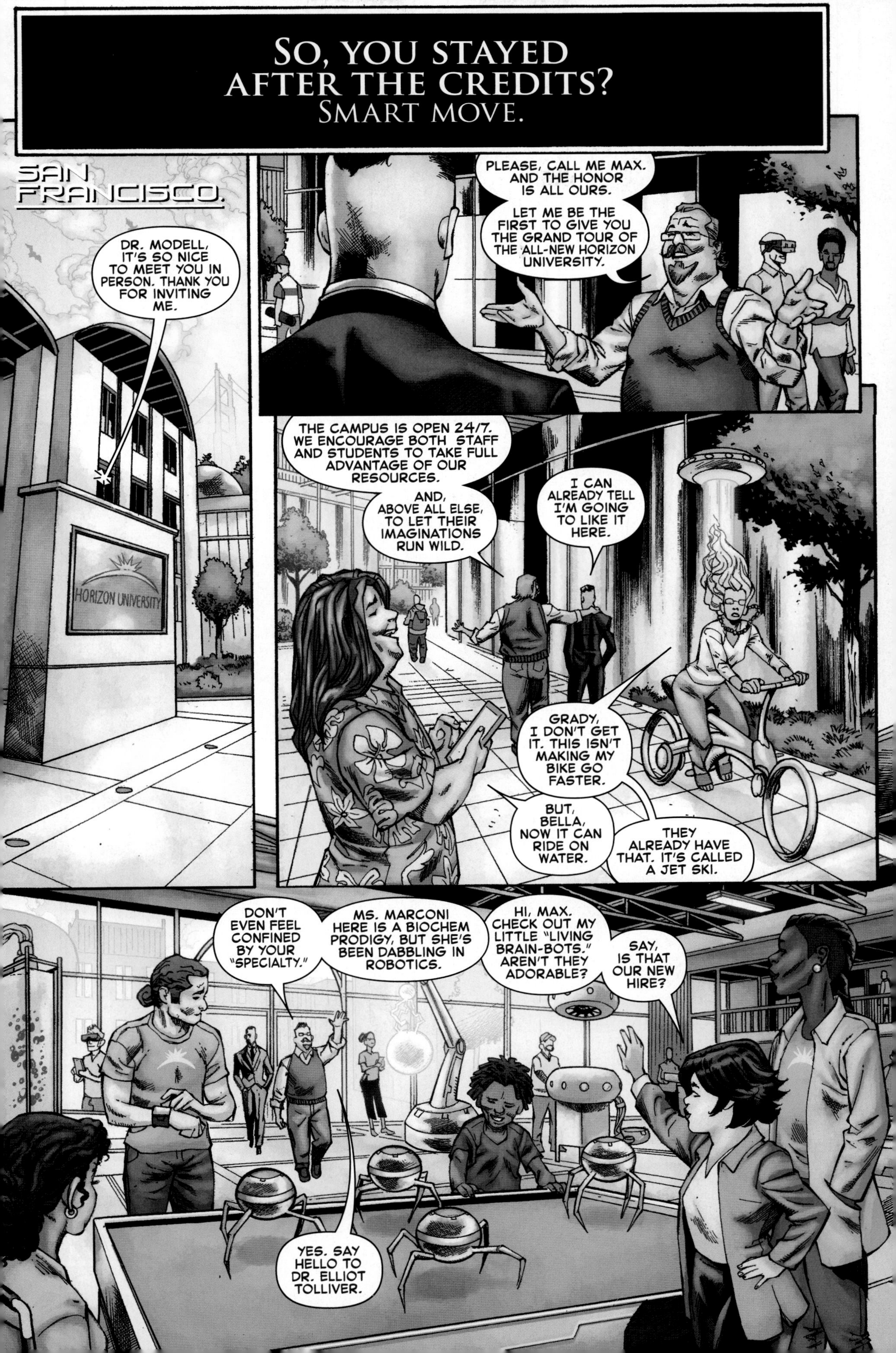
SO, YOU STAYED AFTER THE CREDITS? SMART MOVE.
SAN FRANCISCO.
DR. MODELL, IT'S SO NICE TO MEET YOU IN PERSON. THANK YOU FOR INVITING ME.
HORIZON UNIVERSITY
PLEASE, CALL ME MAX. AND THE HONOR IS ALL OURS.
LET ME BE THE FIRST TO GIVE YOU THE GRAND TOUR OF THE ALL-NEW HORIZON UNIVERSITY.
THE CAMPUS IS OPEN 24/7. WE ENCOURAGE BOTH STAFF AND STUDENTS TO TAKE FULL ADVANTAGE OF OUR RESOURCES.
AND, ABOVE ALL ELSE, TO LET THEIR IMAGINATIONS RUN WILD.
I CAN ALREADY TELL I'M GOING TO LIKE IT HERE.
GRADY, I DON'T GET IT. THIS ISN'T MAKING MY BIKE GO FASTER.
BUT, BELLA, NOW IT CAN RIDE ON WATER.
THEY ALREADY HAVE THAT. IT'S CALLED A JET SKI.
DON'T EVEN FEEL CONFINED BY YOUR "SPECIALTY."
MS. MARCONI HERE IS A BIOCHEM PRODIGY, BUT SHE'S BEEN DABBLING IN ROBOTICS.
HI, MAX. CHECK OUT MY LITTLE "LIVING BRAIN-BOTS." AREN'T THEY ADORABLE?
SAY, IS THAT OUR NEW HIRE?
YES. SAY HELLO TO DR. ELLIOT TOLLIVER.

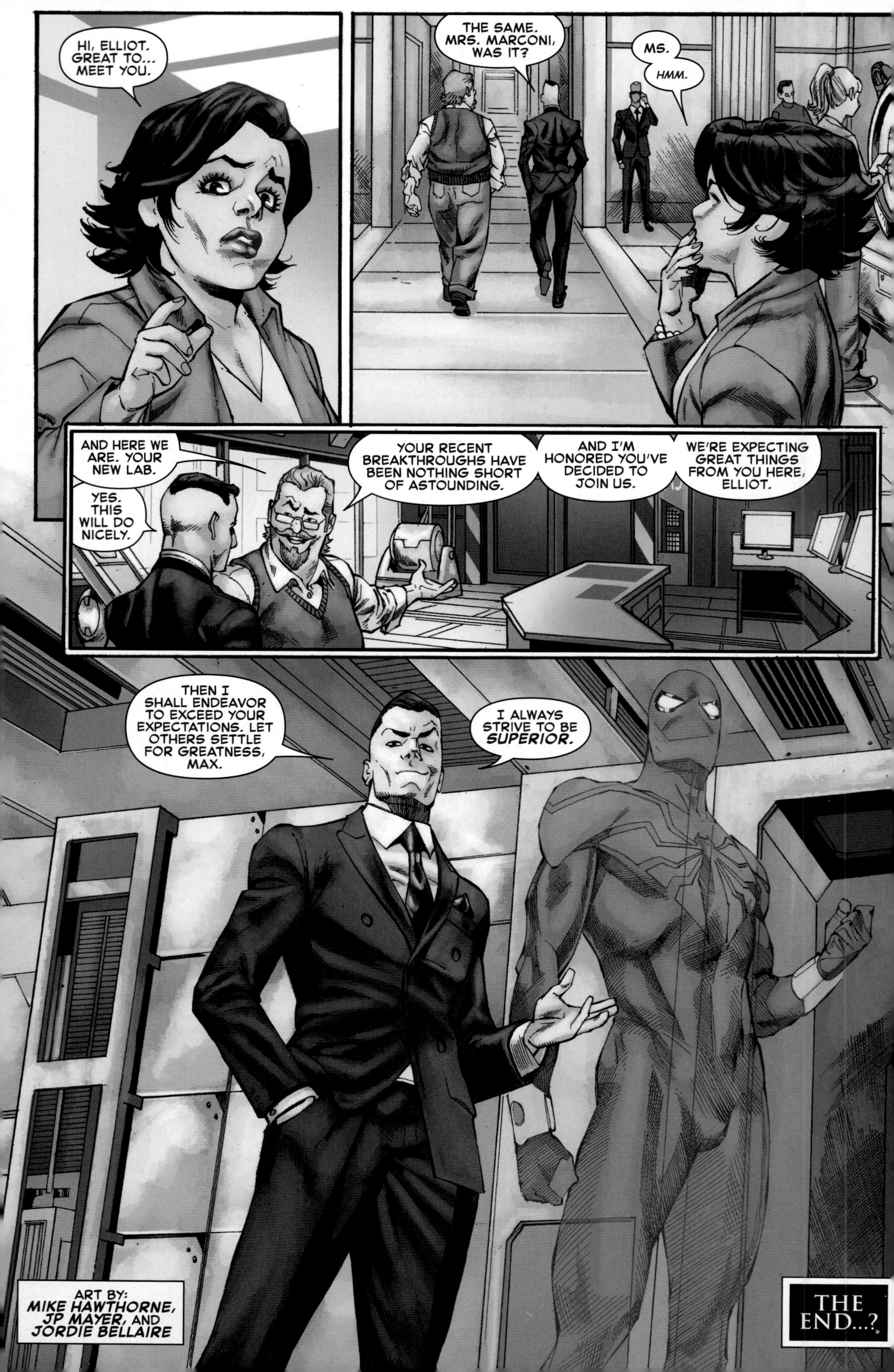
HI, ELLIOT. GREAT TO... MEET YOU.
THE SAME. MRS. MARCONI, WAS IT?
MS.
HMM.
AND HERE WE ARE. YOUR NEW LAB.
YES. THIS WILL DO NICELY.
YOUR RECENT BREAKTHROUGHS HAVE BEEN NOTHING SHORT OF ASTOUNDING.
AND I'M HONORED YOU'VE DECIDED TO JOIN US.
WE'RE EXPECTING GREAT THINGS FROM YOU HERE, ELLIOT.
THEN I SHALL ENDEAVOR TO EXCEED YOUR EXPECTATIONS. LET OTHERS SETTLE FOR GREATNESS, MAX.
I ALWAYS STRIVE TO BE SUPERIOR.
ART BY: MIKE HAWTHORNE, JP MAYER, AND JORDIE BELLAIRE
THE END...?

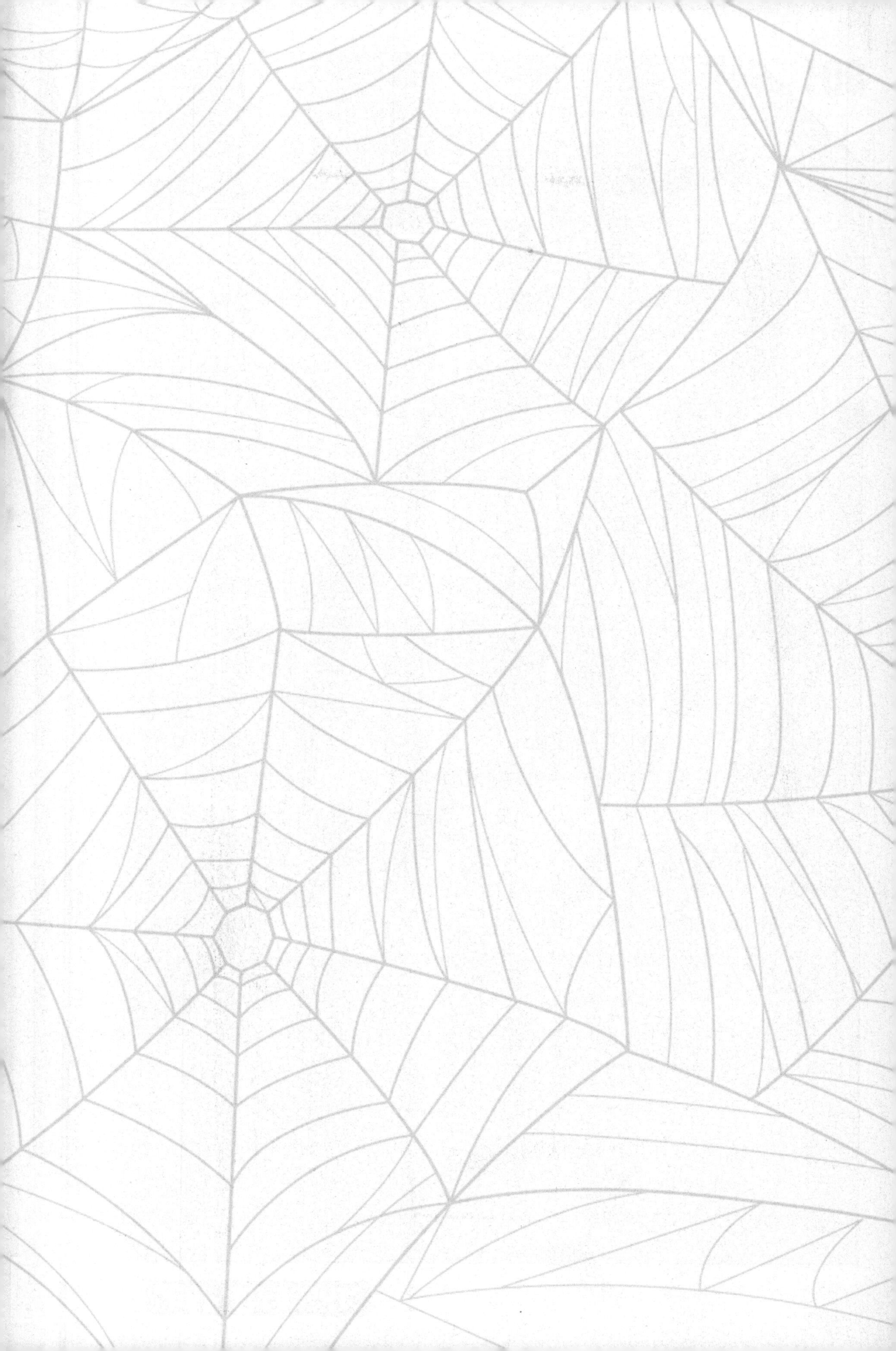

801

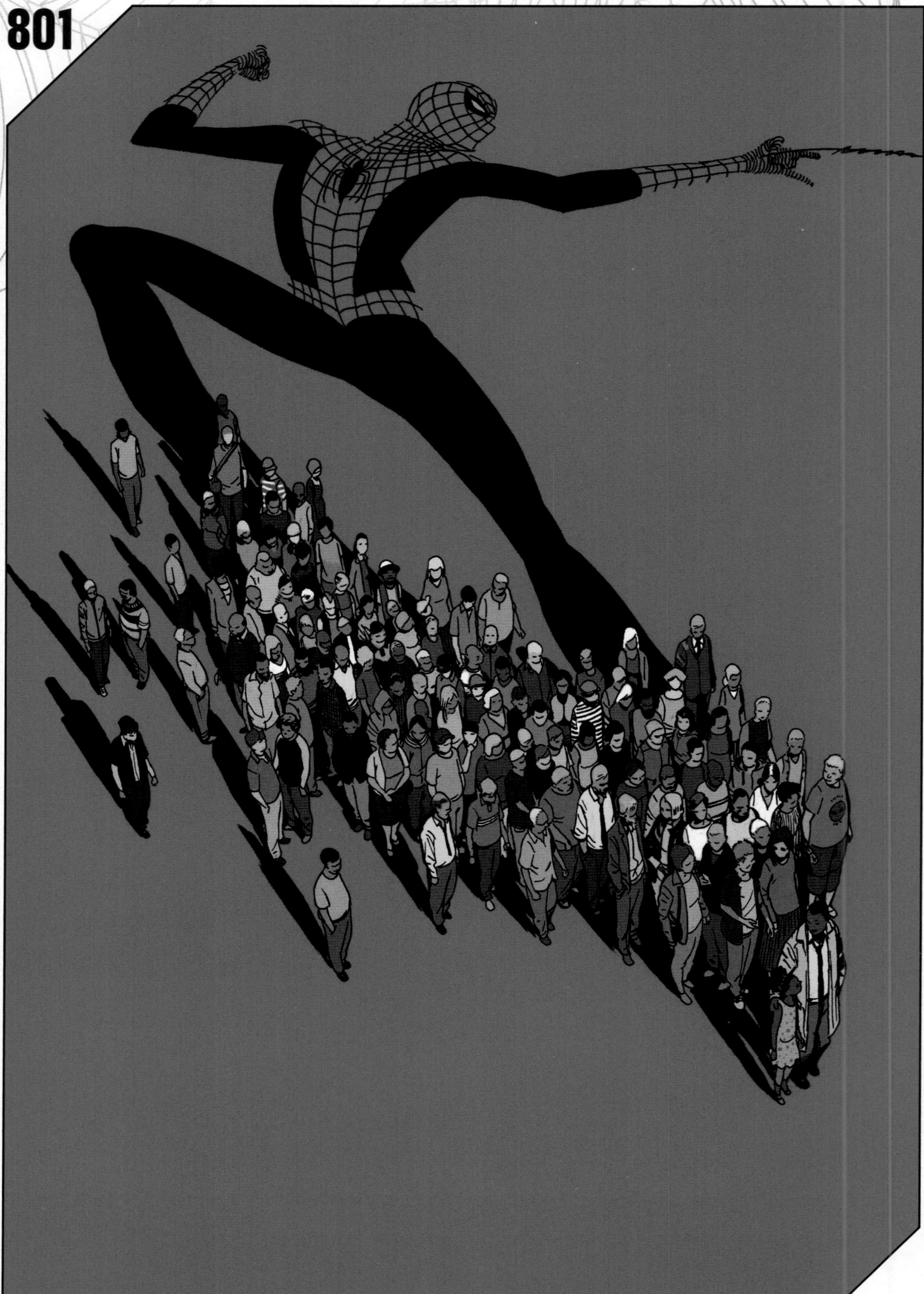

"THERE FOR YOU"

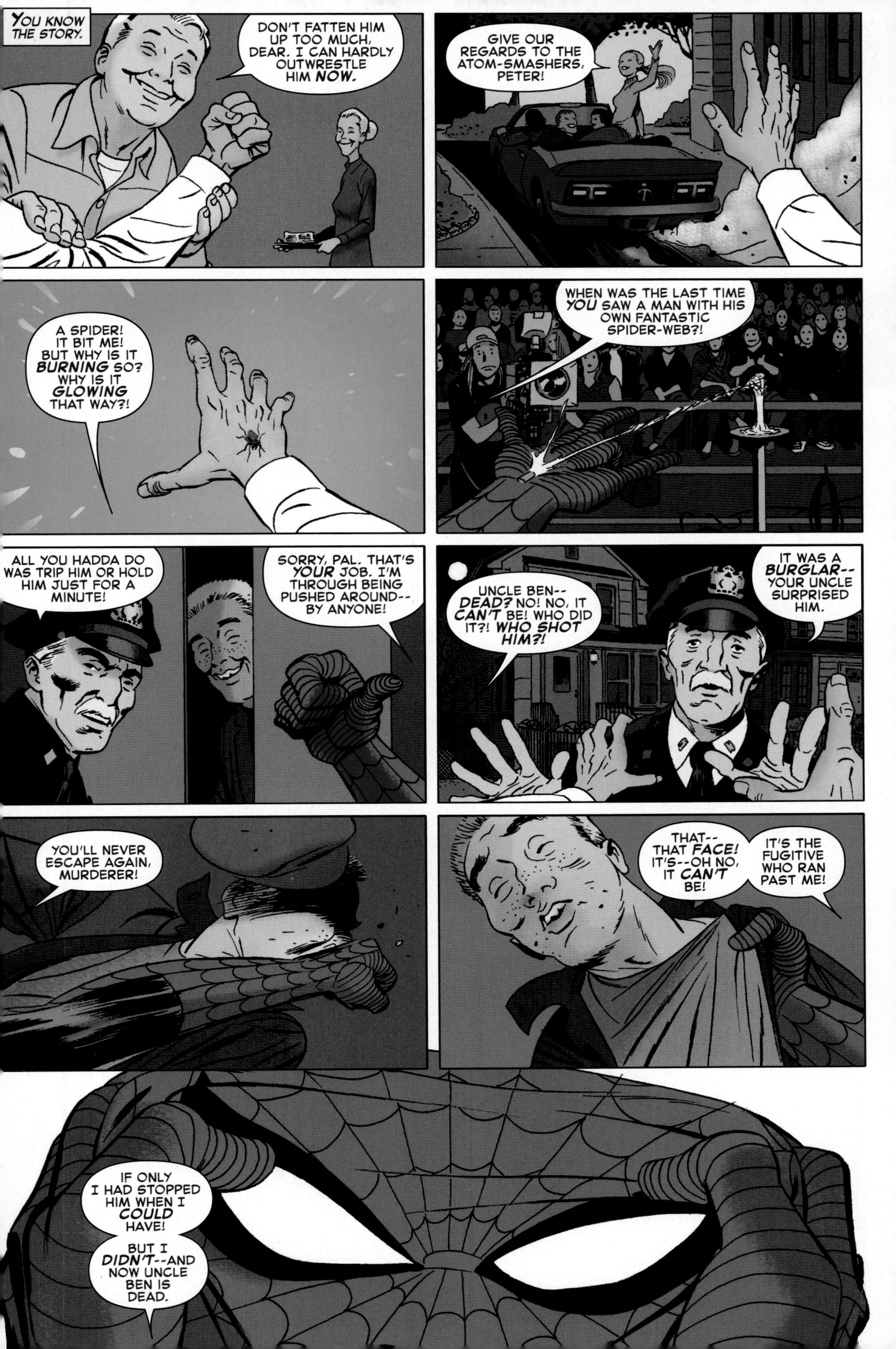
YOU KNOW THE STORY.
DON'T FATTEN HIM UP TOO MUCH, DEAR. I CAN HARDLY OUTWRESTLE HIM NOW.
GIVE OUR REGARDS TO THE ATOM-SMASHERS, PETER!
A SPIDER! IT BIT ME! BUT WHY IS IT BURNING SO? WHY IS IT GLOWING THAT WAY?!
WHEN WAS THE LAST TIME YOU SAW A MAN WITH HIS OWN FANTASTIC SPIDER-WEB?!
ALL YOU HADDA DO WAS TRIP HIM OR HOLD HIM JUST FOR A MINUTE!
SORRY, PAL. THAT'S YOUR JOB. I'M THROUGH BEING PUSHED AROUND--BY ANYONE!
UNCLE BEN--DEAD? NO! NO, IT CAN'T BE! WHO DID IT?! WHO SHOT HIM?!
IT WAS A BURGLAR--YOUR UNCLE SURPRISED HIM.
YOU'LL NEVER ESCAPE AGAIN, MURDERER!
THAT--THAT FACE! IT'S--OH NO, IT CAN'T BE!
IT'S THE FUGITIVE WHO RAN PAST ME!
IF ONLY I HAD STOPPED HIM WHEN I COULD HAVE!
BUT I DIDN'T--AND NOW UNCLE BEN IS DEAD.

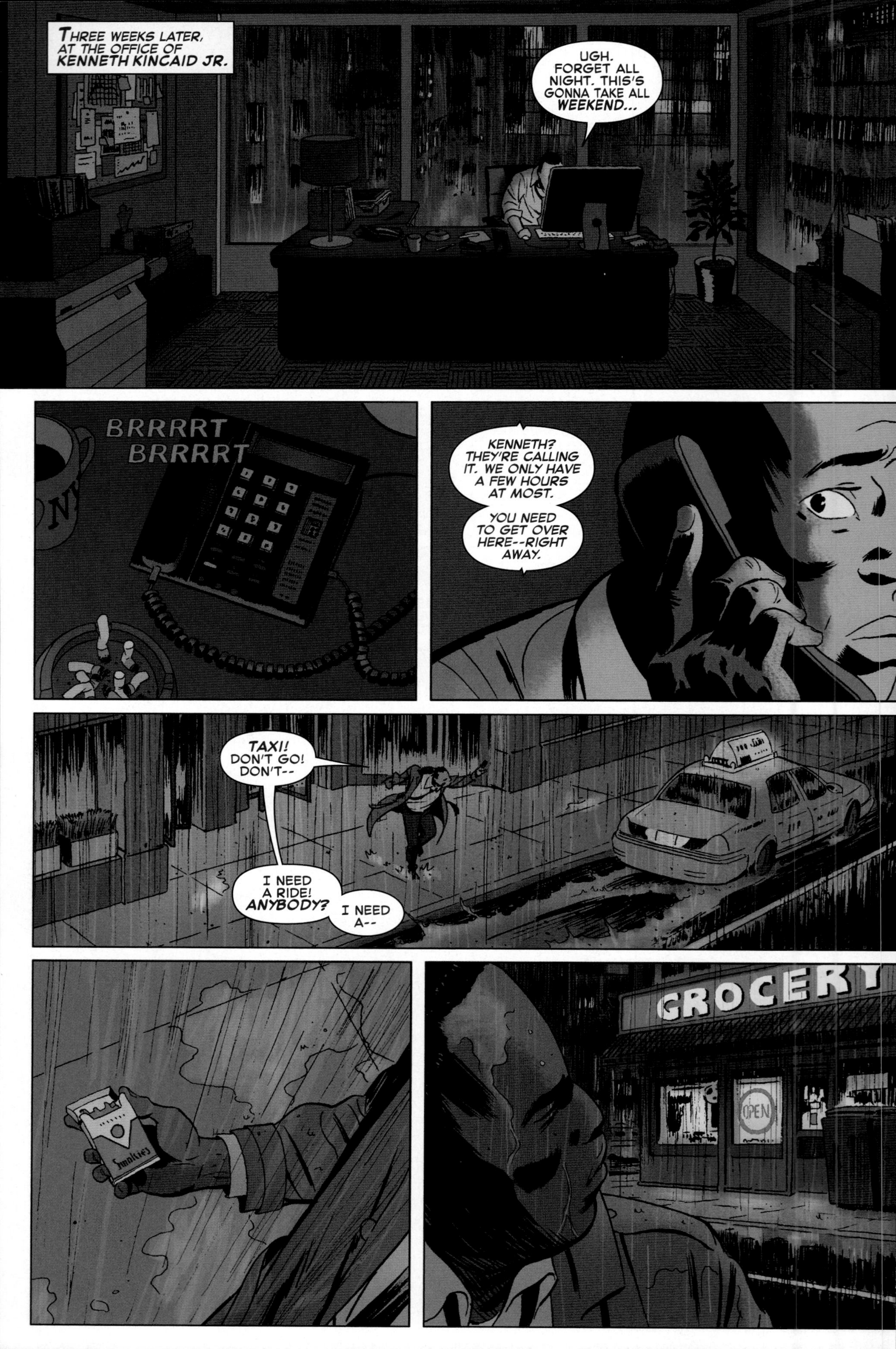
THREE WEEKS LATER, AT THE OFFICE OF KENNETH KINCAID JR.
UGH. FORGET ALL NIGHT. THIS'S GONNA TAKE ALL WEEKEND...
BRRRRT BRRRRT
KENNETH? THEY'RE CALLING IT. WE ONLY HAVE A FEW HOURS AT MOST.
YOU NEED TO GET OVER HERE--RIGHT AWAY.
TAXI! DON'T GO! DON'T--
I NEED A RIDE! ANYBODY?
I NEED A--
Smokies
GROCERY
OPEN

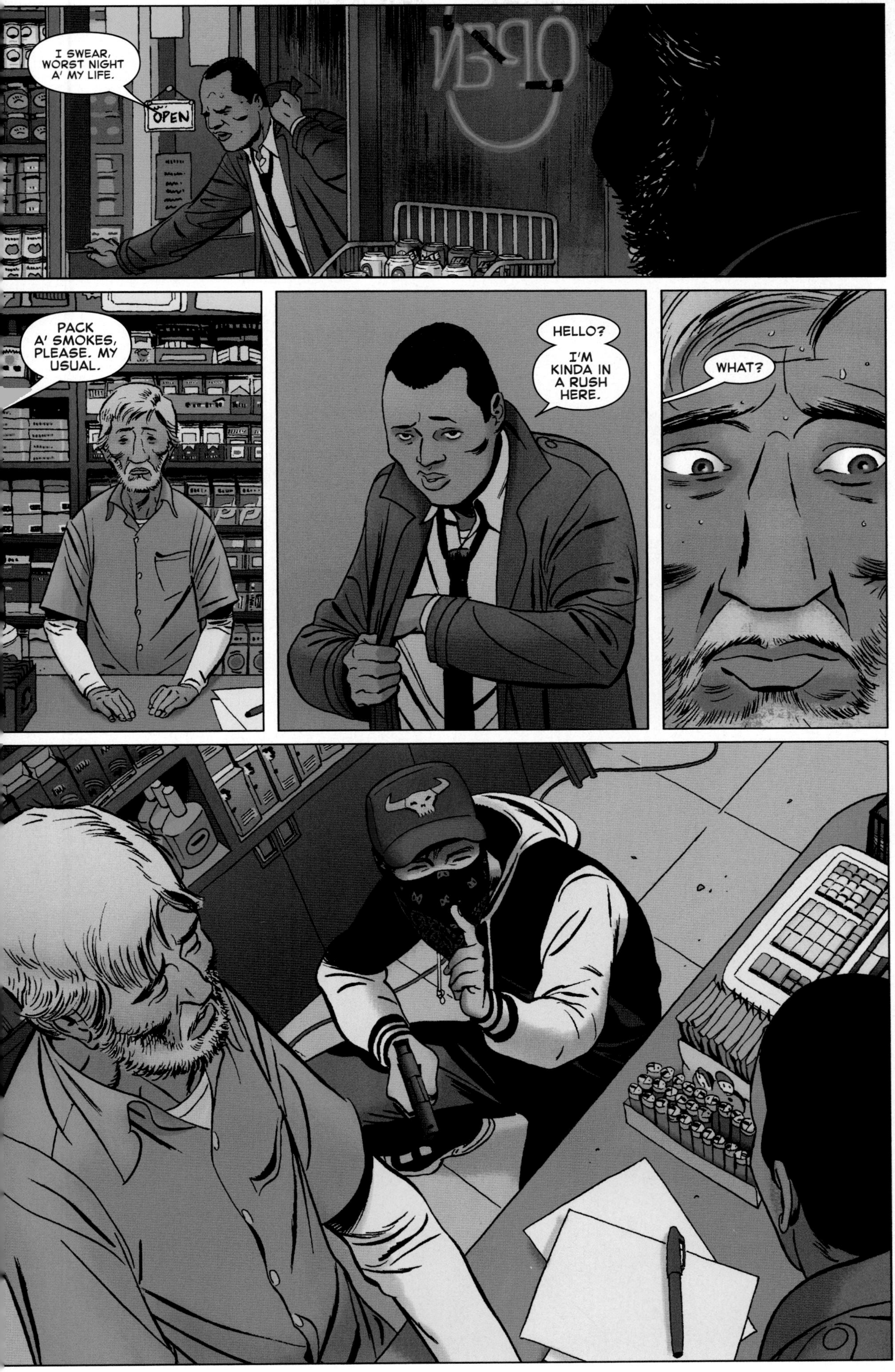
I SWEAR, WORST NIGHT A' MY LIFE.
OPEN
OPEN
PACK A' SMOKES, PLEASE. MY USUAL.
HELLO?
I'M KINDA IN A RUSH HERE.
WHAT?

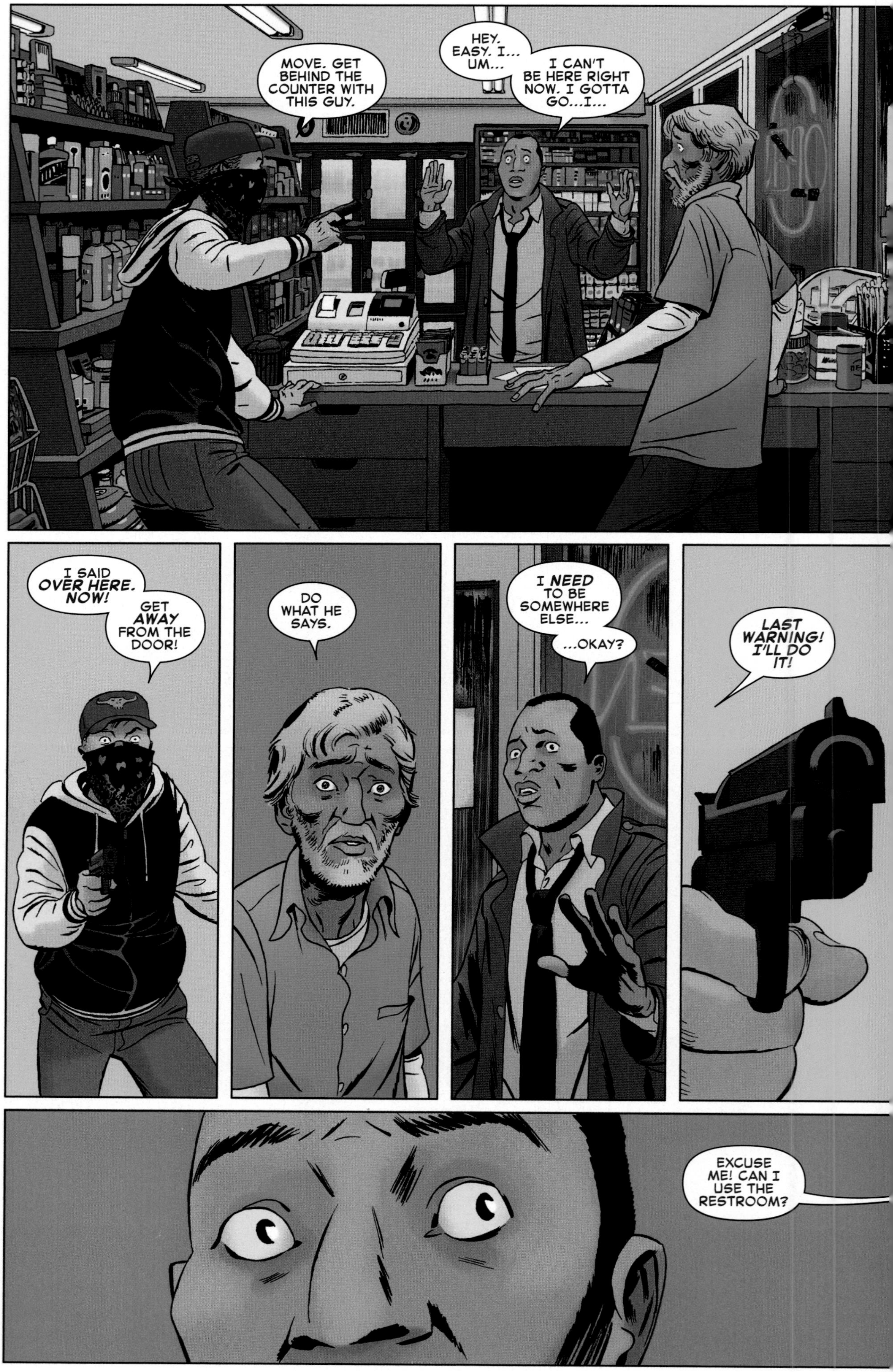

MOVE. GET BEHIND THE COUNTER WITH THIS GUY.
HEY. EASY. I... UM...
I CAN'T BE HERE RIGHT NOW. I GOTTA GO...I...
I SAID *OVER HERE. NOW!*
GET *AWAY* FROM THE DOOR!
DO WHAT HE SAYS.
I *NEED* TO BE SOMEWHERE ELSE...
...OKAY?
LAST WARNING! I'LL DO IT!
EXCUSE ME! CAN I USE THE RESTROOM?

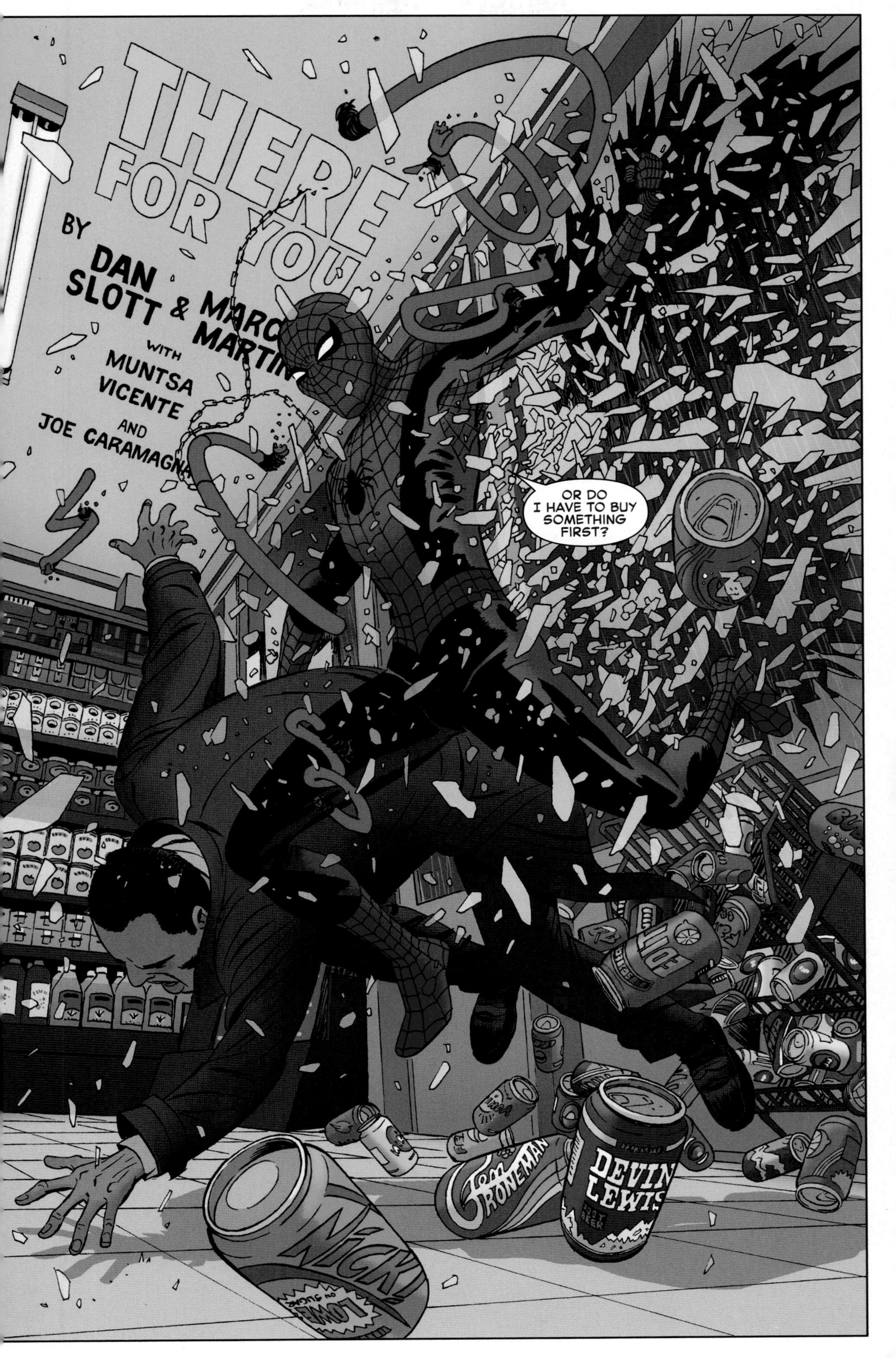
THERE FOR YOU
BY DAN SLOTT & MARCOS MARTIN
WITH MUNTSA VICENTE
AND JOE CARAMAGNA
OR DO I HAVE TO BUY SOMETHING FIRST?
DEVIN LEWIS ROOT BEER
NICK LOWE

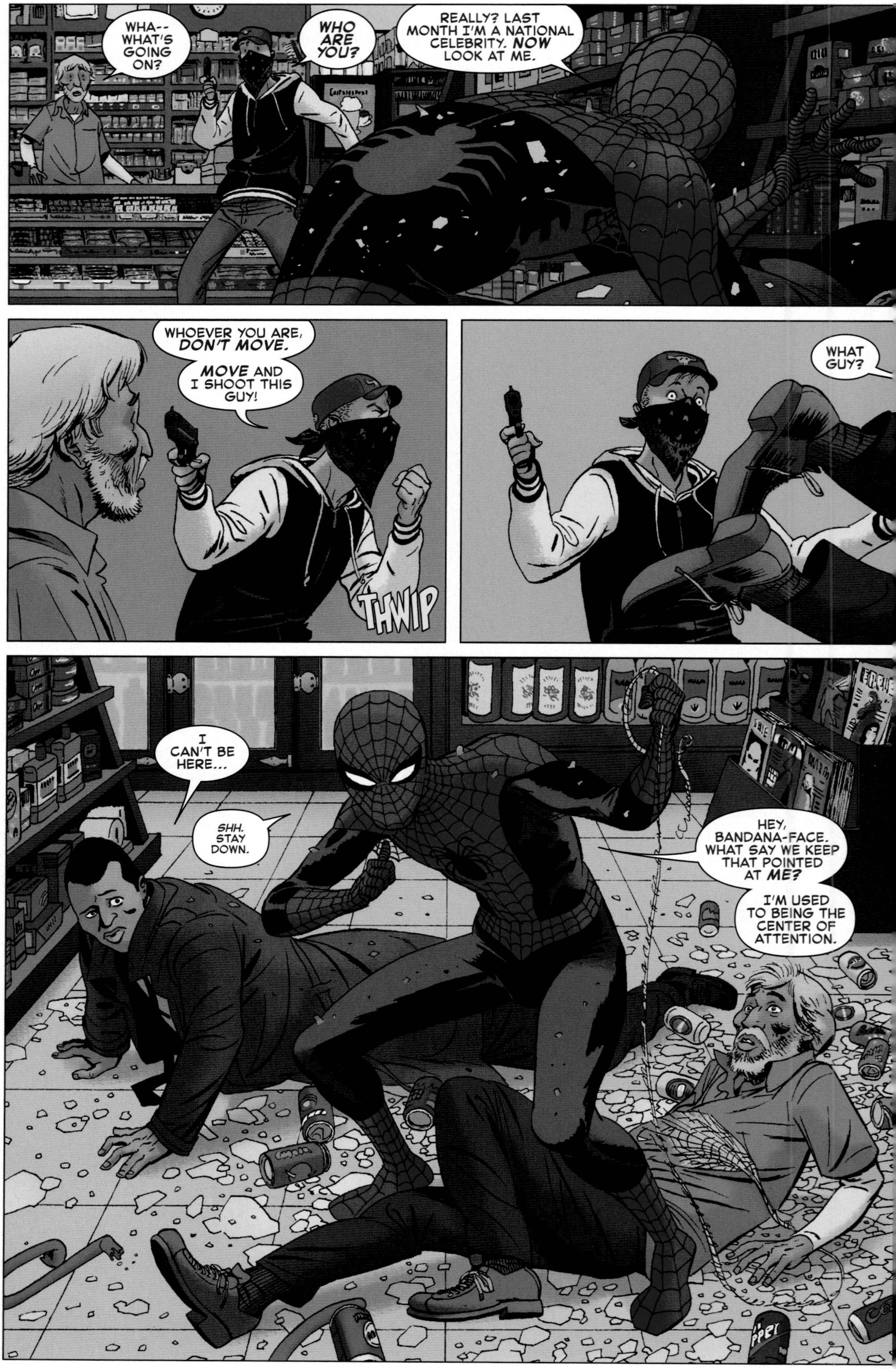
WHA-- WHAT'S GOING ON?
WHO ARE YOU?
REALLY? LAST MONTH I'M A NATIONAL CELEBRITY. NOW LOOK AT ME.
WHOEVER YOU ARE, DON'T MOVE.
MOVE AND I SHOOT THIS GUY!
THWIP
WHAT GUY?
I CAN'T BE HERE...
SHH. STAY DOWN.
HEY, BANDANA-FACE. WHAT SAY WE KEEP THAT POINTED AT ME?
I'M USED TO BEING THE CENTER OF ATTENTION.

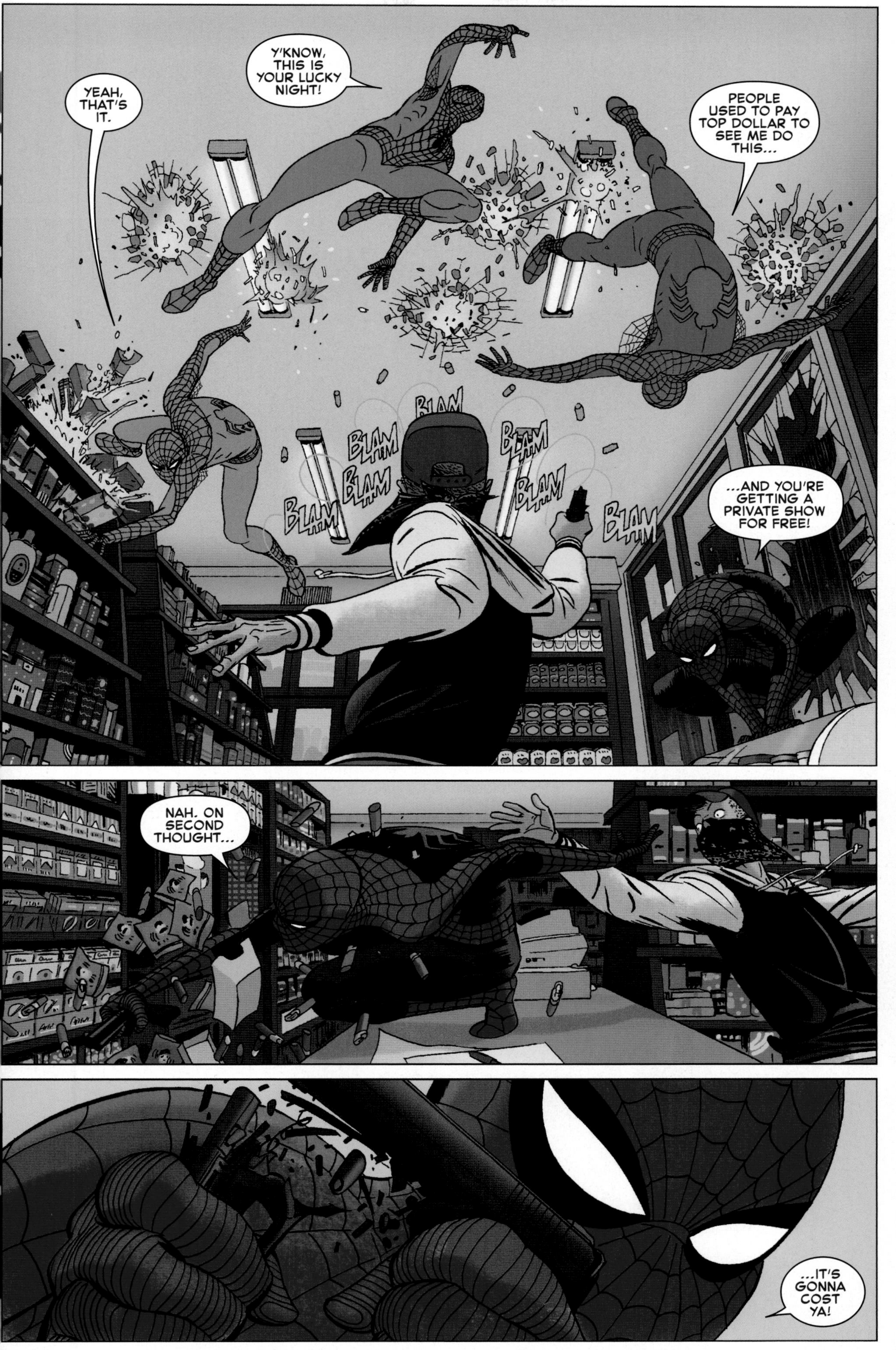
YEAH, THAT'S IT.
Y'KNOW, THIS IS YOUR LUCKY NIGHT!
PEOPLE USED TO PAY TOP DOLLAR TO SEE ME DO THIS...
BLAM
BLAM
BLAM
BLAM
BLAM
BLAM
BLAM
...AND YOU'RE GETTING A PRIVATE SHOW FOR FREE!
NAH. ON SECOND THOUGHT...
...IT'S GONNA COST YA!

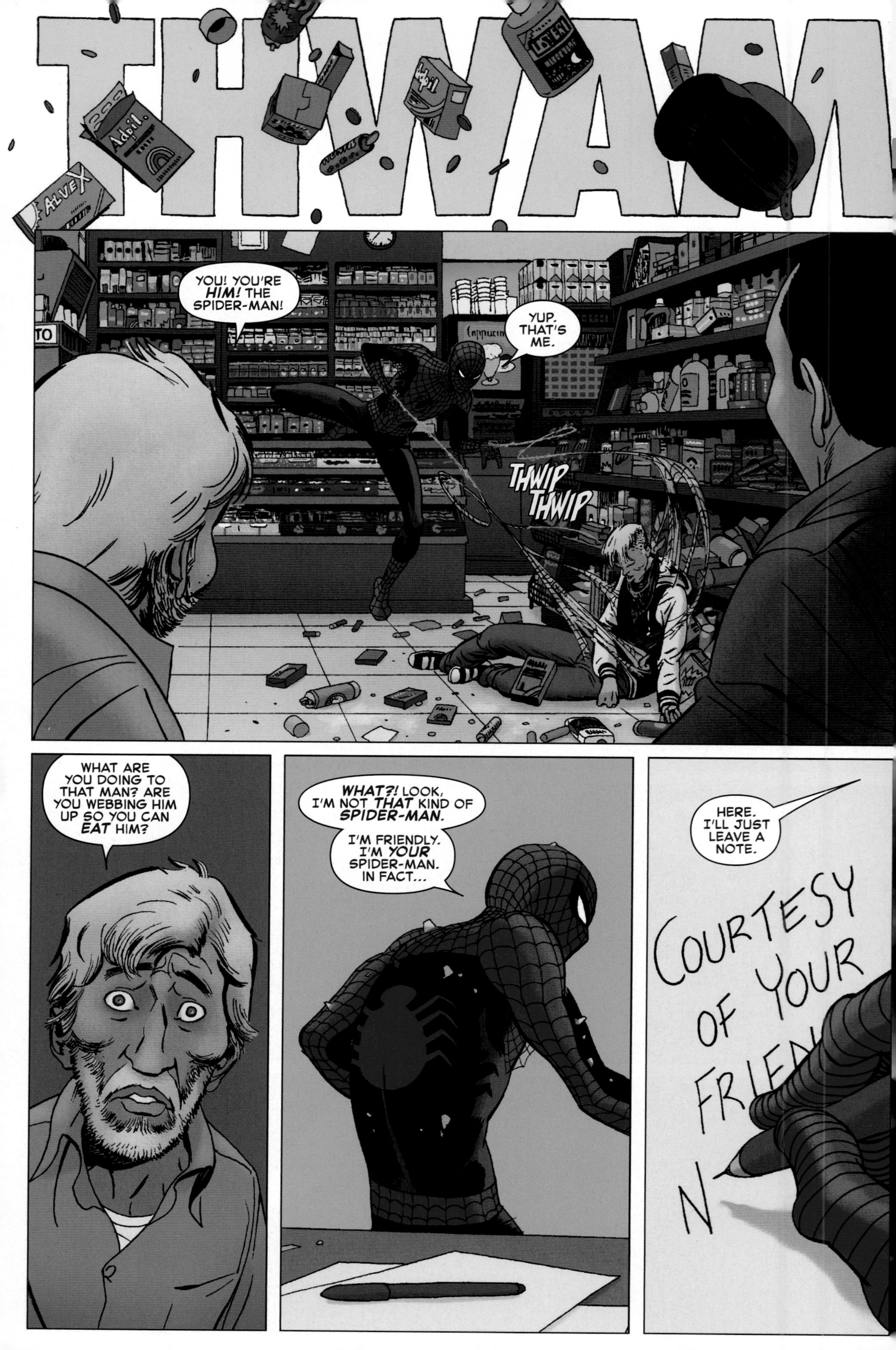
THWAM
YOU! YOU'RE HIM! THE SPIDER-MAN!
YUP. THAT'S ME.
THWIP THWIP
WHAT ARE YOU DOING TO THAT MAN? ARE YOU WEBBING HIM UP SO YOU CAN EAT HIM?
WHAT?! LOOK, I'M NOT THAT KIND OF SPIDER-MAN.
I'M FRIENDLY. I'M YOUR SPIDER-MAN. IN FACT...
HERE. I'LL JUST LEAVE A NOTE.
COURTESY OF YOUR FRIEN
N

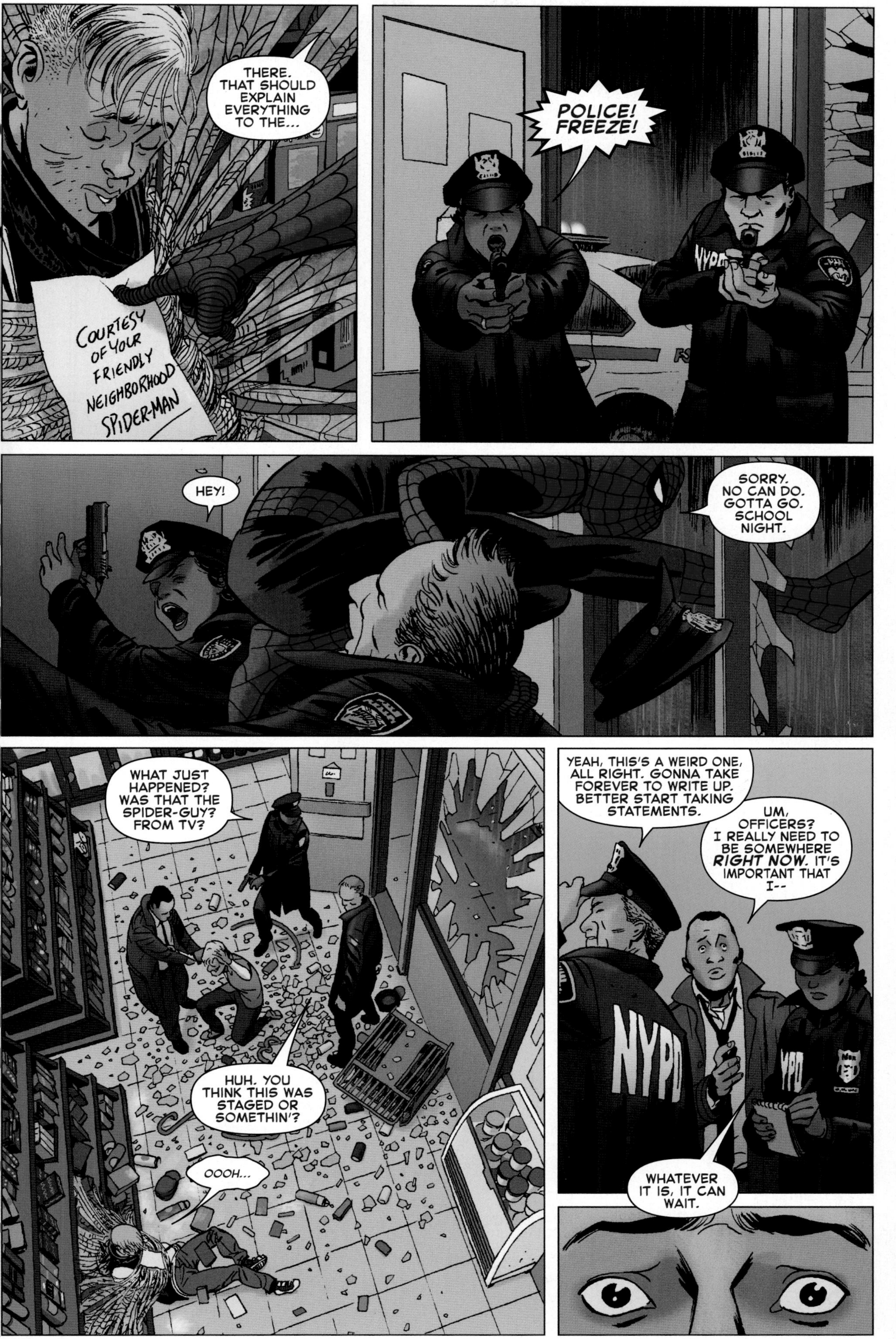
THERE. THAT SHOULD EXPLAIN EVERYTHING TO THE...
COURTESY OF YOUR FRIENDLY NEIGHBORHOOD SPIDER-MAN
POLICE! FREEZE!
HEY!
SORRY. NO CAN DO. GOTTA GO. SCHOOL NIGHT.
WHAT JUST HAPPENED? WAS THAT THE SPIDER-GUY? FROM TV?
HUH. YOU THINK THIS WAS STAGED OR SOMETHIN'?
OOOH...
YEAH, THIS'S A WEIRD ONE, ALL RIGHT. GONNA TAKE FOREVER TO WRITE UP. BETTER START TAKING STATEMENTS.
UM, OFFICERS? I REALLY NEED TO BE SOMEWHERE RIGHT NOW. IT'S IMPORTANT THAT I--
WHATEVER IT IS, IT CAN WAIT.
NYPD

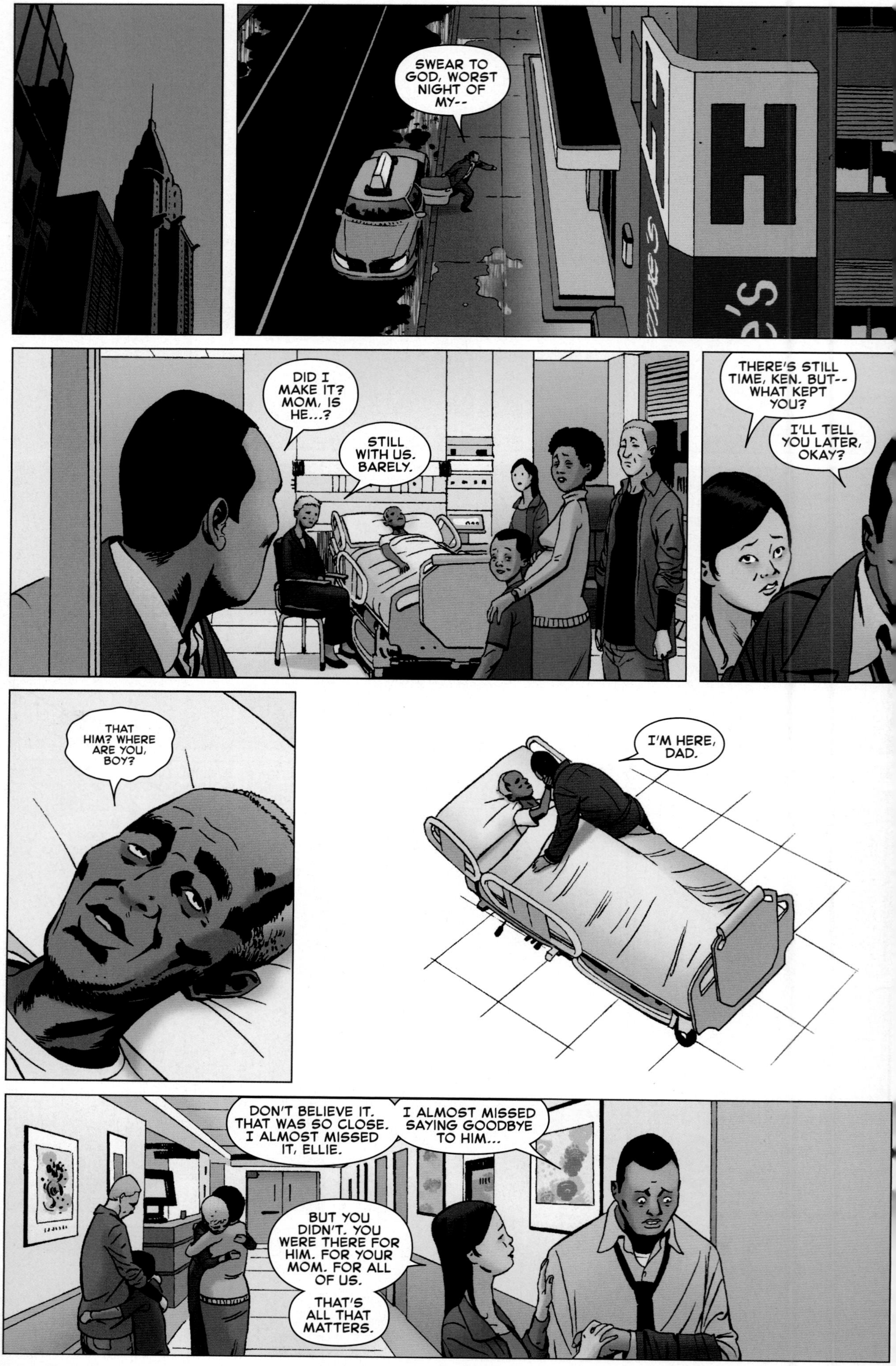
SWEAR TO GOD, WORST NIGHT OF MY--
DID I MAKE IT? MOM, IS HE...?
STILL WITH US. BARELY.
THERE'S STILL TIME, KEN. BUT-- WHAT KEPT YOU?
I'LL TELL YOU LATER, OKAY?
THAT HIM? WHERE ARE YOU, BOY?
I'M HERE, DAD.
DON'T BELIEVE IT. THAT WAS SO CLOSE. I ALMOST MISSED IT, ELLIE.
I ALMOST MISSED SAYING GOODBYE TO HIM...
BUT YOU DIDN'T. YOU WERE THERE FOR HIM. FOR YOUR MOM. FOR ALL OF US.
THAT'S ALL THAT MATTERS.

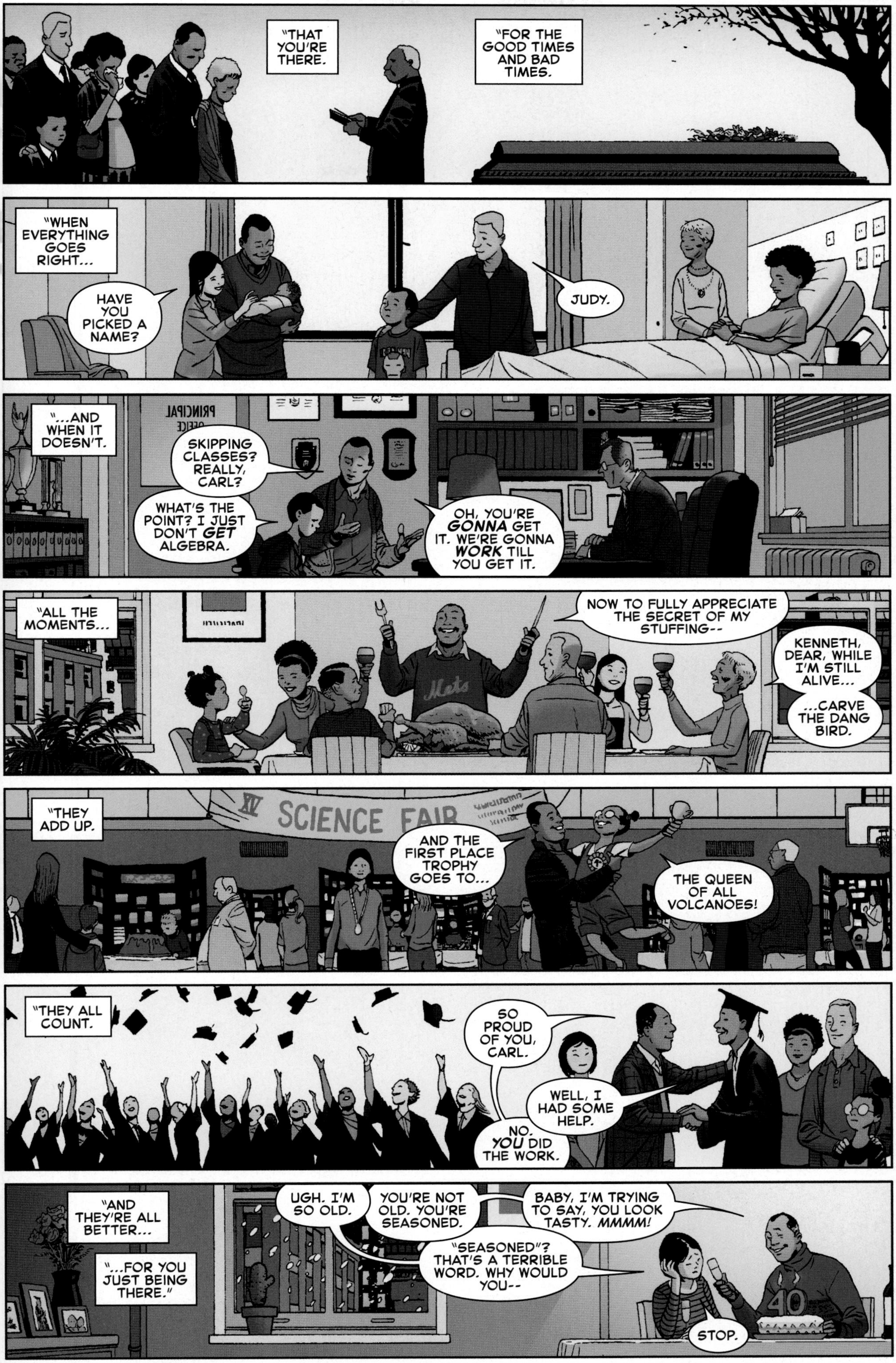
"THAT YOU'RE THERE.
"FOR THE GOOD TIMES AND BAD TIMES.
"WHEN EVERYTHING GOES RIGHT...
HAVE YOU PICKED A NAME?
JUDY.
"...AND WHEN IT DOESN'T.
SKIPPING CLASSES? REALLY, CARL?
WHAT'S THE POINT? I JUST DON'T *GET* ALGEBRA.
OH, YOU'RE *GONNA* GET IT. WE'RE GONNA *WORK* TILL YOU GET IT.
"ALL THE MOMENTS...
NOW TO FULLY APPRECIATE THE SECRET OF MY STUFFING--
KENNETH, DEAR, WHILE I'M STILL ALIVE...
...CARVE THE DANG BIRD.
Mets
"THEY ADD UP.
XV SCIENCE FAIR
AND THE FIRST PLACE TROPHY GOES TO...
THE QUEEN OF ALL VOLCANOES!
"THEY ALL COUNT.
SO PROUD OF YOU, CARL.
WELL, I HAD SOME HELP.
NO. *YOU* DID THE WORK.
"AND THEY'RE ALL BETTER...
"...FOR YOU JUST BEING THERE."
UGH. I'M SO OLD.
YOU'RE NOT OLD. YOU'RE SEASONED.
BABY, I'M TRYING TO SAY, YOU LOOK TASTY. *MMMM!*
"SEASONED"? THAT'S A TERRIBLE WORD. WHY WOULD YOU--
STOP.
40

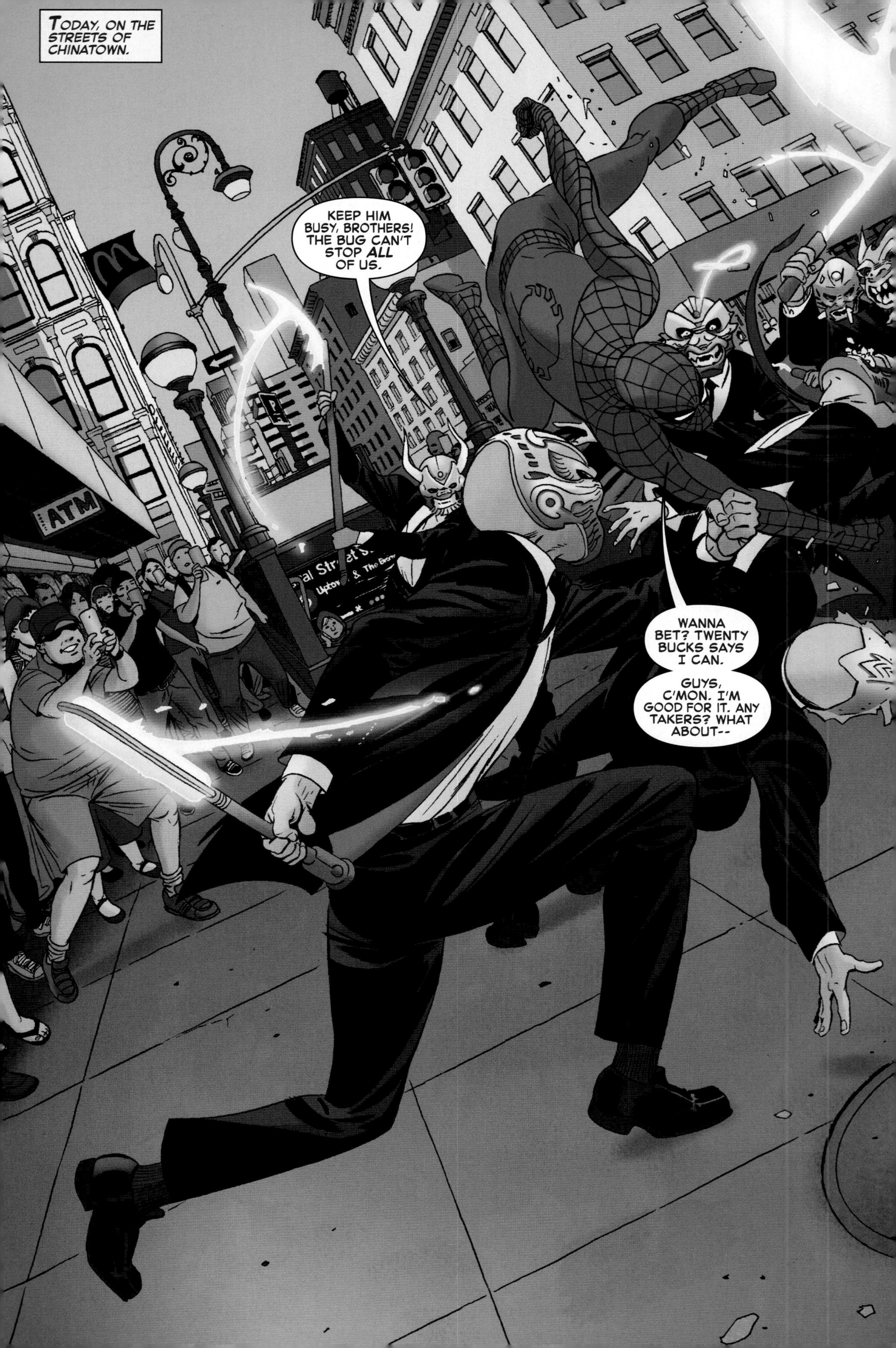
TODAY, ON THE STREETS OF CHINATOWN.
KEEP HIM BUSY, BROTHERS! THE BUG CAN'T STOP ALL OF US.
WANNA BET? TWENTY BUCKS SAYS I CAN.
GUYS, C'MON. I'M GOOD FOR IT. ANY TAKERS? WHAT ABOUT--
ATM

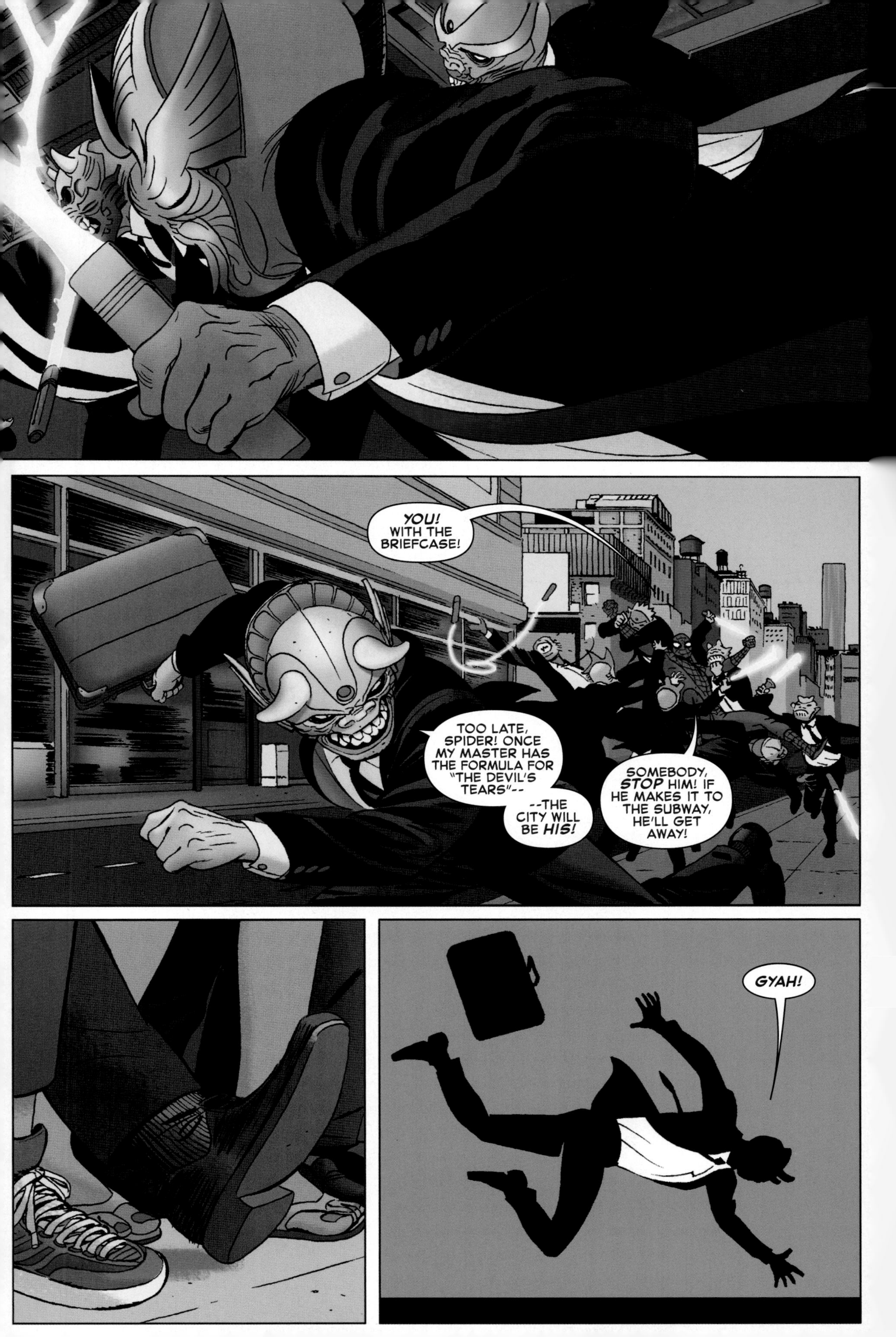
YOU! WITH THE BRIEFCASE!
TOO LATE, SPIDER! ONCE MY MASTER HAS THE FORMULA FOR "THE DEVIL'S TEARS"--
--THE CITY WILL BE HIS!
SOMEBODY, STOP HIM! IF HE MAKES IT TO THE SUBWAY, HE'LL GET AWAY!
GYAH!

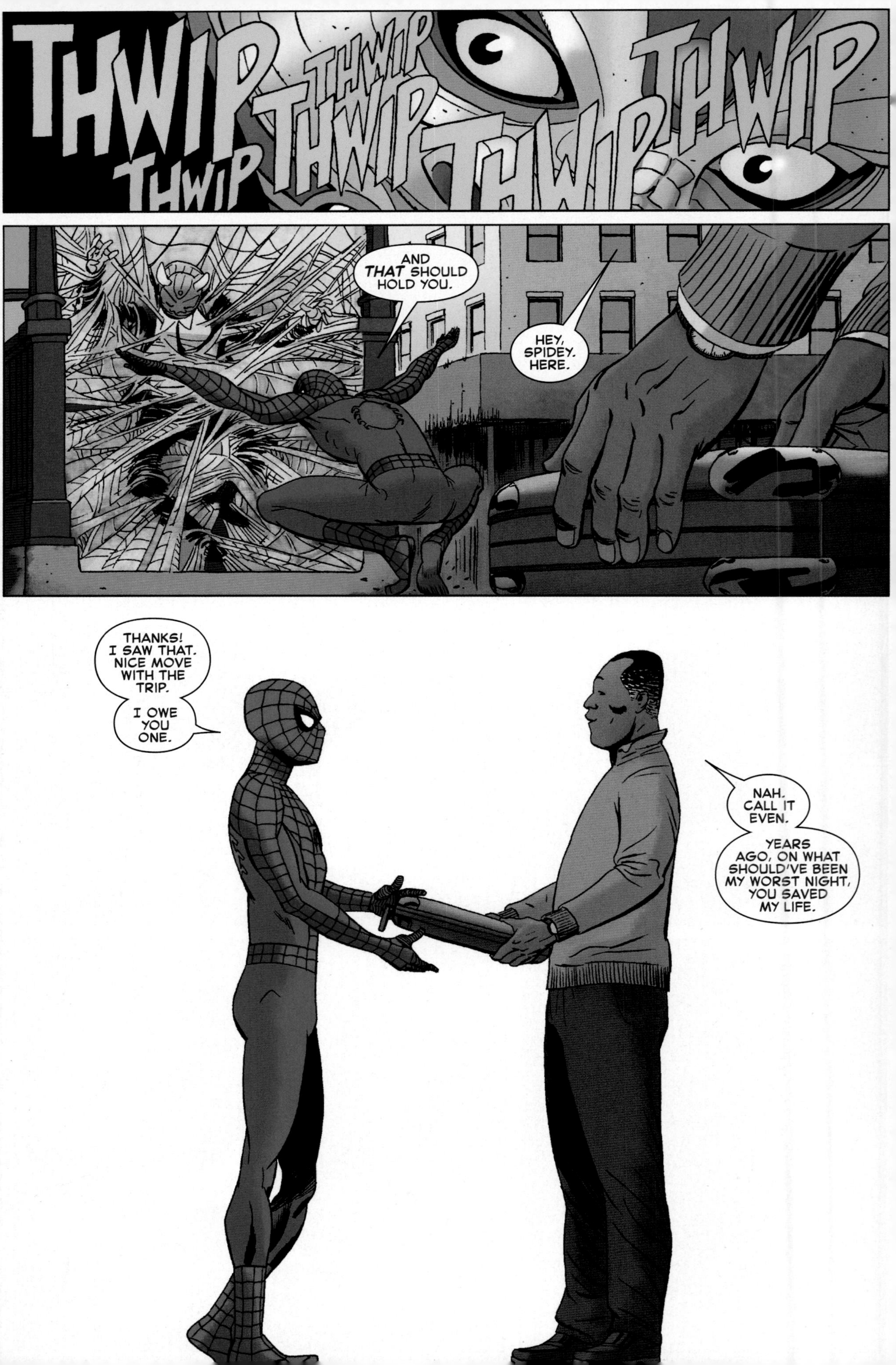
THWIP THWIP THWIP THWIP THWIP THWIP THWIP
AND THAT SHOULD HOLD YOU.
HEY, SPIDEY. HERE.
THANKS! I SAW THAT. NICE MOVE WITH THE TRIP.
I OWE YOU ONE.
NAH. CALL IT EVEN.
YEARS AGO, ON WHAT SHOULD'VE BEEN MY WORST NIGHT, YOU SAVED MY LIFE.

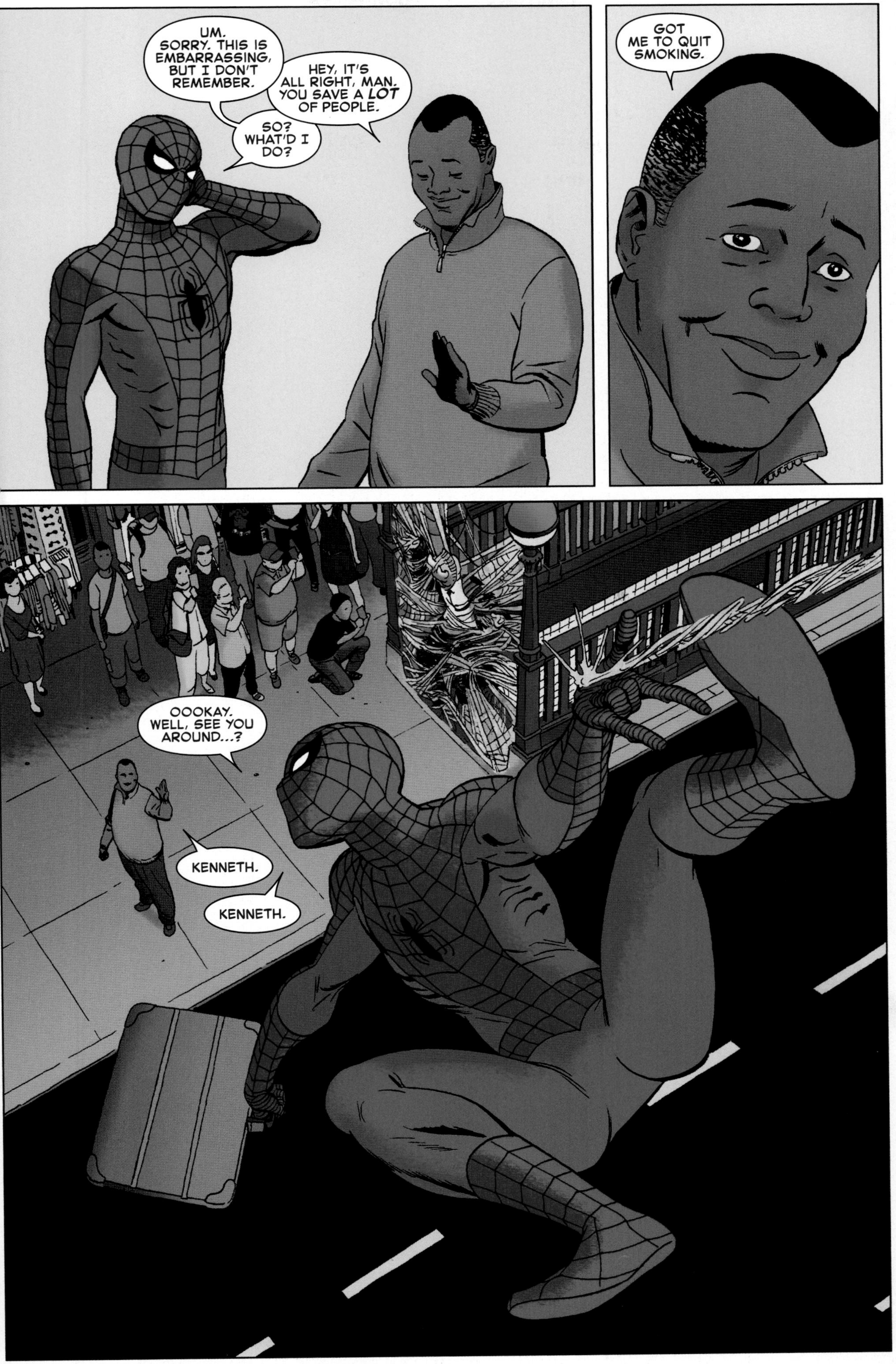
UM. SORRY. THIS IS EMBARRASSING, BUT I DON'T REMEMBER.
HEY, IT'S ALL RIGHT, MAN. YOU SAVE A *LOT* OF PEOPLE.
SO? WHAT'D I DO?
GOT ME TO QUIT SMOKING.
OOOKAY. WELL, SEE YOU AROUND...?
KENNETH.
KENNETH.

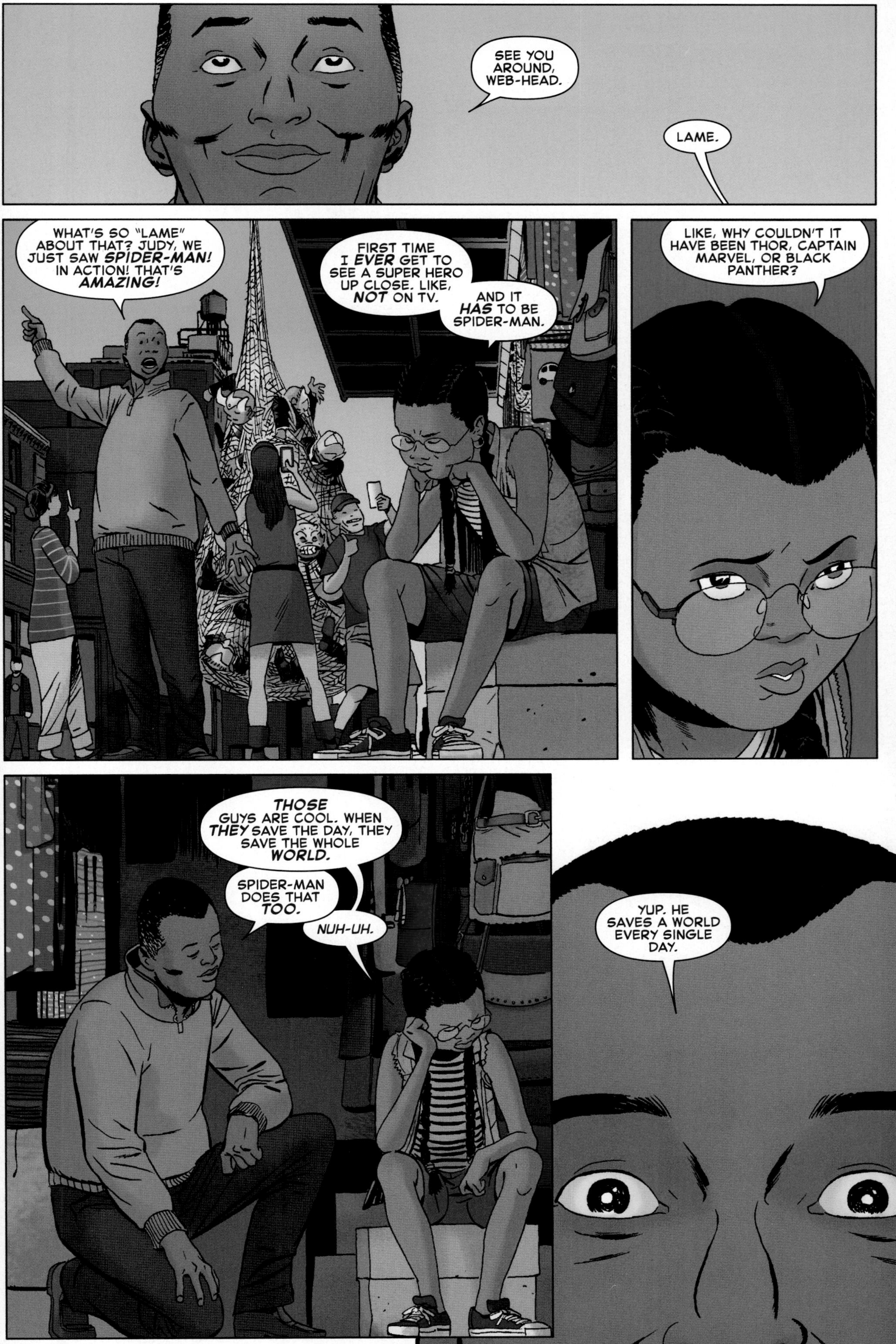
SEE YOU AROUND, WEB-HEAD.
LAME.
WHAT'S SO "LAME" ABOUT THAT? JUDY, WE JUST SAW SPIDER-MAN! IN ACTION! THAT'S AMAZING!
FIRST TIME I EVER GET TO SEE A SUPER HERO UP CLOSE. LIKE, NOT ON TV.
AND IT HAS TO BE SPIDER-MAN.
LIKE, WHY COULDN'T IT HAVE BEEN THOR, CAPTAIN MARVEL, OR BLACK PANTHER?
THOSE GUYS ARE COOL. WHEN THEY SAVE THE DAY, THEY SAVE THE WHOLE WORLD.
SPIDER-MAN DOES THAT TOO.
NUH-UH.
YUP. HE SAVES A WORLD EVERY SINGLE DAY.

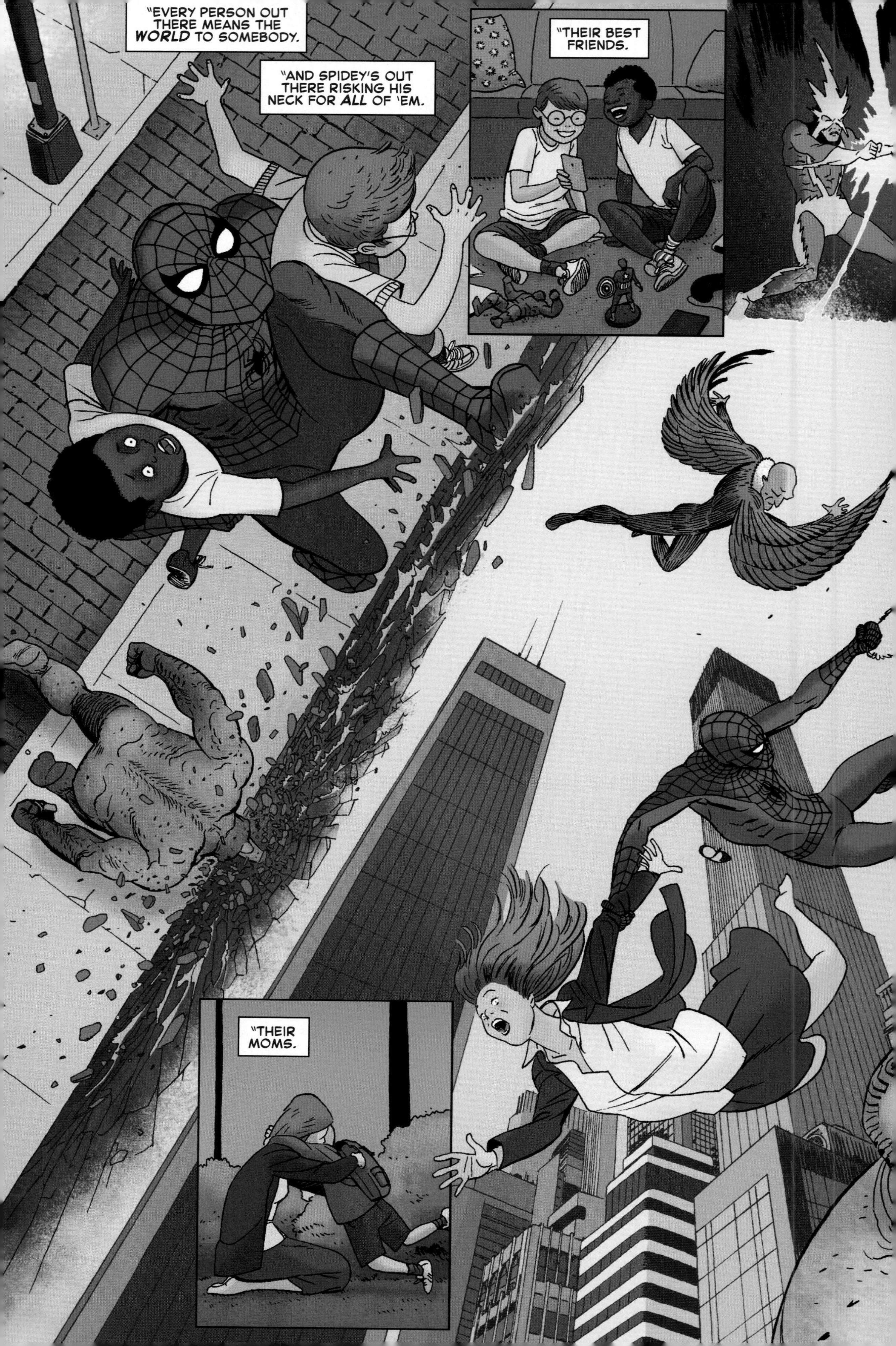
"EVERY PERSON OUT THERE MEANS THE *WORLD* TO SOMEBODY.
"THEIR BEST FRIENDS.
"AND SPIDEY'S OUT THERE RISKING HIS NECK FOR *ALL* OF 'EM.
"THEIR MOMS.

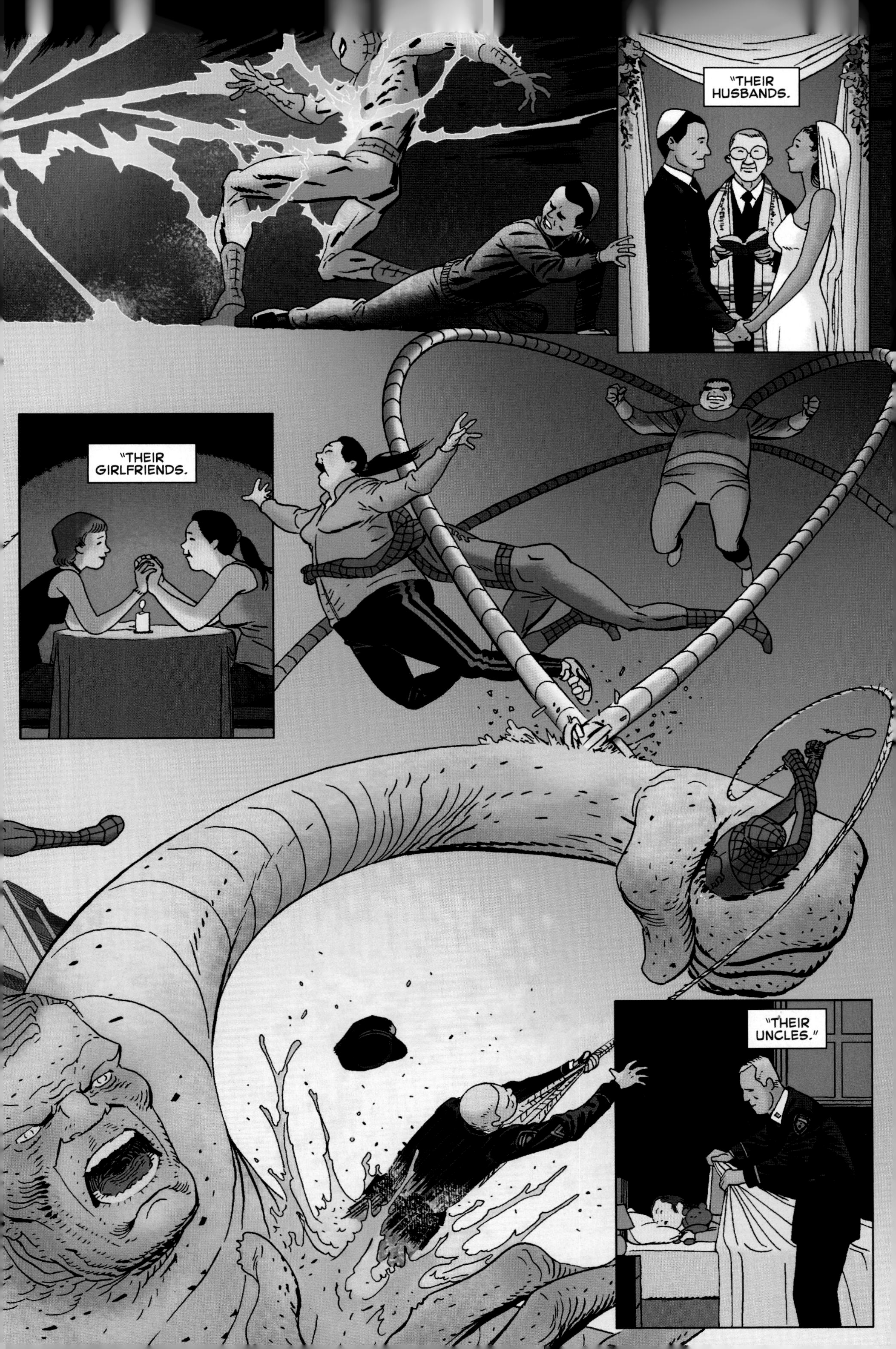
"THEIR HUSBANDS.
"THEIR GIRLFRIENDS.
"THEIR UNCLES."

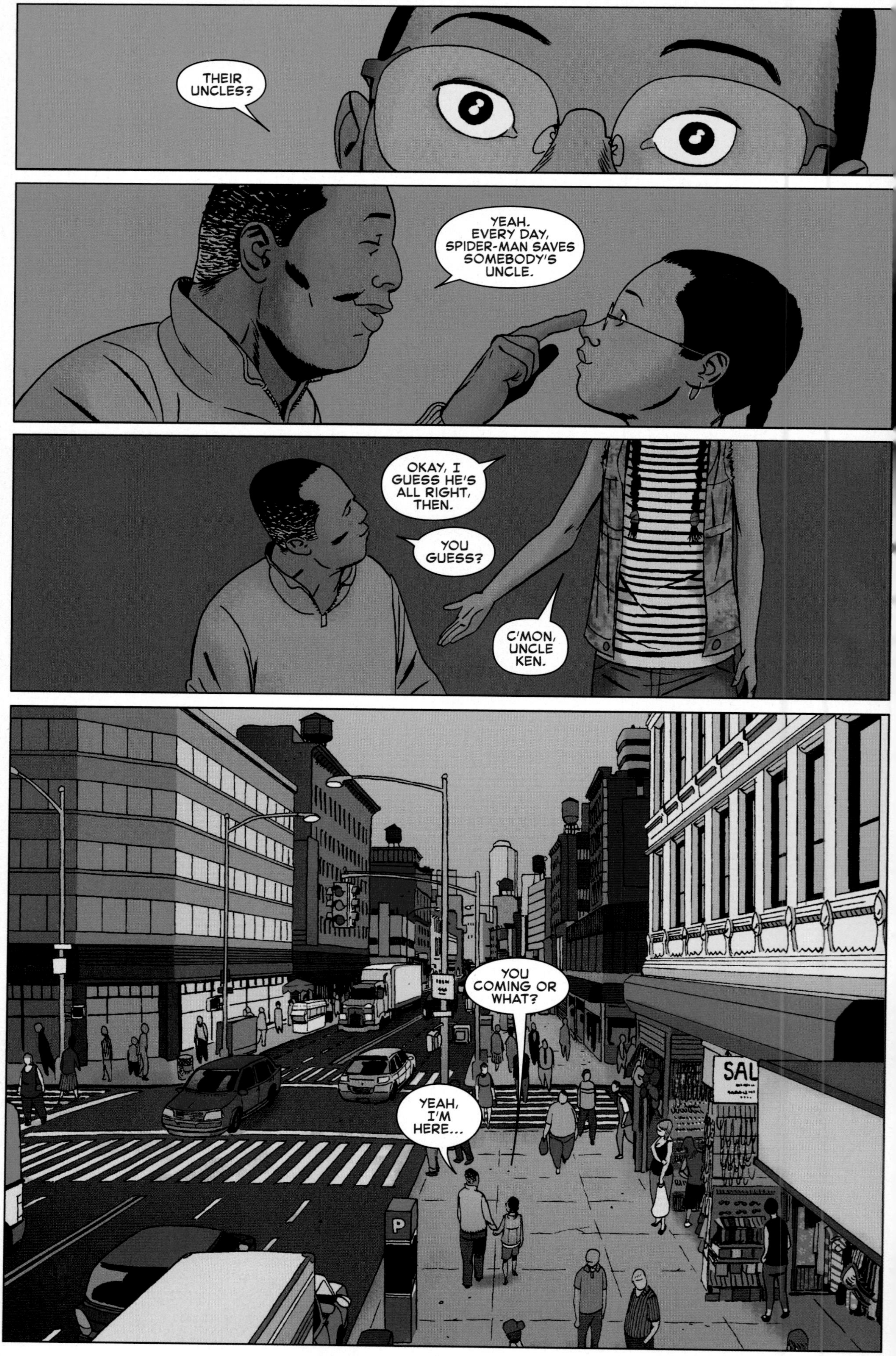
THEIR UNCLES?
YEAH. EVERY DAY, SPIDER-MAN SAVES SOMEBODY'S UNCLE.
OKAY, I GUESS HE'S ALL RIGHT, THEN.
YOU GUESS?
C'MON, UNCLE KEN.
YOU COMING OR WHAT?
YEAH, I'M HERE...

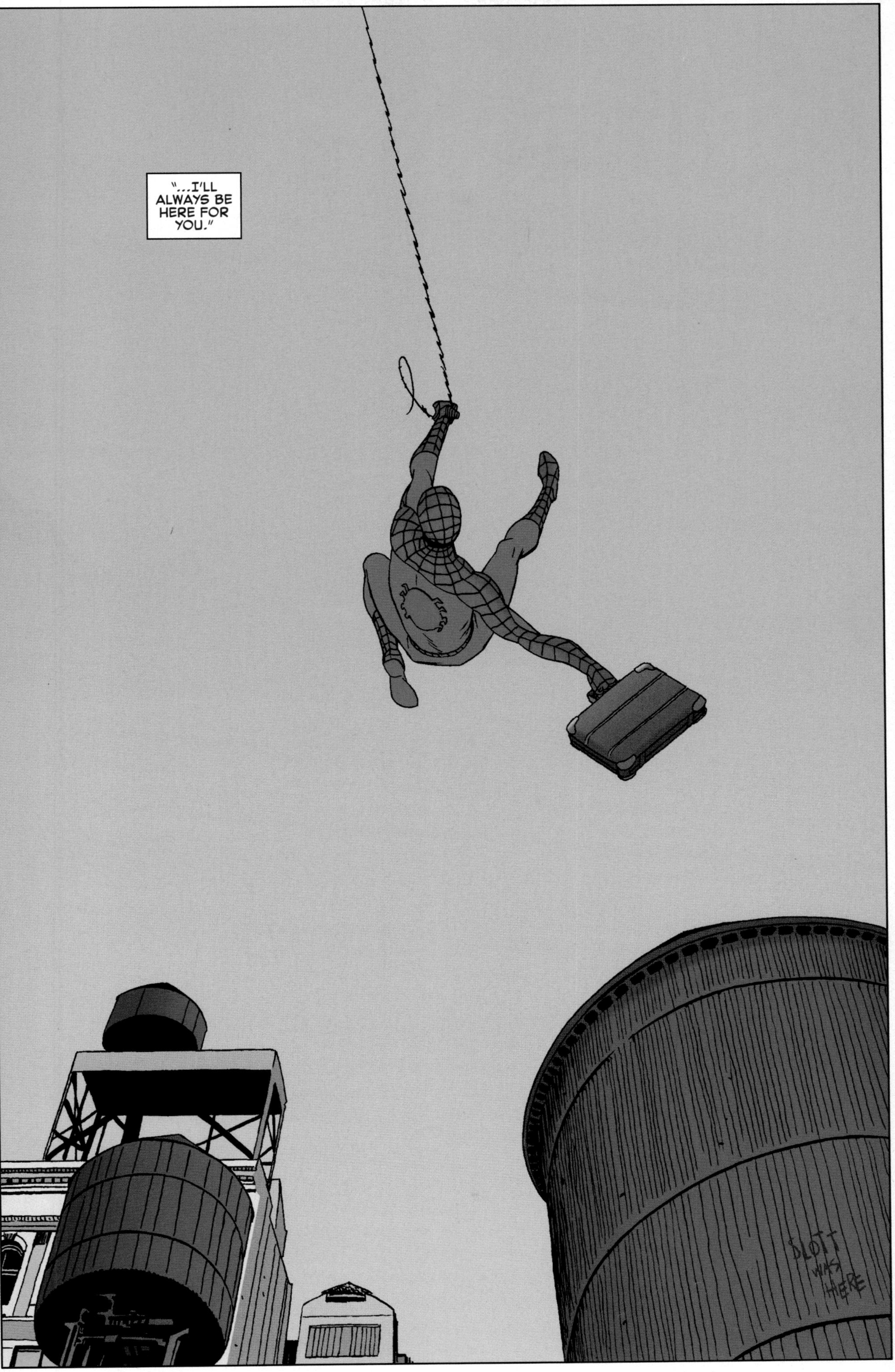
"...I'LL ALWAYS BE HERE FOR YOU."
SLOTT WAS HERE

the AMAZING SPIDER-MAIL

KATHLEEN WISNESKI
ASSISTANT EDITOR

NICK LOWE
with
DEVIN LEWIS
EDITORS

Send e-mail to **SPIDEYOFFICE@MARVEL.COM** (please mark "OKAY TO PRINT")

How about that? Hope you had a hanky with you. I read this lettering earlier this week on the subway heading to work and cried, so I'm with you. Let's talk about Marcos Martin and Muntsa Vicente. If you don't know who they are, go immediately to www.PanelSyndicate.com and check out Private Eye and Barrier or run back to your comic shop to get their work together years ago on AMAZING SPIDER-MAN or DOCTOR STRANGE: THE OATH. You back? HOW AWESOME ARE MUNTSA AND MARCOS?!?!?! They haven't done print comics in several years, so you know it had to be a special occasion to get them back here. And what an occasion this is...

In case this is your first issue of AMAZING SPIDER-MAN, or first in a very, very long time, you should know that this is Dan Slott's last issue as writer. Dan came onto the book about ten years ago and has written more issues of AMAZING SPIDER-MAN than any writer ever. With those issues he, along with some of the best artists in the world, created some of the best Spider-Man stories EVER, to which we can add THIS issue. But before you close the book, Dan wanted to say a few words...

Since I was eight years old, writing SPIDER-MAN has been my dream job. Why would I ever let it go?

When I meet people at signings, there are some readers who say they've started with my run. Maybe with "New Ways to Die," "Big Time," "Spider-Verse" or you name it. But since people heard I was leaving, there've been fans telling me, "Your run is the only Spider-Man I've known my whole life." I have a hard time processing that.

That's when it hits me. It really has been ten years. At a signing for #797, one young reader asked me not to go, because it was like a security blanket to him, knowing my next ASM would always be on the rack waiting for him. Hey, wherever you are, I hope you're reading this. Trust me. Spidey's gonna be in the best of webbed-hands. I've heard Nick Spencer's plans and they're brilliant, funny, surprising and, in every way, amazing.

Meanwhile, me and all the other ASM writers, we're still here for you. All crammed together in your long boxes. We're here whenever you wanna visit, and we'd just love it if you would. We'll always be here for you. And I want to thank you for being there for me these ten years. You guys, you let me have my dream job. Thank you.

Now, I've got a ton of people to thank. I promise I'll be quick! I'm eternally grateful to...

Editor Stephen Wacker, for bringing me on board and having my back. Editor Nick Lowe, who kept me on and kept everything fun. Every assistant editor ever, for EVERYTHING. Senior VP Tom Brevoort, for sage-like wisdom and guidance. My three editor in chiefs: Quesada, Alonso and Cebulski, for trusting me with your flagship character, even when I wrote about brain-swaps and giant spiders.

the AMAZING SPIDER-MAIL

Every penciler, inker, colorist and letterer in all 180 issues. Special thanks to the hardworking crew who came back for the quadruple-sized ASM #800, especially longtime collaborators Humberto and Giuseppe. I miss you both so much!

The stellar creative team on the last year of my run--Stuart, Wade and Marte, you're not just the finest artists working in the industry, you're also the most professional and dedicated people I've ever worked with. I am in awe of you.

My good friend Marcos Martin, for promising ages ago you'd come back for my last story, and then pulling it off (as I knew you would) perfectly.

My two real-life super heroes: Christos Gage, who'd parachute in at a moment's notice to co-write issues while everything was on fire. And Joe Caramagna, who'd letter entire books in ludicrous amounts of time while even the fire was on fire. I'd be dead without you two.

But most of all, Stan Lee, Steve Ditko and John Romita Sr., for creating the world of Spider-Man, my favorite place in all of fiction. I've had so much fun living there--and I can't imagine my life without it. Thank you.

Dan

About four years ago, I took the editorial reins of the Spider-Books and had my first of many long phone calls with Dan Slott. We'd only worked together on a short story while I was X-Editor, so I wasn't quite sure how we'd work together. While there have been times that Dan has driven me crazy, it was always in service to the book and to Spider-Man himself. At the expense of his personal life and often his personal health, Dan devoted 100 percent of himself to making this book the best it could possibly be. Dan bled for this book, and for that, all of us at Marvel will be forever grateful. I count myself very lucky to have been along for some of the ride, and lucky to consider myself Dan's friend.

But you're not off the hook. You have to come back in two weeks for AMAZING SPIDER-MAN #1 where Nick Spencer and Ryan Ottley (along with Cliff Rathburn and Laura Martin) kick off the next era for the web-slinger. And if you glance over on the stands a little further down, you should see the first issue of TONY STARK: IRON MAN, written by our dear friend Dan. He'll add FANTASTIC FOUR to his docket soon as well, so don't miss it.

Happy trails, Dan, and keep swinging!
Nick

#797-801 CONNECTING VARIANTS BY **HUMBERTO RAMOS** & **EDGAR DELGADO**

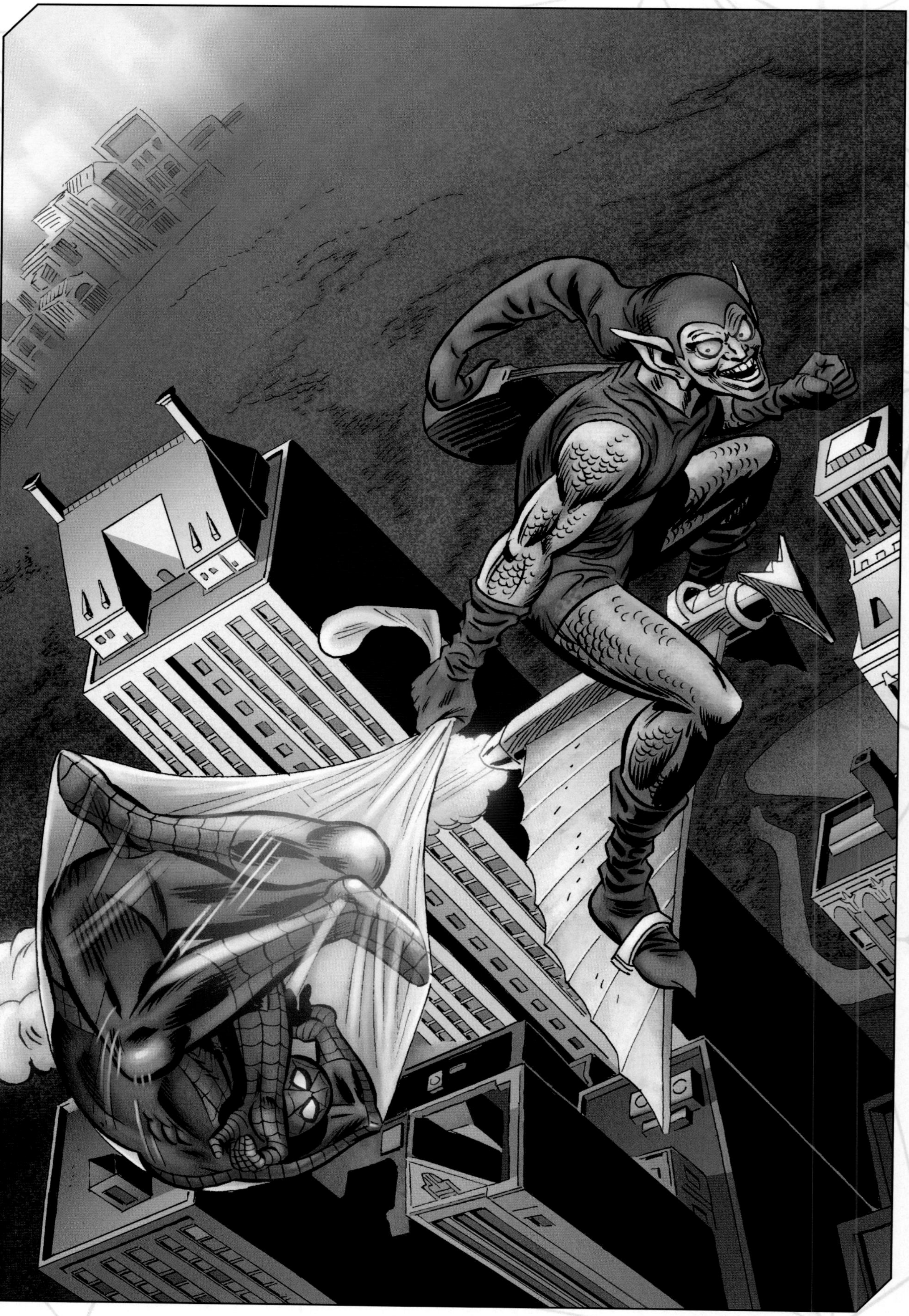

#797 REMASTERED VARIANT BY **ROSS ANDRU, MIKE ESPOSITO & MORRY HOLLOWELL WITH MICHAEL KELLEHER**

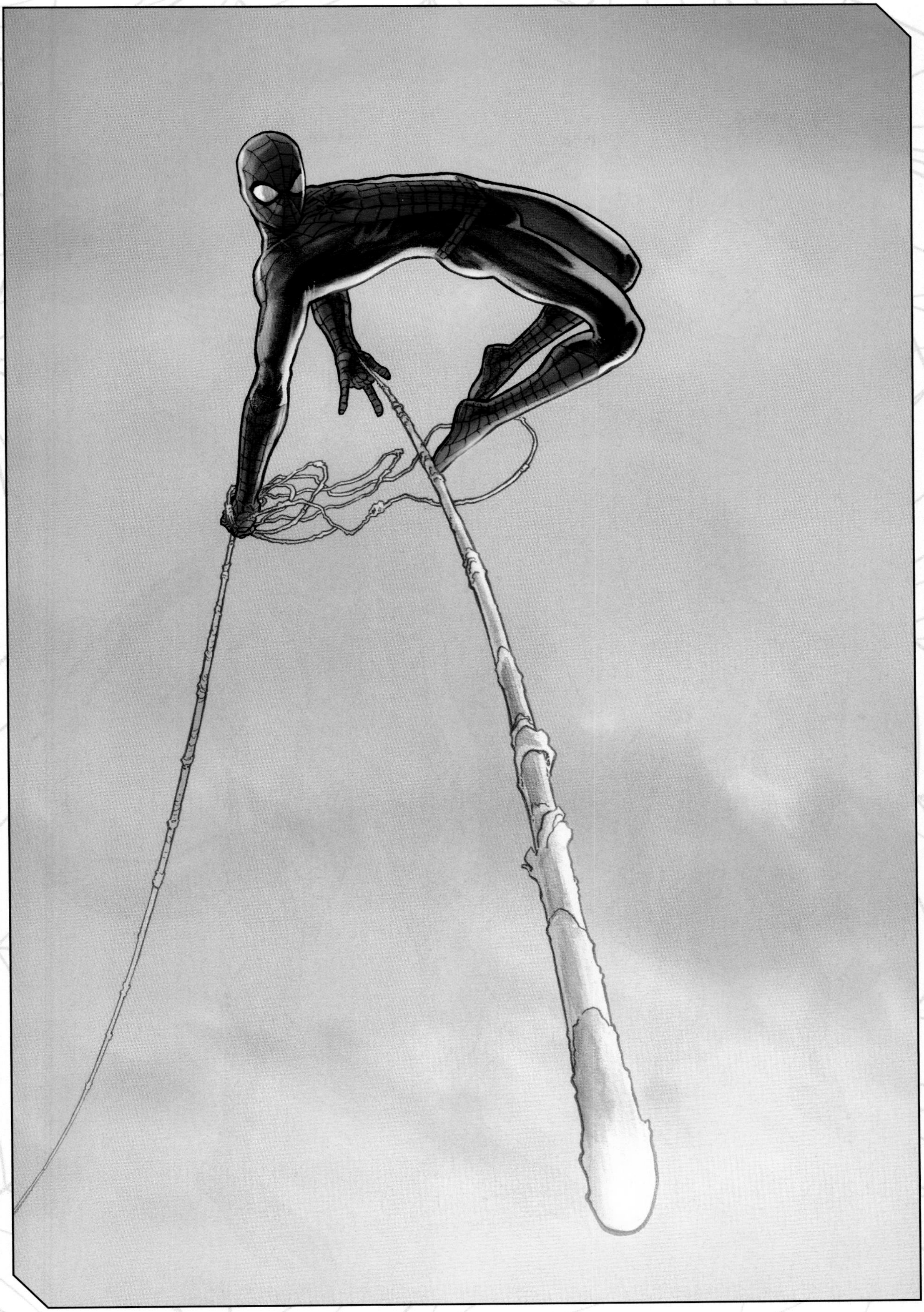

#797 YOUNG GUNS VARIANT BY **AARON KUDER & JASON KEITH**

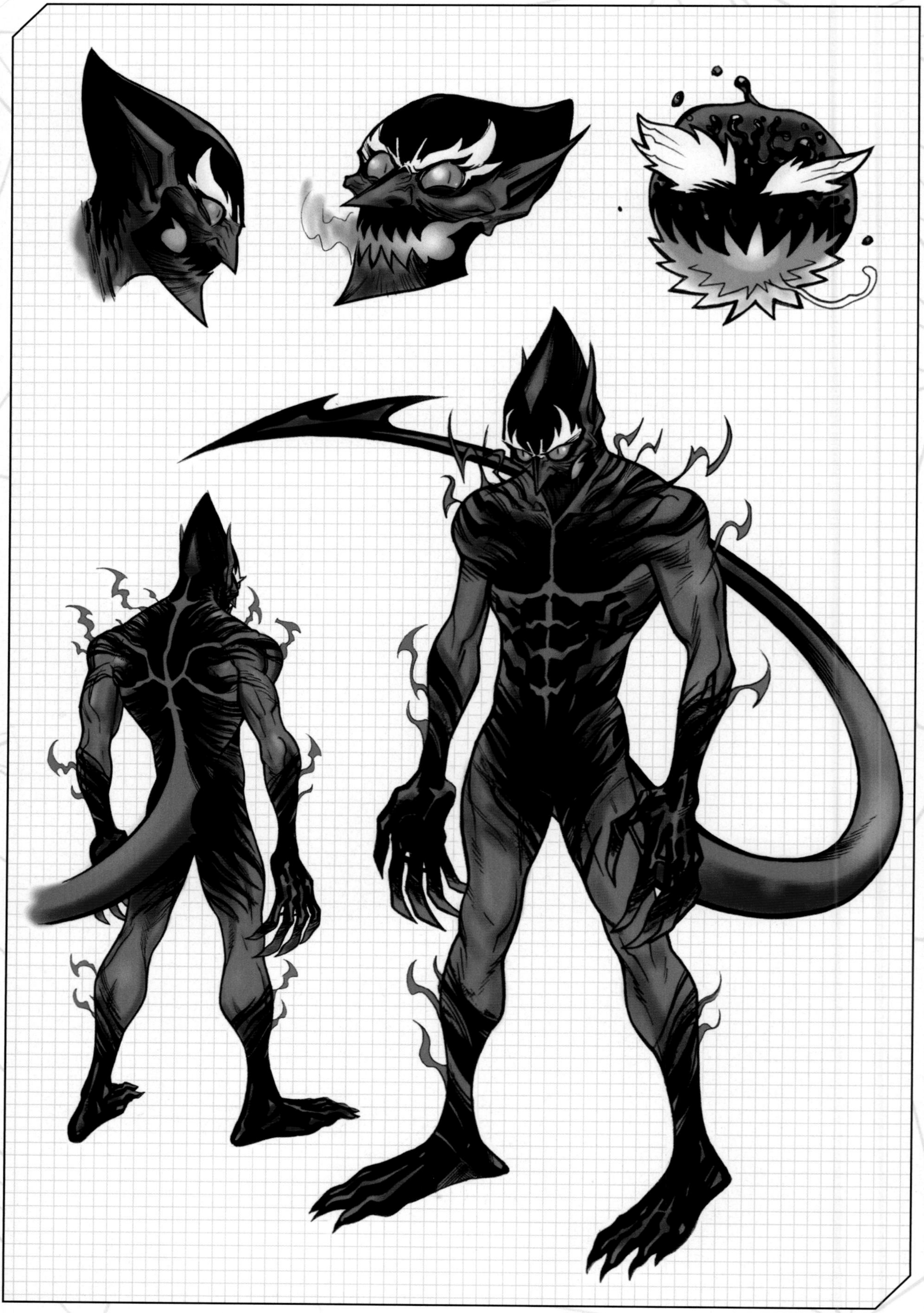

#797 DESIGN VARIANT BY **ED McGUINNESS**

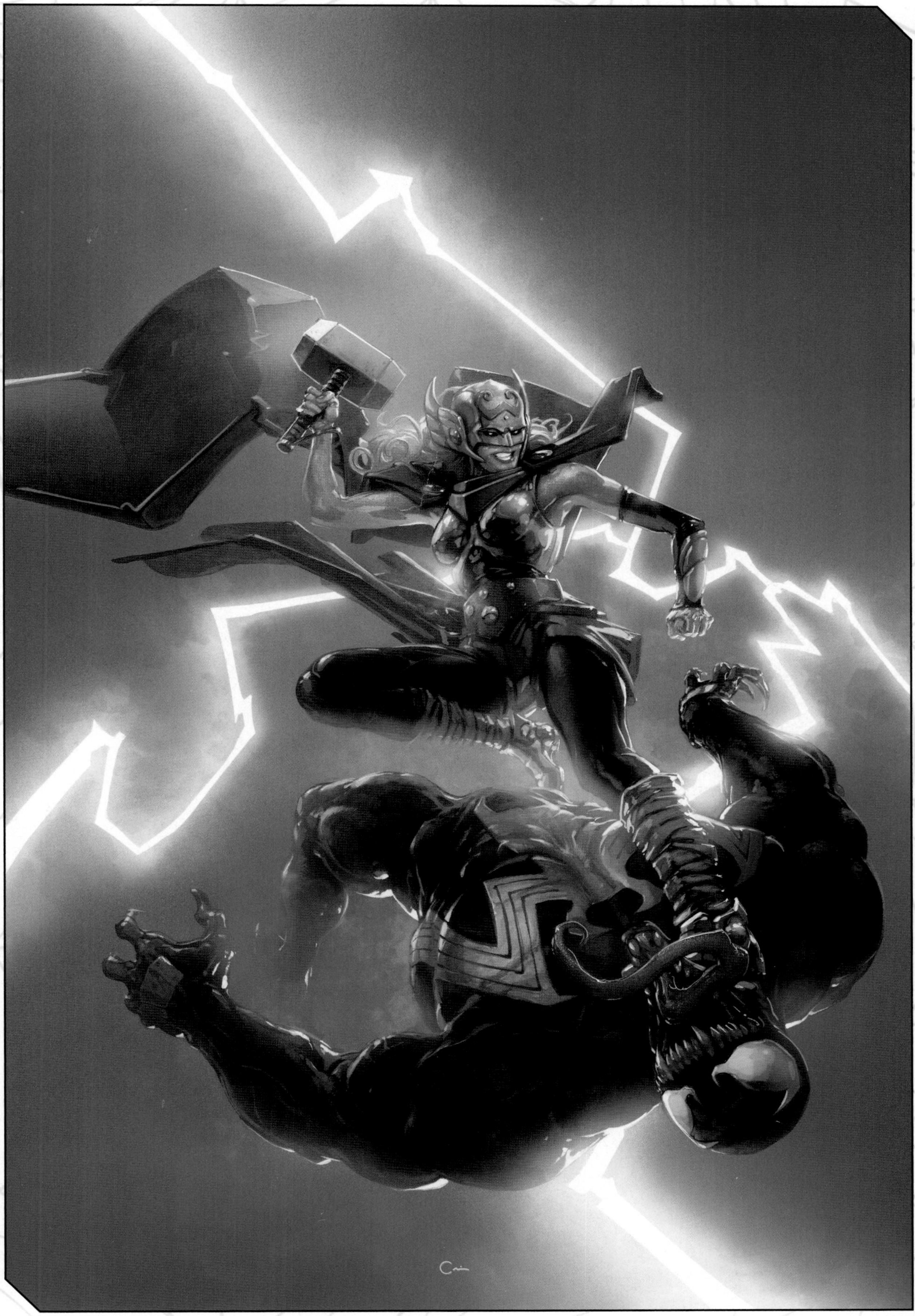

#797 MIGHTY THOR VARIANT BY **CLAYTON CRAIN**

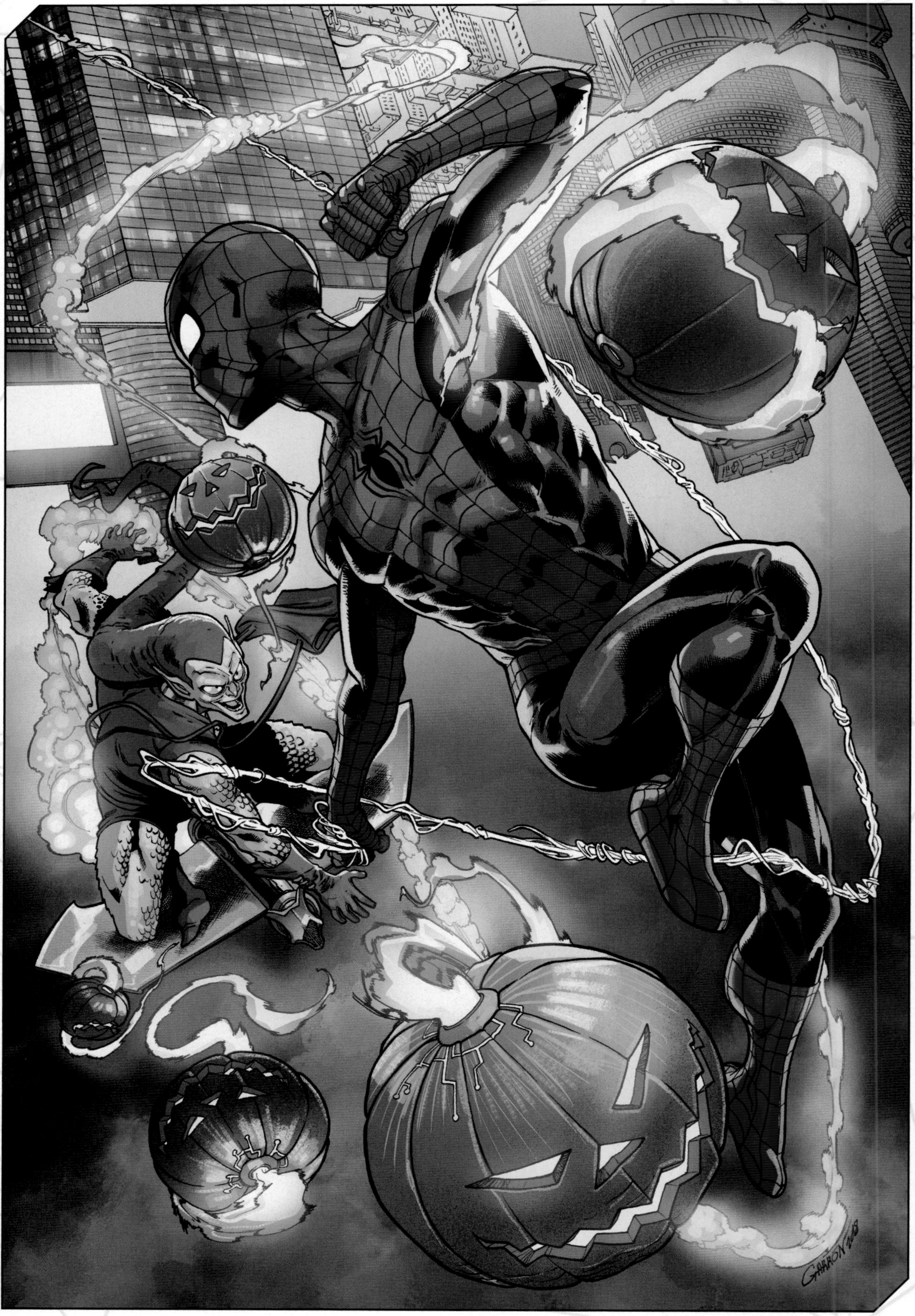

#798 DESIGN VARIANT BY **JAVIER GARRÓN & ROMULO FAJARDO JR.**

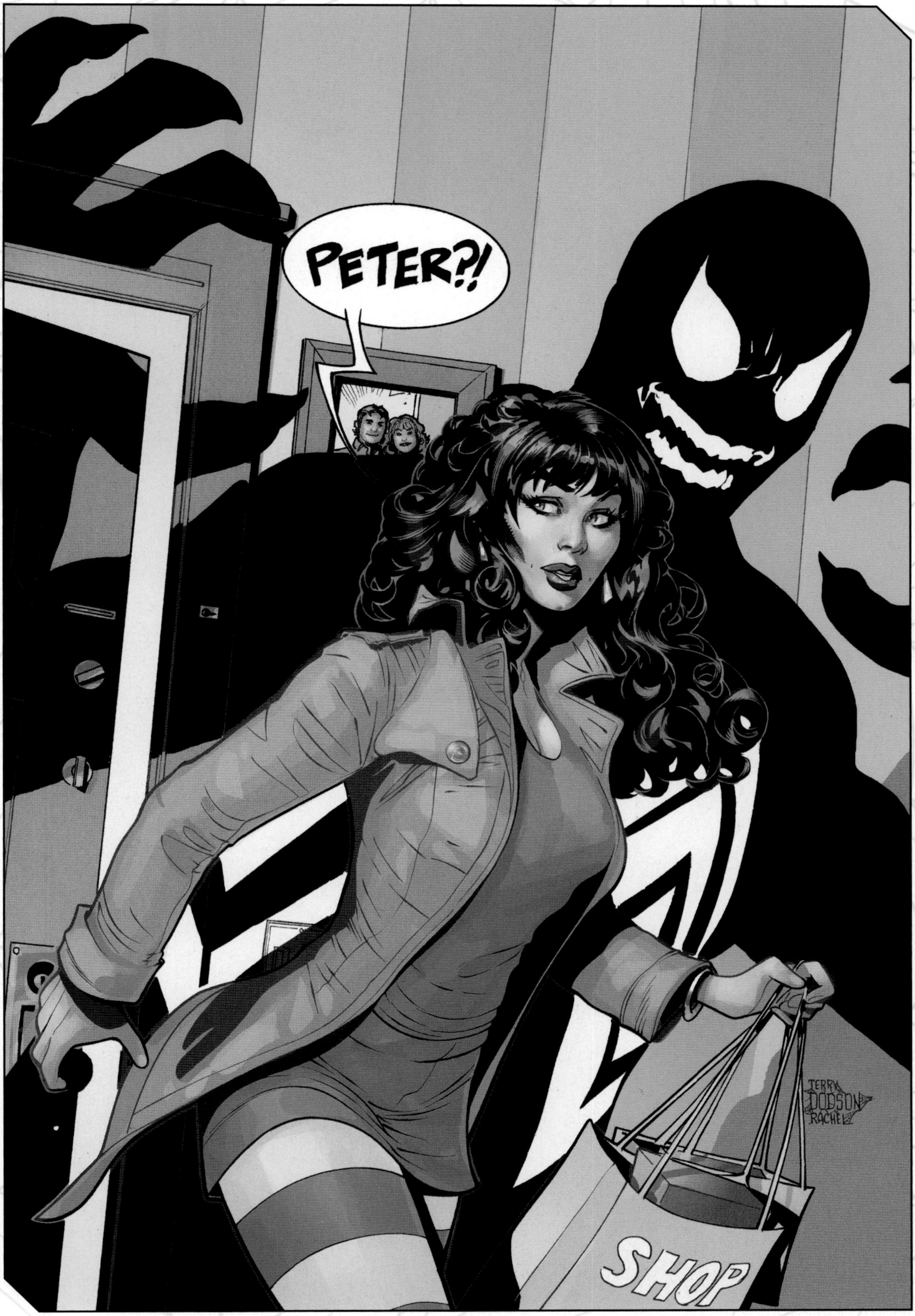
PETER?!
TERRY DODSON RACHEL
SHOP

#797 VENOM 30TH ANNIVERSARY VARIANT BY TERRY DODSON & RACHEL DODSON

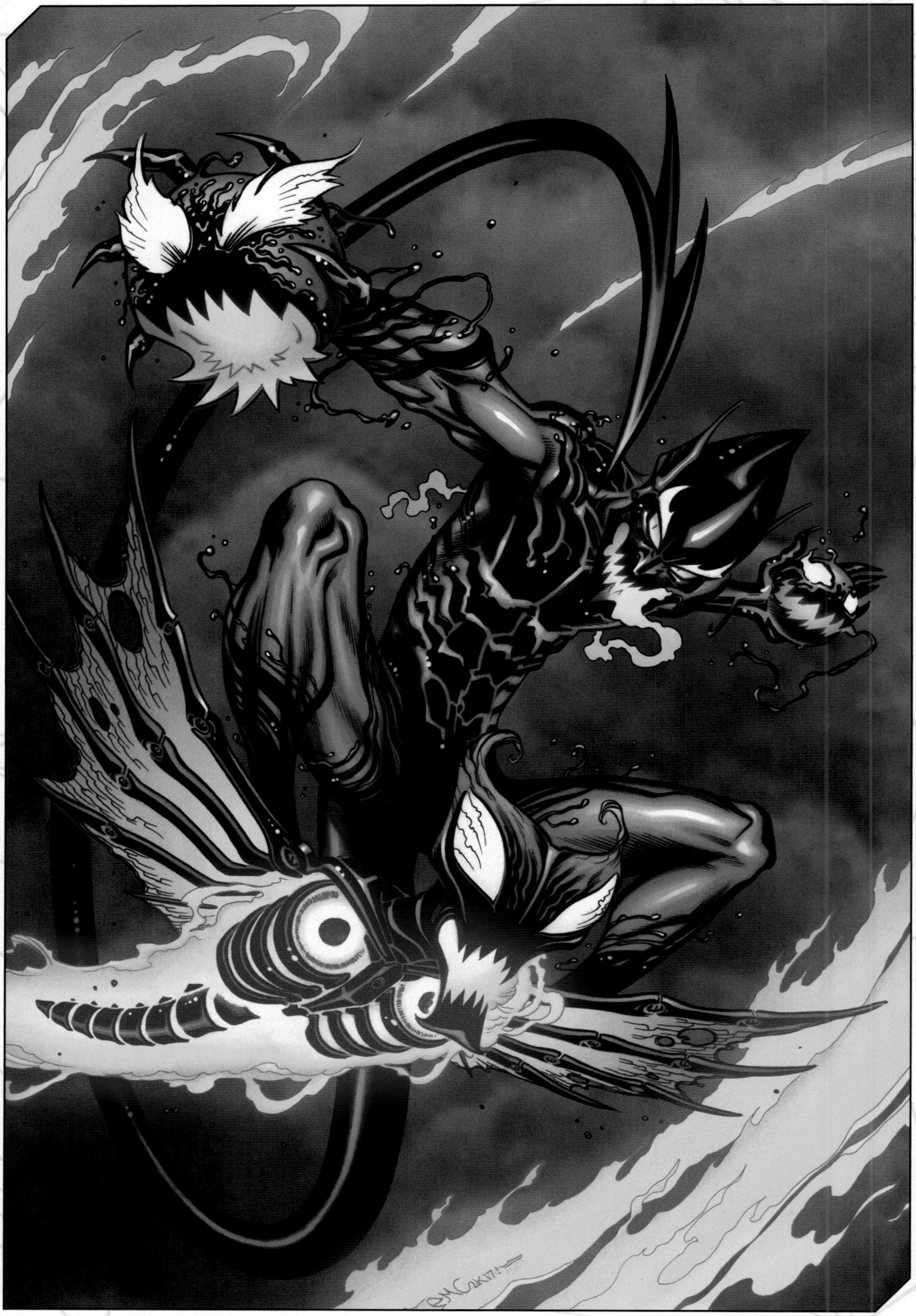

#799 VARIANT BY **ED McGUINNESS & MORRY HOLLOWELL**

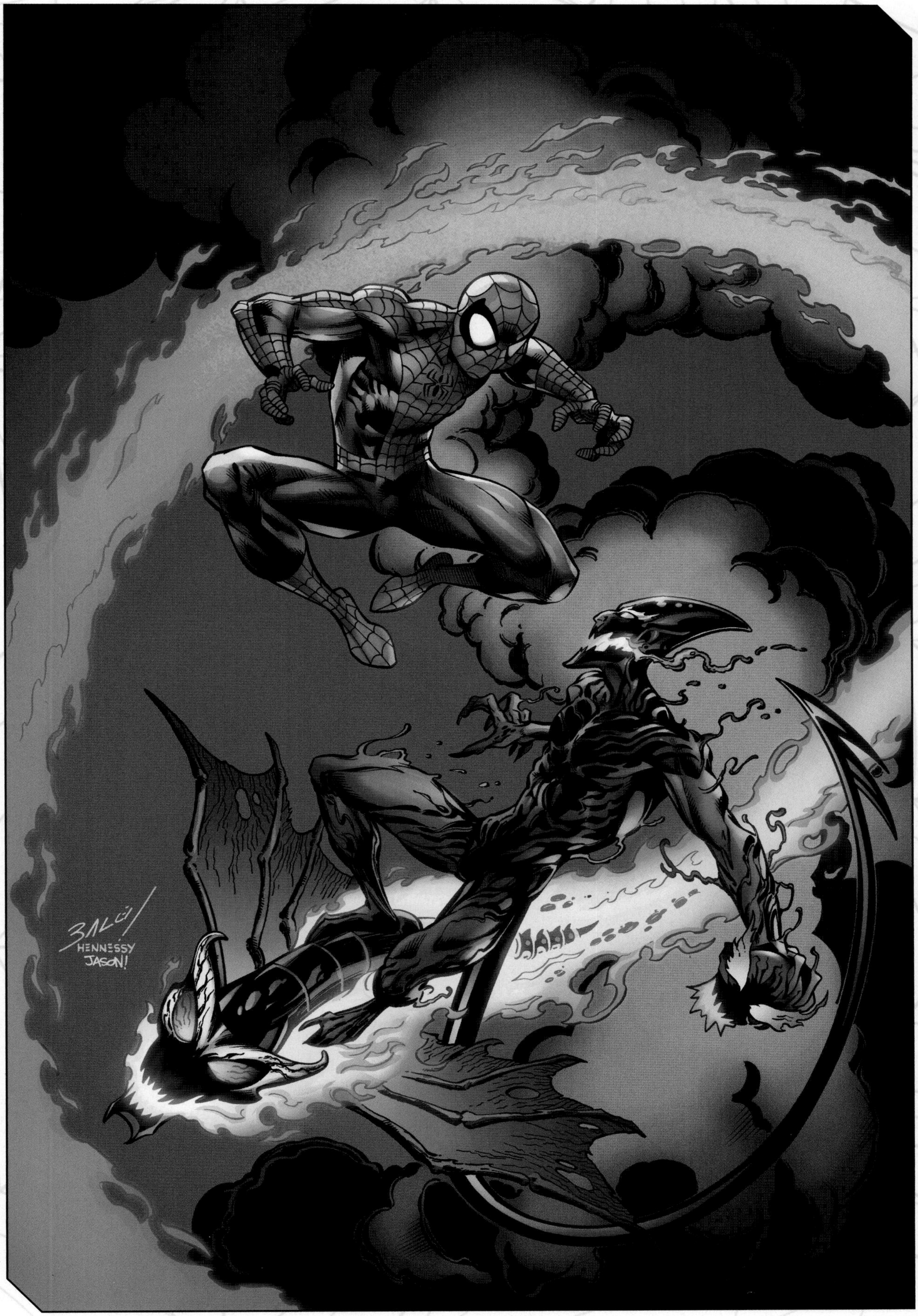
BAGLEY
HENNESSY
JASON!

#800 VARIANT BY MARK BAGLEY, ANDREW HENNESSY & JASON KEITH

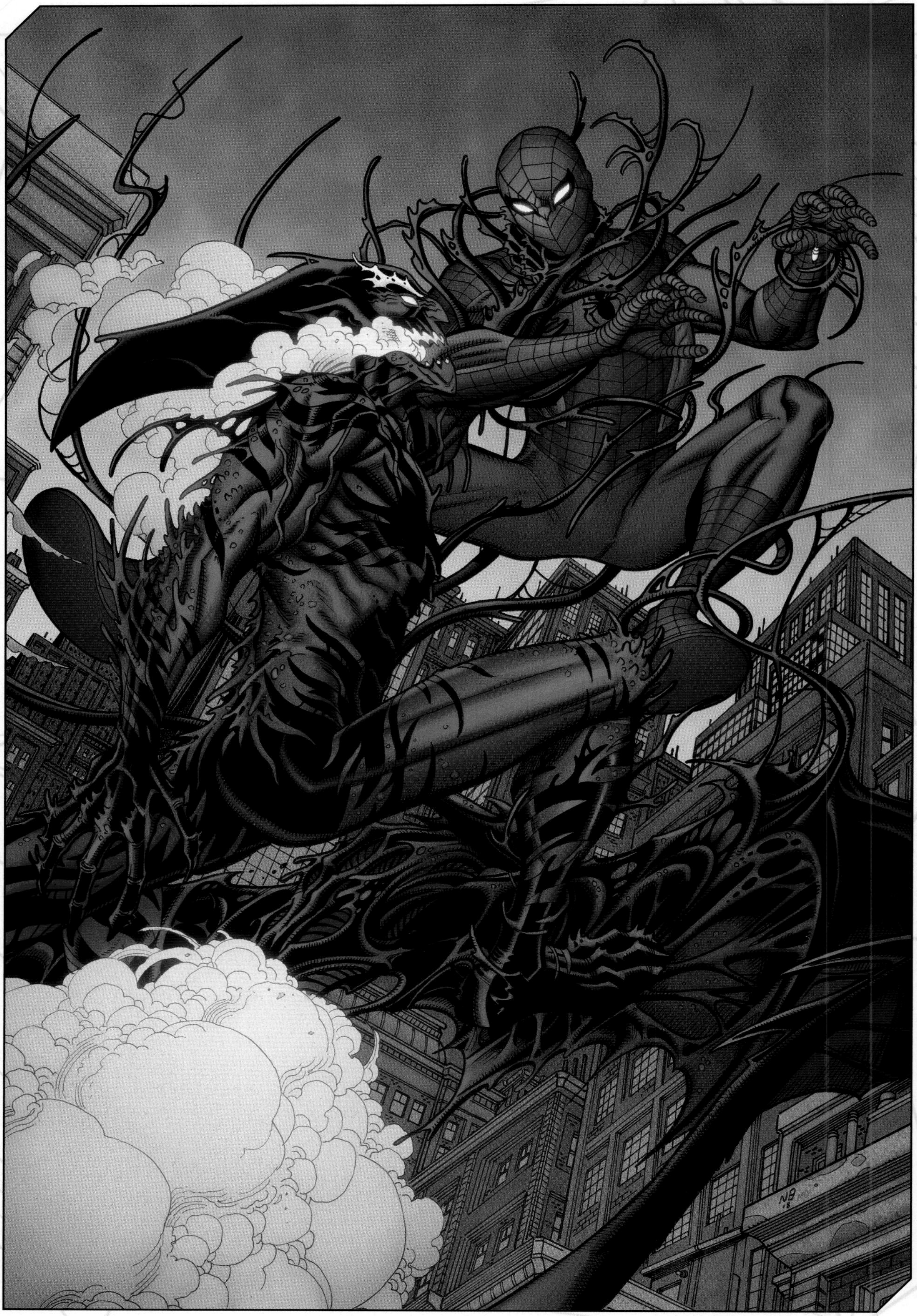

#800 VARIANT BY **NICK BRADSHAW & MORRY HOLLOWELL**

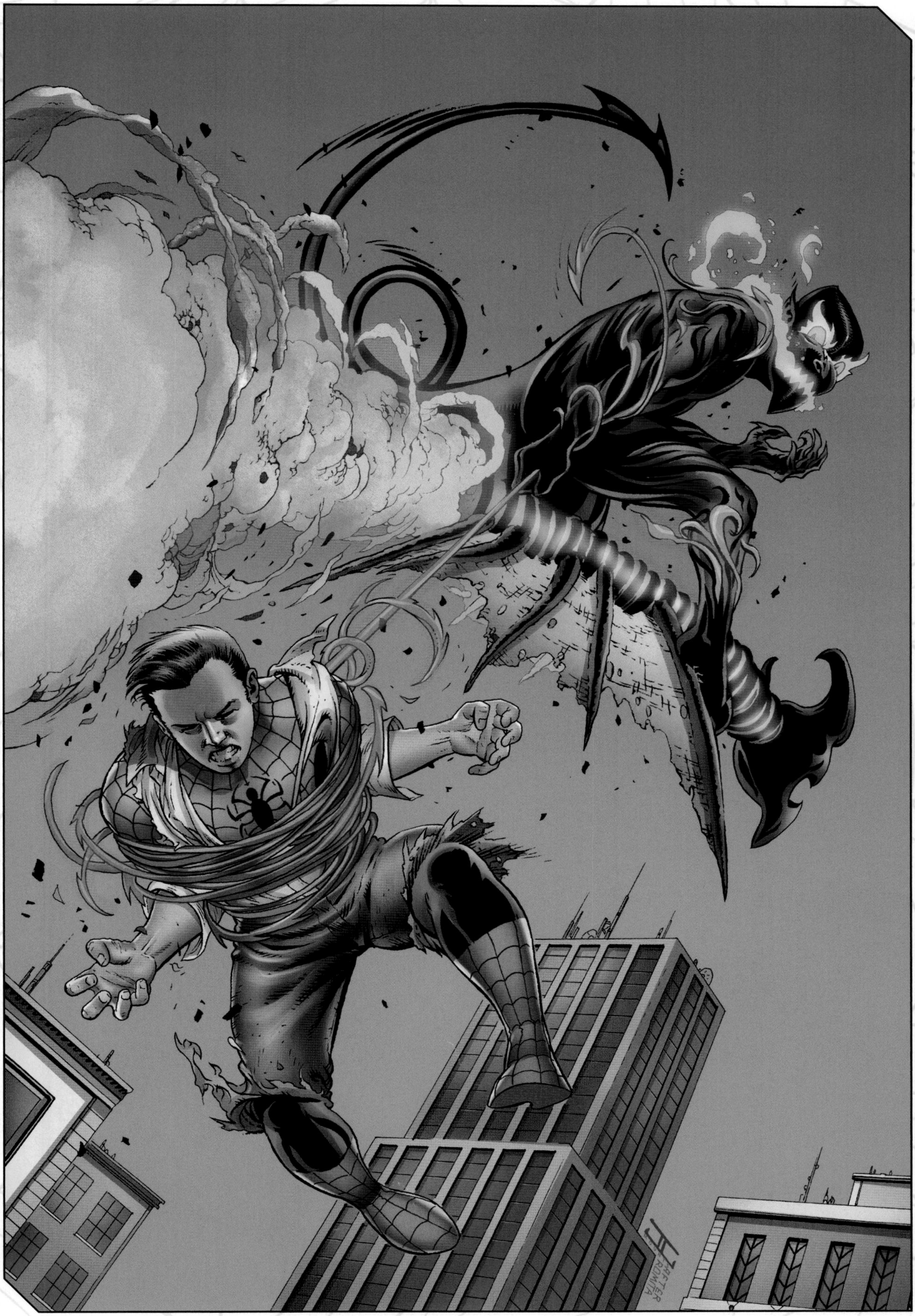

#800 VARIANT BY **JOHN CASSADAY & PAUL MOUNTS**

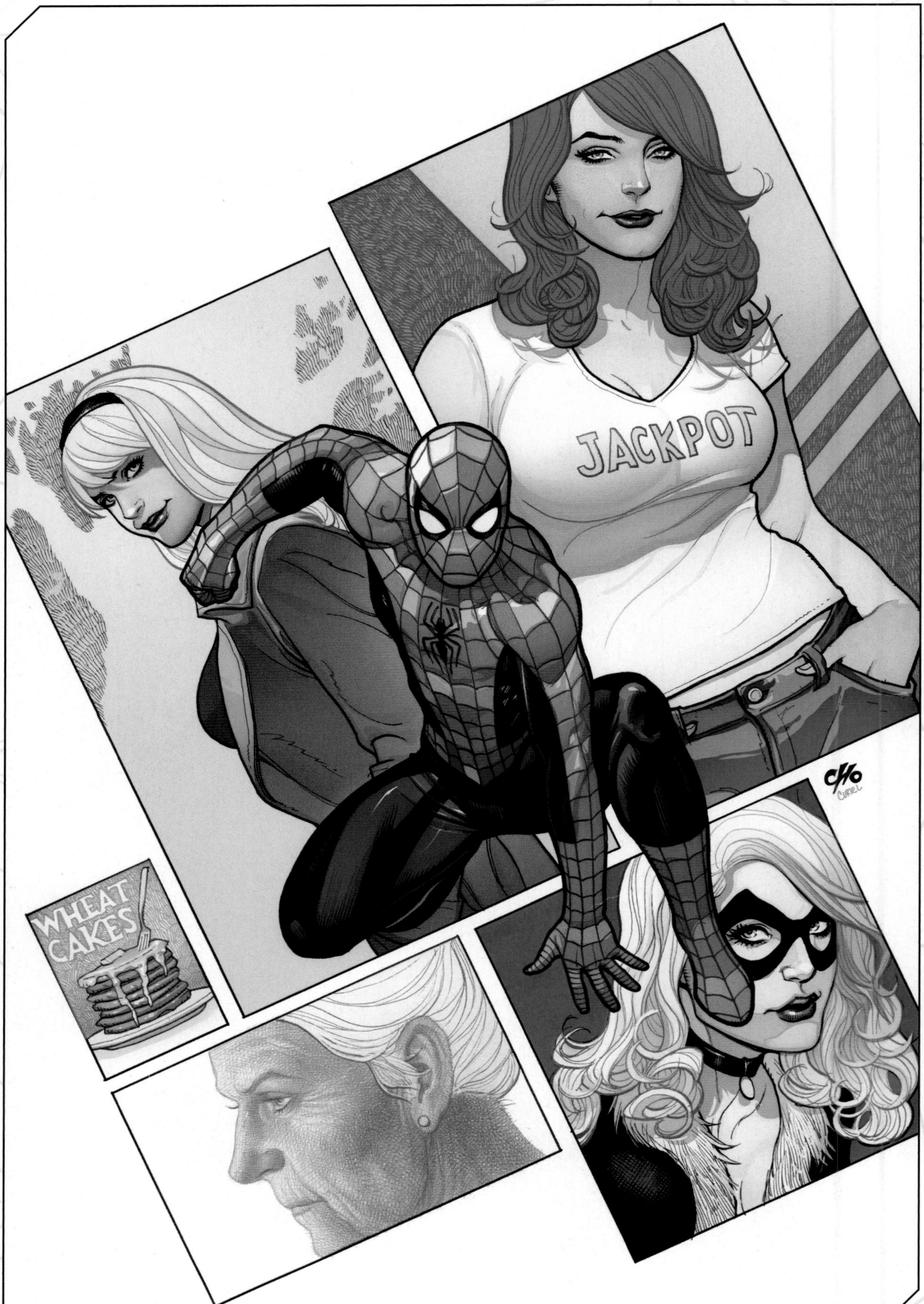
JACKPOT
WHEAT CAKES
CHO
CURIEL

#800 VARIANT BY **FRANK CHO & DAVID CURIEL**

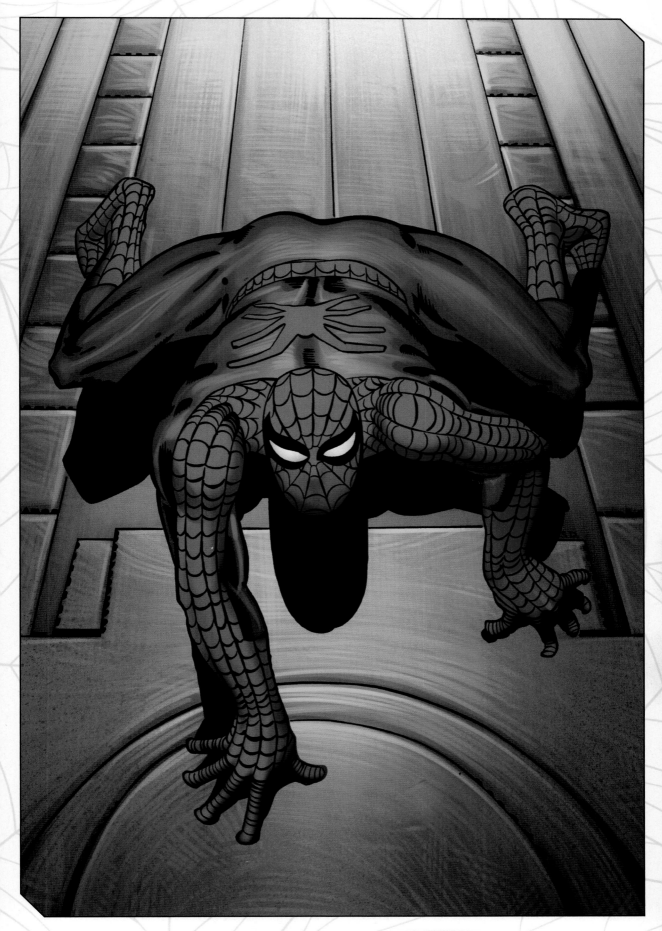

#800 REMASTERED VARIANT BY **STEVE DITKO & RICHARD ISANOVE**

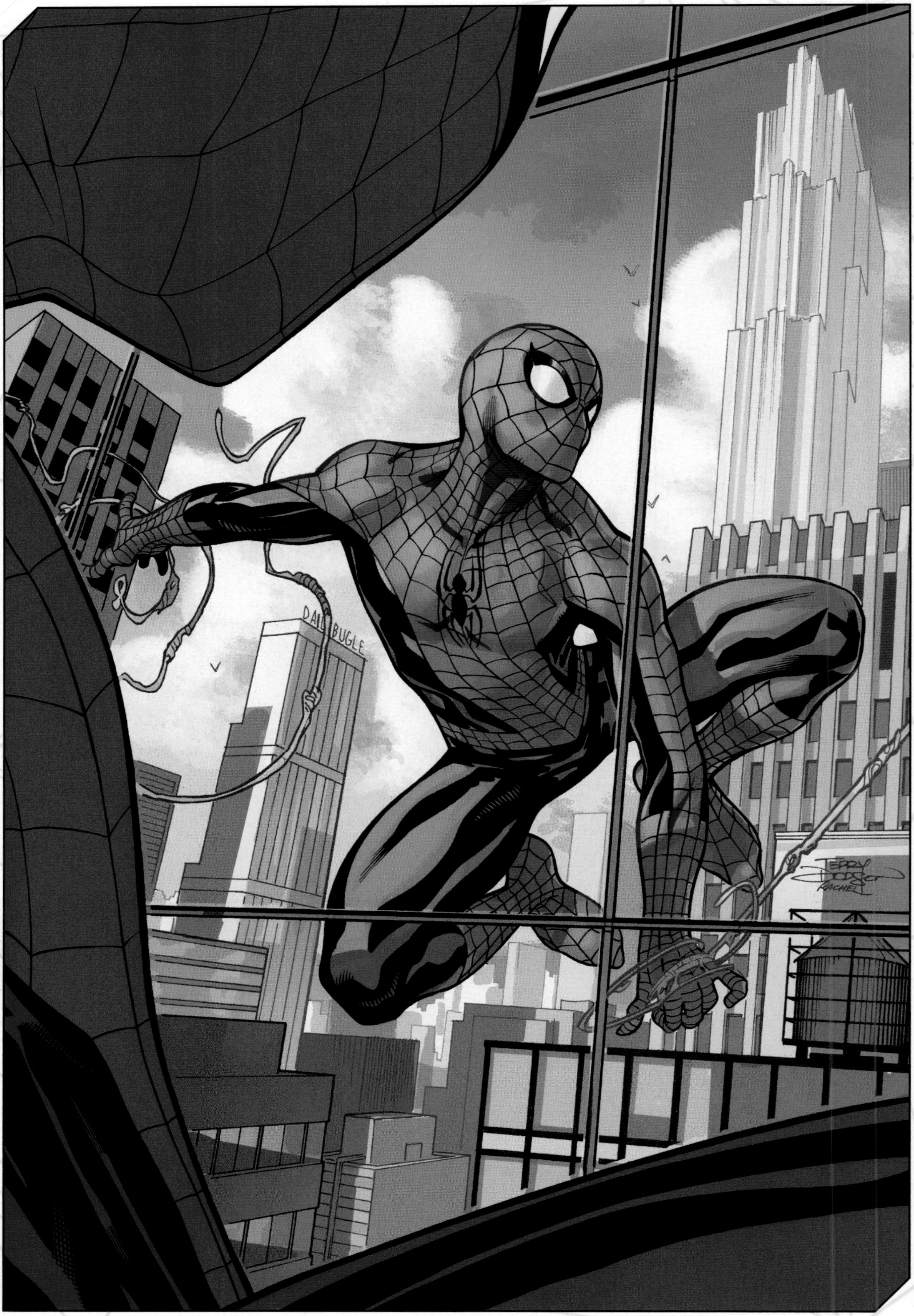
DAILY BUGLE
TERRY DODSON RACHEL

#800 VARIANT BY **TERRY DODSON & RACHEL DODSON**

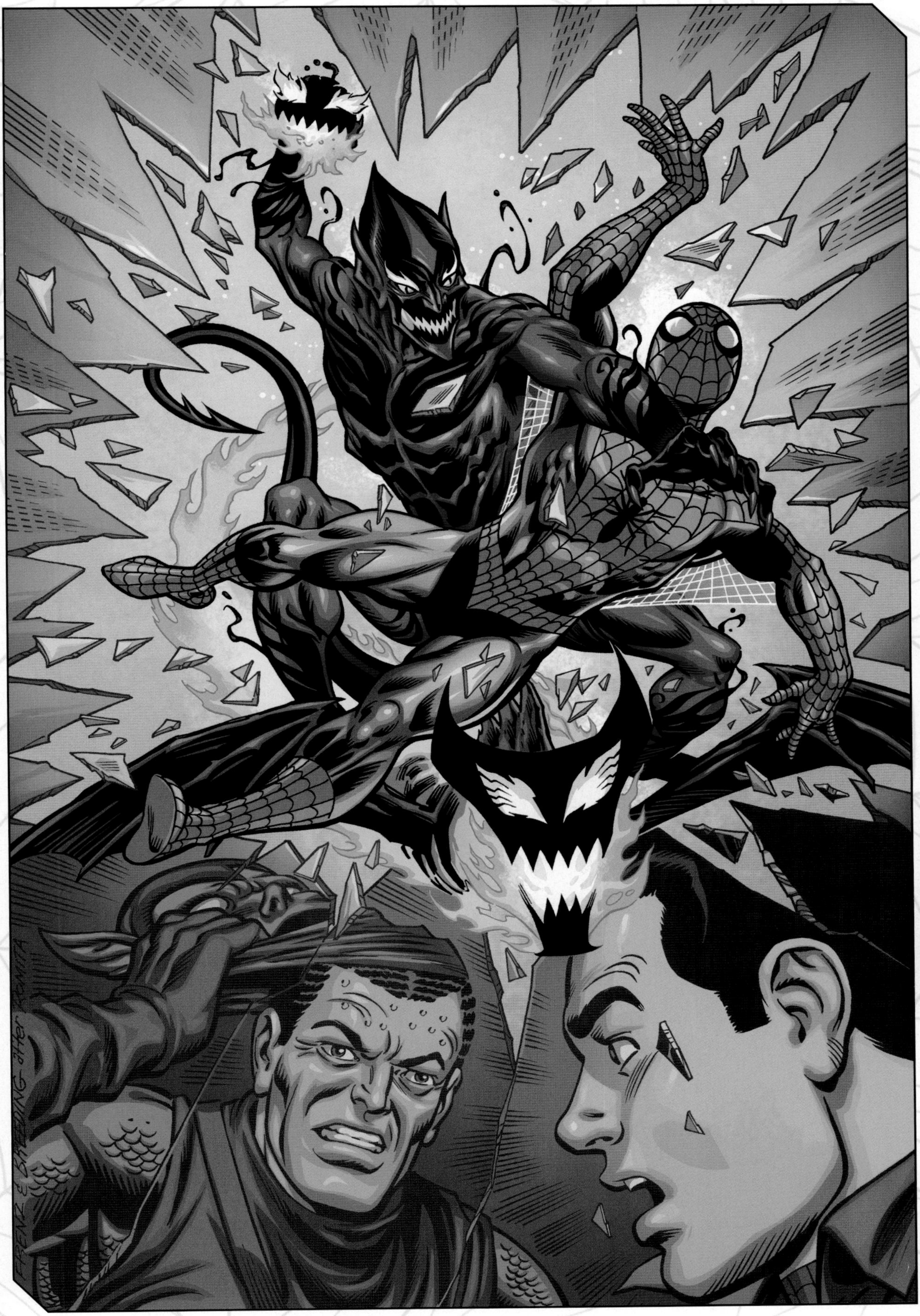
FRENZ & BREEDING after ROMITA

#800 VARIANT BY **RON FRENZ, BRETT BREEDING & DAVE McCAIG**

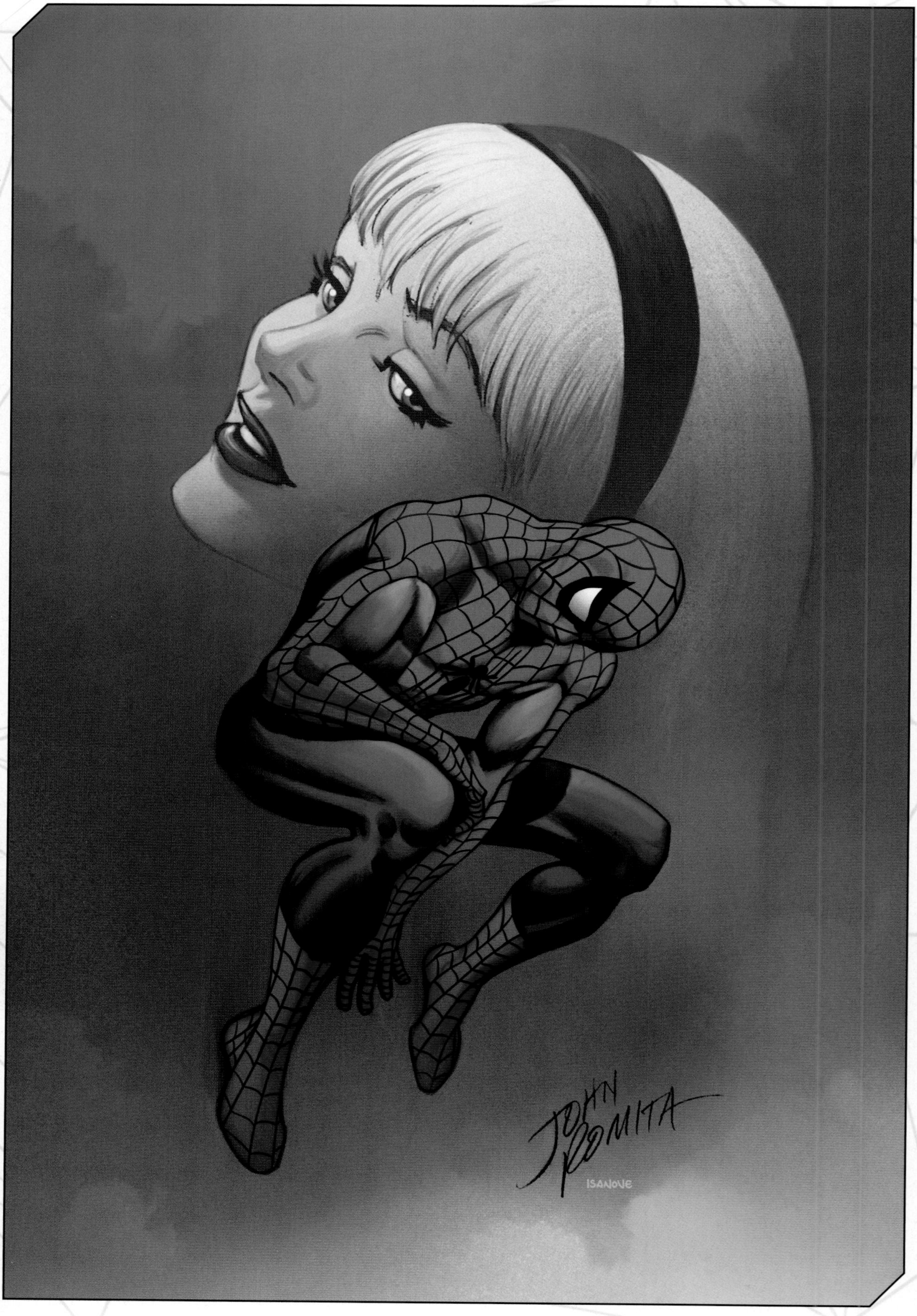
JOHN ROMITA
ISANOVE

#800 VARIANT BY **JOHN ROMITA SR. & RICHARD ISANOVE**

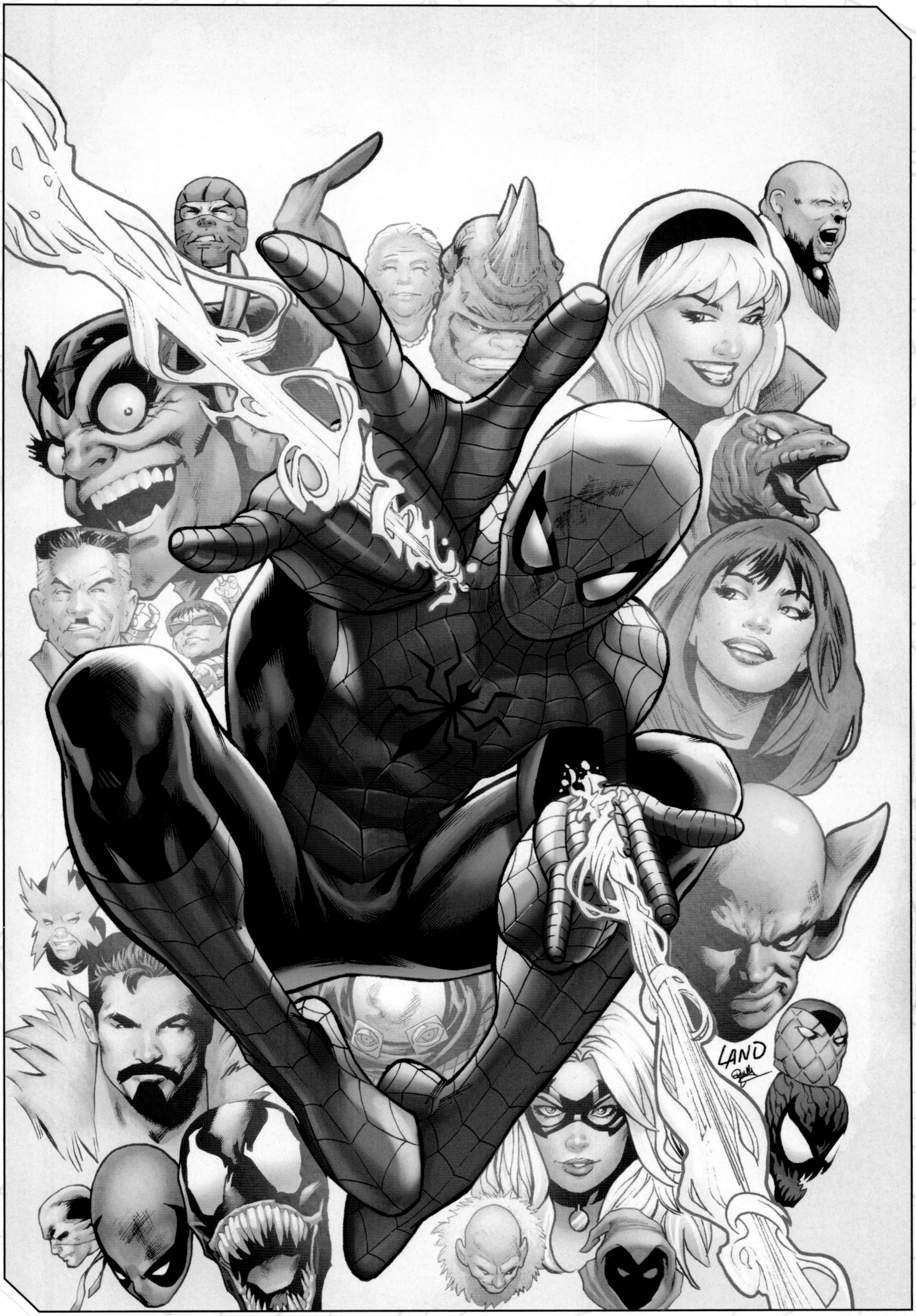
LAND

#800 VARIANT BY **GREG LAND & RACHELLE ROSENBERG**

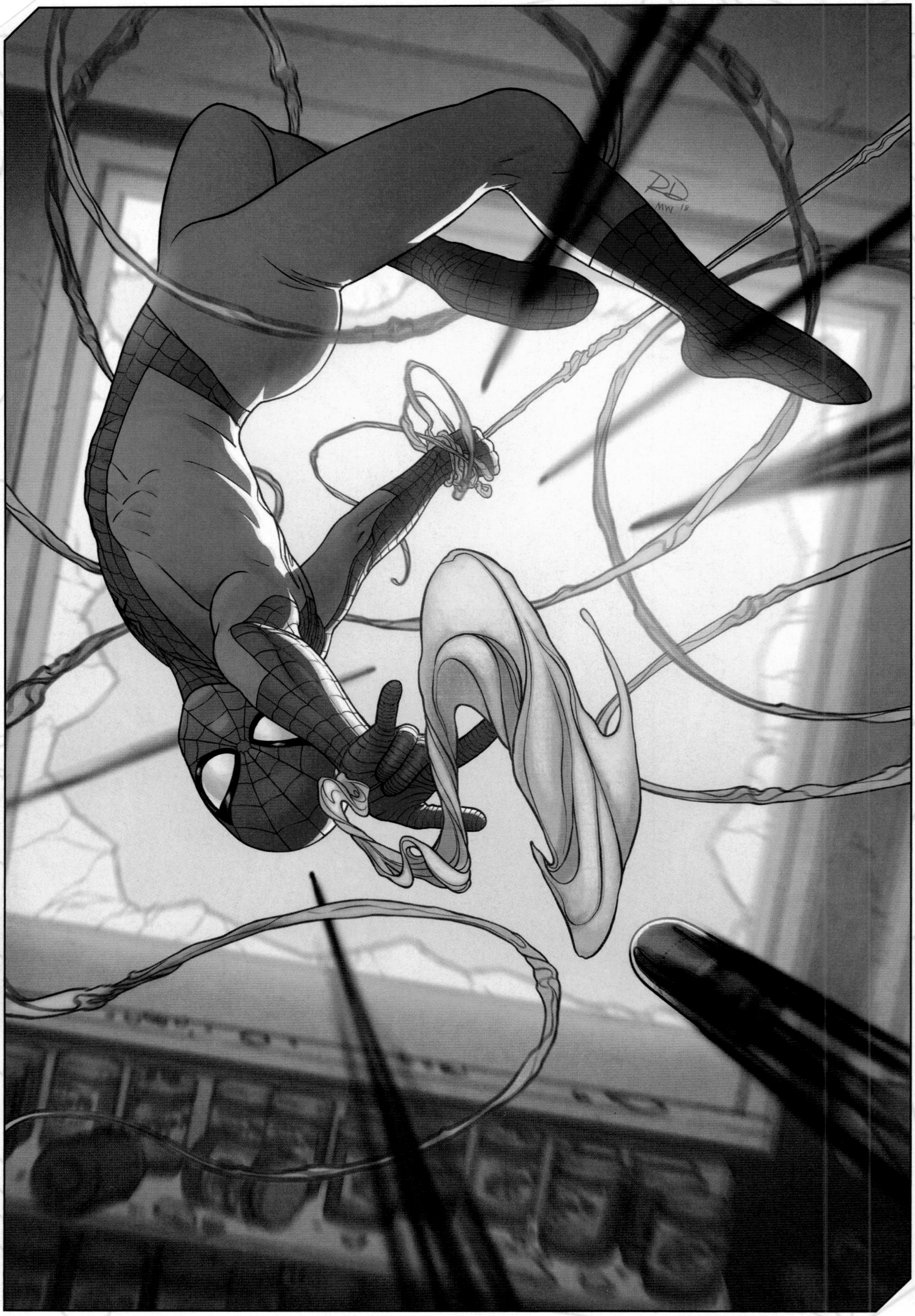
RD
MW '18

#800 VARIANT BY **RUSSELL DAUTERMAN & MATTHEW WILSON**

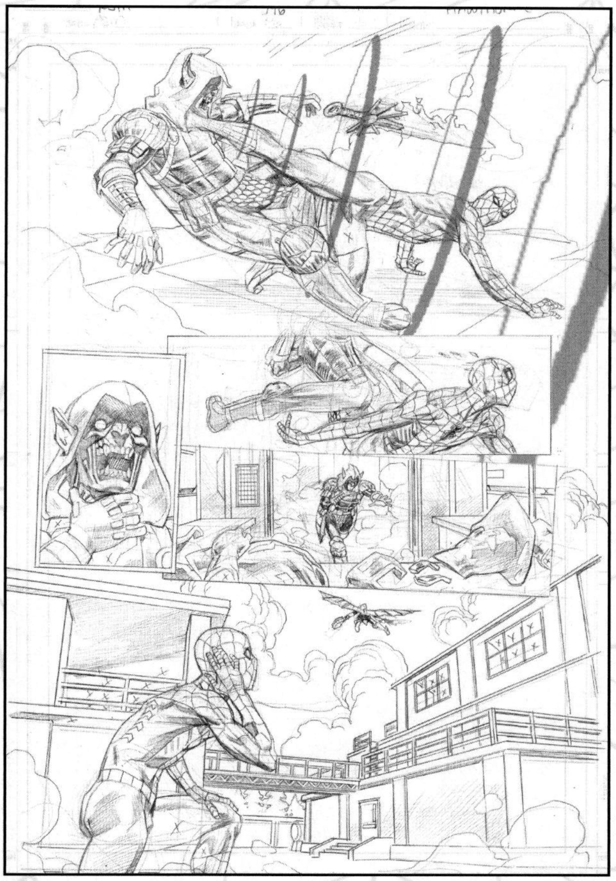

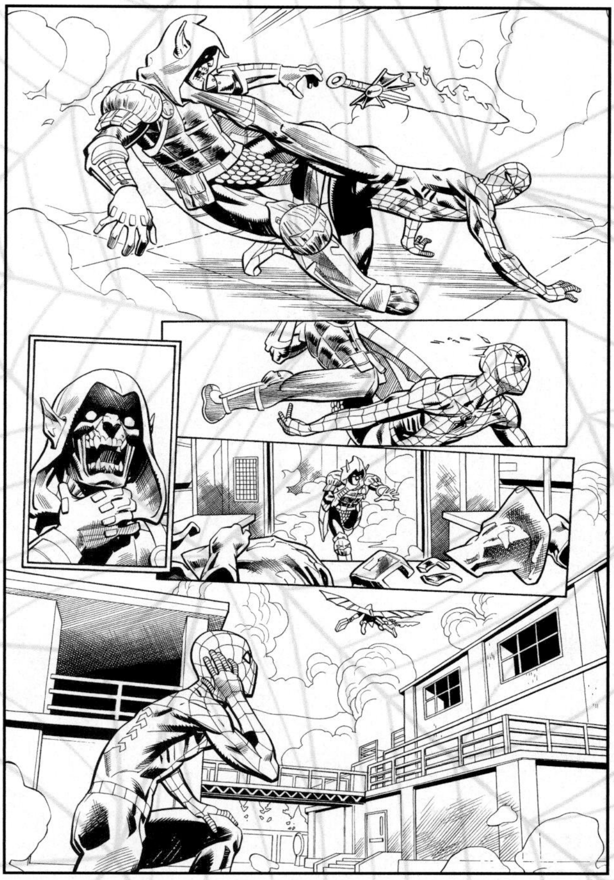

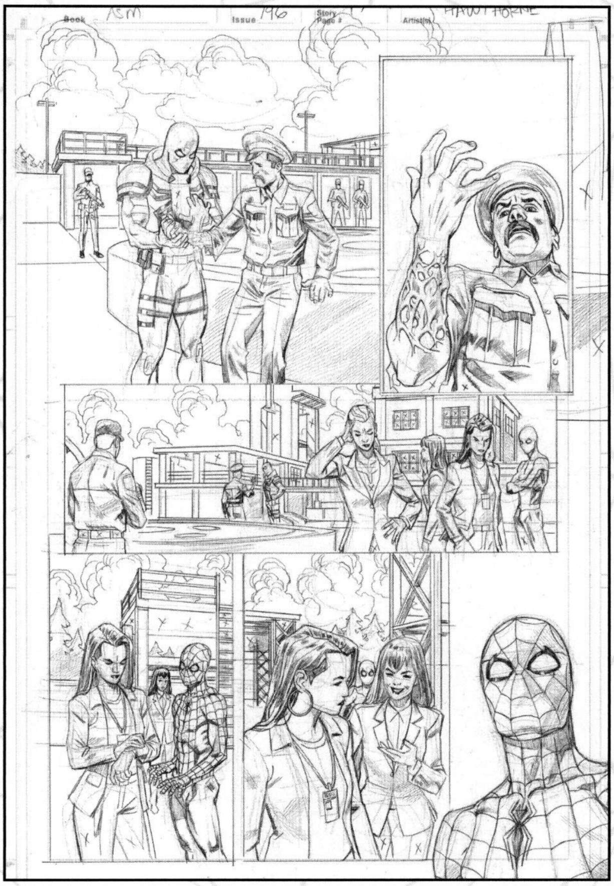

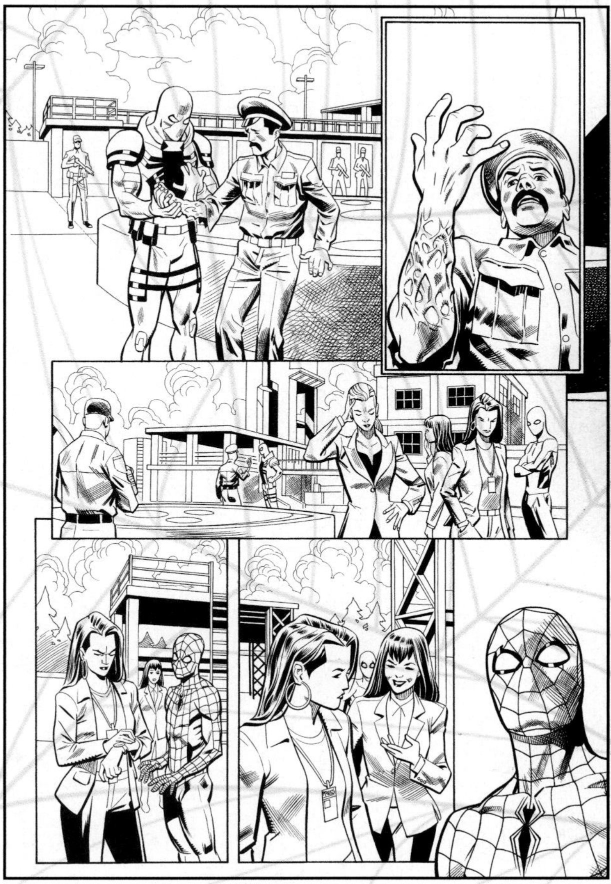

#796, PAGES 16-17 ART PROCESS BY **MIKE HAWTHORNE & TERRY PALLOT**

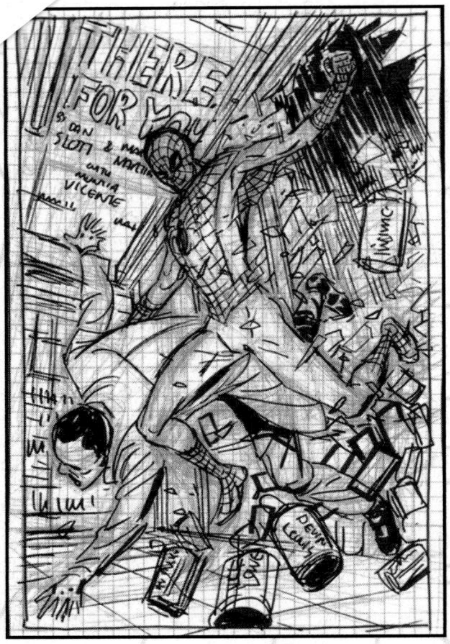
THERE FOR YOU

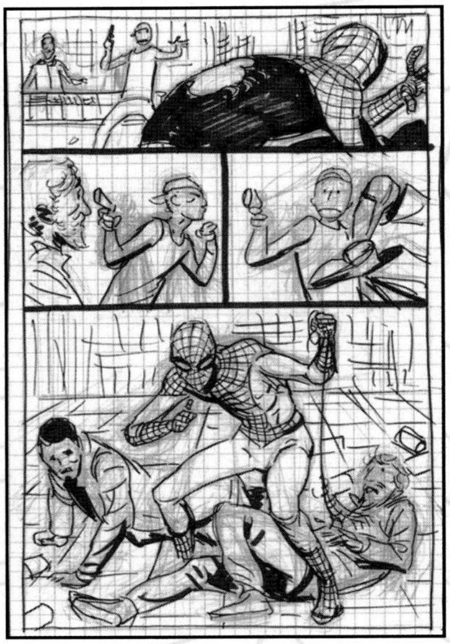

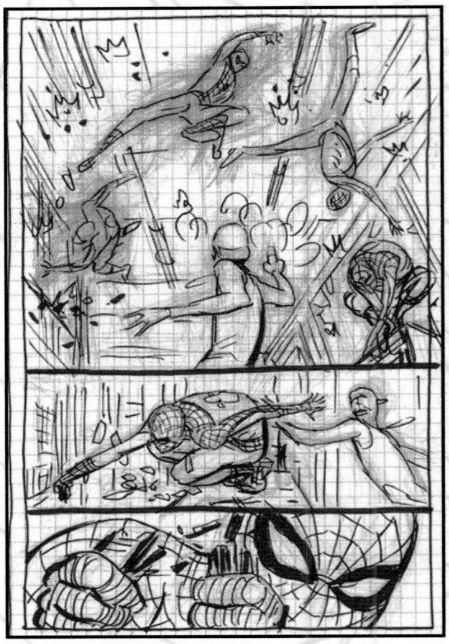

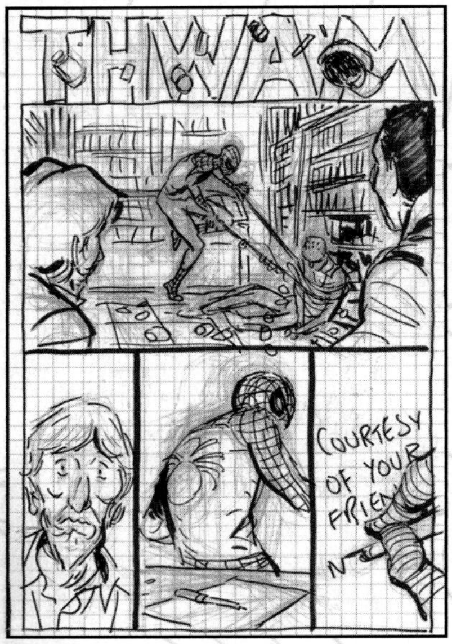
THWAM
COURTESY OF YOUR FRIEN

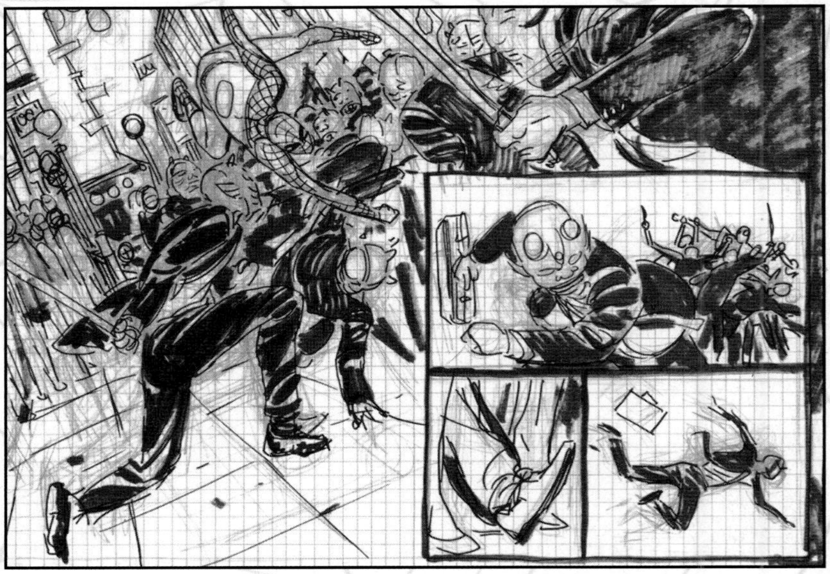

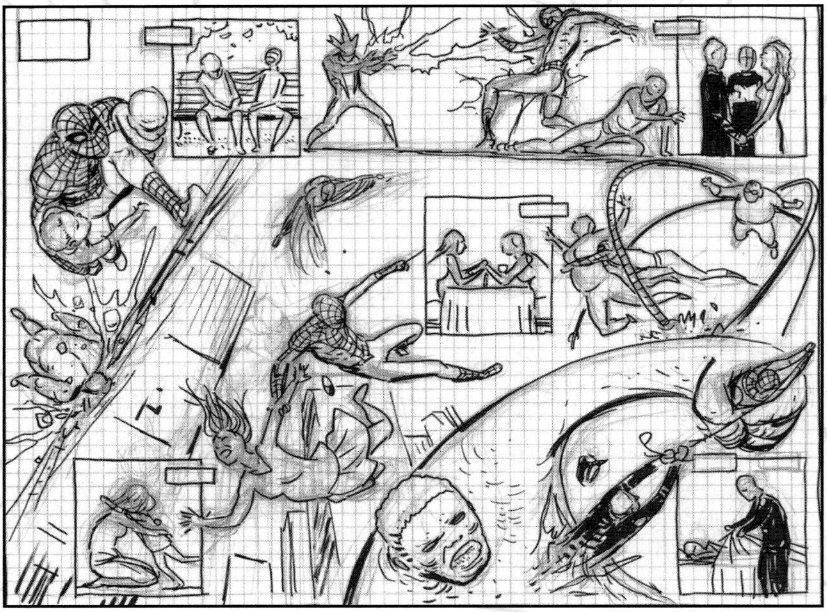

#801, PAGES 5-8, 12-13 & 17-18 LAYOUTS BY **MARCOS MARTIN**

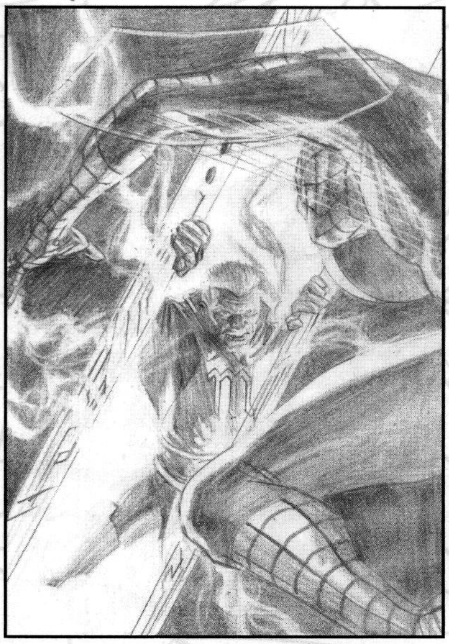
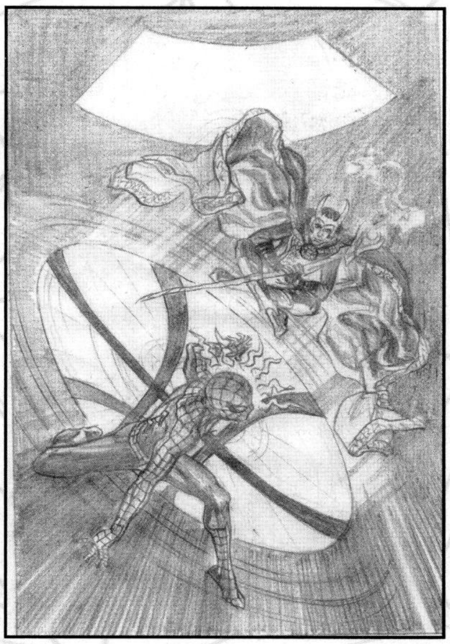
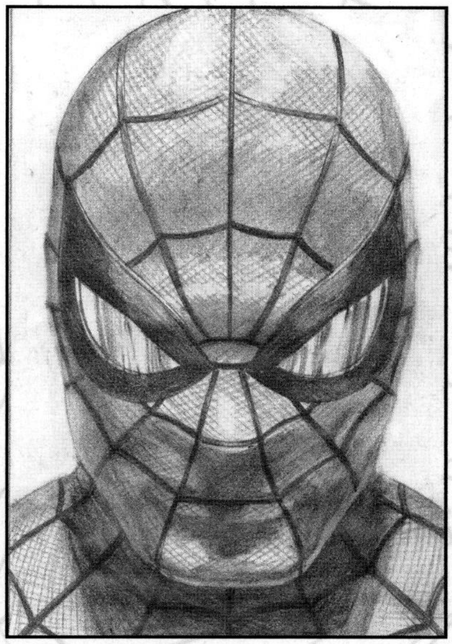
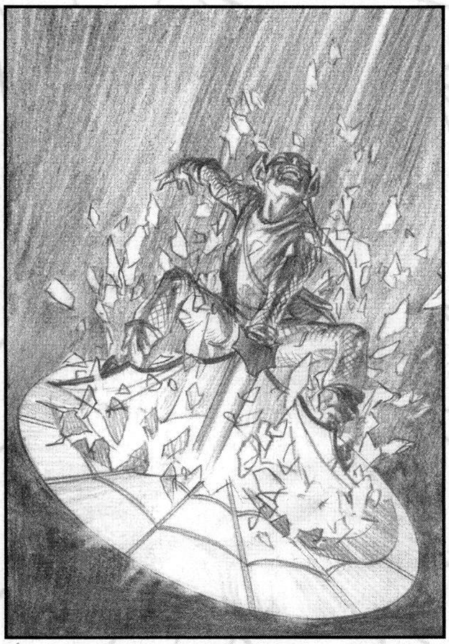
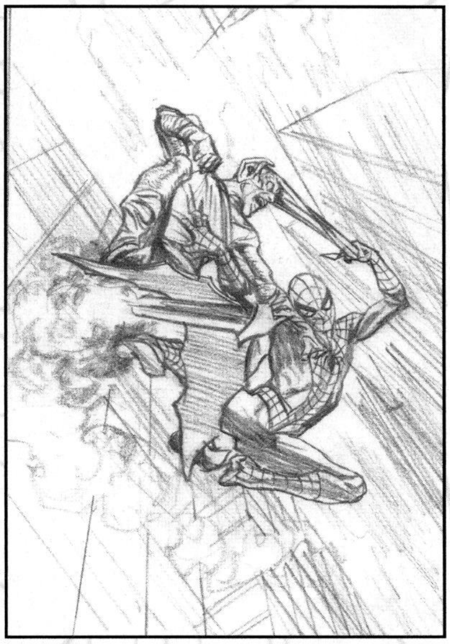
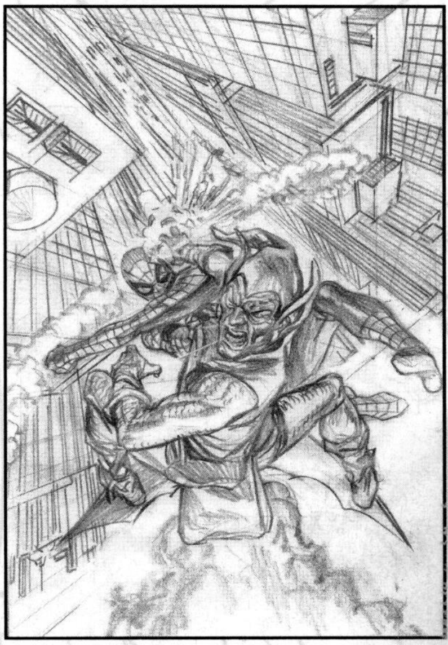
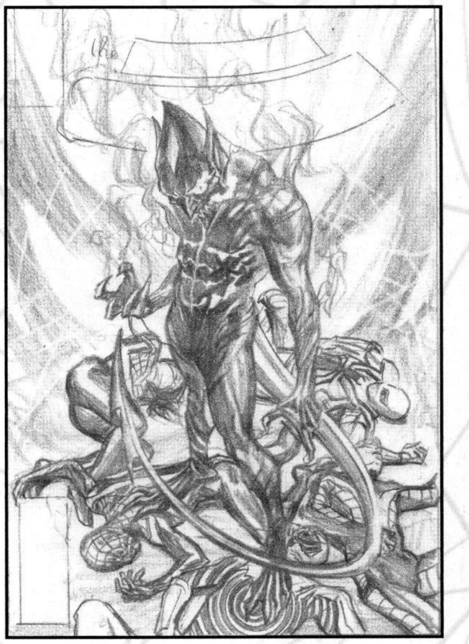
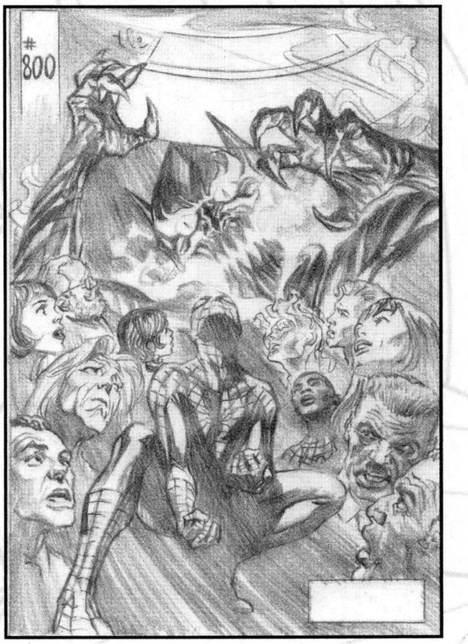
#
800

#794-800 COVER SKETCHES BY **ALEX ROSS**

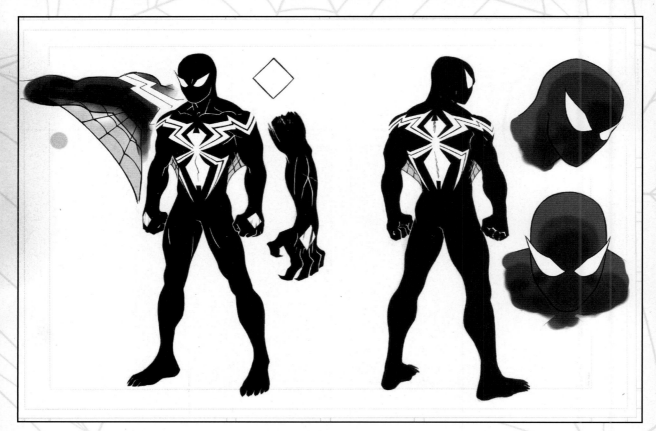

CHARACTER SKETCHES BY **ED McGUINNESS**